Students
Writing
Across the
Disciplines

STUDENTS WRITING ACROSS THE DISCIPLINES

Cyndia Susan Clegg • *Michael M. Wheeler*
PEPPERDINE UNIVERSITY   PEPPERDINE UNIVERSITY

Holt, Rinehart and Winston, Inc.

Fort Worth   Chicago   San Francisco   Philadelphia
Montreal   Toronto   London   Sydney   Tokyo

Pages 104–105, "The End of the World" from NEW AND COLLECTED POEMS: 1917–1982 by Archibald MacLeish. Copyright © 1985 by the Estate of Archibald MacLeish. Reprinted by permission of Houghton Mifflin Co.

Publisher	Ted Buchholz
Acquisitions Editor	Michael Rosenberg
Developmental Editor	Martin Lewis
Senior Project Editor	Charlie Dierker
Manager of Production	Tad Gaither
Art & Design Supervisor	Vicki McAlindon Horton
Text Design	Rita Naughton
Cover Design	Vicki McAlindon Horton
Cover Photography	Gary Logan

Library of Congress Cataloging-in-Publication Data

Clegg, Cyndia Susan.
    Students writing across the disciplines
      p.   cm.
    1. College readers. 2. English language—Rhetoric.
    3. Interdisciplinary approach in education. I. Wheeler, Michael M.
    II. Title
    PE1417.C628 1991
    808'.0427—dc20   90-34305
                                                CIP

ISBN: 0-03-028762-6

Address for Editorial Correspondence Holt, Rinehart and Winston, Inc., 301 Commerce Street, Suite 3700, Fort Worth, TX 76102
Address for Orders Holt, Rinehart and Winston, Inc., 6277 Sea Harbor Drive, Orlando, FL 32887 1-800-782-4479, or 1-800-433-0001 (in Florida)

Printed in the United States of America

1 2 3 4   090   9 8 7 6 5 4 3 2 1

Holt, Rinehart and Winston, Inc.
The Dryden Press
Saunders College Publishing

To the memory of
Everett L. Jones (1915–1990)
educator, mentor, and friend
whose "carry on" has taken us many places

Preface

Students Writing Across the Disciplines shows our commitment to engaging students, both in writing courses and in the entire academic community, in the kind of intellectual discourse that is the principal endeavor of colleges and universities. Since their medieval beginnings, colleges and universities have played two sometimes contradictory roles. They have conferred degrees, virtually certifying professional competence, initially for doctors, lawyers, clergymen, and philosophers, and later with scientific and industrial expansion, for scientists, engineers, businessmen, and teachers. They have also served as centers of learning, creating new knowledge, preserving and transmitting knowledge of the past, reappraising constantly the relationship between old and new. The one role, certifying graduates, is pragmatic and functional; the other, learning, abstract and esoteric.

Writing for college courses resembles the college and university's essentially dichotomous nature. Writing skills—planning, information gathering, recognizing audiences and purposes, organizing, comforming to grammar and paragraph conventions, revising—improve by study and practice; they are a kind of competence that can be learned. Writing course requirements participate in the college and university's credential conferring role. Students who meet this requirement are "licensed" to write in college. "Our English students can write a coherent paper, correct in format and grammar, using and documenting sources," we composition teachers say to our colleagues in other disciplines, and certainly, the goal of mastering writing skills affords a valuable focus for both you, as a student, and us, as writing instructors. But somehow, when skills are our only focus, we all feel cheated. Composition courses, rather than engaging us in college education, seem to be a prefatory rite of passage.

To understand what else a college composition course can do besides certifying a student's writing skills, consider the other role colleges and universities play, as centers of learning. In this role colleges and universities create new knowledge, preserve and transmit knowledge of the past, and re-appraise constantly the relationship between old knowledge and new. But who precisely does this, and how do they do it?

Faculty members like to think of themselves as the custodians of learning—as the college's center—but so too do students and administrators. Some disciplines—at some schools the sciences, at others the humanities—even go so far as to see themselves as the essence of the college or university's endeavor. In reality, as a center of learning, the university's various populations and disciplines are interdependent. Yes, scientists and social scientists may discover more new knowledge, and historians and literature professors may preserve and transmit more of the past, but students in every discipline along with their professors engage in discovering, preserving, transmitting, and reappraising knowledge. And all of us participate in the same ways—through reading, talking, experimenting, thinking, and writing. Participants in the learning enterprise engage in an ongoing discourse with their immediate colleagues in labs, lunchrooms, offices, and dorms; with colleagues at other colleges and universities at conferences and in professional journals; and with writers and thinkers of the past by reading and thinking on our own. By collecting and publishing student essays in *Students Writing Across the Disciplines,* we wish not only to emphasize the important place of students in academic discourse and the value of their writing, but to invite you into the community. By reading fellow students' essays written for courses in various disciplines, by talking about these with classmates, and by writing in response to their ideas, you engage in the challenge and excitement of education in your composition class.

You may ask how one course can address such diversity. All of us who declare majors or teach in our "expert" areas tend to forget that the learning enterprise across the academic curriculum engages us in as many common approaches for reading, thinking, and writing, as it does diverse subjects. Whether we are botanists, psychologists, or literary theorists, we need to be able to recount (transmit) past knowledge; all of us need to know how to summarize—to review—the learning of our forebears. While our approaches for acquiring new knowledge may differ, we need to describe our approaches (experimental methods) to our colleagues, students, and faculty, who may also wish to pursue our line of investigation. The kind of imaginative thinking that allows the physicist to consider discrepancies in data and generate a new theory for subatomic particles resides as well in the student who, after reading recent research on subliminally gratifying stimuli, looks at a psychiatric patient's case history and proposes new treatment.

This textbook invites students and instructors to engage in the whole learning enterprise by both developing competence in writing skills and entering into the academic community's discourse. To assist in reaching this goal, this text is divided into two sections—a short course in writing and reading critically and an anthology of essays students have written for courses across the academic curriculum. The first section includes chapters on:

- Controlling Writing Situations by Attitudes and Good Writing Habits.
- Critical Reading.
- The Writing Process: Prewriting, Drafting, Revising, and Editing.
- Writing from Sources: Quoting, Summarizing, and Paraphrasing.
- Documentation Strategies and Formats: Modern Language Association (MLA), American Psychological Association (APA), Council of Biological Editors (CBE), and Chicago Manual of Style.

The section on student writing includes a chapter on:

- Learning from Student Writing: The most common kinds of essays including scientific reports, position papers, critical analyses, literature reviews, and critiques.

Finally, the Anthology section of Student Writing includes essays from:

- Science.
- Social Science.
- Business.
- Humanities and the Arts.

The essays in the anthology reflect actual course work, some in rhetoric and composition courses, but predominantly in the disciplines. A brief note precedes each essay describing the assignment and the course. Questions drawing attention to writing strategies and encouraging discussion follow. Each section closes with suggestions for writing.

The essays that appear here represent the best work of students at universities, technical and liberal arts colleges, and community colleges across the United States. As editors, perhaps the most surprising thing we found was how consistent assignments were from similar courses at different schools, and how writing tasks crossed discipline lines. The essays here reflect this. Common to all disciplines are critiques, reviews, summaries of relevant literature, and comparative analyses. As a result, this text focuses on how to develop writing and research skills and adapts these skills to the demands of different disciplines.

We would like to thank the following contributors who assisted us in the monumental task of acquiring student essays from their colleagues on other parts of their campuses: David Chapman, Texas Tech University; Mary Cullinan, California State University, Hayward; Grace Ioppolo, UCLA; Gladys Leithauser, University of Michigan; Louis Molina, Dade Community College; Christopher Monte, Manhattanville College; Donald Murray, University of New Hampshire; Linda Robertson, Hobart and William Smith Colleges; James Semones, San Jacinto College; Chris Thaiss, George Mason University; and Lance Wilcox, University of Minnesota.

We are also indebted to those who have helped us develop and refine this book. Kate Morgan and Charlyce Jones Owen, former Holt, Rinehart and Winston editors, provided invaluable assistance in setting the project in motion. Martin Lewis, developmental editor at Holt, Rinehart and Winston, has truly seen this project through manuscript and revision into production. We would also like to thank our reviewers who have provided useful comments: Cathryn Amdahl, Washington State University; Nancy P. Bent, Ithaca College; Alexander Friedlander, Drexel University; Christine Hult, Utah State University; John O'Connor, George Mason University; Margaret Smith, University of Texas–El Paso; Barbara Stout, Montgomery College; and Kimberly Town, Ohio State University.

Contents

Students Writing Across the Disciplines

Writing
for the
Disciplines

Introduction: Taking Control Over Your Writing

ATTITUDES AND WRITING

Whenever we write, we approach the task from the context of our prior writing experiences. This context is built upon the customary ways in which we use writing and the attitudes we have formed toward our limitations and our successes. We use writing in both professional and personal contexts to communicate information to others—in letters to friends and family, in papers to colleagues, employers, and teachers. Some of us write to affect others—to change a congressman's vote, to alter community opinion about a shelter for our city's homeless people, to persuade a prospective employer of our worth. Many of us write for our professions—a business report, a scientific position paper, a lawyer's brief, a social worker's case history, or a student's research paper. Others write in journals and diaries or on miscellaneous scraps of paper to sort out our personal feelings and responses to daily life. For some, writing allows us to express our creativity and unique perceptions about our experiences. For others, writing is a necessary evil—an assignment to complete, an expectation to meet, a job to be done.

Our attitude toward writing depends on the ease with which we write, the success our writing has met, and the criticism we anticipate—either from our readers or ourselves. Effective writers, whether they write for professional or personal ends, exert control over their writing contexts by recognizing their attitudes toward writing, by informing themselves about the subjects about which they are writing, by having an approach for writing—a time, a place, a purpose, and a process—by writing often, and by evaluating their own writing. This text will help you master your writing contexts by including chapters about:

Attitudes Toward Writing
Reading Critically
Process-Centered Writing: A Short Writing Course
Using and Documenting Sources

ATTITUDES TOWARD WRITING: BEING A WRITER

If today you responded to a question on a census form or an application asking your occupation, you would very likely reply "student." At this point in your academic career, you know precisely what being a student requires—attending class, taking notes, reading texts, studying, participating in labs, and taking examinations. Your image alters little as you change from one student task to the next; you still see yourself as a student. If, however, you enroll in a dance class, an acting class, or a music performance class, you become a dancer, a cellist, or an actor. Writing classes require you to become a writer. All the lectures you hear about writing and all the materials you read telling you how to write mean nothing unless you regard yourself as a writer and do what writers do—write. To improve your attitude toward writing—to see yourself as a writer and to be able to write on a regular basis—requires eliminating misconceptions about writing and replacing them with a clear picture of writers writing.

MISCONCEPTIONS ABOUT WRITING

> Whenever I sit down to an empty pad of narrow-lined paper, black fountain pen in hand, I engage in what I call my "procrastination fantasy." Surely, if I wait a little longer, I will know precisely what to write. Words will flow magically from my pen, and the ten-page review I have due next week will be finished in two or three hours. Admittedly, a few undeserved successes as an undergraduate English major fed this fantasy; I wrote papers entitled "Influences of Dostoevsky's *Notes from Underground* on Ralph Ellison's *Underground Man*" and "Why All the Smutz, Mr. Roth?" the night before they were due and received "A's." Unfortunately, I tend to forget that such late night writing also earned me a few "D's." Remembering the "D's" pushes the fantasy aside, and I'm ready to struggle with covering those narrowly placed blue lines with my black scrawl.

This anecdote related by a colleague who writes quite well, reveals three common misconceptions about writing:

- Inspiration directs writing.
- Writing progresses quickly.
- The first written draft is a finished piece.

Understanding these misconceptions can improve your attitude about writing.

Inspiration

In most writers' experience, inspiration is little more than what recent writing research identifies as prewriting activity or preparation. It is the germ of an insight or idea that flowers into words, sentences, and paragraphs, having been fed by reflection, research, and rumination. Each writer prepares to write with activities that are comfortable to her. Suggestions for preparation activities appear in Chapter 3.

Rapid Progress

If writing requires reflection, research, and rumination, then clearly writing requires time—time from thought to hand to paper and time from conception to completion. Less experienced writers may ask how much time experienced writers allow. One novelist reports that she begins her day at 10:00 A.M. and writes four pages; this may take one hour or the entire day. The time required depends upon many factors—the nature of the writing task, the topic's complexity, the writer's comfort with the material, the amount of research required, and the writer's frame of mind. Few writers achieve the writer's three-hour, ten-page review in my colleague's procrastination fantasy on a regular basis. For every four-page hour a four-hour page lies in wait.

First Draft, Finished Piece

All too often students (as opposed to writers) succumb to their schedules' inevitable rigors and submit first drafts as finished pieces, and sometimes, accustomed to saying how poorly students write, professors accept these pieces, read them for content, and put them aside mumbling their confirmed view that students do, indeed, write poorly. Experienced writers know that first drafts reflect a basic writing problem—people think faster than they write. In first drafts we inevitably omit a step in logic or a definition or explanation familiar to us but not to the reader. We use words imprecisely, and we make unconscious mechanical errors. When first we write, we are so close to the materials and so concerned about getting our ideas down, we care little about how a reader will read our writing. Experienced writers rely on the revision process to refine clarity, coherence, completeness of thought, and correctness.

Some Other Misconceptions

The procrastination fantasy touches three principal misconceptions about writing; a few others exist:

- Writers are born not made.
- Every writer works the same way—the right way.
- Some people simply cannot write.

These misconceptions derive from the idea that writers are somehow different from the rest of us. They put writers into a category of "Other" and suggest that all people in that category are similar. Probably the only generalization that can be made about writers is that writers differ. Each develops his or her own approach for writing and labors at a different rate and with different facility, and each encounters a different set of difficulties. Those of us writing in the academic environment also need to know how we individually approach writing and develop practices that allow us to reconcile our writing activities with other demands on our time.

WRITING AND MENTAL PROCESSES

To understand the varying levels of ease and difficulty different writers experience when they work, we can look to how the mind functions. Recent brain physiology studies explain that people process information differently. Studies of people who have lost the function of one brain side or the other show that the left brain processes information in a linear or conventionally "rational" manner and the right side processes information in patterns. Both brain sides have some language facility, but the dominant brain side affects the ease with which certain tasks are performed. The left-side dominant writer may construct plans, design outlines, and write logical arguments with ease. The right-side dominant person may use maps and diagrams to plan his writing and use language creatively, but may have difficulty ordering an essay's linear progress. Furthermore, other tests suggest that some people have greater verbal skills, while others possess greater computational abilities.

This research does not mean that only literary people write and mathematicians compute. (If it did, learning could not be communicated in all disciplines.) The research does help explain why each writer will work with ease at some aspect of writing and struggle with some other. As you recognize your strengths and limitations and allow for them, you will evolve your own approach to writing. This will be more helpful than holding on to those old misconceptions. When we put aside our misconceptions, we can begin to see ourselves as writers. Then, most likely, we will feel about writing as many writers do; we can dislike writing but like having written.

WRITER'S BLOCK

Writing task in mind (or sketched on paper), many of us have sat down to write only to find that those brilliant word strings that moments before flashed through out consciousness cannot find their way onto paper (or screen). We stare at the paper, at the wall, and out the window; we get up for another cup of coffee. Still the words elude us. Recognizing this as writer's block and knowing most writers experience it at one time or another offers little consolation, but perhaps understanding some of its causes and having some tricks to get past it will.

Perfectionism and Writer's Block

While some writers experience serious writer's block that may require professional counseling, for most students the experience is temporary. When students discuss what initially they experience as panic, the panic becomes identifiable as fear of failure. Throughout the educational experience writing receives criticism, judgment, and grades. Students learn to write with instructors as their audience, and pleasing becomes as important as communicating. As a result, student writers find themselves writing in a voice not their own for an audience whose expectations they may not fully understand. This problem is particularly compounded by assuming that the first draft is the finished draft. An inner voice says, "This has to be perfect." Perfectionistic expectations create considerable pressure, and while some pressure may encourage a fine performance, the pressure for perfection usually interferes with truly excellent performance, particularly when it comes to writing.

Self-Esteem and Writer's Block

Not only do the perfectionistic demands we anticipate from others effect a writing block, writing blocks develop when self-esteem becomes tied to writing. Writing is a personal act. Putting to paper personal experiences, observations, ideas, or emotions involves some personal risk, a risk which often makes writing difficult. Writing becomes easier for writers who separate judgment of work from judgment of self. This sounds difficult, but consider what the world would be like if everyone thought the same thoughts and reacted to events in precisely the same way. Dull. When a writer records his personal perspective, he adds to the world's infinite variety. Writing would not be worth doing if everyone experienced the world in the same way. Anticipating our reader's different responses and hoping to share our special perceptions, we write with the knowledge that every reader may not agree with our ideas or share our insights. No writer seriously anticipates that every word or stylistic nuance will meet with every reader's approval and agreement; she anticipates debate and criticism. A reader's critical response neither lessens the written word's value, nor diminishes the writer's worth.

Hints for Overcoming Writer's Block

However well a writer controls perfectionistic demands or separates self-esteem from the valuation of his work, writing blocks still occur. Here are ways some writers overcome blocking.

> I block at introductions so I move on to another section, usually the one that interests me most or that I understand best.

> I put the job I'm working on aside and write whatever comes to mind.

> If I'm writing a paper for a class, I try to envision an audience different from the professor. I can then write for a reason other than the grade.

I consciously write without concern for style, sometimes even without concern for accuracy, so that I can get as much on the page as possible. This draft, barely a rough draft, demands extensive revision but allows me tremendous freedom.

Brief written pieces rarely cause me difficulty; anything over 2,000 words intimidates me. When this happens, I envision a series of short papers, write them separately, then work them together at a later time, when I develop distance.

I change my writing tool. If I block at the typewriter or computer, I pick up pen and paper; sometimes I go the other way—from pen to keys.

I return to my research (either my notes or reading materials), because I am probably not yet ready to write.

I stop writing and start talking, either to a tape recorder or a friend. I find working ideas through verbally focuses my writing.

After I completed my doctoral dissertation (350 pages), I declared a six-month reprieve. Then when I tried writing again, I blocked. The ideas came, but I was unable to formulate them for an academic audience. To retain the ideas, I jotted them on paper scraps. Scraps changed to unlined standard paper sheets; cryptic notes became prose. The occasional notation turned into a daily routine, and I became a journal keeper—and a writer.

I get up from the word processor, put on my athletic shoes, run or walk vigorously for an hour, shower, put on clean clothes, and begin again. If I still cannot write, I pledge myself to an early evening and an earlier start tomorrow.

These suggestions represent ways both professional and student writers cope with blocking. As you look through the above suggestions, you will notice that overcoming writer's block usually involves some changes—an attitude change, a physical change in location or materials, or a shift of focus. If other writers' suggestions do not work for you, develop your own, but keep in mind both the necessity of seeing your first draft as tentative and the importance of allowing enough time between preliminary draft and due date to contend with possible blocks.

GOOD WRITING HABITS

Besides understanding your attitudes toward writing, you can take control of your writing by developing good writing habits. Writing takes both time and discipline. Writing often in a comfortable place at a regular time helps many writers meet deadlines with greater ease. Some practices used by people whose professions require frequent writing can help you develop useful writing habits.

Writing Often

While scientists, attorneys, businesspeople, and journalists often write for deadlines and write with certain tasks in mind—just as students do—most "professional" writers continue writing between tasks and deadlines. They write sketches for future articles or reading notes with fragmentary responses. They record their responses to personal and world affairs. Such writing often takes form in a journal—literally, a daybook—where a writer, unconcerned about audience, can test perceptions and ideas or experiment with style.

Keeping a Journal

Some writers discipline themselves to write daily, but a journal is no mere calendar of daily events. Instead, it offers a qualitative response to experiences. Nor is a journal necessarily a book per se. Some journal keepers may indeed keep records in a single notebook, but others may designate a journal drawer as a repository for miscellaneous papers. Many of us who cannot write without a personal computer's instant editing designate a journal file or disk. Journals reflect a writer's individual interests and experiments with form and style. A journal entry might objectively record research and reading or more personally transcribe a conversation, describe a place, or work through angry feelings. For student writers, keeping a journal provides a good opportunity to become comfortable with putting ideas and experience into writing.

While journal entries are necessarily individual, the following categories of experience often prove fruitful for journal writing:

- intellectual discourse (some newly acquired information and its impact)
- responses to physical surroundings
- investigations of personal belief (religion, politics, morality)
- sensory details from a particularly vivid experience (pleasant or unpleasant)
- emotional self-examination (fears, preferences, prejudices, depression, elation, and their manifestations or causes)
- detailed descriptions of familiar places

Whether by keeping a journal or by attempting to write on some other regular basis, if you adopt the professional writer's practice of writing often, writing will become a more comfortable activity for you.

A Comfortable Place

> Walking through academic halls lined by professors' offices, I balk
> at the persistent clacking typewriters. I gaze in awe at students writing
> away, shoulder to shoulder in the university library's computer room.
> While I do not resemble the Sunday supplement writer who confesses he
> writes better at the kitchen table than in his tidy office, I would find writing
> in the same place I teach, counsel students, and sit on committees impos-
> sible. I need to be able to focus my attention away from other career de-
> mands. On visiting my sunporch office, a friend asked how when writing I
> escape all the place's natural distractions—winter's draft, summer's heat,
> lounging sheep dogs, and all that glaring sunlight. However idiosyncratic, I
> cannot write without natural light, a window-framed view of something
> growing, and a place to sit cross-legged.

Students, particularly those living in college dormitories, rarely write
in circumstances as ideal as the writer above describes, but they can usually
find some compromise if they consider what might be ideal. For example, a
library desk overlooking the university quad could provide light and nature.
Recognizing a need for isolation, some students seek out empty classrooms.
Other students write in dorm rooms, quiet after roommates have gone to
class or to sleep. Many students find a library's quiet crowd reassuring,
while others can work only when television or music fills the background
void. Whatever conditions suit you, discover the place most comfortable for
you, and write there. Write letters, write lecture reviews and book summaries, write in your journal; then writing more time-consuming formal papers
there will be easier.

A Regular Time

Like the novelist who begins writing each morning at ten, find the time
when you write best. Some writers rise with the sun, drink only coffee for
breakfast, and work steadily until noon. Afternoons find them gazing at
walls. Other people can only work when their coffee drinking begins at dinner and their writing at midnight. Studies indicate metabolic differences in
"day people" and "night people" which account for performance variations.
Even when a night person finds it necessary to be at work or class early, that
person's peak performance still comes late in the day. The day person who
stays up late several nights in a row will find concentration difficult and
routine tasks exhausting. Schedules sometime force students to disrupt regular sleep and work patterns, and when this happens, demanding tasks like
writing become even more difficult. Determine when you work best and
regularly schedule writing for that time.

In the last few pages we have looked at the role attitude plays in exercising control over your writing. Effective writing requires putting aside
misconceptions that all writers write the same way and with the same ease.
Developing a positive attitude toward both self and work, finding escape

routes when problems arise, and establishing good writing habits can replace former misconceptions. Writing also requires becoming informed about the subjects our writing will address. The next chapter on reading critically suggests ways to sharpen reading and critical thinking skills. With these skills more firmly in place, both your research using secondary sources—reference tools, books, and journal and magazine articles—and your writing will take a positive direction.

■ TAKING CONTROL OVER YOUR WRITING EXERCISES

1. List the most common reasons you write. For each reason rate the writing difficulty between 1 (very easy) and 5 (very hard). List three causes of your response. Looking over your responses write a brief paragraph explaining what about writing is easy for you and what makes it difficult.

2. You have been asked to write a five-page essay for this class. Your instructor has given no guidelines except the topic—why you are attending college. Imagine yourself writing this assignment successfully. Write a brief description of your writing fantasy—what you write, what happens when you write, what difficulties you encounter, how classmates respond, the teacher's response. When you read it over, how realistic is your fantasy? What misconceptions does it contain?

3. List the positive experiences you have had writing. How have these contributed to your attitude about writing?

4. List your negative writing experiences. How have these contributed to your attitude about writing? Do you have more positive or negative experiences?

5. Have you encountered writer's block? Write a description of what happened, how you felt, and how you overcame it.

6. Buy a book or notebook or set up a computer file with your word processing program to use as a journal. Find something comfortable for you. Set aside time each day for a week to write at least one page. Try writing by:

   • recording a new idea you learned reading or in class, and explain why it is important and what it means to your understanding of the subject
   • explaining a personal religious or political belief
   • describing a special place you remember
   • recording observations about your current physical surroundings
   • recording sensory details about an experience
   • examining an emotion like anger, satisfaction, fear

7. During the first week you keep your journal, investigate your writing comfort. Keep a log recording the writing location, the instrument, the time of day, and your feelings about these. Based on this log, write a short paragraph describing your best writing time and place. Explain why your writing went best there. ■

Reading Critically

2

A close link exists between writing and reading; reading serves as a writer's resource at every stage of the writing process. Reading suggests questions that identify problems for writing and provides information before you write. As you plan, write, and revise, seeing how other writers choose their purposes and shape their writing can suggest problem solving and writing strategies. Also, when you write book reviews, reviews of scientific literature, and critical analyses, the books and articles you read become themselves the subject of your writing. Considering these uses writers make of reading, we will briefly consider here some ways to sharpen your critical reading skills and draw upon your reading for writing.

READING FOR LITERAL MEANING

Written language uses a system of symbols (letters, spaces, punctuation marks) to represent words which in turn represent objects, events, relationships, and actions. When, as children, we learn to read, we learn to manipulate the code; we learn to move rapidly from symbol to concept and back to symbol. Our reading ability increases as we store more and more equivalencies in our memory. A child learns early that r-o-s-e equals a sweet scented flower. Later she learns that a symbol's position in relation to other symbols—its context—also affects meaning. Following a noun or pronoun, r-o-s-e now signals that the action *to rise* happened in the past. While children labor to learn this system of symbols, patterns, and relationships, adults use the system automatically. They assign meaning based on their knowledge of language, reading until a new word or unfamiliar context appears. The unfamiliar sends the reader to the dictionary to expand the code. Reading at this level resembles translation or transliteration, but does not really involve a significant level of comprehension or meaning-making. We truly understand what we read when we integrate it with what we already know through a hierarchical reading that recognizes important generalizations, significant facts and conclusions, and supporting detail.

IDENTIFYING IMPORTANT IDEAS

Using a dictionary to recognize those meanings that the contexts of words do not clarify is only a first step to becoming an effective reader. The second step is to move from reading words and sentences for equivalent meanings to identifying important ideas and distinguishing them from less important ones. Doing this requires you to be an active reader, one who pauses occasionally to question and evaluate as you read. Understanding those structural conventions writing uses (discussed in detail in Chapter 4) can suggest a way to read for important ideas. Most writing uses paragraphs to signal topic shifts. Further, good paragraphs contain both general and specific sentences, with the specific sentences offering comments on the more general ones. We often identify the most general sentence in a paragraph as the "topic" sentence. The remaining sentences "develop" or explain the idea introduced by the topic sentence. Taking a cue from a book or article's title, an active reader looks first for the general sentence (or sentences) which focuses the topic and makes a statement about the topic and then for the specific detail which fulfills the general statement's commitment. The active reader mentally restates the generalization and support in one or two summary sentences. Developing the habit of making mental sentence summaries especially helps when your reading is for a paper or an exam. (In this situation write the summaries in margins or notebooks.)

The paragraph below from a chapter entitled "The Dynamo and the Virgin (1900)" in a great American historian's autobiography, *The Education of Henry Adams,* and the comments following, illustrate using structural cues for active reading. If you were reading this in its original context, you would already know that Adams had earlier introduced the scientist Langley as Adams's own guide to the technological displays at the 1889 Paris exposition, an early world's fair that celebrated new technologies. You would also recognize that when Adams refers to the *scholar, he,* and *Adams,* he is referring to himself in the third person voice.

> <u>Then he [Langley] showed his scholar the great hall of dynamos</u> [electric generators], and explained how little he knew about electricity or force of any kind, even of his own special sun, which spouted heat in inconceivable volume, but which, as far as he knew, might spout less or more, at anytime, for all the certainty he felt in it. To him, the dynamo itself was but an ingenious channel for conveying somewhere the heat latent in a few tons of poor coal hidden in a dirty engine-house carefully kept out of sight; <u>but to Adams the dynamo became a symbol of infinity</u>. As he grew accustomed to the great gallery of machines, he began to feel the forty-foot dynamos as a moral force, much as the early Christians felt the Cross. The planet itself seemed less impressive, in its old-fashioned, deliberate, annual or daily revolution, than this huge wheel, revolving within arm's length at some vertiginous [dizzying] speed, and barely murmuring—scarcely humming an audible warning to stand a hair's-breadth further for respect of power—while it would not wake the baby lying close against its frame. Be-

fore the end, one began to pray to it; inherited instinct taught the natural expression of man before silent and infinite force. <u>Among the thousand
symbols of ultimate energy, the dynamo was not so human as some, but it
was the most expressive.</u>

Formulating a Summary Statement

In the preceding passage the underlined sentences, the most general, establish the topic *dynamos*, and comment that they are, for Adams, symbols of
ultimate energy:

- *Then he [Langley] showed his scholar the great hall of dynamos. . .*
- *. . . but to Adams the dynamo became a symbol of infinity.*
- *Among the thousand symbols of ultimate energy, the dynamo was
  not so human as some, but it was the most expressive.*

Other sentences offer details about the dynamo, and the reverence it evokes:

- *. . . forty-foot dynamos as a moral force. . .*
- *. . . force such as the early Christians felt the Cross.*
- *. . . revolving within arm's length at some vertiginous [dizzying]
  speed, and barely murmuring. . .*
- *The planet itself seemed less impressive. . .*

Combining specific detail with general statements gives the summary
sentence:

> The forty-foot dynamos, revolving silently at dizzying speeds—more im-
> pressive than the earth—for Adams became a symbol of moral force, as im-
> pressive as the Cross to early Christians.

Taken out of context, neither the paragraph nor its summary sentence
give Adams's chapter's full meaning. Since the dynamo is only half the
chapter's focus, as the chapter's title, "The Dynamo and the Virgin," indicates, an active reader would look for the other focus—the Virgin. The paragraph following contains part of the chapter's comparison. Adams here
responds to a trip to the imposing Gothic cathedral dedicated to the Virgin
Mary at Chartres, France. Read the paragraph actively, underlining its most
general sentences and noting the phrases and words offering specific details.

> All the steam in the world could not, like the Virgin, build Chartres. Yet in
> mechanics, whatever the mechanicians might think, both energies acted as
> interchangeable forces on man, and by action on man all known force may
> be measured. Indeed few men of science measured force in any other way.
> After once admitting that a straight line was the shortest distance between
> two points, no serious mathematician cared to deny anything that suited
> his convenience, and rejected no symbol, unproved or unprovable, that
> helped him to accomplish work. The symbol was force, as a compass-needle
> or a triangle was force, as the mechanist might prove by losing it, and noth-

ing could be gained by ignoring their value. Symbol or energy, the Virgin had acted as the greatest force the Western world ever felt, and had drawn man's activities to herself more strongly than any other power, natural or supernatural, had ever done; the historian's business was to follow the track of the energy; to find where it came from and where it went to; its complex source and shifting channels; its values, equivalents, conversions. It could scarcely be more complex than radium; it could hardly be deflected, diverted, polarized, absorbed more perplexingly than other radiant matter. Adams knew nothing about any of them, but as a mathematical problem of influence on human progress, though all were occult [concealed], all reacted on his mind, and he rather inclined to think the
Virgin easiest to handle.

Although a difficult passage, particularly taken out of the entire chapter's context, a summary of it should look something like this.

With their energies hidden, the forces exerted by the Virgin Mary and the dynamo on mankind were interchangeable. But since the Virgin and not the steam engine had built Chartres cathedral, the Virgin had acted as the greatest force the Western world ever felt. Considering their relative impact, then, on human progress, Adams would follow the track of the Virgin's energy.

The difficult decision a reader makes about this passage is what he does with the materials about mechanicians and mathematicians and about radiant energy and the Virgin's energy. Seeing the balance between general and specific sentences should help a reader recognize that mentioning the mathematician's equating symbol and force allows Adams to equate the Virgin as symbol with the Virgin as force. Further, by comparing the Virgin's energy with radiant energy, the historian admits his deficient knowledge of both and his need for study. While these are important parts of Adams's argument, this material is subordinate to the main idea—the great force exerted by the dynamo and the Virgin on western consciousness.

ACTIVE READING—THINKING READING

Uncovering denotative meanings and identifying main ideas and supporting detail takes active readers closer to a writer's meaning than our customary *fast read*. The written word, however, possesses the power to accomplish more than just express a writer's hobbyhorses; the written word is an encounter between a writer, her ideas and purposes, and an audience. Readers fully understand an article or a book when they know not just *what* it says, but how the writer presents herself and her ideas in relation to the audience, and what the writing seeks to accomplish. At this level a reader distinguishes between truth and distortion, information and propaganda, public policy and personal prejudice. Readers become thinkers. Becoming a thinking reader means learning to recognize audiences, writers' personas and purposes, and to evaluate arguments.

RECOGNIZING AUDIENCES

It is easier as a writer to choose an audience and identify its characteristics than it is for a reader to identify another writer's audience. A writer can determine his audience's likely education level, age, socioeconomic group, even sex, when he decides where the writing will be submitted or published. Once a writer identifies his audience, the writing's assumptions, arguments, language, and syntax seek that particular audience's interests and abilities. When we, as careful readers, look for a written work's intended audience, we can look to publication information—publishing house or kind of periodical—in the same way the author uses this information to identify his audience. Internal clues like *diction, tone, argumentative assumptions,* and *evidence* will also lead us to the intended audience.

Diction

Denotative Language and Audience

The words a writer selects relate directly to the audience. At the denotative level, an audience understands only language that relates to its knowledge and experience. Familiar language speaks to everyone. Specialized words from medicine, law, theology, and literary criticism speak to doctors, lawyers, theologians, and critics. Precise language that shuns emotional colorations speaks to logical and reasonable people, regardless of profession.

Connotative Language and Audience

Language is not denotative only; it possesses the capacity to mean beyond the symbolic equivalency to object, action, idea, and relationship. As coin of the realm, words pass from hand to hand, acquiring their own patina. Not just ten cents, dime says cheap, like dime candy. "Give me a dime" asks for a handout. Language's connotative meaning refers to the patina, the social meaning words acquire through use. At the connotative level, language evokes the audience's emotional associations. When a writer uses highly connotative language, he appeals more to his audience's emotion than to its reason.

We can see the impact of connotative language in today's highly volatile and emotional abortion controversy. According to the *Oxford English Dictionary,* when the word *abortion* entered the English language in the sixteenth century it meant any premature delivery of a child. The word's use soon extended beyond the domestic arena to refer to anything "born before its time." In the seventeenth century the word's use shifted to the "imperfect offspring of an untimely birth." Since medicine and midwivery were, at best, rough practices, children born early were often disfigured. As a consequence *abortion* came to mean something disfigured—a monstrosity. Today *abort* still denotes ending anything, particularly a pregnancy, prematurely. For some, *abort* still carries the connotation of disfigurement and monstrosity. Those who favor abortion, then, not only favor ending pregnancy, they favor monstrosity. With the weight of this negative connotative meaning, those who favor legal medical termination of pregnancy, refer to themselves as *pro-choice*. Even the anti-abortion groups avoid the word; they are not anti-*abortion* but *pro-life*.

Connotative language also reflects social, racial, political, or religious stereotypes. When a writer's language relies on these connotations, he expects his audience to share the beliefs at the stereotype's center. A writer referring to liberals as "bleeding hearts" or even "idealists" and conservatives as "hard-minded" communicates not only his own bias, but his expectation that the audience shares his bias.

Tone

Formal and Informal

Words combine with ideas to create the tone of a writing piece. Formal writing creates a distance between the writer and audience by removing most *I*'s and *you*'s, and by using elevated, specialized language. Formal tone suggests a serious, high-minded, probably well-educated audience. Informal tone introduces the personal. When a writer is informal the kinds of stories she relates, the way she presents herself, even the words she uses suggest audience attributes by indicating what she expects them to accept.

Irony, Sarcasm, and Humor

Few readers find identifying formality or informality as difficult as spotting irony, sarcasm, or humor. Irony and sarcasm point to discrepancies between what exists and what ought to be. Seeing the statement "students love exams," a casual reader might think, "Yes, I suppose they do." A more careful reader will look at the context and wonder if this is some extraordinary group of students, or if the writer is looking ironically at the educational system which employs as a central learning device so repellent a tactic. When a writer uses irony he anticipates a sophisticated audience of careful readers. Less subtle than irony, sarcasm (attacking something by saying the opposite) works for wider audiences. Humor reveals far more about audiences than irony and sarcasm because it plays on social group bias. When we laugh at something, we join with people who are of like minds to laugh at the other—the distorted, the unusual, or the exaggerated. When a reader can identify those who are aligned and those who are cast out in humor, the audience is clear.

Argumentative Assumptions

An *assumption* supposes that something is so evident that it requires no explanation or proof. Writing for an American magazine or newspaper, a writer assumes her audience knows the major events of American history, the Judeo-Christian tradition, and the popular culture produced by television, film, and advertising. She cannot assume that the audience shares political views, religious beliefs, or moral values. The assumptions a writer and audience share are apparent more in what goes unexplained than in the position being argued. Writing about abortion for a women's legal journal, a writer would not need to explain to lawyers the value of legal precedent; she could, however, argue that the right to choose abortion is just or unjust.

Evidence and Audience

The audience to which a writer speaks can be seen in the kind of evidence and examples the writer uses to advance his argument. A few years ago *Psychology Today* carried an article by a psychologist asserting that mass media eliminates the boundaries between children and adults because adults no longer share the exclusive store of privileged information about sex, violence, and suffering which was theirs in a reading culture. Writing for an educated, but not necessarily professional audience, he related a few anecdotes and personal observations, but most of his evidence came from historical documents, other social scientists' reported research, and experimental data—all appropriate for the magazine's usual readership.

This psychologist also spoke to a woman's group in a suburban community. Even though his central thesis remained the same as his article's, his evidence consisted of personal observations, anecdotes from television, and descriptions of mother–daughter look-alikes in supermarkets and shopping malls. The kind of evidence he selected for the women's group suggested an audience more interested in fashion, "Falcon Crest," and human interest than in difficult scientific or historical proof. The evidence a writer selects markedly illustrates what the writer believes about the audience.

RECOGNIZING A WRITER'S PERSONA

Diction, tone, assumptions, and evidence all point to a particular audience, but, as the discussion of these suggests, they also reveal the writer's relationship with the audience. The writer's presence in a written work is called a *persona*. One of the most important clues to persona can be found in the tone. In formal writing where the writer and audience are distant, persona is often unrecognizable. The writer, an expert on her topic, speaks as scientist, critic, economist, or historian. If the scientist, critic, economist, or historian is defending a position, the formal expert becomes the reasoned voice of expertise. The closer a writer moves to his audience, the clearer the persona becomes. Repudiating any pretence of objectivity, the persona in personal writing may reveal preferences, prejudices, concerns, and doubts. The writer relies on personal experiences and familiar anecdotes as evidence. For writing in between formal and personal, evidence also identifies the persona. Here, persona emerges from the balance a writer strikes between hard evidence (like statistics, reported data, or historical record) and more human anecdotes and observations. Also, what a writer explains and assumes reveals persona in the same way assumptions reveal audience.

To better understand the difficult idea of persona, look at the next two passages by Joan Didion.

> It was hard to surprise me in those years. It was hard to even get my attention. I was absorbed in my intellectualization, my obsessive-compulsive devices, my projection, my reaction-formation, my somatization, and in the transcript of the Ferguson trial.
> *The White Album*

> Some of us who live in arid parts of the world think about water with a reverence others might find excessive. The water I will draw tomorrow from my tap in Malibu is today crossing the Mojave Desert from the Colorado River, and I like to think about exactly where that water is. The water I will drink tonight in a restaurant in Hollywood is by now well down the Los Angeles Aqueduct from the Owens River, and I also think about exactly where that water is: I particularly like to imagine it as it cascades down the 45-degree stone steps that aerate Owens water after its airless passage through the mountain pipes and siphons.
> *"Holy Water," The White Album*

The *I* in both passages brings the writer into direct relationship with the audience, but the persona differs in each passage. The first passage states directly the writer's self-absorption. The evidence, a series of psychological buzzwords, reveals a neurotic persona hiding behind abstractions. This persona is remote from the reader. The second passage presents facts about Los Angeles water's sources. The detail with which the writer traces the water's movement combined with the author's intrusion "I like to think" shows a persona concerned about a local problem. She is a concerned citizen who lives in Malibu and dines at a Hollywood restaurant. Reading with sensitivity to language makes recognizing a persona far easier. Looking at Didion's diction in the first passage reveals a contrast between the direct statements' simple language and the abstract psychological jargon. This contrast shows a potentially reliable, honest persona distracted by over-intellectualization. In the second passage, the simple concrete language Didion uses to trace the water's path contrasts with words—*a reverence others might find excessive*—whose connotations establish the persona's emotional concern.

DETERMINING PURPOSE

Writers write to tell stories (narration), to recreate for their readers a sense impression of a person, place, or object (description), to explain an idea, an event, a procedure, or a phenomenon (exposition), or to argue a position. Since these are some of the purposes that shape writing, recognizing purposes through identifying description, narration, exposition, and argument is a fairly easy reading task discovered by asking, "*What* is this writing doing?" Recognizing thesis statements and identifying developmental strategies clarify *how* writing proceeds. But the thinking reader needs to know more than *how* writing progresses; this active reader's critical question begins with *why*.

To discover why something has been written, you need first to consider the circumstances surrounding its writing and then look more closely at the author in relation to his subject (point of view). A professor's history journal article on Thomas Jefferson would likely differ from a textbook study. Both would be expository, but the journal article should break new ground. The journal article would seek to change an accepted view; the textbook would advance widely accepted knowledge. A front page newspaper story on nuclear power abuses, although it might cause readers to question the safety of nuclear power, has as its primary purpose objectively informing the audience. An editorial page article can ask the community to vote against a new nuclear power plant after detailing the same abuses as the front page story. Both articles educate, but for different purposes. The description you write about yourself in a letter to a prospective employer seeks a different end than your bio-sketch for the management club newsletter. All these examples show that the place writing ends up—a professor's desk, a college newspaper, a letter-to-the-editor column, a professional journal, or a special interest magazine—gives the reader a clue about purpose.

Point of View and Purpose

After you find purposes related to the circumstances surrounding writing, look carefully at the writer in relation to his subject. A writer's point of view may be either objective or subjective. When a writer writes objectively, he removes himself from the written word and relates facts, events, and data. He assumes the reporter's pose and educational purpose, identifiable to a careful reader by concrete words uncolored by emotional bias. With a subjective point of view, a writer intrudes on his writing's factual content with interpretation, comments, and judgments. If the writer's reaction grows responsibly from his facts, and he argues logically, relying on concrete language appealing to a reader's intellect, such writing changes people's thinking and leads to action. Some subjective writing, however, appeals only to the reader's emotions through stereotypes, highly connotative language, and emotional situations. Such writing seeks to provoke action (or inaction) through positive feelings like compassion, moral virtue, and love and acceptance needs, but also through such negative ones as guilt, indignation, fear, or hatred. Thinking readers need to search subjective writing for emotional appeals to clearly see the writer's purpose.

ASSESSING ARGUMENT

Used loosely, argument refers to what a piece of writing says—its topic, main assertions, supporting evidence or development, and its organizational strategies. Used in this way *argument* refers to any writing. Assessing this kind of argument means making summary statements and describing evidence and organization. Being an active, thinking reader means also identifying formal argument strategies—the kinds used to advance a position on a topic at issue—and recognizing the argument's flaws. Chapter 5 on revising helps you recognize flawed arguments.

CRITICAL ANALYSIS

For a reader to keep in mind all writing's components as he reads may seem overwhelming. Active reading, like good writing, becomes easier the more you do it. At first, a checklist or set of questions might help you sharpen your critical reading. Some questions follow the essays in this book to guide you to important information and writing devices, but making your own questions will focus your critical abilities. Make sure that you have questions to help you identify:

> thesis
> main supporting points
> denotative and connotative language
> tone
> point of view
> assumptions
> audience
> persona
> purpose
> argumentative approach
> kind of evidence
> validity of evidence
> argument flaws

Once you have a checklist, reading critically to discover what a writer is really doing becomes a more focused task. Critical reading is essential for using secondary sources in your writing and developing your own research and writing skills.

■ READING CRITICALLY EXERCISES

1. Create a checklist of two questions for each of the above categories in the critical analysis section.

2. Using this checklist, select an essay from the anthology and write answers to your questions for this essay.

3. Write an essay analyzing the essay used for exercise 2. ■

A Short Writing Course I: Prewriting

Order and simplification are the first steps toward the mastery of a subject—the actual enemy is the unknown. *The Magic Mountain* Thomas Mann

Identifying writing activities and seeing these tasks as part of a patterned behavior—a process—simplifies not only mastering the subject of writing but mastering the discipline of writing regularly. While every writer does not work in precisely the same manner, enough similarities exist to allow us to identify a pattern of writing behaviors which include:

> Planning activities—identifying a writing problem, formulating research questions and working hypotheses, collecting information, focusing, devising a writing plan
> Drafting—writing introductions, developing paragraphs, using specific language, writing conclusions
> Revising and editing—formulating criteria for self-evaluation, making and using a revision checklist, revising, editing, and proofreading

Reading this list from top to bottom suggests that the writing process is a linear, consecutive one. For some writers it is, but for most, writing activities are recursive. This means that paragraphs may take shape simultaneously with focusing. A writer may move from preliminary plan to developing paragraphs and move back to enlarging the preliminary plan before writing an introduction. Revising occurs not just when a writer completes a draft but throughout writing. While writers may move back and forth between tasks and perform some tasks simultaneously, some preparation activities must precede writing just as some writing must precede revision. You will find it easier to make the writing process your own when you better understand the preparation, drafting, and revising activities described in the pages ahead.

WRITING PREPARATION

Writing preparation resembles the phase in legal procedure known as "discovery." During discovery a lawyer questions both her own and the opponent's clients to determine the case's facts, before she brings these facts into "evidence" by presenting them in front of judge and jury. During writing preparation, a writer identifies and focuses the problem his writing will consider, shapes the questions the paper will answer, discovers what he already knows about the subject, researches what he does not know, and formulates a writing plan. Unlike the discovery phase in law, information at this stage is tentative; any new information may significantly alter the writer's plan. Perhaps because information is so tentative at this stage, writing preparation poses difficulties for student writers. Breaking writing preparation into its smaller activities makes it easier.

IDENTIFYING PROBLEMS FOR WRITING

The Closed versus the Open Assignment

The Closed Assignment: Students frequently write in response to an assignment. In this sense the assignment is *closed*. Some professors will outline the type of approach you should take and specify the design of your reading or experiment. The easiest assignment defines the subject, relies on information presented in the course, and suggests an approach for organizing the writing. Here, the writer needs only to rely on discovery to determine what information has been presented in the course relevant to the assignment.

Other writing conforms to conventional patterns adopted in various disciplines. Laboratory reports, reviews of the literature, and book reviews for science and social science courses present research in defined formats. (Chapter 8 considers some of these formats in detail.) Here, while the writing task may be clearly defined (closed), you may still need to consider how to identify and define the problems your experiments and reading will explore, so you may want to consider the prewriting activities for *open* assignments. Learning how to inventory your own knowledge (often called *brainstorming*), evaluate prospective subjects, and develop questions to shape research and writing will prove as useful in these situations as they do for entirely open assignments.

Open Assignments: More often, instructors suggest a general area for consideration and allow students freedom to formulate their writing problem, discover information about the problem, and organize their writing approach. While such freedom may ultimately afford the best learning experience from an instructor's viewpoint, the student often responds that he has no idea what to write about. What this usually means is that he is unsure how to develop from a general assignment a good writing problem, one that is adequately focused and allows investigation. Below are suggestions for proceeding with an entirely open-ended assignment.

Recognizing What You Know—Brainstorming

If you identify with the student who thinks he has no idea what to write about, you can benefit by beginning with an inventory of what you know. An effective technique for discovering what you know on a subject is called BRAINSTORMING. To brainstorm, you list any words or phrases that come immediately to mind. You list rapidly without evaluating each suggestion's feasibility until you have between thirty and forty entries. Then you look back at the list for patterns and possibilities. Brainstorming allows the kind of free associations and word play that actually stimulates creative thinking on a subject. It is particularly effective when it is done with more than one person because a variety of individual interests and associations come into play.

Here is a brainstorm inventory developed by a student whose sociology instructor suggested that a study of toys could offer insight into American values. The instructor offered as guidelines only the general topic and the request that students use both their own observations and the library. Looking at the brainstorm inventory and the assessment following it shows how a good research and writing problem emerged.

A Brainstorm Inventory: Toys and American Values

- G.I. Joe—Barbie
- "He who has the most toys wins"
- games
- competition
- Monopoly
- poor craftsmanship
- self-destruct
- planned obsolescence
- bicycle
- roller skates
- media creates toys
- computer games
- new technology
- individualistic toys
- middle class and sex role stereotypes
- importance of play fantasy "The Hurried Child"
- too many toys
- my nephew at Christmas
- toys do everything
- dolls with beds, strollers, high chairs,
- wardrobes
- fads

- advertising on cartoon shows
- throw-away society
- toys imitate adult activities
- trucks, trains, planes
- toys teach expectations
- toys sold in toy department stores
- bears as fad
- dolls not to play with, but to collect

Assessing a Brainstorm Inventory

A brainstorm inventory may merely list aspects of a potentially interesting problem. Usually, though, groups and categories emerge, and the problem's dimensions take form. The writer reviewed the brainstorm list above looking for similarities and differences and discovered the following categories:

Kinds of Toys: G.I. Joe, Barbie, bicycles, roller skates, dolls with beds, strollers, high chairs, trucks, trains, planes, bears, dolls not to play with but to collect

Kinds of Games: Monopoly, computer games

Characteristics of Toys: poor craftsmanship, self-destruct, planned obsolescence, imitate media, reflect new technology, sex-role identified, too many toys, faddish, fads created by advertising

Characteristics of Society: "He who has the most toys wins," competitive, planned obsolescence, media oriented, technological, individualistic, faddish, throw-away society

What Toys Do: allow children to fantasize, overwhelm little children with abundance (my nephew at Christmas), replace a child's imagination by doing everything for him, allow kids to imitate adult activities, teach children about society's expectations (role models for male/female).

Miscellaneous: advertising on cartoon shows, toy department stores

Finding a Prospective Subject from Brainstorming

This brainstorming inventory and the student's analysis of it suggests several potential considerations for a study of toys and American values:

Board Games and America's Competitive Spirit
Throw-Away Toys in a Throw-Away World
Toys Shaping Stereotypical Sex-roles
Toys Reflecting a Consumer Society's Bad Habits
Toys Robbing Children of Imagination

Criteria for Good Subjects

To determine if a subject will work well for a research and writing assignment, the subject should meet four criteria:

- It should interest the writer.
- It should come within the scope of the instructor's suggested assignment.
- It should indicate a *specific* subject.
- It should be *manageable* within the assignment's allotted time and length.

Looking at the subjects developed from the brainstorm inventory, one person's interests might lead him to consider either sex-role stereotyping, consumerism, or imagination. On reconsidering the instructor's assignment—the relationship between toys and American values—however, only one subject, board games and America's competitive spirit, truly meets the assignment's original limits. If he emphasized *American* consumerism and, quite probably, *American* male and female roles, then he would be looking at issues relating to the assignment's original guidelines. Finally, since imagination extends beyond America, a study of toys and imagination extends beyond the assignment's original limits.

Concern for specificity poses the greatest problem. None of the issues is truly specific, although board games comes the closest. Looking back to the original inventory, we find specifics—Barbie, G.I. Joe, Monopoly, bicycles, roller skates. When these specific words replace "toys," the issues become more focused:

- G.I. Joe and Barbie Related to Stereotyped Sex Roles
- Barbie and America's Consumer Society's Principal Bad Habit; Spending on Created Needs
- Today's Poorly Constructed Bicycles and Skates in Our Throw-Away World

When we revise subjects to meet the criteria of specificity, we usually ensure they will be more manageable. Specificity allows a writer to focus his study and direct research or reading to the problem's requirements. Locating information about specific dolls like Barbie or G.I. Joe is a more clearly defined task than locating information on toys generally. It is also easier to discover our own ideas and responses to a specific, concrete object—one with clearly identifiable characteristics—than it is to a general category. More often than not, when preparing to write on a specific subject, so much information emerges that a writer may select from the information to limit the topic to meet particularly stringent length and time limits.

Identifying Problems Through Library Browsing

We have traced a research and writing problem's development beginning with brainstorming, through categorizing, to identifying effective writing subjects. Brainstorming is only one way to do this. You might also want to draw upon ideas or experiences that interested you enough to include them in your journal, browse through the library's periodical stacks and indexes, or review your assigned course readings. If you have used your journal to respond to important ideas or emotions, you have recorded several subjects that compel your interest at the same time they relate to course materials. Reading, assigned or not, can spur ideas for writing, particularly if you develop the habit of reading critically. (In Chapters 2 and 6 we look more closely at the relationship between reading and writing.) Sometimes merely browsing in a magazine or journal reminds us of issues that interested us once or that we wish to explore further.

While periodical browsing may limit us by our chosen magazine or issue's focus, browsing in an index may suggest the broadest range of potential writing subjects at the same time that it limits these subjects. Depending on whether a writer is more interested in business or psychology, looking at the major index in each field (*Business Periodicals Index* or *The Social Science Index*, respectively) could take the paper on toys in American life in very different directions.

Whatever approach a writer uses to identify a subject for study and writing, testing the prospective subject by the criteria of interest, original assignment specifications, specificity, and manageable limits will make the next steps in the writing process easier.

QUESTIONS TO SHAPE RESEARCH AND WRITING

Once you have defined the area you wish to investigate and write about, you need to refine the direction thinking, researching, and ultimately writing will take. Begin by making a list of statements that you believe to be true about your subject—your assumptions—and then reword these statements as questions. The list below shows some assumptions and the questions that grew out of them for the assigned study of toys and American values, specifically the relationship between dolls and sex-role stereotyping.

> **Assumption:** Sex-role stereotypes have supposedly changed in recent years. In the past men were expected to be strong and willing to stand up and fight; today men can be gentle and nurturing. Women can be assertive and career oriented.

Questions: What does research show about male attitudes toward acceptable identities? Are there differences between a generation ago and now? What does research show about women's attitudes? Are women more career oriented?

Assumption: If boys and girls really are learning less stereotypical lessons, then the toys they play with and the way they play with them will be similar.

Questions: Do boys and girls choose different toys? Do they have different play styles? Would a boy play differently with a G.I. Joe doll than would a girl? How about a Barbie?

Assumption: The G.I. Joe doll probably is not as popular as it was when male identity was more stereotyped.

Questions: What is G.I. Joe like today? How does he compare to the G.I. Joe of an earlier era? What do marketing and sales statistics show about the doll's popularity? Given a choice of toys, would today's child play with this doll? How does the style of play reflect male role identification?

Assumption: Barbie dolls today show girls as more career oriented and less centered on marriage and family.

Questions: What are Barbie dolls like today? What kinds of clothes and accessories do they have? How do these parallel images of women in media? How do these compare with Barbie dolls a generation ago?

These questions that emerge from the assumptions show clear directions a writer can take. Some of the questions can be answered by visiting a toy store, observing Barbie and G.I. Joe, taking notes, and then comparing these doll's imaginary "lives" with observations about real people's lives. Questions on dolls children choose and play styles could best be answered by creating and observing an experimental situation at a school or day care center. If this was what the sociology professor had in mind when she assigned the study, she would very likely give guidelines for effective experiment design. Finally answers to questions about sex roles and changes, or sales statistics, or changes in dolls will receive answers through research into secondary sources—books and periodicals. The time allotted, as well as the assignment's expectations, will designate which questions can be answered and how "research" will proceed.

WORKING HYPOTHESES IN THE HUMANITIES AND THE SCIENCES

When you have decided what questions you want to answer and what resources you will employ to find these answers, you will want to begin collecting information. The most important place to begin is with an idea of where you want your investigation and writing to take you. This idea will take different forms depending on whether or not your research and writing is in the physical and social sciences or arts and humanities.

The Arts and Humanities

Studies in the arts and humanities investigate both creative accomplishments (creative writing, dance, music, or art) and human intellectual endeavors like philosophy and history. How human beings capture, express, or make coherent meaning unifies the arts and humanities. When we write about the arts and humanities we sometimes look at the creative objects and intellectual enterprises themselves and write to interpret or respond to them. Other times we consider the large body of commentary (criticism and interpretation) written by others. When we consider either creative compositions or works responding to them, a series of questions like those presented in the previous section open up our investigation. Frequently a conclusion or series of conclusions (a thesis or theses) emerges as we answer our initial questions. Sometimes the answers to the preliminary questions come in the form of new questions. The process of research in the arts and humanities itself often renegotiates the initial subject and questions. In short, a single working hypothesis may prove limiting.

The Physical and Social Sciences

Research in the physical and social sciences, on the other hand, seeks to establish a *verifiable* body of knowledge about natural phenomena and human behavior. Scientific verification proceeds by a widely accepted method *(the scientific method)* that:

1. Identifies a problem and asks a question or series of questions relating to the problem
2. Formulates an explanation to answer the question and "explain" the problem (a working hypothesis)
3. Collects data, usually through carefully designed and controlled experiments to *test* (or prove) the hypothesis
4. Rejects or accepts the hypothesis, depending on the data

Both generally held scientific theories and individual researcher's knowledge direct the kinds of questions and potential explanations.

If you are researching and writing for science and social sciences courses, you will need a working hypothesis to give you a clear statement of what you expect your research, either from carefully designed experiments (primary research) or from published materials (secondary sources), to "verify."

For example, you are prepared to design an experiment to see how boys and girls choose between and play with Barbie and G.I. Joe. It will not be enough to go in with the question of how their play differs. Instead, you look back to your assumptions, which, in this case, hold that there will be cross-over in the dolls each sex selects, and that play styles will also cross over. The assumptions preceding your questions will become the hypotheses you are testing. Sometimes you will recognize that subsequent questions have redefined your earlier hypotheses—this is fine too. The important thing is to have a statement or statements you are seeking to confirm or disprove—to test. Working in an experimental setting makes it somewhat easier to be objective and to truly test a hypothesis. But this objectivity needs to carry over to research of secondary sources as well—you will need to look at literature that challenges your expectations about changing sex roles as well as the literature that supports your position.

COLLECTING INFORMATION

Primary Sources

Information can be obtained from many sources. Besides a well-designed experiment, first-hand observations, interviews, lectures, and questionnaires are some of the *primary sources* you can use to gain information. In these situations you are the primary investigator—the person who learns first-hand about your subject. As a writer engages with a primary source, the writer observes, questions, and records responses as objectively as possible. Primary sources include:

- a writer's personal experience of an event, a place, a person, or an object
- an interview with another person
- an interview with several people, often in questionnaire form
- a controlled event or experiment

Just as the scientific experiment must be carefully designed, pre-planned, clearly articulated questions get the best possible responses in interviews and questionnaires. If you plan to obtain information from primary sources, you will need to learn special skills for designing experiments, interviewing, and making questionnaires. Physical and social science courses teach experiment design as an important part of the laboratory curriculum. If your primary research is more informal, your library will have excellent guides to designing and administering questionnaires and interviewing. Minimally, the journalists' questions—who, what, where, when, why, and how—can uncover valuable information, but if these are not part of a script prepared with the special expertise of the person you are interviewing in mind, you will waste valuable time and good will.

Secondary sources

If you wish instead to learn what other people have said about your subject, you consult books, articles, and computer data bases—*secondary sources.* Secondary research takes us to other writers' work where they report their observations, investigative results, opinions, and conclusions. While we casually engage in secondary research each time we read the morning newspaper or pick up a magazine, secondary research best finds its home in a library, with such research tools as the card or computer catalogue, subject bibliographies (reference books that list other books and journal articles by subject matter), newspaper and periodical indexes (comprehensive lists of periodical articles published in a given year in either a subject area or a single publication), and the librarians' invaluable ability to direct the research process. Chapter 6 contains more detailed information on accessing your library's resources, taking good reading notes, and using secondary sources in your writing.

Some secondary information not usually stored in libraries is available from government offices, pamphlets published by community service agencies, and special interest group newsletters. Increasingly computer data banks contain information available either to us directly through subscription and modems or indirectly through information-search services at our schools' libraries and computer centers. In our media-intense society, television, film, radio, and video may also prove to be valuable resources.

From the working hypothesis and questions you wish to collect information about, make a specific list of the resources you intend to use. Once you have a clear picture of the sources you intend to use, make a research plan.

Making a Research Plan

The most common research problem, particularly when using secondary sources, is having too much rather than too little information. A good plan can direct the writer through the research maze to the relevant information. A workable plan contains:

  a working hypothesis or governing idea
  a list of potential resources, with questions each resource should
    answer
  a list of alternate words to identify related topics to use for searching in

indexes, catalogues, and data banks (Use your library's copy of the *Library of Congress Subject Headings* to compile this.)
three or four questions that the research will seek to answer

A research plan using personal observation and library resources for the relationship between G.I. Joe and Barbie and sexual stereotyping might look something like this:

Hypothesis: The stereotypical sex roles children learn from Barbie and G.I. Joe have remained constant over the last generation.

Resources: Mattel catalogue, toy stores, published studies on sex-role identification, popular magazine articles on G.I. Joe and Barbie, statistics on dolls' sales since 1950

Related Search Topics: toys and sex-role development, Mattel toy manufacturer, dolls and girls' sex identification, war toys

Questions: • How do these dolls look? What accessories?
• When was G.I. Joe reintroduced in the toy market?
• What have been the sales for Barbie? for G.I. Joe?
• How has Barbie (Joe) changed in recent years?
• How have feminists responded to Barbie? to Joe?

A writer familiar with the library would also list indexes where he would expect to find articles on his subject. A topic as narrow as Barbie would probably not appear in a card or computer catalogue. Articles on sex roles would appear in both *The Social Science Index* and *The Readers' Guide to Periodic Literature,* and articles on business in *The Business Periodicals' Index* and *The Wall Street Journal Index.* Armed with such a plan, a writer can quickly make his way forward to finding information.

FOCUSING

As we read, selecting some information and discarding some, our final essay takes shape. Usually by the time research has given substance to our writing problem, a focus or plan for the written work has emerged. If not, some focusing activities should help.

Sometimes the information a writer collects does not conform to the research plan or the working hypothesis. Here the writer must review the collected information. In the same way he looked at the original brainstorm inventory or the earlier assumptions and questions, the writer must analyze his research. How does the information relate to the working hypothesis? To the research questions? Are new questions necessary? Does the hypothesis require restatement? What information is in agreement? What differences exist? What pieces of information contradict each other? What categories emerge? What patterns appear? What relationships exist? How are causes and effects related? What information should be kept; what is irrelevant? Despite the time involved in research, writers need to be willing to discard information that only marginally applies to the problem. Sometimes this may mean going back to find more information on what originally appeared to be an insignificant aspect of the subject.

Using a Summary Statement

Sometimes formulating a summary statement helps focus collected information. Employing a simple formula can help. To focus, a writer needs to decide precisely what he thinks about his subject, and how the collected information relates to that informed opinion. The formula, "I believe . . . because . . ." can help. Often our knowledge and judgments are so complex that this summary statement can seem cumbersome. Formulating a summary statement, however, requires the writer to make a conclusion from all her thinking and reading, and then select from the collected information the ideas important enough to finish this statement. For example, the student working on Barbie might decide that the doll teaches girls superficial values. This generalization lends little direction to an essay. If, however, she tries, "I believe Barbie teaches superficial values because. . . ," she must formulate reasons that will focus her writing.

> I believe Barbie teaches girls superficial values because her clothing and accessories indicate achievement in terms of physical beauty, career accomplishments through clothing changes, and success through consumer spending.

The summary statement's "I believe" should not find its way into a finished paper, but it provides a starting point.

Thesis Statements

While a working hypothesis that receives confirmation through research may become a paper's thesis, sometimes our abundant and occasionally contradictory information may leave us without a sense of where our writing will go. Some writers need to take time here to formulate an effective thesis statement, even if they will change it later. A thesis statement helps us refocus our thinking and gives our writing a plan. A good thesis statement draws directly on a good writing subject by being specific and imposing limits. A thesis statement also offers comment on the subject. To do this it takes the form of a sentence which offers a comment (a predicate) to the topic (subject). Look at these subjects for essays:

> religious opposition to genetic engineering
> unlawful sports wagering in the NCAA
> the Gramm-Rudman Act
> Barbie, the ultimate consumer

Each is fairly specific, although "genetic engineering" encompasses several different procedures. Two topics, the first and last, impose limits. The first will consider only religious opposition to genetic engineering; the last will consider only Barbie as consumer. But none of these makes a statement *about* the subject. Look what happens when we increase specificity, add further limits, and offer comments.

> Despite its potential for curing genetic disorders, some conservative Protestant groups oppose genetic engineering because they fear man is taking God's creative power into his own hands.
>
> To combat the team dishonesty that college football and basketball betting encourages, the NCAA has recently adopted a stiff set of regulations and penalties which it hopes will deter future collegiate offenders.
>
> The Gramm-Rudman Act offers better hope for eliminating the United States federal deficit than either raising taxes or asking Congress to cut popular programs.
>
> Barbie with all her clothes and accessories teaches little girls that a woman's most important role in American society is being a consumer.

These revised thesis statements focus the prospective paper by:

• stating a specific subject
• limiting the discussion to the study's most relevant evidence
• commenting on the subject

Additionally, these refined thesis statements indicate each paper's controlling approach. The first statement on genetic engineering suggests that the writer would first admit to genetic engineering's potential for curing genetic disorders before discussing conservative Protestant groups' religious reservations. The second will set out the NCAA regulations and penalties and suggest their effect on college football and basketball betting. The third will compare and contrast the relative effects of Gramm-Rudman, increased taxation, and Congressional program cutting on the federal deficit. The last will explain how Barbie teaches girls to be consumers. More than merely focusing a subject, formulating a good thesis statement can take a writer well into the next stage in the writing process—making a writing plan.

ENVISIONING WRITING PURPOSES

Perhaps the most important aspect of planning writing involves shaping a picture of to whom our writing speaks and what our writing seeks to achieve in relation to that audience. Traditionally, writing studies have categorized all written discourse according to its ultimate purposes. Writing whose goal is storytelling is narrative. Expository prose educates through explanation. Argument uses formal logic, inductive and deductive, to objectively convince a reader of the reasonableness of the author's position. Persuasion, like argument, seeks to advance the author's position, but may instead select evidence and language to touch the reader's personal sensibilities as well as his reason.

These traditional categories direct our writing to the degree that they help us think about the larger constraints. Are we going to communicate with our audience by telling a story—ours or an acquaintance's? If so, we will need to attend to the details of event and conversation, and we will need a clear sense of what we want this "story" to communicate to our audience. Narration will require our attention to sequence and descriptive detail. If, on the other hand, we have a body of data amassed through either experimentation or reading, and we need to explain its significance to an audience, narration may not prove too useful. Instead, knowing that we wish to clarify information indicates that our task involves imposing some order for our readers, of showing them how the special knowledge we are examining relates to what they already know. If part of our explanation involves "proving" a particular conclusion, we will need to attend not only to the shape or order we impose on our knowledge through definition, analysis, or analogy, but also to our audience's expectations of logical and reasonable argument strategies. If the audience's expectations do not limit our attempts to prove our conclusions through objective logic, we may consider their particular dispositions and interests and select the evidence and language that will win them over to our point of view.

Audiences and Purposes

While these traditional writing categories afford only a very general overview of the purposes we need to envision when we write, they point to the important relationship between purpose and audience. Unless a writer has a clear audience in mind, she has considerable difficulty knowing exactly what she wants her writing to achieve—what its purpose is. If, for example, you are writing for yourself to clarify an idea, the writing can be cryptic; you can leave out steps in logic or even make up words. If you are writing to explain your idea to someone else, you will need to attend carefully to the explanation and the shape it takes. If your roommate vehemently opposes abortion for religious reasons, you may move from argumentative or explanatory to persuasive writing when you write an editorial on abortion laws for your student newspaper whose audience may include other students who share your roommate's views.

WRITING FOR ACADEMIC AUDIENCES

Some of the writing you do during college will certainly be for friends, parents, or a community audience, but you probably envision most of your writing efforts directed to your instructors—for the purpose of satisfying course requirements. Discussing audience and purpose, then, must seem moot. We would like to suggest that your audiences and purposes are not as limited as they seem. The student essays included in this anthology show this. First of all, that you are reading the writing of other students here draws attention to the fact that students are part of the academic learning community. Students certainly learn from professors' lectures and textbooks, but they also learn from each other just as professors learn from their colleagues through talks at conferences and meetings and their published writings. The essays in this anthology share with you not only the ideas other students wrestle with in their academic experiences, but also the approaches other students have developed for writing about these ideas. While you may not see yourself writing for fellow students, and probably not for publication, your research papers and lab reports frequently may become part of your fellow students' learning experiences by being shared in classrooms, or read at noon seminars, or, increasingly, included in books and periodicals that publish student writing.

Even if you envision yourself writing for fellow students, you probably still feel that your instructors are your primary audience. While some approaches for teaching and some classroom environments may diminish this, you are largely right. Professors read student writing and use it as one means of evaluating student performance, but evaluation is only one motive for assigning written work. If you understand some of the other reasons we, as college professors, ask our students to write, you may find writing for classes has purposes other than evaluating performance.

We ask students to write papers and exams for these purposes:

- To learn information and ideas
- To engage in discussion about information and ideas
- To share information and ideas with other students and faculty
- To give us some measure of your understanding of information and ideas
- To learn and use "professional" writing conventions

Sometimes we give a particular assignment which meets all of these purposes; more often an assignment overlaps one or two purposes. For clarity's sake, we will consider them independently here.

Writing to Learn Within Academia

The first three reasons indicate writing's most important place in the academic curriculum—as a means of learning. Many of us can effectively memorize a formula for physics or chemistry, or a set of names and dates for history, but we also know that we as easily forget the formulas, names and dates if we do not somehow use the formula or fit the names and dates into a pattern of significance. When we write about information not only do we better remember it, but we give information a context and a meaning. When we "discuss" information and ideas, we bring our intellectual capabilities and knowledge to bear on the information and ideas of others and thereby bring them into our sphere of knowledge. When we write these "discussions," we not only give our ideas a place in time, a physical record, but the act of writing, of giving form to our ideas, forces us to work out our own relationship with what we are learning. Furthermore, when we do this with the knowledge that we are writing for others, our peers and professors, we feel a stronger sense of accountability. We ask ourselves if what we say conforms to the standards of understanding, clarity, and truth set by our learning community.

In short, professors ask students to write to learn not just information but to learn the relationship between that information, themselves, and their community. Many essays in each of the broader discipline categories included in this book reflect students exploring these relationships. In "Mathematics: A Two-Way Mirror," Christine Guerrera explores the implications of mathematical problem-solving strategies for understanding the relationship of mathematics and reality. Susan Walton applies a personality theory she studied in her psychology class to Thomas Merton, the American religious writer and poet, by studying his autobiography in "Thomas Merton's Long Climb to Freedom." The paper, "The Hollow Men of Eliot's Time," which shows how Eliot's poem, "The Hollow Men," both reflects Eliot's civilization and speaks to our own, is only part of a learning project where Audrey Peake, along with three other class members, studied Eliot's historic and literary contexts and then taught their classmates about the poet's importance.

Writing with a Professional Voice

While we professors most often assign writing to engage students in learning, we also ask students to write to learn a discipline's professional writing conventions. From their medieval beginnings, colleges and universities have engaged in discovering, preserving, transmitting, and reappraising knowledge. Throughout history writing has been central to this activity. The academic disciplines have developed conventions for written discourse, which, though they change as knowledge and discovery methods change, give some order to transmitting and preserving learning. When students write papers for courses within an academic discipline, they learn the discourse conventions, partly to enable them to move from writing for one professor's class to another's with some ease, and partly to learn how to communicate if they choose finally to become professional scientists, historians, psychologists, business people, and community leaders. Certain kinds of writing may indeed stay inside academic walls, but professionals and community volunteers across the "working world" write reviews, summaries, personnel evaluations, and formal reports.

Several essays in each of the anthology chapters show students using their discipline's discourse conventions. In both the physical and social sciences scientific writing reviews scientific literature. Among the essays that employ this convention are June M. Fahrmann's, "Maternal Smoking" and Cheryl Bromgard's "Dual Career Marriages." Craig Hartman *("Chaos")* and Mary Jimenez *("The Master of the Game")* review books as they would for a magazine or scholarly journal, just as Scott Mersch ("Edward F. Beale: Conflict of Interest in California Indian Policy") and Karim Manassa ("Joe Crail: On the Dam Bandwagon") write using style and publishing conventions for historians. These are only a few examples of this book's many essays where students write quite effectively for a "professional" audience.

Writing for Evaluation

Frequently professors ask students to write papers or exams, particularly exams, simply to show their comprehension of course subject matter. In these instances students address specific questions and show how completely and clearly they understand information they have read or heard in lectures. Sometimes students see essay exams as a subjective measure of their knowledge in opposition to "objective" measures like multiple choice, true–false, or short answer exams. If exams like this ask for a subjective evaluation, the instructor usually expects this to be tied to reasons and facts—to information that can be objectively evaluated. The audience here is usually only the instructor, and the writing's purpose is for the student to convey his mastery of material in relation to the question. A few essays here, Faun Ryser's "Idealism and Materialism," Karen Hyman's and Sarah Hanna's essays on Samuel Johnson's *Rasselas*, and Patty Masters's "Simmel, Durkheim, and Marx" all respond to focused questions with specific information studied in a course.

Academic Audience and Purpose

Earlier we discussed how traditional writing categories relate to purposes. When we consider why college professors ask students to write, however, academic writing's purposes appear both narrower than traditional categories and more varied. Most writing that students do in the academic environment either explains ideas and information or argues logically. On the other hand, this logical and informative writing is shaped by the expectations and needs of various disciplines and varied assignments. Students assuming their discipline's professional voices chronicle scientific discovery to lay groundwork for new experiments (reviews of scientific literature), recommend books to readers' specialized interests when they write for professional journals in their fields, or justify a course of medical or psychological treatment through a case history. Students writing for fellow students (and professors) share their individual insights informed by reading and research about defense strategies, tropical rainforests, genetic testing, advertising, and novels. Its anticipated audience, a discipline's conventions, the assignment, and the subject you write about will all give purpose and shape to your writing.

THE WRITTEN PLAN

Most writers find that they are best able to actually begin drafting when they have some written plan to keep the plan and order in front of them. This plan can be as elaborate as a detailed outline which contains the actual information in fragmentary form that will become sentences and paragraphs. Other writers need only cryptic notes that remind them of their working thesis, their intended purpose and audience, and where in their research and preparation notes the important information can be found. Whichever approach you find works best for you, make a plan, and recognize that the actual drafting may require you to change your initial plan. Like so many other parts of the writing process, planning is recursive; it is subject to revision and modification as writing takes shape.

Outlining

By college, most students have learned elaborate outlining systems. A formal outline requires the writer to analyze his subject, breaking it into topics, subtopics, major points, and minor points, arranged in a system of letters and numbers which looks like this:

        I. _____
            A. _____
                1. _____
                    a. _____
                    b. _____
                2. _____
                    a. _____
                    b. _____
            B. _____
        II. _____
            A. _____
                1. _____
                2. _____

Each outline constituent represents a different aspect of the subject and may be expressed as either a phrase or sentence. Outlines are a valuable planning tool because they force writers to organize and become specific.

A Simple Plan

Sometimes writers can become so concerned about outlining that they have difficulty moving from outlining to writing. In this case, using outlining principles in a simple plan may prove more useful. To do this, consider what outlining accomplishes. First, outlining breaks a subject into component parts, and second, it requires the writer to move from general topics to specific comments. An outline, however effective it proves in organizing information, may not actually suggest how a writer intends to approach his subject. A plan can do both. Here is a plan for a paper on preventing wagering on college sports.

Thesis: To combat the team dishonesty that college football and basketball betting encourages, the NCAA has recently adopted a stiff set of regulations and penalties which it hopes will deter future collegiate offenders.

I. Introduction: Give background to problem
Relate 1985 incident at Tulane
Give Justice Department statistics on
    college sports betting
State thesis
II. Explain the NCAA regulations
III. Explain penalties
IV. Implementation
NCAA institutions self monitor
Clarification of each school's standards of conduct through required policy statement
V. Anticipated positive effects
VI. Detrimental effects from NCAA policy's harshness
VII. Conclusion—weigh advantages against disadvantages and point out importance of integrity—use quotation from Tulane president

Like an outline, this plan breaks the subject into parts—the events leading to NCAA regulations, the regulations, implementation, analysis of effects, and an assessment of the NCAA action. The plan also suggests writing tasks—narrating Tulane events, explaining regulations and penalties, describing the implementation process, and analyzing and weighing positive and negative effects. Clearly, this plan does not have all the writer's information set out in detail. Instead, it makes almost cryptic reference to materials the writer has elsewhere (almost certainly in his research notes).

However a writer formulates his plan, experienced writers recognize that plans are tentative. As they write, new ideas and different approaches suggest themselves; what seemed important initially will yield to a new focus. The writing process's next stage—drafting—builds on all prewriting activities, but also may reintroduce them. At any point in the actual writing, you may find yourself revising your plan, brainstorming, reformulating questions and working hypotheses, or returning to the library for more information.

■ EXERCISES FOR PREPARING TO WRITE

1. Brainstorm on an event in your life that altered your thinking about some important social or political issue. Record every thought or word that comes to mind until you have at least thirty to forty entries.

2. Browse in this book's essay collection to find a topic that interests you. Brainstorm on this topic.

3. From brainstorm lists, identify at least three possible topics. For each topic state three assumptions. Then change these assumptions into questions for research and writing.

4. For one of the sets of assumption/questions, identify information sources and create a plan for gathering information on this topic.

5. Interview a person well informed about your topic. Identify why the person you will interview is an "expert" and what you expect the person to be able to tell you. Prepare a script of questions that relate the person's expertise to your work of research and writing questions before the interview. Be certain the questions are specific so that you obtain good detailed information.

6. Using the *Library of Congress Subjects* make a list of related topics to guide you in using indexes and bibliographies for your topic. Then using the card catalogue or an appropriate current periodical index for your topic, list at least ten possible sources. Check your library's periodical list or card catalogue to find if the articles are available.

7. Prepare a preliminary writing plan for your writing using outlining or a simple plan, and include a thesis statement. Write a brief statement about your audience, purpose, and organizational approach. ■

4

A Short Writing Course II: Producing A Written Draft

Attitudes adjusted, information collected, plan in hand, and strategies for overcoming writer's block reviewed, the only way to move toward a first draft is to write. Even though written pieces conventionally start with introductions, develop their purposes in the body and end with conclusions, writing need not proceed the same way. One writer begins with the part of the project that excites her most; other writers might begin with the section they anticipate as the most difficult. Wherever you begin, realize that what you are writing need not be perfect. Work as rapidly as you can, settling for less than the perfect expression, even leaving out words and phrases if they prove elusive. *The first draft needs to be written with the full intention of revising.*

However you work, the first draft may proceed more easily if you consider that writing consists of:

- making a commitment to the reader
                    and
- fulfilling that commitment

THE COMMITMENT

In the planning process, before beginning writing, a writer has decided what the writing should accomplish and what general pattern to use. The anticipated audience helps shape this decision. A reviewer recommending (or panning) a film or book writes for the specialized audience of the particular kind of film or book. The college professor writing for a professional journal writes for colleagues who share her specialized knowledge. A student writing a research paper writes for the students in the class, his colleagues, as well as the instructor. A good writer forms a clear picture of the particular audience, and then writes to engage its interest. In doing this he makes a commitment to these readers. But commitment to the reader is only part of the writer's commitment; the rest is to his subject, and to his purpose, which mediates between the subject and reader. The relationship looks something like this:

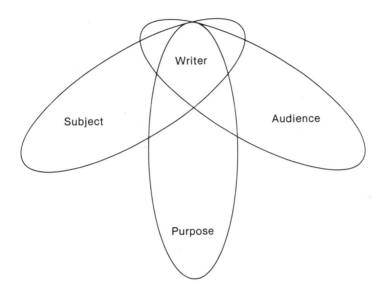

The writer commits to the reader to recreate the Battle of Gettysburg, to explain how fossil fuels destroy the ozone layer, or to draw Chartres Cathedral with words, but she also commits to asking the reader to relive the battle, to take political action for fossil fuel conservation, or to understand the powerful religious devotion that built Chartres. The beginning of a written piece—the introduction—engages the audience and offers the writer's promise. The remainder of the writing fulfills the commitment by presenting details.

INTRODUCTIONS

Engaging the Reader

Effective introductions draw readers into the subject. They can engage human curiosity by presenting astonishing statistics or significant, surprising facts. They can identify a problem by creating a social or political context, or by telling a story where the problem touched individual human lives. An introduction may engage a specialized audience, like muscle physiologists, by surveying the literature and then stating directly the study's significance. On the other hand, an introduction which does not consider audience may alienate readers. If, for example, the muscle physiologist writes about his specialty for *Discover* magazine's popular audience, surveying the literature might discourage their interest. In its concern for engaging a specialized audience, a good introduction brings the audience to the subject.

Introductions—The Writer's Promise

Besides engaging a specialized audience, an introduction offers the writer's promise to the reader, usually as a thesis statement. The thesis statement, which usually restates the working hypothesis, presents a general statement about the written piece's specific subject. Its comment on the paper's subject commits the writer to both the study's focus and to a position. Thus, a thesis statement indicates what the writer is going to say about the subject, without saying "this paper will discuss . . ." In its presentation of the writer's commitment to the reader regarding his subject, the thesis statement brings the subject to the audience.

Consider what commitments the following thesis statements make.

> *It is no exaggeration to state that 19th-century photographers ran as many risks in the dark as they did in the act of finding and taking pictures.*
> "Death in the Darkroom"—Bill Jay

This thesis commits the writer to discussing the dangers a photographer encountered in the darkroom developing film a century ago.

> *The majority of these people [the elderly facing loneliness and isolation] are not seen by a psychiatrist. It is for them that I am trying to outline the changes that have taken place in the last few decades, changes that are ultimately responsible for the increased fear of death, the rising number of emotional problems, and the greater need for understanding of and coping with the problems of death and dying.*
> "On Death and Dying"—Elisabeth Kübler-Ross

Here, Kübler-Ross not only identifies her subject, *changes*, she also commits to the writing task of analyzing how the changes affect the fear of death, rising emotional problems, and coping with death and dying. She also identifies her audience, the elderly, and suggests her purpose of helping her audience.

> *I suspect that each sport contains a fundamental myth which it elaborates for its fans, and that our pleasure in watching such games derives in part from belonging briefly to the mythical world which the game and its players bring to life. I am especially interested in baseball and football because they are so popular and so uniquely American; they began here and unlike basketball, they have not been widely exported. Thus, whatever can be said, mythically, about these games would seem to apply to our culture.*
> "Football Red and Baseball Green"—Murray Ross

The writer, here, commits to explaining the myths embodied in football and baseball, and then to identifying these myths with American cultural myths.

In these thesis statements the writers not only indicate their topic, but their comments make commitments about focus, purpose, approaches to writing, even audience. To do all this, Kübler-Ross and Ross use more than one sentence; Jay uses only one but makes a specific statement. The number of sentences is not as important as making a statement about the topic which indicates the direction the writing will go.

THE BODY—FULFILLING COMMITMENTS

A writer fulfills the introduction's commitments by presenting specific information about the introduction's generalization in a coherent, well-organized manner. She attends to her purpose and audiences and employs organizational strategies and develops her information with the purpose and audience clearly in mind. Writers can improve specificity in both language and paragraph structure. They can make this specific information accessible to the reader using one or many organizational patterns. We will look at some ways to make your writing more specific and give it order.

Specific Paragraphs

Paragraphs punctuate writing to let readers know that the writer is shifting focus. Conventions governing paragraphs are certainly familiar to college students. Even so, paragraph length sometimes proves a problem. Perhaps because we are so accustomed to seeing one-sentence newspaper paragraphs and other printed materials, typed or handwritten paragraphs of more than three or four sentences seem unwieldy. Consequently, student writers often conclude paragraphs without adequate development—adequate specificity.

Becoming aware of the relationship between general and specific sentences in a paragraph can help improve paragraph specificity. A well-developed paragraph usually has only one or two very general sentences; the rest of the sentences offer specific comment on these generalizations, and on each other. To better understand this, look at the following paragraph from Herbert J. Muller's essay "Education for the Future" which appeared in *The American Scholar.*

> Hence there is a wide field for courses on the future. Time and space do not permit a review of the many possibilities, but let us take a look at the already popular subject of the environmental or biological crisis, aggravated by the population explosion. Ecologists tell us that if current trends continue we are headed for disaster, conceivably a world that will become uninhabitable. Together with the possibility of a thermonuclear war, these trends are faced with such immediate threats as the increasing pollution and the urban crisis, the steady deterioration of the central cities in the sprawling metropolitan areas. And behind all these problems is the accepted national goal of indefinite economic growth, even though Americans already consume many times their proportionate share of the world's dwin-

dling natural resources. While one may doubt that such growth can continue indefinitely, neither business, government, nor the public is prepared to accept a program of national austerity, which scientists are insisting is necessary. Almost all economists have assumed that steady growth signifies a healthy economy; only of late have some begun to question it. I would welcome courses in economics for the future.

This paragraph offers specific considerations on future ecological projections to recommend a course on futurist economics. When we look at the relationship between sentences, the degree of specificity is more apparent. Look again at this paragraph arranged by increasing specificity. The most general sentences align at the left margin; each level of specificity is indented.

1) Hence there is a wide field for courses on the future.

2)   Time and space do not permit a review of the many possibilities, but let us take a look at the already popular subject of the environmental or biological crisis, aggravated by the population explosion.

3)   Ecologists tell us that if current trends continue we are headed for disaster, conceivably a world that will become uninhabitable.

4)   Together with the possibility of a thermonuclear war, these trends are faced with such immediate threats as the increasing pollution and the urban crisis, the steady deterioration of the central cities in the sprawling metropolitan areas.

5)   And behind all these problems is the accepted national goal of indefinite economic growth, even though Americans already consume many times their proportional share of the world's dwindling natural resources.

6)   While one may doubt that such growth can continue indefinitely, neither business, government, nor the public is prepared to accept a program of national austerity, which scientists are insisting is necessary.

6)   Almost all economists have assumed that steady growth signifies a healthy economy; only of late have some begun to question it.

1) I would welcome courses in economics of the future.

This paragraph begins and ends with very general topic statements on the desirability of college courses on the future. This particular paragraph is structured like a chain of paper clips with each sentence offering more specific information about the one before it until it gets to two responses to curtailing economic growth—one by business, government, and the public sector; one by economists. At this point the two views are equally specific although they contain different information.

Few writers would write a paragraph intending to structure it like a chain of paper clips. However, seeing that a well-developed paragraph contains sentences at as many as six levels (from very general to very specific) tells you that adding sentences that comment more specifically on previous sentences is a good way to develop an idea.

Specific Language

Specificity can be increased through the language as well as the paragraphs. Language communicates through a balance between abstract and concrete words and general and specific terms.

Abstract and Concrete Words

Abstract words refer to intellectual conceptions—ideas like love, political responsibility, or sexism.

Concrete language refers to something physically apprehensible.

- love
    - a passionate embrace
    - a statement like "I love you"
    - listening to another person's concerns
    - a sacrificial act as mundane as going to a film you do not care to see or as significant as risking your life to save another's

- political responsibility
    - registering to vote
    - reading voter information pamphlets
    - following political debates
    - contributing money to your cause
    - voting
    - writing letters to government officials

- sexism
    - hiring a man instead of a more qualified woman
    - awarding child custody to a mother less qualified than the father
    - expecting girls to become wives and mothers, boys to become scientists or corporate managers

Concrete language refers to an object, a person, or an act which can be intellectually understood but which can also be perceived by the senses—seen, heard, touched, even smelled or tasted.

General and Specific Words

General words may be either abstract or concrete, but they refer to broad categories—college students, colors, religious attitudes, intellectual disciplines. *Specific* words refer to individual cases, but degrees of specificity exist for words as they did for sentences. The examples below begin with general words and increase in specificity.

college students   UCLA students   UCLA undergraduate students   UCLA undergraduate history majors   students in UCLA's History 205

colored   pastel colored   pale sky blue, faded rose   sweet-butter yellow

religious attitudes   Judeo-Christian attitudes   Christian attitudes   Roman Catholic attitudes   Roman Catholic liberation theology in Central and South America

intellectual disciplines   science   natural science   biology   biochemistry   genetics   genetic engineering   recombinant DNA studies

Specific language communicates precisely. With it a writer can paint a vivid word picture for the reader. Without it, a writer can only hope that maybe, just maybe, the students, the colors, the religious viewpoints, or the intellectual disciplines the reader envisions are the same as the writer's intended ones.

Organizational Strategies

Usually when we are ready to write—we have collected information, envisioned our audience, and defined what we want our writing to accomplish—we face the task of imposing some kind of order on what we know. When we think of talk about an idea, we can come to it from many directions and move back and forth from one consideration to another. Either with ourselves or another, we engage in a kind of conversation where we can modify and clarify positions through questions and answers. When our readers read our finished texts, they require some kind of order to be able even to read our meanings. So while writing may function more like our thinking or conversations, where we move back and forth in our own text to refine and develop ideas in response to our questions and further answers, the text we ultimately produce does not have this freedom of recursiveness. When we write we need to give some thought to the kinds of ordering principles that enable our readers to best understand our meanings.

Selecting an Organizational Approach

Organizational patterns we use to order writing do not relate to writing alone. We constantly employ analysis, classification, definition, and comparison to think about our experiences. If your writing is responding to an assignment, the way the assignment has asked you to think about the problem often suggests an organizational approach. If the assignment is more open, the organization you impose on your writing is usually directed by how you are *already* thinking about a subject. Are you considering it in relation to similar knowledge (comparison or analogy)? Are you breaking it into its components (analysis)? Are you assigning it attributes (definition)? Below, we consider some common organizing principles to help you identify how you are thinking about your writing problem and to suggest alternatives you may not have considered.

Common Organizing Principles

Here are some of the most common ways to organize or order thinking and writing. When you write, you will often use several organizing principles in a paper. One approach may govern the writing's overall pattern while other strategies will order sections within the paper. For example, in a scientific report you are likely to use an overall *inductive* pattern with *chronological* organization to review relevant scientific literature and describe experiment design, *classification* to present results, and *analysis* to discuss the results.

Description

Description details the attributes of an event, a person, place, theory, or idea to create a dominant impression. These details, often identified by the strength of their sense impression, can be organized spatially, temporally, or analytically. While we would immediately assume the importance of descriptive writing for discussing art or literature, we need also to remember the important role description plays in scientific writing. In June Fahrman's essay included in the anthology section, "Maternal Smoking: Deleterious Effects on the Fetus," concise spatial and temporal description makes the distinction between placenta and fetus that underlies the experimental findings Fahrman reports:

> . . . less than one week after fertilization, two types of cells can be distinguished; the more rapidly proliferating cells forming a layer over the more slowly dividing cells. This structure is sphere-shaped and is called a blastocyst. A single layer of ectodermal cells, the primitive trophoblast, surrounds the sphere, except at one pole where the rapidly dividing cells have formed the inner cell mass. The inner cell mass composes the beginning of the embryo.

Classification

Classification forms groups based on similarity. It is an essential ordering mechanism employed by writers in every discipline. Scientists classify experimental results, just as psychologists classify behavior, or critics classify literary forms. Classification enables the writer to explain the individual as well as the class. By classifying Claude Monet as an Impressionist painter, and by describing both Monet and Impressionism, a writer can educate the reader about both the man and artistic style.

A good use of classification appears in the anthology's art and humanities section in "Shakespeare's Drag Queens." Here Kathy Silvey classifies some of Shakespeare's comic heroines who dress in men's clothing and identifies the androgynous quality of the class. She then shows how each heroine affects the themes of courtship and love in the individual plays.

Analysis

While classification groups items together, analysis breaks a single entity apart. Classification establishes kinds of music (jazz or classical) and musical forms (ballad or symphony); analysis studies the musical elements of Beethoven's *Ninth Symphony*. Classification may look at kinds of men or forms of bravery; analysis breaks a human into mind and body, and a body into skin, bone, blood, muscle, and nerve. Analysis can enumerate effects or examine events as the product of causes. It may proceed spatially (right to left, top to bottom, outward to inward, small to large) or temporally (first to last or end to beginning). A writer can also present the components of analysis in order of their importance. Analysis appears frequently as a shaping pattern for entire essays. For example, Scott Mersch analyzes Edward F. Beale's Indian policy in California in "Edward F. Beale: Conflict of Interest in California Indian Policy." It can also appear in special sections as when scientific reports include sections entitled "Data Analysis" or here where Brad Werner analyzes NATO in terms of hierarchy and function in "NATO and the SNF Debate":

> NATO's military structure is divided into specialty divisions which enable a smoother operation in its decision-making process. The highest organizational level in NATO is the North Atlantic Council. Comprised of representatives of each allied country, the Council oversees all aspects of the structure. NATO also possesses a Defense Planning Committee and a Nuclear Planning Group (NPG) for treatment of more specific military and nuclear planning issues. True military planning occurs on the level of the Military Committee, the section that advises the North Atlantic Council and the Defense Planning Committee as well as oversees the various strategic commands within the alliance.

Causal Analysis: One special type of analysis looks at cause and effect—particularly in science and history. A strong argument for causation relies on causes which are *necessary, sufficient,* and *contributory.* Look at the following statement about AIDS (Acquired Immune Deficiency Syndrome) and its causes:

> *Exposure to the AIDS virus through blood transfusion, intravenous drug use, or sexual contact causes AIDS.*

- The virus and the means of transmission are *necessary* for a person to contract AIDS.

- The virus and sexual contact are *sufficient* to cause AIDS.
- The virus and sexual contact or blood transfer alone *contribute* to AIDS.

Among the several essays in this anthology where you find students analyzing causal relationships are many that report scientific research including: "Fetal Alcohol Syndrome: The Effects of Ethanol on the Nervous System of the Fetus" (Maria LaPadula), "Tropical Rainforests" (Jeanne Trapani), and "Subliminal Psychodynamic Activation" (Sue di Carlo). Causal analysis also shapes studies in political science, history, and literature in "Gorbachev's Foreign Policy" (Lisa Gentile), "Joe Crail: On the Dam Bandwagon" (Karim Manassa), and "Of Johnson's *Rasselas*" (Sarah Hanna).

Comparison and Contrast
Comparison and contrast studies similarities and differences of two or more like entities to understand the things themselves or to explain something else. For example, we might better understand architect Frank Lloyd Wright's artistic achievement by comparing and contrasting his prairie style houses around Chicago with his Los Angeles Mayan style houses. Or by comparing and contrasting two patients' case histories, a psychiatrist might better understand the particular problems of each. Comparison and contrast proceeds by establishing categories and studying relationships within the categories. To compare and contrast architectural designs, for example, we might consider categories like floor plans, window placement, room sizes, internal ornamentation, external ornamentation, and materials. A writer could examine first one design in terms of these categories, and then the other, or proceed one category at a time, first one design, then the other.

Among the many student essays that use comparison and contrast are Michelle Skraba's "The Crowding Effect in Tadpoles," that looks at contradictory scientific theories, Janet LeRoux's "A Comparative Study of Community Among Public and Private School Teachers," and Laurie Loftus's "Valenzuela and Kafka: The Word 'Killer' and the Word Killer." Because comparison and contrast and comparative analysis appear so frequently in these student essays, you will find a more detailed discussion of it in Chapter 6.

Illustration
We often express what we think and write as generalizations—as the conclusions we reach from experience and observations. Illustration justifies those generalizations by offering the specific, concrete experiences, observations, and instances that go along with them. While it might be of considerable value to have the historian Bruce Catton assert that post Civil War Reconstruction would have been far less devastating for the American South if President Lincoln had lived, this assertion finds far more credibility when Catton describes Lincoln's peace plans that were cast aside by the retribution-seeking faction who assumed power on Lincoln's assassination.

Definition

Definition offers details about a particular term or phrase as a statement of equivalency. "A haiku is a Japanese verse form of three lines containing five, seven, and five syllables respectively." "A molecule is the smallest particle of a substance that retains the properties of the substance." Before Cheryl Bromgard can begin reporting the results of studies of two-career marriages in "Dual-Career Marriages: Roles, Attitudes, and Satisfaction," she defines the dual-career marriage:

> . . . as "one in which both partners pursue careers as well as family roles. Such careers . . . require commitment, have a developmental character and [involve jobs] from which personal rewards are derived." Dual-career marriages need to be distinguished from dual-employment marriages by the wife's academic preparation, motivation for working, and level of career commitment.

Definitions may appear brief, like the ones above, or they may be extended through examples, comparisons, or more extensive lists of attributes. Extended definitions thus build through other development strategies.

Analogy

Analogy identifies an unfamiliar concept, idea, event, or experience by comparing it with a known entity. We understand the unseen atom by analogizing it with the solar system. C. G. Jung, the great psychoanalyst, explained the relationship between the conscious and unconscious mind by using an analogy with land and sea: the sea of the unconscious flows and ebbs against the conscious shore. These examples illustrate that analogy as an organization strategy combines definition with comparison.

Two of the anthology's essays use analogy extensively. Randall Coppinger explains the narrator's complicated role in *The French Lieutenant's Woman* by analogizing him with God in "The Narrator as God in Fowles's *The French Lieutenant's Woman*." In "The Pizza Guy," a study of the influence of Plautus's play, *Menaechmi*, on Shakespeare's *Comedy of Errors*, Brendan Cole uses an analogy between the two plays and bread and pizza:

> Each of these baked goods has the same basic ingredients. For the bread you have flour, water, and salt, and for the pizza dough you have basically the same things but in different proportions. Now let us view the bread and the dough as the comic plot for the two authors. . . . Like the bread, nearly all of Plautus's comedy is based on the ingredients of the plot. . . . Although we see the crust of the pizza, it is easy to understand that crust alone does not make a good pizza. What Shakespeare has done is taken the older concept of bread and reformed and changed it to fit a style that is at the same time different but reminiscent of the older tradition. . . . Spices . . . enhance the pizza in much the same way Shakespeare uses character development, added plot structure, as well as the good old romantic twist to enhance his plays for the Elizabethan audiences.

Chronological Order

Chronology orders material according to time, and while this appears to be a straightforward kind of order (earliest to latest), we frequently combine chronological order with analysis. For example, when Maria LaPadula presents scientific research on the effects of alcohol ("Fetal Alcohol Syndrome"), she presents the earliest research first. She also shows causal relationships. In "Dance Photography" Eileen Coppola shows the development of approaches for photographing dance by working from the earliest to the most recent at the same time that she evaluates the effects of each approach. Similarly, many literary analyses move through a poem or a novel from beginning to end.

Logical Patterns—Induction and Deduction

Inductive arguments reach generalized conclusions from specific evidence. As an organizing strategy, induction presents specific evidence, usually categorized, followed by a generalized conclusion. We typically recognize this as the pattern of scientific argument. Many essays in both the Science and Social Science sections of the anthology employ an inductive organization, particularly those essays that review scientific literature or report original research such as Karen Snyder's "MPTP and Parkinson's Disease" and Nancy Dyer's case study, "Catherine."

Induction and Evidence

Using deductive patterns effectively means giving attention to the quality of the evidence presented. If the evidence consists of personal experience, personal observation, or expert testimony, the evidence source needs to be objective and reliable. Reliable evidence reflects *a representative sample* that is *adequately sized* and *random.*

A Representative Sample: A good study takes as its sample a representative population, or states directly that it is working with a limited population. For example, the University of Michigan frequently inventories freshman student attitudes on politics, sex, religion, and morals. If surveys were of only University of Michigan students, the sample would not be nationally or socioeconomically representative because the University of Michigan's student population is predominantly midwestern and middle-class.

An Adequate and Random Sample: If the study were confined to University of Michigan students, describing only University of Michigan freshman students' attitudes, the sample could still have problems. To be valid the findings must represent attitudes of fifteen percent of the students selected randomly. That is, the sample must be both large enough and wide enough. If fifteen percent of the freshman students were enrolled in History

101, the interviewer still would have a poor sample if he inventoried the attitudes of those students alone. Even though they would make up a large enough sample, the sample would not be random.

Supported Conclusions: Finally a sound inductive argument needs to be careful about its conclusions. They cannot overgeneralize from evidence, nor reflect bias.

Deductive Arguments and Logic

While induction proceeds from specific facts to a generalized conclusion, deduction moves from general premises to conclusions about specific instances. Entire essays are rarely organized deductively. Deduction, however, can order special kinds of knowledge and help a writer elicit his reader's rational responses. To do this it employs formal logic's syllogism to identify an individual instance with a general class.

The *Deductive Syllogism* contains:

THE MAJOR PREMISE, which identifies an individual characteristic with a general group,
All Americans possess constitutionally protected free speech.
A MINOR PREMISE, which identifies an individual with the general group or category,
David Brown is an American.
A CONCLUSION, which assigns the individual the group's attributes,
Therefore, David Brown possesses constitutionally protected free speech.
Stated symbolically,

$$A = B$$
$$\text{and} \qquad C = A$$
$$\text{therefore} \qquad C = B$$

where A is a general category, B is the category's attribute, and C is the individual instance.

Two criteria are used to evaluate whether a formal syllogism conforms to the standards of being "logical"—truth and validity. A statement which is true correlates positively with objective reality; it corresponds with what we know to be true. Validity relates to the syllogism's special place for each term in the syllogism. For a syllogism to be valid, the terms ("A," "B", and "C") and their places are not interchangeable. For example the syllogism,

All Americans (A) possess constitutionally protected free speech (B)
$(A = B)$
David Brown (C) possesses constitutionally protected free speech (B)
$(C = B)$

Therefore, David Brown (C) *is an American* (A)
$$(C = A)$$

cannot be valid, even though the statement "David Brown is an American" may or may not be true. (David Brown may possess protected free speech, but from another country.)

As long as a syllogism's terms remain in their places, the syllogism can also be expressed negatively.

$$
\begin{array}{lll}
\text{No} & A = B \\
& C = A \\
\text{therefore,} & C \neq B
\end{array}
$$

or as an if/then statement,

$$
\begin{array}{lll}
\text{If} & A = B \\
\text{and} \quad \text{if} & C = A \\
\text{then,} & C = B
\end{array}
$$

For deductive argument to succeed, the syllogism must be both valid and true. Just as the good writer must attend to the truth of the conclusions in inductive argument, she must be aware that deductive argument can proceed from false premises. We will look more closely at the problems writers encounter with logical patterns in the chapter on revising.

One essay in the anthology uses formal logic as a means of assessing a critical argument. McKeel Hagerty in "More or Less Reality: An Old Platonic Argument" carefully considers the logic Shakespearean critics use in their studies of *A Midsummer Night's Dream*. If something is either real or unreal, and both the play's forest world and Athens are real, then studies that see one world as more real than the other are misleading.

CONCLUSIONS

Having fulfilled the introduction's promises through specific language and developed paragraphs, the writer still has work left—writing a conclusion. Conclusions reverse introductions, but do some of the same things. While an introduction engages the audience's interest in the subject, a conclusion leads the audience away from specific information about the subject back to the audience's world. In this sense introductions and conclusions are opposite. They are the same because they use some of the same writing devices: a relevant anecdote, startling facts, a generalization about the essay's most important points, a quotation from a recognized authority. It is as important for a writer to have her audience and purpose clearly in mind in a conclusion as in an introduction.

Look again at the muscle physiologist writing for different audiences. If he were writing for a professional audience, an anecdote or startling facts would be singularly inappropriate. Scientific writing conventions require a conclusion to state generalized theory derived from experimental data; a scientific conclusion summarizes how the experimental data verified or failed to verify the experimental hypothesis. The physiologist would not be bound by these same conventions in an article for *Discover*'s popular audience. Here he would have to decide whether he intends to educate the audience or to ask them to take some action based on his presented argument. In the first case, he might choose amazing facts, startling statistics, or even relate an anecdote that would emphasize the importance of what he has told his audience about how muscles work. If, on the other hand, he were appealing to his audience to follow a personal health routine or to ask the government to increase funds for muscle research, the conclusion might restate the most important points and set out a course of action. In each situation, the conclusion's principal function is not just to end the writing, or summarize what has been said. A good conclusion leaves the audience with a clear idea of the importance of what the writer has said.

Actually completing a first draft rarely moves according to the "steps" that this chapter implies. Most writers write a section, revise their writing plan, write again, revise their writing, rework their introduction, and write and revise again. At some point, however, we usually feel as though we have most of what we want to say down, either on paper or computer memory, and we have a "complete" first draft ready for the writing process's last stage—revising. Most writers feel that this is the time to put the draft aside completely and catch up on the unread assignments and unpaid bills or meet those needs for sleep, pizza, or the new Woody Allen film. Even though most writers revise as they work on the first draft, a complete break between a *completed* draft and focused revising activities like the ones presented in the next chapter helps us look at our writing more objectively and makes revision more productive.

■ WRITING EXERCISES

1. Select three paragraphs from your journal and analyze the relationships between the sentences in terms of specificity.

2. Write a paragraph describing your favorite location on campus. Use at least eight sentences with one sentence reaching level six.

3. Rewrite the following sentences, changing general words to specific and abstract words to concrete.

> A beautiful woman walked along the shore.
> Sports are great entertainment.
> Extinction is invisible, but by rebelling against it, we can make it visible.

People poorly understand arms control.
Bad weather makes me feel dreary.

4. Write a first draft for one of the papers you worked through in the last chapter. Do not revise it. If you prefer, find your own subject by browsing, or select a writing assignment following one of the anthology's essays. Whatever way you find a writing subject, be certain to work through some writing preparation exercises. ■

A Short Writing Course III: Revising and Editing

What makes me happy is rewriting. In the first draft you get your ideas and your theme clear, if you are using some kind of metaphor you get that established, and certainly you have to know where you're coming out. But the next time through it's like cleaning house, getting rid of all the junk, getting things in the right order, tightening things up. I like the process of making writing neat.—Ellen Goodman

Journalist Ellen Goodman's apt analogy between revising and cleaning house clarifies the relationship between drafting and revising, and it suggests a reviser's biggest problem—knowing what is junk and what is not. Some of us do not share Goodman's enthusiasm for cleaning house, perhaps because we grew up with mothers who cleaned house avidly. A friend tells how every Friday when she was at elementary school, her mother swept into her room brandishing an oversized wastebasket and tossed away snapshots, school papers, art projects, and outgrown toys. Unlike her childhood room, her house is filled with every book she has ever read, first, second, and final drafts of everything she has written, photographs from every trip; only dirt and refuse find the trash can. As with this friend, one of the most difficult tasks student writers face is parting with anything they have written— even useless words. If your nature is more like our friend's than Goodman's, try her technique: she may not throw anything away, but she puts castoff books and clothes in the basement. Prepare to revise by making a basement file or notebook where you can save your favorite "junk" for an appropriate occasion, develop a way to determine what constitutes junk, and set to cleaning your written house.

REVISION AND EDITING CRITERIA

Experienced writers have little difficulty identifying junk. Experience has taught them to read their own writing as if it were a total stranger's. Objectivity is the first revising tool. The second is criteria for judgment. While writers may develop criteria for their special audiences and purposes, most readers expect writing to be:

complete
coherent
clear
correct

These four C's of good writing provide a useful guide for revising and editing.

When we see that our writing does not meet these criteria—that it lacks completeness or its organization and logic interfere with its clear communication, or its style—language and sentence construction—obstructs rather than engages our intended meanings, we need to go back and rewrite. This may mean moving paragraphs from one place to another within the text, expanding an idea or developing an example, or eliminating a paragraph or sentence that goes off in a direction different from our intended focus. This kind of rewriting (revising) for completeness and coherence requires a global overview of the draft we are working on. It requires reconsidering our ideas, evidence, and purposes.

Editing, on the other hand, reworks smaller units. If our writing does not meet the criteria for clarity and correctness, we need to rework individual sentences, reconsider our language choices, and eliminate spelling and mechanical errors. Few writers can look for this kind of small detail at the same time that they are looking at a paper's larger global issues. We suggest that rereading and revising be broken into smaller considerations, reading and revising for each of the four revision and editing criteria. When we revise, as for other parts of the writing process, we are likely to move back and forth between reading and rewriting, and we will probably work with more than one criterion at a time. To clarify what we do when we revise, though, here we will look at each criterion independently.

COMPLETENESS

In the first reading for completeness, the writer moves rapidly through the text, making sure that the writing covers all the topics in the original and revised plans. He looks to see that his working hypothesis is fully tested and his research questions answered. He concerns himself with whether or not the body has met the introduction's commitments. He looks at the paragraphs to determine if the information is specific. He makes large notes in the margins to indicate where information is missing, or where information does not relate to the introduction's commitment.

Questions for Completeness
- Does the introduction indicate the specific topic and make a commitment?

- Does the introduction interest the reader in the subject?
- Does the writing meet the introduction's commitments?
- Does the writing answer the research questions?
- Does it test the working hypothesis?
- Do paragraphs have some sentences beyond level 4?
- Are generalizations and abstractions illustrated with concrete and specific detail?
- Do all the paragraphs relate to the topic and comment on that topic?
- Are there adequate definitions and summaries of sources to create a common ground between the audience's experience and the writer's knowledge?
- Is the purpose met?

COHERENCE

Once a writer is satisfied that the writing is complete—that the writing's content is satisfactory—she needs to focus more particularly on how the writing works to communicate that content to the reader. Here she needs to look at coherence. The word coherence embraces order, organization, movement through the writing, and logic, so reading for coherence may proceed rather slowly, as the writer considers if paragraphs communicate ideas, if the writing moves from one paragraph and one idea to the next, and if the logic is valid.

Before we can fully consider questions that evaluate coherence, it will be helpful to review some problems writers can encounter with logic and organization.

Reasoning Flaws

Flawed Inductive Arguments

As we discussed earlier, good inductive arguments proceed from evidence gathered from a well-designed investigation whose results represent an adequate, random, broad sample. Despite valid evidence, an inductive argument can also have problems with conclusions. Flawed inductive arguments overgeneralize from evidence, or sometimes, a preconceived conclusion can cause a writer to select data which aligns the conclusion with the preconception. Suppose a nationwide study found that 55 percent of college freshmen used some dangerous drug (alcohol, marijuana, cocaine, uppers, and so forth) at least once a month. An argument concluding from this that college students are drug abusers would be a gross overgeneralization (particularly since alcohol is included). Another flawed conclusion might occur if a study began with the idea that college students engage in promiscuous sexual behavior. An inventory could be designed to ask questions about sexual practices and frequency, but if it omitted questions regarding marital status, or lengths of relationships, the seemingly accurate evidence and the conclusion growing from it would be flawed.

Flawed Deductive Arguments

Deduction begins with a generalization and moves to the specific instance using the syllogism. We saw earlier that for a syllogism to be valid, it must take the form:

$$A = B$$
$$\text{and} \quad C = A$$
$$\text{therefore,} \quad C = B$$

With this is mind, you will recognize that the following is a *valid* deduction.

Men get hurt in relationships with career women.
John is a man.
John will get hurt in his relationship with Samantha, who is a career woman.

The number of career women in good relationships and married suggests that the generalization forming this syllogism's first premise relies more on prejudice than fact. For deductive argument to succeed, the syllogism must be both valid and true. Just as the good writer must attend to the truth of the conclusions in inductive argument, she must be aware that deductive argument can proceed from false premises, or that arguments can pose as logical that are, in fact, *false arguments*.

False Arguments

Sometimes writers seek to influence their audience by using approaches that appear to be arguments but actually appeal to their readers' emotions.

Argument to the Person *(ad hominem)*:   The first such argument avoids the issue and instead discusses the personal life or character of someone involved. Such an approach might ignore a Congresswoman's voting record and argue instead that she should not be re-elected because of her imminent divorce. Or someone might argue that Hemingway's novels and short stories should not be read by high school children because he committed suicide.

Argument to the People *(ad populem)*:   The second kind of false argument might be structured soundly, but its basic premises appeal to its audience's bias. Using this approach, Hitler's arguments for Aryan racial purity appealed to German nationalism.

False Dilemma: A writer also can bewilder his audience by presenting a false dilemma, where he presents only two alternatives, one desirable the other distasteful. We have all heard the statement that unless the United States military intervenes in one country or another, the Communists will take over. Such an argument allows only black or white and admits no possibility of gray.

Appeal to Ignorance: Finally, some arguments assert their own validity because no opposition exists. Such logic says that a university registration system works efficiently because no reliable complaints have been made against it, or that Jim Johns is a fine executive because he has done nothing wrong.

Flawed Analogy

Good analogies need to establish more than one similarity between the things being compared to be convincing. Taken alone, the statement, "People should avoid caffeine because it produces cancer in experimental rats" appears to be a good basis for an argument against people using caffeine. The statement relies on the similarity between human metabolism and rat metabolism, but this analogy relies on only one similarity. To be truly convincing, it would have to establish similarities in dosage, and some statistical indication that humans have problems with caffeine. The more similarities a writer establishes in an analogy, the better and more useful the analogy will be.

Flawed Causal Analysis

As we discussed earlier, without causes which are *necessary, sufficient,* and *contributory,* we cannot truly demonstrate causal relationships. You can see this when you look at the following statement about AIDS (Acquired Immune Deficiency Syndrome):

We can control AIDS by isolating all hemophiliacs and homosexuals.

A valid causal argument cannot be made here because merely *being* a hemophiliac or homosexual is not a necessary, sufficient, or contributory cause of the disease.

Arguments from cause also run into problems when they assert cause when none exists. Until humans understood astronomy, they believed that such cosmic changes as comets caused political unrest. Similar to this, when one event precedes a second, the first is seen as the second's cause. How often have you assigned a cold's cause to a walk in the rain or intestinal flu to a bad meal? This reasoning error sometimes appears in historical writing. Darwin's theory on the survival of the fittest preceded late nineteenth-century laissez-faire economics and may even have influenced the theoreticians, but Darwin did not cause capitalism's vast expansion and abuses during this time—economic policy did.

A more subtle flaw in causal reasoning occurs when a contributory cause is seen as the only cause. A few years ago a teenager committed suicide after listening to rock music advocating suicide. The parents sued the rock group, saying the music caused the suicide. The court ruled that the music alone was not sufficient to cause the boy's suicide. An error in causal reasoning closely related to this occurs when one event is seen as the cause of the second, but actually they both proceed from a common cause. For example, some people argue that crime causes drug abuse, others that drug abuse causes crime. Rather than one causing the other, they may proceed from many complex socioeconomic conditions.

Flawed Definition

A good definition identifies a term as a member of a class and specifies its *essential, distinguishing* characteristics, using precise, denotative language. Poor definitions occur when writers use ambiguous language or define a thing using its own terms (circular definition). An example of a circular definition can be seen in the debate between biologists and Scientific Creationists over evolution. Stephen Jay Gould, a Harvard biologist and evolution spokesperson, points out that "scientific creationism" ambiguously defines itself by misusing "scientific." According to Gould, "Their brand of creationism, they claim, is 'scientific' because it follows the Popperian model in trying to demolish evolution." (This relies on a misinterpretation of philosopher Karl Popper's argument that science's hallmark is the falsifiability of its theories; "science cannot prove absolutely, but it can falsify.") Gould demonstrates that the Scientific Creationists' definition relies on ambiguous use of both *falsify* and *scientific*. Further, the statement that science is the branch of knowledge that studies nature scientifically defines science in its own terms.

Other abuses of definition occur with misused emotional language. In one case, a writer may use a highly connotative word to define a second word, and then use this as an argument's major premise. For example, when a writer argues against abortion from the premise that abortion is *murder*, she abuses definition as much as she would if she opposed capital punishment because it is *murder*. Further, writers may appeal to their readers' emotions by leaving terms undefined. An argument proceeding from terms like *true American, real men, true Christian*, or *concerned Democrat* may pretend definition but invokes stereotypes.

Questions for Coherence

- Does the title reflect the topic and engage the reader?
- Do paragraphs have a topic sentence?
- Are all the sentences in a paragraph on that paragraph's topic?
- When the focus shifts from one aspect of the subject to another, does a new paragraph begin?
- When the focus shifts does the writer use transitional words? *(like-*

wise, similarly, however, although, nevertheless, either, on the other hand, moreover, in addition, because, consequently, next)

- Does the writer link paragraphs through transitional devices like repeating key words and phrases or following organizational patterns like process, cause and effect, or comparison and contrast throughout the paper?
- Are any syllogisms both valid and true? If the writing uses inductive logic, is there enough evidence to support the conclusion?
- Does the writing reach conclusions based on single experiences, that is, does it overgeneralize?
- Does the writing rely on solid evidence rather than emotion and prejudice?
- Does the writing avoid false arguments?
- Does the writing avoid causal reasoning errors?
- Does the writing avoid analogy or definition errors?
- Does the writing avoid substituting prejudice and emotion for reason and argument?

CLARITY

"Clutter," according to journalist and professor William Zinsser, "is the disease of American writing. We are a society strangling in unnecessary words, circular constructions, pompous frills and meaningless jargon." The third reading and revision moves from ideas and structures to language. Here writers must mercilessly cut extraneous words, convert inaction to action, and revive personal responsibility.

Clarity Through Style

To revise for clarity, a writer must have a clear sense of what clear sentences should accomplish.

Clear Sentences Have Concrete Subjects and Active Verbs:

- *not* There were charges of bribery against the players, and they were arrested.
- *but* Tulane police arrested three basketball players for bribery.

They Shun Jargon, Cliches, and Unnecessary Words:

- *not* The bilateral ethics committee composed of both students and faculty is in gear and ready to deal with all problems of cribbing and cheating.
- *but* The faculty-student ethics committee hears cheating cases.

They Opt for Simple English over Bureaucratese:

- *not*   Upon receiving input regarding the incursion of terrorist forces in the attack mode, non-military personnel were retired from embassy positions and Army personnel were deployed in their place.
- *but*   Hearing of planned terrorist attacks, the Army replaced civilians at the embassy.

They Eliminate Unnecessary Prepositional Phrases:

- *not*   The first wave of attack on the causes of this problem focused on the senior employees of the company.
- *but*   The first attack on the problem's causes focused on the company's senior employees.

Revising for clarity demands the writer to opt for simple language and direct statements. It requires him to write with an ear for spoken language and a desire to express ideas rather than impress readers.

Questions for Clarity

- Do sentences have concrete subjects?
- Do I use "I" rather than "one" when I am the subject?
- Where possible, do action verbs replace forms of "to be"?
- Does writing use active rather than passive verbs?
- Does the writing avoid excessive use of expletives (*it is* . . . and *there are*. . .)?
- Does the writing avoid overusing words like *quite* and *very* or doublings like *peaceful and quiet, free and easy,* and so forth?
- Does the writing avoid cliches (words frequently heard or seen in print)?
- Does the writing avoid specialized language inappropriate to audience or subject (jargon)?
- Are sentences overloaded with prepositional phrases?

CORRECTNESS

Finally, a writer reads for mechanical error. Most writers discover many mechanical errors during the first three readings; the glaring sentence fragments, subject-verb agreement errors, and misspellings are usually corrected by the third reading. The remaining errors are the hardest to find because the writer may not recognize them as errors. Here four things can help: a friend, a handbook of standard English usage, a dictionary, and a small notebook. First, read the draft aloud to the friend. Often reading aloud forces a writer to see errors missed in silent reading, particularly sentence construction errors. Next, ask the friend to circle what she thinks are spelling, punctuation, grammar, and word use errors. One person's errors often differ from another's, so writer and friend will recognize different errors. Look up any potential error in the English handbook and dictionary. Record the error and correction in the notebook, so that next time you read for correctness, you look for these particular errors. Also use this notebook to record any errors identified by instructors. After a while this notebook will become an invaluable editing tool.

REVISING AND EDITING—A LAST WORD

The last word in revising is *colleagues*. Those of us who write often know only too well how our writing has improved from the suggestions made by colleagues. Professional writers have reviewers and editors. Your college professor's articles and books are sent out to other professors in their field for evaluation and recommendations. In many writing courses students form "peer groups" that work together, often throughout a course, to read and discuss each other's work. Working together on writing is by far one of the most effective guides to revision. By forming peer groups and using the criteria and questions in this chapter, you can better recognize what "junk" needs to be put in the basement and what seemingly white elephants need to be proudly displayed.

■ REVISING AND EDITING EXERCISES

1. Exchange essays with a classmate. Using the list of questions for completeness and coherence, mark the areas where the student needs to revise. Put necessary comments in the margins.

2. Go through your former written work and list the spelling and mechanical errors you make most frequently. List these errors in a notebook for revising.

3. Using the revision questions, mark problems with clarity and clutter in the example that follows. Rewrite the passage to improve specificity and remove clutter. Or you might reread and revise one of your own essays using these criteria. ■

> Irony in film comedy can be defined as the difference between what is seen and said and what is actually meant. We, the audience, see the entirety of a film and know the truth. The audience can see everything happening in the film while the characters of the film see only what is going on around them. The satiric focus in *Dr. Strangelove* is directed toward the military and its attitudes, the arms race, Soviet and U. S. relations, nuclear war and the doomsday device. In this film Slim Pickens, who is the protagonist, is sent with his men to bomb the Soviet Union. In *Dr. Strangelove* we, the audi-

ence, see that one bomber gets through the Soviet missiles. On their journey they encounter many different obstacles which they must overcome to achieve their goal of bombing the Soviet Union. The antagonists of the film are the President and Mandrake, both played by Peter Sellers. The reason these two are the antagonists is because they want to stop protagonist Pickens from accomplishing his goal, bombing Russia. The values of this film support the launching of a nuclear war. These values, by all means, are unreasonable and are contrary to what the audience feels to be reasonable. So the film's irony has the audience cheering Pickens and their crew on to their Russian target, which will set off the doomsday machine and nuclear war. This is achieved because the whole focus of the movie is to stop the one little bomber which has gone through radar and so many obstacles to get to its destiny. When the President tells the Soviet leader to shoot the plane down, not even caring about the men inside, we start to sympathize with Pickens and his men. The comedy is ironic because we want Slim and his crew to get through the Soviet missiles and bomb them. Even though the result will be total destruction of the earth by the Soviet doomsday machine.

Writing from Sources

6

In Chapter 3, as part of prewriting, we discussed formulating questions for research and writing, developing a research plan, and, briefly, acquiring information. Here we will look more fully at the secondary sources available and at how to identify useful secondary sources. Then we will consider more fully the special reading and writing skills that enable you to incorporate secondary research into your final papers.

COMPUTERS AND RESEARCH

The computer revolution is changing research for many college students, depending on the resources available to them in the laboratories and libraries of their own institutions and their own personal computers. Here, we will briefly describe some of the resources that have become available, even though not all of us have access to them. The most common computer resources are information data bases, data on CD-ROM, and library catalogues.

Information Data Bases

Information data bases are created at research centers in large memory capacity computer banks. They are made available to users outside the research center by subscription. Manuals and accessing and billing procedures are sent to users when they subscribe. When an individual or institution wishes to use the data base, the user usually telephones the main computer from an outside terminal through a modem, a device that communicates computer data over the telephone lines. For most subscription data bases, the host generally charges the user for the time the user's computer is *online*. While some data bases are relatively inexpensive, subscription and computer time on others often exceed most college students' (and professors') personal budgets. Consequently, many colleges subscribe to important data bases and have special arrangements through the various academic departments and the college billing office to make these data bases available to students and bill them directly. The data bases available are too numerous and increase too frequently to even begin to recount them here. You might check with your own major department or university library to learn if any arrangements have been made to access major computer data bases and if these data bases are available to students.

Data on CD-ROM

Increasingly data bases that are relatively permanent are being recorded on CD-ROM. The information is inscribed electronically on a compact disk, like those that have flooded the music recording industry. The CD's data is then read into a computer's memory using a special laser compact disk player. Because a compact disk can store a tremendous amount of information—far more than a regular computer disk—CD-ROM is an efficient data storage resource. The complete works of William Shakespeare, for example, have been put on CD-ROM. A researcher with this resource, the necessary disk player, and adequate computer memory can easily search the complete works for special passages or words and copy data from the compact disk into a word processing or editing program.

The amount of data available on CD-ROM increases yearly and includes invaluable research tools like the Modern Language Association's yearly index to all publications related to language and literature *(MLA International Bibliography)* and the *Oxford English Dictionary*, but, like subscription data bases, CD-ROM is expensive. Unless a user accesses a data base extensively and often, the costs usually outweigh the benefits for the individual user. Many colleges and universities have purchased CD-ROM player technology and data bases, and, through networking systems on their campuses, they have made the data available to students using PC's and modems. Even in these situations the university may charge the student for on-line time.

Computer Library Catalogues

Computer library catalogues represent the computer research technology students are most likely to encounter. Many libraries, including public libraries, have transferred the information once available in the library card catalogue into a computer data base. This data base, besides accounting for a library's holdings, records circulation data, so that the library knows whether or not a book has been checked out, when it is due back, and, in some cases, who has the book. Additionally, many college libraries belong to a library system that allows them to locate books not in their own library that are available at other campuses or even other colleges and universities.

While each library's computer catalogue has its own peculiarities, most libraries have computer terminals, similar to personal computers, where the user indicates on the keyboard what kind of a search he or she wishes to initiate—author, title, or subject. The user then types in the name, the title, or the subject. The computer searches its memory and identifies the title or list of titles that meets the specification. If a user is doing a subject search the exact wording for the category needs to be found in the *Library of Congress Subject Headings* listings, since computers only recognize words already in their data base. After the user has an initial list of titles, he or she can call up a second screen with specific bibliographic information on each of the titles. Some computer catalogue systems have capabilities for printing the results of a computer catalogue search. Furthermore, some computer catalogues are available to students and faculty at their own personal computers through a campus computer network.

LOCATING SECONDARY SOURCES

Even with the tremendous advances in computer data bases available to the personal computer user, the majority of us still need to work in a library a great deal of the time. Using libraries effectively requires beginning with a research plan like the one we discussed in Chapter 3 and knowing what resources a library offers. Your research plan, remember, will have a working hypothesis that your reading will test, questions to identify your subject's limits, alternate topic headings for locating information in indexes and bibliographies, and possibly some potential bibliographical resources. Because libraries' resources and arrangements differ, your reference librarian is the best guide to using your library effectively. Overall, though, you can expect most college libraries to offer the following reference resources in addition to books and periodicals.

Encyclopedias, either generalized like *The Encyclopedia Britannica* or specialized like the *Grove Encyclopedia of Music* or the *McGraw-Hill Encyclopedia of Science and Technology*, give an overview of your subject.

Bibliographies, often focused on a special subject, identify books and articles on specific subjects. The card or computer catalogue will refer you to bibliographies on your subject, under the subheading "Bibliographies," when you consult your general subject heading.

Indexes are bibliographies that concentrate on articles published in magazines and journals, usually during a given year. While a general index like *The Reader's Guide to Periodic Literature* will direct you to articles published in popular magazines, other general indexes like *The Humanities Index* or the *Social Science Index* direct you to scholarly work. Additionally, specialized indexes exist in nearly every field. Most college libraries group the indexes together in a reference room. Becoming familiar with the specific indexes in your own field is essential for locating the kinds of secondary sources required for the research and writing your courses will require.

Abstracts, like *Psychological Abstracts, International Political Science Abstracts,* or *Historical Abstracts,* collect and publish summaries of some of the articles published in a given field during one year. These can be very useful for giving you a sense of the kinds of research and writing being done on a subject, but they are not exhaustive. Reading an abstract can let you know if a source can be useful for your own research, but, because of its brevity, an abstract cannot replace the article as an actual source.

Dictionaries, as you well know, give the meanings of words. Specialized dictionaries exist to help define the language used especially by a given discipline, and biographical dictionaries give information about particular people.

Making and Using a Working Bibliography

Begin locating and collecting information with your research questions and a list of indexes and bibliographies. Allow three or four hours in a block and go to the library with a package of index cards and a notebook. Work your way through the bibliographies and indexes, beginning with the one most closely related to the general area of your course work and research subject. If you are not a biologist, for example, the *General Science Index* will lead to information more accessible to you then *Index Medicus.* If you are more advanced in an area and you need more specialized information you will want to use the more specialized index. For each potential source you identify through catalogues, bibliographies, and indexes, make a separate index card noting:

- author
- title
- publication information
  publisher, city, and year for a book;
  periodical name, year, and month (full date if published more frequently) for an article
- library call number

You will use this bibliography card's information later for documenting your sources, but keeping track of this information from the beginning will save considerable time later.

IDENTIFYING USEFUL SOURCES

Once you have created a bibliography (a list of works you intend to consult), locate your sources. For each source, identify the kind of audience for which it is written, the kind of information it is likely to contain, and then skim the introductions for a thesis and the remainder for key supporting evidence to see if the sources are relevant. Those of us who frequently use secondary sources find identifying sources and skimming (or reading for an overview) second nature. If this is unfamiliar to you, you might consider the following approach.

Getting an Overview

Begin by identifying the kind of information your source is likely to contain. For periodical articles this is somewhat easier than for books. Articles published in popular magazines like *Time, Discover,* or *Psychology Today,* which you have probably identified by using general literature indexes like the *Reader's Guide to Popular Literature,* will give you popularized versions of science, history, and current affairs. Original research by scientists, historians, and literary scholars will be published in scholarly journals. You have probably located these through more specialized indexes. If you are still unsure, the statement of publishing policy on a periodical's title page along with the author's credentials should help. For books, the kind of publishing house can serve as a guide. University presses generally publish original research and scholarly studies while commercial publishing houses publish for a more popular audience. This, however, is not always the case, so you may need to look at prefaces and introductions.

Once you know what kind of publication you are using, instead of plunging ahead into reading, use the following steps:

- Using the title, identify the topic, and then read through the first paragraph to see what limits the writer sets on her topic.
- If the article has an abstract (written summary), use it.
- If the article does not have an abstract, try to imagine what it might be by looking at the first few paragraphs and the conclusion.
- If the introduction and conclusion still do not provide you with a good idea of what the article contains, look for any subtopic or chapter headings, or lacking that, topic sentences.
- Once you have identified the general content, and you feel the source will be useful, read quickly for a general sense and overview, noting the scope of the subject and the direction the writing takes.
- Identify the sections that address your subject and research questions, and then read for specific content.

KEEPING TRACK OF RESEARCH

Once you have identified the usefulness of your source, make reading notes on either index cards or notebook paper. Some writers use index cards (one card for each recorded note); one we know prefers a yellow legal pad for making notes, working consecutively through a source. She staples the bibliography card to the first page and leaves a wide left-hand margin for recording the specific topic, page numbers, and brief comments.

Taking Notes

When you later write your essay you will incorporate your sources by:

> *quoting* them directly
> *paraphrasing*—putting the passage's meaning in your own words
> *summarizing*—recounting the main ideas

The writing that you actually do when you are researching secondary sources uses the same techniques—notetaking for quotation, paraphrasing, and summarizing—and often serves as the building blocks of larger essays. You will make your later writing and documentation easier if you take accurate research notes to begin with. Your research notes will be either

a record of specific evidence
or
summaries of your source and your responses to them

In either case, you identify what you will write down with the working hypothesis you are testing in mind. To do this you cannot simply record everything you read. Instead, you must read your sources for both information and point of view, think critically about what you are reading, and decide about the relevance of your reading to your own project.

When you identify information (evidence) or ideas that relate to your research questions, then make notes. Frequently writers use individual cards for each piece of specific information. Whether you use cards or a notebook, you need a record-keeping system that is consistent. You need a way to clearly identify:

- the source and location in the source of particular information
- what material in your notes is a direct quote
- what information is a summary
- what notes reflect your own responses

For example, you might assign each source a number and include that number on every notecard or notebook entry that you take from that source. (Do not forget page numbers.) To distinguish quotations from summaries, you could indent all quotations and place them in quotation marks. You could indicate your reflections using a different ink or placing them in a different notebook. The actual system that you use is not so important; having a consistent system is.

When you take notes, keep it in mind that recopying pages of data and information is far too time-consuming. Your written notes should record:

- summaries of your source
- specific information like names, statistics, facts or definitions
- relevant statements that you will want to quote directly
- theses, hypotheses, and conclusions from your source

If the information you need from your source is lengthy, more than a paragraph or two, it would be wiser to photocopy the section you need, and then highlight or underline the relevant information. Photocopying is far more accurate than transcribing.

For any notes you make of evidence, hypotheses, or conclusions, or for direct quotation, indicate the context (and page number), and then copy carefully, being certain to preserve all punctuation. Before you go on, make sure the note connects with a bibliography card (a number or title is usually sufficient), and check your copy for accuracy.

Your notes that summarize a source need to identify the main idea, the relevant supporting evidence, and all names, dates, and factual information. Again, before you go on, re-read your entry to make sure that all the information is accurate and sufficient. Writing summaries is such an important skill we will consider it more fully later in this chapter.

A NOTE ON DOCUMENTATION

Whenever you use a source in your writing, whether you quote directly, paraphrase, or summarize, you have an ethical (and in most cases, legal) responsibility to give credit to the source. This can be done by mentioning the author and title directly in your essay or by footnoting. After you complete your writing you will want to refer to the documentation guidelines that appear in Chapter 8.

Using Sources Responsibly

The most important concept about using sources is the idea of *use*. To use a source is to relate your own ideas to the ideas of another writer. While this requires accurately representing what another person has said or written, using a source is more than mere accurate reporting. Using a source means reacting by agreeing or disagreeing; it means combining the ideas from different sources and explaining them to refine a context or definition for your own argument. A source may serve as a foundation for your own ideas, or it may confirm what you believe. By using sources responsibly, we place our own ideas within the context of other writers in our disciplines and become members of a community of knowledge. Students who *use* sources cannot be seriously accused of plagiarism, though they may have documentation problems. To help you use sources responsibly, a distinction between plagiarism and misdocumentation may prove useful.

Plagiarism

To plagiarize is to represent the work of another as our own whether the work comes from some obscure magazine, the catalogue of a paper writing service, or a friend's notebook. Plagiarism is not collaboration—working with peers to generate ideas, to share research, or to edit drafts. Obviously plagiarism is more than failing to give full credit; it involves a serious ethical breech—dishonesty—and grounds for legal prosecution under federal copyright laws.

Misdocumentation

To misdocument is to fail to give adequate credit to a source or to credit a source incorrectly. Most misdocumentation comes from not knowing what to document or what form to use than from deliberate misrepresentation. Careful, accurate research—both bibliography cards and research notes—as well as familiarity with documentation will help you document your sources correctly.

Accurate Documentation

Accurate documentation enables your reader to distinguish between your own ideas and those that derive from sources. At one level documentation allows your reader to distinguish the value of your contributions and ideas; at another level it directs your reader to your source which might discuss the same topic from a different perspective or in greater detail than you do. Good documentation serves both your reader's and your own interests.

With these two interests in mind, the rationale of documentation should be much clearer. To distinguish your ideas from your source's, your documentation needs to make the authorship clear by pointing out any idea that is not your own and by telling your reader where the idea comes from. Therefore, you need to give credit for:

All opinions, insights, research findings, or judgments of others when they are:

- Quoted directly
- Summarized
- Paraphrased

All illustrations, tables, graphs, and charts when they appear in a source.

To help the reader who may wish to read your sources directly, your documentation must indicate the work's title and author, and information about publication. Chapter 8 will consider the actual formats for documentation.

What Not to Document

Information that appears widely in print—facts in encyclopedias, textbooks, newspapers, or magazines—or that receives frequent mention on radio or television does not require documentation. A good guideline for discriminating between something that should or should not be documented is whether or not the information is a widely known fact—a historical or current event, a piece of widely accepted scientific knowledge, or commonly known biography—or the original contribution of a historian, scientist, or writer. "Special" individual knowledge requires documentation; pubicly known "facts" do not.

TAKING NOTES FOR GOOD WRITING AND DOCUMENTATION

Now that you better understand the principles for *using* and documenting your sources, you need to attend to how you will write from your sources— quoting, summarizing, and paraphrasing. Writers quote directly from sources when they will respond to the source author's statement, when the source makes an important point that cannot be expressed in any other words, or when the quotation adds emphasis to the writer's own assertions. In these instances, since the exact words are so important, you have a responsibility to the original source to quote accurately. Any actual quotation should be introduced by a statement that relates the source's ideas to your own. One way of assuring this relationship is to attach every quotation to a sentence in your paper. The quotation itself appears within quotation marks and maintains the source's punctuation. If the quotation is longer than three typewritten lines you may set off the quotation by indenting the entire passage five spaces from each margin, double spacing the entire passage. (If you use indentation, you omit quotation marks.) Quoting longer passages requires consideration in your own writing of their relevance and merit. An essay that only strings quotations together into patch-work writing is not really *using* sources responsibly. Frequently paraphrasing or summarizing a source will better enable you to integrate the source's ideas with your own.

Paraphrasing

A paraphrase restates a passage's exact meaning, but in your own words. Writers use this as a research tool for taking reading notes and again when they present a source in their own writing. A good paraphrase, more concise than the original, clarifies a source's language and ideas for readers. To see how paraphrase works, read Henry Adams's description of Chartres cathedral from *Mont St. Michel and Chartres* and the paraphrase that follows:

> Chartres was intended to hold ten thousand people easily, or fifteen thousand when crowded, and the decoration of this great space, though not a wholly new problem, had to be treated in a new way. Sancta Sofia was built by the Emperor Justinian, with all the resources of the Empire, in a single violent effort, in six years, and was decorated throughout with mosaics on a general scheme, with the unity that Empire and Church could give when they acted together. The Norman Kings of Sicily, the richest princes of the twelfth century, were able to carry out a complete work of the most costly kind, in a single sustained effort from beginning to end, according to a given plan. Chartres was a local shrine, in an agricultural province, not even a part

of the royal domain, and its cathedral was the work of society, without much more tie than the Virgin gave it. Socially Chartres, as far as its stone work goes, seems to have been mostly rural; its decoration, in the stone porches and transepts, is royal and feudal; in the nave and choir it is chiefly bourgeois. The want of unity is much less surprising than the unity, but it is still evident, especially in the glass. The mosaics of Monreale begin and end; they are a series; their connection is artistic and theological at once; they have unity. The windows of Chartres have no sequence, and their charm is in variety, in individuality, and sometimes even in downright hostility to each other, reflecting the picturesque society that gave them. They have, too, the charm that the world has made no attempt to popularize them for its modern uses, so that except for the useful little guide-book of the Abbe Clerval, one can see no clue to the legendary chaos; one has it to one's self.

This is paraphrased as:

The great space of Chartres cathedral, built to hold ten thousand people easily or fifteen thousand when crowded, required a new approach for decoration than earlier cathedrals, particularly because it was built as an agricultural province's local shrine by a diverse society unified only by its faith in the Virgin Mary. Chartres was unlike either Sancta Sofia cathedral, built by the Byzantine emperor Justinian in just six years and decorated throughout with thematically consistent mosaics, or the twelfth-century cathedral at Monreale built by Sicily's rich Norman Kings and decorated with a theologically and artistically unified mosaic series. Local laborers did Chartres' stonework. Chartres' decoration (its stained glass windows) in the transepts and porches came from the nobility, and in the nave and choir, from the middle class. Built by such a diverse society, Chartres has surprising unity, except in its windows, which charm by their variety, individuality, contrasts, and by their remoteness from modern popularization.

The paraphrase relies on the original passage's full meaning rather than its sentence sequence by drawing together references to Monreale, which were separated in the original, and by clarifying the contrast between Chartres and Sancta Sofia and the church at Monreale. Frequently, several sentences are combined into one with moderating phrases. This paraphrase, which contains all the information in the original, simplifies and clarifies the original by changing the language and the sentence structure. It might find its way into a paper comparing architectural styles or one examining the relationship between great architecture's relation to the society which builds it. Used in this way, paraphrasing allows a writer to state the ideas of his source without the jarring shifts in tone and style that come from too frequent quoting. If, however, we were writing about historian Adams's particular vision linking Gothic architecture's artistic achievements with the cult of the Virgin, *summarizing* and emphasizing ideas through brief quotes might be more appropriate.

Writing Summaries

When you write a summary you abstract (remove), a book, article, or passage's main ideas and present them in a shortened form in your own words. Unlike a paraphrase, a summary may focus on certain parts of the original and ignore others. For example, when scientists write reviews of scientific literature they usually emphasize a study's conclusions.

Summaries vary in length depending on their use. A summary may be a few sentences, several paragraphs, or a few pages. One summary may extend throughout an essay, in a book review for example, or an essay may use several shorter summaries, as in a review of scientific literature. When we use summaries as part of research notes, we may be using them only to indicate what a source contains, or we may be explaining the essence of a source's argument so that we can explain it and respond to it in our own writing. Obviously, the purpose we intend for a summary will determine the kind and extent of information we select beyond the source's main ideas.

In the example below of a summary that might be used as part of a longer essay, the writer identifies the source and relates what in the original passage is essential:

> At the beginning of chapter, "The Court of the Queen of Heaven" in *Mont St. Michel and Chartres*, Henry Adams credits Chartres cathedral's architectural achievement to a diverse society brought together by their faith in the Virgin. Unlike such earlier cathedrals as Sancta Sofia and the one at Monreale, Sicily (built and decorated by the single efforts of rich and powerful rulers, the Emperor Justinian and the Norman Kings, respectively), local laborers joined with nobility and the middle class to build Chartres. Although surprisingly unified, Chartres reveals the diverse society that built it in its stained glass windows.

This summary states the source, the main point or thesis, and two principal lines of evidence—the comparison with previous cathedrals and the diverse windows. Finding main points and supporting evidence calls upon the same skills you developed for reading critically—recognizing general sentences and distinguishing concrete details that comment on the generalizations.

Writing summaries requires that you put these generalizations and concrete details into sentences much like the summary sentences you form as you read. A longer summary begins with the source's thesis statement followed by each paragraph's summary sentence and important supporting detail. For a long summary, you must be sure to give the reader links and transitions between diverse ideas or evidence.

Quotations, paraphrases, and summaries rarely serve as ends in themselves; rather, they are the building blocks of larger essays. As you argue or explain, you paraphrase another writer who had addressed the same topic. The summary you write of reported research becomes part of your evidence.

You summarize a plot or an argument before you analyze or critique it. The larger writing task is still your own.

■ EXERCISES

1. For each of the following topics, create a list of alternate subject headings to help you locate information in indexes and catalogues.

   a. ethical controls on scientific experimentation within the scientific community
   b. environmental dangers from genetic engineering
   c. primitive religious customs in American society
   d. alternative child custody judgments' effects on the children of divorce
   e. American labor productivity and the trade deficit
   f. Japanese business management model
   g. preservation programs for Renaissance art in Italy
   h. Elizabethan political policies and Shakespeare's history plays

2. Identify the reference tools in each of the following categories that would give you access to information for each of the topics in question 1.

   a. bibliographies
   b. popular periodical articles
   c. articles in professional journals

3. Create a preliminary bibliography for one of the topics in question 1 and 2 or for a research question you identified in Chapter 3. This should contain at least fifteen entries, with no more than five books.

4. Using your preliminary bibliography, identify the five sources that you believe will be most useful. For these, write a brief explanation of what the title, introduction, and conclusion contributed to your assessment of value.

5. Select one article from your bibliography and write a two-page summary that indicates the article's most important contributions to your understanding of the subject. (Be sure to photocopy the article for your instructor.)

6. Select one section of the article you summarized for question 5 and write a paraphrase for it.

7. Create a set of notecards for the article in question.

8. Be sure to use some notecards for specific evidence and data, and some for summary. Remember to be careful about noting the page numbers and indicating to yourself what is being quoted directly. ■

Documentation

Documentation style varies among the various disciplines, so you will want to clarify with instructors with documentation is preferable for a particular course. Four of the most commonly used formats are those set out in the Modern Language Association's *MLA Style Sheet* and *MLA Handbook,* the American Psychological Association's *Publication Manual,* the Council of Biological Editor's *Style Manual,* and the *Chicago Manual of Style.* The following discussion includes the most important features of these documentation formats with examples of the documentation problems you will most likely encounter. While we can consider only common documentation situations for these formats here, you will find that the manuals address virtually every problem a writer encounters with documenting authorship and publication information.

MLA FORMAT

The Modern Language Association, a professional organization for teachers and scholars in English and European language studies, specifies a documentation format used by instructors and professional journals in literature, linguistics, and foreign languages. This format consists of parenthetical references in the text and a list of works cited.

Parenthetical References in the Text

Parenthetical documentation identifies within your own text the source and the source's page location for materials that you use. Usually, the first reference mentions the author and title in the text and places the page number in parenthesis. Any subsequent reference contains only the page number in parenthesis. When you are using more than one source by different authors, the parenthesis includes the author's last name along with the page number. When using more than one source by the same author, the parenthesis includes the title or a clear abbreviation of the title and page number for subsequent references.

Initial Citation

In *Harlem Renaissance* Nathan Huggins observes that Langston Hughes's manifesto, "The Negro Artist and the Radical Mountain," helped a generation of black writers create their own art (133).

Subsequent Citation When Using More Than One Source

The Harlem poet, Countee Cullen, was "more anxious to use primitive images" than even Hughes (Huggins 161). [*more than one source by different authors*]

or

The Harlem poet, Countee Cullen, was "more anxious to use primitive images" than even Hughes (<u>Harlem Renaissance</u> 161) *or* (<u>Harlem</u> 161) [*more than one source by the same author*]

This format specifies that the parenthetical material be as close as possible to the material to which it refers and that the parentheses precede any punctuation except quotation marks, which they follow. You will also notice that MLA format observes conventional punctuation for titles.

UNDERLINE titles of any work published as a whole—a book; a magazine, journal, or newspaper; a lengthy poem like T. S. Eliot's *The Wasteland*; a play; a movie; or an album.
PLACE IN QUOTATION MARKS titles of works contained within a whole publication—magazine or journal articles, newspaper headlines, poems within a collection, or a song title.

List of Works Cited

A complete list of all the sources to which you have referred in your text follows the last numbered page of your text on a separate sheet of paper. This list will be titled either *Works Cited* or *Works Consulted* depending on which your instructor specifies. ("Works Cited" indicates that the list contains only those titles you have specifically referred to in your writing; "Works Consulted" lists all sources you have read for your work whether you refer to them directly or not.) The entries containing the author's name, the source's title, and publication information appear alphabetically by the author's last name in a double-spaced format. The brief list following illustrates the important format characteristics within brackets.

Works Cited

Barsan, Richard. <u>Non Fiction Film</u>. New York: Dutton, 1973. [*a book*]

Cataldi, Angelo. "Agents Are Bargaining for Trouble." *New York Times* 15 July 1986: E1. [*a newspaper article in section E, page 1*]

Forster, E. M. "Flat and Round Characters." *Theory of the Novel*. Ed. Philip Stevick. New York: Free Press, 1980. 223–231. [*an essay in a collection edited by Stevick*]

Hart, Gary. "The Thai That Binds: New Reflections on Pacific Rim Cultures." *Asian Times* Nov. 1986: 24–26. [*an article in a monthly magazine*]

Kingston, Maxine Hong and Cecilia Chang. *Old China*. New York: Knopf, 1980. [*a book by two authors; name order determined by title page*]

Larkin, Elaine. "Developing Literate Reading." *Modern Fiction Studies* 2 (1975): 208–210. [*an article in a journal that has several issues in a year but numbers consecutively throughout the year. The volume number precedes the year of publication.*]

Leeson, Lee. "Ethnic Considerations in Composition Studies." *Kansas Quarterly* 13.4 (1989): 78–85. [*an article in a journal that pages each issue separately. The volume number is followed by a period and the issue number.*]

Thomas, James. "Yokel Color: Traditional American Humor in the Rural South." <u>New York</u> 1 June 1988: 78–87. [*an article in a weekly magazine*]

Book citations in this list contain:

- The author's name (last name first) followed by a period and two spaces
- The underlined title followed by a period and two spaces
- The city of publication, followed by a colon
- The publisher's name shortened, followed by a comma
- The year of publication, followed by a period

Periodical citations contain:

- The author's name (last name first) followed by a period and two spaces
- The article's title, followed by a period and enclosed within quotation marks; then two spaces
- The periodical title underlined
- The volume number
- The publication date, enclosed within parentheses, followed by a colon
- The pages for the entire article followed by a period

The Harvard Syst

The Harvard syste
references at the e
except that the te:
parenthesis or bot

Dawson (1976

If both the name a
nals and professor

Number-Referen

Instead of parenth
the reader to a list
References are al
ence consistently
signed to a given

This method
consistent res
insights into 1
work by Alts

The documentati
der below. Inform

1. Altschul, S

versity he

in a book]

2. Osler, A. G

N.J.: Pren

3. White, H. :

J. Mol. Ev

ists betwe

numbers]

This kind of docu
tles, and capitali:
names are abbrev
Manual. For both
preceded by a ser

One comm
ences in the orde

You will also notice that the first line of each citation is at the left margin with subsequent lines indented five spaces. This convention is consistant with the *Chicago Manual of Style* format, but in the *APA* format subsequent lines are indented only 4 spaces.

APA FORMAT

The American Psychological Association, a professional organization of social scientists, specifies a documentation format required by most psychology, sociology, communication, education, and economics instructors. This format includes parenthetical documentation in the text that refers to an alphabetical reference list at the ends of the paper.

Parenthetical Documentation in the Text

APA references consist of the author's last name followed by a comma and the year of publication, placed in parentheses immediately following the material taken from the source unless the author's name is used in the body of the text, and then only the year of publication is placed in parenthesis. References to a specific part of a text will also include a page number.

> The earliest study on the differences between men and women and their achievement motives indicated that women have a high motive to avoid success (Horner, 1969). This early data indicating women have a high motive to avoid success relative to men (Horner, 1969) has been repudiated in a recent study by Owens (1988).

The difficulties with this format occur when you have more than two authors, more than two articles published by the same author in the same year, or authors with the same last names.

For more than two authors the first reference will contain all names,

> (Gordon, Williams, Allen, Salkin, & Stein, 1988)

and all later references will have only the first name and *et al.* (*and others* in Latin),

> (Gordon, *et al.*, 1988).

Notice that in parenthetical references and the Reference List the APA format replaces the word "and" with an ampersand ("&").

For an author with more than one publication a year, lowercase letters beginning with *a* follow the date, with the earliest publication receiving the *a*.

> Despite the movement of black males into the middle class, black female single parents still form a ghetto of poverty (Pearce, 1982a).
> Although earlier research found that Black men had increased membership in the middle class significantly, more recent work, which relies on newly

releases
previou

If two auth
initials as w

The Refere

A complete
lows the las
list will be
name and in
information
spaced form
tics within
subtitles are
ticle titles a
Also, two sp

Cowan, R. S.
    ogy fro
    book; c

Gordon, D., V
    marke
    tinuou
    with th

Horner, M. (
    [a mag

Pearce, D. M
    54. [ar
    is und

DOCUMEN

Scientific d
within a sir
documentai
tain to ask
most widel
tem; both a

---

the list of references numerically according to their appearance in the text rather than alphabetically. For example, the first source receives a 1; the second, a 2; the third, a 3, and so on. The reference list then has its first entry numbered 1, its second numbered 2, and so on, regardless of the alphabetical order of authors' names.

CHICAGO MANUAL OF STYLE

Although the *Chicago Manual of Style* includes a discussion of the author-date documentation adopted by both the Council of Biological Editors and the American Psychological Association, when a journal or professor refers a writer to the *Chicago Manual of Style* for documentation guidelines, the journal or professor expects to see a paper that uses notes or footnotes and, most likely, though not necessarily, a bibliography. The notes documenting the text, and corresponding to reference numbers in the text, are called *footnotes* when they appear at the foot of the page and *endnotes* or simply *notes* when they appear at the end of an article or chapter. The *Chicago Manual* prefers that authors use endnotes.

Numbering

Notes should be numbered consecutively throughout an essay beginning with 1. The note numbers in the text follow any punctuation marks (except a dash) and preferably appear at the end of a sentence or at least a clause. The number appears in superscript, a half space *above* the line:

> "This," George Templeton Strong wrote approvingly, "is what our tailors can do."[1] (In an earlier book he has said quite the opposite.)[2] This was obvious in the Shotwell series[3]—and it must be remembered that Shotwell was a student of Robinson.

Note Contents

A note documenting the first reference to a source should include the complete bibliographical information listed below in the order in which they are normally given.

Books

Author's full name
Complete title of the book
Editor, compiler, or translator, if any
Publication information—city where published, publisher, date of publication
Volume number, if any
Page number(s) of the particular citation

Articles in Periodicals

Author's full name
Title of the article
Name of the periodical
Volume (and number) of the periodical
Date of the volume or the issue
Page number(s) of the particular citation

Subsequent References

While the initial reference gives full bibliographical information, subsequent references may be shortened by giving either a shortened title for the work with page reference, or the author's last name and a page reference. If your writing refers to more than one work by a single author, then both name and shortened title will be necessary.

The following example of *Notes* illustrates the *Chicago Manual of Style*'s central format features. The author's name appears in normal order, the first line of the reference is indented five spaces, with the subsequent lines at the left margin. The entire document is double spaced. You will also notice that this format observes conventional punctuation for titles.

> UNDERLINE titles of any work published as a whole—a book; a magazine, journal, or newspaper; a lengthy poem like T. S. Eliot's *The Wasteland*; a movie; or an album.
> PLACE IN QUOTATION MARKS titles of works contained within a whole publication—magazine or journal articles, newspaper headlines, poems within a collection, or a song title.

Explanations about citations appear within brackets.

Notes

1. David Stafford, <u>Britain and European Resistance, 1940–1945</u> (Toronto: University of Toronto Press, 1980), 90. [*a book. Comma follows author's name, publication information placed in parenthesis is unabbreviated, and period follows the page number {which appears without the word "page" or its abbreviation}*]

2. James F. Powers, "Frontier Municipal Baths and Social Interaction in Thirteenth-Century Spain," <u>American Historical Review</u>, 84 (June 1979):655. [*a periodical article. Commas follow both the author's name and the article title; the volume number, 84, immediately precedes the issue date placed in parenthesis and followed by a colon; the page number follows the colon without a space*]

3. James Lost, <u>The Diaries and Correspondence of James Lost</u>, ed. Edward Hughes, 2 vols. (Durham, England: Andrews & Co., 1962), 2:100–212. [*The dia-*

ries and correspondences of James Lost have been edited by Edward Hughes and appear in two volumes. Publication information includes the country as well as the city because confusion might arise over whether the reference is to Durham, North Carolina or Durham, England. The specific reference comes from volume 2, pages 100–102.]

4. Stafford, <u>Resistance</u>, 174. [*shortened title for note 1*]

5. Stafford, 193. [*the same title as note 4*]

6. Lost <u>Diaries and Correspondence</u> 1:150. [*shortened title for note 3 with different volume*]

7. Frank Novak, "The Open University: A Novel Approach to American Education," <u>Time</u>, 14 Nov. 1986, 67–74. [*an article in a popular magazine*]

8. Victoria Myers, The Criticism of S. T. Coleridge: A Serious Study," <u>New York Times</u>, 31 Aug. 1989, Western edition. [*an article in a newspaper. According to the* <u>Chicago Manual</u>, *newspaper articles are rarely listed separately in the Bibliography, and, if they are listed, they follow the format for a popular magazine*]

The Bibliography

The list of sources at the end of a paper is titled *Bibliography*. According to the *Chicago Manual* the most practical and useful arrangement for this is alphabetical order by authors' last names with entries arranged by date when a single author has written more than one work. The bibliography below illustrates the Chicago format conventions, including punctuation:

Bibliography

Barbour, Ian. <u>Myths, Models, and Paradigms: A Comparative Study in Science and Religion</u>. New York: Harper & Row, 1974. [*a book; author, title, and publication information set off by periods*]

Crane, Ronald S. <u>The Idea of the Humanities and Other Essays Critical and Historical</u>. 2 vols. Chicago: University of Chicago Press, 1967. [*a book in two volumes*]

Donegal, L. P., and Joseph Galloway <u>Peace in Ireland</u>. Boston: Nonsuch Press, 1984. [*a book by two authors; a comma follows as well as precedes the given name or initials of the first author*]

————————————————. <u>A Blast of Trumpets</u>. New York: Rinehart Books, 1980. [*same authors as previous entry; note recent date appears first*]

Lost, James. <u>The Diaries and Correspondence of James Lost</u>. Edited by Edward Hughes. 2 vols. Durham, England: Andrews & Co., 1962. [*a two-volume book of works by a single author compiled by an editor; note the full spelling and lack of abbreviation for editor*]

Meltzer, Frances. "On Rimbaud's 'Voyelles'." <u>Modern Philology</u> 76:344–45. [*a periodical article when page numbers immediately follow the volume, a space does not intervene between the colon and the page numbers*]

Powers, James. "Frontier Municipal Baths and Social Interaction in Thirteenth-Century Spain." <u>American Historical Review</u> 84 (June 1979): 605–55. [*a periodical article; periods follow both the author's name and the article title; spaces follow the volume number and the colon because parenthetical information comes between the volume and page numbers*]

Wilburn, Lydia. "Sometimes a Cigar Is Just a Cigar: Freudian Interpretations of Feminist Literature." <u>Harper's</u> May 1989, 16–19. [*an article in a popular magazine*]

You have probably noticed that though the bibliography entry contains essentially the same information as the note, the format changes. The chief differences are that in the bibliography the author's name is reversed, but appears in normal sequence in the note, and that in the bibliography the period replaces the commas and parentheses used in the note. They also differ in their use of page citations: for periodical articles full pagination appears, and no pagination appears for books. The following examples show the basic differences between notes and bibliography in book and article references:

Notes

1. David Stafford, <u>Britain and European Resistance, 1940–1945</u> (Toronto: University of Toronto Press, 1980), 90.

2. James Powers, "Frontier Municipal Baths and Social Interaction in Thirteenth-Century Spain," <u>American Historical Review</u> 84 (June 1979):655.

Bibliography

Powers, James. "Frontier Municipal Baths and Social Interaction in Thirteenth-Century Spain." <u>American Historical Review</u> 84 (June 1979): 649–67.

Stafford, David. <u>Britain and European Resistance, 1940–1945</u>. Toronto: University of Toronto Press, 1980.

The reference formats set forth in this chapter should serve as general guidelines. When you carefully give your reader information about your sources you may encounter some problems this chapter has not fully addressed, for example, multiple authors or unknown authors, works published by organizations or committees, encyclopedias or specialized dictionaries. All of the style manuals referred to in this chapter give hundreds of special circumstances and their preferred documentation. Should you encounter problems please refer to:

MLA Handbook for Writers of Research Papers. Second edition. New York: Modern Language Association, 1984.

Publication Manual of the American Psychological Association. Third Edition. New York: American Psychological Association, 1983.

Council of Biology Editors Style Manual: A Guide for Authors, Editors, and Publishers in the Biological Sciences. Fifth edition. Bethesda: Council of Biology Editors, Inc., 1983.

The Chicago Manual of Style. Thirteenth edition. Chicago and London: University of Chicago Press, 1982.

■ EXERCISES

1. For the preliminary bibliography you prepared for question 3 in Chapter 6's exercises (or for a working bibliography for a paper you are working on), prepare a final bibliography (or List of Works Cited or References) according to each documentation format.

2. For one essay in each of the anthology's discipline areas, write a brief assessment of its documentation. If necessary, correct its documentation format to conform to the accepted format for the discipline. ■

II ANTHOLOGY
Students
Writing
Across the
Disciplines

8

Students Writing in the Disciplines: An Introduction and Three Cases

This book's first section increased your awareness of how writers research, organize, and develop their materials. This section demonstrates how students have applied their skills in writing papers for college courses across the academic curriculum. While the subject matter may change from a literature course to a sociology course, the things we do when we write for all the disciplines—planning, gathering information, drafting, and revising—are similar for every writing task. The student essays in this collection also show that the writing tasks in the various disciplines are quite similar. Outside of scientific reports, which appear exclusively in the sciences and social sciences, students write position papers (arguments), reviews of the literature (reports researched from secondary sources), and critical and comparative analyses (reviews and book reports) for science and art courses as well as for literature and business classes.

LEARNING FROM STUDENT WRITERS

As we discussed in Chapter 3, academic disciplines have developed certain conventions for expediting communication with the discipline. Many of the examples in the anthology reflect these conventions; others, like book reviews, represent a kind of writing that appears not only in all academic disciplines but in popular publications. When you read different essays in the following anthology, you may initially find great diversity, but when you look more closely at the ways the writers solve their writing problems rather than at the essays' contents, several patterns (or structures) appear in all disciplines. These structures can suggest approaches for your own writing. What this means is not that you will copy a writer's thesis and use her evidence, but that you may identify essential structures, adapt these patterns to your own purposes and subject matter, and fit your thesis and evidence on these bones. These patterns are not to be seen as formulas for writing. Some of them, like the scientific report or the critical analysis (book review) reflect conventions that "professional" writing in a discipline uses, but others represent *options* you might like to try in your own writing.

Besides helping you find overall patterns or approaches for your writing, the essays in the anthology can help you see how other students have anticipated audiences, responded to assignments, and developed their own "voices." You will see how fellow students have met the challenge of integrating their own learning experiences and knowledge with their course work. When you read these essays you will want to employ those critical reading skills we discussed in Chapter 2 to help you understand how the writers have responded to assignments, and how they have shaped their knowledge and research to achieve their purposes and reach their audiences. (Following each essay you will find questions to help you with this.)

The next portion of this chapter presents and discusses three student essays to help you recognize some common strategic patterns and understand the choices these students made about audience and purpose. These essays, like those in the anthology chapters, represent typical kinds of writing students do across the academic curriculum.

THE SCIENTIFIC REPORT

In "To Be Successful or Not to Be Successful," Jay Owens presents his research on the differences between college men's and college women's motivations to achieve or avoid success. For a cross-curriculum writing course, Jay and his fellow classmates conducted a limited experiment on male and female attitudes toward success. They modeled their experiment on the work done in the late 1960s by psychologist Matina Horner. While the experiment's scope and design were limited both by Horner's original work and the class's scientific experience, Jay and his fellow students had to develop a working hypothesis, accumulate experimental data, present and assess the data, and reach a conclusion just as they would have to for any scientific experiment. The essay that follows uses the scientific report's conventions to report the "experiment."

Jay's essay begins by stating the research problem—whether the "motive to avoid success," earlier believed to be more prevalent in women than in men, has changed with recent changes in men and women's roles. He then summarizes Matina Horner's research on achievement motivation. In response to recent social changes he proposes his own hypotheses: that the motive to avoid success would be less evident than in Horner's study, but that it would still be more characteristic of women than men. He goes on to describe his experiment—the sample and the test—report the data, discuss the findings, and present the conclusion. Owens's essay conforms to the scientific report's structure.

INDUCTIVE ARGUMENT

Problem
Review of literature
Hypothesis
Experiment description
Data report
Data interpretation
Conclusion

The section identifications appearing below in brackets do not appear in an actual report, although the subtopic headings would.

To Be Successful or Not to Be Successful

Jay Owens

[introduction stating problem]

Conventional wisdom assumes that people strive toward success. However, many people feel uneasy about success and may even try to avoid succeeding when given the chance. This inner anxiety concerning success, known as the *motive to avoid success*, while it has been believed to be more prevalent in female than in male attitudes, should have changed with recent changes of men's and women's roles in society.

[literature review]

In 1969 Matina Horner published an article in *Psychology Today* that explored the differences in feelings concerning success in men and women. She asked a group of college students to respond to the following writing cue: "After first-term finals John finds himself at the top of his medical school class." *John* was changed to *Joan* on the women's tests. Horner then analyzed the papers that were a result of the cue and came to the conclusion that women feel a stronger motive to avoid success. Her research also pointed out that women feel intimidated by men and are extremely reluctant to succeed in a competitive situation with a man.

[hypothesis]
Despite Horner's findings, I began my study with the following hypotheses:

(1) The motive to avoid success would not be as evident in the subjects as it was twenty years ago in Horner's study.
(2) Women would still feel more anxiety about success than men, due to America's male-dominated society.

Test Administration

[experiment description]
Twenty-four college freshman were asked to write an essay in response to a cue similar to Horner's: "After first-term finals John (Joanna) finds himself at the top of his Harvard business school class . . ." Because of recent interest in business we had John attending Harvard business school rather than an unknown medical school. These differences are not large enough to change the experiment drastically. Medicine and business are both considered successful endeavors, and the emphasis on Harvard simply stresses success. The subjects, half male and half female, taken from freshman honors courses were considered very motivated students. The responses to the cue were entirely different in each individual case, but they could be separated into four groups.

Results

[experimental results—data]
The first group of stories showed a definite anxiety concerning success. Approximately 27 percent of the total samples fit into this category. These stories associated success with social problems, drug use, death, or a combination of the three.

The second category contained a story line which meshes with the first group. The motive to avoid success was displayed by characters who cheated or obtained success by other unethical means. Of all the responses, 17 percent fell into this category. It is interesting to note that within this group, 75 percent of the characters were punished for their actions, while only 25 percent actually got away with committing crimes.

The third category is the opposite of the first two. A surprising 25 percent of the total were basic success stories. John worked hard to overcome adversity and succeed. Whenever the subject expressed a doubt whether the success was "worth it," the decision was always affirmative.

The last category contains stories that were a redefinition of success. These characters left the business world, or were mysteriously never in the business world. This category contains 29 percent of the total responses.

Discussion

[discussion]

The experiment represents a very small sample, and cannot be extended as a representation of the entire country, or even of the entire university. However, the results do indicate some patterns that one would expect to see in the larger society.

The responses that were success stories and promoted a positive image of success were 50 percent male and 50 percent female. In this category, sex is not a factor. On the other hand, the negative responses accounted for 46 percent of the total responses. Within this group, 64 percent are male. This points out that men are just as uncomfortable about success as women, thus confirming my hypothesis. Perhaps as more women have entered the job market, men have started feeling more threatened.

Another interesting point about sex differences is seen in the fourth category. Only 40 percent of those who redefined success were male. Perhaps males still see business as a successful, rewarding career, while females find other ways to achieve happiness. This might also indicate that women feel intimidated by the male-dominated business world.

Perhaps the most interesting finding appears in the second category. Here, the character succeeded by unethical means. This group accounted for 17 percent of the total. Within this group, 75 percent were punished for their actions. Death was the usual punishment. Remarkably, the group which did punish its character was 100 percent male, and the group which did not punish its character was 100 percent female. This displays an attitude that the end does not justify the means. Men feel this more strongly than women and may also view cheating as a more severe problem than do women.

Finally, if one divided all the samples into two groups, male and female, 75 percent of both groups would contain the motive to avoid success.

[conclusion]

All of these results display a difference from what Horner found. It seems that women are not more uncomfortable with success than men. Both sexes tend to feel threatened by success and the burden that may come with it. This could be a significant step for women, or it could just show that both sexes are affected as business becomes more competitive. The precise reason for these results requires more careful study. But clearly, Matina Horner's study is both inaccurate and obsolete for today's men and women.

The scientific report's overall inductive pattern is clear in Jay's paper. He presents the specific data before he reaches his conclusions. That Jay acknowledges the sample's limitation in both size and diversity shows his awareness that a conclusion from limited evidence contributes to a weak inductive argument. Besides using induction as an organizing pattern, Jay also uses summary and classification. He summarize's Matina Horner's 1969 article and describes her research methods. After describing his own experiment, he uses classification when he groups his evidence into different categories. These categories emerged when Jay and other members of his research group sat for several hours reading the sample essays. The essays told very different stories, so the research group had to look at patterns of similarity and difference. Jay found the task of reporting and interpreting the data more difficult than actually writing the report since the form for a scientific report is so highly conventionalized.

A POSITION PAPER USING ARGUMENT AND REBUTTAL

Jason Hallman wrote "Is Science Ethical?" for a freshman seminar that considered the assumptions governing scientific research in relation to science's achievements. For this assignment the class read Jacob Bronowski's book, *Science and Human Values*, which identifies the practice of science with the values of democracy. The students were to either agree or disagree with Bronowski's position that science and technology are ethical, and their abuses have resulted from human ethical failures. Jason's essay begins with the position Bronowski stated in one of the book's essays that no "sharp boundary" exists between science and technology. Jason goes from there to the assumption that if truth is the ethical imperative of science, it must also be technology's imperative since Bronowski equates science and technology. Jason is here developing a deductive argument that uses the syllogism:

> Technology is the same as science.   (Major premise)
> Science is ethical.   (Minor Premise)
> Therefore, technology is ethical.   (Conclusion)

Remembering the discussion of logic in Chapters 4 and 5, you will recognize that this is a "valid" syllogism. Jason goes on to establish the syllogism's truth by offering evidence that supports science's worth. He then counters the position that science is ethical with evidence from astronomy and physics, chemistry, and biology and medicine. In doing this he shows that his initial syllogism is not true and thereby disputes his initial argument.

In the first part of his argument, Jason has constructed a critique of the position that science is ethical by disproving his major deductive premise. He then moves to rebut this view by demonstrating that in those same areas where science has failed mankind, new action is being taken to remedy serious problems. He can, thus, reach the conclusion that, "It is the very nature of science and the scientist to take care of the problems which science and technology inevitably bring about as a by-product of change."

The pattern for Jason's essay, which looks like this,

Introduction
Position A summary
Position A opposing evidence
Rebuttal position (B) summary
Position B supporting evidence
Conclusion

is one pattern for an argumentative essay discrediting one position and advancing an alternative.

Is Science Ethical?

Jason Hallman

In his essay "The Creative Mind," Jacob Bronowski defines science, ". . . as the organization of our knowledge in such a way that it commands more of the hidden potential in nature." This raises the question of whether the applications of science (technology) should be considered as science; Bronowski addresses that issue in the same essay when he states that, "It [science] admits no sharp boundary between knowledge and use." Obviously Bronowski considers technology to be the logical extension of science and, in fact, an inherent part of science.

To evaluate whether science and technology are ethical we turn to the meaning of ethics. Rather than formulate principles for use as ethical guidelines, a more general philosophy of ethical behavior will suit the purposes of this discussion. The problem encountered when dealing with specific precepts concerns the precept's applicability in all situations. This dilemma grows into the quagmire of ethical relativism, the assertion that there can be no generalization of ethics because there are no infinitely common ethical questions or answers. In response to this theory of ethics a number of other ethical attitudes have arisen. The scientist has remained through the ages almost aloof from this turmoil of philosophical controversy, although at times it has certainly inflicted its unwanted presence on him. This distant stance has been sustained by an obligation to truth as an end in itself. The very nature of science centers around a quest for greater understanding, and this has in turn created a sense that scientists cannot rise above the truth which they are seeking to uncover. Of course, this has been subject to exceptions, but for the most part has been the underlying factor

responsible for developing the ethical imperatives which have preserved the integrity of science.

[position A]

The history of science clearly demonstrates this encompassing drive
for truth. Modern science began with the first astronomical model by
Claudius Ptolemy. This theory was fundamentally flawed because of
limited means of observing celestial movement beyond the moon.
Fourteen hundred years later, the Polish astronomer Nicolaus Coperni-
cus discovered Ptolemy's error, and postulated the heliocentric view as
opposed to Ptolemy's geocentric view of the solar system. Unfortunately, the Roman Catholic Church proved unreceptive to such her-
esy, and condemned the theory. The invention of the telescope enabled
Galileo Galilei to prove the fact that the planets orbited the sun, yet
the Church forced him to recant his position and retire. This was perhaps the first instance of a scientist facing a sizable ethical dilemma.
The same understanding of truth allowed Galileo to indulge the
Church their token victory, enabling him to recant what he knew to be
true. The Church's refusal to accept the truth did nothing to change its
nature. He realized that Truth needs no defense, and that time would
vindicate him when in the face of insurmountable evidence, the
Church would concede the Truth.

Following the Copernican Revolution science blossomed steadily
with little opposition. Its applications were quietly utilized in industry
while humanity clearly benefited. With the advent of the Industrial
Revolution in England, however, science once again was often viewed
as a threat. The Luddite movement typified this hostile attitude and
eventually adopted violent methods of opposing industrial progress.
The eventual success of the Industrial Revolution and the integration
of many new technologies into society caused a new brand of concern
about science to emerge. It would eventually result in the cultural division between "humanistic" academia and "scientific" academia which
Sir Charles Snow proclaimed in 1959.

[position A critique]

World War I brought these latent concerns to the forefront. Science
was named as the progenitor of the modern machines of war. Poison
gas, machine guns, tanks, artillery: all were seen as resulting from scientific advances. Sadly, the accusation was not unreasonable. The
Great War exposed the world to slaughter on a scale never before con-
templated—someone was to blame for the carnage! World War II drew
even more attention to the role of scientists in the destruction of human life. Nazi rocket scientists unleashed the fury and devastation of
the V2 "buzz bomb" on London civilians, and the United States un-

leashed the fury and devastation of nuclear bombs on Hiroshima and Nagasaki. Much of the blame was placed upon the scientific community—without whom the fury and devastation would not have been possible.

Following the war, America and the Soviet Union became absorbed in the Space Race. Amazing advances in astronomy and physics were made, and science was granted a brief reprieve. All the sciences progressed as government funds became increasingly available and universities began sponsoring major research efforts. Amidst increasingly cautious public sentiment, the computer revolution swept in and modern technology firmly entrenched itself in our lives. As people began examining some of the "disconcerting ways" science was making itself known, they began questioning whether obligation to the truth was still maintaining science's integrity. Recently we often ask whether the modern scientific community has deserted this ideology and replaced it with lower motivations. What began as a mere query has now grown into an urgent probe of fact and motive throughout the scientific community. Examination of modern science and technology itself does not yield very optimistic results. In fact, the current state of affairs would apparently indicate that perhaps the foes of science are correct in their indictment. Take, for example, the field of astronomy and physics: two years ago America's prodigy, the space shuttle, exploded because of shoddy engineering and a politically motivated launch schedule. Where was anything similar to an attitude of objective responsibility? Nuclear reactors annually generate thousands of tons of radioactive waste which will be with us for at least as long as our concept of forever allows. Where is responsible foresight? Chernobyl spread contamination across the globe when human error nearly caused its core to melt down. Rather than forcing governments on an international scale to eliminate nuclear weapons, scientists are engaged in creating even more efficient doomsday devices like the MX missile. Where is their obligation to truth?

On the side of chemistry, science has yielded chemical weapons of virulently deadly potency. Unlike nuclear weapons, these have actually been used during recent years in the Gulf War. Pesticides have been developed and put to use without sufficient impact studies as to their effect on the environment, the food chain, or even humans. In order to circumvent stricter production requirements, chemical engineering companies move their plants to third world nations, where they can afford a Bhopal occasionally. Where is any sign of moral conscience now? As increasing fossil fuel use brings on the global warming trend, where are the petroleum engineers? They are exploring cheaper ways to extract crude oil from anywhere they can think of! Pollution from virtually every aspect of chemical processes down to the finished product itself wreaks havoc on the environment, from acid rain to ozone deterioration. Where is the sense of respect and wonder for the natural world?

In biology and medicine, we find inhumane research being carried on, even in fields themselves inherently filled with unresolved ethical dilemmas. Biotechnology and genetic engineering contain potential pitfalls we are only beginning to recognize. Our current medical capabilities often call for doctors or even laymen to make decisions of divine proportions. Where is a sense of perspective on human limitations? The issues we could raise are nearly endless—these have served as a mere sampling—but sobering nonetheless. Again, where in all this is a feeling of an obligation to the betterment of humanity?

[position B]

Is there any defense to be made for where science has brought us today? Perhaps the views above do not reflect the progressive nature of science discussed earlier; perhaps these issues do warrant a more comprehensive view. Today, the space shuttle Discovery was successfully launched into space, after two years of self-evaluation on the part of the entire American space program. We have not yet been able to solve all of the problems connected with nuclear power, but recently it has been suggested that fusion reactors will eventually be able to actually destroy the radioactive waste products of fission without generating any of their own. While pesticides do have obvious dangers, and the companies which produce them have perhaps not been as careful as they should, an awareness of this is bringing about a perceptible change in their attitudes and actions. As unlikely as it may seem, one of the largest research undertakings of the world's petroleum industry has been to find alternatives to fossil fuels in many areas of industry and other fields. Awareness in the scientific community and in the public of environmental problems has led to discussion and implementation of plans to solve this significant issue. While it is true that we are uncertain of many of the ramifications of biotechnology and genetics, the answer is not to close these fields off, but to explore them with caution and that sense of responsibility to the truth. With every problem medicine presents us with, there exist hundreds of unimpeachable benefits to offset the relatively few problems. Even these have been recognized and an attempt made to deal with them in a satisfactory manner. Ethics committees, peer review, and outside consultants are but a few of the ways modern medicine is still seeking the truth.

The scientist and warfare deserve to be addressed separately. War is an area which by nature is incompatible with ethical behavior. Science has been brought into the theater of war not by scientists, but by warriors. It is not my place to question their participation in such endeavors. It is useful to note though, that since the first use of the Bomb, and since the creation of biological and chemical weapons, none of the major world powers have used any of these in their various conflicts. A part of this reluctance must be ascribed to the efforts of the scientific community to prevent their use.

[conclusion]

What I have tried to establish here is the concept that science is a dynamic process. That it IS still guided by the same attitudes and sentiment outlined earlier. It is the very nature of science and the scientist to take care of the problems which science and technology inevitably bring about as a byproduct of change. Science originates the problem and the solution. Such an awareness and sense of responsibility is not found in any other pursuit, and it is the essense of ethical behavior.

You have seen how Jason used organizational and argument strategies, but what about the other considerations that went into this essay? Jason wrote this in response to an assignment that focused on a reading assignment. Some, but not all, of the information Jason used here was in his source, Bronowski. He also drew upon his own general knowledge about science. To do this he used brainstorming on science and technology's successes and failures. Obviously, he had a tremendous span of scientific time to draw upon and organize. He orders this material by looking at the development of science—he uses a chronological approach. He finds science's greatest abuses in recent time, so there he categorizes scientific abuse.

Jason chose to survey scientific morality, but he could instead have selected one category of misuse and developed his evidence and argument in greater detail. His choice was probably shaped by the audience he was writing for and his purpose. Jason was writing for other students in his seminar, who would also be familiar with the overview of issues he discusses. The essay's focus is more on the argument—the position—than on research into detailed examples. Advancing his position—his argument—is the essay's central purpose. He seeks in the fullest sense to answer his, and Bronowski's question, "Is Science Ethical?"

A CRITICAL ANALYSIS

A critical analysis does not necessarily have to present an argument evaluating something's worth; it may, instead, explain how the object of the critical analysis works by considering its parts and their interrelationship. Most critical analyses in the anthology's essays are book reviews, but Joy Bianchi's paper on a poem also uses this approach. In the essay " 'The End of the World' by Archibald MacLeish," Joy Bianchi explains MacLeish's poem by describing each of the poem's features and suggesting its meaning. She identifies the poem as a sonnet (a fourteen-line poem written in iambic pentameter—twenty syllables alternating weak and strong stresses) and adopts the sonnet's organizational principal of octave (eight line group) and sestet (six line group) as the organizational principal for her analysis. Besides the poetic form she also considers other poetic elements: imagery, diction, and meter. The shape of Joy's paper looks like this:

> Summary
> Part A (octave)
> Description, component 1 [imagery]
> Assessment, component 1
> Description, component 2 [diction]
> Assessment, component 2
> Decription, component 3 [meter]
> Assessment, component 3
> Part B (sestet)
> Description, component 1 [imagery]
> Assessment, component 1
> Description, component 2 [diction]
> Assessment, component 2
> Conclusion

This structure could serve as well for a critique of a short story, novel, film, television series, or rock concert, or to explain a scientific experiment's structure or evaluate a patient's case history.

"The End of the World" by Archibald MacLeish

Joy Bianchi

The End of the World

Quite unexpectedly as Vasserot
The armless ambidextrian was lighting
a match between his great and second toe,
And Ralph the lion was engaged in biting
The neck of Madame Sossman while the drum
Pointed, and Teeny was about to cough
In waltz-time swinging Jocko by the thumb—

Quite unexpectedly the top blew off:
And there, there, overhead, there, there hung over
Those thousands of white faces, those dazed eyes
There in the starless dark the poise, the over,
There with vast wings across the cancelled skies,
There in the sudden blackness the black pall
Of nothing, nothing, nothing—nothing at all.
    Archibald MacLeish

The end of the world. This simple statement provokes a torrent of thoughts: [summary] death, fear, confusion. MacLeish recognizes the anxieties brought on by these thoughts, and tries to portray his connotations of them in his English sonnet entitled "The End of the World."

The poem is divided into two main parts, an octave followed by a sestet. [A: description 1] The octave's circus world is filled with images of animals and funny people doing strange things: Ralph the Lion, engaged in biting Madame Sossman by the neck, little coughing Teeny, and Jocko swinging by the thumb. A struggle to read, nothing in the octave seems to make sense.

[A: assessment 1] Chaotic imagery strong here heightens the feeling of panic and raises misunderstanding. MacLeish describes a jumbled disconnected world on the verge of annihilation, a world contrary to the one we know, precariously balanced on the earth's longevity. MacLeish's deliberate confusion and play on words in this octave clearly demonstrate the lack of reason and normalcy which could precede "The End of the World."

[A: description 2] MacLeish starts off right away with his play on words in line 2 when he writes of "the armless ambidextrian" who "was lighting a match between his great and second toe." First of all, the task of lighting a match between two toes on one foot seems to be an impossible feat. Secondly, an ambidextrian is a person with the ability to use both hands equally well. If he lacks arms, he must also be missing hands. Obviously a person is not an ambidextrian if he has no hands. This [A: assessment 2] example illustrates the underlying feeling of complication and paradox. Nothing is as it should be.

Inconsistent meter within the poem also manifests the chaotic feeling and lack of normalcy. Quite unexpectedly, the [A: description 3] poem starts off with a dactylic trimeter and then varies into the expected iambic pentameter in the first octave. The emphasis on the first word *Quite* is followed by the two weak syllables *un* and *ex. Pect* is strong, whereas *ed* and *ly* are weak. The rest of the line continues with these dactyls of strong-weak-weak. These [A: assessment 3] differences of rhythm force the reader to slow down and inspect the alteration in each line.

[part A assessment and transition] The first octave seems to express a dismal, yet almost comic and childlike view of the world near its end. Then, "Quite unexpectedly, the top blew off": this last line in the first octave sets the change in motion for the second part of the poem, the sestet. The "top blowing off" gives a graphic image of destruction, and the colon after the word *off* indicates that more is to come.

And come it does. The sestet [B: description and assessment 1] deviates abruptly from the rambling phrases of the octave to a much more serious and desolate tone. [B: decription 2] MacLeish writes of the thousands of white faces and dazed eyes, indicating surprise and shock. In stark contrast to the white faces exists the blackest black: "starless dark . . . vast wings across cancelled skies . . . sudden blackness . . . black pall." A very thick and heavy black, it is described as "hung over" and "hovering."

The severe sestet contrasts starkly to the octave with its childlike rendition of silly thoughts and strange occurrences.

[B: assessment 2] This dark sestet seems to tease the light "nursery rhyme" poetry of the octave, just like a teasing child who frightens a sibling afraid of the dark by turning out the lights. It seems to say that when the end of the world arrives, we will be like frightened and helpless children.

When a teacher wants to make a point, he usually repeats what he wants his students to know several times for emphasis. MacLeish wants the sestet to stand out as the poem's main part. The very first line of the sestet stops the reader with the repetition of the word *there*. "And there, there overhead, there there hung over . . ." Three out of four lines in the body of the sestet also begin with the word *there*. *There* functions gramatically to point out something. It is a strong word connected with direction. If someone asks where to look for something, the answer would be to "look over *there*."

[conclusion] The repetition of the phrase "Quite unexpectedly" in the first part of the poem has a binding effect on the octave and sestet: it begins and ends and binds together the "unexpected jumble of phrases" with their meaning. The apparently meaningless confusion is subtly described "here," in the octave, but the meaning of the poem is hidden *there,* in the sestet. The meaning of the poem is summed up with a realization that things are not what they appear to be. What should have made sense is now confused; the armless ambidextrian, for instance. Where once events might have existed and meant something, now they have disappeared. Nothing is crucial because in the end life's value will be moot. The significance of four *nothings* in a row

in the last line draws the reader in, forces him to read the words, to acknowledge their presence and their meaning: nothing has value; there
is nothing left, "nothing at all." The final line of MacLeish's sonnet is
his depiction of the end of the world as well as the end of the poem.

Joy uses literary analysis's specialized vocabulary, particularly when
describing poetic form and meter. Writing for an introductory literature
course, Joy's language shows her learning the "professional" conventions for
literary analysis. She writes here for her peers. If she were writing for students outside of her academic discipline, she would have chosen a vocabulary more familiar to a broader audience. Another choice Joy made was to
use the poem's form as her own organizing principle. She could instead have
summarized the poem's meaning line by line and then treated each poetic
device (meter, imagery, diction, etc.) separately. Joy's organizational choice
strengthens her writing's appeal to an audience conversant in literary discourse conventions.

Comparative Analysis

Joy chose to explain MacLeish's poem by a close analysis, but she might also
have looked at the poem in relation to another writer's sonnet or other
poems by MacLeish. Had she chosen this approach, she would have written
a *comparative analysis*. The shape of such an essay would look like this:

Introduction (including thesis)
Brief summary poem A
Component 1-A
Component 2-A
Component 3-A
Component 4-A, etc.
Brief summary poem B
Component 1-B
Component 2-B
Component 3-B
Component 4-B, etc.
Similarities A & B
Differences A & B
Conclusion

A comparative analysis looks at the relationships between like parts of
two or more similar things. A comparative analysis requires at least one
common ground—the same hypothesis, the same focus of investigation, the
same researcher, or in the case of literary analysis, the same author or the
same genre. Also, it must consider the same analytical components for each
thing. A comparative analysis usually serves some purpose other than ex-

plaining how the two things work. A comparative analysis usually clarifies the objects' common ground. By comparing two case studies a psychologist not only could show differences and similarities in each patient's symptoms, but could increase understanding of their behaviors. A study of two critic's readings of Shakespeare's *Macbeth* would inform the reader about both the play and any critical controversy. Had Joy considered MacLeish's poem in relation to another sonnet, she might have illustrated how sonnet form can effectively communicate irony.

Two organizational strategies can be used for comparative analyses. Like the example above, a writer can either analyze one object, then the other, and follow the analyses with a discussion of the similarities and differences. Or, he can focus on one analytical component at a time, looking at both (or all) objects of consideration. Such an approach would look like this:

Introduction (including thesis)
Brief summary A & B (etc.)
Component 1 A & B (etc.): similarities and differences
Component 2 A & B (etc.): similarities and differences
Component 3 A & B (etc.): similarities and differences
Component 4 A & B (etc.): similarities and differences
Conclusion

Critique

Another choice Joy Bianchi might have made in her literary study would have been to combine her analysis with judgment about the poem's merit or effectiveness. Had she done this she would have written a *critique*. When evaluating something, saying, "I like it" or "I didn't understand it" is not enough. A critique explains *why* something works or does not work. A writer needs to bring to a critique all his analytical skills—a clear understanding of the analysis's objective, specified analytical components, careful observation, or, in the case of a book review, a critical reading. To this he will add standards for judgment. These are called critical *criteria*.

Criteria and Evaluation

Learning what constitutes "good work" in any field of endeavor is part of that field's education. Each academic discipline has both assumptions that govern its investigations and standards by which its work is evaluated. The standards of objectivity and verifiability that govern scientific research differ from an artist's creativity and originality. A discipline's standards and assumptions usually become the criteria we use when we write evaluations of experiments, patients, creative works, or published research. As a student in an academic area, you will need to familiarize yourself with your discipline's assumptions. We will look at one example to suggest how cues for developing criteria come from course work.

Often a professor will ask students to write a book review. A good clue for criteria for such a review often comes from how other course materials have been presented. For example, an American social history class discussed David M. Potter's book *People of Plenty,* which refines Frederick Jackson Turner's hypothesis that the frontier shaped the American character by replacing Turner's *the frontier* with Potter's *abundance* (abundance shaped the American character). The class discussion emphasized that Potter's book's value lay in breaking new ground in social history by combining accurate historical observations with vital work done on national character by anthropologists, social psychologists, and psychoanalysts.

The book that the students have been asked to review argues that the privileges accorded white male landowners by the Constitution shaped the American character. Besides looking at the relationship between the thesis and the evidence (always an important consideration for historical studies), a critique of this book would be wise to consider whether the book meets the criteria the professor had previously introduced: "breaking new ground," "accurate historical observations," and the presence of "vital work done on national character by anthropologists, social psychologists, and psychoanalysts."

Besides summarizing the book, the critique would consider each of the criteria and the textual evidence which shows the writer either meeting or failing to meet the criteria. Each criterion becomes an analytic component and thereby gives shape to the essay. The pattern for such a critique would look something like this:

Introduction
Summary
Analysis
Component 1 (criterion 1)
Textual evidence for or against criterion 1
Component 2 (criterion 2)
Textual evidence for or against criterion 2
Component 3 (criterion 3)
Textual evidence for or against criterion 3
Conclusion which gives overall estimation of the work

We have considered a special critique, the book review, because book reviews and reviews of literature appear in all disciplines in this collection of student writing. Book reviews are not the only kind of critiques that students write, however; they write critiques of performances, case histories, and scientific experiments. These critiques differ in the criteria they evolve and in the evidence they present, but their overall approaches are remarkably similar.

STUDENT WRITER'S CHOICES

We have closely considered the choices three students have made, as well as a few other options for writing analyses, to suggest how you can learn from the essays included in the following pages. Jay Owens, Jason Hallman, and Joy Bianchi have envisioned their audiences and made choices about evidence, language, and structure to help them reach these audiences and achieve their goals. The patterns we found in their writing are one way of explaining one aspect of their choices. Hopefully, when you look at the work of fellow students in the pages ahead, you will find options for your own writing in the choices they have made. You may also decide that some of their writing strategies will not work for your audiences and purposes. Like Jay, Jason, and Joy, you will make choices and adapt approaches to your own special needs.

■ EXERCISE

The essay following examines the relationship between John Fowles's novel *The French Lieutenant's Woman* and the film. As you read the essay, answer the following questions. When you have finished prepare a model or descriptive pattern like the ones we have been working with in this chapter. ■

■ QUESTIONS

1. Sandbach narrows the focus of his analysis to what common aspect(s) of the film and book?

2. What criteria for evaluation does Paragraph 3 establish?

3. In what direction will these criteria take a discussion of literature or film?

4. Where does the essay apply these criteria to the book? Where to the film?

5. What other analytical components besides novel and film are used for applying the critical criteria?

6. Besides the criteria introduced for evaluating serious and escape literature, what other criteria does the author introduce? Do the criteria for a discussion of film differ from those for literature?

7. To what kind of conclusion does the comparative analysis of film and novel lead? What other possibilities did the study allow?

8. Where does the writer use summary? How effective are these summaries in developing the comparative analysis? ■

The French Lieutenant's Woman's *Endings*

Robert Sandbach

In John Fowles's novel, *The French Lieutenant's Woman*, one can see the creation for all intents and purposes of a double ending. The first ending is a romantic convention or seemingly "happy" ending that is more characteristic of escape literature, whereas the second ending, or "sad" one, could be perceived as characterizing serious literature and being, therefore, more realistic. In Harold Pinter's screenplay for the movie, *The French Lieutenant's Woman*, the viewer also feels a sense of ambiguity at the end for, like the novel, the movie presents us with alternative endings. The "happy" ending takes place within the frame of the movie between Sarah and Charles, while the "sad" ending occurs in the outer frame between Anna and Mike, the actors who play Sarah and Charles. Both the book and the movie present us with alternative endings, but because of the different expectations of the book audience and the movie audience one ending, the "sad" or realistic one, works better for the book and the other ending, the "happy" one, works better for the movie.

Fowles's novel actually presents the reader with three possible endings, the happy one, the sad one, and a very inconclusive ending which is suggested in chapter 55. In chapter 55 we find Charles on board a train to London where he encounters John Fowles, the author. Fowles considers the idea of ending the novel at this point but realizes that this would be very inconclusive, and, therefore, I will not, as Fowles did not, consider this as an ending at all.

In order to determine which ending works better for the novel, the reader must first come to terms with Fowles's purpose for writing it. Basically, what it comes down to is the question of whether the novel should be read for escape or be considered as a more serious piece of interpretive literature. This question prompts me to ask another question. Why do we read literature, or more specifically, *The French Lieutenant's Woman*, at all? What are the expectations of the reader? Laurence Perrine suggests that,

> Unless it [literature] expands our minds or quickens our sense of life, its claim is not appreciably greater than that of video games, bridge, or ping pong. To have a compelling claim on our attention, it must yield not only enjoyment but understanding (3).

My feeling on the matter is that the immature reader who lives exclusively on an escape diet, would choose the first ending of the novel primarily because this type of reader seeks to find a happy outcome in everything. The problem with this as Laurence Perrine suggests, is that as for television, where the happy outcome is a given, it "sends the reader away undisturbed and optimistic about the world . . . It creates superficial attitudes towards life . . . distorts our view of reality and gives us false expectations" (7). While there are plenty of novels that are suitable for such reading endeavors, such as Harlequin Romances, the *French Lieutenant's Woman* has a theme which requires that it be read for both "enjoyment and understanding," or as a serious piece of interpretive literature. Only when the reader realizes that Fowles is not dealing with the story of a romance involving two lovers, but rather is attempting to illustrate the concept of personal growth, will he/she understand that the novel is not focusing solely on entertainment as escape literature does, but rather on a broader, more encompassing generalization about life as interpretive literature does.

The first or happy ending is presented to the reader in chapter 60. After Charles discovers that Sarah is living in London under the assumed name of Mrs. Roughwood, he goes to see her. Sarah, however, is not won back easily by Charles, for after some discussion she states,

> I do not wish to marry, I do not wish to marry because of my past, which habituated me to loneliness. . . . I do not want to share my life (Fowles 353).

Charles then states, "Then you have not only ruined my life. You have taken pleasure in doing so" (354). At this point, it seems as if this ending will not provide any form of reconciliation, but Fowles, who here defers to the conventions of the Victorian novel, probably felt compelled to include it. The scene closes, and the romantic convention appears as Sarah brings out their young child, Lalage, and the couple, finally, after the long period of separation and problems, is reunited. While this ending is "happy," it is, quite frankly, too happy. It sends the reader away, as Perrine suggests, with a distorted view of reality, and, more importantly, this ending fails to convey the message or theme that Fowles presents throughout the novel. I think Fowles was dissatisfied not only with this ending for his novel but with this type of ending in general. He probably saw the foolishness of and the problems with such endings and broke away from this convention by including his second ending. At this point his intention in including both endings is now clear; it serves to illustrate his dissatisfaction with Victorian literature's conventional ending.

Fowles's second ending appears in chapter 61 and begins with Fowles, himself, setting his watch back fifteen minutes in order to restart the scene in the middle of the argument between Sarah and

Charles. This time, however, the sight of the child does not effect a reconciliation; for after seeing it, Charles "threw her one last burning
look of rejection, then left the room." Charles not only leaves the
room, but he leaves Sarah and his child with the understanding that
there is no hope for a relationship between them. This ending works
with and continues to develop the theme of personal growth which we
find prevalent throughout the novel, and even though it is not as happy
as the first ending, Fowles urges the reader not to consider it, "a less
plausible ending to their story." According to Laurence Perrine, two
justifications exist for sad endings. First of all, "many real life situations have unhappy endings; therefore, if literature is to illustrate life,
it must present defeat as well as triumph" (48). Secondly, "the unhappy ending has a peculiar value for writers who wish us to ponder
life" (48). In light of this, it becomes apparent that the first ending of
the novel is "wrapped up" and does not cause the reader to exercise
his/her mind. The second ending, however, leaves the reader actively
thinking, wondering and pondering this idea of human growth; therefore, because it fulfills the expectations of the good reader, it is justifiably the better ending.

The expectations of a movie-going audience run contrary to those
of a good reader. While the good reader strives to be challenged and
therefore stimulated, the typical movie-goer seeks a passive activity directed solely toward entertainment. Observing the conservative nature
of Hollywood films in "Genre Films and the Status Quo," Judith
Wright notes,

> Genre films have been the most popular (and thus the most lucrative)
> products ever to emerge from . . . the American film industry. . . . We
> may trace the amazing survival and proliferation of the genre films to
> their function . . . viewers are encouraged to cease examining them-
> selves and their surroundings, and to take refuse in fantasy (Wright
> 49).

Very rarely will one find a movie that is both sad and successful at the
box office at the same time. Therefore, Pinter's dilemma is clear. How
could he convert the novel to a movie and make it successful? What
Pinter did was very clever, for he created an inner frame, the movie
based on the novel involving Sarah and Charles, and a very convincing
outer frame that involved a seemingly real-life affair between Anna
and Mike, the actress and actor who played Sarah and Charles respectively. As a result of this framing technique, Pinter was able to present
his audience with the happy ending to the inner frame, the movie, and
a sad ending for the outer frame, Anna and Charles's affair.

Perhaps given the expectations of a Hollywood audience, Pinter
should have left the second ending of the movie out altogether. Several
of my classmates and I left the movie with ambivalent feelings not

knowing quite what to think. Basically, we, like most movie audiences, did not expect to see a sad ending. The primary function of all big Hollywood productions is, bottom line, to make money, and in order to do so, they must entertain. Would the average movie viewer pay two or three time to see Rocky lose or Rambo die? I think not, and Pinter realized this and wrote the inner ending accordingly; however, his second ending fails to meet the audience's expectations.

The happy ending is the resolution to the inner ending of the movie—the relationship between Sarah and Charles. After a heated argument, Charles says, "No. It is as I say. You have not only planted a dagger in my breast, you have delighted in twisting it." As Charles now heads for the door, Sarah attempts to stop him, and he pushes her to the floor. Realizing his mistake, Charles rushes to her side to assist her, and much like the first ending of the novel, the conflict is resolved. However, whereas in the novel the expectations of the reader are not met by this ending, the movie-going audience is satisfied with such a resolution.

With the inner frame of the movie resolved, Pinter now faced developing the ending for the situation between Anna and Mike. At this point, Pinter could have opted for a double happy ending, but I feel he realized that since this scenario was so true to life, he was no longer bound by the conventions of film. Anna and Mike could not have stayed together for, after all, they were not Sarah and Charles. Both of them were married, and Mike had a family. As Fowles did in the novel, in the screenplay Pinter attempted to make a film far more serious with the inclusion of the second ending. Just as Fowles dealt with the convention of the novel, Pinter began with the conventions of film making, and he, again like Fowles, tried to break from these conventions by including the sad ending. Unfortunately, because of the movie audience's expectations, Pinter's attempt was not as effective and may even detract from the film. While it is fairly simple to see what Pinter did "on paper," it is not readily apparent to or accepted by a movie audience. The film creates a strong expectation for romance, where after some trials and tribulations, the couples resolve their differences, concede that they do indeed love each other, and kiss passionately as "Love Lifts Us Up Where We Belong" plays in the background. This expectation itself counters the discouraging sad ending where lovers split. What Pinter might have done, rather than leave the whole outside frame out, was to place the sad ending of the outer frame before the happy ending of the inner frame. Although this probably would have taken away from what he was trying to achieve, it may have made the movie more appealing to his audience.

In *The French Lieutenant's Woman* both Fowles and Pinter attempt to illustrate the conventions of their respective fields. When reading the book or watching the movie, the reader or viewer must keep in mind that he/she is experiencing fiction, and both Fowles and Pinter illustrate how reality can be manipulated through art. Both men make us aware of the conventions of their respective art forms, and both men broke away from the traditional, expected conventions. In both cases the sad ending proves to be more realistic, but it is not, in terms of audience response, the movie's best ending as it is the novel's.

Works Cited

Fowles, John. *The French Lieutenant's Woman.* New York: Dell, 1975.

Perrine, Laurence. *Literature: Structure, Sound and Sense.* New York: Harcourt Brace Jovanovich, Inc., 1974.

Wright, Judith Hess. "Genre Films and the Status Quo." *Film Genre Reader.* Ed. Barry Keith Grant. Austin: University of Texas, 1986.

Science

9

Scientific writing that communicates scientific knowledge within the scientific community frequently takes the formal scientific report's form. But scientific writing also may wrestle with the implications science holds for the wider human community. When science classes require students to write up their laboratory experiments, however informally, or when term papers assume the form of more formal reviews of scientific literature, college students are learning the professional scientist's conventions and language. Position papers and book reviews engage students in thinking and writing about the ideas that scientific research generates. The essays here reflect both kinds of scientific writing—the structured scientific reports and the essay of scientific ideas—done for classes in biology, chemistry, biochemistry, mathematics, scientific writing, and English composition.

Reviews of scientific literature summarize scientific experiments and data reported in professional scientific journals. Merely summarizing, however, is rarely enough. The material must be organized by some synthesizing principle—agreement and disagreement, history, or relevance. In formal scientific reports reviews of the literature provide background for new experiments. Four essays here—"Maternal Smoking: Deleterious Effects on the Fetus" by June M. Fahrman, "Fetal Alcohol Syndrome: The Effects of Ethanol on the Nervous System of the Fetus" by Maria LaPadula, "The Crowding Effect in Tadpoles" by Michelle Skraba, and "MTPT and Parkinson's Disease" by Karen Snyder—represent reviews of professional literature, but each review reflects different principles of organization and selection. Laurie Tennyson adapts the literature review's conventions to popular sources in "The War Against Cancer Is Nearly Won."

Reviewing scientific literature represents only one way students use secondary sources in their scientific writing. Students also take positions on controversial scientific issues and refer to secondary sources to support their positions. Important issues like the ethical problems in genetic screening, animal research, and cloning receive consideration in Lisa Soice's "Concepts Involved in Genetic Screening," Chris Rasmussen's "A Great Tradition," and Andrea Jahn's "Is the Research and Development of Cloning and Recombinant DNA Technology Necessary for the Advancement of Humankind?" While these papers do consider alternative positions, they martial their evidence toward emphatically supporting one viewpoint. Jennifer Murphy ("Winning at All Costs") and Jeanne Trapani ("Tropical Rainforests") assemble a much broader scientific background for their readers and advocate a course of action only in their conclusions. Eric Wolford uses scientific literature to describe an injury and treatment alternatives in "Anterior Cruciate Ligament Injury."

Students write not only about what science has explored and discovered but about what science is and how it works. Christine Guerrera constructs a convincing argument on the nature of mathematical problem solving in "Mathematics: A Two Way Mirror." John Dagg, Ted Bretter, and Craig Hartman review important books about science in "Carl Sagan: On the Romance of Science," "DNA: Honesty, Credibility and Perjury," and "*Chaos*."

DNA: Honesty, Credibility, and Perjury

Ted Bretter

Ted Bretter's essay critiques two studies of early DNA research, *The Double Helix,* by James Watson, whom science acknowledges as the discoverer of DNA, and *Rosalind Franklin and DNA* by Anne Sayre. Written for a rhetoric class, this review considers both the history of DNA research and the quality of each writer's argument.

Many scientists made contributions toward the discovery of DNA. Anne Sayre and James Watson have written two separate accounts of this discovery. These two accounts differ in their descriptions of both the character of Rosalind Franklin and the conclusions she arrived at from her research. Studying these two accounts lends insight into the credibility of science and scientific writing.

In science there are many ways to attack a puzzle. Different scientists using separate methods normally share information to find a puzzle's answer. In the DNA puzzle several different research methods and the information produced from them enabled Watson and Crick to discover DNA's structure—a double helix. However, all the scientists studying DNA did not willingly share their information.

Rosalind Franklin and Maurice Wilkins, both proficient in X-ray crystallography, were researching DNA through the different patterns they saw in their X-ray photographs. Franklin, the leader in the study of X-ray crystallography, used meticulous procedures in her DNA studies, which we will see differed from the studies of Watson and Crick. Franklin and Wilkins examined the A and B forms (dehydrated and hydrated) of DNA for thickness, length, and angles of various molecules and atoms in the structure.

James Watson and Francis Crick worked together studying DNA in a completely different manner. Because Wilkins and Franklin were already studying DNA, Watson and Crick could not study it directly because of the English sense of fair play. Instead they were assigned other projects, but they did study and think about DNA in their extra time. They did not use the crystallographic method because they were not very experienced in this field. Rather, they sought the research and opinions of other scientists and made their own conclusions from this. Later they applied this information to model building as trial and error of models became an effective scientific instrument.

Watson and Crick discovered the structure of DNA in April of 1953. This discovery could not have been made without the help of many other scientists from whom Watson and Crick received information. Watson was parasitic in the way he used other people's research. He admits this when, in beginning his written account of DNA's discovery, he says he first received information on DNA from a lecture by Maurice Wilkins where Wilkins said they were looking at a crystalline structure.[1]

When Linus Pauling discovered the a-helix of polypeptide chains, Watson and Crick quickly read Pauling's accounts of it to see if they could find anything useful for their DNA study.[2] Watson said, "We knew what to do: imitate Pauling and beat him at his own game. Pauling's success with the polypeptide chain had naturally suggested to Francis that the same tricks [Pauling used] might also work on DNA."[3] They then went to Wilkins and asked him questions about Pauling's data and its relation to DNA. "Maurice had told Francis [Crick], however, that the diameter of the DNA molecule was thicker than would be the case if only one polynucleotide chain were present. This made him think that the DNA molecule was a compound helix composed of several polynucleotide chains twisted about each other."[4]

Watson and Crick continuously went from person to person finding out whatever information they could. Together they went to a lecture by Linus Pauling, and Watson alone went to a lecture by Rosalind Franklin. According to Jacob Bronowski, who also was at the lecture, Franklin stated that DNA was probably a helix with a definite phosphate backbone on the outside.[5] Anne Sayre verified this when she stated that this conclusion was clearly written in Franklin's notes for the lecture.[6] Watson, however, denied hearing this and said Franklin opposed the theory of a helical structure. Watson and Crick then had questions about the three-dimensional positioning of inorganic ions, so they quickly consulted Linus Pauling's book, *The Nature of the Chemical Bond*, where they found what they were looking for.[7]

From the work of Pauling, Franklin, and Wilkins, Watson and Crick were able to develop their first model of DNA. When Rosalind Franklin came to see it, she told them they had gone wrong with the water content and also in using MG^{++} to hold the chains together.[8] She then told them the correct water content. Later Watson and Crick came up with a backbone structure, and Watson commented on its correctness:

> Moreover, there was no longer any fear that it would be incompatible with experimental data. By then it had been checked out with Rosy's (Rosalind Franklin) precise measurements. Rosy, of course, did not directly give us her data. For that matter, no one at King's realized they were in our hands. We came upon them because of Max's membership on a committee [where he received a summary of all the work completed in Randall's lab] . . . Max saw no reason not to give it to Francis [Crick] and me.[9]

Watson actually admits to taking Franklin's work and using it without her knowledge.

The last problem in discovering DNA's structure was the bonding of the bases. Watson was able to figure out that Adenine bonded with Thymine, and Cytosine with Guanine, by interpreting Erwin Chargaff's rule. In order to figure how A bonded with T, and G with C, he read J. M. Gulland's and D. O. Jordan's papers on DNA which said that the bases would connect by hydrogen bonds.[10] Then Watson received help from Jerry Donahue, who changed Watson's first and incorrect bonding pattern of the Enol forms to the correct bonding of the Keto forms.[11] Finally Watson and Crick were able to develop their correct model for DNA's structure.

In the beginning of the race to find DNA's structure, Rosalind Franklin was ahead of Watson and Crick. She was producing data and hypotheses either ahead of them or at the same time. Not until the end of the race, when positioning of the bases and their bonding was studied, did Watson and Crick move past Franklin. According to Crick,

> Rosalind Franklin was only two steps away from the solution. She needed to realize that the two chains must run in opposite directions and that the bases, in their correct tautomeric forms, were paired together. She was, however, on the point of leaving King's College and DNA.[12]

What Crick is saying here is that Franklin was on the verge of discovering DNA's structure and that if she had not left King's and been emotionally upset, she might have come up with the answer. Closely analyzing Watson's book, *The Double Helix*, alongside Sayre's *Rosalind Franklin and DNA* securely supports the idea that Franklin would probably have been DNA's discoverer had it not been for her emotional state and departure from King's College.

If we look at the two different accounts produced by Sayre and Watson, we must ask ourselves which writer is more credible and trustworthy. *The Double Helix* contained many facts and statements shown incorrect in *Rosalind Franklin and DNA*. Watson simply presented his argument, while Sayre backed hers up with facts and references. Most of the facts pertaining to where Watson received his information were not considered by Sayre, so we can assume these are true, especially because Watson quite candidly admits that he did little of the actual research. Watson, however, denied Franklin some of the important credit she deserved.

How could Watson say Franklin was anti-helical when both Jacob Bronowski and Anne Sayre said that Franklin, at her lecture, did state DNA was probably helical? Sayre even backed this up with a quote from Franklin's notes on the lecture. Franklin wrote:

> The results suggest a helical structure (which must be closely spaced) containing probably 2, 3, or 4 co-axial nucleic acid chains per helical unit, and having the phosphate groups near the outside.[13]

Watson also tried to discredit Franklin by suggesting she was asked to leave King's College. Sayre contests this and defends her claim with evidence. First she quotes from Watson's book where Watson stated that Franklin deserved to be fired from King's because she was hindering the study of DNA. Watson continued making it seem as though Franklin was practically ordered to leave King's. Sayre then states that Franklin decided to leave on her own. She supported this with a quotation from a letter she received from Franklin just before Franklin left King's College. Franklin wrote:

> When I got back from my summer holiday I had a terrific crisis with Wilkins which nearly resulted in my going straight back to Paris . . . I went to Paris for a week in January to decide whether or not to go back. Got it all fixed up to work with Vittorio on liquids, and then thought it was probably silly after all. Somehow I feel that to take such a big step backwards wouldn't work so I went to see Bernal, who condescended to recognize me, made himself pleasant, and gave me some hopes of working in his biological group one day.[14]

Franklin continued in her letter about the benefits that would be offered if she went to work for Bernal. This clearly indicates that Franklin was not asked to leave King's and that she chose to leave so she could work in a better environment than King's, even though she would have to drop her DNA research. Sayre's use of textual examples is more convincing than Watson's aspersions.

In Watson's account, he continually made Franklin look egotistical and selfish to the readers because she would not share her information with him. This frustrated him, so he emphasized this point. I see two contradictions that reflect Watson's bias about Franklin. Watson said in his book:

> Maurice had received a letter from Linus asking for a copy of the crystalline DNA X-ray photographs. After some hesitation he wrote back saying that he wanted to look more closely at the data before releasing the pictures.[15]

This showed Wilkins was hesitant in handing out his information to Pauling. Why did Watson not jump on this and insult Wilkins? This was because Wilkins gave him some help. Wilkins's holding back of this information from Pauling actually made Watson happy because this would slow Pauling down in the race for the solution. Watson was saying that anyone who withheld information from him was unscientific, selfish, and deserving of criticism. However, if they withheld information from his competition, they should be praised. His self-interest discredits his objectivity towards Franklin.

Another instance involving withholding information is when Watson hears that Pauling is going to visit London. Watson immediately becomes fearful that if Pauling were to visit Cambridge, then Watson would have had to talk with Pauling and reveal some of his [Watson's] discoveries regarding DNA. Watson is even more frightened by the fact that if Pauling visited King's College, he might get some information which was unavailable to Watson himself. This depicts the same type of self-interested bias Watson showed in the previous example. However in this case, it is Watson himself who is very hesitant in giving out information. Watson is then extremely happy when he finds out that Pauling was not accepted into the country because his passport was revoked.[16] This also discredits his integrity.

Watson's book not only took away some of the credit Franklin deserved, but also directly insulted Franklin as a person. Watson made Franklin look like a mean and selfish woman. Sayre then makes her seem just the opposite. I am able to believe Sayre's account of Franklin's personality more than Watson's, partially because of the way she showed how Watson discredits Franklin. A second reason for finding Sayre more credible is because of the way she gives plausible explanations for Watson's bias against Franklin. The fact that Sayre did not take away any scientific credit from Watson also makes her account more credible.

Sayre provides several reasons why some scientists did not get along with Franklin. Sayre speaks of two professors who both taught Franklin and made the same comment about her. Sayre says:

> [Professor] Norrish saw her as highly intelligent, intellectually bright, and eager to make her way in scientific research, but he saw her, too, as stubborn and difficult to supervise, and not as easy to collaborate with. There is no reason to argue with him; Rosalind could be all these things.[17]

Sayre also gives reasons why Wilkins did not get along with Franklin when she says that Franklin's argumentative nature immediately made Wilkins dislike her, not because he was against females, but that he was just against arguing.[18]

Sayre finds the final cause for Franklin's poor reception among scientists in King's College's structure. King's College, historically a male college, was now accepting females. However, that women were not treated as equals was made obvious by the facts that women could not eat in the dining area with the men, and they were not allowed in the Men's Club. This sex bias made it almost impossible for Rosalind Franklin to meet on a nonprofessional basis with her colleagues.[19] Sayre says:

Professional fraternization on an informal level is the leaven which in many cases, if not most, raises professional relationships to that point where they become comfortable and satisfying; without it they tend to remain stiff, uneasy, and coldly impersonal.[20]

Because the informal meeting could not take place at King's, Franklin developed a cold and impersonal relationship with Wilkins.

By looking at Franklin's personality and the environment at King's, Sayre indicates why scientists might not have liked Rosalind Franklin. Watson obviously did not like her, and this caused him to be biased against her. Sayre seems very credible because she does not make Franklin seem perfect and lays on Franklin some of the blame for her hostile reception.

Sayre also shows her objectivity when she does not try to take credit for the discovery of DNA away from Watson. She says science is a group effort, and she has no argument against the way Watson and Crick got to the solution by using other people's information.[21] She agrees that Watson did deserve the Nobel prize.[22] She also recognizes the fact that Watson and Crick were the ones who came up with the problem's final solution.[23]

There is one final reason which makes Sayre the more trustworthy writer, and this comes from two more statements in Watson's book. When the structure of DNA was found, Rosalind Franklin came to Cambridge to see it. When she showed her data and agreed with Watson and Crick's structure of the molecule, Watson said, "Her past uncompromising statements on this matter thus reflected first-rate science, not the outpourings of a misguided feminist."[24] Why would he insult her throughout most of the book calling her a feminist, and then take it back saying she was actually a great scientist? He then stated in his epilogue, "Since my initial impressions of her [Rosalind Franklin] both scientific and personal, were often wrong, I want to say something here about her achievements."[25] He then goes on complimenting her work. Right here he is admitting that his impressions are incorrect and that his book has many fallacies about Franklin's work and personality.

Sayre is the more credible writer. Watson showed he was not trustworthy several times in his book. Sayre showed this when she took actual passages from *The Double Helix,* and then proved them wrong using resources like Franklin's notes, other people's views, and her personal letters from Franklin. Sayre also proved her trustworthiness by proving she was not biased against Watson. She did this by not degrading Watson's work and methods. She gave him full credit for what he deserved. She also showed some fault in Franklin that might have caused these people to dislike her. No matter how much Watson disliked Franklin, his criticism is unsupported.

From the comparison of these two books we learn that for a writer to be credible in an argument, he or she should analyze the other side closely and identify fallacies. The writer must also not be biased to make his own side appear perfect. By showing the strengths and weaknesses of both sides, the author shows the reader that he or she is not prejudiced. To be credible it would be advantageous to follow Sayre's approach.

Endnotes

1. Gunther Stent, ed., *The Double Helix,* by James D. Watson (New York, W. W. Norton & Co., Inc., 1980) p. 23.
2. Ibid., p. 25
3. Ibid., p. 32
4. Ibid., p. 34
5. Ibid., Jacob Bronowski's article, 1968, p. 201
6. Anne Sayre, *Rosalind Franklin and DNA* (NY: W. W. Norton and Co.) p. 128
7. Watson p. 51
8. Ibid., p. 59
9. Ibid., p. 105
10. Ibid., p. 105
11. Ibid., p. 110
12. Ibid., Crick's article, 1974, pp. 143 & 144
13. Sayre p. 126 (which she got from Franklin's actual notes)
14. Ibid., pp. 137, 138
15. Watson p. 15
16. Ibid., pp. 70, 71
17. Sayre pp. 58, 56
18. Ibid., p. 106
19. Ibid., p. 97
20. Ibid., p. 97
21. Ibid., p. 157
22. Ibid., p. 188
23. Ibid., p. 193
24. Watson p. 124
25. Ibid., p. 132

■ THE WRITER'S ASSIGNMENT

Use your reading of Sayre as an opportunity to consider what is meant by her statement, "Interpretation reflects the interpreter." Reading Sayre's account in conjunction with Watson's book gives you a good opportunity to explore what that statement means because the two writers interpret the same thing—the character of Rosalind Franklin—in very different ways. You can learn much about what it means to be a credible writer from thinking about which interpreter you ultimately decide is the more credible and why. I would like to read your reflections on these issues. ■

■ UNDERSTANDING WRITING STRATEGIES

1. What distinguishes Watson and Crick's DNA research from that of Franklin and Wilkins? How does Bretter present the two approaches for

his reader? What kinds of assumptions does this presentation indicate about Bretter's audience?

2. What does Bretter's summary of DNA research suggest about scientific progress? What is Bretter's judgment about this?

3. What criteria does Bretter use to evaluate Crick and Watson's book, *The Double Helix* and Sayre's *Rosalind Franklin and DNA*?

4. What is the material in Watson that contradicts Sayre regarding Franklin's role in discovering DNA? What use does Bretter make of this?

5. Why does Bretter find Sayre more credible than Watson?

6. What does Bretter's essay achieve for you as a reader? Has Bretter envisioned his audience well? How do you see this?

7. What kinds of commitment does the introduction make? How do you see this? Does the essay fulfill these commitments?

8. Does the conclusion redirect the reader to the promises of the introduction? What might the writer have done for a more effective conclusion?

9. What does this essay suggest about the ways scientific discovery proceeds? ■

■ SUGGESTIONS FOR WRITING

1. Write an essay that defines science and takes a position on scientific objectivity using Bretter's essay on DNA's discovery as part of your evidence.

2. Rewrite the conclusion to relate better to both the introduction and the essay's contents. ■

Carl Sagan: On the Romance of Science

John K. Dagg

John Dagg examines scientist Carl Sagan's contributions to the popular understanding of science. His essay, written for a course emphasizing writing for the sciences, considers how Sagan's books have confronted religion and myth.

> We have examined the universe in space and seen that we live on a mote of dust circling a humdrum star in the remotest corner of an obscure galaxy. And if we are a speck in the immensity of space, we also occupy an instant in the expanse of ages (Sagan, *Cosmos* 21).

Man's idea of the universe has changed greatly since ancient times. He once saw himself as the center of all the Cosmos, surrounded by gods, mystery, and order. Science appears to have taken this security away from man—leaving him dangling in a seemingly lonely, empty, and uncaring universe. Modern man is faced with the search for the significance of his existence.

Carl Sagan is an American scientist and author who is trying to show man that he is probably not alone in the universe and that he is firmly footed on science and not hanging from a broken ideology. Perhaps the "meaning in life" is indeed the search for the meaning of existence. Sagan writes:

> For myself, I like a universe that includes much that is unknown and, at the same time, much that is knowable. A universe in which everything is known would be static and dull, as boring as the heaven of some weak-minded theologians. A universe that is unknowable is no fit place for a thinking being. The ideal universe, for us, is one very much like the universe we inhabit (*Broca's Brain* 18).

The universe is, of course, somewhat large, and the question of whether or not we can actually "know" it is difficult to answer. The human brain has a limited amount of memory space and to know the universe would naturally take vast amounts of memory. Man has developed books and computers to help solve this problem. Sagan compares the problem of comprehending the universe with understanding a grain of salt. This would be an awesome job if it were not for some known regularities in the nature of atoms that neatly sum up much repetitious information. The only way to understand the universe, then, is to seek out the regularities of nature—this process is called *science*. Man is a curious animal, and his ability to find and use these laws has been the single largest factor in his success as a species.

> Human beings are, understandably, highly motivated to find regularities, natural laws. The search for rules, the only possible way to understand such a vast and complex universe, is called science. The universe forces those who live in it to understand it. Those creatures who find everyday experience a muddled jumble of events with no predictability, no regularity, are in grave peril. The universe belongs to those who, at least to some degree, have figured it out (*Broca's Brain* 19).

Therefore, science is man's key to knowing the Cosmos, and to know the Cosmos is to know the ultimate potential of mankind.

Man is star stuff that is contemplating itself. The heavy elements were produced in the stars from helium and hydrogen. These elements constitute planets. On Earth, some combinations of these atoms formed molecules, which could, quite by accident, make crude copies of themselves. Occasionally these "combinations" made a faulty duplicate that was actually better suited to the environment than was the parent. Different species of these crude creatures arose, some better suited to survive than others. Life and natural selection had come into being. These creatures became increasingly complex and, after billions of years, one of the resulting animals was man. The evidence for this time-consuming process is conclusive, and Carl Sagan declares, "Evolution is a fact, not a theory" (*Cosmos* 27). Man is a part of the Cosmos that has evolved to self-awareness.

This "fact" of evolution causes problems for some Western religions. Most people are frustrated with the idea of infinity because the human mind simply cannot comprehend it. In an effort to resolve this problem, man created God and proposed that He was the beginning and created the universe from nothing. However,

> The question naturally arises—and many ten-year-olds spontaneously think of it before they are discouraged by their elders—where does God come from? If we answer that God is infinitely old or is present simultaneously in all epochs, we have solved nothing, except perhaps verbally. We have merely postponed by one step coming to grips with the problem. A universe that is infinitely old and a God that is infinitely old are, I think, equally deep mysteries. It is not readily apparent why one should be considered more reliably established than the other. Spinoza might have said that the two possibilities are not really different ideas at all (*Broca's Brain* 337)

Hence, science and religion were developed for the same reason—to answer how, and perhaps why, a finite being is intertwined with the infinity of the Cosmos.

Science unfortunately brought with it a danger to the very species that created it. Technology, which has helped man to come to know his universe better, could, if misused, destroy him. To choose probing the Cosmos over self-destruction should be an easy task for a species that has fought to survive for so long—yet this does not turn out to be the case.

> The choice is stark and ironic. The same rocket boosters used to launch probes to the planets are poised to send nuclear warheads to the nations. The radioactive power sources on the Viking and Voyager derive from the same technology that makes nuclear weapons. The radio and radar techniques employed to track and guide nuclear missiles and defend against attack are also used to monitor and command the spacecraft on the planets and to listen for signals from civilizations near other stars. If we use these technologies to destroy ourselves, we surely will venture no more to the planets and stars. But the converse is also true. If we continue to the planets and the stars, our chauvinisms will be shaken further. We will gain a cosmic perspective (*Cosmos* 339).

The value of space exploration is quite clear: It may be the only way that man can safely use his acquired knowledge. In nearly all of his books, Carl Sagan emphasizes that man is at a critical point in his history—he can fool-heartedly annihilate himself or he can use his technology for peaceful and meaningful activities. Once the exploration of space is seriously undertaken, man will realize just how infantile it is to endanger his unique and precious world.

Perhaps one of the most important occurrences in man's exploration of the universe will be contacting an extraterrestrial intelligence. Knowing that man is not condemned to a solitary existence in such vastness would be comforting and exciting. Man has always wished to find that other beings inhabit the universe. Since his beginning, man has said that gods dwelled in the heavens. More recently, man believed there were Martians digging canals on Mars. A large interest in unidentified flying objects has also arisen. Although these beliefs are likely to be falsely founded, they do show that man does not wish to be alone. Carl Sagan relates what he believes the impact of a real contact with an extraterrestrial race would be like in *The Cosmic Connection*.

> The scientific, logical, cultural, and ethical knowledge to be gained by tuning in to galactic transmissions may be, in the long run, the most profound single event in the history of our civilization. There will be information in what we will no longer be able to call the humanities—because our communicants will not be human. There will be a deparochialization of the way we view the Cosmos and ourselves. There will be a new perspective on the differences we perceive among ourselves once we grasp the enormous differences between us and beings elsewhere—beings with whom we have nonetheless a serious commonality of intellectual interest.

The benefits of making such a connection with another civilization might also include the answer to overcoming the dangerous stage of development our civilization is going through. The knowledge that self-destruction can be avoided would be of enormous value alone—it would prove that man is not doomed and that his struggle for existence is not in vain.

The human race, however, cannot depend on this "cosmic connection" to deliver it from its desperate situation. The technology that could be used to destroy man is controlled by very few and understood by even fewer. If people do not try to learn these sciences, they cannot possibly hope to stop their misuse. The obvious answer to this problem is to strive for a more science-literate culture. If society actively participates in the enforcement of the proper use of science, the chances of human survival are vastly increased. The advantages of such an educated society would go beyond even this:

> In addition to the immense practical benefit of having a scientifically literate public, the contemplation of science and technology permits us to exercise our intellectual faculties to the limits of our capabilities. Science is an exploration of the intricate, subtle, and awesome universe we inhabit. Those who practice it know, at least on occasion, a rare kind of exhilaration that Socrates said was the greatest of human pleasures. It is a communicable pleasure. To facilitate informed public participation in technological decision making, to decrease the alienation too many of us feel from our technological society, and for the sheer joy that comes from knowing a deep thing well, we need better science education, a superior communication of its powers and delights (*Broca's Brain* 45).

Hence, science need not be the downfall of the human race—it could, if used wisely and universally, preserve and enrich human existence.

As promising and rewarding as science has proven to be, many religions attempt to denounce its achievements. The best example of this conflict is between the theories of evolution and creation. Although evolution is supported by a wealth of evidence, some religions stubbornly refuse to acknowledge it as a fact. It is interesting to note that, even against logic and common sense, religions still have a strong following. Carl Sagan analyzes this oddity in *Broca's Brain:*

> But religions are tough. Either they make no contentions which are subject to disproof or they quickly redesign doctrine after disproof. The fact that religions can be so shamelessly dishonest, so contemptuous of the intelligence of their adherents, and still flourish does not speak very well for the toughmindedness of the believers. But it does indicate, if a demonstration were needed, that near the core of religious experience is something remarkably resistant to rational inquiry (*Broca's Brain* 332).

This "resistance to rational inquiry" expresses man's fear of discovering that there is no God. Science has severely scarred religion. The fact that religion still has an immense following shows that man does not want to lose the security of an all-powerful, watchful, and caring figure. Man is so afraid of being alone that he will even deceive himself.

There are two ways of viewing the Cosmos: by means of superstitious beliefs and by means of science. The superstition method is by far the easier of the two; however, it is also ultimately less satisfying.

> Those afraid of the universe as it really is, those who pretend to nonexistent knowledge and envision a Cosmos centered on human beings, will prefer the fleeting comforts of superstition. They avoid rather than confront the world. But those with the courage to explore the weave and structure of the Cosmos, even where it differs profoundly from their wishes and prejudices, will penetrate its deepest mysteries (*Cosmos* 332).

The scientific technique of explaining the universe is vastly more fulfilling. It challenges and intrigues the human mind rather than allowing it to be clouded with absurd suppositions of fancy.

> It is by far the best tool we have, self-correcting, ongoing, applicable to everything. It has two rules. First: there are no sacred truths; all assumptions must be critically examined; arguments from authority are worthless. Second: whatever is inconsistent with the facts must be discarded or revised. We must understand the Cosmos as it is and not confuse how it is with what we wish it to be. The obvious is sometimes false; the unexpected is sometimes true (*Cosmos* 333).

These rules are hard to follow for most people—scientists included. The rewards of following this outline are immense, as the greatest achievements of mankind have shown.

A major theme found throughout many of Sagan's works is the denouncement of what he calls "pseudosciences." Many of these false and often ridiculous "beliefs" are created as a method of obtaining money from unwary people. Some of these pseudosciences include astrology, science-religions, and the occult. Sagan emphasizes that there is no need for such institutions when what science can offer is much more amazing and truthful. In *Broca's Brain*, Sagan gives a list of what he sees as good substitutes for pseudosciences—sciences (*Broca's Brain* 75). Many of the "borderline sciences" that Sagan attacks are clearly hoaxes. He explains why it is that some people are so easily deceived by these "sciences":

> In many cases we are not unbiased observers. We have an emotional stake in the outcome—perhaps merely because the borderline belief system, if true, makes the world a more interesting place; but perhaps because there is something there that strikes more deeply into the human psyche. If astral projection actually occurs, then it is possible for some thinking and perceiving part of me to leave my body and effortlessly travel to other places—an exhilarating prospect. If spiritualism is real, then my soul will survive the death of my body—possibly a comforting thought (*Broca's Brain* 88).

This characteristic of the human mind must be kept in check by scientists so that their wishes do not influence their decisions. One area particularly vulnerable to this weakness is in the search for life elsewhere in the Cosmos. Carl Sagan writes, "If we are alone, that is a truth worth knowing also" (*Broca's Brain* 68). Hence, perhaps the most important asset to the scientist is an unprejudiced and critical mind.

One of Carl Sagan's greatest concerns is a product of evolution—aggression. In order for a species to survive, it must be physically superior to other species. A common form of animal aggression is territoriality. Now, however, these animal instincts in man could prove to be the destruction of his and countless other species. A single act of rage could result in global disaster. Perhaps the only way to control this fault is to look to the Cosmos and see the world in a "cosmic perspective." Carl Sagan poses the question "Who speaks for Earth?" in his book *Cosmos*. The answer is, of course, no single person or group of people, but rather all of Earth's inhabitants.

> We are the local embodiment of a Cosmos grown to self-awareness. We have begun to contemplate our origins: starstuff pondering the stars; organized assemblages of ten billion billion billion atoms considering the evolution of atoms; tracing the long journey by which, here at least, consciousness arose. Our loyalties are to the species and the planet. We speak for Earth. Our obligation to survive is owed not just to ourselves but also to that Cosmos, ancient and vast, from which we spring (*Cosmos* 345).

Carl Sagan's message is clear: Man is a very rare and special occurrence in the Cosmos. After a long climb up the ladder of evolution, it would be tragic to waste a ripening civilization on narrow-minded pettiness. The common use and understanding of science is man's only hope of continuing as a species. Carl Sagan gives modern man hope for the future and sees science as a way to fill the vacuum left by faltering ideologies.

Works Cited

Sagan, Carl. *Broca's Brain*. New York: Random House, 1979.
———————— *The Cosmic Connection*. Garden City, N.Y.: Anchor Press, 1973.
———————— *Cosmos*. New York: Random House, 1979.

■ THE WRITER'S ASSIGNMENT

A central purpose of this course is to relate major scientific and philosophical developments. Study one scientist of your choice. Read some of his own original writings. . . . Using your readings as sources for ideas and documenting your uses, develop a paper discussing [science's] influence.   ■

■ UNDERSTANDING WRITING STRATEGIES

1. What are the principal books Dagg refers to? From this essay, what do you determine as the topic of each book?

2. On what principles does Dagg organize his essay?

3. How effective is Dagg's technique for giving an overview of Sagan's work?

4. What other ways might Dagg have organized and developed his essay?

5. What assumptions does Dagg make about his audience's views on scientific validity?

6. Does Sagan have a bias about the place of scientific knowledge for modern humanity? Does Dagg have a bias?

7. In what ways does the essay show science's influence on philosophy?

8. How does Dagg adapt the assignment to his own writing interests?

9. How complete and effective is Dagg's documentation?   ■

Mathematics: A Two-Way Mirror

Christine Guerrera

Written for a mathematics course, Christine Guerrera's position paper argues that as a problem-solving strategy mathematics is a human invention rather than a natural phenomenon awaiting discovery.

Mathematics is one of the oldest of disciplines. Despite its maturity, however, it lacks a certain basic understanding of itself. Within the field there is no agreement as to whether mathematics is invented or discovered. Those who believe it is discovered often cite examples of concepts that were simultaneously discovered by two or more people.[1] These arguments sound convincing, but may be explained in terms of social climate or, as I hope to argue, the functioning of the human mind itself. The argument, on the other hand, of those who believe in invention may be summarized as follows:

> The realization that physical theories may change or may be modified (Newtonian mechanics vs. Einsteinian mechanics, for example), that there may be competing theories, that the available mathematics may be inadequate to deal with a theory in the fullest sense, all this has led to a pragmatic acceptance of a model as a 'sometime thing', a convenient approximation to a state of affairs rather than an expression of eternal truth.[2]

It is this point of view that I wish to support, although I will have to leave the field of mathematics in order to do so.

We, as conscious animals, are equipped with a mind that is adapted to interpret the information we receive from our senses into a working idea of our universe. The mind itself is an abstract entity that cannot be scientifically explained. Some of its interpretive functions, however, can be located and studied in the brain. We know, for instance, that our neurons receive stimulation from the sensory neurons, and translate the information into an electrical and chemical message that is sent to a designated area in the brain, where it is presumably interpreted. We can tap into this interpretation by means of studying the reaction which is evoked by the information. With this in mind, the Gestalt psychologists conducted pattern (design) recognition experiments. Here, they ran into the problem of explaining how a subject can recognize a pattern even if it has been moved, rotated, or otherwise slightly altered. They concluded that we see not only the parts, but the relations between the parts of a figure. We group figures, according to their features and the relations between them, into categories. A category is made up of all the possible variations, i.e. slight alterations, of the figure. When we see a variant of the figure, then, we are able to identify it according to its category. This categorization applies for conceptual as well as visual material and for alterations that cannot easily be defined.[3]

Since we do not know what consciousness is, and since mathematics certainly involves conscious thought, we must turn to another theory to pick up where Gestalt psychology leaves off. The German tradition of hermeneutics provides this bridge. Hermeneutics is a theory of interpretation that asserts that, "the whole can be understood only in the context of its parts and that the parts can be understood only in the context of their whole."[4] This theory encompasses that of the Gestalt psychologist, but it also stresses the importance of context. For them the whole is greater even than the object or concept in question. The "whole" that affects the interpretation of an object includes both the object and subject of the interpretation, as well as the context of each.[5] We may consider mathematics to be an interpretation with the universe as its object and the human mind as its subject. According to the hermeneutic model, we must consider the context of both the universe and the human mind if we are to understand mathematics.

The universe, as I have said, is the object of the mathematical interpretation. The only way we can know about the universe is through math and the natural sciences. Since it is this way of knowing that we are investigating, we cannot use any knowledge we have about the universe to aid us. In this case, it is impossible to consider the context of the object.

We have, however, no better acquaintance than with the subject, the human mind. We can fulfill at least part of the hermeneutic tradition by studying the context of the human mind as the subject of the mathematical interpretation. We can begin by studying the situational context of the mind, culture. We do not think in a vacuum. From the moment we are born we are bombarded with the beliefs, values, and assumptions of our culture. We digest these so well that it is a major task of philosophers to determine what assumptions are *a priori* and, in fact, whether or not there is such a thing. Something as basic as time is not assumed in all cultures. The Hopi, for instance, do not believe in a time continuum. They believe, instead, in the manifested and the manifesting. The manifested includes our past and present, as well as anything that is objective and exists outside of the mind. The manifesting is the subjective within the mind, including dreams and the future.[6] It is difficult for us to divorce ourselves from our assumption of the time continuum, but if you try you will see that the Hopi philosophy makes sense. Obviously any interpretation of the universe we make will be very different from that of the Hopi because they are built on two very different foundations. The point here, however, is to illustrate the degree to which our thought depends on our culture.

The context of the human mind involves more than culture. It also involves the brain itself and how it, as an organ, functions. We know that the brain processes information through neural pathways and we know, from the Gestalt psychologists, that our mind is predisposed to recognize patterns and relationships. We can proceed, now, to investigate the types of patterns and relationships the mind recognizes by studying its creations. It seems logical, in other words, to assume that the patterns and relationships created by the human mind reflect those it recognizes. Structuralism takes just that approach.

Structuralism began in the study of linguistics where it asserted that language is a system of relationships. It was conceived with the Sapir-Whorf hypothesis in mind, which states that our thought is governed by the structure of our language. Structural linguistics sought to identify the structure of our language that molds our thought. Levi-Strauss was a major influence in this field and he proposed that, "binary opposition is the most extensive structural universal of all languages."[7] He was thinking in terms of both the sound and the meaning of language, referring to such dualities as voiced/unvoiced phonemes, male/female, animate/inanimate, etc. This idea of binary opposition can be seen readily in mathematics in terms of such concepts as positive and negative, inverses, paired operations such as addition/subtraction and square/square root, commutativity, and the binary language used in computers. It is important to remember, however, that structural linguistics assumes that the structure of the language determines thought, so the structural linguist would assert that it is the mathematician's language, not his mind, that determines what form mathematical theories will take. It is also important to point out that there is much more to mathematics than binary oppositions.

The assertion that language molds our thought is a bold one, and many people are reluctant to accept it. For this reason there evolved from structural linguistics a new field, called psychological structuralism. It was, in fact, Levi-Strauss who revised his own theory to create psychological structuralism. He may be summarized as follows:

> Levi-Strauss is not content with finding a mere similarity between the structure of language and that of other institutions. He is eager to establish

their identity by tracing them back to their common source, namely, the unconscious structure of human mind. This unconscious mental structure will be regarded as the ultimate ground of all structures in his psychological structuralism, the same pivotal role played by the structure of language in his linguistic structuralism.[8]

Since language, like mathematics, is a creation of the mind, this seems to be a logical step. This step, in fact, permitted the recognition of a new structural principle to add to that of binary opposition. This structural principle is called homology, and refers to analogy or equivalence. It allows for the combination of binary oppositions. We may now have a string of analogous binary oppositions, which is to structure our world in terms of similarities. This way of thought has been seen in pre-Socratic thought and that of "primitive" societies.[9]

A final development of structural thought, according to psychological structuralism, occurred with Socrates, in his search for definitions. In the course of this search, he distinguished between universalities and particulars. This development marked the introduction of the hierarchy to Western thought.[10] The concept of the hierarchy is indispensable to us. We use it in the classification of animals, in the structure of our college (college, department, particular course) and in countless other human institutions. It can be seen very plainly in the Venn diagrams of set theory, which itself can be applied to countless situations.

The hierarchy, in terms of mathematics, is more than just a model within the field. It is crucial to the very development of the field. Socrates used the hierarchy to develop deductive reasoning.[11] This form of reasoning builds from true statements on one level to true statements on another level. The importance of the hierarchy can be seen in the familiar argument:

All men are mortal.
Socrates is a man.
Therefore, Socrates is mortal.

It is deductive reasoning, finally, that is crucial to the development of mathematics. Mathematics uses the same logic as does philosophy; they even employ the same system of representing statements, implications, etc. It is this logic of deductive reasoning that makes possible the very foundation of mathematics, the mathematical proof. The mathematical proof allows us to build a "valid" system of relationships from a very few basic assumptions. We look for these relationships because, according to Gestalt psychology, our mind is predisposed to see patterns of relationships. This is how we organize all of the information we receive into a form that we can understand. We are able to create these patterns of relationships for ourselves because our minds work in terms of the hierarchy which, according to structural psychology, is a consequence of the evolutionary state of the human mind. It seems logical, to my human mind at least, to conclude that mathematics is not an eternal truth of the universe that we humans are gradually uncovering. It is instead a human creation designed to allow the human mind to understand its universe. If our minds had evolved differently, I believe we would have had to have found an entirely different way of understanding our universe.

What about the simultaneous discoveries mentioned earlier? When we take the discovery in context, the chance of simultaneous development is really not that remote. First of all, the historical and cultural context of the people developing theories and concepts limits them to only certain point of view. On top of this, they are working with almost identical instruments, namely their minds, which further increases the chance of simultaneous developments in the same direction.

I am not asserting that there is no one reality out there for us to understand. I am saying, however, that mathematics is only one way of understanding it. Consciousness itself may be only one way of understanding it, and mathematics is a subclass of consciousness. Within mathematics we often see conflicting theories that explain the same thing equally as well. An obvious example is Euclidian and non-Euclidian geometry. This contradiction should be seen not as a fault but an advantage. We are already limited to a very narrow view of reality. If, however, we have as many vantage points as possible within that view we are much more likely to get a good idea of the whole. No one theory is capable of explaining the universe accurately. If we are able to build a composite of theories, however, we may come closer to the overall picture. This is the same philosophy that stands behind the study of myths. In a given culture there are often various contradicting myths that explain the same phenomenon. By analyzing all of the versions it is possible to differentiate between the insignificant details particular to the story and the larger concepts considered important by the culture, which could not have been expressed in one story.[12] I believe that much the same approach can be taken with mathematics.

It is important to remember that mathematics reflects not only the universe we live in, but the mind that tries to interpret it as well. In this way it serves as a two-way mirror. Consider the illustration on page one of *Gödel, Escher, Bach* by Douglas Hofstadter. It is a block of wood carved in such a way that light shining from above will leave a shadow of a B, from the right will leave a shadow of a G, and from the left will leave a shadow of an E. We can consider the block to the the human mind and the wall on which the shadows fall to be the universe. The shadows left behind tell us at the same time about the wall and the block. This illustration was intended to represent how we can see the same idea represented in music, art, and mathematics. The same analogy can be made, I believe, for conflicting theories of mathematics. For this reason I believe that math should be used, not only to understand our universe, but to understand the human mind as well. Perhaps one day psychological structuralism will recognize the worth of this tool.

Endnotes

1. Philip J. Davis and Reuben Hersh, *The Mathematical Experience*, (Boston, Birichauser, 1981), pp. 52–53.
2. Ibid., pp. 78–79.
3. Ulric Neisser, *Cognitive Psychology*, (New York, Appleton-Century-Crofts, 1966), pp. 50–59.
4. T. K. Seung, *Structuralism and Hermeneutics*, (New York, Columbia University Press, 1982), p. 200.
5. Ibid., pp. 200–203.
6. Benjamin Lee Whorf, *Language, Thought and Reality*, (Cambridge, Mass., The M.I.T. Press, 1956), pp. 58–64.
7. Seung, p. 14.
8. Ibid., p. 17.
9. Ibid., pp. 19–29.
10. Ibid., p. 30.
11. Ibid., p. 33.
12. Edmund Leach, "Genesis as Myth," *Genesis as Myth and Other Essays*, (London, Cape, 1969), pp. 7–9.

■ THE WRITER'S ASSIGNMENT

Write a paper supporting your view on whether math is invented or discovered. ■

■ UNDERSTANDING WRITING STRATEGIES

1. The author lays groundwork for her argument about mathematics. What is this groundwork? What does this suggest about the essay's audience?

2. Where does the author move from background to argument? How does she do this?

3. What is structuralism? How does structural linguistics serve as an analogy for mathematical language?

4. Along with binary opposition, what other concepts drawn from philosophy and psychology are important for understanding mathematics?

5. What logical patterns appear in this essay?

6. What is the author's conclusion about the nature of math? How does the argument she has presented up to this point prepare you for this?

7. The final paragraph sets up an analogy to tie together the argument's strands. How well does the writer help you envision the woodcarving? Is this analogy adequate to illustrate the essay's arguments? How well does this *conclude* the essay? ■

■ SUGGESTION FOR WRITING

Not all of us are experts on mathematics even though we have spent many hours being taught math. Using your own math class experiences evaluate whether or not math teachers, as evidenced by their teaching methods, and textbooks support or discredit Guerrera's hypothesis. ■

Maternal Smoking: Deleterious Effects on the Fetus

June M. Fahrman

Reviews of the literature appear in all published scientific reports, so science courses frequently require students to master their conventions. Written for a biology class, June Fahrman's essay summarizes and integrates published studies on maternal smoking's effects on the unborn child. Her paper demonstrates her understanding of the literature and her ability to select information relevant to her subject.

The placenta, lifeline between fetus and mother, has been the subject of various studies aimed at determining the mechanisms by which substances in the mother's bloodstream affect the fetus. For example, cigarette smoking is clearly associated with an increased risk in the incidence of low birthweight infants, due both to prematurity and to intrauterine growth retardation.(5) Smoking during pregnancy also has been associated with offspring who have significantly lower IQ scores, shorter stature, and an increased occurrence of minimal brain dysfunction.(7) In addition, these infants are at higher risk of perinatal mortality and their mothers at increased risk of placenta previa and abrupto placenta. These deleterious effects of smoking on fetuses have been seen with as little as five cigarettes per day or continued exposure to a smoke-filled environment (even if the mother does not smoke). Laboratory studies indicate a lowered Po_2 level and an elevated Pco_2 level in both mother and fetus when exposed to cigarette smoke.(6)

Studies demonstrating possible mechanisms such as decreased blood volume capacity in smoker's placentae, thickening of the trophoblastic basement membrane, increased cadmium levels, increased thiocyanate levels and vasoconstriction, provide adequate evidence about the relationship between smoking mothers and these harmful effects, yet women continue to smoke during their pregnancies.

The focus of this paper will be a review of the most recent studies surveying placental changes in smoking mothers, effects on the fetus, possible mechanisms of change, and a hypothesis addressing the possibility of individuals transplacentally exposed to maternal smoking being at greater risk of cancer in adult life, preceded by a brief section summarizing placental development.

DEVELOPMENT OF THE PLACENTA

At the morula stage of development, less than one week after fertilization, two types of cells can be distinguished; the more rapidly proliferating cells forming a layer over the more slowly dividing cells. This structure is sphere-shaped and is called a blastocyst. A single layer of ectodermal cells, the primitive trophoblast, surrounds the sphere, except at one pole where the rapidly dividing cells have formed the inner cell mass. The inner cell mass composes the beginning of the embryo.

As the continually changing ovum passes into the uterus it will implant on the seventh to eighth day after ovulation. The trophoblastic cells, with their invasive capacity, aid the blastocyst in sinking into the endometrium which then encloses it and forms the decidua capsularis.(1)

After implantation, mesodermic cells grow out beneath the primitive trophoblast, which, by proliferation, forms villous projections into the surrounding decidua.(2) Each villus consists of a mesodermic core covered by two layers of trophoblastic cells. The outer cells are called syncytial trophoblasts and have dark staining nuclei.

Trophoblastic cells have marked invasive capacities and grow right through the walls of maternal blood vessels, establishing contact with the maternal blood stream. In the recently implanted blastocyst the rim of the trophoblastic cells, with the underlying mesodermic stroma, constitutes the primitive chorion.(3) The amnion becomes evident at this time also.

By the end of the fourth week, the vessels of the fetus and those of the chorion make connections and form the fetal-placental circulation. The villi absorb nutrients and oxygen from the maternal blood in the intervillous space and subsequently transport the substances to the fetus through the umbilical vein and its villous branches. Waste products from the fetus are carried into the maternal blood via two umbilical arteries which are continuations of the fetal hypogastric arteries. The villi are oxygenated directly from the maternal blood and exhibit infarction whenever the maternal circulation around them ceases.(4) The placenta functions as an endocrine gland for both the mother and the fetus in its production of chorionic gonadotropic hormone, progesterone and estrogen, as well as functioning in respiration, nutrition and excretion for the developing fetus.

MATERNAL SMOKING AND PERINATAL EVENTS

Perinatal events associated with maternal smoking during pregnancy have been the subject of numerous studies over the past thirty years. One study, by M. Meyer et al.(13), reported the following events:

Birthweight: Out of a total of almost 113,000 births, grouped by race and geographic factors, increased risks of low birthweight infants for smoking women were evident. Within every group, the higher the smoking level, the greater the proportion of babies weighing less than 2500 gm. Compared with nonsmokers, the increased risk of low birthweight varied from 30 to 170 per cent for light smokers and from 90 to 340 per cent for heavy smokers.

Gestation: Births occurring at less than 37 to 38 weeks are considered to be preterm. The earlier the birth, the greater the chance for impaired survival and fetal death. For mothers who smoked less than one pack per day, the risk of preterm delivery increased from less than one per cent to 56 per cent, with a median increase of 25 per cent among 37 subgroups. For smokers of greater than one pack per day, the risk increased 12 to 106 per cent, with a median increase of 69 per cent, compared with nonsmoker rates.

Perinatal Mortality: In this study the risk associated with smoking less than one pack per day and of smoking greater than one pack per day were evaluated separately for fetal deaths at greater than 20 weeks gestation and perinatal deaths. In women smoking less than one pack per day the median increase in risk over nonsmokers was 24 per cent for fetal deaths and 22 per cent for perinatal deaths. For smokers of greater than one pack per day the median increases for risk were 55 per cent for fetal, 35 per cent neonatal, and 44 per cent for perinatal deaths.

Placental Complications: Several investigators have reported increased incidence in placenta previa, abrupto placenta, and bleeding during pregnancy among mothers who smoke. This study reported the median increase of placental complications as 28 per cent and 85 per cent for the two smoking levels of less than one pack per day and greater than one pack per day, respectively.

PROPOSED MECHANISMS

Speculation abounds as to the mechanism involved by which maternal smoking reduces fetal growth. Reduction in maternal blood flow, inhalation of carbon monoxide, nicotine, cadmium, and cyanide have been indicated.

Cyanide

In smoking individuals cyanide is absorbed from the smoke and detoxicated to thiocyanate in the body. Thiocyanate levels were measured in venous blood samples taken from mothers within 24 hours before delivery and again on the 4th day after delivery, in an investigation done by A. Meberg et al.(8) Cord blood samples were taken at delivery from the placental portion of the cord. It was shown that smokers had significantly higher levels of serum thiocyanate than those of nonsmokers (Fig. 1). In the 21 nonpregnant,

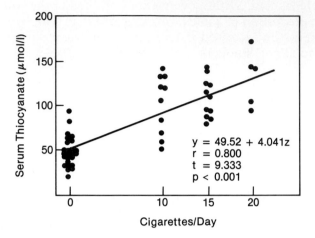

FIGURE 1. Relation between serum thiocyanate concentrations at delivery in 51 women and their smoking level during pregnancy.

SOURCE: Meberg A. et al.

nonsmoking controls, serum thiocyanate concentration was 55 ± 15.5 μmol/l. Those levels were similar to that in the pregnant nonsmokers.

A correlation between the thiocyanate levels of the mother and the umbilical cord is seen in Fig. 2, and in examining the weight of the new-

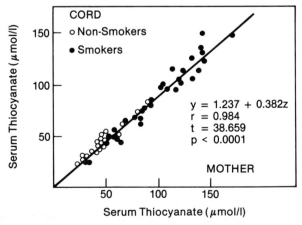

FIGURE 2. Relation between maternal serum thiocyanate concentrations and umbilical cord serum thiocyanate concentrations in 26 women smoking 10–20 cigarettes daily during pregnancy and in 25 non-smoking controls.

SOURCE: Meberg A. et al.

borns, an inverse relationship existed between birthweight and thiocyanate levels (Fig. 3).

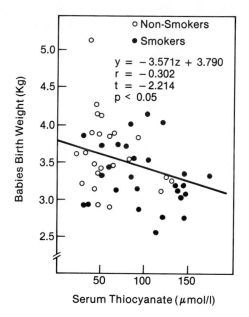

FIGURE 3. Relation between maternal serum thiocyanate concentrations at delivery in 26 women smoking 10–20 cigarettes daily during pregnancy and in 25 non-smoking controls, and the birth weights of their infants.

SOURCE: Meberg A. et al.

The question here was that of whether the fetal thiocyanate levels reflects only passive diffusion of thiocyanate from the mother, or that cyanide detoxification takes place in the fetus itself. This leaves the exposure to toxic cyanide levels in utero a possible risk factor for the fetus of smoking mothers. The conclusion was reached that smoking itself interferes with fetal growth in a dose-related manner.

Structural Placental Changes

W. J. VanDerVelde et al.(11), reported structural changes in the placenta. Less vasculosyncytial membranes, lower volume densities of the fetal vessels, and a thickening of the basement membrane of the trophoblast at the ultrastructural level were found in placentae of smoking mothers. Similar villous basement membrane thickening was demonstrated by Sen & Langley (1974) in pre-eclampsia, intrauterine growth retardation, and in placentae associated with intrauterine death, but in that study smoking habits were not mentioned.(11) It would seem clear that there is a decreased effectiveness of placental exchange and this would contribute to the pathophysiology of maternal smoking.

In addition, this group is looking at cadmium as a possible toxic agent causing placental changes. Cadmium is a known constituent of tobacco smoke. A reduction in birthweight after cadmium exposure in animals has been described (Sutoe et al., 1980).(11)

Carbon Monoxide and Nicotine

Another study, in which the diminished fetal reactivity with smoking was examined(10), carbon monoxide and nicotine with combined effects are discussed. Infants of smoking mothers have been demonstrated to have higher levels of carboxyhemoglobin than nonsmoking control subjects. As a result, the oxyhemoglobin dissociation curve would be shifted to the left. Before a given amount of oxygen could be released from hemoglobin, fetal oxygen tension would have to be lowered. In other words, a state of relative fetal hypoxia would exist. At the same time, nicotine, its effects mediated by maternal catecholamines, has been demonstrated to reduce uterine blood flow.(10) This may lead to decreased uteroplacental sufficiency.

Adult Life and Possible Cancer Risks

A final hypothesis(14) from Richard B. Everson is worth noting. The following is the summary direct from the hypothesis.

Studies which provide evidence suggesting that cancer could result from transplacental exposure to maternal smoking include animal experiments showing that: (1) compounds present in tobacco smoke and cigarette smoke condensate itself are active placental carcinogens; (2) the fetus has greater sensitivity to some carcinogens than the adult, so that estimates of doses necessary for transplacental carcinogenesis cannot be accurately predicted from effects in adults; (3) carcinogens administered transplacentally can increase sensitivity to later carcinogenic exposures; and (4) many (at lower doses, probably most) tumors resulting from transplacental exposure are not evident until adulthood, and their morphology and sites do not differ from those of spontaneously occurring tumors. Studies in man have shown that components of tobacco smoke can reach the fetus, and that human fetal tissues are capable of activating carcinogens similar to those in tobacco smoke. These findings suggest that conditions causing transplacental carcinogens in animals may be duplicated in man by prenatal exposure to maternal smoking, and that resulting tumors could occur in adulthood. In view of the widespread prevalence of smoking during pregnancy, epidemiological studies of cancer in adults should investigate the possible role played by maternal smoking in increasing cancer risk.(14)

CONCLUSION

In summary, abundant evidence exists as to the harmful effects maternal smoking may have on the fetus. These include low birthweight, low IQ scores, minimal brain dysfunction, shorter stature, perinatal mortality, and premature birth. A conclusion may be drawn from the culmination of these studies that the risks are dose related. There is also suggestion of increased cancer risks for these children later in life. Possible mechanisms for these deleterious effects include the impact of the following: structural changes in the placenta, cyanide, cadmium, carbon monoxide, and nicotine.

Regardless of the mechanism(s), the message is clear; smoking should be contraindicated for pregnant women. As smoking is without beneficial effects for the mother, this seems a minimal request for the health of another.

As more data has become available on the effects of passive smoking, rising insurance costs due to smoking-related illnesses, decreased productivity in the workplace, and the greater than 350,000 smoking-related deaths per year, one would not find it unreasonable to question a society that allows this unhealthy fixation to continue at the risk of its entire membership. Education may be the one hope for reduction. As in all areas of health care, if more preventive education was available, less crisis intervention would be necessary.

Glossary

1. **abrupto placenta**—Partial or complete premature separation of a normally implanted placenta.
2. **catecholamines**—Pyrocatechols with an alkylamine side chain; examples of biological interest are epinephrine, norepinephrine and dopa.
3. **hypoxia**—Decrease below normal levels of oxygen in air, blood, or tissue, short of anoxia.
4. **minimal brain dysfunction**—Also referred to as hyperactivity and/or attention deficit disorder.
5. **neonatal period**—Newborn; related to period immediately succeeding birth through the first 28 days.
6. **perinatal period**—Period before delivery from the twenty-eighth week of gestation to the first seven days after delivery.
7. **placenta previa**—Placenta that is implanted in the thin, lower uterine segment and that is typed according to proximity to cervical os.

References

1. Netter, M. D., Frank H., *The Ciba Collection of Medical Illustrations,* Volume II, Reproductive System, p. 217.
2. *Ibid.*
3. *Ibid.,* p. 218.

4. *Ibid.*, p. 219.

5. Saunders, W. B., *Conn's Current Therapy 1988*, p. 862.

6. Jensen, Benson & Bobak, *Maternity Care, The Nurse and the Family*, Second Edition, p. 296.

7. Committee on Technical Bulletins, 1979; Korones, 1981.

8. Meberg, A., Sande, H., Foss, O. P. and J. T. Stenwig, 1979, Smoking During Pregnancy—Effects on the Fetus and on Thiocyanate Levels in Mother and Baby, *Acta Paediatr Scand* 68:547–552, 1979.

9. Lehtovirta, P., & M. Forss, 1978, The Acute Effect of Smoking on Intervillous Blood Flow of the Placenta, *British Journal of Obstetrics and Gynaecology*, October, 1978. Vol 85, 729–731.

10. Phelan, Jeffrey P., Diminished Fetal Reactivity with Smoking, 1980, *American Journal of Obstetrics and Gynecology*, 136:230–233, 1980.

11. VanDerVelde, W. J., et al., Structural Changes in the Placenta of Smoking Mothers: A Quantitative Study, *Placenta* (1983), 4, 231–240.

12. Asmussen, I., Ultrastructure of the Villi and Fetal Capillaries in Placentas from Smoking and Nonsmoking Mothers, *British Journal of Obstetrics and Gynaecology*, March 1980. Vol. 87, 239–245.

13. Meyer, M., et al., Perinatal Events Associated With Maternal Smoking During Pregnancy, *American Journal of Epidemiology*, 1976, Vol. 103, No. 5, 464–476.

14. Everson, Richard B., Hypothesis, Individuals Transplacentally Exposed to Maternal Smoking May Be At Increased Cancer Risk in Adult Life, *The Lancet*, July 19, 1980, 123–127.

■ THE WRITER'S ASSIGNMENT

This upper-level biology course required a review of the literature, which then led into a report of an original research project. This paper represents the literature review requirement. ■

■ UNDERSTANDING WRITING STRATEGIES

1. What studies does this essay review? What is the subject of each of these studies? What organizing principle governs Fahrman's order in discussing these?

2. Assuming that Fahrman's sources all use standard scientific report format, what parts of those studies does she draw upon for her review?

3. Fahrman wrote this for a class assignment that prepares her for scientific report writing. What writing characteristic would likely be valued in an assignment like this?

4. On what criteria would this essay be evaluated if it were part of a report submitted to a scientific journal? Explain how this essay does or does not meet criteria for scientific writing.

5. Reviews of the literature serve an important function in scientific re-

search. What is this? Why must researchers review previous literature before they present their own experimental findings? ■

■ SUGGESTION FOR WRITING

Rewrite this essay for a popular health magazine's audience. ■

Chaos

Craig Hartman

James Gleick's book *Chaos* chronicles the men and events that have shaped the new scientific study of chaos. Craig Hartman's review of *Chaos,* written for a honors cross-disciplinary writing course, presents a concise overview of the book's very difficult subject and places it in its scientific context.

During the past few years an increasing amount of attention has been focused on the making of a new science. Scientists of all sorts, primarily physicists, have created a new and revolutionary method of understanding, or at least trying to understand, the complexity of nature and the world around us. The science is called chaos, and its implications are nothing short of mind-boggling. What was until now unexplainable, chaos explains: the onset of turbulence, the prediction of weather, the formation of clouds, currents, and snowflakes. Chaos presents patterns where before there were none. Chaos ties together phenomenon which were traditionally completely unrelated. Most importantly, chaos provides order where only disorder could be seen. The most enthusiastic advocates of chaos argue that it will be one of the twentieth-century's three most significant scientific contributions, along with quantum mechanics and relativity.

In his book *Chaos,* James Gleick chronicles the events of the past twenty years which have shaped this new science, and the men responsible for these events. He begins with what is considered the starting point of the new science, Edward Lorenz's Butterfly Effect, and ends with a discussion of the newest discoveries and the future of chaos. But most importantly, he explains in depth the incredibly fascinating equations, theories, and concepts which are the heart of chaos, and the brainwork behind them all. For example, Mitchell Feigenbaum's theory of universality. Using only a hand-held calculator, this incredibly gifted physicist proved that simple equations from a simple system can be applied to a totally unrelated system to produce a complicated solution. Though this theory was at first greeted with extreme skepticism, it soon became the basis for finding order in otherwise unrelated irregularities.

Chaos is a conceptual science, more abstract than concrete, and is therefore especially difficult to explicate. Nevertheless, Gleick does a remarkable job and manages to concisely relay to the reader the most significant aspect of the science, while somehow clarifying abstractions which seem unexplainable.

Gleick was also quite qualified to write his book. Hired in 1978 as a scientific specialist for the *New York Times*, he has been an editor and reporter ever since. Within the last few years, namely 1986 and 1987, a number of articles began appearing in scientific journals and magazines concerning the growing science of chaos. Gleick happened to be one of the primary authors involved with such publications, as he authored over a dozen articles on different facets of chaos in less than two years. The timing of his book was perfect, as a growing interest in the new science called for an all-encompassing publication including both the history and explanation of chaos. In *Chaos*, Gleick achieves both of the above.

Though his audience is obviously the scientific community, the book is not impossible to read. A general knowledge of basic physics and calculus is really all that is needed to understand and enjoy the information which is so effectively presented. However, a strong scientific background is necessary in order to fully appreciate the significance and understand the implications of such a science.

Other scientific writers agree that *Chaos* is an exceptional chronicle of the evolution of the new science, particularly effective in Gleick's use of the founding scientists' own words. But not even Gleick himself goes so far as to place some far-reaching importance on the science of chaos. For this reason, it is difficult to judge exactly how relevant the whole thing is, or if it's just another interesting, yet useless, piece of scientific rhetoric. In any case, it certainly presents a whole new philosophy on science's relationship with nature, and after reading this book, it is impossible to look at the world in quite the same way again.

Notwithstanding the questionable relevance of it all, Gleick's work is an outstanding piece of scientific journalism. It is written objectively, and thus Gleick is not attempting to justify the science or define its place in the scientific community. He is simply compiling all attainable information on chaos and presenting it to the public to judge for themselves. Accordingly, it would not be fair to consider Gleick's failure to comment on exactly how important chaos is as a shortcoming of the book itself, for he never intended to offer such an evaluation. In fact, it is actually better that the public, especially the scientific community, be given the opportunity to evaluate an objective account of what chaos is, and then decide if it has a dramatic impact on the way science should work. And this is exactly what has been done.

The opinions expressed toward this subject vary considerably. For instance, William M. Schaffer, a well-known and respected ecologist, was profoundly affected by the emergence of chaos. After becoming an adamant advocate of the science, he was unable to continue any research in the type of ecology he had spent most of his career in. Instead, he moved to the mountains and began a whole new study on the behavior of animals based on principles strongly associated with methods used in the study of other chaotic systems.

On the other hand, more conservative scientists tend to dismiss chaos as "interesting, but impractical." Nonetheless, this is a common attitude historically taken by conservative scientists in light of a revolutionary discovery.

Research in chaos will certainly continue, and it will probably be some time before anyone is actually sure of its implications. Still, the research already done by such people as Feigenbaum is recognized and respected in the scientific community. Therefore, chaos has already made its mark, and it seems only logical that advancements will continue to be made, and someday chaos will stand as a true science: a way of explaining the complex world in which we live.

If this is the true progression of science, *Chaos* will stand as the original documentation of how it was all done, and who did it. If it turns out that the new science is merely another irrelevant collection of useless theories concocted by modern scientists frustrated with the relatively stagnant scientific period of the late 1900s, then *Chaos* will stand as another perfect example of how scientists are occasionally wrong. Either way, *Chaos* will not be a piece of scientific journalism that is easily forgotten. The scientists involved and the discoveries made are simply too significant.

Said one colleague of Gleick's, "the scientific community cannot afford to overlook the implications inherent in James' [Gleick] work. Even if chaos eventually leads nowhere, the mere thoughts and concepts presented by such a distinguished group of scientists are invaluable. Besides, it might prove to be the answer we've all been looking for."

If it does prove to be the answer, Gleick will be highly praised for his contribution to the understanding of chaos. The exciting thing is that new applications are made almost every day. Almost any modern science journal will contain some comment on strange attractors, fractional dimensions, a possible universal constant, or an editorial on a particular scientist's contribution to the new path of science, such as Benoit Mandelbrot's concept of fractals. Chaos is particularly important in modern science because there really doesn't seem to be anywhere else to go. All that can be explained has been explained; only the wild, disorderly, chaotic systems are still left unexplained. But scientists are discovering that most of the natural world fits under that classification. So, there is still much to be done in the world of science; still much to be explained. And it looks as though chaos may well be the medium through which it can be done.

■ THE WRITER'S ASSIGNMENT
Review a current science book by first summarizing the book's contents and then placing the work in its scientific context. ■

■ UNDERSTANDING WRITING STRATEGIES

1. What kind of commitments does the introduction make about the subject matter?

2. What are the summary's principal points? How well does this familiarize you with the book?

3. What organizing principle does Hartman use for the summary? What suggests this?

4. What does Hartman's discussion of the author, Gleick, contribute to the review?

5. How does Hartman evaluate *Chaos,* the book, and chaos, the science?

6. What criteria does Hartman use for his evaluation of the book?

7. How well does this review establish the book's scientific context? What demonstrates this?

8. Does this review give a clear picture of the book and stimulate a reader's interest? On what do you base your response? ■

■ SUGGESTION FOR WRITING

Write a review for a book on science, either popular or technical, where you both summarize the main ideas and indicate their and the book's importance. Before you write establish your own criteria for evaluation. ■

Is the Research and Development of Cloning and Recombinant DNA Technology Necessary for the Advancement of Humankind?

Andrea Jahn

Andrea Jahn, writing for a biology class, argues in favor of controversial research on cloning and recombinant DNA. Her essay reflects current ethical ferment about scientific issues, a ferment that illustrates the difficulty of value-neutral science and science's willingness to confront issues in college classes.

There is much controversy surrounding the research and developments in genetic engineering today. The discovery of recombinant DNA and cloning has triggered passionate responses from biologists, sociologists, members of the clergy, philosophers—people from all walks of life—and has raised some significant ethical, political, and social issues.

The word "clone" comes from the Greek "klon," meaning twig or slip, which refers to asexual reproduction, also known as vegetative reproduction. Cloning simply means that sex is not part of the process of generation. Genetic engineering is the artificial manipulation of life, and recombinant DNA is a laboratory technique for splicing together genetic material from unrelated organisms to manufacture novel forms of life.

One of the first examples of cloning was done around 1892 by a man named Hans Adolph Eduard Driesch. By using blastomere separation, he obtained two separate embryos that had originally come from one cell. He used sea urchins which were in a two blastomere stage (right after fertilization when the cell divides in half), put them in a container, and shook the container so hard that the two cells became detached. He discovered that both of the cells developed as whole embryos although they were dwarfed. This was probably because the blastomeres were smaller than the original undivided egg. The philosophical implications of doing this were so dumbfounding that Driesch left experimental embryology and became a professor of philosophy.

Another method of cloning is that of nuclear transplantation. This was first successfully achieved in the frog, *Rama pipiens*. The process begins with the destruction of the nucleus (by ultraviolet light) in an unfertilized egg. A nucleus is also taken from an intestinal cell of a tadpole by microsurgery. The intestinal cell nucleus is then carefully injected into the cytoplasm of the nucleus deficient egg. Mitotic divisions occur and what develops is a new tadpole. There is only a 1% success rate for this procedure. The reason for failure appears to be that the surgery often mechanically damages the nucleus or the egg or both, and the egg with the transplanted nucleus does not develop.

The cloning of mice by nuclear transplantation is done in a slightly different way. First, the blastocysts from the donor parent are isolated and removed from the membranous envelope. Then, cells from the inner cell mass—the part of the blastocyst destined to give rise to the embryo itself—are isolated and dissociated into single cells. At the same time, freshly fertilized eggs are taken from the recipient mouse. A nucleus from a single cell from the inner cell mass is removed and transplanted into the zygote. These transplanted cells are cultured in vitro, where about 35% divide and produce new blastocysts. These are then implanted into a foster mother, where there is further development.

While the technology of in vitro culture has made remarkable strides, it is not yet possible to culture a mammalian embryo for the entire fetal period. To obtain a cloned mouse, the embryo must be implanted in the uterus of a female.

The discovery of DNA led to the discovery of recombinant DNA, which is the actual manufacture of new forms of life. Recombinant DNA technology can yield clones of DNA itself. Recombinant DNA technology procedures are dependent upon the process of cell cloning, which is here described.

Bacteria can be grown in dishes containing a nutrient medium. If the nutrients are adequate and conditions such as temperature are appropriate in the culture dish, bacteria will flourish in vitro. Millions of bacteria, called a colony, can grow from a single bacterium. If there was only one progenitor cell and all the cells were produced by ordinary cell division, then all the members of the colony are genetically identical and the colony is known as a clone.

Scientists have found ways in which DNA molecules from one source can be combined with DNA molecules found in bacteria to produce clones which are literally new forms of life.

This procedure begins with a chemical scalpel, called a restriction enzyme, which is used to split apart the DNA molecules from one source. After the DNA has been cut into pieces, a small segment of genetic material—a gene, or a few genes in length—are separated out. Then the restriction enzyme is used to slice out a piece from the body of a plasmid, a short length of DNA found in bacteria. The piece of DNA from the first source and the body of the plasmid develop "sticky ends" as a result of the slicing process.

The ends of both segments are then hooked together, forming a genetic whole consisting of material from the two original sources. Finally, the modified plasmid is used as a vector to move the DNA into a host cell, which is usually a bacterium. The cells divide and they replicate not only their own DNA but also the foreign DNA into the bacteria's genetic material. The clone of bacteria, consisting of many millions of cells, has now made many millions of identical copies of the foreign DNA.

Techniques have been developed for attaching fragments of human genetic material to some bacteria's DNA. It is done in the same way as the procedure just described.

An example of useful recombinant DNA technology is the production of human insulin made through bacterial clones done with a human gut bacterium, *E. coli*. There is an uncertain supply of insulin derived from animals for diabetes patients, while a great number of *E. coli* containing human genes can be grown relatively cheaply.

Today, scientists are using cloning procedures to gain insight into biological phenomena such as differentiation, immunobiology, aging, and cancer. When asked "Why clone a frog?", Robert Gilmore McKinnell, Professor of Genetics and Cell Biology at the University of Minnesota, replies, "Why try to understand differentiation?" The uses of cloning are for scientific and research purposes, to improve mankind, to wipe out disease, to extend the life span. There are innumerable things that can be done in research using the technology of recombinant DNA. The ability to clone farm animals could have tremendous advantages.

Frogs, salamanders, mice, carrots, and fish have all been cloned, and cattle embryos have been fragmented surgically, resulting in genetically identical offspring, but no humans have ever been cloned, although the technology is here. The only obstacles against applying this animal technology to humans are convention, decency, and the law. There will always be some people willing to defy convention or break the law and some people will probably succeed in cloning a human. It would be a very difficult procedure if it did work. Most scientists do not want to clone humans. The process must be done with a fertilized egg and to most this would be unethical and immoral.

The opponents of cloning appear to be misled in their factual information about the subject. One man actually wrote a book on the assumption that a man had had himself cloned. The book *In His Image, The Cloning of a Man*, by Rorvik, has factual errors of biology. A U.S. District Court judge ruled the book a fraud and a hoax. This incident ignited the media into providing misinformation about cloning.

Some of the opponents of cloning do have some ethical and social issues to raise. Should we "play God"? Is there really a need to change the heredity of a cell? Why should we create new forms of life, isn't that God's domain? Is there a reason to fuse cells from two different species? These are legitimate questions, and they are not easy to answer.

The issues of scientists creating a superrace of Einstein-like people is hardly possible considering no human has ever been cloned yet and the funding for this would be extraordinarily high. There is barely enough funding to keep the research going as it is today.

One issue which I believe has probably caused the most controversy is that corporations, or people, have the legal right to own and sell all new forms of life they create. Is owning and selling other life forms ethical? Has our technology reached such a point that we believe this is acceptable to do? It is a legal right now. I believe that at this point in our technology we have to ask ourselves if continued research is necessary for humanity.

My opinion is that the technology that has been utilized so far has been very useful for humanity. If there is a way to combat cancer or slow down aging or increase the world food supply, we should use these methods to improve ourselves and the world that we live in. However, I do not think that the cloning of humans is useful to ourselves or the world. Why make more people when the world is already overpopulated?

I feel that there should be adequate funding so that research can be continued, although I think that many things take priority over recombinant DNA research. We need to improve our natural resources—the water supply, the environment. We need ecological research. Cloning research could aid in the world food supply, combat diseases, and help in other ways as I have already mentioned. We therefore need funding for these areas.

I believe that the controversy surrounding cloning and recombinant DNA technology will continue for a long time. We must ask ourselve a simple question: If penicillin or the polio vaccine were not discovered, where would we be today? When a new technology arises we must research it and utilize it to help humanity.

Bibliography

Our Uncertain Heritage: Genetics and Human Diversity
    by Daniel L. Hartl
Who Should Play God?
    by Ted Howard and Jeremy Rifken
Cloning of Frogs, Mice, and Other Animals
    by Robert Gilmore McKinnell
The Ultimate Experiment: Man-Made Evolution—DNA
    by Nicholas Wade

■ THE WRITER'S ASSIGNMENT

Write a position paper in which you present and decide between two points of view, and then defend your choice.   ■

■ UNDERSTANDING WRITING STRATEGIES

1. Jahn begins by providing a background for her argument. What information does she provide? How does she organize this information?

2. What relationship exists between cloning and recombinant DNA?

3. What two points of view does Jahn present? Where do you find each clarified?

4. How objective is Jahn's presentation of each viewpoint?

5. How does Jahn defend her choice?

6. How does she discredit her opposition?

7. How convincing is the analogy between polio and penicillin research and DNA and cloning research? ■

■ SUGGESTION FOR WRITING

Remembering that an argument from analogy is only as effective as the number of terms they share, mentally compare and contrast the polio/penicillin research with the DNA and cloning research in terms of research conditions, positive and negative consequences, social benefits, and ethical considerations. Write an essay opposing Jahn's position using this extended analogy. ■

Fetal Alcohol Syndrome: The Effects of Ethanol on the Nervous System of the Fetus

Maria LaPadula

Using a historical perspective, Maria LaPadula reviews and integrates studies on Fetal Alcohol Syndrome and the fetal nervous system published in scientific journals.

"Behold, thou shalt conceive, and bear a son and now drink not wine or strong drink . . ." (Judges 13:7).

Ever since biblical times there has been a intuitive feeling that the use of alcohol during pregnancy may be deleterious to the unborn child. In 1899 Sullivan reported the first empirical work on the fetal effects of maternal drinking during pregnancy (Striessguth, et al., 1980). Female alcoholics in the Liverpool jail had a stillbirth and infant death rate of 56%, more than double that of nonalcoholic female relatives. Noting that the outcomes of successive pregnancies were increasingly adverse as a woman's alcoholism progressed, Sullivan concluded that "maternal intoxication" was the main source of damage to the fetus (Streissguth et al., 1980). Despite this early observation, little research was reported during the next fifty years.

French researcher Alexandre Lamache was the first to draw recent attention to the possibility that maternal alcohol abuse might have adverse effects on the developing fetus (National Institute of Alcohol Abuse and Alcoholism, 1983). In 1967 Lamache reported on 3,352 children with "physical or psychic anomalies." Among these, 1,245 children were the offspring of alcoholic parents, and Lamache noted that these children often had growth retardation, mental deficiency, and congenital abnormalities. In 1968, Lemoine, Harousseau, Borteyru, and Messuet, also in France, described similar features in 127 children born to alcoholic mothers.

Similar observations were made in the U.S. in the early 70's by a Seattle group under David W. Smith. They described a distinct dysmorphic condition associated with maternal gestational alcoholism, which they named Fetal Alcohol Syndrome (FAS). Research activity regarding FAS has rapidly increased, and by 1982 more than 800 papers had been published (National Institute of Alcohol Abuse and Alcoholism, 1983).

According to Sterling Clarren et al. (1985) in 1980 the Fetal Alcohol Study Group of the Research Society on Alcoholism defined criteria for FAS diagnosis. The group based the criteria on a review of 245 cases by Clarren and Smith (1978). Signs in each of the following categories indicate FAS:

A. Prenatal, and/or postnatal growth retardation (weight, length, and/or head circumference below the tenth percentile when corrected for gestational age).
B. Central nervous system involvement (signs of neurologic abnormality, developmental or intellectual impairment).
C. Characteristic facial dysmorphism with at least two of the following signs: microcephaly, microphthalmia and/or short palpebral fissures, poorly developed philturm and thin upper lip, and flattening of the maxillary area.

The reported prevalence of FAS varies widely depending on the location and the population under study. The overall prevalence has varied from .4 per 1,000 in Cleveland to 2.1 per 1,000 in Boston. In Seattle, where the syndrome was first identified, one study indicated a prevalence of 1.3 per 1,000. Estimates from Europe have ranged from 1.6 per 1,000 in Sweden to 2.9 per 1,000 in France. The overall prevalence of FAS is in the range of 1 to 3 per 1,000. Estimates of FAS frequency among offspring of females identified as alcohol abusers are somewhat more consistent and higher than the above figures, ranging from 23 to 29 per 1,000 (Clarren et al., 1985).

When a pregnant woman takes a drink, since alcohol has a molecular weight of 600–1,000, it readily crosses the placenta (Striessguth et al., 1980). Alcohol levels in the fetus are at least as high as they are in the mother.

Therefore, the fetus stays drunk as long as the mother does. Studies have shown that chronic consumption of 89ml of absolute alcohol (6 drinks per day) puts the fetus at risk for FAS.

Human clinical and neuropathological findings suggest that ethanol may affect the developing brain within the first three months of gestation (Sulik & Johnston, 1983). On the basis of normal developmental sequences, for the full syndrome to develop, maternal drinking between the third and ninth weeks of gestation is decisive. Sulik and Johnson report that a prospective study of 163 selected offspring of 1,529 alcoholic mothers conducted by Hanson et al. (1978) suggested that the strongest relationship between maternal drinking and fetal outcome seems to exist in the month preceding recognition of pregnancy (i.e., during the first two to three weeks following fertilization).

Recent studies stress the neurological and neuropsychological abnormalities as FAS's most important functional disturbances (Streissguth et al., 1980). This paper will deal specifically with the effects of ethanol on the nervous system.

Alcohol is but one of a multitude of possible pregnancy risks: other cofactors include maternal characteristics, medical disorders, and pregnancy complications. In addition, alcoholics frequently abuse other drugs, such as caffeine and nicotine, and may have unbalanced diets. Animal studies thus allow much greater control and greater certainty in inferring a causative role for alcohol as a teratogen.

One experiment done with rats revealed that prenatal exposure to ethanol alters the organization of hippocampal mossy fibers (West et al., 1981). The hippocampus is a brain region that is ideally suited for studying the effects of prenatal exposure to ethanol. It is unique in the precision of the laminar organization of its neurons. Since hippocampal afferents terminate on distinct segments of the dendrites of pyramidal and granule cells, subtle structural changes can be detected. Previous studies have shown that ethanol adversely affects the hippocampus in fetal and adult rats and humans. This study shows that the exposure of rat fetuses to ethanol during a period equivalent to the first and second trimesters in humans results in abnormal neuronal circuitry in the central nervous system.

Nulliparous female Sprague-Dawley rats were mated with proven studs and isolated after vaginal smears showed them positive for sperm. One group was given free access to a liquid diet containing 35% ethanol-derived calories. This liquid, delivered in calibrated feeding tubes, was given to the rats from days 1 to 21 of pregnancy. The rats were then placed on normal diet until term. The mean daily calorie intake was $66.37 = 2.61$kcal, and the mean daily ethanol consumption was $12.15 = 1.15$g/kg (West et al., 1981). A second group was pair-fed an equal volume of the same diet except that ethanol was replaced by isocaloric amounts of a solution containing maltose and dextrin. This controlled for possible neuronal alterations due to reduced caloric intake by the ethanol-fed mothers. After sixty days of age, six animals, randomly selected from each group, and six normal rats were deeply anesthetized with sodium pentobarbital. Their brains were excised and processed according to a modification of the Timm's Sulfide Silver procedure.

In normal rats, the densely stained, dark brown mossy fiber terminal field occupies much of the hilus of the dentate gyrus and then forms a hook-shaped suprapyramidal bundle that courses through the stratum lucidum of the region inferior to approach the border of the region superior (West et al., 1981). An infrapyramidal bundle also exists and is confined primarily to an area near the hilus corresponding to hippocampal subfield CA3c of Lorente de Nó. Prenatal exposure to ethanol results in a dramatic change in mossy fiber topography. In all six ethanol-exposed rats a band of distal infrapyramidal mossy fibers in hippocampal subfield CA3a at middle and temporal levels of the hippocampus were found (West et al., 1981). These aberrant fibers appeared to be a continuation of the normal distal infrapyramidal band. Also, there were small, dark granules scattered through an infrapyramidal area corresponding to hippocampal subfield CA3b. None of the pair-fed control animals had obvious alterations in mossy fiber topography. Thus, rats exposed to ethanol throughout their gestation were found to have abnormally distributed mossy fibers in temporal regions of the hippocampus.

The granule cells of the dentate gyrus are the major recipients of massive projections from the enthorihinal cortex. They project to the hippocampal pyramidal cells, forming a major excitatory intrahippocampal pathway (West et al., 1981). There is evidence that the granule cells are involved in a behavior-dependent gating process that regulates the pattern of information processing to hippocampal field CA3. The organization of the mossy fibers may play a physiologically significant role in the transfer of information from the enthorihinal cortex to the hippocampus. Alterations in neuronal connections, such as those between granule cells and pyramidal cells in the hippocampus, may have a profound effect on an area of the brain which, in humans, is thought to play a role in memory. "These distortions in neuronal architecture may be responsible for some of the serious mental impairments, although one can only speculate about the specific causes of the mental retardation seen in FAS" (West et al., 1981).

Another experiment conducted by Kathleen Sulik and Malcolm Johnston (1983) studied the effects of ethanol on the CNS of mice. Female mice, eight to twelve weeks old, were placed with males for one hour in the morning. The time of copulation plug detection was considered 0 days, 0 hours of gestation. Two injections of 25% ethanol in saline were administered in doses of .015ml/gm maternal body weight. The injections were four hours apart. Pregnant females were sacrificed by cervical dislocation and the uteruses were removed. The embryos were then processed for Light Microscope (LM) or Scanning Electron Microscope (SEM) analyses. Twenty-four hours after exposure there appeared to be an overall decrease in size relative to somite number in treated embryos as compared to controls (Sulik & Johnston, 1983). The forebrain (prosenephalic) region of the neural plate appeared to be particularly small. The forebrains of the treated embryos were narrow and pointed in the anterior end. Also, the anterior extremity of the ethanol-exposed neural plate was narrow and pointed. Since gastrulation is occurring at the same time of alcohol exposure, and the mesoderm is responsible for inducing and maintaining the neural plate, an adverse effect of the mesoderm could result in a deficient neural plate development (Sulik & Johnston, 1983).

In the course of development the brain goes through several periods of rapid growth during which it is extremely vulnerable to exogenous insults (Diaz, 1980). In humans, the period of rapid development, known as the brain growth spurt, begins at mid-gestation, peaks by the third trimester, and ends by the third postnatal year. In rats, brain growth spurt occurs during the first fifteen days after birth with a peak at postnatal days six to eight. In this experiment Diaz used rats that had undergone an artificial rearing procedure in which the neonate is provided the required total daily nutrition independent of the mother. On gestational day 26, half of the litter mates were infused with an ethanol milk formula: 3% ethanol by volume on the first day, 5% on the second day, 1% on the third day, and 5% on the fourth day. After the fourth day the experimental group was given a milk-only formula. On gestational day 40, the rats were killed, and their brains were removed.

Immediately after ethanol administration, the pups experienced continuous body tremors that at times were very severe. This tremor period lasted three to five days after discontinuation of ethanol. The experimenters also noticed that the ethanol had a marked effect on brain growth, particularly on the cerebellum (the cerebellum grows at a faster rate than the rest of the brain during this spurt). The blood-alcohol levels induced in these rats were high, but still within the range seen in human female chronic alcoholics (Diaz, 1980). Since alcohol passes the placenta easily, and since fetal blood ethanol levels approximate those of the mother, it is likely that the fetus of a drinking mother would experience such high levels of ethanol exposure.

Neuropathological observations suggest that the effects of ethanol on the developing nervous system result from errors in neural migration (Dow & Riopelle, 1985). Migratory events are a very early component of neurogenesis and involve interactions of neurons with a matrix upon which they move and extend processes. These events depend on the ability of the neuron to interact with the extracellular matrix of growth and with diffusible tropic factors in its environment. Dow and Riopelle looked at matrix interaction and process formation in vitro in order to examine directly the effects of ethanol on embryonic neurons. Dissociated neuronal cultures were prepared from eight-day chick embryo dorsal root ganglia (DRG) and spinal cord.

Dow and Riopelle hypothesized that teratogenic influences during early neurogenesis might act (1) by influencing the survival of neuron-extending processes toward targets, (2) by preventing the interaction of neurons with neurite-promoting molecular species in the extracellular compartment, (3) by inhibiting the attachment of neurons and their processes to immobilized templates, (4) by altering neuronal metabolism to prevent process extension even though receptor interactions are appropriate, or (5) by disrupting cellular production of neurotrophic materials during critical periods of development before target connectivity is established (Dow & Riopelle, 1985).

The results of the study suggest that the attachment of neurons to immobilized substrates, their survival, and receptor interactions with neurotrophic materials in the extracellular environment are not influenced by ethanol. However, process formation and neuron production of neurotrophic factors are inhibited by ethanol, in a dose-dependent manner, at concentrations lower than those previously shown to have toxic effects in vivo and in vitro. Thus, ethanol may alter specific metabolic characteristics of developing neurons (Dow & Riopelle, 1985).

St. Sandor of Rumania also studied the effects of ethanol on early meophogenesis in laboratory animals (Jones & Smith, 1985). He reported deformed brain vessicles, spinal cord abnormalities, abnormal development of somites, and retardation of general growth in developing chick embryos. St. Sandor also demonstrated ethanol-induced dysmorphogenesis in albino rat embryos (Jones & Smith, 1985).

In guinea pigs, whose neural development is complete at birth, shallow fissures, abnormally flat gyri, and cellular lesions in the cortex and basal ganglia were found in the offspring of mothers given oral doses of ethanol (Striessguth et al., 1980). Thus, it is evident from all of these studies that ethanol has adverse effects on the nervous system of animal fetuses.

Ethanol's effect on human fetuses is now well established by extensive studies. As a teratogen, ethanol produces pre- and postnatal growth deficiency, an unusual facial pattern, anomalies of joint position and function, cardiac defects, microcephaly, and mental deficiency in humans (Clarren et al., 1978). Clarren et al. (1978) suggests that in utero exposure to ethanol can produce structural brain abnormalities as well as abnormally small brains. The brains from cases 1 and 2 were derived from routine neuropathologic evaluation. Cases 3 and 4 were ascertained among eleven infants who had died and who were examined without knowledge of maternal alcohol intake. Coronal sections of the cerebral hemisphere and horizontal sections of the brain stem and cerebellum were made after the brains were fixed in formalin for ten to fourteen days. Representative blocks were selected for microscopic study, and then these blocks were embedded in paraffin and sections were stained with hemotoxylin and eosin. The following cases are Clarren's descriptions upon observing the brains:

CASE 1:
A female infant born at 32 weeks gestation to a chronic alcoholic, and had the typical features of FAS. The infant died at 6 weeks. The head circumfer-

ence was 27 cm at birth and did not grow during the six weeks of life. The brain was microencephalic and weighed 140 gm, which is the mean weight for 25 weeks gestation, and far below the 380 gm anticipated mean weight for 38 weeks gestation.

There was a massive sheet of tissue that covered the left cerebral hemisphere, crossed the midline frontally and extended onto the right frontal lobe. Microscopically this tissue consisted of neuronal, and glial cells connected to the superficial cortical layers by numerous bridging bands. The cortex beneath the leptomemingeal, neuroglial heterotopia was uniformly thinned and disorganized. In scattered regions the cortex lost all of the usual laminations and the neurons adopted bizarre arrangements. Other cerebral defects included scattered ectopic neurons in the white matter of all lobes, and the absence of a corpus callosum. In addition, the cerebellum was quite small.

CASE 2:
This male infant was born at term. The mother reported drinking as much as a gallon of wine at a time, several times a week.

The birth weight of the infant was 3.2kg. He had hydrocephalus noted at birth and facial abnormalities including short palpebral fissures, maxillary hypoplasia and micrognathia. The neurologic exam elicited no evidence of cranial nerve function. The infant died at 10 weeks of age due to cardiopulmonary arrest.

The brain weighed 660 gm, which is appropriate for age. The pallidum was thinned and the ventricles were moderately dilated. Ectopic neurons were scattered through the frontal and temporal white matter. The cerebellum was very small and poorly shaped. The brain stem and cerebellum weighed 16.5 gm, which is less than 25% of the anticipated weight for these structures. Neither a pons nor a medulla could be identified grossly or microscopically. The anterior wall of the fourth ventricle was composed primarily of glial tissue with occasional nonidentifiable neuronal clusters.

CASE 3:
This infant was stillborn at 29 weeks gestation. The mother reported drinking alcoholic beverages at weekly intervals, sometimes consuming less than one drink at a time. The conceptus had short palpebral fissures, a flat midface, and micrognathia. The brain showed microscopic evidence of hydrocephalus.

One of the most frequent malformations Clarren et al. (1978) observed in these cases was neuronal heterotopia, which is a sheet of aberrant neural and glial tissue that covers part of the brain surface and may partially incorporate the pia mater. Also, in most of the cases extensive brain disorganization resulted from errors in neuronal and glial migrations. Thus, we can see the ethanol damages the nervous system quite extensively in the human fetus.

Peiffer et al. (1979) also studied the brains of human fetuses exposed to ethanol. The following are their observations.

CASE 1:

A four and a half year old male born at term, both of whose parents were alcoholics. The third ventricle of this brain was small and bridged by two broad massae intermediae. The ventricular lamen was absent in its posterior dorsal part and was replaced by a sagittal strip of ependymal cells.

CASE 2:

A six month old male born at term. The mother reported drinking for three years. During the first three months of pregnancy she drank 4 to 5 bottles of beer and almost one liter of 40% ethanol daily. The brain displayed some hydrocephalus. The thalami were joined by markedly enlarged massa intermedia. Heterotrophic gyri were observed in the cerebellar white matter near the tonsils. The cerebral and cerebellar white matter showed retarded maturation.

CASE 3:

This was a female infant whose mother reported drinking heavily for eleven years. A hydrocephalic configuration of the head appeared in the sixth week. At both the parietal and occipital lobes the parasagittal cortex was extremely thin and partly ruptured. The olfactory bulbs were absent. Small arachnoidal cysts could be observed parietally and frontally. There was no corpus callosum or anterior commissure. The pons and medulla oblongata were very small. The spinal dura appeared ballooned in the sacral region. The microscope examination of the frontal lobe showed an indistinct separation between the six cortical layers and between the gray and white matter. In the microgyri regions the nerve cells were irregularly scattered or arranged in columns.

CASE 4:

A fetus of the twentieth gestational week. The mother reported drinking for nine years. After opening the skull there was a cystic, fluid-filled cavity without identifiable brain tissue. Preparation under water revealed only thin, floating membranes instead of brain. Neither basal ganglia nor pons nor medulla oblongata could be observed.

These observations, like Clarren's (1978), demonstrate that an embryo's nervous system is extremely susceptible to the teratogenic influences of ethanol.

Streissguth reports that evaluated neurobehavioral developments in twelve infants with alcohol-related physical birth defects and a history of maternal alcohol abuse and compared them with twelve normal infants. These two groups were examined at a mean age of one year without knowledge of the mothers' prenatal drinking history. Both the mental and motor scores were twenty points lower in the alcohol group, a noticeable difference. Furthermore, the alcohol group had significantly higher frequencies of postnatal growth retardation and microcephaly (Streissguth, 1985).

Wisniewski et al. (1985) reported five neuropathologic assessments in patients exposed to gestational alcohol. His findings were similar to those of Clarren (1978, 1985) and Peiffer (1979). All of the brains were microencephalic; one had agenesis of the cerebellar vermis.

Of the eleven children who were first diagnosed as having FAS ten years ago, two are dead and one is lost to follow-up (Streissguth, 1985). The remaining eight all remain growth deficient with respect to height, weight, and head circumference. None of the eight children had normal intellectual development; four are mildly handicapped, and four are seriously handicapped. Of the four mildly handicapped children, IQ scores are in the borderline to dull-normal range. They are enrolled in regular and remedial classes; two out of the four repeated one grade. The four seriously handicapped children are mildly to moderately retarded intellectually. They attend classes for the mentally retarded; two can read and write at a primary level, and the other two can barely write their names.

Alcohol is clearly a teratogen. The animal and human studies have clearly demonstrated that ethanol's effects on the fetal nervous system are devastating. These children, if they survive, will be physically and mentally handicapped for life. Most of the studies described similar malformations stemming from errors in migration of brain cells both neuronal and nonneuronal. The most common abnormalities of the nervous system resulting from prenatal ethanol exposure include microcephaly, hydrocephalus, agenesis of the corpus callosum, neuronal heterotopia, and mental retardation.

Although it is obvious that alcohol is a teratogen, the mechanisms through which the effects are produced remain unclear. The question of whether it is the direct effect of alcohol on morphogenesis or the effect of a breakdown product, such as acetaldehyde, or an unknown toxic agent of the alcoholic beverage awaits further study.

Since the alcohol's effects on the fetus are clearly known, and the mechanisms through which the effects are produced is in the process of being studied, the next logical step would be to increase the public's awareness to the problem. On June 1, 1977, following the first federally sponsored workshop on FAS, Ernest Noble, then director of NIAAA, issued a health caution on FAS, warning that consuming six drinks a day corresponded to adverse effects and that the effects at a lower level remained uncertain (National Institute of Alcohol Abuse and Alcoholism, 1983). On November 15, 1977, Kennedy urged the Bureau of Alcohol, Tobacco, and Firearms (BATF) to initiate rule-making to require that labels be put on bottles regarding alcohol use during pregnancy. In 1979 BATF decided against bottle labeling partly because of the complexity of the message that would be required.

Since 1979 public awareness of FAS has increased dramatically. Journal and magazine articles have repeatedly warned the public of alcohol's adverse effects on the fetus. Despite public knowledge, FAS remains a worldwide problem.

Bibliography

Clarren, Sterling K., Alvord, Ellsworth, & Sumi, Marc (1978). Brain malformations related to prenatal exposure to ethanol. *Journal of Pediatrics, 92,* 64–67.

Clarren, Sterling K., Bowden, Douglas M., & Astley, Susan (1985). The brain in the fetal alcohol syndrome. *Alcohol Health and Research World, 10,* 20–23.

Clarren, Sterling K., & Smith, David W. (1978). Fetal alcohol syndrome. *New England Journal of Medicine, 298,* 1063–1067.

Diaz, Herman (1980). Impaired brain growth in neonatal rats exposed to ethanol. *Science, 208,* 751–753.

Dow, Kimberly & Riopelle, Richard (1985). Ethanol neurotoxicity: Effects of neurite formation and neurotrophic factor production in vitro. *Science, 238,* 591–592.

Espiret, C. & Argiles, J. M. (1984). Ethanol and acetaldehyde concentrations in the rat foeto-maternal system after an acute ethanol administration given to the mother. *Archives Internationales de physiologie et de Biochimie, 92,* 339–344.

Jones, Kenneth & Smith, David W. (1985). Recognition of the fetal alcohol syndrome in early infancy. *Lancet, 3,* 999–1001.

Jones, Kenneth, Smith, David, & Streissguth, Ann P. (1973). Pattern of malformation in offspring of chronic alcoholic mothers. *Lancet, 1,* 1267–1270.

Larsson, G., Bohlin, A. B., & Tunnell, R. (1985). Prospective study of children exposed to variable amounts of alcohol in utero. *Archives of Disease in Childhood, 60,* 316–321.

National Institute of Alcohol Abuse and Alcoholism. (1983). *Fifth Special Report to the US Congress on Alcohol and Health,* 69–79.

Peiffer, J., Majewski, F., Fischbach, H., Bierich, J. R., & Volk, B. (1979). Alcohol embryo and fetopathy. *Journal of the Neurological Sciences, 41,* 125–137.

Streissguth, Ann P. (1985). Psychological and behavioral effects in children prenatally exposed to alcohol. *Alcohol Health and Research World, 10,* 6–12.

Streissguth, Ann P., Clarren, Sterling K., & Jones, K. (1985). Neural history of the fetal alcohol syndrome: A ten year follow-up of eleven patients. *Lancet, 2,* 85–91.

Streissguth, Ann P., Landesman-Dwyer, Sharon, Martin, Joan C., & Smith, David W. (1980). Teratogenic effects of alcohol in humans and laboratory animals. *Science, 209,* 353–361.

Streissguth, Ann P., Herman, Cynthia, & Smith, David W. (1978). Intelligence, behavior, dysmorphogenesis in the fetal alcohol syndrome. *Journal of Pediatrics, 92,* 363–367.

Sulik, Kathleen & Johnston, Malcolm C. (1983). Sequence of developmental alterations following acute ethanol exposure in mice. *The American Journal of Anatomy, 166,* 257–269.

West, J. R., Hodges, C. A., & Black, A. C., Jr. (1981). Prenatal exposure to ethanol alters the organization of hippocampal mossy fibers in rats. *Science, 211,* 957–959.

■ UNDERSTANDING WRITING STRATEGIES

1. Like Fahrman's essay on maternal smoking, LaPadula's essay reviews scientific literature on her topic. How does LaPadula's review of the literature compare with Fahrman's in the ways each organizes and presents sources?

2. Is this paper's purpose simply to present the results of studies on alcohol's effects? On what do you base your response?

3. The author argues, as much scientific research does, from an analogy of research with animals to human effects. How does she justify this analogy?

4. What conclusions does LaPadula reach about alcohol's effect? To what degree do her conclusions go beyond each of her individual sources? How well does she indicate the limitations of each of her sources as well as their conclusions?

5. What kind of social contexts does the author offer for the scientific research she synthesizes?

6. What is LaPadula's argument? What role does *all* the evidence play in developing this argument?

7. How necessary is each piece of evidence? Could this essay have omitted some of the evidence for a scientific audience? If so, what?

8. What evidence would you omit if this were for a popular audience? Why?

■ SUGGESTIONS FOR WRITING

1. Scientific language is concrete, specific, and unemotional, but the case histories this essay includes represent substantial human pain. Look up the scientific terminology in a medical dictionary and write a description to help a reader visualize children affected by Fetal Alcohol Syndrome.

2. Using LaPadula's paper as a source, write an objective and scientifically accurate position paper appealing for funds for further Fetal Alcohol Syndrome research.

Winning at All Costs

Jennifer Murphy

Jennifer Murphy reports her research from both scientific journals and popular magazines on anabolic steroids and their use by athletes to achieve high performance. This essay, written for a women's biology course, illustrates how writing can personalize even the most abstract scientific topic.

Testosterone, a hormone necessary to build muscle, occurs naturally in large quantities in men, but only in small amounts in women. It triggers the masculine changes that occur in men during puberty—lowering of voice, growth of body hair, maturation of the penis and testicles, production of sperm, broadening of the shoulders, development of aggressiveness, and development of sex drive. Anabolic steroids are forms of testosterone artificially created in laboratories. They were designed for men who had testosterone deficiencies. They also have been used to treat aplastic anemia, Fancomi's anemia, and severe burn patients. Now an estimated one million U.S. American athletes have driven the use of anabolic steroids for nonmedical reasons to epidemic proportions.[1] These drugs, like any others, have addictive forces and long- and short-term effects that are unable to be overlooked. The use of anabolic-androgenic steroids poses many ethical questions making one wonder whether or not they should be used. The Federal government and other organizations are cracking down on steroid abusers, hoping to reduce the obtainability of steroids and to promote fair play in competition.

WINNING AT ALL COSTS

The performance-enhancing, physique-building, euphoric, and libido-enhancing effects of steroids may constitute a powerful addictive force for athletes. If athletes train hard, eat well, and supplement their program with the use of anabolic steroids, obvious enhancement of skeletal muscle mass and muscle strength will be noted. A recent study revealed that athletes who combined (stacked) moderate doses of different steroids showed gains of more than 9% in lean body mass (controls had no gain) and strength gains of 18% (controls gained 12%) in 30 weeks.[2] Athletes can see themselves progress day by day. Former Ms. America, Tina Plackinger, found herself getting bigger and stronger at a much faster rate with the use of anabolic steroids. She became known as the "bodybuilding queen of the Midwest."[3] Not only athletes but also various medical associations recognize the improvements in performances and physiques of athletes who use steroids. For example, the American College of Sports Medicine (ACSM) states its position on steroids, "concurrent use of steroids and training with a proper diet may enhance athletic performance."[4]

The use of anabolic steroids creates the ultimate training conditions for the user. Athletes experience a state of diminished fatigue (euphoria) which enables them to train for hours on end. Upon cessation, this euphoria can yield to depression. Addiction comes to those users who want to maintain the euphoria and avoid depression.

Medically, steroids are often prescribed to men who have an irregular deficiency in the production of testosterone. When taken by normal adults, anabolic steroids can strongly increase the libido. Testosterone, also known as "sexual TNT,"[5] is found to have a triple effect on the psychosomatic sexual mechanism in normal women, causing (1) a heightened susceptibility to psychosexual stimulation; (2) increased sensitivity of the external genitalia, particularly of the clitoris; and (3) intensified sexual gratification as demonstrated by more and deeper orgasms. The majority of weight-trained women who reported using self-prescribed steroids for more than two years reported clitoral enlargement and increased libido.[6] In normal men libido-enhancing effects of testosterone therapy include increases in sexual acts and feelings, erotic fantasies, orgasms, and spontaneous erections. Male self-prescribers experience a temporary decrease in libido when the drugs are discontinued and this may contribute to habituation.

Too often athletes will take more than one drug to receive the full effect of the steroids. Stacking is another means of drug abuse and possible addiction that users undergo. Athletes often stack steroids to ensure physical progression from the drugs. Stacking can take the form of using two or more oral agents together, or more often, using oral and injectable steroids during the same cycle. Heavy users often take other prescription drugs, believing that other drugs promote the effects of the steroids, and desiring to fight off the adverse effects of steroid use.

When all of these so-called "good effects" are overpowered by the fact that steroid use is a killer, athletes have to quit. With quitting comes associated withdrawal symptoms. Depression is one word that could sum up what athletes experience upon cessation. All of a sudden hormone flow stops, and with it goes all the synthetic energy and power. The artificial steroids cut off the natural body supply by inhibiting normal secretions. Normal body testosterone drops below normal. The body nitrogen level drops drastically so that the water weight gained is lost rapidly, so quickly that all gains disappear within weeks, to an even lower level than prior to ingestion. An athlete coming down off of steroids sees his body shrinking and growing weaker before his eyes . . . "the gains just fading away, the muscle poundage just peeling away."[7] They start receiving questions like, "Are you sick?" Depression sets in. Along with this depression come other symptoms, including temporary loss of libido and reductions in lean body mass and strength. These symptoms can induce the user to quickly resume using steroids and may add to the potential for habituation and addiction. If steroid use does not stop, certain long-term effects are unavoidable.

Steroid users, both male and female, are gambling with the health of their livers and hearts. Hepatic effects consist of Hepatomas (liver cancer) and Peliosis hepatis. Hepatoma or hepatocellular primary liver cell cancer accounts for 80%–90% of all liver cancers. This disorder is associated with an increase in the size of the liver and with pain or tenderness. Peliosis hepatis is a condition of the liver which is characterized by "widespread and often cystic hepatic sinusoidal dilation."[8] Blood pools are noted in the liver.

Recently, a twenty-one-year-old male weightlifter, who was taking heavy doses of steroids, had a massive heart attack. He had no family history of heart problems and he was not abusing any other drugs. This example just proves the degree of danger one is in if one uses steroids. Fluid retention, hypertension, clotting abnormalities, " 'roid rage," (described later), decreased high-density lipoprotein cholesterol (HDL-C) levels, and increased low-density lipoprotein cholesterol (LDL-C) levels create a potential for devastating effects on the cardiovascular system. Studies show that high-density lipoprotein cholesterol concentration has a strong correspondence with coronary artery disease. A detailed analysis of the plasma lipoprotein profiles of male and female athletes using anabolic steroids shows that they are adversely affected. This fact is reflected by the results of a study carried out by Jonathan C. Cohen and his co-workers when they took 61 subjects, all regular steroid users, and 40 weight-trained athletes, none of whom had ever taken steroids (reference), and compared their ages, weights, total cholesterol levels, and HDL-apoprotein A-I (apoA-I) levels.

Seeing the statistics, there are noticeable differences between the users and nonusers. (See Fig. 1.) It is known that a serum total HDL-C concentration below 38.7 mg/100ml carries a high risk for the premature development

Group	Age (yr)	Weight (kg)	Total Cholesterol *	HDL-C *	HDL2-C *	HDL3-C *	ApoA-I *	ApoA-II *	HDL-C/ Total Choles.	HDL3-C/ HDL-C	ApoA-I/ ApoA-II
STEROID USERS											
Male Mean	29.3	93.2	291.1	23.5	1.8	21.7	54.6	25.0	0.08	0.92	2.18
Female Mean	31.0	65.6	216.4	30.6	0.0	30.6	73.5	29.0	0.14	1.00	2.50
REFERENCE											
Male Mean	27.4	81.9	182.9	52.0	16.1	35.9	92.3	39.5	0.28	0.68	2.34
Female Mean	27.2	56.0	172.8	00.2	19.0	47.2	142.1	38.1	0.38	0.71	3.72

*All of the concentrations listed here are in mg/100ml.

These statistics are also mean averages of steroid users and the reference group.

FIGURE 1. Characteristics and lipoprotein profiles of steroid-using, weight-trained athletes and reference groups of non-steroid-using male weight trainers and sedentary women

of coronary artery disease. All the current (male and female) users had HDL-C concentrations below this figure, whereas none of the reference group exhibited such an abnormality.

Suggestions have been made that the HDL2-C fraction of HDL-C protects against atherosclerosis, deposition of fatty substances in and fibrosis of the inner layer of the arteries. In male users, HDL3-C made up 93% of total HDL-C levels, compared with 68% HDL3-C in the male reference group. A disturbing fact from this study was that female users had no HDL2-C serum. This is troubling because females usually have higher levels of HDL2-C than men. Also in this study, HDL-C apoA-I levels, associated with obstructive coronary artery disease, were 69% lower in male users than in the male reference group.[9] (Footnote refers to all statistics and conclusions from this study.)

The long-term effects of steroid abuse like heart and liver diseases affect all users. The short-term effects, however, vary slightly. In some of the best male bodybuilders in the world, one can look to see stretch marks across their biceps, pectorals, and shoulders. Stretch marks are small tears in the skin that develop when body growth is too fast for the skin to accommodate. Also noted is an increased incidence of severe muscle ruptures and tendon and ligament tears. Taking anabolic steroids causes structural damage to the ligaments, tendons, and connective tissue because one's muscles strengthen disproportionately to one's tendons and ligaments. Male users also experience a decrease in testicle size and sperm production, leading to sterility. Enlarged or growing breasts, premature baldness, and prostatic hypertrophy all accompany the use of steroids in men. Just ask ex-bodybuilder, Michael Murray, "Was it worth it?" He will answer, "No way in hell!"[10]

"My God! Is that a man or a woman?" Some people find themselves asking this question when looking at a steroid-using female. Steroid-free bodybuilder Gladys Portuges says, "A male hormone injected into a male equals a man. A male hormone injected into a female equals a freak!"[11] She estimates that out of the top 30 female bodybuilders, 15 to 20 are possible users and ten are pretty heavy users.[12] Former Ms. America, Tina Plakinger, became a steroid abuser and attained all the typical symptoms experienced by a female user, symptoms like lowered voice, new facial hair, diminished breast tissue, and an enlarged clitoris. Women say, "I cheated the system—so what? I did what I had to do to win." Later these women will pay with deformed faces, bodies, and babies. Even if a woman stops using steroids for ten years, she still has a good chance of giving birth to a deformed baby.

Kids, not only adults, are now starting to use steroids to enhance physical performance, look good in muscle shirts, or get girls on the beach. This is ironic because once they get the girls, their male parts will not work to keep them. Steroids cause impotence and testicular shrinkage. Adolescents who use steroids are in the most danger because use causes premature fusion of the epiphyses of long bones, leading to stunted growth. Ex-bodybuilder Michael Murray used steroids at sixteen and says, "My heavy use of steroids at that early age permanently stunted my growth. I'm 5'6", and all the other males in my family are over six feet."[13] With these physical effects come psychological changes in the steroid user.

High serum androgen levels can stimulate verbal and physical aggression and create a potential for violence in steroid abusers. Two Harvard researchers interviewed 31 steroid users and found seven with psychotic symptoms. (Occasional psychotic episodes in heavy steroid users are known as " 'roid rages."[14]) Four were found to have madman characteristics.[15] Dr. Bob Goldman, in his book, *Death in the Locker Room*, tells of a Navy man with a previously flawless record who began using steroids and soon after robbed six homes and burned three of them to the ground. Both males and females experience raging aggressiveness from steroid use. When studied primates were given steroids, they seemed to exert a major influence on social rank and dominance, both which are related to fighting. This fact shows that steroid use produces aggressiveness in its users.

Steroid use has always posed a question of ethics. What good is a championship if it is tainted? Even if steroids did not have harmful effects on the body, there would still be a conflict as to whether or not they should be used. Steroids offer an unfair advantage over the "natural athlete." The main reason the United States Powerlifting Federation developed an official stand against steroids was to provide fair competition. The majority of competitors use steroids because they do not want their opponents to have an advantage. Right beside the question of fairness in competition is the ethical question as to whether or not physicians should prescribe these drugs to athletes or even monitor the health of users. One who did and quit is Robert B. Kerr. He originally prescribed the drugs to steer athletes clear of black market steroids of dubious quality and minimize the medical risks of taking steroids by prescribing so-called safe types and dosages. He was outwitted by his patients when they went to the black market and used far more than his prescribed dosages. Plakinger, for example, admits to popping ten Anavar pills daily—two and a half to twenty times the dosage doctors give to sick patients—and shooting up 200 mg of Deca-Durabolin weekly—six times the dosage used to treat illness. Most physicians agree that getting the athlete to adhere to recommended dosages is the biggest problem when prescribing to and monitoring the health of an anabolic-androgenic steroid user.

Tony Millar, a physician from Australia, publicly admits to prescribing steroids for his patients/athletes because he feels his reasons are valid. He believes that "athletes who want to take anabolic steroids are best protected by receiving prescription pharmaceuticals rather than resorting to black market drugs that may be veterinary, contaminated, or of dubious composition."[16] He feels that care for the athlete must come first, and where winning is the only goal, an athlete will use steroids with or without a physician's cooperation. Many physicians disagree with Millar when they say, "There is no reason to prescribe steroids because the first rule of medicine is to do no harm to the individual, and there is no safe way for an individual to use these drugs or for a physician to guarantee the absence of long-term adverse effects."[17]

Team physicians are placed under a different kind of pressure. On one hand they are obligated to report steroid users to coaches or athletic department administrators, and then see that efforts to rehabilitate the user are implemented. On the other hand some team physicians are full believers in the "winning at all costs" syndrome, discounting the dangers and believing that the benefits are worth the risks. Team physicians, more often than not, are sports fans. This fact ends up playing an important role in the use of anabolic steroids. When anabolics first appeared, team physicians willingly prescribed them, hoping that a way had been found to bypass some of the long, arduous years of training and diet that are required to produce champions. Who could blame them for wanting their team to excel? Patriotism also plays an important role in the widespread use of anabolic steroids. The feeling of physicians is that if they can in any way help an American athlete bring home the gold, they have somehow struck up points for their country.

Steroids are easy to obtain. Plakinger says, "Buying the drug was no problem. It's real available. You can get any drug you want in the gym."[18] The gym is not the only place to get steroids. It is a known fact that 80% of the anabolic steroids used by U.S. athletes are bought on the black market.[19] Athletes get bad information from the steroid pushers who are making big money from steroid sales. Athletes do not get the sound information that should be coming from physicians. Tom Gitchel, chief of the state and industry section in the Office of Diversion Control of the Drug Enforcement Administration (DEA), estimates that there might be 10,000 questionable U.S. outlets, perhaps 15 manufacturers, 15 importers, and approximately 500 distributors handling the U.S. traffic.[20]

Federal agencies are finally starting to crack down on the criminals who are making unspeakable amounts of money from the illegal sales of anabolic steroids. "Last May, federal agents arrested 34 illegal steroid dealers across the country. The bust, they claimed, shattered an international drug network that controlled 70% of the $100-million U.S. black market in steroids."[21] Agencies like the Food and Drug Administration (FDA), Federal Bureau of Investigation (FBI), Drug Enforcement Administration, and U.S. Customs all have contributed to the seizure of millions of dollars worth of anabolic steroids and related drugs. Those who decide to risk the chances of being caught and sell steroids anyway, end up paying the price of extended periods in jail and enormous fines. "A Florida man was indicted on twenty-one felony counts of violating the act. The man, whose mail order steroid business netted him $400,000 profit in under two years, was sentenced in 1986 to six years in prison and fined $210,000."[22]

Some officials are proposing the idea of reclassifying anabolic steroids as controlled substances like cocaine and narcotics, which are more tightly regulated. Reclassification would help control the wide abuse of steroids for many reasons. Heavy penalties for violation of the Controlled Substances Act would discourage some potential dealers from trafficking in anabolic steroids. Because manufacturers of controlled substances must adhere to strictly enforced record-keeping procedures, it would be harder to divert supplies from manufacturers to black market outlets. Another good reason for reclassification would be the fact that physicians could be monitored, allowing the enforcers to see which doctors are prescribing anabolic steroids to their patients/athletes. The addicting effects steroids have on users is another reason such easy attainability should be hindered. Perhaps the greatest impact of reclassification would be on junior high and senior high school students, who seem to think that steroids have no medical relevance at all. These juvenile abusers would no longer be able to obtain them without a prescription.

In the eyes of sports groups like the National Collegiate Athletic Association (NCAA), the International Olympic Committee (IOC), and the U.S. Powerlifting Federation (USPF), prescribing anabolic steroids for nonmedical purposes is illegal. In order to protect the concept of fair play in these organizations, one must pass certain drug tests before being considered eligible to compete. To ensure passing these tests, an athlete must train steroid-free, the whole objective of the steroid testing philosophy. In the past two years, some fifteen powerlifters, about a dozen collegiate football players, fourteen bodybuilders, and over twenty track athletes worldwide got caught.[23]

International Olympic Committee steroid tests are delicate screens and confirmational tests. A gas chromograph converts urine into gas, screening out traces of forbidden drug compounds. A mass specrometer confirms the presence of the specific steroid according to each steroid's individual structural blueprint. Subjects are watched while urinating, so that no substitution can be made. In the past, it was possible for athletes to discontinue synthetic steroids to pass a test and meanwhile to slow their physical decline by using pure testosterone to maintain strength and size. Now there are procedures available to test the ratio of testosterone to epitestosterone (a breakdown product) to ensure that artificial testosterone has not been used. Normally urine contains a testosterone to epitestosterone ratio of one to one. If this ratio exceeds six to one, an athlete is disqualified.

Modern detection exists in the nanogram range (that's one billionth of a gram!). This degree of specificity is expensive. Specialized steroid tests cost anywhere from $100 to $200. Detectability depends on method of ingestion, types of drugs, duration of use, level of body fat, cellular attraction of metabolites (breakdown products), and whether or not stacking occurred. Injected steroids are easier to detect and trace for longer periods of time. Oil-based steroids are detected over a broad range. They are detectable for four to seven months after cessation. Water-based steroids, which stop producing anabolic effects much faster, are correspondingly quicker to leave one's urine. They are detectable for four to five months after discontinuation. Oral steroids are more limited and could be eliminated from the urine within four to eight weeks. To ensure a testosterone to epitestosterone ratio of six to one or less, an athlete must be off all oil- or water-based testosterone for at least three months (water) and up to six months (oil). A user should also refrain from estrogen inhibitors because of possible rebound properties relative to testosterone.

As one can plainly see, the use of anabolic-androgenic steroids has its advantages and disadvantages. They obviously enhance one's athletic performance and build one's body. Steroids also create a euphoria that generates the ultimate training conditions. A stronger libido experienced by the athlete may also constitute to their advantages. On the flip side, steroids cause serious liver, heart, and reproductive side effects in users. Raging aggressiveness may also result. Steroids also give "chemical athletes" an unethical advantage over the "natural athlete." Pressure is placed on physicians who prescribe these drugs to athletes. Are they doing the right thing? Many organizations are trying to put a stop to the abuse of steroids through Federal reclassification and drug testing. If athletes only could stop and realize that what they are doing to their bodies could be stopped through the cessation of steroids. They should realize that with the extra effort, time, and patience, they could achieve the same results, but without the nasty side effects.

Notes

[1] William N. Taylor, MD, "Synthetic Anabolic-Androgenic Steroids: A Plea for Controlled Substance Status," *The Physician and Sportsmedicine*, 15 (1987), p. 142.

[2] Taylor, p. 144.

[3] David Groves, "The Rambo Drug," *American Health*, (1987), p. 81.

[4] Taylor, p. 144.

[5] Taylor, p. 143.

[6] Taylor, p. 143.

[7] Taylor, p. 143.

[8] Bob Goldman, *Death In the Locker Room* (Indiana: Icarus Press, 1984), p. 125.

[9] Jonathan C. Cohen and W. Mieke Faber, "Altered Serum Lipoprotein Profiles in Male and Female Powerlifters Ingesting Anabolic Steroids," *Muscle and Fitness*, 14 (1986), pp. 131–135.

[10] Michael Murray, "What Steroids Did to Me," *Muscle and Fitness*, 48 (1987), p. 21.

[11] Joyce Vedral, PhD, "It Breaks My Heart," *Muscle and Fitness*, 48 (1987), p. 120.

[12] Groves, p. 45.

[13] Murray, p. 21.

[14] Taylor, p. 146.

[15] Groves, p. 48.

[16]Calvin Miller, PhD, "Anabolic Steroids: An Australian Sports Physician Goes Public," *The Physician and Sportsmedicine*, 14 (1986), p. 167.

[17]Marty Duda, "Do Anabolic Steroids Pose an Ethical Dilemma for U.S. Physicians?" *The Physician and Sportsmedicine*, 14 (1986), p. 174.

[18]Groves, p. 45.

[19]Groves, p. 45.

[20]Virginia S. Cowart, "Would Controlled Substance Status Affect Steroid Trafficking?" *The Physician and Sportsmedicine*, 15 (1987), p. 152.

[21]Groves, p. 87.

[22]Cowart, p. 154.

[23]Jeff Everson, "The Long Arm of Steroid Tests," *Muscle and Fitness*, 48 (1987), p. 31.

Bibliography

Cohen, C. Jonathan and Faber, W. Mieke. "Altered Serum Lipoprotein Profiles in Male and Female Powerlifters Ingesting Anabolic Steroids." *Muscle and Fitness*, 14 (June, 1986), 131–135.

Cowart, S. Virginia. "Would Controlled Substance Status Affect Steroid Trafficking?" *The Physician and Sportsmedicine*, 15 (May, 1987), 151–154.

Everson, Jeff. "The Long Arm of Steroid Testing." *Muscle and Fitness*, 48 (May, 1987), 31+.

Duda, Marty. "Do Anabolic Steroids Pose an Ethical Dilemma for U.S. Physicians?" *The Physician and Sportsmedicine*, 14 (November, 1986), 173–175.

Goldman, Bob. *Death In the Locker Room*. Indiana: Icarus Press, 1984.

Groves, David. "The Rambo Drug." *American Health*, (September, 1987), 43–47+.

Lambert, Mike. "We Can Stop Steroids: An Australian Sports Physician Goes Public." *The Physician and Sportsmedicine*, 14 (November, 1986), 167–170.

Murray, Michael. "What Steroids Did to Me." *Muscle and Fitness*, 48 (December, 1987), 21+.

Nightingale, L. Stuart. "Anabolic Steroid Use by Athletes." *American Family Physician*, 36 (September, 1987), 349–350.

Strauss, H. Richard. "Controlling the Supply of Anabolic Steroids." *The Physician and Sportsmedicine*, 15 (May, 1987), 41.

Taylor, N. William. "Synthetic Anabolic-Androgenic Steroids: A Plea for Controlled Substance Status." *The Physician and Sportsmedicine*, 15 (May, 1987), 140–147.

Vedral, Joyce. "It Breaks My Heart." *Muscle and Fitness*, 48 (May, 1987), 120–123.

Weider Research Group Report. "Drug Testing: How and Why It Works." *Muscle and Fitness*, 48 (July, 1987), 162–164.

Weider Research Group. "Drug Testing: The Odds Against Steroids: A Billion to One." *Muscle and Fitness*, 48 (August, 1987), 122–124.

■ THE WRITER'S ASSIGNMENT

Write a paper on a topic related to the course title: "Biology: A Feminine Perspective." ■

■ UNDERSTANDING WRITING STRATEGIES

1. What kind of background information does Murphy provide for her discussion? What audience will find this background information most useful?

2. This essay analyzes the physical and psychological effects of steroid therapy. What benefits do steroids provide? How do they damage users?

3. What other considerations besides effect does the essay address?

4. Where is the feminine perspective in this essay?

5. How would a feminine perspective on steroid use differ from a masculine one?

6. What kind of information do the introduction and conclusion provide to engage the reader in a particular course of action? How effective is the writer's appeal?

7. Before you read this essay what did you know about anabolic steroids and their use? How did this essay extend your knowledge? How did this essay affect your opinions?

8. Under what conditions might an athlete be convinced to use anabolic steroids? Under what conditions can you envision yourself being convinced to use anabolic steroids? ■

■ SUGGESTIONS FOR WRITING

1. Murphy says, "Some officials are proposing the idea of reclassifying anabolic steroids as controlled substances like cocaine and narcotics, which are more tightly regulated." Write a position paper advocating this reclassification.

2. Murphy's sources generally are health and sports magazines. What is the scientific case? Write a review of the literature on anabolic steroids from scientific journals. ■

A Great Tradition

Chris Rasmussen

Chris Rasmussen's essay opposes scientific research that uses animals for toxicity studies. Appealing to the conscience of a general reader, Rasmussen's essay, while scientifically accurate, considers the implications of science rather than scientific studies. The essay's approach parallels the one Andrea Jahn uses in her position paper for a biology class, but Rasmussen wrote this for a writing course.

"Suds-o Detergent will get your whole wash clean and fresh smelling too!! This product brought to you through the deaths of three million animals. Now we will return to our movie already in progress. . . ." Did that commercial sound a little bit out of the ordinary to you? Perhaps it's because you've never seen how many wasteful deaths are caused to bring a product to you. As you can imagine, it does not make the best marketing technique.

The deaths I'm talking about are due to a liquid diet that approximately 2,700 animals are put on every day, to ensure product safety for consumers. This diet may include motor oil, detergents, food additives, cosmetics and many other appetizing items. In scientific circles it is called the "LD50" or Lethal Dose 50% or Median Lethal Dose. I call it just plain "torture."

Scientifically it is defined as the traditional "technique for assessing acute toxicity of new substances." The LD50 seeks to discover the amount of a substance, administered in a single dose that will kill half a test group of animals within a specified time period. More directly, half a group of 40–100 animals are deliberately poisoned for up to 2 weeks until they die.

Generally this custom is performed on any new products which are going to be marketed or which will cross state lines. The procedure goes like this: three groups of at least 10 animals (one per dose level) are administered excessive doses of the substance in question. It is either inhaled, painted on their skins or forced down their throats. They then suffer the effects until half their number die. The survivors are killed and dissected. The LD50 is derived from the number of deaths occurring at each dose level. I've never been a guinea pig, but I can see where this might be a painful experience.

Researchers generally try to defend their time-honored practice of the LD50 by saying that they only do so to satisfy government regulations. They do not realize that many agencies, such as the Food and Drug Administration (FDA) and the Pharmaceutical Manufacturers Association (PMA), are now protesting its use.

Linda A. Grassie, a spokesperson for the FDA, said that "although the FDA requires acute toxicity data, it has no regulations requiring the use of the LD50 test." She went on to say, "There is general agreement that the LD50 test is often credited with greater quantitative and scientific accuracy than it merits." At a FDA workshop in D.C. one scientist stated that "the only reason the LD50 is still being used, although most agree it is an anachronism, is tradition." Yet despite this, the Department of Health, strangely not the government department under whose jurisdiction the animal tests are controlled, and many other agencies still requires the tradition to be passed on.

The LD50 is generally recognized as bad science because the results can vary significantly, whether due to the animal's age, sex, diet, species, lab conditions etc. . . . . Even if we could control all of these factors, there is still the problem of applying these results to humans. No matter how specific the LD50 value might be, it cannot be directly applied to man. The value given is basically the dose it would take to commit suicide. It requires extrapolation to be useful to man; this is just another chance for error.

Another fault of the LD50 is its inability to project long-term effects of the material tested. As we have seen through our often disastrous history (for example with asbestos, Agent Orange, or Thalidomide) it is long-term exposure that can be most dangerous for humans. Even with this auspicious test, we are still not adequately protected. Every year thousands of consumers are injured by products tested on animals. Lung lesions due to talc products, blindness from mascara and hair loss due to hair coloring have all resulted from faulty testing.

If the results are so questionable and the reasons for its use so weak, why is it still handed down through the years like some treasured heirloom? It is not because there are not any replacement tests. The fact is, due to recent advances in modern technology, there are many new alternatives.

The "in vitro" technique, or the use of toxicity testing on "out of animal" cell, tissue or organ cultures has shown promising results. More recent substitutes are computer and mathematical models to study the LD50. These are simply any physical, chemical or conceptual systems that faithfully reproduce the responses of an organism to a specific substance. Assay techniques use the living material to detect or measure the effect of harmful substances on animals. If these aren't acceptable to the world of science, there are tests that involve fewer animals and are sufficient for most toxicity testing. The "Limit Test" requires the single administration of some preselected dose. Interpreting the results is easy, if no deaths or ill effects occur, no further testing is needed. The "LD50 Approximation" uses carefully controlled observation of the signs of toxicity and determination of the target organs. Still there are those who maintain the ritual. The government has proposed that the severity of an experiment should be balanced against its potential benefits. According to this definition, the amount of pain suffered by an animal subjected to the LD50 should be fulfilling some great purpose. This is just not the case. The LD50 is used in testing many generics or copies for products already on the market. This introduction of new items is purely for commercial reasons rather than for any real need. If it is not for science, nor for medicine, are commercial profits an allowable excuse for the deaths of 2–4 million animals per year?

The assessment of suffering in a lab animal is often difficult due to their relatively limited ability to talk. Pain is a sensation experienced by everyone, large or small, young or old, but seemingly not by animals. In their case it is just not readily observable. It is therefore left to the researcher to decide, and he is clearly most interested in having his practices unhindered. The researchers are not required to seek accreditation for their experiments at any bureau or agency. This probably explains the abundant repeat testing. The labs are not required to follow any specific regulations. They are however *encouraged* to follow guidelines for care of laboratory animals published by the National Institutes of Health.

The Federal laws regulating the use of animals in research are a little lacking. The current Federal Animal Welfare Act fails to actually cover the treatment of animals *during* the experiment. In addition "the majority of USDA inspectors that are in charge of the administration of the act have no special training in animal welfare and are unfamiliar with the lab setting."

The anti-cruelty laws in existence vary from state to state. A number of these were modeled after the Model Penal Code provision that deals with animal cruelty and does not apply to activities carried out for scientific research. Many laws can only be enforced *after* the mistreatment has occurred, and it *can* be difficult to remedy death. Often the offender has to be proven to have had purposeful intent in the act for any legal action to take place. It is fairly difficult to establish Fred the researcher's inherent dislike for white bunnies. Any fines paid, rather than going to further animal research, are given to the state to salt the roads in the winter. Finally your local policeman is not really interested in investigating some fanatic's alleged mistreatment of animals.

The safety of our future generations *should* be ensured and testing products which will directly affect our lives *should* be continued, but not at the cost of so much useless destruction. I suggest that instead, we pass down a reverence and respect for life, because the LD50 is one tradition we can do without.

■ UNDERSTANDING WRITING STRATEGIES

1. How does the introduction engage the audience? What does it commit the writer to accomplish in the essay?

2. Where is the thesis, or position statement?

3. Does the evidence and language present an objective view of LD50? Where do you see this?

4. On what grounds does Rasmussen identify the use of LD50 as "bad science"?

5. What kinds of argument strategies does Rasmussen use? Are any of these misused?

6. What criteria does Rasmussen use to judge the use of LD50? Explain how he relates these criteria to the evidence.

7. What course of action does the essay advocate? Is this course justified by the evidence presented?

8. What objections might be raised to Rasmussen's position? Where in the essay does he anticipate and respond to these objections?

9. The assignment for this essay probably asked the student to go to sources outside of his own experience, but that documentation was not necessary. What information probably comes from outside sources? What might be the sources for this kind of information? What is the justification for not documenting them?

10. Where would you have liked to know more about Rasmussen's sources and what they had to say? Why? ■

■ SUGGESTIONS FOR WRITING

Using animals in scientific rescarch has become highly controversial and emotionally charged. Locate a position paper from an animal rights group and one advocating using animals. Evaluate their assumptions, arguments, evidence, and biases. Write a paper reviewing and critiquing these studies using the criteria of objectivity and necessity. ■

The Crowding Effect in Tadpoles

Michelle Skraba

Writing to fulfill a review of the literature requirement for a biology class, Michelle Skraba narrows this review's focus to comparing contradicting theories about crowding effect in tadpoles. This approach allows her to select material from the published literature while it gives her an approach for her summaries.

The environment plays a very influential role in each of our lives. We are shaped in many ways as a result of the limitations and demands our surroundings place on us. For example, the climate controls how we dress, the quality of the land influences what crops we grow and where we live. We are not always aware of how readily our environment affects our lives. If one turns to a small-scale model, he can see that even the lives of tadpoles are subject to the effects of their small laboratory environment.

Since the late 1800's, researchers have been able to conclude that the growth rate during early development is altered as a result of environmental influence. Much research has been conducted in an effort to demonstrate that crowding leads to retarded growth in tadpoles. Specifically, *Rana pipiens*, the grass frog, has been used because of its expediency. The eggs are large and easy to observe, develop nicely under laboratory conditions, and artificial fertilization permits synchronous development of large numbers of eggs at the same time. Eggs are produced by mature female frogs once a year and can be ovulated through the use of pituitary injections from December or January through March (Kerr, 1988). *Xenopous laevis*, the South African Clawed toad, is also used in studies of the influence of the environment on development, differing slightly from *Rana pipiens*, in development. This paper will consider only the species *Rana pipiens*.

Although it has been recognized that crowding of tadpoles inhibits their growth, the mechanism for the cause of this so-called "crowding effect" has not been demonstrated. Researchers are divided with respect to their support for explanations for the crowding effect. One side promotes the idea that a water-borne inhibitor is responsible for the retarded growth in crowded tadpoles. The other side maintains that growth is suppressed as a result of the amount of interaction between tadpoles in a crowded environment. Support for each faction exists in the literature at present. Despite being divided, both groups affirm that lack of food and temperature changes do not play a role (Gromko, Mason, Smith-Gill, 1973).

The "crowding effect" elicits some very specific changes in the developing tadpole. Growth of the tadpole under optimal conditions is very slow between fertilization and hatching, proceeds with logarithmic increase of bulk for about two weeks, and then declines in rate up to the beginning of metamorphosis. The crowding of many individuals together causes little change in the initial rate of logarithmic increase, but brings on the decline in rate much sooner and more severely than in isolated individuals (Adolph, 1931). In addition, it is also important to note that the crowding effect does not impact on all members of a population equally. Some crowded tadpoles develop at the same rate as uncrowded tadpoles, while other members of the population show all degrees of retardation, including mortality (Rose, 1959).

Of the two existing theories to explain these developmental changes, much research explains the so-called "water-borne inhibition theory." This is an idea that the environment grows worse due to a water-borne inhibitor; a "biological conditioning of the environment" (Nakata, et al. 1982). Within this realm, investigators believe that the "crowding effect" is caused by an inhibitory substance or cell produced by the tadpole and released in its feces. Richards provided the evidence for this by comparing growth of tadpoles in fresh water to that of tadpoles in crowded water as well as to that of tadpoles in fresh water to which the gut content of a single large tadpole was added.

Her results show a marked decrease in growth for the tadpoles in crowded water and in water with the gut contents. Thus, the inhibitory substance is a product of the tadpole.

Researchers have isolated this substance from tadpole feces but are unable to designate just what type of cell it is. A round, vacuolated cell in the intestinal tract, it may be in the yeast, fungi, algae, or protozoan categories. Some researchers believe it is a cell produced in the gut of crowded tadpoles. Others believe the substance is an alga-like cell. Richards noted upon microscopic examination that the cells are non-motile and colorless, with a heavy outer coat. They vary in diameter from five to 19 micrometers and generally have one (sometimes two) nuclei. These inhibitory products may be removed from the water by heating, freezing and thawing, centrifugation, filtration, or sonication (Richards, 1958).

In her work with *Rana pipiens*, Richards made some additional discoveries with respect to growth inhibition. She found that tadpoles whose growth had been inhibited by keeping them in crowded water immediately began to grow when they were placed in fresh water. In addition, she noted that when crowded water was allowed to stand at room temperature for eight days before testing, it lost some of its effectiveness, and after standing 26 days at room temperature it lost it all (1958).

From those researchers who believe that growth inhibition is caused by a component of tadpole feces, there exist two additional hypotheses. Some investigators believe that the cell is confined to the feces and transferred by consumption. Richards concluded, "Tadpoles maintained in water conditioned by large tadpoles of the same species had a reduced growth rate because they eat fecal material containing a peculiar type of cell which is probably responsible for the inhibition" (Richards, 1958). Yet others contend that the cell is diffusable in water. In one experiment, tadpoles were reared in two plastic boxes that confined six tadpoles to two liters of water. One box allowed their fecal material to be lost through the bottom, and the other did not. In both situations, growth of the tadpoles was slow. The animals that could not ingest their own fecal material did not grow any better than the tadpoles that were in direct contact with their fecal material (Akin, 1966). This experiment illustrates the hypothesis that the inhibitory substance is not confined to fecal material.

In the second theory, researchers believe that inhibition of growth in a crowded colony of tadpoles is a result of things other than an inhibitory cell. Investigators hypothesize that the crowding effect is a result of density. These experiments involved both "diffusable density variables" (the presence of a diffusable growth-inhibiting substance) and "effective density variables" (the volume of water that the tadpoles can move around in). Gromko, Mason, and Smith-Gill found that, ". . . the time to metamorphosis, and the variability in the population were found to be functions of density" (Gromko, Mason, Smith-Gill, 1973). These investigators divided sibling tadpoles into three groups, each with the densities systematically varied in four pans. Two of the three groups were set up so that plastic screens separated the tadpoles from their feces. The researchers saw a crowding effect in both the presence and absence of the screen. In addition, growth and differentiation retardation was seen in all three groups, ruling out the "inhibitory substance theory." The most likely explanation is that the crowding effect is mediated by effective density of the population (Gromko, Mason, Smith-Gill, 1973). In other words, at high effective densities, interactions among tadpoles are causing the crowding effect.

Still other investigators maintain that behavioral interference adversely affects growth and differentiation in *Rana pipiens*. Adolph, in his studies of tadpole growth rate, concluded, ". . . the composition of the water itself has no significant influence on growth." He also found that the ingestion of food per individual is much reduced by crowding. He states, "The effect is therefore exerted upon the behavior of the tadpole toward food." The tadpoles spend less time feeding because they are more involved with the behavior of other tadpoles in the environment (Adolph, 1931).

CONCLUSION

It is obvious that many controversies remain regarding the crowding effect. Although extensive research has been done in this area, investigators are divided in their support for a theory to explain the crowding phenomenon. Richards, Akin, and Rose are researchers who promote the "inhibitory substance" theory. Conversely, Adolph, Gromko, Mason and Smith-Gill uphold theories involving effective density and behavioral interference. Since it is not clear which is the main cause of the crowding effect, the possibilities of both causes should be considered at present.

Tadpoles are not the only organisms that illustrate developmental changes as a result of a crowded environment. Similar effects can be noted in insects, snails, fish, bacteria, hydra, planarians, protozoans, and many others. For this reason, people should be concerned. This crowding effect can play a major role in the economic well-being of our society. For example, in the fish industry, this phenomenon could hurt productivity by decreasing the size and increasing the mortality of fish raised in fisheries. Just as we are shaped by our environment, so, too, are other organisms in their environments.

Bibliography

Adolph, E. 1931. The size of the body and the size of the environment in the growth of tadpoles. *Biological Bulletin*, 61:350–375.

Akin, G. 1966. Self-inhibition of growth in *Rana pipiens* tadpoles. *Physiological Zoology*, 39(4):341–356.

Gromko, M., Mason, F., and S. Smith-Gill. 1973. Analysis of the crowding effect in *Rana pipiens* tadpoles. *Journal of Experimental Zoology*, 186:63–72.

Nakata, K., Sokabe, M., and R. Suzuki. 1982. A model for the crowding effect in the growth of tadpoles. *Biological Cybernetics*, 42(3):169–176.

Richards, C. 1958. The inhibition of growth in crowded *Rana pipiens* tadpoles. *Physiological Zoology*, 31:138–151.

Richards, C. 1962. The control of tadpole growth by alga-like cells. *Physiological Zoology*, 35:285–296.

Rose, S. 1959. Failure of survival of slowly growing members of a population. *Science*, 129:1026.

Rose, S., and F. Rose. 1961. Growth controlling exudates of tadpoles. *Symposium of the Society for Experimental Biology*, 15:207–218.

■ THE WRITER'S ASSIGNMENT

This upper-level biology course required a review of the literature, which then led into a report of an original research project. This paper represents the literature review requirement. ■

■ UNDERSTANDING WRITING STRATEGIES

1. How does the introduction engage the reader in the topic's importance?

2. How does the introduction suggest the paper's limits and organization? What organizing principles does the writer use?

3. What are the two views about growth inhibition caused by tadpole crowding?

4. How does Skraba use her literature? Does she quote directly? Paraphrase? Summarize? Find an example of each and explain what kinds of considerations affected her writing choices.

5. Like the introduction, the conclusion emphasizes the topic's importance. How effectively does this work for you as a reader? ■

MTPT and Parkinson's Disease

Karen Snyder

Writing for a biochemistry class, Karen Snyder explains how a drug-induced syndrome parallels Parkinson's Disease. She associates Parkinson's neurological damage with the drug's chemical composition and toxic effects by describing published experiments and reporting their results.

Many of the intricacies of neural degeneration in Parkinson's Disease have been recently brought to light by 1-methyl-4-phenyl-1,2,3,6-tetrahydropyridine (MPTP). MPTP was discovered to be a contaminant of 1-methyl-4-phenyl-4-propionoxypiperidine (MPPP) when some young drug abusers injected MPPP as an "alternative to heroin" (Heikkila, Nicklas, & Duvoisin, 1986, p. 149). Subsequently, they developed symptoms of Parkinson's Disease. These unfortunate cases have allowed science to advance in its understanding of Parkinsonism, by inducing MPTP into a variety of animal subjects in controlled settings and by observing the effects on human subjects who had injected it during their abuse of drugs (Calne et al., 1985; Kopin, 1986).

The effects of MPTP were first seen in 1973 when a college student attempted to synthesize demerol (MPPP) in a laboratory. Although he was successful in doing this, and continued to synthesize MPPP over several years, his procedures eventually became sloppy. Later, it was determined that the hastily synthesized MPPP had become contaminated with MPTP (Kopin, 1986). Presumably, in the young man's growing addiction to the mixture of cocaine and MPPP, his progressively urgent needs to create more of it caused impatience with accurate laboratory procedures. The drug mixture initially produced only some tremor and rigidity. However, the symptoms increased to severe mutism and paralysis. What looked like catatonic schizophrenia was actually MPTP-induced Parkinson's Disease (Kopin, 1986). The patient's carbidopa and bromocriptine treatment was overshadowed by his ongoing abuse of drugs and eventual death by overdose. Postmortem examination of the student's brain tissue revealed Parkinsonian degeneration of the substantia nigra (Kopin, 1986). Several years later, a group of teenagers in California injected MPPP, and again the drug was found to be contaminated with MPTP (Kopin, 1986; Knoll, 1986). These incidents, along with scientific experimentation on MHPP, MPPP, and MPTP in rats led to the conclusion that it was MPTP and its metabolites which led to the onset of Parkinson's Disease. Subsequently, much research and controversial data have evolved concerning MPTP.

CHARACTERISTICS OF IDIOPATHIC PARKINSONISM

Parkinson's Disease is characterized primarily by the degeneration of the nigrostriatal pathway, in which the dopamine-secreting neurons have their cell bodies (Carlson, 1986; Calne et al., 1985). Because the neurons project to the caudate nucleus in the basal ganglia, the organism's motor system is heavily affected when degeneration occurs. Deficits occur in posture and co-ordinated, spontaneous movement, resulting in "akinesia, rigidity, tremor, flexed posture and mutism" (Porrino et al., 1987).

Carlson (1986) suggests probable damage to locations outside of the substantia nigra, such as the neurons in the ventral thalamic-motor cortex pathways, and Jellinger (1986, p. 1) claims that Parkinson's Disease "basically affects pigmented neuronal systems of the brainstem often as part of a more widespread process."

PARKINSONISM AND MPTP: COMPARISONS AND CONTRASTS

Like idiopathic Parkinson's Disease, MPTP-injected organisms show degeneration of the substantia nigra, accompanied by motor deficits. Gibb et al. (1986) have noted that MPTP also affects other areas, including the ventral tegmental area. Yet in another study, damage to this area was found to be variable (Jenner et al., 1986).

As much as MPTP-induced toxicity parallels the idiopathic disease, certain characteristics differentiate the two. After injections of MPTP, the onset of symptoms is abrupt, as opposed to the gradual onset seen in Parkinsonism. Furthermore, if the neurotoxicity of MPTP is treated, the degenerative process will stabilize at one level, whereas the idiopathic disease is characterized by a progressive decline, even with treatment (Kopin, 1986).

Within the central nervous system, MPTP neurotoxicity appears to affect the organism in a more limited way. No destruction in the noradrenergic systems occurs, particularly in the location of the noradrenergic cell bodies, the locus ceruleus (Kopin, 1986). Further, Lewy bodies do not appear in the cytoplasm, and the cholinergic complex in the substantia nigra and the serotonin groups are not destroyed (Gibb et al., 1986). Gibb et al. also point out that the caudate nucleus and putamen in the basal ganglia remain unaffected by MPTP, and agreed with Jenner et al. (1986) that the substantia innominata remains normal, as opposed to the damage done to these areas by Parkinson's Disease.

Perhaps because MPTP damages the Parkinsonian central location of vulnerability, the substantia nigra, and because it lacks toxicity upon some of the related Parkinsonian areas of vulnerability, as mentioned above, MPTP induces a powerful but limited version or Parkinson's Disease. MPTP's effect on only part of the whole Parkinson syndrome may lead to information about why the symptoms from MPTP may be stabilized with treatment, and why in some cases (Jenner et al., 1986; Kopin, 1986) even full recovery may occur.

METABOLIC ACTION OF MPTP

MPTP's toxicity is not direct; it is metabolized twice before becoming the toxic substance which acts upon the organism. Once injected, MPTP is converted into 1-methyl-4-phenyl-1,2,3-dihydropyridinium (MPDP), by monoamine oxide type B (MAO-B). This process is thought to occur in the astrocytes, and some experiments have found MAO-B specifically in the mitochondria of the glial cells (Riederer et al., 1986).

The conversion of MPDP to MPP+ (N-methyl-4-phenylpyridine), MPTP's second metabolite, is controversial. While some studies show results suggesting that MPDP is also oxidized by MAO-B (Cohen, 1986; Kopin, 1986), Smith, Ekstrom, Sandy, & DiMonte (1987) argue that this second conversion occurs by some other mechanism such as "an enzyme or some other factor in the liver cells independent of monoamine oxidase" (Smith et al., 1987, p. 743).

In any case, MPP+ is formed and still outside of the substantia nigral neuron. MPP+ is able to enter the neuron through the catecholamine pump (Cohen, 1986), a "sodium dependent, high-affinity uptake process" (Kopin, 1986, p. 140).

Kopin (1986) also found that the reason catecholamine neurons are selectively destroyed by MPP+ is that they take up 6-hydroxydopamine, which evidently characterizes MPP+. Therefore, MPP+ is capable of accumulating within the neuron at the same rate, and to the same degree, as dopamine. Once MPP+ collects inside the nigral neuron, it "generates free radicals by interaction with neuromelanin, dopamine, or other granular reducing agents normally sequestered from the mitochondria. The free radical, MPP, may generate superoxide and/or other toxic oxidase molecules which overwhelm the scavenger antioxidant capacity of the nigral neurons, causing cell death" (Kopin, 1986, p. 141). Heikkila et al. (1986) further support this hypothesis that MPP+ is particularly toxic to the mitochondria in dopaminergic neurons. They found that MPP+ was so selective and potent that it led to decreased cellular respiration and eventual death. Smith, Sandy, & DiMonte (1987), however, argue that oxygen radicals and lipid peroxidation are *unlikely* to occur during MPTP conversion to MPP+, claiming that the evidence is unconvincing. They credit any presence of lipid peroxidation in substantia nigra to the breakdown of dying cells in that area, thereby viewing it as a result of the degenerative process, rather than a cause.

Another hypothesis explains MPP+'s toxic effects differently, by claiming that the highly polar MPP+ cannot cross the blood-brain barrier. However, an intermediate ion formed in the metabolism of MPP+, dihydropyridinium, separates from MPP+ and forms an oxidation center which is capable of metabolizing dopamine into toxins, which then kill nigral cells (Kopin, 1986).

Neuromelanin: A Factor in Toxicity

Some studies implicate cell pigment's role in MPTP toxicity. Neuromelanin, an irregular polymer made during the oxidation of catecholamines, appears to bind very effectively with MPP+ (D'Amato et al., 1987). Kopin's (1986) findings that lipid soluble drugs have high concentration in melanin-containing neurons, and that MPTP is attracted to artificial neuromelanin support this hypothesis. Furthermore, Kopin suggests that the free radicals produced during interaction with neuromelanin lead to toxicity, so that once MPTP is metabolized and taken into the neuron as MPP+, it appears to become toxic through reactions with the cell's pigment. The *exact* process of MPP+'s neurotoxicity, however, is still unclear; further research is needed to clarify the details of the neuromelanin hypothesis, and/or to propose alternative hypotheses.

Neuromelanin in Different Species

The varied results obtained from studies of MPTP toxicity on different species also implies the role of high-content neuromelanin. Monkeys, whose brains contain large amounts of this pigment, have been shown to be the best subjects in some studies, showing high susceptibility to low doses of MPTP (Cohen, 1986; Knoll, 1986; Mytilineou & Cohen, 1986). Yet Kopin (1986) shows monkeys to develop Parkinsonian symptoms only after several administrations of MPTP and suggests dogs as ideal subjects, instead, as they were heavily affected after only one dose. The effects on both species, however, may be significantly connected to the presence of high neuromelanin. In contrast, the lack of neuromelanin in rodents may account for the lesser effects of MPTP injections in rats, gerbils, and Guinea pigs, as well as their rapid recovery from toxicity (Heikkila et al., 1986; Kopin, 1986; Mytilineou & Cohen, 1986).

Mice are the exception, however, as they *do* show the effects of MPTP toxicity. Kopin (1986) claims that norepinephrine decreases are seen, but adds that the effects are generalized beyond the substantia nigra, and that normal chemical balance is resumed after several months. By contrast, Heikkila et al. (1986) found that MPTP's effects on mice included not only decreased levels of catecholamines, but also destruction of the nigrostriatal pathway, the ability of these neurons to take up dopamine, and some damage to the pars compacta. Because these results parallel results seen in primates and humans, they suggest mice as the subjects for MPTP toxicity research. Whether or not neuromelanin presence in the brains of mice is responsible for MPTP's effect is not clear.

GLUCOSE UTILIZATION

Generally speaking, changes in functional activity correspond with changes in energy use. The study of the utilization of glucose, the brain's only source of energy, allows for mapping changes in metabolism in local areas of the brain (Porrino et al., 1987).

However, the evidence of two major glucose utilization studies in monkeys contradict each other. Schwartzman and Alexander (1986) found neurological changes in MPTP-treated monkeys similar to those in monkeys with idiopathic Parkinson's Disease, by using $2[^{14}C]$ deoxy-D-glucose (2-DG) to determine the metabolic rate of glucose utilization in local cerebral areas (1CMRg). Results suggest increased 1CMRg in the substantia nigra, along with the globus pallidus, ventral tegmental area, olfactory tubercle, and the medial and cortical nuclei of the amygdala. The fields of projection of the dopaminergic neurons, the striatum and cortex, showed a decrease in 1CMRg, therefore implying a decrease in the functional activity.

Porrino et al. (1987) also used the 2-DG method, but chose to wait at least three months before observation, so that the degenerative process would have opportunity to become full-blown and stable. The authors suggest that, after this waiting period, tests measured true Parkinsonian symptoms, whereas testing sooner probably would have produced results showing the immediate pharmacological affects of the toxin. Their results suggested that local cerebral glucose utilization (LCGU) was *reduced* in the substantia nigra, which paralleled the neuronal loss in this area. Decreased LCGU was also found in the subthalamic nucleus, the caudate nucleus, the putamen, and areas outside of the basal ganglia, including the ventral tegmental area.

They note *increases* in LCGU only in part of the globus pallidus, which they suggest connects with the subthalamic nucleus in a reciprocal fashion, accounting for the motor deficits seen in both MPTP-induced and idiopathic Parkinson's Disease (Porrino et al., 1987).

Saccadic eye movements were observed in MPTP-treated monkeys, similar to those in Parkinson's Disease (Brooks, Fuchs, & Finocchio, 1986), and another study noted "failure of upgaze and abnormal pursuit eye movement" (Schwartzman & Alexander, 1985, p. 137) Porrino et al. (1987) point to decreases in LCGU in the mediodorsal nucleus of the thalamus and the cortical frontal eye fields as the explanation for these Parkinsonian deficits.

TREATMENT: L-DOPA AND DEPRENYL

Deprenyl appears to be the best treatment for MPTP-induced Parkinson syndrome in animal studies. It inhibits or blocks MAO-B from oxidizing MPTP into the toxic MPP+, and when given in conjunction with L-DOPA, retards the degenerative process (Cohen, 1986; Corsini, Pintus, Bocchetta, Piccardi, & Zompo, 1986; Heikkila et al., 1986; Knoll, 1986; Mytilineou & Cohen,

1986; Riederer et al.,1986; Youdim & Finberg, 1986). In blocking MAO-B's action of metabolizing MPTP to MPP+, deprenyl inhibits further destruction of neurons in the substantia nigra and other related areas. L-DOPA is administered so that dopamine can be metabolized from it, in order to compensate for the lack of dopamine being metabolized by the destroyed nigrostriatal cells.

L-DOPA WITH OTHER DRUGS

There are claims for other drugs as effective treatment of MPTP toxicity, such as chloroquine, by blocking the MPP+ interaction with neuromelanin (D'Amato et al., 1987), and 4-phenylpyridine (Irwin, Langston, & DeLanney, 1987) and [N-(2-aminoethyl)-p-chlorobenzamide]-HCl (DaPrada et al., 1986), by blocking metabolism of MPTP into MPP+. However, Knoll (1986, p. 109) points out that "deprenyl inhibits tyramine uptake, whereas other MAO inhibitors increase the effect of tyramine." He goes on to say that deprenyl is the only MAO inhibitor which does *not* produce the "cheese effect"—a serious side effect of hypertension after consumption of a high quantity of free-amine foods. Therefore, he suggests administration of deprenyl, along with L-DOPA, as a safe and effective treatment for humans with Parkinson's Disease (Knoll, 1986). Presumably, the same would hold true from MPTP-induced Parkinsonism.

AGING

Aging seems to affect the consequences of treatments for Parkinson's patients. The body seems to become more susceptible to symptoms and less able to recover from symptoms when treated as it ages. In 1984, Parkinsonism was thought to be irreversible (Javich & Snyder, 1984), yet recent studies show cases where MPTP-injected humans had only passing symptoms, completely recovering from any signs of the disease (Calne et al., 1985; Jenner et al., 1986). Calne et al. (1985) then speculated that the disease must gradually wear down the dopaminergic neurons, with aging. Calne's subjects had youth on their side; therefore, the disease had only temporary effects on them.

Another study by Langston et al. (1987) found that the effect of equal doses of MPTP on older mice were approximately three times greater than the effects on younger mice. They attributed this to an increased MPP+ production, and, therefore, a greater dopamine depletion in the older subjects. Could it be that in older organisms there are more glial cells in the CNS, due to natural and/or diseased-based dying of CNS neurons, leading to the filling in of glial cells? More glial cells raises the likelihood of MAO abundancy, assuming that this is their primary location. MAO abundancy, in turn, would allow for a higher degree and faster rate of oxidation of MPTP into the toxic MPP+. Observation of the aged organism would show a greater amount of dopaminergic neuronal destruction, as compared to a youthful organism of the same species.

If the glial cells become more abundant in old age, then a little toxin would go a long way, making the organism susceptible to the disease, whether endogenously or exogenously initiated.

Calne et al. (1985) point out another important consideration: the variation between individuals in their rates of metabolism and the strength of their immune systems. This could account for variations and contradictions seen in studies of the same species. For example, monkeys were found to be highly susceptible to MPTP-toxicity in some studies (Cohen, 1986; Knoll, 1986; Mytilineou & Cohen, 1986) but not in others (Kopin, 1986). In humans, the variation in immune systems may be part of the reason for some young people having passing symptoms from MPTP (Calne et al., 1985) while others are affected quite heavily (Heikkila et al., 1986).

CONCLUSIONS AND SUMMARIES

In conclusion, MPTP is able to have toxic effects on the substantia nigra, but the effects on other related Parkinsonian areas are unclear. MPTP's powerful yet limited toxicity is paralleled by its clinical symptoms; they appear abruptly, and are reversible, or at least able to be stabilized. Idiopathic Parkinson's Disease, on the other hand, has a gradual onset, and is progressive even with treatment.

The mechanisms by which MPTP has its toxic effects are not yet fully understood. The best evidence, however, indicates MAO-B as the oxidizer of MPTP to MPP+. Smith et al. (1987) make clear their disagreement regarding this pathway, but their alternative hypotheses seem weak and in need of clarification.

While several drugs are being researched for treatment of Parkinson's Disease, deprenyl stands above the rest. Some of the others have been shown to be effective, but deprenyl has the advantage of being the safest, particularly in humans (Knoll, 1986). It also appears to be the generally accepted drug for treatment, as almost every reference discusses its use. Until some of the other drugs are further researched, deprenyl appears to be the best answer to Parkinson's Disease, whether brought on by endogenous or exogenous factors.

References

Brooks, B. A., Fuchs, A. F., & Finocchio, D. (1986). Saccadic eye movement deficits in the MPTP monkcy model of Parkinson's disease. *Brain Research, 383,* 402–407.
Calne, D. B., Langston, J. W., Martin, W. R. W., Stoessl, A. J., Ruth, T. J., Adam, M. J., Pate, B. D., & Schulzer, M. (1985). Positron emission tomography after MPTP. Observations relating to the cause of Parkinson's disease. *Nature, 317,* 246–248.

Carlson, N. R. (1986). *Physiology of Behavior.* Newton, MA: Allyn & Bacon.

Cohen, G. (1986). Monoamine oxidase, hydrogen peroxide, and Parkinson's disease. *Advances in Neurology, 45,* 119–125.

Corsini, G. U., Pintus, S. P., Bocchetta, A., Piccardi, M. P., & Zompo, M. D. (1986). Characterization of [3H]MPTP binding sites. *Advances in Neurology, 45,* 153–158.

D'Amato, R. J., Alexander, G. M., Schwartzman, R. J., Kitt, C. A., Price, D. L., & Snyder, S. H. (1987). Neuromelanin: A role in MPTP-induced neurotoxicity. *Life Sciences, 40,* 705–712.

DaPrada, M., Kettler, R., Keller, H. H., Bonnetti, E. P., & Imhof, R. (1986). Rol6-6491: A new reversible and highly selective MAO-B inhibitor protects mice from the dopaminergic neurotoxicity of MPTP. *Advances in Neurology, 45,* 175–178.

Gibb, W. R. G., Lees, A. J., Wells, F. R., Barnard, R. O., Jenner, P., & Marsden, C. D. (1986). Pathology of MPTP in the marmoset. *Advances in Neurology, 45,* 187–190.

Heikkila, R. E., Nicklas, W. J., & Duvoisin, R. C. (1986). Studies on the mechanism of the dopaminergic neurotoxicity of 1-methyl-4-phenyl-1,2,3,6-tetrahydropyridine. *Advances in Neurology, 45,* 149–152.

Irwin, I., Langston, J. W., & DeLanney, L. E. (1987). 4-PP and MPTP: The relationship between striatal MPP+ concentrations and neurotoxicity. *Life Sciences, 40,* 731–740.

Javich, J. A., & Snyder, S. H. (1984). Uptake of MPP+ by dopamine neurons explains selectivity of Parkinsonism-inducing neurotoxin, MPTP. *European Journal of Pharmacology, 106,* 455–456.

Jellinger, K. (1986). Overview of morphological changes in Parkinson's disease. *Advances in Neurology, 45,* 1–18.

Jenner, P., Rose, S., Nomoto, M., & Marsden, C. D. (1986). MPTP-induced Parkinsonism in the common marmoset: Behavioral and biochemical effects. *Advances in Neurology, 45,* 183–186.

Knoll, J. (1986). Critical role of MAO inhibition in Parkinson's disease. *Advances in Neurology, 45,* 107–110.

Kopin, I. J. (1986). Toxins and Parkinson's disease: MPTP Parkinsonism in humans and animals. *Advances in Neurology, 45,* 137–144.

Langston, J. W., Irwin, I., & DeLanney, L. E. (1987). The biotransformation of MPTP and disposition of MPP+: The effects of aging. *Life Sciences, 40,* 749–754.

Mytilineou, C., & Cohen, G. (1986). Tissue culture model for studying MPTP toxicity to dopamine neurons. *Advances in Neurology, 45,* 145–148.

Nicklas, W. J., Youngster, S. K., Kindt, M. V., & Heikkila, R. E. (1987). MPTP, MPP+ and mitochondrial function. *Life Sciences, 40,* 721–729.

Porrino, L. J., Burns, R. S., Crane, A. M., Palomba, E., Kopin, I. J., & Sokoloff, L. (1987). Changes in local cerebral glucose utilization associated with Parkinson's syndrome induced by 1-methyl-4-phenyl-1,2,3,6-tetrahydropyridine (MPTP) in the primate. *Life Sciences, 40,* 1657–1664.

Riederer, P., Konradi, C., Schay, V., Kienzl, E., Birkmayer, G., Danielczyk, W., Sofic, E., & Youdim, M. B. H. (1986). Localization of MAO-B and MAO-B in human brain: A step in understanding the therapeutic action of L-deprenyl. *Advances in Neurology, 45,* 111–118.

Schwartzman, R. J., & Alexander, G. M. (1985). Changes in the local cerebral metabolic rate for glucose in the 1-methyl-4-phenyl-1,2,3,6-tetrahydropyridine

(MPTP) primate model of Parkinson's disease. *Brain Research, 358,* 137–143.

Schwartzman, R. J., & Alexander, G. M. (1986). Changes in the local cerebral metabolic rate for glucose in the MPTP primate model of Parkinson's disease. *Advances in Neurology, 45,* 171–173.

Smith, M. T., Ekstrom, G., Sandy, M. S., & DiMonte, D. (1987). Studies of the mechanism of MPTP cytotoxicity in isolated hepatocytes. *Life Sciences, 40,* 741–748.

Smith, M. T., Sandy, M. S., & DiMonte, D. (1987). Free radicals, lipid peroxidation, and Parkinson's disease. *The Lancet, 1,* 38.

Youdim, M. H. B., & Finberg, J. P. M. (1986). MAO type B inhibitors as adjunct to L-DOPA therapy. *Advances in Neurology, 45,* 127–136.

■ UNDERSTANDING WRITING STRATEGIES

1. How was MPTP-induced Parkinson's disease discovered?

2. What is the nature of the controversy over MPTP and Parkinson's disease?

3. For what audience is this paper written? What indicates this audience?

4. What kinds of knowledge have researchers obtained by studying chemically induced Parkinson's disease? What does this indicate about why scientists would pursue these studies?

5. Besides merely summarizing and linking in a chain a series of studies, the author selects information from the studies and creates her own order. What topics does this essay discuss? What relationships exist between the topic and the way the writer has ordered them?

6. What direction for further work does the conclusion suggest?

7. What importance does the conclusion suggest for this body of research?

8. This essay's language is highly technical. Why and to what degree is this necessary? ■

■ SUGGESTIONS FOR WRITING

Compare this essay with one of the other literature reviews (Skraba, Fahrman). Using the criteria of clarity, completeness, and coherence, write a critique of the two essays. Be certain to include a clear explanation of what each essay says. ■

Concepts Involved in Genetic Screening

Lisa Soice

This position paper, written for a biology class, describes possible abuses of genetic screening yet supports genetic screening for diseases which may be prevented if forestalled. Soice draws on magazine articles for her evidence.

We all have a different genetic makeup, which means some of us may have a predisposition to such illnesses as manic depression, sickle cell anemia, or emphysema. Recently, scientists have identified genes that influence a person's health. In fact, Collaborative Research, a research company in Bedford, Massachusetts, claims that it is only two years away from a complete map of the 23 pairs of human chromosomes.[1] This will allow scientists to pinpoint all the genes associated with human illness. Today, however, most probes cannot pinpoint a bad gene; they can only detect sequences of healthy genes, called markers, found near a bad one.[1] Finding an abnormal gene in such an indirect way is expensive and time-consuming. Researchers need to study many relatives, including one of them who has the sought-for disease. This is a long process and because the marker can be inherited without the defective gene, findings may be misleading.[1] Once scientists are able to home in on a defective gene, people will be aware of the genetic defects they and their children carry. But is this really so wonderful? My paper will consider the ethical and discriminatory issues that genetic screening raises. I support genetic testing for diseases in which humans may prevent or forestall the severity of a disease by adopting different health habits. I do not advocate mandatory genetic screening for all people. People should decide for themselves if they want to know if they have a particular genetic disease. Some people who are at risk for developing Huntington's Chorea say they would rather live their lives without knowing if they inherited the gene because knowing would be too hard to bear. Genetic screening raises many other questions. I will consider the most prominent ones.

Arguments arose several years ago over genetic screening of industrial workers. Researchers believed they could find tests to predict who is most susceptible to harm from toxic substances in the work place. With this knowledge, those workers with alphs-1-antitrypsin (AAT) deficiency, which predisposes them to lung cancer and emphysema, could be excluded from jobs that had exposure to asbestos or cotton dust.[2] Industries are very interested in this type of genetic screening because it helps them conform to the Occupational Safety and Health Act (OSHA) which requires safe work places. Genetic screening would also reduce the number of work related lawsuits. The Johns-Manville Company had to declare bankruptcy in 1982 because of the numerous lawsuits filed by employees who developed asbestosis and other diseases. Industries could also carry this screening a step farther by excluding people because they are at high risk for disease not related to occupational exposure. Companies may justify these actions by arguing that because they put time and money into training an employee, they have the right to screen out sickly job applicants.

Unions, women's groups, and civil liberties groups strongly oppose genetic screening. They view it as racist, invasive of privacy, anti-labor, antiegalitarian, and threatening to democratic ideals.[3] I strongly agree with the opponents of genetic screening. The screenings discriminate and may be unjustly applied. Instead of industries making the workplace safer, they may hire only those people whose genes promise to make them invulnerable. They could discriminate against people from certain ethnic and racial groups, where some diseases, such as sickle cell anemia in blacks, are more prevalent. Some of the rare genetic defects have already prompted cases of discrimination. The American Air Force had a discriminatory case against them when they barred people with sickle cell trait from the Air Force Academy. This was obviously a mistake because carriers do not have the disease themselves and are a danger only to their offspring.[4]

It seems that genetic screening would create unemployment. What would happen to people's pride and sense of community if they could be barred from work? Kenneth Miller, medical director of the Worker's Institute for Safety and Health, told Congress in 1982, "The social costs of unemployment incurred by the discriminatory nature of this screening method far outweigh the nonexistent benefits to the health and well-being of the individual."[2] Not only would it be costly, but it would be unjust to discriminate against people that are capable of contributing so much to society before they become ill, or for that matter, to discriminate against them even when they have a disease that is not debilitating, as with diabetes.

Another controversial area in genetic screening involves the use of genetic test results by health and life insurance companies. Health insurance plans may use genetic testing either to exclude people from enrolling in them or to charge them higher premiums. This would create a terrible situation for these people. Not only would they have to deal with the emotional trauma of knowing they carry a gene for a serious illness, but they would also be facing potentially large medical costs not offset by insurance.

Life insurance is a little different. Life insurers have traditionally excluded people because their health is poor or they are at risk of becoming seriously ill. For example, smokers pay higher rates than non-smokers.

Such insurance discrimination already faces people at high risk for AIDS. Some states have passed laws forbidding insurance companies to require that high risk individuals submit to an AIDS test, while other states permit insurance companies to require the AIDS antibody test. In Minnesota insurance companies will ask if the individual has had a recent blood test or if they have an immune deficiency disorder. If the individual answers affirmatively, the insurance company can require them to take an AIDS test. Some researchers believe that AIDS testing may be setting a precedent for genetic screening.

Prenatal genetic screening can indicate diseases that won't strike until the unborn child reaches midlife or old age. How does a couple deal with the news that their unborn baby will be prone to schizophrenia in adolescence or Huntington's Chorea in old age? Should an abortion be performed if the child is at a certain percentage risk of contracting the disease? If so, who should decide—the doctor or the parents? If people start aborting affected fetuses, medicine may reduce its search for cures. I feel that a couple should be able to choose prenatal screening. I would want my baby to be tested for severe genetic defects and those diseases that could be fended off by taking preventive measure, but I would need to keep in mind that a predisposition is an estimate based on probabilities. Having an abortion for a relatively minor risk would be sad.

Clearly, genetic screening raises numerous ethical questions as well as the potential for discrimination. The purpose of genetic tests should be prevention, with test results available only to those who undergo testing, at least until genetic screening is better perfected and more reliable and until ethical and legal guidelines exist. As a society we need to wrestle with the recourses available to people who have and carry genetic diseases. The sooner we start resolving these difficult issues, the better off society will be, because genetic testing is no longer merely hypothetical.

Works Cited

1. McAuliffe, K. "Predicting Diseases," *U.S. News & World Report* (May 25, 1987) 64–67.
2. Kolata, G. "Genetic Screening Raises Questions for Employers and Insurers," *Science* (April 18, 1986) 317–319.
3. Hunt, M. "The Total Gene Screen," *The New York Times Magazine* (Jan. 19, 1986) 33;50–59.
4. "Genetic Interfering," *The Economist* (July 19, 1986) 17–18.

■ THE WRITER'S ASSIGNMENT

Write a position paper in which you present and decide between two points of view, and then defend your choice. ■

■ UNDERSTANDING WRITING STRATEGIES

1. How effective is the introduction's explanation of genetic screening? Do you understand what it is? Why can it be done scientifically?

2. What commitments does the introduction make to the reader?

3. What are some areas where genetic screening may prove beneficial?

4. On what grounds do various groups oppose genetic screening?

5. What reasons, or evidence, does Soice offer to substantiate her opposition to genetic screening?

6. How effective is the analogy between genetic screening and AID's testing? Explain your position.

7. Is this paper more persuasive or more reasoned? Explain your position.

8. This essay actually takes several positions, or positions on several aspects of the topic. What are they? How do they relate to the views of groups opposing genetic testing?

9. On what grounds does Soice oppose genetic screening? ■

■ **SUGGESTIONS FOR WRITING**

The questions above suggest potential writing topics: What Is Genetic Screening?—The Benefits of Genetics Screening—The Ethical Choices After a Genetic Test—are a few. From your responses to the reading questions select a topic where you feel Soice needs to expand her ideas, and write a paper that both expands her position and considers and answers the opposing view. ■

The War Against Cancer Is Nearly Won

Laurie Tennyson

In this essay, written for a cross-disciplinary writing course, Laurie Tennyson recounts recent advances in the war on cancer reported in the popular press. She gives a popular audience access to important scientific information through clear definitions and explanations.

Will people always live in fear of the dreaded plague—cancer? Today the word cancer is associated with death. Is the cure beyond the reach of present technology? Chemotherapy and radiation therapy may, in the very near future, seem quite primitive in light of recent breakthroughs in cancer treatment research. Some of the world's leading scientists and cancer researchers believe "this is one of those very rare times in the history of biology in which [they] seem ready to make a quantum leap" (Ross 127). Dr. Lewis Thomas, chancellor of Memorial Sloan-Kettering Cancer Center in New York, believes cancer could end before this century ends and that a cure "could begin to fall into place at almost any time starting next year or even next week. . . ." (Ross 127). Similarly, Dr. Vincent T. DeVita, director of the National Cancer Institute, believes that it is possible that "by the year 2000 we may not have cancer. . . . The speed of advance has been enormous" (DeVita, quoted by Ross, 127).

According to Walter S. Ross, in his book *Crusade,* research in immunology has led to many promising developments in cancer treatment. One new method now being studied, according to Ross, is monoclonal antibodies. These were found almost by accident to effectively combat cancer. Two scientists, George Kholer and Cesar Milstein, were conducting research with antibodies at MRC Laboratories of Molecular Biology in Cambridge, England. They were interested in making synthetic antibodies. These scientists created a hybrid cell, known as hybridoma, which can produce a single antibody in relatively huge quantities (Ross 130–131). Ross described clinical research of the hybridoma:

> Several cancer patients have been successfully treated with the new antibodies, made specifically for their tumors. The first to be reported in 1982, was a sixty-seven-year-old man at Stanford University Medical Center in Palo Alto, California. He had been suffering from B-cell lymphoma, a rare cancer of the lymphatic system. Despite two years of treatment with chemotherapy and interferon, the disease had spread to the liver, spleen, bone marrow, and blood. He was in intense pain.
>
> Dr. Ronald Levy and associates were able to culture antibodies from the man's blood and make hybridoma cells that cloned a large supply of these (monoclonal) antibodies. The process took six months. Then the antibody was injected into the patient. Within three weeks the patient's enlarged lymph nodes shrank, the liver and spleen were reduced to normal proportions and other tumors disappeared. A year and a half later, the man was still disease-free. (Ross 131)

Ross went on to say that this therapy didn't work as well in Dr. Levy's other patients who had other kinds of tumors, but these antibodies offer other possibilities. They are able to carry radioactive substances or—in the case of chemotherapy—poisonous drugs directly to the cancerous cells, and normal cells will be spared the hazardous effect of these poisonous drugs.

Another method being studied which has shown encouraging results in defeating cancer is Interleukin-2 (IL-2). John Inglis reports studies conducted by Steven Rosenberg and colleagues at the National Cancer Institute in Bethesda, Maryland, in his article "Natural 'Anti-Cancer' Cells Found," in the *New Scientist* journal, Volume 1462. According to Inglis, immunologists have discovered a variety of lymphoid cells, several of which can kill other types of cells. Under the right culture conditions, they can kill tumor cells. These are called cytotoxin (cell-killing) cells. In their search for the cells responsible for "immune surveillance," immunological research has revealed that lymphoid cells communicate by the release of hormone-like substances called lymphokines. This substance bonds to lymphoid cells' surface and "activates" them. These activated cells are called T-cells (Inglis 16).

Rosenberg and colleagues observed a striking characteristic in lymphoid cells taken from normal animals or people and activated by a particular lymphokine called IL-2. These cells not only acquired the ability to kill tumor cells in vitro, but also to distinguish between tumor cells, which they killed, and normal cells form the same donor, which they did not kill. When these "lymphokine-activated killer" (LAK) cells are injected into mice with tumors in the lungs, the tumors disappear (Inglis 16).

Rosenberg reported optimistic results at a meeting at the National Cancer Institute, in clinical trials of the treatment with IL-2 activated LAK cells in people with advanced cancer. After treatment one patient had complete regression and had been tumor-free for four months at the meeting date. In a second patient three of five tumors had regressed. A third patient did not improve. The lymphokine treatment had minor side effects, such as chills and an indefinite feeling of discomfort, but was generally well tolerated (Inglis 16).

Another study conducted by Rosenberg and his colleagues is described in an article in *Science News* entitled "A One-Two Punch for Cancer." This clinical study with IL-2 activated LAK cells involved twenty-five patients with advanced and untreatable cancer of various types. The treatment transfuses the patients with the immune system stimulator, IL-2, along with the patient's own previously collected white blood cells. Of these 25 patients, in ten months after therapy, one was cancer-free, tumors shrank by more than 50 percent in eleven patients, and 10 patients had a partial response (One-Two Punch . . . 359).

Another method, under investigation at Boston University Medical Center, is a hybrid protein produced by modifying a diphtheria toxin. Bernard Davis of Harvard Medical School calls this new protein a " 'magic-bullet' with a vengeance," according to J. A. Miller in "Toward a 'Magic-Bullet' for Melanoma" (*Science News* 199). John R. Murphy and colleagues are targeting this modified diphtheria toxin against malignant melanoma cells. They have observed impressive results. This new hybrid protein, still a potent killer, attaches only to melanoma receptors rather than binding to diphtheria-sensitive cells (Miller 199). This hybrid protein kills human malignant melanoma cells in laboratory cultures and does not harm other laboratory-grown cells which are sensitive to diphthcria but lack the melanoma receptors. Murphy and his colleagues injected guinea pigs with a dose 1000 times the lethal dose of diphtheria and observed no ill effects (Miller 199).

The *New York Times* reports some admirable studies of the Tumor Necrosis Factor (TNF). TNF was first discovered in the early seventies by

Dr. Jan Vilcek, a microbiologist at New York University Medical School. The discovery was made when laboratory animals, after being injected with bacteria, produced a substance which attacked bacteria and tumors ("Rare Anticancer Agents Made in Laboratories" 18:5). "Rare Anticancer Agents Made in Laboratories" touches on the background and recent development in the study of TNF. According to this, the agent TNF was so rare that some scientists doubted its existence. Dr. Rik Derynck of Genentech, Inc. in South San Francisco, found barely detectable amounts of TNF in the bloodstream, yet it can now be produced in the laboratory ("Rare Anticancer . . ." 18:5). Dr. Seth Rudnick of Biogen (genetic engineering), Cambridge, Massachusetts, reports that when a mouse with tumors was injected with TNF, "each tumor literally breaks apart" ("Rare Anticancer . . ." 18:5). This agent attacks and kills bacteria and tumors without damage to healthy cells.

Joanne Silberner argues—although weakly—that TNF's dangerous side effects are too great to promote its use in human cancer treatment. Silberner reports studies in "The Dark Side of Tumor-Fighting Protein" that show the TNF is essentially identical to another body protein, cachetin, which causes "debilitating weight loss" in people with chronic infection or cancer. Silberner also relates a study by researchers at Rockefeller University which suggests cachetin is one of the major causes of bacterially induced shock. They found that when cachetin action was blocked, the effect was blocked as well (Silberner 132). Stanford University researchers Frank Torti reports that studies show cachetin to cause weight loss in patients even when food intake remains constant. Torti speculates that this protein mobilizes energy to fuel the body's fight against infection or cancer (Silberner 132). For this very reason, Anthony C. Cerami of Rockefeller believes cachetin is "good" in small amounts. Cerami believes the key is in finding the correct dosage. "Losing weight for one week won't hurt that much," Cerami says, "The limiting factor will be shock" (Silberner 132). In Japan, human trials with TNF have reported a slight fever as the only side effect (Silberner 132). On the brighter side of Silberner's "dark side," Dan Longo of the National Cancer Institute says that these findings suggest special ways to use TNF, such as employing an antibody to the protein to prevent shock (Silberner 132). The benefits which could be reaped from TNF in the war against cancer appear to be far greater than the possible dangers.

Cancer research is clearly more intense today than ever before with numerous treatment methods presently being studied around the world. Discussed here were only a few of the many promising methods under investigation. Evidence suggests that cancer may soon be a manageable condition and not the feared killer it is today. The battle is nearly won.

References

"A One-Two Punch for Cancer." *Science News*, December 7, 1985, p. 359.

Inglis, John. "Natural "Anti-Cancer Cells Found." *New Scientist*, June 27, 1985, p. 16.

Miller, J. A., "Toward a 'Magic Bullet' for Melanoma." *Science News*, September 28, 1985, p. 199.

"Rare Anti-Cancer Agents Made in Laboratories." *New York Times*, January 1, 1985, Section A, 18:5.

Ross, Walter S., *Crusade: The official history of the American Cancer Society*. Arbor House: New York, 1987.

Silberner, J., "The Dark Side of Tumor-Fighting Protein." *Science News*, August 31, 1985, p. 132.

■ UNDERSTANDING WRITING STRATEGIES

1. Like several other essays in this section, this essay reviews several published articles. What kinds of sources does this essay review?

2. Assuming that many of the sources used scientific report format, what parts of the original essays does this essay select?

3. Does the essay have a bias? That is, does it select evidence that proves a point, or does it report both sides of a position? Where do you see this?

4. Recognizing that inductive arguments require evidence that reflects a significant sample, how strong is Tennyson's evidence?

5. For what audience is Tennyson writing? How does the use of scientific terminology indicate this?

6. What audience do the introduction and conclusion suggest?

7. What changes would you make in this essay to create a review of the literature for a scientific report? ■

■ SUGGESTIONS FOR WRITING

Is the case for a cancer "cure" as encouraging as Tennyson suggests? Present an argument that either contradicts or confirms Tennyson's position by presenting at least two more articles. This will require you to take a position, review Tennyson's findings, and then present your own evidence in the context of Tennyson's arguments. ■

Tropical Rainforests

Jeanne Trapani

Jeanne Trapani's essay supports American intervention to preserve tropical rainforests which developing nations are destroying for economic gain. Written for English Across the Curriculum, this research paper presents evidence from published studies in science, economics, and political science supporting her position.

Most North Americans, Europeans, and North Asians will probably never see a tropical rainforest; these giant nurseries can only survive in the relatively narrow belt around the globe between the Tropic of Cancer, about 25° North of the equator, and the Tropic of Capricorn, about 25° South. Even here, their very existence is threatened by encroaching development and get-rich-quick schemes initiated by man. In a mere 200 years, we've managed to destroy almost half of the world's rainforests (Caufield "Reporter" 41), forcing into extinction countless species of plants and animals, and eliminating assets, many of which we are not even aware!

Unfortunately, reversing the trend is not easy. Rainforests (or rather, industries associated with their destruction) are tremendous sources of income for the countries that control them, and trying to convince these people to preserve the forests can be frustrating. The "notion that rainforests are global treasures that should be preserved for the good of mankind does not sit well in rainforest countries. . . . [They] don't like being told to live in harmony with nature by countries that appear to be enjoying sweet fruits of centuries of assault upon the natural world" (Caufield *Rainforest* 239).

All is not lost, however; some of the government and local people are working with conservation organizations, writing legislation, creating parks and reserves, and performing studies in the rainforests to find lucrative alternatives to the current financial advantages the destruction of the forests yields. Hopefully, enough will be done (soon) so that our children and grandchildren can experience the benefits of the forests that we've been able to experience.

Walking in one of these rainforests is surprisingly easy once you get past the dense outer brush so often depicted in the jungle scenes in movies. Inside the forest, the floor is almost bare; the litter layer generally measures less than an inch. You do have to be careful of tree roots, however. Soil conditions being poor, many rainforest trees have shallow roots, many of which grow right along the ground (Caufield *Rainforest* 67). But if you watch where you're walking and nowhere else, it's going to be a relatively dull journey.

Most of the activity in a rainforest goes on in the upper layers, starting about 60 feet up, where the foliage is. (It might behoove you to stop walking before looking up.) The uppermost layer, the canopy, consists of the broad leaves of the various species of slender-trunked evergreens (most of which you could hug with no problem) whose height reach 100–150 feet (Mohlenbrock 31), mere dwarfs when compared to the 400-foot Giant Redwoods of California, but just as spectacular in their own right. This dense canopy foliage, along with secondary canopy foliage from the 50–80 foot trees (Caufield *Rainforest* 46), allows only minimal sunlight through even at midday, thus explaining the sparse vegetation on the forest floor (Lee & Taylor 62).

Extending from the canopy to the floor is a layer of vegetation that requires little light, consisting mainly of climbers, vines, and epiphytes (Caufield *Rainforest* 46). These plants are the true backbone of the forest; they support many of the shallow-rooted trees (that in turn support them) and keep them from falling over. (Unfortunately, the reverse is also true: when a tree dies naturally, it eventually falls, pulling several others with it as a result of the intertwining vines.) One of the amazing things about this layer of the forest is that many of the plants have no ground roots, yet are not parasitic; they derive enough water and nutrients directly from the rainwater and the air around them to allow them to grow as big around as a basketball (Mohlenbrock 31). In fact, if these plants had to depend on getting their nutrients from the aforementioned poor soil, they would not survive. Consequently, the nutrients in a rainforest are almost exclusively found in the vegetation, contributing to problems with agriculture that will be discussed later in the paper (Norris 23).

This has not always been the case; tropical rainforests used to dominate the better soils as well. Forty-five million years ago, the ground that supports most of our cities today was supporting tropical rainforests; pollen grains of verified tropical plant species have been found as far north as Alaska (Caufield *Rainforest* 34). Over the millennia, the rainforests receded naturally until about a few thousand years ago when they came to cover only about five million acres, or 12–14% of the earth's surface (Caufield "Reporter" 41) within the tropical boundaries recognized today. Although these tropical boundaries still prevail, the total acreage for the forests has diminished markedly. As was previously mentioned, during the past two hundred years, man has devastated almost half of the world's rainforests (Caufield "Reporter" 41), with figures now indicating that only 7% of the earth's surface currently supports them. (WWF 1). Today, only thirty-seven countries have an immediate interest in rainforest economics (they have significant rainforest areas), with 57% of the remaining forests growing in Latin America, 25% in southeast Asia and Pacific Islands, and 18% in West Africa (Caufield *Rainforest* 37). However, because of the biological and ecological variety and abundance found in them (and the assets stemming from these), we all have a stake in their future.

It is estimated that tropical rainforests support 66% of earth's plant and animal species (Iker 25), with Amazonia (the region surrounding and including the Amazon River in South America) supporting a full 10% by itself (Lovejoy & Salati 211). Well over half of the known plant species live only in such forests, while 80% of the insect world and 90% of all known primate species (monkeys) are also only found there (WWF 5).

Unfortunately, relatively little is known about these giant gardens; they have only recently (within the past twenty-five years or so) become a topic of study. Because the forests experience no distinct seasons (averaging 80°F, they experience no cold spells, and with 160–400 inches of rain annually, they experience no dry spells), the trees produce no rings by which we can even determine their age (Caufield *Rainforest* 33). And while we are aware of the vast diversity of plant and animal life in the forests, "the majority of its species are unknown to science, and of those that are, the details of their distribution and ecology are scantily known. . . . [The forest] is not uniform in species composition. . . , the collection of any scientific data is slow (Lovejoy "Conservation" 1). Although the number of species is high, it does not follow that the number of individuals of each species is equally high. In fact, the spacing between some individual tree samples is often several acres. For example, a one square mile stand of trees in a temperate zone may contain only one species, or two, or five, or even ten, while a one square mile stand of rainforest in Colombia can support over 1,100 species! Panama alone boasts as many plant species as all of of Europe (WWF 2), and North America supports a scanty 700 tree species while tiny Madagascar supports 2,000 (WWF 5). With so many species occupying so little land, it's understandable why the individual samples are few and far between, but knowing this doesn't make collecting samples any easier!

Why did we begin collecting samples? Scientific curiosity? Certainly the rainforests provided a heaven-on-earth for botanists, biologists, and ecologists, but true concern for the rainforests started spreading only a few decades ago when it became apparent that (1) rainforests contain valuable resources and (2) they don't re-establish themselves as quickly (or at all) if too large an area is destroyed (about 360 square yards) (Caufield *Rainforest* 54).

One of the great myths attributed to tropical rainforests is that they contribute vast amounts of oxygen to the atmosphere, and if they were to suddenly disappear, we would all suffocate. Nothing could be further from the truth. In fact, the intact rainforest is an extremely efficient closed system, recycling all nutrients with little or no waste. The oxygen that the vegetation expels through photosynthesis is used just as quickly to aid with decomposition. Thus, generating oxygen can not be considered a direct asset. If the rainforests are destroyed, however, any possible role they play in pulling CO_2 from the atmosphere will be eliminated, and if they are burned or flooded, these practices will pull oxygen from the air and release CO_2, thus increasing its density in the atmosphere (WWF 9).

The rainforest does possess assets, though, that are well worth mentioning. The first and foremost I have already expressed: the number and diversity of species it supports. Plants, insects, and monkeys have already been mentioned, but fish, amphibians, and birds also depend on the rainforests for survival. About one-third of the birds familiar to us in the United States winter over in the tropical forests of Mexico, Central America, the Caribbean Islands, and South America, including tanagers, thrushes, mockingbirds, warblers, and orioles (Norris 23). And largely because of the rainforests, the 3,000 freshwater species of fish in the Amazon (Caufield *Rainforest* 244) are able to provide a full 50% of all animal protein required by the people who live there (Lovejoy "Conservation" 6). In 1980, a study was led by Dr. M. Goulding (American biologist) that showed an unusual relationship between approximately 75% of these fishes (Lovejoy "Amazonia" 330) and the floodplain forests. It seems "many fishes swim into these forests at the time of high water and feed on fruits and seeds and other living matter which fall into the water. This transfer of nutrients from the terrestrial to the aquatic ecosystem permits a higher fish biomass than would otherwise be possible" (Lovejoy "Conservation" 6).

A second asset of the rainforest is its contribution to medicine. One quarter of all American prescription drugs contain some rainforest plant (Lee & Taylor 62), yet "fewer than 1% of tropical forest species have been screened for their use in life-saving drugs" (WWF 7). Imagine the potential! Seventy percent of the 3,000 plants identified by the National Cancer Institute as having anti-cancer properties are rainforest species. The Madagascar periwinkle alone provides chemists with sixty alkaloids from which medicines can be derived. Some of these medicines reduce blood pressure, some lower glucose concentration in the blood, and two are anti-tumor agents, one of which yields a 99% chance of recovery from lymphocytic leukemia, and the other allows 58% of all Hodgkin's disease patients' survival beyond ten years after treatment, compared with only 2% in 1961. Derivatives from South American liana species are used to treat multiple sclerosis, Parkinson's disease, and other muscle disorders, and without them, tonsillectomies, eye surgery, and abdominal surgery would be impossible. South American ipecac cures amoebic dysentery; West African strophanthus gratus yields the heart medication strophanthin which has fewer side effects than digitalis; tetrodotoxin, which is derived from several Central American frog species, is an anesthetic 160,000 times as strong as cocaine, and wild yams in Mexico yield cortizone and diosgynin (the active ingredient in birth control pills) (Caulfield *Rainforest* 219–21). It's probably safest to say that just about everyone who has used Western medicine has benefited from the tropical rainforests.

Still another asset of the rainforest is its climate control. Scientists now "widely accept that rainforests directly influence climate and, indirectly, global weather patterns. . . . Some scientists believe that the spreading of the Sahara is due in part to the shrinking of equatorial forests" (Lee & Taylor 61–2). This theory is based on research that has proven that rainforests generate up to one-half of their own rainfall (Lovejoy "Amazonia" 331), and the fact that after a large area has been deforested, local rainfall is reduced. (In Central Panama, which has been totally deforested, the average

annual rainfall has fallen 17 inches in the past fifty years [Lee & Taylor 62].)
In addition to helping control precipitation, the forests contribute to climate
control. Forests, with their vast vegetation, are able to absorb more of the
sun's energy than open land. Deforestation, then, can disrupt local weather
patterns by warming air which was previously kept cool (WWF 9), but it
may also have global implications. Forests, by their very nature, return
water vapour to the atmosphere; the larger the forest, the greater (and faster)
the return. This water vapour in turn determines cloud formation; where
trees thin out, there is less cloud. Because cloud formation provides a major
form of heat transfer, deforestation would affect the global heat balance, and
the planet could experience a temperature increase of 2°–3°C, enough to partially melt the polar icecaps (Salati et al. 68) and endanger coastal cities
worldwide.

Yet another asset of the rainforests is the abundance and variety of
food and consumer goods they can (and do) provide. From oils, gums, resins,
latexes, waxes, rattans, bamboo, pesticides and dyes some such manufactured products as wicker furniture, lubricants, glue for postage stamps, golf
balls, chewing gum, toothpaste, shampoo, and make-up (WWF 10). Perhaps
more interesting is the fact that "all of the world's main crops have been derived from wild relatives. Of the dozen or so which provide 90% of the
world's food, one-half are descended from tropical forest plants" (WWF 5).
Rice and maize are two of them. Others include coffee, tea, potatoes, pea-
nuts, chocolate, pineapples, bananas, oranges, and lemons (WWF 5–6).
Rainforests also provide plants in the natural state for cross-breeding purposes in the never-ending search for disease-resistant genes. A case in point
refers to a project undertaken in the late 1960's by the International Rice Research Institute in the Philippines. Researchers screened 10,000 varieties of
cultivated rice to find a gene that was resistant to grassy stunt virus, the
only major rice disease for which there was no known protection. When this
proved futile, they turned to their collection of wild rice seeds. Only two
seeds of one species found in India possessed the sought-after gene. So the
researchers trekked to India to find more seeds, but to no avail. In the eighteen years since that discovery, no other source of resistance to grassy stunt
virus has been found. Consequently, every modern rice plant (for cultiva-
ting) has a gene derived from one of those two seeds (Caufield "Rainforest"
227–28)!

Unfortunately, the rainforests' assets have not been enough to convince the majority of the governments controlling them that they should be
preserved. Most of these governments are struggling with problems of feeding their people and paying off their (usually very large) foreign debts
(Channel 4 News), as well as colonizing for military and political reasons
(WWF 11).

All of the reasons the rainforests are being destroyed lead back to economics. The two main culprits are logging, whether selectively or for timber, and ranching/farming. Selective logging for woods such as mahogany

and teak is nice in theory, but doesn't work well in the real world. For instance, generally, when 10% of a stand of trees is selectively harvested, another 30–48% is damaged from bulldozing and other logging operations (Caufield 162). The sad thing is, though, these harvested woods are used for luxury items such as hardwood veneers for furniture, house moldings and railings, coffins, and even chopsticks (WWF 18). Surely there are alternatives!

More productive in the short term is logging for timber; the immediate financial return is simply higher. In fact, timber logging earns more money from the rainforests than any other activity. Twenty percent of the world's industrial wood comes from rainforests, and all hardwood logs and over half of hardwood sawn timber in world trade comes from rainforests (Caufield *Rainforest* 150). Ironically, because the rainforest countries lack equipment to process raw timber, the income derived from exports must be used to import sawn timber, plywood, and paper (Caufield *Rainforest* 152).

In Latin America, the main reason for clearing forest lands is to create cattle ranches. Now, with the forest taken away, the soil is very poor, mainly because the land here is billions of years old and has become weathered and infertile. Two-thirds of the tropic soils are acidic and low in nutrients, usually being hard and clay-like or sandy and shallow, inviting erosion (Caufield *Rainforest* 65). Consequently, cattle ranches must be very large; each head of cattle needs at least twelve acres to produce marketable beef (Caufield *Rainforest* 145). And who buys all this beef? The United States buys 75% of all Central American beef exports. In 1960, the average annual beef consumption per American was 85 pounds, and we imported no beef. By 1978, we were importing 10% of our beef as we each consumed 122 pounds annually (Caufield *Rainforest* 108).

Sadly, to create the large cattle ranches, many of the "developers" use the "slash-and-burn" technique, which is to cut the trees and burn them in the field. The people just don't have the means or the time to clear the forest in a more conventional manner. So, not only are barren lands being created, but the original natural resources are being wasted! I say barrren lands are being created because after three to five years, even these original twelve acres are not enough to sustain even one head of beef; the old "pastures" are deserted and new "pastures" are created; more trees are destroyed. Obviously, the soil here is not suitable for conventional cattle ranching, but as long as there is money to be made, the industry will continue. It should be pointed out that attempts have been made to improve the quality of the soil. But adding nutrients and otherwise incorporating temperate-zone farming have failed due to the amount and intensity of rainfall which causes massive run-off and erosion (Caufield *Rainforest* 132).

As was touched on earlier, part of the problem in dealing with deforestation is with the governments of the rainforest countries. Often they will cite over-population as a need to clear the forests for colonization, and even encourage migration into forest areas (WWF 16). But population is not a real problem in the countries experiencing the most severe deforestation. Most often, it's just poor people looking for land to support them (WWF 15). In most Latin American countries, for example, the easiest way to establish title to unoccupied land is to clear it. In legal terms, deforestation is an improvement to the land (Caufield *Rainforest* 111). However, like the cattle ranchers, these small farmers soon experience crop failure due to soil conditions, and so move on to clear another patch of forest (WWF 16).

Yet another reason for deforestation is the creation of hydroelectric dams. The potential energy in the Amazon Basin alone is estimated to be equivalent to an oil well producing five million barrels of oil a day and never running dry. Brazil now pays twenty-five million dollars a day to import oil, so the incentive to develop hydroelectric power is certainly there! However, clearing for dams is often prohibitively expensive, so the reservoir area is merely flooded, and the trees left to decompose (rot) in the water. Besides the incredible stench produced by the newly released hydrogen sulfide (a by-product of decomposition), the water becomes acidic and corrodes the cooling system and turbine casings of the machinery. Also, water weeds infiltrate the system, fish are killed, and breeding sites for malaria are created (Caufield *Rainforest* 17–22). Clearly, more study needs to be done on this subject before more damage is done!

The destruction that the rainforests have been forced to endure in the past two centuries has been devastating, and in many cases, irreversible. Each day, 144,000 acres of rainforest are cut. In a year, this amounts to an area the size of Nebraska (Lee & Taylor 61). India, Bangladesh, Haiti, and Sri Lanka have already lost all of their primary forest (Caufield "Reporter" 41). In fact, the deforestation of Haiti is a primary cause of poverty there (Lee & Taylor 62). According to the Food and Agriculture Organization of the U.N. (in the most comprehensive study done to date), almost one-fifth of the world's remaining rainforests will be gone by the year 2000. At current reduction rates, Nigeria and the Ivory Coast in Africa will be completely deforested; Thailand will lose 60% of its forests; in Latin America, Costa Rica will lose 80%, and Honduras, Nicaragua, and Ecuador will each lose over 50% (WWF 3).

But, it's been pointed out, "if Americans were able to virtually deforest New England, and have that area heavily forested today, what then is the basis for concern about tropical deforestation?" (Lovejoy "Amazonia" 334). First of all, New England has several advantages: better soil, more viable seeds (allowing a major seed bank in the soil, so reforestation is possible even without parent plants present), lower species number, and simpler biological arrangements. All of these contribute to a faster and more complete recovery, and all are absent in tropical forests (Lovejoy "Amazonia" 334).

As if loss of the forest itself is not enough, its absence invariably leads to negative effects including the aforementioned reduced cloud cover, reduced rainfall, a change in global weather patterns, and erosion of soils so complete that nothing can grow there, creating wastelands and causing mudslides and floods. Accompanying all this is a reduction (or loss) of the dependent animal life. Deforesting the floodplain where many of the fish feed, for example, would certainly reduce fish productivity (Lovejoy "Conservation" 6), and the siltation from the run-off would reduce it even more. (Siltation has other devastating consequences as well: the Panama Canal will be impassable to large ships within fifteen years due to the nearby deforestation caused by small farmers [WWF 9].) Forest tribes are also affected by encroaching "developers." Anthropologists estimate that in 1500, the Amazon Basin supported six to nine million indigenous people. By 1900, the number had fallen to one million, and since then, about half of the 230 tribes have become extinct, so that today less than 200,000 indigenous people survive in the area (Caufield *Rainforest* 86). It is believed that at least one tropical species (be it plant or animal) becomes extinct each day, and with specialization high in the tropics (a bird may only feed on one type of plant or insect, for instance), it's only logical to conclude that many species will be doomed to go the way of the dinosaur unless something is done to halt the process (Lee & Taylor 62).

Two things are needed to save the rainforests: education and money, and a third, research, can perhaps help restore some of them. Because it would be ludicrous to expect deforestation to cease on its own, some of the rainforest countries have recognized that they may do well to declare some forested areas as parks or reserves. Encouragingly, Bolivia, Ecuador, Venezuela, Indonesia, and Brazil have all set up such reserves. The problems arise, however, in determining where the parks should be and how large they should be. It was decided among the researchers that the parks should be located in the areas that remained rainforests during the last ice age (Iker 25), and a twenty year study to determine the minimum critical size necessary for survival of the most species is currently underway in Brazil as a co-effort of the Brazilian government and the World Wildlife Fund (WWF 20). In the study, different sized "islands" are created as the forest around them is removed, and before-and-after comparisons are made. Hopefully, the project will yield conclusions about the mechanics of extinction, the smaller reserves (about two square acres) going through change very quickly and providing preliminary conclusions, the larger reserves (about twenty-five square acres) giving slower but more sophisticated results (Iker 29).

Other studies being done by private organizations include precipitation research, surface run-off and groundwater research, forest agriculture studies, river and floodplain studies, and actual animal tracking and monitoring. One such group, Conservation International, essentially "bought" four million acres in the Bennie Reserve in Bolivia by paying off a foreign bank loan for the country in return for the protection of the Reserve (Channel 4 News).

But still more needs to be done. More local governments need to become involved as in the Congo, where ten million trees have been planted in a drive to stop deforestation. And in Haiti, where thirteen million trees have been planted in the past four years, farmers are encouraged to grow trees for timber as well as subsistence fuel (Lee & Taylor 62). Commercial and development banks need to be convinced to stop subsidizing the beef cattle industry in Central America, and need to be encouraged to investigate the environmental impact of the projects they finance (Norris 23). Industry that does not harm the forest (rubber tapping, harvesting fruits and nuts, collecting vines and rattan for fiber, etc.) needs to be developed (WWF 21). Local people need to be educated about the dangers of deforestation and the relative futility involved in the practice. (Conservation groups are already strong in Costa Rica, Indonesia, and Brazil [WWF 19].).

As individuals, we can encourage our legislators to finance tropical forest conservation; we can encourage local businessmen to sell only tropical wood and timber products that have come from forest areas or plantations grown for that purpose; we can discourage the sale of tropical animal life; we can contribute financially to conservation organizations; we can learn as much as possible and spread the word to our friends and neighbors; we can remember that a tree is a terrible thing to waste.

Bibliography

Caufield, Catherine. *In the Rainforest*. NY: Knopf, 1985.

———. "A Reporter at Large." *New Yorker* 14 Jan. 1985: 41.

Channel 4 News. "The Bennie Reserve in Bolivia." 8:45 AM, 9 Oct. 1987.

Iker, Sam. "Islands of Life." *Mosaic* 13 (1982): 24–30.

Lee, John, and Ronald Taylor. "Ravage in the Rainforest." *U.S. News and World Report* 31 March 1986: 61–62.

Lovejoy, T. E, J. M. Rankin, R. O. Bierregaard, K. S. Brown, L. H. Emmons, and M. E. Van der Voort. "Ecosystem Decay of Amazon Forest Remnants." In *Extinctions*. Ed. M. H. Nitecki. Chicago: Univ of Chicago Press, 1984; 295–325.

Lovejoy, T. E., and E. Salati. "Precipitating Change in Amazonia." Ch. 8 in *The Dilemma of Amazonian Development*. Ed. E. Moran. Bloomington: Univ of Indiana Press, 1983. 211–220.

Lovejoy, T. E. "The Science of Amazon Conservation." Washington, DC: World Wildlife Fund, ND.

———. "Amazonia, People and Today." Ch. 18 in *Key Environments: Amazonia* Ed. G. T. Prance and T. E. Lovejoy. Oxford: Pergamon Press, 1985. 328–337.

Mohlenbrock, Robert H. "Olympic Rain Forest, Washington." *Natural History* Mar. 1986: 31.

Norris, Ruth. "The Silent Forest." *Backpacker* 14 (1986): 23.

Raloff, Janet. "Plan Unveiled to Save Tropical Forests." *Science News* 26 Oct. 1985: 261.

———. "Pressure on Central American Forests." *Science News* 14 Jan. 1986: 14.

Salati, E., T. E. Lovejoy, and P. B. Vose. "Precipitation and Water Recycling in Tropical Rainforests with Special Reference to the Amazon Basin." *The Environmentalist* 3 (1983): 67–71.

World Wildlife Fund. *Pamphlet on Caring for Tropical Forests*. Washington, DC: World Wildlife Fund, ND.

■ THE WRITER'S ASSIGNMENT

Write an eight-page research paper using at least ten sources. Your essay must do more than simply record or describe information; it must use information to demonstrate a specific point or support an argumentative position. ■

■ UNDERSTANDING WRITING STRATEGIES

1. What position or positions does this paper take? At what point do you become aware of this (these) position(s)?

2. How does the introduction engage the reader? What kind of commitment does it make about the subject?

3. After Trapani clarifies the issues with which she is concerned, she offers the reader background. What is this? How necessary is this information for the reader? What writing strategy does she use here?

4. Why are rainforests important?

5. What is their role in relation to the balance between oxygen and carbon dioxide? Why is this important?

6. How does Trapani organize her information on rainforests' value?

7. How does Trapani conclude her study? What part does the last paragraph play in this conclusion? ■

■ SUGGESTIONS FOR WRITING

Trapani's essay illustrates a central problem in ecological consciousness— the tension between short-term economic benefits and long-term ecological goals. Proceed from Trapani to study other ecological battlegrounds like whale killing, refuse disposal, and oil transporting. Write a paper explaining this tension between ecological and economic benefits using these issues to illustrate your explanation. ■

Anterior Cruciate Ligament Injury

Eric Wolford

Eric Wolford's essay analyzes and evaluates a common sports injury and recommends treatment. Written for a course in sports medicine, this study presents a comprehensive review of the literature both from physiology and medicine.

Late in the second half, down by ten points, the Chargers' Dan Fouts elects to throw twenty yards downfield to his all-pro tight end, Kellen Winslow. The ball is thrown high. Stretching and making the reception, Kellen Winslow is hit violently from the front and the side by two Raider defensive backs, Lester Hayes and Vann MacElroy. Seeing the precarious extending and twisting of Winslow's leg, Charger fans cringed with fearful anticipation. Diagnosed quickly as having suffered an acute anterior cruciate ligament lesion, Kellen Winslow was carried off the field, leaving one question in the minds of sports fans and announcers, "Will he ever play again?"

Recent findings in the field of medical research have led to considerable advancements in the diagnosis and treatment of various pathological conditions. One example of this is the management of lesions to the anterior cruciate ligament (ACL) (King et al., 1986).

Because knee injuries are the most common injury in all sports, with 60% of all knee injuries coming from football, and because the ACL has now become the most prolific and "serious" knee injury, according to the Rochester School of Medicine, it merits a much more diligent investigative effort (DeHaven, 1986).

Until recently, injuries to this structure may well have eluded proper diagnosis and treatment, thus jeopardizing or ending the future of an aspiring athlete. However, the development of new sophisticated forms of diagnosis, surgical repair, and rehabilitation has brought a new outlook to this problem (King et al., 1986).

ANATOMY

The anterior cruciate ligament runs from the anterior part of the tibial plateau, just medial and posterior to the anterior tibial spine, and goes posteriorly and laterally to attach to the posterior-most portion of the medial aspect of the lateral femoral condyle (Roy and Irvin, 1983). It is composed of two fibrous parts; a small anteromedial band (AMB) and a posterolateral band (PLB), connected by a soft tissue along their length, permitting separate movement. This very complex geometric configuration allows various parts of the ACL to be tight, while other parts are laxed (Appenzeller, 1981). During analysis of injury, determining which aspect ot the ligament is injured is very instrumental in achieving an accurate final diagnosis and prescription (King et al., 1986). Blood supply to the ligaments is delivered by the inferior and superior middle geniculate arteries. At this time, it doesn't appear that blood supply is of any major concern to ligament repair, bar its total absence (Roy and Irving, 1983).

FUNCTION

Until recently, the importance of the function of the ACL has been played down or not realized. However, current orthopaedic research concludes, "The anterior cruciate ligament is the essential stabilizer of the knee" (King et al., 1986). Roy and Irvin, authors of the textbook, *Sports Medicine*, concur with this conclusion, saying, "It (the ACL injury) is probably the most serious injury that can affect the high performance athlete and has meant the end of many a promising career" (Roy and Irvin, 1983).

Central in support of the knee joint, the functions of the ACL are as follows: prevention of anterior luxation of the tibia, hyperextension, prevention of tibial rotation, especially during running and cutting, and resistance of acute valgus and varus stresses to the knee, the major of these being prevention of anterior tibial luxation in either flexion or extension (Moynes, 1975).

As was mentioned earlier, only certain parts of the ligament are involved throughout the range of motion of the articulation. The AMB, the smaller of the two bands, is taut and provides resistance from about 70° of flexion to full flexion. At 90° flexion, the AMB provides 85% of the resistance. The PLB, on the other hand, is taut in extension and up to 20° of flexion. This is the principal structure of the ACL that is responsible for prevention of hyperextension. A general laxity in both fibers occurs at 40°–50°, leaving the joint suceptible to injury (King et al., 1986).

In fact, one study reported that the greatest amount of injuries found in healthy individuals occurs within 45°–35° of flexion (Bassett, 1986).

CAUSES OF INJURY

Injuries to the ACL occur in almost all groundbased sports. Sports of greatest public attention (football, basketball, hockey, soccer, skiing) appear to be those with highest probability of ACL injury. The ACL lesion is a complex injury which occurs through usually one or a combination of the following mechanisms: hyperextension, hyperflexion, internal rotation of the tibia with external rotation of the body, external rotation of the tibia with forced flexion, an anteriorly driven force on the tibia, valgus or varus forces, and often deceleration as in basketball (Apenzeller, 1981). The most common of these mechanisms for injury is hyperextension with a rotational component (Roy and Irvin, 1983). Due to the very nature of football (jagged cuts, cross cuts, violent forceful blows, blind collisions) it is no wonder that this sport has been the cause of the greatest frequency of knee injuries—and more specifically, the greatest frequency of ACL ruptures.

Sports such as football and basketball have common environments for ACL danger; however, recent research has discovered another mechanism for injury that might not normally be suspected. Injury to the ACL may be caused by active/passive loads during fallback recovery seen in expert skiiers or ski jumpers. The tendency to lean back too far when landing after a long jump or during a tight tuck on a downhill run often leads to a violent flexion of the quadricep, as recovery is attempted. This violent flexion, the active load, to re-establish the body's vertical dimension, often luxates the tibia, the passive component, causing an unfortunate tear in the skiier's ACL. Surprisingly, this type of injury occurs undramatically, without even the release of the skiier's binding (McConkey, 1986). For example, a 32-year-old former ski racer was practicing slalom through ski gates. To save seconds and improve his time, he assumed a "jet" posture crossing the finish line. After breaking the finish beam, he drew himself back to an upright posture. During this apparently innocent maneuver, something snapped deep within the knee. The skis were tracking forward and there was no binding release. Surgery identified acute ACL rupture (McConkey, 1986). Important in this injury is that it only occurs in expert skiiers because of the skill and power required to make the move (McConkey, 1986).

Another undramatic impetus for ACL injury (in that it often goes undetected) is ACL degeneration over a period of time. During an activity, an athlete may take a fall, hearing a small "pop" sound from his knee. Free of swelling and diagnosed as being uninjured, the athlete continues with his career. Over the course of a couple of years, the athlete notices a slow loosening or instability in his anterolateral or anteromedial mobility, culminating in frequent bucklings of the knee.

Arthroscopic surgery will often show severe ligament degeneration. Apparently, the original small pop that was diagnosed as no injury was in reality a small lesion that, left untreated, spread across the rest of the ligament, causing a career-terminating injury (Roy and Irvin, 1983).

ANALYSIS AND EVALUATION

The diagnosis of an ACL lesion has for many years posed a problem to health care professionals. Accuracy and consistency with this type of injury has been virtually nonexistent. According to one M.D., "Acute disruptions of the ACL are probably the most undetected lesion in knee injuries" (King et al., 1986).

It has been said that the history of a knee injury is worth 80% of the diagnosis (DeHaven, 1986). Questions such as these—Was there contact? Was the foot planted? Was there a "pop" sound? Did the knee give way? Was there swelling or hemarthrosis? Was there or is there any pain? Have you had a previous knee injury?—are common preliminaries in formulating a diagnosis (Tibone et al., 1986). Classic or salient symptoms of an ACL injury are the popping sound during the instant of injury, hemarthrosis within 12 hours of injury, limited range of motion (ROM), and anterolateral or anteromedial instability. Resulting pain may or may not accompany the injury. Following accumulation of data, based on patient's history and simple observations, the next step is to apply various tests to the joint that exploits any pathological states of the ACL. The Anterior Drawer Test, the Lackman Test, and the Pivot Shift Test provide professionals with the most effective techniques for on-the-spot evaluation (Tibone et al., 1986).

The Anterior Drawer Test is designed to test the AMB portion of the ACL (King et al., 1986; Roy and Irvin, 1983). After having the patient lie in the supine position with the injured leg bent 90 degrees at the knee, and 45 degrees at the hip, the professional, sitting on the patient's foot of the injured leg, places his hands posteriorly and high on the tibia, pulling anteriorly on the tibia. Looking specifically for anterior luxation of the tibia, the professional compares the injured leg and luxating movement with the uninjured leg (Roy and Irvin, 1983).

The Lackman test, frequently called the most sensitive indicator of ACL lesions, is designed to best test the PLB of the ACL (King et al., 1986). Similar to the Anterior Drawer Test in all but angle of bend at the knee, the Lackman test with a five to ten degree bend at the knee detects any tibial luxation on the femur or loosening of the joint anteromedially and anterolaterally (King et al., 1986). The scale of measurement of a positive test is a bit subjective and is as follows: +1 for some luxation, +2 for complete luxation, and +3 for extreme joint luxation (Bilko, 1986).

The Pivot Shift Test is designed to demonstrate anterolateral rotator instability and can be used to detect both acute and chronic situations (Roy and Irvin, 1983). Using the Pivot Shift Test of MacIntosh, the athlete lies supinely while flexing his leg at the hip 35–40 degrees with the knee fully extended. The foot and tibia are inwardly rotated. A valgus force is applied to the lateral side of the knee while the leg is being flexed. While valgus force is being applied, lateral to medial rotation is attempted and looseness is compared to the uninjured leg (Roy and Irvin, 1983). Combining these test with the historical background of the injury, the professional should have a strong basis for evaluation.

Often detection of the ACL weakness cannot be affirmed by any of these methods, yet still injury is suspected. To further test the integrity of the ACL and from a different angle, various performance tests have been created.

In Linkopin, Sweden, numerous tests were used to test the dysfunction of the ACL in either unoperative or post-operative athletes. Test were administered mostly on soccer players with similar abilities and similar ages.

Compared to a healthy control group, those with ACL injuries performed significantly less well in the figure eight run, the spiral stair run, and the slope run—all of which place a large strain on the knee. Running and hopping straight ahead surprisingly resulted in no significant difference (Tegner et al., 1986).

In a test completed in Inglewood, California, at the Centinela Hospital Medical Center Biomechanics Laboratory, a significant difference was found between the cutting index of injured and uninjured limbs during cross cut tests (Tibone et al., 1986). Poor femoral external rotation, inability to cross cut, illustrates the anterolateral instability often found in ACL injuries (Tibone et al., 1986). Pre- or post-operatively, these tests can further the quality of one's diagnosis or prognosis.

On the edge of sports medicine technology, recent research and development has created a new and revolutionary evaluation technique called "Magnetic Resonance Imagery" (MRI) (Richer et al., 1986). Formed at U.C.L.A., MRI uses a permanent magnet system and a combination of solenoidal surface coils and thin, sectioned high resolution scanning techniques. Images depict structural anatomy. At face value, this technique appears very attractive. It is non-invasive, without ionizing radiation, it is able to accurately define anatomy and pathoanatomy, and very importantly, is much less expensive than arthroscopy (Richer et al., 1986).

To determine the effectiveness of this test, 105 patients were tested with MRI and then later, with arthroscopy, the unanimously accepted authority for ACL diagnosis. Remarkably, in testing ACLs for injury, MRI recorded 100% in areas of sensitivity, specificity, accuracy, and positive and negative predicted values. With this ability to detect noninvasively, complete, acute, or degenerative ACL injuries, professional diagnosis without surgery can prove extremely accurate (Richer et al., 1986).

As mentioned previously, arthroscopy is the final word before surgery, its effectiveness is outstanding. A tiny camera views the inside of the pathological area, allowing the professional to see the actual damages. In an attempt to remain focussed, I will not branch off into arthroscopic surgery (King et al., 1986).

TREATMENT

"Treatment of the acute or chronic lesion to the ACL may be the most controversial area in sports medicine at the present time," according to Jean-Pierre Cuerrier, Ph.D. Treatment of the diagnosed ACL injury may take one of two courses, surgical or non-surgical (Hawkins et al., 1986). Many variables must be considered before definite steps in either direction are taken. The age, level of demand that will be placed upon the knee, future activity, severity of joint laxity, and the desire, commitment, and motivation to endure rehabilitation following surgery, if surgery is chosen, are the major considerations. Non-surgical treatment involves a strengthening and protecting of the injured knee and a possible addition of a protective brace (see appendix 2, regarding braces). In the case of younger, below 40 years old, active individuals, with a significant lesion of the ACL, the non-surgical approach may lead to future complications (King et al., 1986). According to Cabaud, "The anterior cruciate deficient knee is a handicap which is never compensated for satisfactorily by bracing or rehabilitation" (King et al., 1986). It has been proven that ACL instability only increases with time. This degenerative progression may lead to a multitude of serious damages, including articular cartilage deterioration and osteoarthritis. The results by Fetto and Marshall's tests are perhaps the best long-term evidence of the shortcomings of the non-surgical approach. In a follow-up study on non-surgically treated ACL lesions, after three years not one knee was rated above the good category, and after five years, seldom did a knee report better than poor (King et al., 1986).

Lack of surgical success has understandably been the reason for the tendency toward the non-surgical approach. However, recent findings prove this statement to be inaccurate. An increased understanding of the function of the ACL, combined with a newly developed vast repertoire of surgical procedures, has led to a definite increase in the popularity of surgical intervention. These procedures may be classified as either intra-articular or extra-articular repair.

The intra-articular approach can be further broken down into three categories: primary repair, inert structure substitution, and prosthetic implantation (King et al., 1986). Primary repair involves re-establishment of the severed ligament, using sutures. This is, more simply, a retying of the torn ligament. The primary repair approach seems to be the approach with least success, due mainly to the inability of the weakened fibers to withstand early rehabilitation stress (King et al., 1986).

Another approach to intra-articular repair involves the use of certain inert structures that simulate the function of the ACL (King et al., 1986; Tegner et al., 1986). In a recent 1984 questionnaire study, 80% of surgeons surveyed recommended this type of ligament reconstruction (augmentation of an inert tissue) (Bilko, 1986). The most common tissue chosen for this repair, indicted from the survey, was the patellar tendon at 64%. Second was the semitendinosus, at 20%, and third was the iliotibial band at 16% (Bilko, 1986).

In the patellar tendon procedure, the medial 1/3 of the tendon is excised near the proximal end and re-routed from its distal insertion through the joint cavity and anchored to the later condyle of the femur. It is important to emphasize that this procedure, as well as all the rest, attempt to simulate the function of the ACL by duplicating anatomical position, tibial and femoral attachments (King et al., 1986).

The use of inert structures for intra-articular repair has become a very popular technique, scoring a large number of successes. An article entitled, "Anterior Cruciate Ligament Reconstruction, with the Patellar Tendon, " in the *Journal of Orthopedic Research*, May, 1986, reported an 80% success rate in patellar tendon ACL reconstructions, out of 45 patients. Success included return to pre-injury status, following a rigorous rehabilitation program (Bell, 1986).

The third type of intra-articular approach is the use of prosthetic ligaments. Materials such as polyethylene, polyglycolic acid sutures, and carbon fiber implants have been used to artificially simulate the function of the ACL. The general success of this type of repair is unfavorable. This has been mainly due to the inferior tensile strength of the artificial ligament (King et al., 1986).

The second type of surgical procedure is the extra-articular type. Also utilizing inert structures, extra-articular repair attempts to provide stability for the knee, outside the cavity of the knee joint, beneath the collateral ligaments, as opposed to the in-cavity approach of the intra-articular procedure. Extra-articular repair uses as its inert structures the iliotibial band, the biceps femoris, and the pes anserinus. Reasonably successful, the extra-articular procedure often leaves over time a residual laxity in the knee, due to a stretching of the structures involved in the rehabilitation period. Because of this, extra-articular repair has been used most successfully as an augmentation to intra-articular repair (King et al., 1986).

One surgeon reported with this type of combination (intra-articular and extra-articular) a 92% success rate in return to normal activity without any recurring instability (Gibson et al., 1986). Forty percent of surgeons surveyed used this combination technique as their number one course in reconstruction of the ACL (Bilko, 1986).

An interesting development using a computer knee model for analysis of a new type of ligament reconstruction is showing favorable signs of potential success. Called the Muller Anterolateral Femoraltibial Ligament (ALFTL) Reconstruction, its hope is to aid in the knee's resistency to internal rotation. Its ultimate use is in conjunction with ACL intra-articular repair, providing most of its support during 20 to 30 degrees of flexion, an area where both bands of the ACL are laxed. In re-construction, it is to be attached just anterior the linea aspera and at a level superior and lateral to the geniculate vessels. It is important to note that the implanted strip be posterior the geniculate vessels for the best 20 to 30 degree knee stability. The computer results appear beneficial. Using the regular, unaffected knee as a point of reference, ACL and ALFTL reconstruction provided a 16.8% and 25.5% increase in strength at 15 and 30 degrees of flexion, respectively. Again, because these tests were all computer run and since there have been no in vivo experiments to support its claim, these extra-articular surgical results will have to be looked at conservatively (Gibson et al., 1986).

The very latest in anterior cruciate ligament reconstruction possibilities is described in this year's 1986 O'Donahue award winning article, "Anterior Cruciate Ligament Allograft Transplantation," found in the *American Journal of Sports Medicine*. The most revolutionary idea on the market,

ACL allograft involves the transplanting of an ACL from a cadaver to the injured person (Nikolaou et al., 1986).

Because the ACL is such a complex structure, multiaxled, composed of fibers of different lengths and directional orientations, with attachment sites differing in size, shape, and geometric orientation, and radical orientation changes in flexion and extension, Nikolaou believes that cadaveric ACL is the perfect graft material. Fifty-six mongrel dogs were used to test this type of transplantation. A specially designed instrument was used to remove the ACL with a cylindric bone plug attached at the femoral end and a triangular bone plug attached at the tibial end of the graft. This bone-ligament-bone type of transplantation hopes to be as secure as the original ACL. A potential problem with this type of transplantation is regarding the cryopreservation degenerations to the cadaveric ACL. However, this study found the tensile strength of the cryopreserved grafts were 96% of fresh ACL grafts (Nikolaou et al., 1986).

After 36 weeks following the transplantation, the dogs with the allografts appeared to be functionally normal. Arthroscopic surgery confirmed the positive results regarding the joint's acceptance of the transplantation (Nikolaou et al., 1986).

Two concerns of major importance in cadaveric ACL transplantation are the immunologic reactivity of the graft material and the long-term strength and viability of the transplant. Current work in allograft transplantation has determined that cryopreservation of the graft prior to use dramatically reduces the antigenicity of the ligament-bone complex without affecting the structural integrity of the ligament. Other studies have shown that ligaments preserved in this manner may be safely stored for up to one year (Nikolaou et al., 1986).

The very promising results of this study leads many to believe that the use of cadaveric ACL allografts can be considered for future clinical use. Key to its success in the future, is availability of and quality of graft material (Nikolaou et al., 1986).

REHABILITATION

In the post-operative knee, the extreme importance of a well-designed rehabilitation program should not be diluted. According to Russell R. Zelko, M.D., "If a proper rehabilitation program is not available, the function of the involved extremity may be significantly impaired even though the surgical repair may have been completely successful" (Zelko, 1986). An ACL study group searching for better solutions to the problem of ACL repair concluded regarding rehabilitation, "The importance of rehabilitation in treatment of ACL injuries cannot be over-emphasized enough. At least 50% of the ultimate success of the surgery depends upon the rehabilitative effort" (Bilko, 1986).

The basic philosophy of rehabilitation is the same following nonurgical and surgical treatment. This involves the prevention of progressive instability, postponement of the onset of degenerative changes, reinstatement of the preinjury level of performance, and protection from reinjury (King et al., 1986).

Depending upon the severity of the injury, surgeons today say that 10–12 months of rehabilitation are required following major surgery (Zelko, 1986). With a variety of rehabilitative techniques available, I will briefly outline a 12-phase program that has emerged recently as one of, if not the best rehabilitative process in the field today. The following program boasts a 95% success return to athletics rate (Zelko, 1986).

In the initial stages of rehabilitation, an emphasis is placed on a protection of the vulnerable ligament from forces of approximately 60 lbs. or more. This precautionary measure is often referred to as "the protective umbrella" (Zelko, 1986; King et al., 1986).

Phase I: For the first six weeks following surgery, the injured extremity is immobilized in a cast. Still, in this state, therapists attempt, as soon as possible, to begin isometric quadricep contractions, with either electric stimulation or voluntary contractions. Other exercises starting soon thereafter include straight leg raises, flexing at the hip, hip abduction on both sides, leg extension while lying prone, and dorsi flexion, planter flexion, eversion, and inversion. The latter is important for calf strengthening, since the gastronemius crosses the knee joint and thus provides added support and protection to the injured area (Zelko, 1986).

Phase II: For the next two weeks, the goal of rehabilitation is careful improvement of range of motion, as well as development of muscular control of the injured limb. With the cast off, painless flexion and extension in a whirlpool should begin daily. Crutch walking, placing no more than 50 lbs. of pressure on the affected leg at once, is very important at this stage for redeveloping muscular control.

Discouraging the use of a protective brace during rehabilitation, this process places the element of safety on the supervision and good design of the program. Careful instruction and observation during every phase of the program, especially the first four phases, should provide better protection than the brace, while eliminating the patient's reliance on this crutch, the knee brace (Zelko, 1986).

Phase III: According to Matthew C. Morrissey, the most important muscle group to rehabilitate after serious ACL surgery is the hamstring muscle. Preventing anterior tibial luxation and limiting tibial rotation, the hamstring muscle, he states, supports the ACL better than any other muscle (Morrissey, 1986). In this phase, 8–12 weeks following surgery, an increased emphasis is placed on hamstring isotonics. A progressive resistance technique is used on the hamstring. The previous exercises are re-emphasized, and swimming is added two days a week. Slowly, and safely, the theory is to build up both duration and intensity of exercise. Important to note is that at the sign of swelling, exercise should be halted, and ice should be applied immediately until swelling is reduced (Zelko, 1986).

Phase IV: Called the "crutch-weaning stage," at 12 to 14 weeks, the patient is taught normal and proper gait patterns. This propriety is emphasized to eliminate improper walking patterns or habits. Swimming is increased to three to four times a week, while exercises in phases I and II are lessened. Stationary cycling is added (Zelko, 1986).

Phase V: By this time in rehabilitation, the patient should have near full painless extension within three to five degrees of full extension. Forced extension or hyperextension should be avoided. During this two-week period, walking should normalize considerably and a new exercise, toe raises off of a step, should be added (Zelko, 1986).

Phase VI: Because of the possibility of mental burn-out, it is wise to take two weeks off, maintaining just precautionary measures. From the 20th week to the 24th week, leg presses on a machine should be done. Although leg presses seem to provide an extreme stress on the knee joint, because of the physical directions of the forces, these leg presses are much less likely to provoke reinjury than active resistant leg extensions. The leg extensions create a pseudo-rotational force of the tibia about the femur, luxation, while the leg presses direct the forces straight through the femur and tibia to the foot, without the luxational element. Also added at this stage are situps and mild jogging (Zelko, 1986).

Phase VII: This phase is called a "re-education period." The therapist analyses the biomechanics of the patient's exercises and corrects the "bad habits" that have developed. Leg curls for the hamstring and leg presses are emphasized (Zelko, 1986).

Phase VIII: For the next six weeks, 30th to 36th weeks, there is the introduction to and stressed importance on a new exercise—power squats. King calls it the most fundamental exercise for all ground-based sports (King, 1986). *National Strength and Conditioning Association Journal*, June, 1984, describes power squats as the most important exercise for the concentric and eccentric build-up of the quadricep muscle and especially important in the reconditioning of an atrophied muscle. Because this involves free weights, a great amount of technical training and caution is imperative. Stretching every day should also begin at this phase (Zelko, 1986).

Phases IX and X: During this portion of the rehabilitative program, enough progress should have been made to allow a conclusive prognosis to be made regarding the patient's return to athletics. Faster straight running, jumping, cycling, and painfree zig-zag running all should be done by the patient in this phase. By now, the 36th through the 40th week of rehabilitation, the knee should be strong enough to begin, with light weights, active resistant isokinetic extension (Zelko, 1986).

Phases XI and XII: These last two stages mark the transition phase of the program from cautious exercises and rehabilitative techniques to high performance activity simulating the athlete's pre-injury activities. In this transition zone, figure eight test and agility tests are given and evaluated. Harder zig-zag running is prescribed while the therapist evaluates body mechanics and leg power and intensity. Guided imagery is recommended to help build the athlete's confidence and to better help the athlete see himself actively participating in his sport. Upon the athlete's passing of various performance tests, cutting, cross cutting, figure eight, agility tests, power and strength tests, and speed tests, the athlete may begin participating in his sport again (Zelko, 1986).

Many patients find that through the course of this rehabilitative process they not only regain their speed, but often find improvement in their times in the 40-yard dash (Zelko, 1986).

Important in the process of rehabilitation are protection and dedication. Full measures of these attitudes will certainly increase the probability of success dramatically.

CONCLUSION

Consisting of two anatomically complex and functionally different bands (AMB and PLB) and being extremely instrumental in support of the knee, the ACL, when ruptured, has understandably caused much confusion and controversy in the medical field, as well as pain and atheletic frustration in the lives of certain athletes.

Due to recent medical findings regarding the importance of the ACL to the functioning of the knee joint, the ACL injuries have become very salient and thus are meriting much investigation. Recent inquiries into the causes and remedies of ACL injuries have benefitted professionals by providing them with more conclusive and efficient diagnostic techniques, surgical procedures, and rehabilitation programs. The continual improvements of these techniques, procedures, and programs indicate a bright future in this area of sports medicine. A pathology that once implied definite physical restrictions and possible disability can now be handled with expertise and precision (King, 1986).

Bibliography

Appenzeller, Otto; Sports Medicine. Baltimore, Urban & Schwarzenberg, 1981.
Beck, Charles, M.D.; Drez, David M.D.; Soma, John, M.D.; "Instrumental Testing of Knee Braces," American Journal of Sports Medicine, August, 1986.

Bell, Larry, M.D.; "Reconstruction of the Anterior Cruciate Ligament with the Pa-
teller Tendon," Journal of Orthopedic Research, June, 1986.

Bilko, Thomas, M.D.; "Current Trends in Repair and Rehabilitation of Acute Anterior Cruciate Ligament Injuries," American Journal of Sports Medicine, March,
1986.

Brown, B. J.; Complete Guide to Prevention and Treatment of Athletic Injuries. West
Nyack, NY, Parker Publishers, 1972.

Cooluille, Mark, M.D.; Lee, Christopher, M.D.; Crutto, Jeremy, M.D.; The Lenox
Hill Brace, American Journal of Sports Medicine, July, 1986.

DeHaven, Kenneth, M.D.; "Athletic Injuries: A Comparison by Age, Sport, and Gender," American Journal of Sports Medicine, June, 1986.

Gibson, Michael, M.S.; Mikosz, Richard, M.S.; Reider, Bruce, M.D.; Andriacchi,
Thomas. Ph.D.; "Analysis of the Muller Anterolateral Femoraltibial Ligament
Reconstruction, Using a Computerized Knee Model," American Journal of
Sports Medicine, May, 1986.

Hawkins, Richard, M.D.; Misamore, Gary, M.D.; Merritt, Thomas, M.D.; "Follow
Up of the Acute, Nonoperative, Isolated Anterior Cruciate Ligament Tear,"
American Journal of Sports Medicine, June, 1986.

King, Steve, M.S., A.T.C.; Buttewick, Dale, M.A. A.T.C.; Cuerrier, Jean-Pierre, Ph.D;
"The Anterior Cruciate Ligament: A Review of Recent Concepts," The Journal
of Orthopedic and Sports Physical Therapy, August, 1986.

Morrissey, Matthew, M.D.; "Hamstring Weakness After Surgery for Anterior Cruciate Ligament Injury," Journal of Orthopedic and Sports Physical Therapy, May,
1986.

Nikolaou, Pantelis, M.D.; Seaber, Anthony; Glisson, Arnold; Ribbock, Beth, M.S.;
"Anterior Cruciate Ligament Allograft Transplantation." American Journal of
Sports Medicine, August, 1986.

Richer, Murray, M.D.; Mandelbaum, Bert, M.D.; Finnerman, Jerry, M.D.; Hortzman,
Steven, M.D.; "Magnetic Resonance Imagery as a Tool for Evaluation of Trau-
matic Knee Injury," American Journal of Sports Medicine, May, 1986.

Roy, Steven; Irvin, Richard; Sports Medicine, Inglewood Cliffs, Prentice-Hall Incorporated, 1983.

Tegner, Yelverton, M.D.; Lysholm, Jack, M.D.; Lysholm, Makatta, R.P.T.; "A Performance Test to Monitor Rehabilitation and Evaluate ACL Injuries," American Journal of Sports Medicine, March, 1986.

Tibone, James, M.D.; Antich, J., M.S.; Fanton, Gary, M.D.; "Functional Analysis of
Anterior Cruciate Instability," American Journal of Sports Medicine, June,
1986.

Zelko, Russell, M.D.; "Knee Rehabilitation Following Anterior Cruciate Ligament
Injury and Surgery," Journal of Athletic Training, Fall, 1986.

■ UNDERSTANDING WRITING STRATEGIES

1. For what audience is this paper written? What in the paper's language
and evidence indicates this?

2. Why is the anterior cruciate ligament an important concern for this audience? How does the paper focus on that concern?

3. Most long studies such as this contain smaller sub-studies. What are they here?

4. Could the order of the sub-parts be changed? How?

5. What are the alternative treatments for this injury? How does Wolford present them?

6. How thoroughly does Wolford present his source studies? Why does he present Nikolaou's and Zelko's studies in greater detail than the others?

7. What does the conclusion accomplish? How does it do this? ■

■ SUGGESTIONS FOR WRITING

You have submitted this article to a journal, and they have returned it to you saying they would like to publish it, but they need you to cut it preferably to 2,500 words, maximum 3,000 (ten pages, maximum twelve). The content, however, should remain substantially the same. Revise this paper to meet their specifications. ■

Social Sciences

10

The social sciences study human institutions and behavior with science's objectivity and proclivity for experimentation. In the social sciences, writing frequently adopts scientific conventions; consequently reviews of scientific literature and experiment reports represent a substantial part of social science writing, particularly in psychology and educational psychology. But not all work in the social sciences is experimental in the formal sense. Social scientists observe existing institutions and write to explain them and relate them to other institutions past and present, particularly in sociology, political science, and anthropology. When students engage in research and writing for social science courses, they write to address the field's important ideas, but also to learn the voice of professionals in their disciplines. This chapter's essays show students writing to learn about their disciplines and learning their discipline's writing.

Reviews of professional literature appear in the essays by Cheryl Bromgard ("Dual Career Marriages: Roles, Attitudes and Satisfaction") and Sue di Carlo ("Subliminal Psychodynamic Activation"). Sallyanne Jones-Waldinger also reviews professional literature but only as a part of a formal report of original psychological research in "Color Encoded as a Verbal Label." Janet M. LeRoux reports her observations and relates them to theory in "A Comparative Study of Community Among Public and Private School Teachers," an essay that reflects how the social sciences use observations and theory.

The relationship between observation and theory represents an important kind of writing in the social sciences—the case history. Case histories provide substantial bodies of data in psychology and sociology, but they also form an important part of clinical work. The four case histories here show students working both practically and theoretically. Nancy Dyer's "Catherine" and Deborah Sanders's "The Case of Luke" relate observations in a clinical setting to theoretical studies as a means to recommending treatment. Dennifer Kann and Susan Walton apply personality theory to autobiography in "*Personality Today Magazine* Presents, The Hiding of Anne Frank: A 'Ghost Interview' with Karen Horney" and "Thomas Merton's

Long Climb to Freedom: *The Seven Storey Mountain* in Terms of Allport's Personality Theory." Janice Abrams's "The Impact of Religion on the Rate of Suicide" relates theory to statistical rather than personally observed data.

Relating observation to theory asks students to develop and apply criteria. The writing task then is similar to that of the formal critique. Book reviews and article reviews, formal critiques, develop and apply criteria to evaluate their subjects. Sheila Alexander and Pam Bruton critique education journal articles in "Teaching Vocabulary Through External Content Clues" and "The Concept-Text-Application Approach." Mary Jimenez's "*The Master of the Game* by Strobe Talbott" and David Woolner's "Locarno Diplomacy: Germany and the West, 1925–1929" both review books, adapting the professional book review journal's style.

Besides primary experimental research, social science disciplines like history and political science combine secondary and primary sources in their professional writing. When students in these disciplines write "term papers" synthesizing diverse secondary sources, they are learning their discipline's discourse. Angela Womack's "Native Americans and the Reservation System" and Robin McDavid's "NATO—A Credible Alliance?" are term papers that rely on popular sources, while Brad Werner's and Lisa Gentile's essays, "NATO and the SNF Debate" and "Gorbachev's Foreign Policy," more closely approach published political science articles because of their breadth and their sources' origins in the work of political scientists.

Not all students write with a "professional" goal or audience in mind. In the social sciences as in all disciplines students write to exercise newly discovered intellectual muscles. Essays or exam responses like Patty Masters's "Simmel, Durkheim, and Marx: Three Views on the Individual in Contemporary Society," Elizabeth Rose's "Transforming Stories," and Robert Fleischman's "The Realities of Fantasy" represent students writing to learn and discover.

The Impact of Religion on the Rate of Suicide

Janice Abrams

For an introductory sociology class, Janice Abrams replicates the work of nineteenth-century sociologist Emile Durkheim using statistics on suicide in twentieth-century America. Explaining and evaluating statistical data represents an important writing skill for the social sciences.

In studying the social causes of suicide, Emile Durkheim undertook what would later be considered a statistical analysis of the effect various religious confessions had upon suicide. He not only considers the number of suicides for each religion, but also accounts for different time frames and diverse social environments found in dissimilar countries as further weight of the stability of the occurrence of suicide.

He points out that without exception, Protestants commit suicide far more than either Catholics or Jews. And generally, the rate of suicide for Jews falls below that of Catholics. It must be remembered, he notes in reference to Jewish suicides, that ". . . Jews live more exclusively than other confessional groups in cities and are in intellectual occupations" (155).

As both Protestants and Catholics prohibit suicide as a matter of doctrine, Durkheim sees the essential difference between the two in the fact that free inquiry is inherent to Protestantism, whereas Catholicism embraces considerably more structured practices of belief. Durkheim points out that free inquiry is not the culprit leading directly to an increase in suicides. Rather, free inquiry develops as a result of a perceived lack, or degeneration of traditional beliefs. Protestantism allows far more individual freedom because it provides fewer common beliefs and practices in comparison to the Catholic Church. Durkheim states: "we thus reach the conclusion that the superiority of Protestantism with respect to suicide results from its being a less strongly integrated church than the Catholic church" (159). And this integration factor reflects too, on Judaism; Durkheim notes, "Judaism, in fact, like all early religions, consists basically of a body of practices minutely governing all the details of life and leaving little free room to individual judgement" (160).

Durkheim confirms this explanation by looking at the Anglican church, where Protestant suicide is least prevalent. He notes the similarity between the hierarchies of the Anglican and Catholic churches and enumerates several actual religious requirements. He also discusses the fact that of all Protestant countries, England provides the largest number of clergy per layman, indicating a more strongly integrated religious society.

Durkheim concludes that ". . . as a rule suicide increases with knowledge" (168). However, he is quick to point out that knowledge itself is not a causal factor. He states: "Man seeks to learn and man kills himself because of the loss of cohesion in this religious society; he does not kill himself because of this learning. It is certainly not the learning he acquires that disorganizes religion; but the desire for knowledge wakens because religion becomes disorganized" (169).

It may be said that an integrated religion decreases the tendency toward suicide, but this is not because of religion's inherent views on the morality of the matter of suicide or due to the special nature of any particular religious concept. Rather, "If religion protects man against the desire for self-destruction, it is not that it preaches the respect of his own person to him with arguments sui generis; but because it is a society" (170). It is a society binding man to man by commonly accepted beliefs and practices.

How do Durkheim's findings relate to today's statistics tying suicide with religion? Below is a table derived from a random 600 cases of a 2000-case contemporary general social survey. Columns 1-5 represent (consecutively): Protestant, Catholic, Jew, None, and other. Row 1 indicates a positive response; Row 2, a negative response to the question: "Do you think a person has the right to end his or her own life if this person is tired of living and ready to die?"

Rows: Suicide	Columns: Religion				
	1	2	3	4	5	All
1	45	28	3	18	1	95
	12.33	17.18	21.43	51.43	14.29	16.27
2	320	135	11	17	6	489
	87.67	82.82	78.57	48.57	85.71	83.73
All	365	163	14	35	7	584
	100.00	100.00	100.00	100.00	100.00	100.00

At first glance it would seem that this table completely contradicts Durkheim's findings, as 21.43% of all Jews favored suicide compared to 17.18% of Catholics and only 12.33% of Protestants. In spite of the percentages of these three groups, Durkheim's main premise that suicide is caused by the disintegration of society (religion, family, etc.), still holds true. This is evidenced by the phenomenal jump in "yes" responses from the fourth group with no professed religion (51.43%), and purportedly no structure in religious life. If one refers to the tables on prayer and on church attendance (see works cited), it is quite clear that the more devout one is, regardless of the religious confession one holds to, the more protected one is from the very notion of suicide.

Several factors could have contributed to the shift toward suicide, percentage-wise, for Catholics and Jews. Perhaps in the late 1800's, those people who perceived a lack in the rigid structure of the Catholic church and who may have been susceptible to the "free inquiry" allowed by the Protestant church, today would simply opt instead for the freedom of no religious affiliation.

The advent of the Second Vatican Council in the 1960's, which commenced an era of great change in the Catholic church, certainly contributed to what appeared to some faithful Catholics as a total disintegration of their beliefs. This could result in either a surge of egoistic suicide, where man no longer finds a basis for existence in life, or anomic suicide, with man's activities suddenly lacking the regulation that the pre-Vatican I Church amply provided.

Especially today, with the ecumenical movement solidly founded, Catholics and Protestants more freely move between denominations. Perhaps dissatisfied Jews feel that they have nowhere to move but outside of faith community boundaries totally, exposing them to higher rates of suicide than when they were integrated into a strong congregation.

In contemporary society there seems to be no stigma for choosing to be free of any religious affiliation. The seeming protection that Protestants today enjoy may be due in part to the fact that those who remain faithful to Protestantism are caught up in the conservative movement that has emerged in the last decade. Protestants driven by the likes of Rev. Jerry Falwell and Rev. Pat Robertson feel a common fervor that binds.

Of course, overshadowing all of these explanations dealing with the numerical discrepancies between the 1800's and the present is the fact that while Durkheim dealt with the numbers of actual deaths attributed to suicide, our tables are based on living human beings' speculations of the possibility and conditions of their own suicides. Also the respondents to the contemporary social survey are all Americans, living in an incredibly unrestricted society. And we are examining only one aspect of life in an increasingly complex and changeable world where other factors certainly influence the rate of suicide.

Works Cited

Durkheim, Emile. *Suicide.* New York: The Free Press, 1951.

■ THE WRITER'S ASSIGNMENT

Durkheim produced a sociological masterpiece by exploring nineteenth-century data about suicide in Europe. Using up-to-date data about suicide in America assembled by the National Opinion Research Center, replicate a part of Durkheim's study. Select a set of findings, explain the findings, and then explain the theoretical significance of those findings.   ■

■ UNDERSTANDING WRITING STRATEGIES

1. What background does Abrams give for her study?

2. What conclusions does Abrams select from Durkheim?

3. How do Durkheim's conclusions shape Abrams's study?

4. What context does Abrams offer for presenting her data?

5. What explanations does Abrams offer? How does she justify her interpretation?

6. What assumptions does Abrams have about religious conviction?

7. What relationship exists between assumptions, objectivity, and evidence in Abrams's essay?

8. Do you find an adequate justification for Abrams's conclusions in the data? What other conclusions would you have reached? ■

■ SUGGESTIONS FOR WRITING

Abrams makes several statements about religion in America—movement between denominations, disintegration in Catholic belief, increased Protestant conservatism. Examine and then review the literature and statistics on one of these topics. ■

Teaching Vocabulary Through External Content Clues

Sheila Alexander

Sheila Alexander critiques two articles published in professional education journals in this essay written for an education class. Both articles make practical suggestions for teaching reading and vocabulary at the elementary school level.

Ryder, R. J. (1986). Teaching vocabulary through external context clues. *Journal of Reading, 30,* 61–65.

SUMMARY

In his recent article, Randall J. Ryder (1986) states, "students' use of context may be responsible for most of their vocabulary learning" (p. 61). These context clues are either internal or external clues. "Internal clues are the morphological elements of a word (such as affixes and roots); external clues are syntactic and semantic elements within and among sentences" (Ryder, 1986, p. 61). Readence, Bean, and Baldwin (1985) refer to the internal clues as the process of morphemic analysis. Ryder (1986) states that students receive more instruction in and have a better understanding of internal context clues than they do external clues. He describes a four-step method of teaching external context clues, which is based on the belief that "context clue instruction occurs over many years at all grade levels" (Ryder, 1986, p. 62).

The first step Ryder (1986) describes makes use of pictures to introduce the concept of context. Using a word that is unfamiliar to the students, the teacher first shows them a sentence and underlines the new word as she reads the sentence orally (Ryder, 1986). The teacher then shows the students a picture which provides them with a clue to the meaning of the new word (Ryder, 1986). The students are asked to look at the picture and give the teacher a list of words, which is placed on the blackboard, that describe the actions or the features in the picture (Ryder, 1986). After the teacher has pointed out the meaningful clues in the picture, the children are asked to give a definition of the new word and to show the pictorial clue that helped them with the definition (Ryder, 1986). "As students become familiar with this activity, the teacher exhibits fewer visual clues" (Ryder, 1986, p. 63).

Ryder's (1986) next step makes use of sentence context. This step contains three steps in itself. The first step uses a sentence which directly defines the word (Ryder, 1986). After the teacher reads the sentence, identifies the new term, and gives the definition of the term, the children point out the clues in the sentence that help define the word (Ryder, 1986). The second step provides fewer direct clues (Ryder, 1986). The process of identifying the meaning of the new word is the same as in step one. Readence, Bean, and Baldwin (1985) refer to this type of clue as a descriptive context clue. The last step uses the surrounding sentences to provide the meaning of the word (Ryder, 1986). Once again, the process of identifying the meaning is the same as in steps one and two. One type of clue that Readence, Bean, and Baldwin (1985) identify that Ryder (1986) does not is contrast clues. This is where "the word is compared with some other word or concept, often an opposite" (Readence, Bean, and Baldwin, 1986, p. 92).

The third step that Ryder (1986) describes uses whole paragraphs to provide the meaning of a word. To begin with, the teacher underlines the main clue in the paragraph (Ryder, 1986). The students then derive the meaning of the word based on the underlined clues (Ryder, 1986). When the students can do this efficiently, the process is reversed. The teacher defines the word and the students locate the context clues in the paragraph (Ryder, 1986).

The final step makes use of multiple paragraphs to derive the meaning of the new word (Ryder, 1986). This process is basically the same as the process in step three. The teacher underlines the clues found in the surrounding paragraphs and the students define the word based on these clues (Ryder,

1986). The process is once again reversed when the first process is mastered (Ryder, 1986).

Ryder (1986) bases this technique on three general assumptions. First, "students learn best when initially provided with concrete examples" (Ryder, 1986, p. 62). Second, "students should be taught how to use context clues with the materials they commonly read in their classrooms" (Ryder, 1986, p. 62). Third, students must continue receiving instruction on the technique as they come across more difficult texts (Ryder, 1986).

EVALUATION

The technique described in this article will be very beneficial to this writer. It is extremely important that students are taught how to use context clues. Many times this is the only way to define a word without using an external reference. The method that Ryder (1986) describes is very clear and can be easily put into action. One point that this writer finds as odd is the fact that the fourth step is never clearly defined as the fourth step. Ryder (1986) mentions a second step within the third step that this writer sees as the fourth step. This conclusion is based on Ryder's statement that the technique ends "with a stage where students locate in consecutive paragraphs the context clues of a single word" (Ryder, 1986, p. 62). Overall, this article gives excellent suggestions for teaching students to use external context clues.

APPLICATION

A program based on Randall Ryder's (1986) technique would be excellent to implement into a class for special needs learners. A learning disabled child, or even an educable mentally retarded child, would benefit greatly from such a program. A special needs learner must have some sort of concrete experience in order to understand a concept. Ryder's (1986) technique provides these concrete experiences through the use of pictures. Although each step would have to be taken very slowly, the special needs child would eventually develop an understanding of the use of context clues. Once this child understands and learns to use context clues, he will have a tool which he will use for the rest of his life.

References

Readence, J. E., Bean, T. W., & Baldwin, R. S. (1985). *Content area reading: An integrated approach*, 2nd ed. Dubuque, Iowa: Kendall/Hunt.

Ryder, R. J. (1986). Teaching vocabulary through external context clues. *Journal of Reading, 30,* 61–65.

■ UNDERSTANDING WRITING STRATEGIES

1. What is Ryder's method for developing context summarized by Alexander?

2. How did Alexander structure her presentation of Ryder's method?

3. On what criteria does Alexander evaluate Ryder?

4. What purpose does this essay serve?

5. To what audience besides an instructor might an essay like this be addressed?

6. What kinds of changes in the essay would make it appeal to an audience broader than an instructor? ■

■ SUGGESTIONS FOR WRITING

Revise this essay to appeal to a different audience—a weekly newsletter for reading teachers, parents, or even an education magazine. ■

Dual-Career Marriages: Roles, Attitudes, and Satisfaction
Cheryl Bromgard

Cheryl Bromgard's extensive literature review summarizes and integrates published studies on the relationship between sex role attitudes and both marital and career satisfaction in dual-career marriages. Written for a psychology class, this essay abstracts important definitions and relevant findings from social and psychological studies published in professional journals.

Two-career marriages are more prevalent than ever in today's society. In 1980, (Benokraitis, 1985) nearly 50% of American families were dual-earner families, with the number expected to increase to 80% by 1990 (cited in Hanson & Bozett, 1987). Wives have gone to work for a variety of reasons, including boredom, financial need, and fulfillment of personal career goals. Change from traditional marital and family structure presents new roles and attitudes, new problems, and new factors which will contribute to a well-adjusted, successful marriage.

Rapoport and Rapoport (1971) define the dual-career marriage as "one in which both partners pursue careers as well as family roles. Such careers . . . require commitment, have a developmental character, and [involve jobs] from which personal rewards are derived" (p. 468). Dual-career marriages need to be distinguished from dual-employment marriages by the wife's academic preparation, motivation for working, and level of career commitment (Thomas, Albrecht, & White, 1984). Husbands and wives are affected differently by these structural changes.

Wives have traditionally been the primary caretakers of the household and children. Therefore, when working outside the home, married women are faced with dual roles to fill, sometimes with little help from their husbands, and with high demands on their time. According to Rapoport and Rapoport (1976), role overload and role strain are two of the most common problems experienced by married women who work full-time (cited in Smith & Reid, 1986a).

Married women with jobs may feel that they are torn between their two roles, or that they may not be able to perform well in both roles. Keith and Schafer (1985) found that dissatisfaction with roles, disagreement over roles, and perceptions of less competent role behavior were significantly correlated with greater distress and depression in working married women.

Bird and Bird (1986) found that career-oriented women reported that empathy from husbands reduces role strain. Smith and Reid (1986a) believe that the sharing of domestic and child care roles is the best way for spouses to support their dual roles. They found, however, that although husbands and wives agreed on the idea of domestic role-sharing, their behaviors differed from their ideals. The wives still performed the majority of the traditionally female household duties. In addition, they found that the wives felt that their husbands should share in domestic roles because of the pressure to share and to be equal, and apparently felt that they were the enforcers of the egalitarian standard.

Wives, although advocating the idea of role-sharing in the marriage, still held onto traditional beliefs about the overriding importance of their domestic and maternal responsibilities (Smith & Reid, 1986a). Yogev (1981) speculated that the traditional pattern still existed in the home not only because the husbands might be reluctant to help, but also because the women do not want their husbands to share these responsibilities equally. Yogev (1981) states, "It is important for them to have this unfair division so it will enable a wife to feel that she is the *mother* in the family" (p. 868).

Regardless of the wife's employment status, it appears that the husband is still seen as the primary supporter of the household. More than a third of the wives in Smith and Reid's (1986a) study stated that although they are employed full-time, they felt that the husband was more or mostly responsible for the breadwinner role.

Hanson and Bozett (1987) believe that a predominant difference between men and women is that "fathers' roles remain limited, and mothers expand their roles from that of full-time wives, mothers and homemakers, to include being wage-earners also" (p. 13). Some research does indicate that men are increasing the amount of time they spend in performing housework and child-care duties (Pleck, 1979), but it is more the exception than the rule.

It appears that men's attitudes towards helping in the home are changing, but their actions do not always follow their ideas. Smith and Reid (1986a) found that, although husbands agreed on the idea of equitable role sharing, most of their employed wives still performed the majority of the household and child care duties. When husbands did share more in the duties, the main reason they gave was because they actually wanted to help, not because their wives pressured them to do so. Conversely, the wives believed that their husbands did help because they pressured them to do so.

In another study, the researchers found that male parents with employed wives spent about the same amount of time per week on child care and even less time on household chores than did men with wives who stayed at home (Googins & Burden, 1987). Additionally, the more a man works, the less involved he is with his children, whether or not his wife works (McHale & Huston, 1984).

Husbands have not participated in what has been considered traditionally "women's work" for a number of reasons: traditional attitudes about appropriate sex roles, and social, economic, and employment policies and practices that assume husbands are breadwinners and wives are homemakers and child-rearers (Smith & Reid, 1986a). When husbands do become more involved at home, it may be for different reasons. A husband's love for his wife might make him want to help (Crouter, Perry-Jenkins, Huston, & McHale, 1987), as might his sense of fairness (Smith & Reid, 1986a). Hoffman (1983) suggests that marital conflict is associated with husbands' increased involvement in family work (cited in Crouter et al., 1987).

Fathers may also become involved with their children as a result of negative pressure from their wives (Crouter et al., 1987). This negative pressure can have aversive results. Stanley, Hunt, and Hunt (1986) indicated that dual-earner fathers are less satisfied with their work, marital relationships, and personal lives than single-earner fathers. Hoffman (1983) suggests that marital conflict is associated with husbands' increased involvement in family work (cited in Crouter et al., 1987).

Despite the stress caused by dual-earner marriages, husbands and wives do find successful way of coping and adjusting to the changes from traditional family structure. Researchers have studied many factors predictive of successful adjustment. Model (1981) found that the higher the wife's status and income relative to her husband's, the more likely she was to be employed and he to share in the household duties.

Smith and Reid state that one of the best ways to alleviate the difficulties caused by role strain and role overload is for the wife and the husband to assume co-responsibility for the domestic and child-care roles, not just for the husband to occasionally help the wife perform the tasks (1986a). In an in-depth study, Smith and Reid (1986b) found that a majority of couples who not only believed in equal role-sharing, but who also identified themselves as role sharers, did actually divide domestic and child-care tasks on an equitable basis.

Rapoport and Rapoport (1976) have suggested equity as an alternative to the ideal of egalitarianism (cited in Rachlin & Hansen, 1985). Equity refers to a feeling of fairness derived from the individual's perception of the overall balance of rewards and costs in the relationship, whereas egalitarianism refers to the completely equal division of all the household responsibilities (Rachlin & Hansen, 1985). Rachlin and Hansen (1985) surveyed the perceptions of marital adjustment, marital satisfaction, and general well-being among dual-career couples, with the specific goal of finding differences between the sexes. They found that women in egalitarian/equitable relationships report the highest feelings of adjustment, satisfaction, and well-being, whereas no significant difference was found between the husbands in equitable versus inequitable marriages. This outcome may indicate that a feeling of equity is not as important to husbands because of beliefs about traditional family structure.

An issue related to egalitarian attitudes toward role-sharing is perception of sex-roles. Baruch and Barnett (1981), while surveying a group of middle-class couples with preschool children, found that the more nontraditional the parents' attitudes, the more involved the fathers were in caring for their children. These results indicate that a change from traditional attitude can have an impact upon male involvement in the home.

Thomas et al. (1984) identified several factors predictive of higher marital quality in dual-career couples: more positive regard, more emotional gratification between the spouses, more effective communication, and greater interaction between the spouses. The researchers feel that the most important issues involve satisfaction with intimacy between the couple.

Ladewig and McGee (1986) tested a multivariate model of marital adjustment among men and women in dual-earner marriages to find relevant predictors of marital adjustment. The researchers hypothesized that a higher level of occupational commitment, while possibly hurting marital adjustment directly, would indirectly create a more supportive family environment, and thus help marital adjustment. The researchers found that females associated a higher level of occupational commitment with a more supportive family. Additionally, the women's level of occupational commitment was perceived to be aversive to marital adjustment, while the men's level of occupational commitment was not.

How the dual-career couples perceive their problems and their ability to deal with them is also important in predicting marital quality and adjustment. Levels of communication and relation efficacy made significant contributions to the prediction of marital adjustment, while perceived severity of hassles did not (Meeks, Arnkoff, Glass, & Notarius, 1986). The superiority of relational efficacy as a predictor of marital adjustment is consistent with Lazarus' (1966) hypothesis that stressful outcomes are not only a function of a person's coping resources, but, more importantly of the individual's appraisal of those resources (cited in Meeks et al., 1986). The results of Meeks' and his colleagues' (1986) study suggest that a couple's management of daily hassles depends not only on the couple's skills, but also on their perceived ability to cope with these dilemmas.

Occupational competition is almost always detrimental to a dual-career marriage (Bird & Bird, 1987). However, Hall and Hall (1979) concluded that competition is less likely to occur if the husband achieves the greater success and recognition, though they admit this can lead to jealousy if the wife feels she has helped advance his career at the expense of her own (cited in Bird & Bird, 1987).

Good communication is obviously important to the success of any marriage. Rosenfeld and Welsh (1985) hypothesized that higher levels of self-disclosure would lead to better understanding and better adjustment in a dual-career marriage. Self-disclosure constitutes "high quality" communication, which is the most relevant communication for the well-being of the marital relationship.

Characteristics predictive of high levels of self-disclosure have been identified with individuals in dual-career marriages. Dual-career partners generally obtain higher levels of education than single-career partners, and higher levels of education have been positively associated with both perceptions of spouse equality and with a high value placed on self-disclosure (Komarovsky, 1967, cited in Rosenfeld & Welsh, 1985; Rice, 1979, cited in Rosenfeld & Welsh, 1985). Secondly, dual-career couples have been shown to emphasize the quality of their time together, not the quantity (Shaevitz & Shaevitz, 1979, as cited in Rosenfeld & Welsh, 1985).

The change from traditional family structure to that of a dual-career family also has an impact upon the children in the family. In general, the children of dual-career parents rated their families relatively high on the components of family strength, and a majority of them also felt that their parents respected each other (Knaub, 1986). Knaub (1986) also listed several benefits given by these children of dual-career parents: positive role models, financial security, and the opportunity to develop independence. Knaub (1986) noted an interesting observation of the children's perceptions of traditional household duties. Knaub (1986) found that 51% of the children in her study disagreed with the statement that the "things mother does around the house are traditionally feminine and those that father does are traditionally masculine" (p. 436).

The current research on dual-career couples has obvious importance in social work and therapy. Two-career couples are dealing with new roles and attitudes and nontraditional values, which counselors need to be aware of to effectively help them to adjust. Rachlin and Hansen (1985) state two steps necessary for the couples to achieve a sense of equity in their marriage: it is important to clarify and make explicit their values and expectations regarding the family and their part in it, and the individuals need to learn and to implement strategies of negotiations and compromise. Additionally, couples need to learn skills to promote intimacy to influence development and satisfaction in the relationship (Hoffman & Hoffman, 1985).

In summary, the research conducted on two-career marriages and the corresponding results provide useful methods for studying both troubled and well-adjusted two-career couples. Two-career marriages are very prevalent in American society, and the numbers will continue to increase.

As the numbers do increase, more research should be focused on the effects on children of two parents working, as well as on the couple themselves. Finding what skills help a two-career adjust certainly seems beneficial for the children's development. The acquisition of this knowledge can also help teachers, school counselors, and social workers in working with children growing up in these dual-career homes. This research can give insight into one of the most important social changes of the century, and thus further research is warranted, and should prove important.

References

Benokraitis, N. (1985). Fathers in the dual-earner family. In S. M. H. Hanson & F. W. Bozett (Eds.), *Dimensions of fatherhood*. Beverly Hills, CA: Sage.

Bird, G. W., & Bird, G. A. (1986). Strategies for reducing role strain in dual-career families. *International Journal of Sociology of the Family, 16*, 753–758.

Bird, G. W., & Bird, G. A. (1987). In pursuit of academic careers: Observations and reflections of a dual-career couple. *Family Relations, 36*, 97–100.

Baruch, G. K., & Barnett, R. C. (1981). Fathers' participation in the care of their preschool children. *Sex Roles, 7*, 1043–1055.

Crouter, A. C., Perry-Jenkins, M., Huston,T. L., & McHale, S. M. (1987). Processes underlying father involvement in dual-earner and single-earner families. *Developmental Psychology, 23*, 431–440.

Googins, B., & Burden, D. (1987). Vulnerability of working parents: Balancing work and home roles. *Social Work, 32*, 295–300.

Hall, F. S., & Hall, D. T. (1979). *The two-career couple*. Reading, MA: Addison-Wesley Publishing Company.

Hanson, S. M. H., & Bozett, F. W. (1985). Fatherhood and changing family roles. *Family and Community Health, 9*, 9–21.

Hoffman, L. W. (1983). Increased fathering: Effects on the mother, In M. E. Lamb & A. Sagi (Eds.), *Fatherhood and family policy* (pp. 167–19). Hillsdale, NJ: Erlbaum.

Hoffman, L. W., & Hoffman, H. J. (1985). The lives and adventures of dual-career couples. *Family Therapy, 12*, 123–149.

Knaub, P. K. (1986). Growing up in a dual-career family: The children's perceptions. *Family Relations, 36*, 431–437.

Komarovsky, M. (1967). *Blue-collar marriage*. New York: Random House.

Keith, P. M., & Schafer, R. B. (1985). Role behavior, relative deprivation and depression among women in one- and two-job families. *Family Relations, 34*, 227–233.

Ladewig, B. H., & McGee, G.W. (1986). Occupational commitment, a supportive family and marital adjustment: Development and estimation of a model. *Journal of Marriage and the Family, 48*, 821–829.

Lazarus, R. S. (1966). *Psychological stress and the coping process*. New York: McGraw Hill.

McHale, S. M., & Huston, T. L. (1984). Men and women as parents: Sex role orientation, employment, and parental roles with infants. *Child Development, 55,* 1349–1361.

Meeks, S., Arnkoff, D. B., Glass, C. R., & Notarius, C. L. (1986). Wives' employment status, hassles, communication, and relational efficacy: Intra- versus extra-relationship factors and marital adjustment. *Family Relations, 34,* 249–255.

Model, S. (1981). Housework by husbands: Determinants and implications. *Journal of Family Issues, 2,* 225–237.

Pleck, J. H. (1979). Men's family work: Three perspectives and some new data. *The Family Coordinator, 28,* 481–488.

Rachlin, V. C., & Hansen, J. C. (1985). The impact of equity or egalitarianism on dual-career couples. *Family Therapy, 12,* 151–164.

Rapoport, R., & Rapoport, R. N. (1971). *Dual-career families.* Baltimore: Penguin Books.

Rapoport, R., & Rapoport, R. N. (1976). *Dual-career families re-examined.* New York: Harper & Row.

Rice, D. G. (1979). *Dual-career marriage: Conflict and treatment.* New York: Free Press.

Rosenfeld, L. B., & Welsh, S. M. (1985). Differences in self-disclosure in dual-career and single-career marriages. *Communication Monographs, 52,* 253–263.

Shaevitz, M. H., & Shaevitz, M. H. (1979). *Making it together as a two-career couple.* Boston: Houghton-Mifflin.

Smith, A. D., & Reid, W. J. (1986a). Role expectations and attitudes in dual-earner families. *Social Casework, 76,* 394–402.

Smith, A. D., & Reid, W. J. (1986b). *Role-sharing marriage.* New York: Columbia Press.

Stanley, S. C., Hunt, J. G., & Hunt, L. L. (1986). The relative deprivation of husbands in dual-earner households. *Journal of Family Issues, 7,* 3–20.

Thomas, S., Albrecht, K., & White, P. (1984). Determinants of marital quality in dual-career couples. *Family Relations, 33,* 513–521.

Yogev, S. (1981). Do professional women have egalitarian marital relationships? *Journal of Marriage and the Family, 43,* 866–890.

■ THE WRITER'S ASSIGNMENT

Literature Review Research Paper: Students are to report what scientific researchers have discovered doing research. Students accomplish this goal by summarizing and paraphrasing research findings and not by presenting personal opinions. A useful approach for format is to begin by stating the magnitude of the problem. Secondly, the writer needs to categorize or group the kinds of studies or approaches (or treatments) he finds in some sensible way which offers a framework to the paper. The concluding paragraph often summarizes all the studies in such a way that the writer might say: "The majority of the studies suggest that . . ." Documentation should meet APA specifications. ■

■ UNDERSTANDING WRITING STRATEGIES

1. How does the introduction focus the topic?

2. How does Bromgard limit her study? Why would she choose these limits?

3. What kinds of conflicts do women with jobs experience? How can distress and depression be alleviated?

4. What attitudes exist about husbands' roles? How are these affected by a dual-career marriage?

5. How does Bromgard order the studies she presents?

6. Assuming that most studies Bromgard reports follow standard scientific report format, what information does she appear to select from her sources?

7. What kinds of solutions does Bromgard suggest for the "problems" she has introduced? Does the evidence support these as "solutions"?

8. What other factors besides husbands' and wives' attitudes and behaviors does Bromgard examine? ■

■ SUGGESTIONS FOR WRITING

Bromgard presented a vast body of literature fairly objectively. Using her evidence, write a position paper on dual-career marriages. Maintain the objectivity of this essay, but argue a side using evidence. ■

The Concept-Text-Application Approach

Pam Bruton

Written for an education class, Pam Bruton's essay critiques a professional journal article on teaching reading in elementary school.

Wong, J., & Hu-pei Au, K. (1985). The concept-text-application approach: Helping elementary students comprehend expository text. *The Reading Teacher, 38,* 612–618.

SUMMARY

"The concept-text-application or CTA approach is a means for organizing lessons to improve elementary students' comprehension of expository text." (Wong and Hu-pei Au, 1985, p. 612). The CTA lesson requires lots of planning by the teacher, but the majority of the teachers who have used such a lesson have found that the planning really paid off. The students became excited and were ready to participate fully in the lesson.

Wong and Hu-pei Au (1985) briefly describe the three phases of a CTA lesson. "The initial concept assessment/development or C phase is a prereading discussion during which the teacher tries to find out what the students already know about the topic" (Wong and Hu-pei Au, 1985, p. 613). This phase of a CTA lesson relies heavily on a student's prior knowledge. Pearson and Tierney (1985) refer to this step as a before reading activity in which the students rely upon their schema to participate in the discussion. During this phase, the teacher will also introduce any unfamiliar vocabulary that the students may need to know to help them understand the text.

The second phase of a CTA lesson is the text or T phase. It is at this stage of the lesson that the teacher focuses the students' attention on the reading of the text. The teacher must "set purposes for reading" (Wong and Hu-pei Au, 1985, p. 613) at this time. Wong and Hu-pei Au (1985) suggest that the reading task should be broken down into small subcomponents. The students read a small section and the teacher checks for comprehension through guided discussions. These steps are repeated until the entire section is completed and understood. It may be beneficial to the students to develop a graphic organizer that would help them to combine the C and T phases.

Wong and Hu-pei Au (1985) state that the main purpose of the application or A phase is "to encourage students to make use of their new knowledge" (p. 613). This phase requires students to use their higher levels of cognitive thinking. They must be able to summarize what they have read and then evaluate the text. Pearson and Tierney (1985) refer to these activities as "post reading," (p. 2). It is during this stage that students must try to fit everything together into one big picture.

CTA lessons help the teacher and the students to focus on the main idea of expository text. They are also very useful in teaching primary students how to "read to learn" (Wong and Hu-pei Au, 1985, p. 617). Herber and Nelson-Herber (1987) are proponents of this idea. They believe that if students are taught *how* to learn what is important in content material, they will become independent learners. CTA may be the answer for helping to develop a generation of just this type of learners.

EVALUATION

Wong and Hu-pei Au (1985) have developed a very interesting approach to teaching expository material to elementary students. The three phases of a CTA lesson are not difficult to understand and they can easily be utilized in a classroom. The flexibility of a CTA lesson should appeal to both the teacher and the students.

Wong and Hu-pei Au (1985) and Pearson and Tierney (1985) all agree that there are three phases to studying expository material. Wong and Hu-pei Au (1985) refer to the stages as CTA, while Pearson and Tierney (1985) have named the stages before reading, during reading, and post-reading activities. The only major discrepancy between these two styles occurs in the placement of setting purposes for reading. Pearson and Tierney (1985) have placed this step in the before reading stage and Wong and Hu-pei Au (1985) feel that it belongs in their T phase.

Wong and Hu-pei Au do not hesitate to point out the one major drawback to their CTA approach. The amount of time required for planning a CTA lesson may frighten teachers away from using this approach.

APPLICATION

A CTA lesson can be utilized in every content area of the classroom. But in order for it to be successful, the students must have some prior knowledge of the subject. It is the responsibility of the teacher to activate this prior knowledge in order to begin a CTA lesson. Once the students' prior knowledge has been evoked, it is time to introduce new concepts and vocabulary that they will need to help in understanding the text. It is this C phase that lays the foundation for the CTA lesson.

After the students have been properly motivated and their curiosity has been aroused, it is time to introduce them to the text. Once again, the teacher must set the purposes for reading to help the students focus on the main ideas. The material must be broken down into small segments. By doing this, the teacher can assure success in comprehension of the material. This task is accomplished through guided questioning and discussions. Each time a new section of material is completed and reviewed, the teacher must help the students to connect it to the previously read sections. Thus, each short segment becomes one whole unit.

The application phase is a summary of the information that has been read and discussed. The students should evaluate what they have read at this time. It is during the evaluation of the text material that the teacher will be able to see how well the students picked up on the main idea of the material. It is the opinion of the writer that assimilation or accommodation of the new material occurs during this phase.

A CTA lesson would be a very useful tool for teachers to utilize in teaching difficult expository material. It has been proven to be successful in helping students to read to learn, in increasing comprehension and in "making reading challenging and interesting" (Wong and Hu-pei Au, 1985, p. 618). If teachers can help students to become interested in their content area texts, the job of teaching that material will become easier and much more rewarding for both the teacher and the student.

References

Herber, Harold L., & Nelson-Herber, Joan. (1987, April). Developing independent learners. *Journal of Reading, 30* (7), 584–588.

Pearson, David, & Tierney, Robert J. (1985). Tour guides to schema. *TAIR Newsletter, 28,* pp. 1–3.

Readence, John E., Bean, Thomas W., & Baldwin, R. Scott. (1985). *Content area reading: An integrated approach,* (2nd ed.). Dubuque, IA: Kendall/Hunt.

Wong, JoAnn, & Hu-pei Au, Kathryn. (1985, March). The concept-text-application approach: Helping elementary students comprehend expository text. *The Reading Teacher, 38* (7). 612–618.

■ UNDERSTANDING WRITING STRATEGIES

1. What is Wong and Hu-pei Au's method for developing context summarized by Bruton?

2. How did Bruton structure her presentation of the method?

3. On what criteria does Bruton evaluate the journal article?

4. What use does Bruton make of Pearson and Tierney (1985)?

5. What purpose does this essay serve?

6. To what audience besides an instructor might an essay like this be addressed?

7. What kinds of changes in the essay would make it appeal to an audience broader than an instructor? ■

■ SUGGESTIONS FOR WRITING

Write a comparative analysis of Bruton's and Alexander's essays. Direct your thesis toward the relative effectiveness of the writing. ■

Subliminal Psychodynamic Activation

Sue di Carlo

In this literature review, written for a psychology class, Sue di Carlo both summarizes and evaluates published studies on the relationship between subliminal psychological stimuli and either psychological adaptation or psychological disturbance. The research she considers attempts to scientifically test Freud's personality theory. However brilliant Freud's work is, some contemporary psychologists have challenged it for its nonexperimental basis. Di Carlo's paper effectively represents the controversy and evaluates the often conflicting experiments.

"Subliminal stimuli with certain kinds of psychodynamic content (i.e., content related to unconscious wishes, defenses, anxieties, and fantasies) can trigger psychopathology, stimuli with other psychodynamic content can dissipate pathology or otherwise enhance adaptation" (Silverman et al., 1982, p. 8). It is this hypothesis that has generated laboratory research for the past twenty plus years which has discovered the effects of such unconscious fantasies in psychotic, neurotic, character-disordered, and "normal" populations.

The initiative for Lloyd Silverman to investigate subliminal activation of fantasies and wishes was a desire to bring into the laboratory some of the psychoanalytic theories so difficult to support emphatically in a clinical setting. A clinician may form a hypothesis or inference as to the causative agent for a certain pathology, yet so many variables enter into this treatment setting it is difficult to know, with any degree of certainty, just what is underlying the pathology or to know the specificity of the positive effects of therapy. The data from clinical studies is empirical and based on the verbal interchange between patient and therapist. Such empirical data can be interpreted in a variety of ways and underlying dynamics can be suspected but not supported with statistical evidence.

Psychoanalytic propositions postulate that behavior is due to unconscious motivation resulting from experiences and perceptions formed in infancy and childhood (Silverman, 1976). Yet, it is exactly these unconscious motivations that guide our behavior and perceptions of reality during adult life. Data supporting psychoanalytic theory is limited by the inability to control variables in a clinical setting. More specifically, in psychoanalytic theory "psychopathology emerges as a reaction to the presence of unconscious libidinal and aggressive wishes" (Silverman, 1976, p. 622). It is when these wishes and desires and fantasies begin to threaten an individual that anxiety and pathological symptoms appear.

Silverman postulated that if aggressive wishes were unconsciously stimulated, results from such a conflict would be manifested in observable behavior. Conversely, if those unconsciously stimulated wishes and fantasies were temporarily satisfied, there would be a resulting decrease in observable pathology (Silverman, 1976).

"A number of psychoanalytic clinicians had posited that schizophrenic symptoms were most immediately the result of unconscious conflict over aggressive wishes. This seemed like a particularly worthwhile psychodynamic relationship to address. . . " (Silverman et al., 1984, p. 113). This hypothesis was tested under laboratory conditions in sixteen experiments, twelve of which originated in Silverman's laboratory. Subliminal exposure to stimuli designed to exacerbate conflict over aggressive wishes in populations of schizophrenics did lead to intensification of pathology as noted in dependent variables (Silverman, 1976, 1982). The lab conditions and design of the experiments generally consisted of a subject population of male schizophrenics being shown a "neutral" stimulus by looking into a tachistoscope (i.e., *People Are Walking*). This verbal message is shown at 4ms—a rate so rapid as to preclude conscious processing. Generally the stimulus was perceived as flicker of light. After this stimulus pathological thinking and behavior were measured in what is called a baseline measurement. The subjects are then shown the critical aggressive stimulus of *Cannibal Eats Person*, or some similar verbal message designed to arouse aggressive impulses. Accompanying these verbal messages and shown milliseconds following the verbal stimulus are pictures congruent with the verbal message. The original behavior and thought measurements are repeated, and the difference in scores indicate either the increase or decrease of pathological thinking. These intensifications of symptomology were seen to offer support to the psychoanalytic proposition that schizophrenic symptoms were the result of unconscious conflict over aggressive impulses. The intensification of thought disorder seemed to lend support to this theory.

As many of the above mentioned experiments of aggressive stimulus were doctoral dissertations and studies of the 60s, I was not able to read them but accepted these reported results as supporting evidence. In a more recent attempt at replication Litwack (1979), as part of a broader study, investigated the aggressive stimulus of *Cannibal Eats Person* shown to 30 hospitalized male chronic undifferentiated schizophrenics. Their length of hospitalization ranged from one to ten years. As in the previous mentioned studies the patient was first exposed to "neutral" stimulus, baseline assessment of pathology was taken, then critical stimulus was administered followed by critical assessment. The message *Cannibal Eats Person* elicited an increase in behavior pathology to a degree that approached significance. I have found that very often in these studies "approached significance" is referred to in other papers as support for the effectiveness of the stimulus in eliciting behavior change. These results are based on a comparison with control stimuli of *People Are Walking*. These increases in pathology level are fleeting (Litwack, 1979; Silverman, 1984) and slight. This study (Litwack, 1979) failed to replicate Silverman's finding that pathological thought is exacerbated.

A more recent study (Porterfield, 1985) also dealt in part with aggressive stimuli (i.e., *Tiger Eats Person*) designed to stir up aggressive conflicts. He found no significant differences and raised some questions regarding the original experiments. He pointed out that most replications and support has come from dissertations and from Silverman's own laboratory findings. He finds problems with diagnosis, as the diagnostic system in the 60s and 70s was different from today's DSM III's more stringent requirements for a schizophrenic diagnosis. He cites a study (Klein, 1982) where it is shown that only 28 percent of a sample of patients diagnosed schizophrenic under DSM II criteria carried the same diagnosis under DSM III. Porterfield reasons, therefore, that Silverman's populations were extremely heterogeneous and the hypothesis for the etiology of schizophrenia was hardly specific to this disease. He also did not use Silverman's Nonverbal Pathology Rating Scale to rate behavior, as he states it has "No demonstrated association with schizophrenic pathology beyond its face validity as an inferential index of anxiety" (Porterfield, 1985, p. 632). Problems with this rating scale are also addressed in another paper. Porterfield's dependent variables measured only the pathological thought of the population, as this is a central component in this disease. His dependent variables were Rorschach tests for cognition and the Stroop Color Word Test. Neither of these were used by Silverman. Porterfield also eliminated the pictorial element of the stimulus and used more rigorous analysis. This study can hardly be called a failure to replicate as the design differed in so many aspects. Yet, the study clearly did not reveal any sign of increasing through pathology after exposure to aggressive stimuli.

Dr. Silverman then turned to investigating the ameliorative effects of subliminal psychodynamic activation and "advanced the thesis that unconscious oneness fantasies can enhance adaptation if, simultaneously, a sense of self can be preserved" (Silverman et al., 1982, p. 1). The oneness stimulus, specifically *Mommy and I Are One*, stimulates a fantasy of these symbiotic wishes being gratified. The psychoanalytic theory being investigated was that "the manifest pathology of adult schizophrenics is viewed as an expression of 'symbiotic-like' wishes and the defenses against these wishes" (Silverman et al., 1984, p. 118).

I have read seven of these studies. Basically, the design remained the same as to baseline assessments, critical stimulus at 4ms and critical assessment, although with the passing of years they have all become more sophisticated. The Silverman (Silverman et al., 1975) study of forty schizophrenics showed significant improvement on all seven dependent variables from pre to post measurements for all subjects, and yet only one half of these subjects had received the symbiotic stimulus while the other half had received the control. One of the problems I saw in this study was the choice of dependent variables. Ward Behavior Pathology was assessed by the head nurse on a 30-

item inventory which assessed maladaptive behavior. I have trouble with a single observer. Second, a head nurse might not always be objective and reports might really come from a daily log book. Also, as this experiment ran for days, there are numerous experiences in the other twenty-three hours per day which might equally affect behavior. The Interview Pathology Assessment was administered by an advanced clinical trainee (also a single observer) for a twenty-minute interview. The other dependent variables seemed more definitive.

This study was run over a six-week period and the stimulus was applied three times weekly. The subjets received either the *Mommy and I Are One* or *People Are Walking*. The latter is considered to be a neutral stimulus. Although there was significant improvement for all patients, the experimental stimulus effects were not significant, although they showed a trend toward significance. The data was interpreted as "provides further support for the theoretical proposition that activating symbiotic fantasies in 'differentiated' schizophrenics can reduce psychopathology" (Silverman et al., 1975, p. 388).

Another study using a neutral control, *Mommy and I Are One* and *Mommy and I Are Two*, produced significant effects for reducing pathological behavior on the Nonverbal Assessment Scale but not on the thought processing scale (Mendelsohn, 1981). The stimulus that improved functioning significantly and to a more powerful degree was the *Mommy and I Are Two* stimulus. This effect was explained as the idea of separateness in the "two" stimulus gratified the schizophrenics' need for symbiotic gratification yet protected the fragile self against threat of merging. This same explanation was offered in an investigation (Kaye, 1975; cited in Mendelsohn, 1981) of the stimulus *My Girl and I Are One*. This also proved to be more powerful in ameliorating pathological symptoms. The reason is again that while this stimulus activates the symbiotic fantasy it also protects the schizophrenic from loss of differentiation. Jackson (1983) refers to a study (Cohen, 1977) investigating effects of *Mommy and I Are One*, *Daddy and I Are One*, and *Girlfriend and I Are One* on female schizophrenics. The results showed both "Daddy" and "Girlfriend" reduced pathology to a degree that approached significance whereas the Mommy and I stimulus did not. This was viewed as support for the oneness fantasy theory on the basis of Lidz' (1973) observation that fathers of schizophrenic daughters often form symbiotic relationships with the afflicted child in infancy.

The specificity of oneness was investigated (Kaplan et al., 1985) in a population of 128 hospitalized schizophrenic men. This study utilized neutral stimulus and control stimulus, *Mommy and I Are One*, *Mommy Is Always with Me*, *Mommy Feeds Me Well*, and *I Cannot Hurt Mommy*. The design, as with most studies, showed a neutral stimulus, took a baseline assessment, showed a critical stimulus and then a critical assessment. The differences between the experimental and control stimulus were then measured on the assessment scales. Results showed significantly less pathological thinking, a trend toward less pathological nonverbal behavior, and significantly greater self-esteem. There was no significant finding on the other stimulus. These findings "clearly support the view of those psychoanalytic clinicians who maintain that it is specifically symbiotic experiences that can be ameliorative to schizophrenics" (Kaplan et al., 1985, p. 665).

This is just a sampling of approximately fifty studies. The problems which come to mind after reading these and reading others are listed below.

Drugs: Nowhere in the literature has the vision of these schizophrenics been checked nor has the 4ms timing of the tachistoscope been adjusted for individual differences. The fact that masking has not been utilized questions this 4ms time (Bornstein & Masling, 1984). I wonder about the effects of neuroleptic drugs on vision. Chlorpromazine had anticholinergic activity and anticholinergics can produce blurred vision (Merck Manual). Yet neither the type nor amount of medication has been controlled in these studies.

Populations: There is a wide grouping of schizophrenic subtypes in these studies, some paranoid, some undifferentiated, and perhaps some acute. I wonder if all would process the stimulus, experimental as well as neutral and control, in the same manner. Imagine a paranoid schizophrenic sitting down in front of a machine which he has been told will show him flickers of light which may help him relax. I would think he would view this machine as a very suspicious apparatus and would become more guarded and rigid. He is then administered the neutral baseline stimulus of *Men Looking, People Talking,* or *Boys Are Standing*. Regardless of whether this information is processed consciously or too rapid for awareness, I believe that any of these messages would be extremely threatening. The initial baseline assessment for the pathological thinking and nonverbal behavior could actually include an escalation of symptomology as a result of this "neutral" stimulus. The experimental stimulus of *Mommy and I Are One* and the ensuing critical assessmnent could then really indicate a return to normal pathology. I found this question partially addressed in one study (Litwack, 1979) and in one paper (Giovacchini, 1984).

Dependent Variables: The Nonverbal Pathology Rating Scale was designed by Silverman and assesses the patient's behavior while he is responding to the cognition test. Many of the behaviors listed in this scale are questionable as being specifically pathological (Porterfield 1985, Tebes 1981; cited in Werman's 1984 paper). I attach a copy of this scale. I agree that it does indicate anxiety, but the results of this are supporting a psychoanalytic theory specifically for the etiology of schizophrenia. I also attach a copy of the Story Recall Task measuring thought pathology. This scale has also been used extensively in the schizophrenic studies and was designed by Silverman.

Controls: I would feel that the specificity of ameliorative effects of the oneness fantasy as it applies to a schizophrenic population and then lends support to a psychoanalytic theory of the population would have to be tested against the saame stimulus effect in a "normal" person. Results of so many of these studies are neither consistent nor predictive. Sometimes behavior is improved, sometimes cognition is improved, sometimes a trend is shown, yet all are interpreted as support for this theory.

These same stimuli do not affect behavior or cognition if presented supraliminally. The explanation for this is that as it is not in conscious awareness the defenses of the person are not raised to ward off the threat of merging or conflict of such a symbiotic desire. Previous to the start of all these experiments a differentiation task (Adpectine Rating Scale) is administered to assess the degree of differentiation of the patient from his mother. In other words, are his self-boundaries stable and strong enough not to be severely threatened by such a merging? This variable has been found (Silverman et al., 1982, p. 75) to affect the behavior and cognition scores. The less differentiated subjects actually show increased pathology whereas the more differentiated subjects show ameliorative effects. All of the studies done since this realization have been done on relatively differentiated schizophrenics. Yet Mendelsohn (1981) indicated that these differentiation scores change and decrease after exposure to the oneness stimulus. How then can six weeks of exposure be beneficial only to differentiated subjects?

Statistics: Silverman has been criticized (Allen & Condon 1982; Porterfield 1985) for using one-tailed *t* tests rather than the more robust Anovas. Porterfield's (1985) study using Anovas did not find results. None of the papers that I read used one-tailed *t* tests as stated in Allen & Condon (1982), but many did utilize a 2-tailed *t* test.

Experiences: One study utilized a Family Relationship Interview and Picture (Jackson, 1983) to help interpret data. It found that the male schizophrenics who reported one parent as active and involved in the family, the more likely he was to reduce pathology to the stimulus involving that parent. This was the study utilizing the Daddy and Mommy stimuli. We now have added specificity as to real experiences or perceived experiences lending weight to the effect of oneness fantasies. The Family Picture Test in this same study supported this observation. These correlations did not appear for the female schizophrenic.

Defenses: Conscious reactions to these stimuli were assessed as to the strength of defenses (Litwack, 1979). They were divided into nondefended responses in which the subject recognized and verbalized the content of the message. The other group was composed of subjects who viewed the message defensively, either avoiding or denying the overt content. It was indicated that the people who described the messages without defensiveness showed a pathological reaction to the subliminal stimuli where the opposite was true for the defensive group. This study had assessed the effect of the stimulus *I Am Losing Mommy*. Regardless of the stimulus, it now seems that defenses play a part in responses.

"The authors have specifically related the poststimulus behavior of their subjects to the activation of unconscious fantasies of oneness. But such an assumption can only be made appropriately when the investigator is cognizant of all the significant variables, dependent and independent, related to his experiment. This does not, I believe, hold true for the work cited by the authors" (Vernon, 1983, p.182). On the basis of the reading I have done and the tables and charts I studied, I do not feel that strong support for SPA (subliminal psychodynamic activation) effects on behavior or thought process is evidenced in these studies. Yet, do these stimuli affect behavior to any degree? I am not convinced in either the oneness or the aggression studies with schizophrenics, yet other groups of studies have recently been conducted that seem to provide stronger support.

Effects of SPA have been assessed on depressed hospitalized and noninstitutionalized females. These results are even less consistent than the schizophrenic studies. One study (Nissenfeld, 1979) showed significant reduction in pathology after the oneness Mommy stimulus. This was followed by a failure to replicate these findings (Oliver and Burkham 1982; Dauber 1984). In the latter study the control stimulus decreased scores of depression on the Beck scale more than did the oneness stimulus. In a second part of the Dauber (1984) study the stimulus *Mommy and I Are Two* was weakly supported as being effective in reducing depression. There have not to date been any studies on the effects of SPA on depressed men.

In his book *The Search for Oneness*, Silverman refers to a study (Silverman et al., 1974) in which the oneness fantasy along with desensitization was used in helping bug-phobic women overcome their fear of insects. After four sessions utilizing these two therapies, he reports the experimental group receiving the oneness stimulus showed more improvement on the ability to make contact with the insects and on an anxiety observer scale. A later study (Condon & Allen, 1980) disputes these findings on the basis of statistics used and anxiety scores being rated by one observer. They repeated the study with a tighter control and found that the subjects in all conditions manifested significant improvement on all variables such as bug approach and anxiety. There were no differential effects found for the experimental oneness stimuli compared to the control stimuli.

Effects of oneness fantasy seemed more convincing when applied to a population of smokers attempting to break the habit. These people volunteered for the experiment through a newspaper ad and were randomly assigned to either *Mommy and I Are One* stimulus or control *People Are Walking*. In addition to the stimulus all subjects were to receive another group-oriented behavior therapy program (Palmatier, 1980). Subjects were randomly assigned to groups and met twelve times over an eighteen-day period for one hour. The dependent variables were abstinence rates as reported by phone at four weeks and at 12 weeks. These self-reports were independently verified by someone familiar with the smoker (70 percent of the cases were verified). There appeared a significant ($p = .01$) difference between the two groups at four weeks, with the experimental group showing 67 percent still abstinent as opposed to 12.5 percent for the control group. At twelve weeks the differences were no longer significant. The problems with the study in my mind would be the self-report aspect and the failure to match groups for amount smoked and length of habit. Does the oneness fantasy affect behavior? In this study, it seems to have an effect on motivated people, yet I do not see an attempt at replication.

The most interesting study and in my opinion the strongest support for the positive effects of oneness fantasies affecting behavior comes from a study done in Israel (Ariam & Siller, 1982). The *Mommy and I Are One* stimulus was translated into two Hebrew translations "as being the most similar in emotional meaning to the original English phrase" (Ariam & Siller, 1982, p. 345). *Teacher and I Are One* was added to the study as was *People Are Walking in the Street* as the control. In the Street was added to the control for the length of the message after translation into Hebrew.

These stimulus were given to 72 normal Hebrew-speaking 10th-grade students. These students were divided into four groups, each receiving the assigned subliminal stimulus four times a week over a period of six weeks. The students were matched for sex, mathematics class, and previous math grades. Improvement in math was the dependent variable and measured by the final math exam. A one-way Anova shows a significant treatment effect and a significant effect of improvement in math scores for both the *Mommy and I Are One* stimuli as compared with the control group or *Teacher and I Are One*. As two other math tests administered within the six-week period did not reflect this significant difference, it has been proposed that "sufficient time or exposure or both are needed in order to permit the *Mommy and I Are One* effect to take place" (Ariam & Siller, 1982, p. 347). The children were reported to be highly invested in this program and most appeared for debriefing. Again, I wonder if motivation is a variable to be considered in assessing effects of subliminal activation.

A similar study was conducted at a boarding school for emotionally disturbed adolescents in the U.S. (Bryant-Tuckett & Silverman, 1984). Dependent variables were the California Reading Achievement Test, arithmetic achievement, self-concept, homework assignments completed, independent classroom functioning, and self-imposed limits on T. V. and report card grades. These adolescents were exposed to the stimulus or control five times a week for six weeks. Students were matched for I. Q. and age. Behavior variables mentioned above were recorded by teachers and counselors blind to the study. A 2-way Anova revealed significant differences after the six weeks on all variables except reading grade on report card. The failure of this variable to reflect significance was explained as the grades on the report cards encompassed six weeks time prior to the beginning of the study as well as the six weeks of the study. Therefore any improvement was hidden by previous grades.

It would seem that these studies do offer support as to the enhancing effect of the oneness stimulus. The latter study indicates increased adaptive behavior throughout the experiment as expressed in teacher reports of homework completion and time spent working independently, whereas the Ariam-Siller report indicates significant improvement only after the completion of six weeks. The Ariam-Siller study only assessed math exam scores whereas the Bryant-Tuckett study also assessed behavior variables. Perhaps slight behavior improvements throughout the six-week period finally became evident in the math final grade.

On the basis of this suggested effectiveness I can imagine an interesting scenario—Don't forget your lunch, did you take your daily vitamins and SPA!

Despite the controversies in print covering problems with design, statistics, or hypothesis as to psychodynamic explanations, I am still left with a fairly consistent trend, in the direction of a significant p value for the oneness stimulus being ameliorative regardless of population being tested. It seems something is affecting behavior. Perhaps an extraneous variable not controlled for or perhaps it is a universal phenomenon of Mahler's symbiotic phase. Back to the original question—Can subliminal stimulus affect behavior? Silverman (1982, p. 145) refers to strong support on the basis of the effect of a neutral stimulus. The Litwack (1979) study shows a correlation between conscious perceptions and effects of subliminal activation of fantasies on behavior.

In conclusion I do not feel convinced of SPA efficacy in supporting psychoanalytic theory in the etiology of schizophrenia. I am not convinced as to the effects of libidinal conflicts being activated in the dart throwing studies (not covered in this paper). Silverman himself (Silverman et al., 1975, p. 389) states his caution in viewing SPA as a therapeutic treatment. "Yet I cannot say that there is nothing working here but confounding variables. However, to ascribe to symbiotic processes, fusion states, or oneness fantasies a central dominant position explaining complex structural defects and characterological processes as well as making them responsible for therapeutic change, including resolution of the effects of infantile trauma and the acquisition of psychic structure, strikes me as unidimensionally oriented and oversimplified" (Giovacchini, 1984, p. 158). For me, the question must remain open pending more consistent findings.

References

Allen, G. & Condon, T. (1982). Whither subliminal psychodynamic activation? A reply to Silverman. *Journal of Abnormal Psychology, 91,* 131–133.

Ariam, S. & Siller, J. (1982). Effects of subliminal oneness stimuli in Hebrew in academic performance of Israeli high school students: Further evidence on the adaptation enhancing effects of symbiotic fantasies in another culture using another language. *Journal of Abnormal Psychology, 91*, 343–349.

Bornstein, R. & Masling, J. (1984). Subliminal psychodynamic stimulation: Implications for psychoanalytic theory and therapy. *International Forum for Psychoanalysis, 1*, 187–204.

Bryant-Tuckett, R. A. & Silverman, L. (1984). Effects of subliminal stimulation of symbiotic fantasies on academic performance of emotionally handicapped students. *Journal of Counseling Psychology, 31*, 295–305.

Cohen, R. (1977). The effects of four subliminally introduced merging stimuli on the psychopathology of schizophrenic women. Unpublished doctoral dissertation. Columbia University.

Condon, T. & Allen, G. (1980). Role of psychoanalytic merging fantasies in systematic desensitization: A rigorous methodological examination. *Journal of Abnormal Psychology, 89*, 437–443.

Dauber, R. (1984). Subliminal psychodynamic activation in depression: On role of autonomy issues in depressed college women. *Journal of Abnormal Psychology, 93*, 9–18.

Giovacchini, P. (1984). The quest for dependent autonomy. *International Forum for Psychoanalysis, 1*, 153–166.

Jackson, J. (1983). Effects of subliminal stimulation of oneness fantasies on manifest pathology in male vs. female schizophrenics. *Journal of Nervous and Mental Disease, 171*, 280–289.

Kaplan, R., Thornton, P. & Silverman, L. (1985). Further data on the effects of subliminal symbiotic stimulation on schizophrenics. *Journal of Nervous and Mental Diseases, 173*, 658–666.

Kaye, M. (1975). The therapeutic value of three merging stimuli for male schizophrenics. Unpublished doctoral dissertation. Yeshiva University.

Klein, D. (1982). Relationship between current diagnostic criteria for schizophrenia and the dimensions of premorbid adjustment, paranoid symptomology and chronicity. *Journal of Abnormal Psychology, 91*, 319–325.

Lidz, T. (1973). *The origin and treatment of schizophrenic disorders.* New York: Basic Books.

Litwack, T. (1979). Fear of object loss, responsiveness to subliminal stimuli and schizophrenic personality. *Journal of Nervous and Mental Disease, 167*, 79–90.

Mendelsohn, E. (1981). The effects of stimulating symbiotic fantasies on manifest pathology in schizophrenics. A revised formulation. *The Journal of Nervous and Mental Disease, 169*, 580–590.

Nissenfeld, S. (1979). The effects of four types of subliminal stimuli on female depressives. Unpublished doctoral dissertation. Yeshiva University.

Oliver, J. & Burkham, R. (1985). Comments on three recent psychodynamic activation investigations: Reply to Silverman. *Journal of Abnormal Psychology, 94*, 644.

Oliver, J. & Burkham, R. (1982). Subliminal psychodynamic activation in depression: A failure to replicate. *Journal of Abnormal Psychology, 9*, 337–342.

Palmatier, J. (1980). Effects of subliminal stimulation of symbiotic merging fantasies on behavior treatment of smokers. *Journal of Nervous and Mental Disease, 168*, 715–720.

Porterfield, A. (1985). Failure to find an effect of subliminal psychodynamic activa-

tion upon cognitative measures of pathology in schizophrenia. *Journal of Abnormal Psychology,* 94 (4): 630–639.
Silverman, L. (1984). Unconscious oneness fantasies: Experimental findings and implications for treatment. *International Forum for Psychoanalysis, 1,* 107–152.
Silverman, L. (1976). Psychoanalytic theory: The reports of my death are greatly exaggerated. *American Psychologist, 31,* 621–637.
Silverman, L., Lachman, F. & Milich, R. (1982). *The search for oneness.* New York: International Universities Press, Inc.
Silverman, L., Levinsen, P., Mendelsohn, E., Ungaro, R., & Bronstein, A. (1975). A clinical application of subliminal psychodynamic activation. *Journal of Nervous and Mental Disease, 161,* 379–392.
Tebes, J. (1981). Subliminal psychodynamic activation: A critical review and analysis. Unpublished manuscript. State University of New York, Buffalo.
Werman, D. (1984). Psychological research, its pitfalls and the wish for natural science rigor. *International Forum for Psychoanalysis, 1,* 181–186.

■ UNDERSTANDING WRITING STRATEGIES

1. What is subliminal psychodynamic activation? Why has it been an important area of investigation?

2. What was Silverman's hypothesis?

3. How were the experiments designed to test Silverman's hypothesis?

4. What is the relationship between Silverman's and later work with schizophrenics?

5. How does di Carlo order the studies she reviews?

6. Explain the difference between the cues "Cannibal eats person" and "Mommy and I are one." How would each affect behavior? What reasons does di Carlo give from her studies for this?

7. What problems does di Carlo find with these studies? How does she evolve her criteria for evaluation?

8. On what grounds do Silverman's colleagues criticize his work?

9. What are di Carlo's conclusions? How well does she account for all the evidence she has presented?

10. What kind of knowledge does di Carlo assume her audience to have? What does she give you to clarify her topic? What did you need beyond di Carlo's assistance? ■

■ SUGGESTIONS FOR WRITING

Using a dictionary of psychological terms, a general introduction to Sigmund Freud's work, or Freud's own short book, *An Outline of Psychoanaly-*

sis (widely available), come to terms with Freud's ideas of the unconscious, relationships between mother and children, the causes of mental illness, and love and aggression.

Write a paper explaining why, based on Freud's theories, any of the cues di Carlo discusses would affect behavior. You might, for example, explain the differences between "Mommy and I are one" and " Teacher and I are one" or between "Mommy and I are one" and "Mommy and I are two." You might also critique the assumptions and designs of the studies that use these cues.　■

"Catherine"

Nancy Dyer

In a social work practice course, Nancy Dyer worked as part of a team of mental health experts. Here she met Catherine, studied her case history, and monitored her treatment. This essay documents the practicum's experiences by describing Catherine, presenting relevant theoretical studies, recommending treatment, and evaluating Catherine's progress.

IDENTIFYING DATA

Patient Name: Catherine　　Date of birth: 4/30/55
Residence: Westchester　　Marital status: single　　Religion: Catholic

PRESENTING PROBLEM

In Catherine's words: "I need to deal with my impulses." This is Catherine's fourth psychiatric hospitalization. She has suffered from anorexia, bulimia, and alcoholism. Although she reports never having acted on her feelings, she does state that she has experienced recurrent suicidal ideation for approximately ten years.

HISTORY OF PROBLEM

Catherine feels her difficulties began about the age of 13, which was the year that her parents divorced. She experienced anorexia symptoms and behaviors and lost 30 pounds over a three-month period following the divorce, leaving her 20 pounds underweight. She describes the next seven years as ones characterized by binge drinking, although she does not recall specifically how or why she began abusing alcohol. She describes a binge as "getting drunk to the point of blacking out every couple of weeks." Catherine attended college and developed a relationship with a man to whom she became engaged. At age 20, she broke off her engagement but is vague about the reason other than she was not sure if she was ready for marriage. Catherine then continued to binge, alternating between food and alcohol, for the next ten years. In the past three years, she has been hospitalized three times for increasing suicidal ideation, bulimia, and alcohol rehabilitation. Over the past three years she has been involved in Alcoholics Anonymous, Overeaters Anonymous, and individual psychotherapy.

Four months before admission to New York Hospital, her therapist went on vacation. Catherine lost 40 pounds in the six weeks during and after the vacation and then binged to a point of gaining 25 pounds. This approximate cycle went on for two months. Catherine experienced several crises one month before her admission to New York Hospital: her O.A. sponsor dropped her, her A.A. sponsor left the area, and an employer she admired quit his job. She reports that she soon found herself spending $50–75 per day on food and vomiting eight to ten times per day. Catherine and her therapist agreed that she needed hospitalization to control her behavior and increasing suicidal ideation.

FAMILY AND PERSONAL HISTORY

Catherine is the fifth of six children and is described by her parents as having been a "model child. " Her younger sister, often referred to in the family as her "twin," is 13 months younger. Her mother is Baptist and a teacher, and her father is Catholic and a retired dentist. There appears to be a history of depression and alcohol abuse in the family with references to Catherine's father and maternal aunt. Catherine describes her father as both affectionate and tyrannical and her mother as cold and submissive. She has felt a need to be protective of her father and tried to please him. Her father, however, has been critical of Catherine and of any expression of emotion. Although Catherine has felt quite connected to her father, he states he has never felt particularly close to her. Her mother has spoken of a suspicion of sexual abuse between the father and Catherine but is reluctant to elaborate. Of note was Catherine's upset over her parent's divorce while the other siblings all felt that it was for the best.

Catherine describes herself as having experienced various "mood swings" throughout her life that can last "months, weeks, or hours." When she is feeling "up," she channels her energy into vocational and academic activities or into a rigid exercise program. She has felt during these times that she is able to "help the world." However, she also finds herself feeling very alone during these periods. When she is feeling "down," she experiences depressive episodes and drops out of any activity or relationship in which she is involved. Her binging increases, and she feels more paranoid and suicidal.

Catherine describes a history of many intense but brief relationships that are broken off when they feel "too close." She has no long-term friendships. Her sexual history includes heterosexual and homosexual experiences and a brief period of prostitution. She now considers herself bisexual. In the past ten years she has had 30 different jobs and lived in 20 different places. Catherine says that she leaves jobs when feeling frustrated or "stifled." She has been involved in dozens of self-help, religious, and political groups including transactional analysis, Buddhism, and Greenpeace. She tends to rise to the top of these organizations and then drop out.

ASSESSMENT

An assessment of Catherine and the difficulties that brought her into the hospital has been a challenging undertaking. While she initially stated that her reason for coming to the hospital was to control her impulses around eating and alcohol abuse, those behaviors did seem to be under better control through structured management and routines. Catherine also spoke with what appeared to be a good deal of insight and understanding about the difficulties she had had in the past and the feelings she had experienced around various events. But if there was so much understanding, what brought her to a long-term unit? Catherine connected with many issues on an intellectual level but the emotional connection and expression seemed to be absent (Goldstein, 1984). As I spoke more with Catherine and the treatment team, it became clearer that her treatment would include not only the control and understanding of her impulsive behaviors but also the exploration of her sense of identity, her relationships, and her feelings.

After a six-week evaluation period, Catherine had a case conference in order to more formally discuss and decide on several questions such as diagnosis and treatment plan. As Catherine met the criteria for borderline personality organization, we could more clearly begin to explore the development of her difficulties and the treatment methods that could be utilized.

Otto Kernberg, Margaret Mahler, and James Masterson provide several theories that can be considered while developmental processes are assessed for borderline patients. Kernberg (Goldstein, 1984) points to identity diffusion, where the child is unable to integrate good and bad self- and object-representations during the developmental stage of approximately 4 to 12 months of age. The individual becomes fixated, primitive defenses like splitting dominate, and other ego functions like control of drives and aggression are impaired.

Mahler (Goldstein, 1984) emphasizes that difficulties arise in the rapprochement subphase (approximate age, 15 to 22 months) of the separation-individualization process. This is a conflicted period for the child who wants to both assert his autonomy and maintain the mother's emotional support. A mother's failure to support as well as separate prevents the child from internalizing a solid sense of self, object relatedness, and other ego functions.

Masterson (1980) suggests that the lack of support from the mother for separation during the rapprochement phase leads to an experience of abandonment depression which re-emerges throughout the individual's life. Mastery and autonomy are associated with rage, emptiness, rejection, passivity, and guilt. Maladaptive coping mechanisms are developed to deal with these feelings (Goldstein, 1984) rather than healthier ego functions.

The above mentioned theories provide a framework for examining the development and recurrence of Catherine's difficulties. Her younger sister was born at a time when Catherine may have been deprived of the attention she needed from her mother during her attempts at separation and autonomy; she may have been "forgotten" by her mother or treated in the same way as the newborn infant. The issue of separation and abandonment comes up again during the "second" separation phase at adolescence; at age 13 Catherine's parents divorced and Catherine was the family member most affected. In addition, the events that led up to her current hospitalization revolved around the losses of several important supports. Catherine's way of coping, drinking and binge/vomiting (both oral gratifications), have been self-destructive, although she has utilized various organizations to help her control these behaviors.

Interpersonally, Catherine's life has been conflicted and empty. She seems to have gotten "double messages" from her father about the expression of feelings and describes her relationship with her mother as one of deprivation or, at least, resentment. Perhaps the need to protect her father came from a measure of identification with him. Currently, she states that she has "given up" on having any kind of relationship with her father and has grown closer to her mother over the past few years. Her growing neediness on the unit could be an explanation of her desire for, as well as disappointment in, her mother's nurturance.

Catherine describes her relationships as ones that become intense quickly but then ultimately end in frustration. Similarly, she gets very involved in various organizations, rises to leadership positions, and then drops out. She seems to want to "belong" immediately with little tolerance for frustration and, eventually, with disappointment.

Catherine's use of community organizations and groups has been both adaptive and maladaptive. She has utilized Alcoholics Anonymous, Overeaters Anonymous, political organizations, and been active most recently in the Catholic church. While these groups have provided structures for certain behaviors, they may also be external controls that keep Catherine from the experience and expression of feelings. She has also expressed somewhat delusional thoughts about "saving the world" when involved in political and religious organizations. On the unit, she was elected to the patient government within a few weeks, while most patients are not involved until six to eight months into their treatment. Belonging to groups and organizations may also provide Catherine with a clearer sense of identity or role. Roles are often equated with status (Hollis and Woods, 1981) and Catherine's self-esteem could have been connected to her roles as helper, protector, or leader.

Catherine also appears to feel conflicted about the sexuality. Feelings about herself as a woman, discomfort with her body, and perhaps, fear about herself sexually may be expressed through her bulimia and anorexia which alters and does damage to the body. There may also be confusion about her sexual identity as suggested in her current feeling of being bisexual. In addition, she states that her parents assume she is heterosexual and that she does not discuss sexual issues with them.

An assessment of Catherine is complicated. However, as I think about her treatment, I have kept in mind several main issues: (1) the lack of a clear sense of identity, (2) fears around separation and abandonment, (3) a difficulty with the expression of feelings through words rather than action, (4) intense feelings of dependency, and (5) the depth of her emptiness that has not been filled through relationships, jobs, etc.

INTERVENTIVE PLAN

Our treatment plan for Catherine included short- and long-term goals. These goals were developed in cooperation with Catherine, and although she agreed with all of the individual goals themselves, she felt anxious about how these goals would be met. Our interdisciplinary treatment team recommended that Catherine stay on the unit for approximately one year.

Long-term Goals

1. Establish and maintain independent functioning.
2. Eliminate self-destructive behavior such as anorexia, bulimia, and alcohol abuse.
3. Develop long-term peer relationships.
4. Develop vocational and avocational interests.
5. Develop more satisfying family relationships.
6. Develop discharge plans: living arrangements, geography, job.

Short-term Goals

1. Control and explore eating disorders.
2. Control and explore alcoholism.
3. Explore nature of and difficulties with interpersonal relationships.
4. Explore suicidal ideation.
5. Evaluate use of external structures as defensive versus adaptive.

6. Evaluate extent and/or direction of family work.
7. Encourage verbalization of feelings; i.e., anger, depression.
8. Evaluate for recreational and vocational activities.

While the number of goals developed with Catherine may seem extensive, it has been important to spell the issues out clearly in order to provide her with direction and structure in a treatment that may last a year or more. The goals are flexible but are underlined with the more general goals of facilitating Catherine's coping with the demands of her self, significant others, and environment (Pinkus & Mishne, 1982).

These goals will be addressed in a variety of settings including individual psychotherapy, group therapy, therapeutic activities, family therapy, and in the milieu. Some issues will be addressed through verbalization and discussion and others will be addressed more behaviorally with management plans.

Example

Before coming to New York Hospital, Catherine had been controlling her bulimia with "food commitments" as required by O. A. In a very ritualistic way, she would recite what types of food she would eat during the day. She felt that this then freed her from thinking about food and/or bingeing. The staff asked her not to commit her food but to instead work with the dietician around a reasonable diet and to talk with staff when she felt urges to binge and/or vomit.

C- Nancy, can I talk to you for a minute?
N- Sure, what's going on?
C- I feel like I could just go into the dining room and eat everything in sight.
N- Did this come up out of the blue or did something happen?
C- Well, Cathleen just pulled off one of her usual numbers and forgot to pick me up from session. When I asked her what happened she made it sound like it was my fault she forgot.
N- You really seem angry. Did you tell her how you were feeling?
C- Not really. She doesn't like me and I know if I say anything she'll just blast me.
N- It sounds like you sat on your feelings and now you feel an urge to binge. Is that the connection?
C- I think so. I know I should talk to Cathleen but my gut reaction is to go eat.
N- Well, it looks like you're trying hard not to binge by talking to me and controlling your impulse. The next step might be to talk to Cathleen.
C- Yeah, I feel a bit better about the bingeing but I don't know about Cathleen.

N- Well, think about it and maybe we can talk more about it later.
C- Okay. Thanks a lot.

Anne Freed (1980) discusses several characteristics of interventions with borderlines that I utilized in the above interaction:

1. Empathy and acceptance of ambivalence.
2. Focusing on active rather than passive problem solving.
3. Support for controlling impulses.
4. Using my own ego functions in clarifying the situation.
5. Support for both of us cooperating with our contract—she agrees to come to staff when impulsive and we agree to be available to her.

The hospital generally is in agreement with the unit's policies and procedures around individual patient's treatments, and we act fairly autonomously. Administrative pressure is applied around issues like justifying the length of hospitalization, documentation, and concrete goals. However, discharge planning has become more complicated over the past year as it has been harder to find half-way houses for patients. The hospital has been reluctant to either establish new facilities or organize around finding alternatives in the community. In addition, the finance department has been lax about informing patients of insurance problems and has often forced individuals into crisis situations and potential premature discharge.

PATIENT/WORKER RELATIONSHIP

Both the patient and the worker bring a variety of values, orientations, behaviors, and feelings into the therapeutic relationship (Kadushin, 1983). The worker needs to be able to observe and explore these issues for herself and encourage open discussion of them if or when they emerge in treatment. Rather than resist or deny differences or similarities between worker and patient, the worker needs to be aware of how they can or should be introduced into treatment. For borderline patients this is especially important as so many of their coping mechanisms revolve around denial, projection, devaluation, and splitting.

Example

C- I'm feeling kind of nervous about visiting this weekend with my friend Susan.
N- What's making you nervous?
C- Well, Susan and I were lovers for awhile a couple of year ago. We're still friends but I felt kind of awkward about her meeting me here.
N- You were lovers? What was your relationship like?

Catherine then went on to describe their relationship in intimate detail. She took awhile to get back to her original concern, feeling awkward about seeing Susan while in the hospital. I had not done much to help her refocus on this issue.

In retrospect, I do not think I handled this interaction well and wonder what some of the reasons might be in terms of the sexual aspect of the discussion. Did I feel seduced, or was I the one encouraging her to focus on their relationship rather than on her original concern? Catherine may have been touching on questions about my own sexuality and rather than exploring that away from the specific interaction, I was perhaps using Catherine's time for my issue. Patients may not be coming to the hospital to deal with their sexual identity, and workers need to be clear about their own hidden agendas (Dulaney and Kelly, 1982).

I am also aware of the potential for conflict around the different values of the worker and client. I often get frustrated with the patients' high levels of dependency and extreme difficulty with taking responsibility for seemingly simple things. Although I am in the "helping services," I am also aware at times of my impatience with such persistent requests for help. This is at the core of borderline pathology, and I have found it helpful to discuss my feelings with my supervisors in order not to act out my frustration with a patient.

Transference and countertransference are reactions that a worker needs to be especially aware of in working with borderline patients. These reactions can be powerful tools either for the cultivation of pathology or the greater understanding of a patient's difficulties.

Example

> N- Catherine, it sounds like you're avoiding the extent of your own anger at people by saying you feel too intimidated by them to be open about your feelings.
>
> C- Yeah, I know. That's why I like talking with you, Nancy. You understand me so much better than anyone else.
>
> N- You've mentioned that to me quite a few times. What makes you feel that way?
>
> C- I don't know, you just do.
>
> N- I think it might be helpful at some point to really take a look at what our relationship brings up for you.

Catherine had been seeing me in a very idealized way over the previous few weeks; I could do no wrong and understood everything. Several staff members were finding Catherine difficult to reach while I was finding her easier to work with. Catherine and I later explored our relationship and how she was able to create a situation where she could feel supported by me and not have to deal with any less positive reactions or feelings. This was also a pattern that had occurred in several relationships before coming to the hospital. By openly looking at both our realistic and unrealistic reactions to each other as a reflection of her ways of relating to people (Reid, 1977), we used transference and countertransference as a therapeutic tool.

CRITIQUE

The accuracy of my assessment of Catherine has generally been supported by Catherine's own understanding of critical issues as well as through discussion with the entire treatment team. In several areas she has presented some typical borderline traits such as unstable relationships, self-destructive behavior, suicidal ideation, identity disturbance, and unstable mood. However, I have also wondered about my lack of a strong reaction to her either positively or negatively. This may be a reflection of her emptiness, or it may be attributed to my own issues, but I am curious about that missing intensity of reaction that I usually experience with the borderline patients I work closely with.

I also think that a complete assessment of her relationships with her siblings, especially her "twin" sister, could be beneficial. Although I do not work directly with the family in session, I do have contact with them in a multi-family support group and that might be a forum to observe or discuss family relationships.

I have also become more aware of Catherine's fragility as her treatment has progressed. After originally presenting a rather "put together" image of herself, the gradual removal of some of her internal and external defenses has uncovered a tremendous amount of fear and confusion. She has recently been experiencing what she calls "panic attacks" that appear to have no specific cause and bring on hyperventilation, tears, and anxiety. Catherine seems frightened and somewhat paranoid at these times, although she does seek out staff contact. She states that she thinks it is a reaction to a build-up of the issues that she is facing. Catherine has been very needy over the past month, almost to the point where it feels like she is asking for staff for any reason she can find.

It is hard to judge whether our treatment plan and goals are appropriate since we are working within a long-term framework, but both Catherine and the staff feel that important issues are emerging. It has been difficult for Catherine, and she has been open about questioning just how much she really wants to change if it means giving up feelings and behaviors that are familiar. There are several different modalities being used in working toward her goals. With so many different people involved, it has been critical for us to communicate regularly and openly about Catherine's work and our reactions to her. This has helped her pull together a more complete picture of herself and her relationships.

In addition to some of the things already mentioned, I think I would have addressed her perceptions about the different key people involved in her treatment at an earlier point. There may have been something gratifying in knowing that she saw me in such an idealized way that kept me from confronting it. While I may have been appropriately fostering a connection, I may also have been making it more difficult to explore her relationships in the long run.

The next few steps with Catherine may include trying to understand what these panic attacks are about. We may need to be focusing more specifically on what issues she feels are building up and on an alternative way for expressing herself. Related to this could be her recent desire for more staff contact. This could be an adaptive coping mechanism or an avoidance of personal responsibility. There also seems to be a question about how much she is using her peers for support and contact. She sees herself as a "caretaker" in the community and may be having difficulty revealing this other side of herself. We need to think about how much support and how much confrontation Catherine needs right now.

Working with Catherine has been challenging and educational. While her problems are severe, I feel she is motivated toward changes and open to examining herself with help from staff and peers.

References

Dulaney, D. P., & Kelly, J. (1982, March). Improving services to gay and lesbian clients. *Social Work, 27* (2), 178–183.

Freed, A. O. (1980, November). The borderline personality. *Social Casework, 61,* 548–558.

Goldstein, E. G. (1984). *Ego psychology and social work practice.* New York: The Free Press.

Hollis, F., & Woods, M. E. (1981). *Casework: A psychosocial therapy* (3rd ed.). New York: Random House.

Kadushin, A. (1983). *The social work interview* (2nd ed.). New York: Columbia University Press.

Masterson, J. F. (1980). *From borderline adolescent to functioning adult: The test of time.* New York: Brunner and Mazel.

Pinkus, H., & Mishne, J. M. (1982, November). The missing system in social work's application of systems theory. *Social Casework,* 547–553.

Reid, K. E. (1977). Non-rational dynamics of the client-worker interaction. *Social Casework, 58,* 600–606.

■ UNDERSTANDING WRITING STRATEGIES

1. Sociology and psychology frequently use case histories both for practice studies and research studies. What characteristics would a good case history have?

2. What kinds of special knowledge shape the ways in which information is presented in case histories?

3. What organizing principles shape this case history?

4. What other elements compose this study?

5. Assessment requires grounds or "criteria." What grounds shape Dyer's assessment?

6. What evidence does she draw from the case study and relate to the terms of her assessment?

7. What is the relationship between Dyer and Catherine? How does Dyer evaluate this?

8. On what grounds does she critique their relationship?

9. This paper serves important purposes for the author and the course instructor. What are they? How might this paper serve a large community? ◼

■ **SUGGESTIONS FOR WRITING**

Eating disorders seriously afflict a significant number of young women in a society that admires thinness amidst tremendous commercial pressure to indulge. Catherine indicates a deeper dimension to this problem. Write a paper helping young women understand bulimia, using Catherine's experience and treatment as *part* of your evidence. ◼

The Realities of Fantasy
Robert Fleischman

Considering a mental health issue for his English composition class, Robert Fleischman argues that negative consequences of playing the popular game *Dungeons and Dragons* reside in the player's frame of mind rather than the game itself.

Steven was 16 and played Dungeons and Dragons. The longer he played, the more he seemed to change. The posters of Cheryl Ladd came down and were replaced by ones of demons. The occult seemed to dominate Steven's life. Then one day, Steven killed himself with carbon monoxide from the family car.

What could have brought this youth to commit suicide? Steven's sister accuses the fantasy game Dungeons and Dragons as the main catalyst for his demise. She claims that the game is "a door into the occult" and placed her brother's life in danger. The upset sibling then blames the game for her brother's disturbed thinking, instead of investigating whether he had emotional and mental problems before playing the game.

Other cases like this one have been documented over the past seven years. People played fantasy games, notably Dungeons and Dragons, and committed suicide. The distraught families make loose accusations that the game is the cause of all the problems and grief, without giving consideration that the game player may have problems of his own that were not easily seen.

Dungeons and Dragons, like many other fantasy games, is a game that relies mostly on imagination. Although the game has rules and requires the use of dice and recording statistics, imagination is what makes the game enjoyable to play. In the game, the player's character becomes an extension of himself, thus allowing him to do things possible only in the realm of the mind.

Currently, four million people play fantasy games with the majority of the players being adolescent males. There are 5,000 teenage suicides a year in this country; therefore, the coincidence of a teen who commits suicide and plays fantasy games is likely to happen.

From the fear of this coincidence, two organizations have risen to inform and protect the public from these games.

The National Coalition on Television Violence or NCTV has made attempts to have bans put on Dungeons and Dragons, but nothing has ever come of it. The bans were refused and a warning to be printed on the game was denied. Evidently, there isn't as large a threat posed to society as the organization seems to think.

Another group called Bothered About D&D or BADD has also tried to call attention to the game. Patricia Polling, its founder and president, had a 13-year-old son who she claims committed suicide because of the game. The boy was an avid player, but was also known to have personal and family problems. After this tragic incident, Mrs. Polling formed the group. This group has also tried to have legislation passed on the game, but to no avail.

After close examination of the deaths accused of being linked with Dungeons and Dragons, a striking coincidence is found. None of the deaths were actually confirmed as being caused by Dungeons and Dragons. The majority of deaths occurred after family arguments or arguments with friends. Surprisingly, the games are blamed instead of the families. Since 1979, 29 suicides were linked with Dungeons and Dragons but were found having nothing to do with the game after subsequent investigations.

According to Dieter Sturm, the spokesman for TSR, the maker of Dungeons and Dragons, "the overwhelming majority of kids who play Dungeons and Dragons after all do not commit suicide, which suggests that the ones who did may have been troubled in other ways." Evidently, there is a connection between mental stability and playing fantasy games.

Dungeons and Dragons has its more positive aspects. Dr. Joyce Brothers says that "the game is just a game as long as you have fun." Dungeons and Dragons can be used as a useful outlet for built-up tensions and emotions without using violence. As long as the game does not reach obsessive proportions, no problem exists.

Playing Dungeons and Dragons allows a person to leave the boundaries of reality. If a person is unstable emotionally, he could lose touch with everyday life. The game could then become necessary to keep the player's sanity in check. Other facets of the person's life might suffer. A lack of care for improvement may throw his lifestyle out of acceptable proportions. This lack may alarm families who blame the game for the deformation, when in fact the person is abusing the game instead of abusing something else, such as controlled substances. Emotionally unstable individuals should be warned not to let the game become an obsession. Excess in anything is not healthy.

However, for the majority of people who play, instability is not a problem and neither is the game. Just because a person reads Hansel and Gretel does not mean a person is going to throw someone in an oven. Likewise, playing Dungeons and Dragons does not make a person want to kill himself or another person.

The hysteria that has set in is a grave misjudgment made by many panic-stricken people grasping at straws as to why a member of their family would commit suicide. The families refuse to accept that something was wrong with the player and not the game.

Religion takes these misfortunes and uses them as an excuse to stop the occult. Many churches see the game tempting unwary people into satanism and witchcraft. The suicides have no evidence of being linked to the occult. The suicides were committed with guns, carbon monoxide, and hanging. There is no evidence of any satanic or occult methods of death.

The Association for Gifted-Creative Children encourages playing Dungeons and Dragons. The Association says that the game encourages the reading of Shakespeare, Tolkien, and Asimov, authors whose novels are supposed to improve a person's mind.

The evidence points to the fact that playing Dungeons and Dragons or any other fantasy game does not corrupt the player. In many cases, it may improve the player's mind and encourage intellectual growth. Playing the game provides a pleasant emotional outlet and actually lets a person forget reality for a short time. The only problems created by the game are the problems created by the players. Obsession can lead to disastrous results. While used in moderation, it can be fun and helpful.

■ UNDERSTANDING WRITING STRATEGIES

1. Fleischman examines logically flawed arguments here. What kinds of problems does he find?

2. What kind of evidence does he offer to rebut these arguments?

3. How do you assess the validity of this evidence?

4. What kind of strategy does Fleischman use in his introduction to engage

the reader? What kinds of commitments do this and the next few paragraphs make?

5. What background does Fleischman give about *Dungeons and Dragons*? What does this background suggest about his audience?

6. What does the conclusion accomplish? ∎

∎ SUGGESTIONS FOR WRITING

Television, film, rock music, pornography, and now fantasy games, receive blame for corrupting young people. Always the controversy is intense and the arguments emotional. Find two opposing articles in the popular press on one of these subjects and one article in a professional journal. Write an objective essay in which you explain the issues in the controversy, and evaluate the ways in which opponents construct their arguments and martial their biases. ∎

Gorbachev's Foreign Policy

Lisa Gentile

This research paper, written for a political science course, International Security and Arms Control, analyzes and evaluates Gorbachev and his role in Soviet foreign policy. Gentile draws upon Gorbachev's own writing as well as books and articles by political analysts and biographers.

Our talent, while imperfect, to foresee the future consequences of our present actions and to change our course approximately is a hallmark of the human species, and one of the chief reasons for our success over the past million years. Our future depends entirely on how quickly and how broadly we can refine this talent. We should plan for and cherish our fragile world as we do our children and our grandchildren: there will be no other place for them to live. It is nowhere ordained that we must remain in bondage to nuclear weapons.
(Sagan, 1985, p. 330)

At a time in history when the nuclear threat is so great that humans are forced into psychological denial, every possible avenue of security must be explored in order to ensure the survival of the human race and the planet. Until now arms control has done little to reduce that threat and to make the people of the world feel secure. A select group of individuals hold the reins in the arms control race. Superpower leaders are the key individuals who can make or break arms control progress.

Before speculating on the possibilities for the future, one must first become familiar with influential policy makers, foreign policy, and military doctrine. None of these is isolated from the others, and they must be viewed simultaneously in order for a clear picture of the current and future political situation to emerge. Today, Mikhail Gorbachev has become one of the principal characters in the international theater. In his role as a Soviet political leader, and most importantly, reformer, Gorbachev is in one of the most powerful positions of any human being on the earth. He is in the position to define for the world the future of arms control and to redefine perceptions on international security. In order to determine which way Gorbachev can and will affect the future of arms control, first, it is important to briefly review the past U.S.–Soviet arms control efforts. Then, one must get to know Mikhail Gorbachev, the person, the communist, the General Secretary, and the reformer. Furthermore, one must survey the domestic roots of Soviet foreign policy, Soviet military doctrine, and Gorbachev's foreign policy and "new political thinking." Last of all, one must determine whether Gorbachev has already accomplished or will initiate new ojectives in arms control, and then, if so, whether he can foresee any changes in Soviet military doctrine. This paper seeks to probe into the policies and positions of Mikhail Gorbachev and the implications for arms control.

A BRIEF SKETCH OF U.S.–SOVIET ARMS CONTROL EFFORTS

In the nuclear era, arms control has been one of the utmost concerns in foreign policy formulation, but few agreements have been made which are considered to be real or significant progress. Before World War II, the Rush Bagot Agreement of 1817 between the United States and Great Britain stood as the most successful and permanent of any international arms control agreements. Since World War II, the successes and failures of arms control negotiations can be placed in five distinct periods as outlined by Blacker et al. (1984, p. 94). In the year following World War II, the first period, the United States attempted but failed to control nuclear weapons. During the second period between 1946 and 1954, the continuing failure is described as "an era of largely ritualistic gestures, rhetorical battles, and arms buildups" (Blacker et al., 1984, p. 94). In the third period, the mid-50s, the two superpowers moved closer to a possible agreement on disarmament but failed again narrowly. In the fourth period from 1957–1968, the United States and the Soviet Union reached common ground and made serious efforts to constrain their nuclear competition, the Limited Test Ban Treaty of 1963 and the Nonproliferation Treaty of 1968 being the most notable achievements. During the last period from 1968 until the present, negotiators have focused their efforts on actual limitations on and reductions of strategic delivery systems. Because of detente in the late 1960s and early 1970s, the number of negotiations between the U.S. and U.S.S.R. have increased dramatically, and since then, there have been two SALT agreements, the Strategic Arms Reduction Talks, the Mutual and Balanced Force Reduction Talks, and the Intermediate Nuclear Forces Treaty. As displayed by this outline of arms control since World War II, it is evident that success has been very limited. In the cases when treaties have been signed and ratified, specific individuals have played a very pronounced role in the final outcomes, and without their input into decision-making, history would be written very differently. Major U.S. players in arms control have been presidents, like John F. Kennedy and Richard Nixon, political advisors like Zbignew Brzezinski, Henry Kissinger, and Paul Nitze, and lawmakers like Senator Henry Jackson.

Little is discussed of the primary Soviet actors in arms control. It has become increasingly clear that Mikhail Gorbachev's reforms have turned the tides in U.S.–Soviet relations. Without him, there may not have been an INF Treaty. Without his ascendancy to the office of General Secretary of the Communist Party, arms control may have taken a backseat to other matters on the foreign policy agendas of both the Soviet Union and the United States for the duration of the 1980s. Therefore, further inquiry into the man and his life may be useful.

MIKHAIL GORBACHEV—BACKGROUND

Mikhail Sergeyevich Gorbachev was born on March 2, 1931, in the agricultural village of Privolnoye (which means "free" in Russian) in southern Russia. The Stavropol region was the Russian equivalent of the American West. Before the Bolshevik Revolution, many peasant families who were freed by the Emancipation Act of 1861 immigrated to this area where they settled and became farmers. During the purges of the 1920s and 30s, these people were called "kulaks" which meant anyone who owned two cows or a nice house, and they were a major obstacle to the consolidation of Stalin's power. Born during Stalin's reign of terror in the region of Stavropol which was characterized by its large number of kulaks and "middle peasants," Gorbachev learned either first-hand or later through family members of the slaughter of many people of his region, including one of his own relatives.

"Little is known of the role of Gorbachev's grandparents in these great events . . . [but] it is almost certain . . . that the Gorbachevs supported the Bolsheviks. Not only was grandfather Andrei a party member, he also took a leading role on the government side in the collectivization of Soviet agriculture in the late 1920s and early 30s" (Morrison, 1988, p. 26). His father, Sergei Andreyevich, later became a young supporter of the regime. He served in the army during the war and later worked as an economist and party local official. His mother, Maria Panteleyvna, is now around 77 years old and still lives in Privolnoye. It is thought that Gorbachev is an only child since there is no knowledge of any siblings. "Although Russian peasant families are traditionally rather large, this does not apply to the late 1920s and 1930s. In these years of rural discontent, collectivization, terror and starvation, the rural birthrate declined sharply and infant mortality rate rose" (Medvedev, 1986, p. 22).

When Gorbachev was eleven years old, the Germans rolled into Stavropol and occupied the area through autumn and winter. These events left a great impression on the young Gorbachev as they did on most Russians who experienced the destruction of World War II. Later, when talking with a Western official, he remembered "being shocked to see the full extent of the damage done to the villages and town during the war." In the same conversation, he expressed some irritation that the United States and Canada had helped the Western European nations rebuild after the war but that the Soviet Union had had to do its own reconstruction . . ." (Butson, 1986, p. 29).

Gorbachev was part of the first generation of young Russian peasants to gain formal education. Life in the Gorbachev family was not easy, and they were very poor, even by the living standards in their area. "While he was attending high school, he spent his vacations working on a combine in the local grain fields. Sometimes the harvest ran late into the season, and it was bitterly cold on the primitive Soviet combines . . . and young Gorbachev had to wrap himself in straw to try to keep warm" (Butson, 1986, p. 29).

At the age of fourteen, he joined the Komsomol, the Youth Communist League. He was already beginning to display the talents which make him so widely respected and hailed as a great leader. Among his many talents, he demonstrated "an ability to make his points forcefully and articulately before an audience, an excellent memory for detail, a single-minded enthusiasm for tasks in hand and, by no means least, an ability to impress his superiors with his solicitude and evident loyalty to them" (Morrison, 1988, p. 43). His work for the Komsomol and on the collective facilitated his rise to prominence in the party bureaucracy. It was this combination plus his Stavropol background, rather than his academic record, which allowed his entrance into Moscow State University, the most prestigious and important center of higher education in the Soviet Union in 1950. Known for his diligence and persistence not his brilliance, Gorbachev knew he had to rid himself of his provincial, "country bumpkin" image. His choice to study law is puzzling to many who study his life, but most speculate that he decided early on about his personal, political ambitions. At the university, being aware of the importance of political connections, he organized and became the head of the Komsomol and is remembered as one who was "overly prone to giving speeches about duty to party and country" (Butson, 1986, p. 30). It was at Moscow University where Gorbachev made some of his most crucial connections, most notably that with his Czech roommate, Zdenek Mlynar. "If Gorbachev has become 'westernized' in his appearance, manners, dress and the image he projects of tolerance and cordial behaviour, all the small signs which mark him as different from the usual Komsomol and Party boss, it was probably Mlynar's doing. It was this mixture of cultured image and political orthodoxy which attracted his Party patrons like Suslov and Andropov and made them regard him as the epitome of the new style Party man which the country required" (Medvedev, 1986, p. 43).

Following Stalin's death in 1953, Gorbachev dramatically changed his position on Stalin and became very outspoken about him. He referred to the injustices inflicted upon the "middle peasants" during collectivization, mentioning his own relative who had been arrested at the time. He also began to recognize that Stalin had made mistakes in domestic policy, especially in agriculture. Some might question this abrupt change, but "in fact, the suddenness of Gorbachev's change of attitude toward Stalin was obviously more apparent than real. As Mlynar makes clear, in private conversations without mentioning Stalin's name, the young man from Stavropol had all along harbored plenty of reservations about Soviet life under the dictator" (Morrison, 1988, p. 77).

After graduating from law school in 1955 at age 24, Gorbachev returned reluctantly to his native region to be deputy chief of a department in the city Komsomol organization in Stavropol. He earned several promotions very quickly. By 1962, he was in a very serious post as a party organizer in agriculture, and after enrolling in evening classes, graduated with a diploma in agronomy in 1967. With the changing of the guard from Khrushchev to Brezhnev in 1964, Gorbachev's career advanced solidly and rapidly. By 1970, he was the first secretary of the Stravropol regional party and was emerging onto the national scene as a member of the nation's parliament. "From all accounts, Gorbachev was unusually popular during his term as party leader in the Stravropol region," mostly due to his innovative problem-solving techniques and his efforts to raise living standards (Butson, 1986, p. 38). Gorbachev may appear to have burst full-blown onto the world scene from out of nowhere, but there were glimpses of a new type of political leader in the making during his Stavropol years.

After the death of Fyodor Kulakov in 1978, Gorbachev's ties to the Suslov wing of the party became apparent because of his replacement of Kulakov as secretary of the Central Committee with special responsibility for agriculture. As opposed to Nikolai Tikhonov and Konstantin Chernenko, Mikhail Suslov's camp consisting of Gorbachev and his friend, Yuri Andropov, was not in full support of Brezhnev. Andropov, Suslov, and Kulakov all began their political careers in the Stavropol region, and "because of this unusual intersection of so many political power lines in an outlying region of Russia, Kremlinologists often speak of the 'Stavropol connection' " (Morrison, 1988, p. 81). Also during his years in the Stavropol Krai, he encountered another up-and-coming regional politician who also began his career in the Communist youth league. Eduard Shevardnadze's "reputation as a tough opponent of official corruption and his willingness to use such unorthodox methods as public opinion surveys and television programming to root out and expose violators of 'socialist legality' must also have earned him the respect of the Stavropol Krai leader" (Morrison, 1988, p. 99).

At the beginning of December 1978 he arrived in Moscow. By October 1980, he was a member of the Politburo, and in 1982, while Andropov served as the General Secretary, Gorbachev was promoted to the post of Central Committee secretary in charge of all Soviet economy. "Gorbachev's loyalty to Andropov evidently arose from a feeling that in the former KGB chief the Soviet Union had, for the first time, a leader who truly grasped the enormity of the economic problems facing the country" (Morrison, 1988, p. 120). After Andropov's death in February 1984, "Gorbachev's youth, which had hitherto been an advantage in his promotion, told against him" (Narkiewicz, 1986, p. 222). Because of their insecurity about losing their comfortable positions, older members of the party preferred the aged Chernenko to the younger man Gorbachev. Nevertheless, Gorbachev became the second most important person in the party and the government and was appointed chairman of the Commission for Foreign Affairs at the Supreme Soviet in 1984. On a trip to Great Britain, he was heralded as the most influential leader in the Kremlin and he "impressed everyone not only with his intelligence and his sense of humour, but even more with his 'western' appearance" (Narkiewicz, 1986, p. 223).

Gorbachev, addressing the Central Committee at the end of 1984 after his visit to the West in which he saw first-hand the efficiency of Western economic management, "told his audience, 'we cannot remain a major power in world affairs unless we put our domestic house in order.' Three months later he found himself the man burdened with directing that task" (Morrison, 1988, p. 130). Within four hours of the communique announcing Chernenko's death, Gorbachev was unanimously elected to the post of General Secretary. It was March 1985, and he was now filling the number one position in the Kremlin. He was different from the previous leaders because he was the first to come into direct contact with Communist party officials in most Eastern and Western countries, and he had also travelled to Mongolia, Vietnam, Britain, and Northern America. Another characteristic which sets him apart from all those before him is the "simple chronological fact that he is the first Soviet leader in seven decades of Communist rule to have been born after the Bolshevik Revolution of 1917" (Morrison, 1988, p. 26). Although some claim that age was a major factor in the novelty of such a leader as Gorbachev and that he was chosen primarily because of a desire to contrast youthful leadership with that of Ronald Reagan as the U. S. president, it should be pointed out that both Lenin and Stalin were in their forties when they took power. Undoubtedly, as Elliot (1987) states, "he is the product of a system which does not encourage radical innovations or original free thinkers; yet that system allowed a man from a peasant family, who began his career at 15 as an assistant operator of a combine harvester, to reach the top. Managerial efficiency and loyalty to the current party line are the qualities most likely to have taken Mikhail Sergeyevich Gorbachev to the Kremlin" (pp. 24–25).

GORBACHEV'S RADICAL REFORMS

When Mikhail Gorbachev rose to the office of General Secretary on March 10, 1985, he inherited an ailing economy and society which was in desperate need of reform. The system which is in place today is one that developed under the leadership of Stalin, a system in which economic problems of industrialization were attacked through a process of mobilization and centralization. This meant the collectivization of agriculture and the imposition of hierarchical planning in industry. Undoubtedly, the system was successful in terms of rapid growth in the last 40 years, but there were inherent economic, social, and political problems in it, for example, in terms of incentives, distribution, waste, inefficiency, laziness, and corruption. "The most serious economic problem" as Butson (1986) avows, "and the one with which Gorbachev has been most closely identified, is the Soviet Union's chronic inability to feed the more than a quarter of a billion people who live within its borders" (p. 133). It is this system which Mikhail Gorbachev endeavors to reform through the policies of *glasnost* and *perestroika*. Within a year of March 1985, "the entire country would be immersed in a heady and disturbing turmoil of *glasnost* and *perestroika*, words whose meanings . . . were virtually unknown to the outside world, and were obscure even to Soviets" at the time of Chernenko's death (Morrison, 1988, p. 132).

Since Gorbachev became the number one man in the Soviet Union, critics and supporters alike have emphasized his personality and image. Assuredly, Gorbachev has introduced a new style of leadership in Soviet politics, in terms of his personality projection, his dealings with the media, and his presentation of new and divergent policy measures. Yet, one must attempt to peer beyond the style and packaging of Gorbachev's new institutions to what is really meant by "reform." Under Brezhnev, reform became a "weasel word" and "reforms and experiments served as *substitutes* for policies rather than their foundation . . . That is why Gorbachev talks of the need for radical 'reform'—not to imply necessarily that he wants to turn the whole system upside down, but simply to indicate that he means business in a way that Brezhnev did not" (Dyker, 1987, p. 2). In this sense, reform means a policy of gradual social and economic changes rather than revolutionary ones.

Gorbachev's vision was a grand one and is encompassed in the following outline:

An arms-control agenda that proposed to eliminate nuclear weapons by the end of the century, and in 1987 made possible the first superpower agreement outlawing a class of nuclear armaments.

An across-the-board relaxation on freedom of expression, centered upon his famed *glasnost* policy, and an unprecedented thaw in the arts and journalism.

Civil rights reforms, including the release of large numbers of political prisoners, easing of restrictions on foreign travel, and revision of the Soviet criminal code.

Economic reforms—the perestroika program—that place greater emphasis on individual incentives and the market-place as a means of improving a notoriously stagnant economy.

Gradual movement toward greater "democratization" in Soviet society, including worker election of managers and secret ballots in lower-level Communist Party elections.

A complete reorganization of the Soviet foreign policy and propaganda establishment, resulting in startling improvements in relations with the rest of the world and in the Soviet Union's public image. (Morrison, 1988, p. 142).

During his first year in power, Gorbachev implemented large changes in the personnel of the Politburo and the government and rapidly formulated policies on economic development for the next fifteen years. "Perhaps [his] most evident innovation in personnel policy was the appointment of the first woman in the top leadership for over two decades" (Elliot, 1987, p. 41). He directed a bloodless purge of middle and senior level officials, sweeping thousands of bureaucrats into retirement or into prison for corruption.

Gorbachev's policy of *glasnost* refers to a new openness in the media and it allows for more open criticism of leadership. In his attempt to return to the Leninist tradition, Gorbachev frequently grants interviews with the press and has made unprecedented efforts to make contact with the people. *Glasnost* often acts as a substitute for multiparty politics. Morrison (1988) cites Gorbachev's explanation that "we do not have any opposition parties . . . That is why [criticism and self-criticism] are essential for the normal functioning of both the party and society" (p. 145). Under *glasnost*, censorship has been reduced to military secrets, pornography, and direct attacks on the socialist basis of the society. The film and book industries have blossomed. And, the right to emigrate has been extended so that 9000 Soviet Jews left in 1987, the highest figure since 1979, and many more Soviets have been permitted to travel abroad.

Improving the Soviet economy being the main objective, Gorbachev called for an economic program involving strict standards of discipline, the massive replacement of obsolete equipment, a dramatic improvement in technology, and increased efficiency in the use of energy and other natural resources. As Gorbachev (1987) describes it, "*perestroika* is an urgent necessity arising from the profound processes of development in our socialist society . . . [and its essence] lies in the fact that it unites socialism with democracy" (p. 25). Turning to Lenin as an inspiration and ideological source of *perestroika*, he evolved the concept gradually, consulting scientists and experts before formulating documents which were based on a thorough analysis of the economic situation. "Stripped of the verbiage, much of Gorbachev's 'new thinking' on economic change is little more than a demand for harder work and more sensible behavior" (Morrison, 1988, p. 159).

Though *perestroika* has taken on every connotation from socialist revival to capitalist flirtation, Gorbachev insists that his reforms are socialist ones and that the socialist basis of society will not be undermined. In other words, therefore, this process of reform must be a slow and gradual one occurring within the framework of the existing system. In a July 31, 1986, speech, Gorbachev summarized his view of *perestroika*. "He insisted that the dogmas which some Soviet scholars put forward as 'eternal truths of socialism' should not be allowed to become obstacles to progress, and condemned people who see 'restructuring' as a 'shaking of our foundations, almost a renunciation of our principles'. Rather, he argued, it was time to face up to the full complexity of what was being tackled" (Elliot, 1987, p. 44).

THE DOMESTIC ROOTS OF SOVIET FOREIGN POLICY

Soviet foreign policy is deeply rooted in the domestic situation. "The main purpose of foreign policy is to preserve and/or develop the state's internal social, political, and economic order" (Kavan, 1986, p. 166). As in any country, the nature of the relationships between internal and external affairs provides a significant clue to the future development of foreign policy. According to Ploss (1980, p. 79, 80), internal factors which are determinants of a government's transactions in the international field are the following: (1) economics; (2) politics; (3) ideology; (4) personality of leaders; and (5) chance. The primary and utmost determinant is the economic element in domestic politics. It was Lenin who said initially that "the very deepest roots of both the internal and foreign policy of our state are shaped by economic interests" (Ploss, 1980, p. 79). Others like Keeble (1985) argue that "economic policy has come second only to the security of the Soviet state as a factor in Soviet foreign policy" (p. 4).

If the policy of any state is truly determined, in the final analysis, by its economic system, then restructuring of the economic system should cause change in foreign policy. The changes in international relations to be brought about by new foreign policies are derived from the required domestic reforms. "For the sake of a successful domestic reform certain changes in foreign policy may be needed" (Kavan, 1986, p. 165).

SOVIET MILITARY DOCTRINE

"Much of the continuing American debate on nuclear strategy hinges on the debaters' interpretations of the USSR's intentions and strategic capabilities. Few issues in the field of international security have been so little studied and so hotly debated as Soviet military doctrine" (Blacker & Duffy, 1984, p. 210). There are diverse conclusions by experts concerning Soviet strategy and doctrine. Some, like George Kennan, argue that the Soviet policies are predominantly defensive and based on a history of inferiority and insecurity, while others like Richard Pipes insist that the Russians are Clausewitzean expansionists whose policies are primarily offensive and aggressive.

> To a large extent, the disagreements arise from attempts to define Soviet policies in a language derived from the American experience. The language of American strategic analysis is alien and inappropriate to the Russian experience of war. If we make the intellectual effort to understand the strategy of the Russians in their terms rather than ours—as a product of Russian history and military tradition—we shall find that it is usually possible to reconcile the conflicting conclusions of the experts.
> (Dyson, 1985, p. 95)

We must investigate beyond our limited experience in order to understand Soviet military doctrine and strategy. The question one must ask is what are the sources of Soviet defense policy, military practice, and notions of security. "Unraveling the puzzle requires one to travel through a maze of connections linking historical biases, strategic concepts, images of war, the process by which weapons are acquired, and even the prism through which [Western] military efforts are viewed" (Legvold, 1987, p. 97). The military power of the Soviet Union has been a domestic priority for a long time. Czar Peter administered the entire nation in hopes of a single goal which was to create a mighty military machine. Soviet leaders since the time of Stalin have placed great emphasis on the importance of military power, forcing their society to sacrifice greatly in order to possess it. Such practices contrast with Lenin and the revolution's purpose which was to destroy this subordination of society to military need, leading one to believe that these military strivings might have been responses to an imperative imposed upon the Soviets by the massive arms build-ups by their Western counterparts.

"Wars and the preparation for war have always been central to Russian life . . . The Russians have suffered from recurring, deep-rooted, and often justified fears of invasion" (Jones, 1983, p. 95). At the outset of the nuclear age, Soviet strategists prepared for the possibility of limited nuclear war. They had seen worse destruction than that which was inflicted at Hiroshima in air bombings during the World War. Unpredictability and uncertainty were intrinsic to the nature of war from the Russian's perspective. Initially, Soviet strategy was based on the premise that there was such a thing as a legitimate use of nuclear weapons and the international political scene had not seen a revolutionary change in the advent of nuclear weapons.

After the French pulled out of NATO, weakening the NATO conventional force in Europe, and the U.S. adopted the policy of flexible response in the early 60s, the Soviets had a conventional option. "Soviet leadership could now take seriously the wartime objective of avoiding nuclear devastation" (Legvold, 1987, p. 107). From that time on, Soviet nuclear strategy was predicated on a second-strike use of force. By the time of Brezhnev's death, Soviet leaders were beginning to feel that their borders were secure from attack. By the late 1970s, Brezhnev, Gromyko, and others had begun to alter some of the most enduring notions underlying Soviet military policy. First, Brezhnev formally repudiated strategic superiority. Second, he denied the possibility of victory in the event of a nuclear exchange. Last, in 1982, he announced a no-first-use doctrine. MccGwire, a leading expert on Soviet military doctrine, maintains that these policies are not just words without substance and credibility. "The Soviets' overarching objective is to promote the long-term well-being of the Soviet state" (MccGwire, 1987, p. 37). The purpose of these measures and the change in doctrine was to avoid nuclear devastation of the Soviet Union in a conventional war with Europe or Asia. According to Blacker & Duffy (1984), "above all else, the Soviets seek to prevent nuclear war" (p. 215). Osgood (1983) points out that "Soviet military writings describe nuclear flexibility as destabilizing—because it may make the use of nuclear weapons more likely" (p. 126). Therefore, one can rest assured that contemporary Soviet military doctrine is derived from a position which states that nuclear war is non-winnable and should be prevented at all costs.

THE MILITARY AND THE ECONOMY

Before Khrushchev, Soviet leaders believed that power was based principally on military strength, which may have been true at one time, but Khrushchev recognized change in the nature of power politics and expressed his position that power must be founded on an economic base, and this position is widely accepted today and advocated extensively by Gorbachev. Since he rose to prominence, he has said that "unless something is done to correct current economic trends, the Soviet Union will not enter the twenty-first century a great power worthy of the name. Military might will not do it alone. Indeed . . . the economy must be attended to if the base of Soviet military power is to be preserved" (Legvold, 1987, p. 102).

Unquestionably, the military is closely tied to the economy. With the decline in industrial and technological growth and the increasing failures of the Soviet economy to meet consumer needs, some are concerned that the weight of the military burden is too heavy and may be causing the economy to crumble. These same concerns were aired by Andropov, signalling that pressures were mounting even before Gorbachev's rule. One of the surest ways to halt the Soviet Union's economic decline would be to break the stranglehold that the Soviet military-industrial complex has on the rest of the economy. The growth in Soviet nuclear forces is largely a reaction to U.S. policies, and the Soviet economy cannot as easily cope with the arms race. Some in Washington have advocated using the arms race in order to break down the Soviet economy and weaken the country as a world power. The enormous military expenditures through which the Soviet Union achieved parity with the U.S. in the 1970s became less fruitful than anticipated. While the Soviet Union's military power increased in the 60s and 70s, its political power declined. If military expenditures are gutting and weakening the economy and the objective of domestic policy is to make the economy stronger, it follows that defense expenditures should decrease and arms control measures are inevitable.

GORBACHEV'S FOREIGN POLICY

Some Western politicians argue that Soviet foreign policy is one of expansion and world domination, but Soviet historians "explain the pre-revolutionary expansion of Russia as unification, or both pre- and post-revolutionary expansion as defensive action against invasion from Asia and from the West, particularly from Germany which has invaded Russia twice this century. The memory of the second German invasion and the war which followed still dominates the Soviet political mentality" (Medvedev, 1986, p. 225). As mentioned previously, even Mikhail Gorbachev's political mentality has been shaped by his personal experience as a youth under German invasion. Since Soviet foreign policy derives its basic elements from domestic policy, Gorbachev's foreign policy evolved out of his domestic program of *perestroika*. With revival of the economy at the top of Gorbachev's priority list, "Soviet dependence on the Western capitalist countries for the development of high technology and for vital commodities like grain, meat, sugar and butter to prevent domestic malnutrition contributed to a reorientation of foreign policy priorities" (Medvedev, 1986, p. 227). Policy is now being guided by practical interest rather than by ideology, and there is more to be gained from stability than from conflict.

In terms of international affairs, Gorbachev has stated from the beginning that he supported a new and open approach to the rest of the world. He has followed through thus far on a reform of foreign policy which he calls "new political thinking. " As the term implies, before altering foreign policy and in order to provide consistency with new programs and proposals, policy-makers must change their way of thinking. Though to the outsider these new Soviet policies may sound like propaganda, one must also acknowledge, however, that "governments and the men who form them do modify their ideas as the world evolves" (Legvold, 1988, p. 8). Immediately after World War II the Soviet leaders believed that war with the United States was extremely conceivable and probably inevitable. Nikita Khrushchev was the first leader to deal with these weapons after realizing their full implications. Only then was the notion of the inevitability of war suppressed and the avoidance of war made an underlying goal of policy. Most recently, after critical analysis and reevaluation of Lenin's and Stalin's philosophies and their applicability for basic policy assumptions in the 1980s, Gorbachev has further altered the military doctrine; and now, a fundamental "theme of [his] foreign policy is the complete repudiation of the Leninist doctrine of an inevitable, final, physical battle between capitalism and communism. He has stated repeatedly that this doctrine is suicidal and has been renderred obsolete and inoperative by weapons technology" (Naylor, 1988, p. 38).

As Robert Legvold (1988), a leading Sovietologist, states, "to doubt the capacity of Soviet leaders to change their minds, therefore, reveals a frail grasp of history. Rather than being put off by the Madison Avenue quality of Gorbachev's phrase, one would be wise to consider the possibility that for real and good reasons the evolution of concepts continues, not as a sudden break with the past, but as a natural progression" (p. 9). When national priorities are redefined and the goals and aspirations of a whole country are reexamined, it follows that the world will witness a chain effect on behavior also.

A basic tenet of the "new political thinking" in foreign policy begins with dialogue. Gorbachev feels that there cannot be understanding without it. Within his first few months in office, he displayed "an astonishing foreign policy festival" in which he met in a series of one-on-one meetings with foreign dignitaries such as Francois Mitterand, George Bush, Helmut Kohl, and Margaret Thatcher (Morrison, 1988, p. 132).

Before looking at the areas of "new political thinking" which Gorbachev outlines in his bestseller, *Perestroika*, one must first grasp the importance of domestic priorities and continuity and change. "Gorbachev from the beginning has made it plain that the problems facing him and his colleagues at home take precedence over, indeed dictate, Soviet engagement in the outside world" (Legvold, 1988, p. 10). His success on the home front is contingent upon avoidance of excessive foreign policy distractions or entanglements such as third-world wars. As pointed out earlier, strengthening the dilapidated economy is first and foremost. All domestic and foreign policies should be derived from such an aspiration.

In terms of continuity with the past and in keeping with the old establishment, the basic core of policy has not changed enormously. Like his predecessors, he has endeavored to normalize relations with China, he seeks to gain leverage over Americans through relationships with Western rulers, and he continues to focus his concerns on the United States. Also, while he denies the inevitability of war with the United States, his foreign policy, consistent with others since the 1920s, is "based on the proposition that international relations are crucially determined by the struggle between socialism and capitalism" (Kavan, 1986, p. 169). "What has clearly changed is the style of Soviet policy under Gorbachev. From his skillfully conducted press conferences to his free-wheeling conversations with Western political leaders, . . . [he] has altered the look of Soviet policy . . . and has brought a deftness to diplomacy" (Legvold, 1988, p. 12). Contrary to what many skeptics suggest, the changes are more than cosmetic. For longer than a decade, the intellectual elite of the Soviet foreign policy establishments have been formulating the very same ideas and concepts which Gorbachev now presents so eloquently to the Soviet public and to the world. "The current conceptual ferment did not spring into being on the strength of Gorbachev's personality alone. As noted earlier, altered images of the world do not occur overnight. Meaningful change is usually a cumulative process" (Legvold, 1988, p. 13).

When focusing on Gorbachev's new foreign policy innnovations, they can be divided into four areas: (1) security, (2) interdependence, (3) the third world, and (4) socialist relations. In a break from the past, Gorbachev has reworked the concept of security. First, he has accepted a more progressive, extended definition of national security. Stability, as he contends, is based on economics and politics as much as it is military might. Second, he is the first Soviet leader to say that his country cannot pursue its own security at the expense of others, particularly that of the U.S. Foreign policy strategists have begun to "speak about the link between Soviet national security and the security of other nations—the link between national and mutual security" (Legvold, 1987, p. 103). Gorbachev says that true security is nonexistent unless it is extended to everyone. In the nuclear age, insecurities produce uncertainty and mistrust.

Under the leadership of Gromyko, foreign policy had always been founded on the view of a bipolar world in international affairs. Gorbachev selected as his foreign policy minister his longtime associate from his days as a regional manager of the Komsomol, Eduard Shevardnadze. Gorbachev, Shevardnadze, and their entourage prefer the modern multipolar approach to international relations. This multipolar vision of the world supplements the concept of interdependence. Interdependence among countries is the second major aspect of the "new thinking," interdependence in the sense that "one side's loss is not necessarily the other side's gain . . . These are realities . . . that also diminish the historic competition between East and West" (Legvold, 1988, p. 15).

With respect to the Third World, less and less attention will be devoted to developing countries at a time when Soviets have their own economy and industrialization to worry about. "For Gorbachev the Third World has become a far less inviting place, one filled with headaches and troubles capable of embroiling the superpowers and spilling over to contaminate whole areas of foreign policy" (Legvold, 1988, p. 15). For the first time, the Soviet leader is aware what involvement in heightened conflicts in the Third World can do to relations with the United States, although for the past 10 years Soviets have been more and more discouraged with the problems facing the developing world.

Legvold asserts that the most fundamental change in policy is in the realm of socialist relations. In his realization that no Communist party can possess any monopoly on truth, Gorbachev speaks "of the need to treat others' approaches to socialism as a genuinely important and valid contribution to the common store of knowledge" (Legvold, 1988, p. 17). In dealing with the communists of Western Europe, Gorbachev has downplayed ideological differences and stressed economic integration of socialist markets.

There is no doubt that Soviet foreign policy has been dramatically reformed under Gorbachev, and the forces have been set in motion which many claim are irreversible. The area of arms control may be a gauge for what is truly occurring in international politics and U.S.–Soviet relations. Because of *glasnost, perestroika,* "new political thinking," and a reassessment of military doctrine, arms control is one area of policy which has represented promising dialogue and changes in the present and future.

ARMS CONTROL UNDER GORBACHEV

Over the last few years, Soviet political and military strategists have begun to explore the implications for arms control on alternative defense postures in Europe. They have started to reassess the military history of the Soviet Union and have arrived at a more defensive, less offensive conventional force posture. The signing of the INF Treaty in 1987 signals that Gorbachev has come to the realization that he must address the conventional balance in Europe. With Gorbachev in power, the U.S.S.R. has dramatically stepped up arms control efforts. He led the Soviets back to the negotiating table in the Strategic Arms Reduction Talks and the Intermediate Nuclear Force discussions. Also during his term, there have been new conventional arms limitations talks, the Conference on Security and Confidence Building Measure and Disarmament in Europe, and the Committee on Disarmament. Until Gorbachev's time, verification was a widely disputed and controversial issue in arms control negotiations. Advocating such a practice, he claims "there can be no disarmament without verification and that verification without disarmament makes no sense" (Gorbachev, 1986, p. 74).

Under Gorbachev, military strategy has proposed a new characteristic called "reasonable sufficiency. " This means that the military would be solely composed of that which was reasonably necessary in order to ensure sufficient defense for the country. First, it would include a nuclear arsenal capable only of a second strike. Second, conventional forces would be prepared for defense of the nation. Third, they would not conduct major offensive operations. Last, interventionary forces would be capable of deterring an aggressor in regional crises but insufficient to support a regime which could not defend itself alone.

According to Gorbachev (1987), "the fundamental principle of the new political outlook is very simple: nuclear war cannot be a means of achieving political, economic, ideological or any others goals" (p. 140). He says that there can be no winner in the arms race and therefore, proposed on January 15, 1986, an entire program for the eventual complete disarmament of nuclear powers in the world by the year 2000. In July 1985, he had announced a six-month long unilateral moratorium on underground testing of nuclear weapons. Having appealed to the United States to do the same, but without a positive response, in January 1986 he extended the ban on testing for another three months.

Gorbachev (1987) affirms that "security is a political issue, not a function of military confrontation. Failure to understand this can only result in war with all its catastrophic consequences" (p. 230). Gorbachev has placed disarmament and security as a high priority central direction to his foreign policy. In terms of international security and based on his new perspective on the interdependencies of the world, he has made some very concrete and far-reaching proposals in the military sphere "in order to build an all-embracing system of international security" (Legvold, 1988, p. 56). They are:

- the renunciation by the nuclear powers of war—both nuclear and conventional—against each other or against third countries;
- prevention of an arms race in outer space, cessation of all nuclear weapons tests and the total destruction of such weapons, a ban on and the destruction of chemical weapons, and renunciation of the development of other means of mass annihilation;
- a strictly controlled lowering of the levels of military capabilities of countries to limits of reasonable sufficiency;
- disbandment of military alliances, and as a stage toward this—renunciation of their enlargement and of the formation of new ones;
- balanced and proportionate reduction of military budgets. (Legvold, 1988, p. 56)

Outer space weapons have become a prominent issue in the arms control debate due to the Reagan proposal of the Strategic Defense Initiative. "Soviet arms control policy since 1983 has consistently emphasized that before any progress can be achieved toward the conclusion of a new agreement to limit the arms race, the United States must abandon its commitment to the development of strategic weapons technologies" (Dallin & Rice, 1986, p. 149). As Narkiewicz (1986) points out, because of the state of the economy, "Soviet leaders would like to put more money into people's pockets and less into defense; it is for this reason that Gorbachev had said that they will not develop a 'Star Wars' program of their own" (p. 228). They simply cannot afford it.

Although Gorbachev seeks a disarmament agreement, he will not unilaterally disarm; and he still recognizes the importance of defense. He sees the acquisition of parity as something which has strengthened socialism and the position of the Soviet Union. The preservation of such a balance is crucial to safeguarding peace and international security.

CONCLUSION

Though in many ways, the Soviet Union of today is more the result of a historical drama played out at a time of Gorbachev's birth than to the initial seizure of power by the Bolsheviks in 1917, Gorbachev, in a revolutionary style and manner of his own, is attempting to travel back and to recharge some of the basic Leninist, Bolshevik roots of Soviet socialism. In the evolution of ideas, a gear in the evolutionary mechanism of humankind, the Soviets are learning along with the rest. They are learning primarily from their own involvement in a changing international environment. In my estimation, Legvold's (1988) assessment is accurate that the "Gorbachev era will turn out to be one of the great turning points in the history of Soviet foreign policy" and maybe even the history of mankind (p. 13).

In conclusion, the reforms have taken place under Gorbachev out of utter necessity. Change in foreign policy has occurred out of fundamental necessity, and therefore arms control objectives have been redefined out of necessity. One might even say that Gorbachev's role as a leader has been directed primarily by necessity. The Soviet Union and the rest of the world were ready for a new style and a new approach which had been in the works for some time. However distinctive Gorbachev's personal effect on the course of events has been, he has not created but has facilitated change. The deeper impulse to change stems from a continually evolving external international global setting. At the present, the future of arms control appears promising in light of the changes in the Soviet Union and the reworking of perceptions about the world and arms control. With a relaxation of tensions and a new and less hostile administration in the United States under Bush, arms control agreements resulting from START talks as well as conventional weapons talks could prove to be very reassuring, concrete, and significant. Only through increased dialogue and genuine attempts to understand and trust each other can the United States and the Soviet Union move towards meaningful progress in arms control. Gorbachev or no Gorbachev, the forces are in motion in the Soviet Union. Through increased cooperation, it may be possible for both the U.S. and U.S.S.R to halt the incessant arms race which wastes resources and human potential, and we may be able to place a hold on the military-industrial complexes before they put a hold on us and run our economies into the ground. Time remains to tell.

Works Cited

Blacker, Coit D. and Gloria Duffy (Eds). (1984). *International Arms Control: Issues and Agreements.* Stanford: Stanford University Press.

Butson, Thomas. (1986). *Gorbachev: A Biography.* New York: Stein and Day Publishers.

Dallin, Alexander and Condolezza Rice (Eds). (1986). *The Gorbachev Era.* Stanford: Stanford Alumni Association.

Dyker, David A. (Ed). (1987). *The Soviet Union Under Gorbachev: Prospects for Reform.* London: Croom Helm Ltd..

Dyson, Freeman. (1985). On Russians and Their Views of Nuclear Strategy. In Charles W. Kegley, Jr. and Eugene R. Wittkopf (Eds). *The Nuclear Reader: Strategy, Weapons, War* (pp. 95–99). New York: St. Martin's Press.

Elliot, Iain. (1987). The Consolidation of Gorbachev's Political Power—A Springboard for Reform? In David Dyker (Ed). *The Soviet Union Under Gorbachev* (pp. 21–56). London: Croom Helm.

Gorbachev, Mikhail. "Nuclear Disarmament by the Year 2000." *New York Times.* February 5, 1986 (p. 5).

Gorbachev, Mikhail. (1987). *Perestroika: New Thinking for Our Country and the World.* New York: Harper & Row, Publishers.

Gorbachev, Mikhail. (1986) *Speeches and Writings.* Oxford: Pergamon Press.

Jones, David. (1983). "Military Organization and Deployment." In James Cracraft (Ed). *The Soviet Union Today: An Interpretive Guide* (pp. 95–112). Chicago: *Bulletin of the Atomic Scientists.*

Kavan, Zdenek. (1986). "Gorbachev and the World—the Political Side." In David Dyker (Ed). *The Soviet Union Under Gorbachev.* London: Croom Helm.

Keeble, Curtis (Ed). (1985). *The Soviet State: The Domestic Roots of Soviet Foreign Policy.* Boulder, Colorado: Westview Press.

Legvold, Robert. (1988). *Gorbachev's Foreign Policy: How Should the U.S. Respond?* New York: The Foreign Policy Association.

Legvold, Robert. (1987). War, Weapons, and Soviet Foreign Policy. In Seweryn Bialer and Michael Mandelbaum (Eds). *Gorbachev's Russia and American Foreign Policy.* (pp. 97–132). Boulder, Colorado: Westview Press.

Medvedev, Zhores. (1986). *Gorbachev.* Oxford: Basil Blackwell Ltd.

MccGwire, Michael. (1987). *Military Objectives in Soviet Foreign Policy.* Washington, D.C.: Brookings Institution.

Morrison, Donald. (1988). *Mikhail S. Gorbachev: An Intimate Bibliography.* New York: Time Inc.

Narkiewicz,Olga A. (1986). *Soviet Leaders: From the Cult of Personality to Collective Rule.* New York: St. Martin's Press.

Naylor, Thomas H. (1988). *The Gorbachev Strategy: Opening the Closed Society.* Lexington, Massachusetts: D.C. Heath and Company.

Osgood, Eugenia. (1983). "Military Strategy in the Nuclear Age." In James Cracraft (Ed). *The Soviet Union Today: An Interpretive Guide* (pp. 123–136). Chicago: *Bulletin of the Atomic Scientist.*

Ploss, Sidney. (1980). Studying the Domestic Determinants of Soviet Foreign Policy. In Erik P. Hoffman and Frederic J. Fleron, Jr. (Eds). *The Conduct of Soviet Foreign Policy.* New York: Aldine Publishing Co.

Sagan, Carl. (1985). Nuclear War and Climatic Catastrophe: A Nuclear Winter. Reprinted from *The Cold and the Dark* in Charles W. Kegley, Jr. and Eugene R. Wittkopf (Eds). *The Nuclear Reader: Strategy, Weapons, War* (pp. 312–330). New York: St. Martin's Press.

■ THE WRITER'S ASSIGNMENT

Develop a topic broadly related to the course using approaches we have studied. This 10–12-page paper should use bibliographic sources other than those assigned in the course. Endnotes should be used to indicate sources, and you should include a bibliography if you have consulted sources that are not indicated in notes. ■

■ UNDERSTANDING WRITING STRATEGIES

1. The essay gives the largest subtopics in headings. What are the constitu-

ent elements of each of these? What organizational principles govern the ordering of these elements?

2. Look at the references for the section on Gorbachev's life. How many sources does the author use for this section? What seems to determine how she uses these sources? For example, does she summarize one and then go on to another, or does a topic govern her selection?

3. What information in the section on Gorbachev's life contributes significantly to understanding the Soviet leader? What information could be omitted?

4. To what degree does personality shape Soviet policy? To what degree does the domestic situation shape it?

5. Gentile shapes much of her argument from studying causes and effects. What patterns of influence does she trace? Does she impose this pattern or do her sources? What indicates this?

6. What are the central tenets of Gorbachev's "new political thinking"?

7. What is the place of arms control in the "new political thinking"?

8. What conclusions does Gentile reach? How do these unify her discussions?

9. Gentile's paper has a clear opinion of Soviet foreign policy. What is it? How does she construct her argument to reflect this opinion?

10. How does she use her sources to strengthen her position? ■

■ SUGGESTIONS FOR WRITING

Gentile refers throughout her paper to critics of Gorbachev and *glastnost*. What are their criticisms? Select one area of criticism, and write a position paper explaining and, if possible, justifying the objections. Obviously, you will wish to select a relatively narrow subject, but use at least three or four different sources. Work as Gentile has to synthesize your sources. Find where they agree and disagree, and where they introduce different arguments and evidence. In your paper, explain the similarities and differences. ■

The Master of the Game
by Strobe Talbott

Mary Jimenez

Mary Jimenez reviews Strobe Talbott's book on Paul Nitze's influence on American foreign policy, particularly during the Reagan administration. This essay, written for a political science class entitled American Foreign Policy, effectively summarizes the book and evaluates its importance.

The last forty years or so of American foreign policy, especially in regard to the Soviet Union, have been characterized a great deal by ambiguity and internal struggle. This can be seen historically by way of chronological developments in the Soviet–American relationship and the administrations which contributed to these developments. In his book, *Master of the Game*, Strobe Talbott recognizes the significance of the history of American foreign policy and its culmination in the Reagan Administration and, particularly, the debate over SDI. Talbott's focus, however, is not the history of foreign policy itself, but rather an ever-present, if not always prominent, figure in that history. Paul Nitze's own life, specifically his career in relation to U.S.–Soviet relations, parallels and personifies the evolution of U.S. foreign policy. Talbott, using his own themes, illustrates how Nitze utilized his own experience to ultimately become, in Talbott's own words, "more than just master of the game . . . [but] also a victor."

One of the most important aspects of *Master of the Game* was Paul Nitze's personal character and the way it affected his manner of working.

> He has many proteges, but he has never expected them to sit at his feet and absorb his wisdom. He has always wanted them to challenge him, to argue with him. . . . He has always been an aristocrat in his bearing and his background, but an intellectual egalitarian in the way he deals with people. . . . For him, 'argumentative' is a compliment. . . . The more disagreement, the better the discussion (Talbott 10).

Talbott portrays Nitze almost favorably by noting how Nitze's argumentative characteristics and manner of discussing and examining a problem exhaustively were extremely instrumental in much of the progress the U.S. had in negotiations with the Soviets. During the negotiations for the SALT treaty, Nitze persistently worked very hard with his own colleagues and with the Soviet negotiators in order to achieve the goals he thought were necessary, namely, a treaty of "unlimited duration" (129), and addressing of the problem of Soviet throw-weight (125), and, an area in which he felt he could better succeed, strategic defense (125). However, Nitze ultimately felt that, in a rush to reach an agreement, "Kissinger had acquiesced in a number of provisions in SALT I that were ambiguous or disadvantageous to the U.S., or both" (134). In this way, SALT I became a disappointment for Nitze.

Another personal characteristic of Nitze's was that if there seemed to be no solution to the problem at hand, he would persistently and sometimes solitarily go back over it until he found a different angle to look at or until some different sort of solution was possible. For example, during the INF negotiations, Nitze realized that "INF was going nowhere, [and he] decided to set out on his own for a different destination" (174). This realization resulted in the "walk in the woods" formula of negotiating one-on-one with Kvitsinsky in the informal setting of a mountainside. The significance here is that Nitze took it upon himself to try to succeed where he felt that the others were failing.

Another example of Nitze's relentless persistence can be found toward the end of the Reagan Administration. At this time, his way of constantly working when others had lost their motivation provided a stark contrast to many members of the soon-to-be exiting Administration.

> As long as there was any chance at all of making progress, Nitze would press ahead. This never-say-die, it's-not-over-till-it's-over determination was characteristic of the man, but not of the government he served. A grudgingly valedictory mood had long since begun to settle over Washington . . . Those who saw the Administration as having deserved its setbacks and stumbled into its successes often singled out Nitze's efforts on behalf of progress in arms control as the exception that proved the rule (393).

Despite the fact that Nitze was often considered an excellent negotiator, Talbott illustrated throughout this account of Nitze's career that Nitze was indeed the "most dogged negotiator." Nitze encountered an unbelievable number of disappointments which ultimately contributed to an almost bitter and sarcastic attitude that infrequently surfaced during his dealings with Congress, his colleagues, many members of the Executive Branch, and the Pentagon.

> He almost never got the jobs he wanted when he wanted them. He was turned down for, or at the last minute deprived of, as many assignments as he received. He was constantly being sounded out for attractive jobs, only to be blackballed by someone higher up in the government or off to one side of Congress (11).

Talbott further discusses that many times it was personality which turned people off to him—no matter what he was saying or even how important it was. A prime example of this occurred in Plains, Georgia, where Jimmy Carter hosted a series of "seminars" to discuss policy issues and also to informally interview possible candidates for positions in his future Administration. At this particular seminar, Nitze was present, along with a number of his former colleagues and other prominent intellectuals. In contrast to the relaxed setting of Carter's home, Nitze launched into an intense presentation of Soviet civil defense, the doctrine of nuclear deterrence, and U.S. defense policy. From that, Carter received a very negative impression of Nitze, one which cost Nitze a senior position (149).

Probably one of the most recurrent themes in Talbott's book is the division within the U.S. government toward its foreign policy and the fact that Nitze was the personification of that ambivalence. This was seen in the intro-governmental controversy over such issues as the doctrine of Mutually Assured Destruction and Soviet parity with the U.S.. This was also seen in the way the current interpretation of the ABM Treaty had evolved from the interpretation at the time of its ratification as a result of the controversial issue of "exotics" and furthermore, SDI. Those in the government who wanted to proceed with development and testing of "space-based exotic ABM's" found loopholes in the ABM Treaty justifying their position. Even Nitze himself, the only member of the Administration at that time who had been directly involved in the ABM negotiations, became convinced of the validity of this new position.

> But on the question of development and testing, Nitze initially wavered and eventually ended up agreeing with Sofaer . . . Nitze became convinced that despite what he and the other American negotiators believed they had accomplished in SALT I, Sofaer was right: The Soviets had never unambiguously agreed to a provision banning the development and testing of space-based exotic ABM's; therefore, no such ban was established by the treaty. . . . [He] now persuaded Nitze that the ABM Treaty had been the object of a thirteen-year-old misunderstanding on Nitze's own part as well as everyone else's (244).

Later, the Reagan Administration's own ambiguity regarding the ABM Treaty interpretation was made public as it announced that it supported the broad interpretation of Sofaer and, at the same time, adopted the compromise that this new interpretation would be accepted as law, while the old interpretation would still be kept on as policy (247). This compromise was a suggestion by Nitze to Schultz in order to keep the political damage of accepting the new interpretation at a minimum.

Finally, it seems that the underlying purpose of Talbott in writing this book is to illustrate the similarities and, to a greater extent, the differences between Paul Nitze and President Reagan. In addition, Talbott points out how Nitze and the other members of the Executive Branch were all part of a covert scheme to deceive the President. They all outwardly appeared to support SDI for the same reasons Reagan did. In truth, however, they were divided up into two opposing factions whose own objectives for SDI were quite different from the President's. All of these members of the Administration, Nitze included, had learned early on that to oppose Reagan or try to undermine SDI in any way was asking for trouble. The only possible way of achieving any other objectives was to go along with Reagan, or at least, appear to do so. This was, in effect, the game at which Nitze became a master. He was able to appear as if he supported the President's objectives for SDI when he really was working for his own more realistic aspirations of such a program.

According to Talbott, the life and career of Paul Nitze serve as a parallel to the evolution of American foreign policy. Nitze was both directly and indirectly involved with many important negotiations regarding nuclear weapons and proved to be highly influential in shaping the actions of the presidents whom he served. It seems as if Talbott's purpose in *Master of the Game* was also to criticize Reagan and his administration by exposing the internal as well as external controversies of the SDI program. By depicting a certain ambivalence present in many administrations and the internal struggles, prominent chacteristics of U.S. foreign policy, Talbott revealed that despite the change SDI initially seemed to present, U.S. foreign policy objectives remained consistent with those of the "old era." SDI was not as revolutionary as many had thought.

▌ UNDERSTANDING WRITING STRATEGIES

1. How does the introduction both create a context for Talbott's book and indicate its focus?

2. What principle does Jimenez use to order her own discussion of the book? Why is this a valuable strategy for a book review?

3. What bias does she suggest the author, Talbott, has about his subject, Nitze?

4. What insights does Jimenez offer about Talbott's authorial purposes beyond simple biography?

5. What does Jimenez accomplish beyond merely summarizing Talbott's book? ▌

▌ SUGGESTIONS FOR WRITING

Read four or five book reviews in well-respected journals or magazines like the *New York Review of Books*. What seems to be the purpose or purposes of book reviews? Do reviews differ in popular magazines and professional journals? Write a guide for writing book reviews in the social sciences for your fellow students. Be sure to consider the use of summary, paraphrase, and quotation, along with such concerns as content, purpose, style, and format. ▌

Color Encoded as a Verbal Label

Sallyanne Jones-Waldinger

In her experimental psychology course, Sallyanne Jones-Waldinger conducted an experiment to determine whether her subjects remembered colors by their names or the perceived hue. This paper reports her original research. Conforming to scientic report format, she begins with a literature review, followed by a description of her experiment, a report of experimental results, a discussion of these results, and a conclusion.

A modification of Allen's study of short-term memory for colors and color names was used to determine if color is encoded as a verbal label. Subjects in the Experimental Group were exposed to four levels of consistency for color and color name. Two control groups received only colors or only color names. Four trials were given per subject, and all groups had a specific recall task. Results indicated that (1) no significant difference existed between recall of colors or color names and (2) that no significant difference in recall scores between consistency levels was present. The discussion focuses on the possibility that color is encoded as a verbal label and a visual image, and that this may vary between subjects.

In 1807, through an attempt to modify Newton's color circle, Thomas Young developed a subsequent theory of sensory function. Newton's (as cited by Levine and Shefner, 1981) color circle described the process of color mixture, which was initially revealed to him through the refraction of light using a prism. In discovering that short light wavelengths could undergo the greatest refraction, and long wavelengths could undergo the least refraction, Newton developed the color spectrum. The color red, the shortest wavelength, begins the spectrum, and it is followed by orange, yellow, green, blue and violet. As colors progress on the spectrum their original light wavelengths are longer. Newton's color circle (as cited by Kaufman, 1974), which made use of all of the colors in the color spectrum, provided rules for color mixture. If two colors which were closely placed on the color spectrum were mixed, a "neutral" color would result. All neutral colors could be located on the spectrum. Colors which were far apart in spectral order would yield a color not found in the spectrum. For instance, the mixture of red and yellow will produce orange, a color which can be located on Newton's color spectrum. However, the mixture of spectral colors red and blue will result in purple, a color not found on the spectrum.

Through modification of Newton's color spectrum theory, Young (as cited by Levine and Shefner, 1981) unknowingly described the trichromatic theory of color vision. Young proposed that the human eye contained three primary "fibres" which, when stimulated by the appropriate light wavelengths, produced specific color sensations. According to Young's theory the "fibres" of the eye were red, green, and violet, and each was sensitive to its respective light wavelengths. Basing his assumption on Newton's development of the color circle, Young observed that by appropriately mixing three spectral colors one could produce any desired color. Thus, the conclusion that color vision must be based upon three specific color receptors.

In publicizing Young's theory, Helmholtz (as cited by Kaufman, 1974) developed yet another theory of color processing in humans. Basing his assertion on Young's conclusions, Helmholtz too theorized that the eye contained three primary fibers which receive specific light wavelengths. However, Helmholtz chose to change Young's choice of "fibres" from red, green, and violet to red, green, and blue, in keeping with Newton's original color spectrum. Helmholtz concluded that although these fibers were sensitive to all wavelengths of light, the "red" fiber was most strongly receptive to red wavelengths, the "blue" fiber to blue light wavelengths, and the "green" fiber was most sensitive to green wavelengths. These fibers, today identified as cones, acted as color information transmitters to the brain upon stimulation by light.

In the development of the Young-Helmholtz Theory of Color Vision, Helmholtz designed hypothetical excitation curves based on visual pigment absorption (Levine and Shefner, 1981). A series of psychophysical experiments have provided evidence to back the assertion that vision is trichromatic in humans.

Brown and Wald (1964) performed experiments on the human eye using a microspectrophotometer to measure the exact amount of light wavelengths which entered a single cone. Marks, Dobelle and MacNichol (1964) performed such experiments on various primates, and found that primates have three major types of cones. The levels of light absorbance, 450 nm, 525 nm, and 550 nm, are very similar to the levels of human cone wavelength absorbancy determined by Brown and Wald (1964).

Although there is empirical evidence to support the presence of trichromatic vision in humans, another theory of color vision offers another approach to the field of color processing and detection. In 1878 Ewald Hering (as cited by Hurvich and Jameson, 1957) proposed the Opponent-Process Theory of color vision. As a result of experiments with color afterimages and complementary colors, questions had arisen which indicated that the Trichromatic Theory failed to provide explanations for various visual processes.

Afterimages occur upon staring at a color for 30 seconds or more and then shifting to a white figure. The afterimage itself is the impression of that color which is complementary to the color originally focused on. For example, if one were to stare at a blue square for 30 seconds and then shift to a white square, presumably a yellow impression should exist. This concept of complementary colors simply describes the relationship between two colors that together produce white when combined.

Hering (as cited by Haber and Hershenson, 1973) theorized that if colors operate in a complementary manner, then so too must human color perception. Thus, Hering's development of the Opponent-Process Theory provided for three color "substances," one which perceived blue and yellow, one red and green, and one which perceived black and white light wavelengths. The opponent process actually occurs within each substance; if the blue/yellow "substance" were to respond positively to blue wavelengths, the yellow would then respond negatively.

Present supporters of the Opponent-Process Theory agree with the contemporary supporters of the Trichromatic Theory in that the "substances" once referred to by Hering, as well as the "fibres" discussed in the Young-Helmholtz Theory, are the cones which lie in the retina of the eye. Contemporary Opponent-Process Theory bases itself upon the use of cones to signal light brightness and the resulting nulling of an existing opponent process.

Experiments conducted by Hurvich and Jameson (1957) provide evidence to support the Opponent-Process Theory. After being presented with a monochromatic stimulus, subjects were to add green or red light until the stimulus appeared to be "neither red or green." The amount of green light added received a positive sign while the amount of red light added was given a negative sign. The experimenters also performed this task using the blue/yellow opponent process. Hurvich and Jameson (1957) developed the Chromatic Response Function by plotting the amounts of light added as a function of light wavelengths of the original stimulus. Results indicated that the amounts of light added were equal between the red/green and blue/yellow processes. Furthermore, results also showed that the stimulus wavelengths within the red/green and blue/yellow opponents directly opposed one another.

The results of Hurvich and Jameson (1957) serve to substantiate Hering's model of the Opponent-Process Theory. Moreover, these results provide an explanation for color afterimages. Staring continuously at a green circle will "null" the opposing red process. Switching from a green circle to a white circle will suddenly "release" the nulled red process, and thus result in a red impression, or afterimage.

In 1983 C. K. Allen attempted to determine if humans encode colors as verbal labels of visual images. The process of encoding involves the separation of a stimulus into specific aspects or characteristics which can be stored and presumably recalled. Allen's experiment was based on the presumption of short-term memory existence in humans, as the retention interval in his experiment was only thirty seconds.

The concept of differentiation between short-term memory and long-term memory was introduced by D. O. Hebb in 1949. Hebb's assertions received little attention, as convincing empirical evidence did not yet exist

(Peterson and Peterson, 1959). However, experiments conducted by Peterson and Peterson (1959) provided positive evidence to substantiate Hebb's 1949 claim of short-term memory existence. The experimenters orally presented three-letter clusters to subjects, while rehearsal was prevented through performance of a retention interval subtraction task. The period of retention interval was varied, and results showed that the length of retention interval and percent of correctly recalled letter clusters were positively correlated. Thus, the results of Peterson and Peterson (1959) implied that some differentiation between short-term memory and long-term memory did indeed exist.

Miller (1956) has postulated that short-term memory and chunking work together to increase the capacity of short-term memory. Chunking simply describes the linking together of letters to form words, or the linking of words to form sentences. This process of chunking facilitates the expansion of short-term memory capacity regardless of the type of stimuli.

Bower and Karlin (1977) determined that recognition of faces was based on the encoding of specific traits or facial characteristics. Bower and Karlin's experimental stimulus was a series of pictures of faces. Subjects were to judge each picture about the sex, likeability, or honesty of the face presented. Recall in subjects evaluating honesty and likeability was significantly higher than recall in those subjects who evaluated sex. Bower and Karlin (1977) proposed that these results could be related to the larger amount of processing, or encoding, necessary to determine honesty and likeability.

Another aspect of visual sensory store lies in Neisser's (1975) concept of iconic memory. This term describes the persistence of a visual impression after it has been removed. Sperling (1960, as cited by Haber and Hershenson, 1973) explained that what a subject actually saw, and what was perceived may in reality be two different things. Moreover, Sperling proposed that the visual impression subjects recall may contain more than was originally presented, and that perhaps an overlap in impressions could occur. Using a "partial-report" technique Sperling (1960) demonstrated that if recall in iconic storage tasks was delayed beyond one second, recall dropped significantly. However, Shiffrin and Gardner (1972) attained experimental results which indicated that iconic memory storage was greater than indicated by Sperling (1960).

The presence of an auditory sensory storage has been examined through the modality effect. Broadbent, Vines, and Broadbent (1978) concluded that subjects who received a stimulus auditorily, or vocalized the stimulus words, were superior in recall to those who received a silent-visualized presentation of the experimental stimulus. Engle and Roberts (1982) further substantiated the results of Broadbent et al. (1978) by extending recall delay in modality effect experiments to sixty seconds. Auditory recall scores were still significant, although the filler task itself could not be auditory or vocalized.

It is possible that a slight modality effect was present in C. K. Allen's (1983) experiment of short-term memory for colors and color names, thus resulting in higher recall scores.

The use of "release from proactive inhibition" to increase recall scores has become prevalent among short-term memory researchers. Keppel and Underwood (1962) concluded that in Peterson-Peterson short-term memory tasks, proactive inhibition is a confounding variable. So, to compensate for subjects' increase in recall errors due to proactive inhibition, Wickens, Born, and Allen (1963) interjected a shift condition into short-term memory experiments. Results indicated that "release from proactive inhibition," in this case a shift from one mode of presentation to another, did yield significantly higher recall scores.

C. K. Allen (1983) also implicated a "release from proactive inhibition" when studying short-term memory for color and color names. Subjects were presented with either colors or color names for three trials, and on the fourth trial half of the subjects were shifted to the opposite condition. The other half of the subjects remained with the original stimulus condition. Results indicate that the interaction between the shift and no shift conditions was significant. Thus, it was concluded that proactive inhibition does indeed develop to colors as well as color names. However, Allen's conclusion fails to answer his original question concerning the way in which persons encode colors. Allen's (1983) stimuli (color vs. color names) were continually matched throughout the experiment. Recall scores can be no indication of whether the color or color name was encoded; a correct color/color name recall would merely indicate that one of the two was encoded. Allen's (1983) defense for his use of "release proactive inhibition" to increase recall of colors and color names is effective, if one is studying the *recall* of colors and color names and methods to improve recall. However, Allen states that his purpose is to reveal how persons *encode* colors and color names. For this purpose his methods are not effective.

The present experiment was an attempt to answer Allen's (1983) originally posed question "Is color encoded as a kind of visual image or a verbal label or both?". The critical component of inconsistency between color and color name was added in hopes that it would allow the experimenter to measure whether the actual color presented was encoded, or if the color name (verbal label) was encoded.

Subjects in the Experimental Group were exposed to a color vs. color name condition in four varying levels of percent consistency. A second group of subjects was exposed to the color names only, while a third group received only colors. Both of these groups acted as controls.

The proposed hypothesis stated that if color is indeed encoded as a verbal label, then those subjects in the Experimental Group should have high recall scores (of color names) regardless of the various consistency conditions. Furthermore, if color is encoded as a verbal label and not a visual image, subjects in Control Group B (those who receive color names only) should also have significantly high recall scores.

The present experiment also attempted to control for the possible presence of a slight modality effect in Allen's (1983) study. The counting task in the retention interval period was extended from thirty to sixty seconds on the basis of the findings of Engle and Roberts (1982).

"Release from proactive inhibition" was not a consideration in the present study, as the technique would have acted as a confounding variable in attempting to conclude how persons encode color.

METHOD

Subjects

The subjects for this experiment were twenty-four female undergraduates who were randomly selected from the Manhattanville College population. All subjects were randomly assigned to one of three groups, and all subjects were tested in only one group. The Experimental Group contained twelve subjects while Control Group A and Control Group B each contained six subjects.

Materials

Twelve highly discriminable colors and their appropriate color names were used in developing the experimental stimuli. The color names selected were not those of primary colors, and were not easily identifiable. The twelve colors and color names selected are as follows: lavender, mauve, sand, amber, indigo, turquoise, jade, olive, scarlet, salmon, lemon, and pumpkin.

All stimuli were presented on 5 × 8 in index cards.

The stimuli for the Experimental Group was composed of four separate 5 × 8 in index cards. On each card three different 2 × 5 cm colored strips were pasted. Each individual strip was placed horizontally so that the three color strips together formed a vertical row. Typed in boldface print onto each color strip was the name of one color. The color name typed onto each card was determined according to the specific experimental percent consistency condition being tested. Thus, the four stimulus cards for the Experimental Group were as follows:

Card I.   100% Consistency: Three color strips labeled with their appropriate corresponding color names.

COLOR OF STRIP	COLOR NAME LABELED
lemon	lemon
scarlet	scarlet
jade	jade

Card II. 67% Consistency: Three color strips, two of which were labeled with their appropriate color name, and one of which was labeled with a clearly incorrect color name.

COLOR OF STRIP	COLOR NAME LABELED
pumpkin	pumpkin
salmon	salmon
lavender	indigo

Card III. 33% Consistency: Three color stips, two of which were labeled with incorrect color names, and one of which was labeled with the appropriate color name.

COLOR OF STRIP	COLOR NAME LABELED
olive	lavender
sand	mauve
turquoise	turquoise

Card IV. 0% Consistency: Three color strips, all of which were labeled with incorrect color names.

COLOR OF STRIP	COLOR NAME LABELED
indigo	olive
mauve	amber
amber	sand

On each stimulus card a three-digit number was typed in boldface print directly below the color strips. The number varies for each stimulus card in the experimental condition.

The four stimulus cards for Control Group A were each composed of three color names only. Each stimulus card contained the same color names as did the corresponding cards for each condition in the Experimental Group. All color names were typed in boldface print onto a 5×8 in index card. The color names were typed one beneath another, so that the three together formed a vertical row. Centered below the color name was one three-digit number. The number on each card was the same as that on the corresponding card in the experimental condition.

The four stimulus cards for Control Group B were each composed of three color strips only. Each stimulus card contained the same color strips as did the corresponding card in the experimental condition, and the color strips were placed horizontally so that the three together formed a vertical row. The same three-digit number centered below corresponding cards in the previous two groups was typed below the color strips in Control Group B.

A metronome, set at one beat per second, operated throughout the period of experimental testing.

A stopwatch was used to time the retention interval period and the intertrial intervals.

Procedure

Five random orders of presentation were established. These random orders are as follows:

1. 100%, 0%, 67%, 33%
2. 33%, 67%, 0%, 100%
3. 0%, 67%, 100%, 33%
4. 33%, 100%, 0%, 67%
5. 67%, 100%, 0%, 33%
6. 100%, 67%, 0%, 33%

Prior to testing all subjects received and signed a consent form.

Subjects were randomly assigned to one of the three groups, and each subject was tested in only one group.

Those subjects placed in the Experimental Group were exposed to stimulus cards containing both color and color name. Two subjects were exposed to one of the six random presentation orders, for a total of twelve subjects.

Those six subjects randomly placed in Control Group A were exposed to the stimulus cards containing only color names. Each subject received one of the six random presentation orders listed on the previous page.

Those six subjects placed in Control Group B were exposed to colors only. They too received one random presentation order apiece.

Prior to the presentation of any stimulus cards, subjects in the Experimental Group and Control Group A received the following instructions:

1. Upon presentation of a stimulus card they were to read aloud, in correct order, the color names that they saw on the card.
2. To then read aloud the three-digit number typed at the bottom of the card, and to add three to that number.
3. To continue adding three to that number until told to "stop."
4. Upon being told to stop, they were to attempt to recall the color names they read aloud prior to counting.

Those subjects in Control Group B were exposed to colors only, and received the following instructions prior to testing:

1. Upon presentation of a stimulus card they were to assign a color name to each color that they saw.
2. To then read aloud the three-digit number that was centered beneath the three color strips, and to add three to that number.
3. To continue adding three until told to "stop."
4. Upon being told to stop, to attempt to recall the color names that they assigned each color strip prior to counting.

A metronome, set at one beat per second, operated throughout all testing periods. All subjects were exposed to each stimulus card for four seconds. Oral repetitive additions of three continued for sixty seconds. Immediately following the retention interval, subjects were given twelve seconds to recall color names or color labels. The next trial began eighteen seconds after the previous recall period ended. Subjects received three practice trials which were not scored.

Each trial was scored individually. Subjects received one point for each correctly recalled color name or color label. One additional point was added if all color names or color labels were recalled in the correct order. Scoring ranged from zero to four points.

A one-way Analysis of Variance was calculated between the recall scores of the Experimental Group, Control Group A and Control Group B.

A one-way Analysis of Variance was also calculated between the recall scores in the four consistency conditions in the Experimental Group.

RESULTS

The mean score for subjects in the Experimental Group was 2.85, with a standard error of 2.61. The mean score for Control Group A was 2.79, and the standard error was 3.58. Subjects in Control Group B had a mean score of 3.62, with a standard error of 4.50.

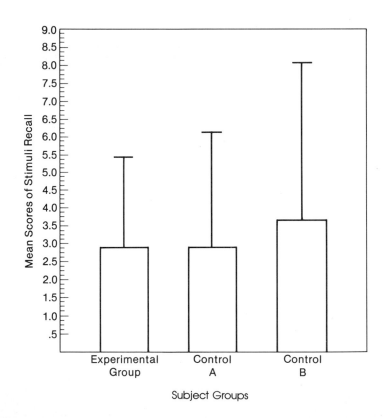

FIGURE 1. Mean Color/Color Name Recall Scores for the Experimental Group, Control Group A and Control Group B

Means and standard errors were also calculated for the recall scores in the four percent consistency conditions of the Experimental Group. In the 100% consistency condition the mean score was 3.33, and the standard error was .271. The mean score for the 0% consistency condition was 2.66, while the standard error was .338. For the 67% consistency condition the mean score was 2.41, and the standard error was .317. The mean score for the 33% consistency condition was 3.00, and the standard error was .332.

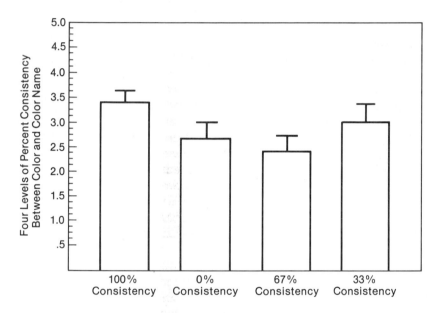

Four Levels of Percent Consistency Between Color and Color Name

FIGURE 2. Mean Recall Scores in Four Levels of Percent Consistency Within the Experimental Group

A one-way Analysis of Variance between the Experimental Group, Control Group A and Control Group B yielded an F value of 3.067. At $df_{bg} = 2$ and $df_{wg} = 21$ the critical value at .05 was 3.47. As the obtained F value of 3.067 failed to exceed either critical value, the null hypothesis H_o: $u_1 = u_2 = u_3$ was retained.

A one-way Analysis of Variance calculated between the scores in the four levels of percent consistency yielded an F value of 1.465. At $df_{bg} = 3$ and $df_{wg} = 44$, the critical value at .05 was 2.84. The obtained F value of 1.465 failed to equal or exceed either of these critical values, and the null hypothesis H_o: $u_1 = u_2 = u_3 = u_4$ was retained.

DISCUSSION

The results obtained from a one-way Analysis of Variance calculated on re-call scores between the Experimental Group, Control Group A and Control Group B indicated that no significant difference in recall ability was present between the subjects who were exposed to color, color name, or color and color name. Moreover, a one-way Analysis of Variance performed on recall scores between 100%, 67%, 33%, and 0% levels of consistency showed that no significant difference existed between any of these four groups of recall scores.

Although no significant differences were found between recall scores in the Experimental Group, Control Group A, and Control Group B, it is im-portant to note existing trends in the data. The mean score of those subjects who assigned color labels to color strips (Control Group B) was 3.62. Obvi-ously this score is higher than the mean score of the Experimental Group and Control Group B, which were 2.85 and 2.79, respectively. Although the mean score for Control Group B was not statistically significantly higher, it does point to the possiblity of achieving statistically significant results if ex-perimental methods were manipulated. The use of a greater number of mea-sures within each trial might serve to produce results which show that subjects who assign color labels to colors do have a significantly higher label recall. Despite the rather common use of a four-point scoring scale among researchers, such a scale mandates that scores must be more "drastic" or se-vere to achieve statistically significant results. Miller (1956) has suggested that short-term memory has the capacity for retention and recall of seven items, plus or minus two. Hence, the addition of three or four color/color name stimuli to each stimulus presentation card may result in significantly different results.

Individual recall scores within each subject group must also be consid-ered in the analysis of data. In both the Experimental Group and Control Group A were scores that appeared to be drastically different than those of other subjects within the group. In the Experimental Group one subject had a total score of six of sixteen possible points, or a mean score of 1.50. A sec-ond subject had a total score of seven of sixteen possible points, or a mean score of 1.75. Had these subject scores not been used in the calculation of the overall mean for the Experimental Group, the overall mean score would have equaled 5.10. Although the omission of these two scores would not have resulted in significantly different mean recall scores between the Ex-perimental Group, Control Group A and Control Group B, it might have sig-nificantly altered the differences between percent consistency conditions within the Experimental Group.

The presence of scores which appeared to be drastically low in relation to other individual scores within the percent consistency conditions may have also acted to change results, as well as the F value, within the Experi-mental Group. For instance, in the 100% consistency condition, seven subjects received scores of four (recalled all color names in the correct order), and four subjects received scores of three (recalled all color names). However, one subject received only one point in the 100% consistency condition. It is also important to note that this did not occur within all consistency conditions, but rather only in the 100% and the 0% consistency conditions. Had subjects of this low-scoring nature not participated in the study, results within the Experimental Group may have shown that significantly different recall abilities did exist between the four levels of percent consistency.

To control for such a possibility, in a follow-up study of how persons encode colors, subjects should be given a memory test prior to presentation of stimuli. On the basis of memory test scores the experimenter could assign subjects to specific groups rather than relying on random placement, so as to balance the distribution of high and low short-term memory retention/recall subjects. Moreover, a larger number of subjects within each group should aid in controlling for drastically low recall scores and their effect on the overall mean score.

A particular trend which occurred within Control Group B points to yet another area of future investigation. Those subjects who received colors only, and were required to assign appropriate color labels to them, had a tendency to overlap in recall material. More specifically, subjects in Control Group B who recalled incorrect answers tended to recall color labels assigned to colors in *previous* trials rather than in the present trial. It seems that these observations are consistent with those of Neisser (1975), which led to his development of the iconic memory concept.

Although Shiffrin and Gardner (1972) obtained experimental results which indicated that iconic memory storage was greater than the one-second recall duration that Sperling (1960) obtained, it has not been documented that iconic memory storage is significantly effective in retention intervals of sixty seconds. Thus, it is highly unlikely that recall of color labels in Control Group B could be attributed to the concept of iconic memory. However, Sperling (1960) also proposed that the visual impression which subjects may recall could contain more than was originally presented, and that perhaps an overlap in impressions could occur. Noting the trend of subjects in Control Group B to recall the color label assigned to stimuli presented on previous stimulus cards, Sperling's (1960) proposal of impression overlap would indeed seem possible. Further investigation of such a proposal might be facilitated by *not* randomizing stimulus card presentation order, so as to effectively measure not only correct/incorrect response, but also exact recall response. It is possible that the impression overlap in recall could be determined to be statistically significant, and consistent with Sperling's (1960) proposal.

Results of the present study indicated no significant difference in recall ability between those subjects presented with color, color name, or color *and* color name. Moreover, varying levels of consistency did not yield significantly higher or lower recall scores. Hence, experimental results failed to support the proposed hypothesis that if color is encoded as a verbal label, subjects in the Experimental Group would have higher recall scores regardless of the implication of percent consistency relationship. Moreover, the recall scores of color names by subjects in Control Group A failed to support the hypothesis that if the color is encoded as a verbal label subjects who receive only color names should have significantly higher recall scores.

Based on the non-significant results obtained, it would seem that the answer to C. K. Allen's (1983) originally posed question "Is color encoded as a kind of visual image or verbal label, or both?" is probably both. This conclusion is consistent with the findings of Paivio (1969) who had college students rate a series of nouns for their ability to arouse "a mental picture, or sound, or other sensory picture." Paivio's (1969) results, which served to form his Dual-Coding Hypothesis, showed that some words convey more of a mental image while others convey a label.

It is possible that color and color names convey more of an image than a label, and that this factor resulted in a higher mean recall score in Control Group B, despite the fact that the mean score was not statistically significant. A future study should include the proposed hypothesis that some subjects are more verbally oriented while others are more image oriented. Such a study should include extensive research on left and right brain hemisphere dominance, as it is possible that hemisphere dominance effects image and label orientation. Moreover, such a study might succeed in answering C. K. Allen's (1983) question, in showing that color may be encoded as a verbal label and a visual label, and that this concept may vary between subjects. A modified experimental recall task using a chart of color strips and printed color names would allow subjects to recall the stimulus in a more natural way, as opposed to predisposing them to transfer recall to a verbal label in a recall task of verbal nature. Furthermore, a chart recall method would allow the experimenter to record the impression overlap in recall responses within the subject group only receiving color strips, whereby facilitating the study of Neisser's (1975) concept of impression overlap in iconic memory.

References

Agrawal, R. (1982). Rehearsal in short term memory as a function of load of information, age and intelligence. *Journal of Psychological Research, 26,* 76–83.

Allen, C. K. (1983). Short term memory for colors and color names. *Psychological Reports, 53,* 579–582.

Boerse, J. & Crassini, B. (1984). Investigations of perception and imagery using color-after-effects. *Perception and Psychophysics, 35,* 155–164.

Bower, G. H. (1970). Imagery as a relational organizer in associative learning. *Journal of Verbal Learning and Verbal Behavior, 9,* 529–533.

Bower, G. H. (1970). Organizational factors in memory. *Cognitive Psychology, 1,* 18–46.

Bower, G. H. & Karlin, M. B. (1977). Depth of processing pictures of faces and recognition memory. *Journal of Experimental Psychology, 103*, 751–757.

Broadbent, D., Vines, R. & Broadbent, M. (1978). Recency effects in memory as a function of modality of intervening events. *Psychological Research, 40*, 5–13.

Brown, R. & McNeill, D. (1966). The "tip-of-the-tongue" phenomenon. *Journal of Verbal Learning and Verbal Behavior, 5*, 325–337.

Brown, P. K. & Wald, G. (1964). Visual pigment in single rods and cones of the human retina. *Science, 144*, 45–52.

Christie, D. F. & Phillips, W. A. (1979). Simple drawing and pattern completion techniques for studying visualization and long-term visual knowledge. *Memory and Cognition, 7*, 360–367.

Delaney, H. D. & Logan, F. A. (1979). Item similarity and proactive interference in short-term memory. *Bulletin of the Psychonomic Society, 14*, 288–290.

Engle, R. W. & Roberts, J. S. (1982). How long does the modality effect persist? *Bulletin of the Psychonomic Society, 19*, 343–346.

Gellar, E. S. (1982). Studying short-term storage of expectation with reaction time. *Bulletin of the Psychonomic Society, 19*, 343–346.

Haber, R. N. & Hershenson, M. (1973). *The Psychology of Visual Perception.* New York: Holt, Rinehart and Winston, Inc.

Hurvich, L. M. & Jameson, D. (1957). An opponent-process theory of color vision. *Psychological Review, 64*, 384–404.

Kaufman, L. (1974). *Sight and Mind: An Introduction to Visual Perception.* New York: Oxford University Press.

Keppel, G. & Underwood, B. J. (1962). Proactive inhibition in short-term retention of single items. *Journal of Verbal Learning and Verbal Behavior, 1*, 153–161.

Levine, M. W. & Shefner, J. M. (1981). *Fundamentals of Sensation and Perception.* Reading, Mass.: Addison-Wesley Publishing Co.

Marks, W. B., Dobelle, W. H. & MacNichol, E. F. Jr. (1964). Visual pigments of single primate cones. *Science, 143*, 1181–1183.

Miller, G. G. (1956). The magical number seven, plus or minus two: Some limit on our capacity for processing information. *Psychological Review, 63*, 81–97.

Neisser, U. & Becklen, R. (1975). Selective looking: Attending to visually significant events. *Cognitive Psychology, 7*, 480–494.

Paivio, A. (1969). Abstractness, imagery, and meaningfulness in paired-associate learning. *Journal of Verbal Learning and Verbal Behavior, 4*, 32–38.

Peterson, L. R. & Peterson, M. J. (1959). Short-term retention of individual verbal items. *Journal of Experimental Psychology, 58*, 193–198.

Reid, G. & Marisi, D. Q. (1982). Overt rehearsal in short-term motor memory. *Perceptual and Motor Skills, 55*, 229–230.

Shiffrin, R. M. & Gardner, G. T. (1972). Visual processing capacity and attention control. *Journal of Experimental Psychology, 93*, 72–82.

Underwood, B. J. (1957). Interference and forgetting. *Psychological Review, 64*, 49–60.

Underwood, B. J. (1969). Attributes of memory. *Psychological Review, 76*, 559–573.

Wickens, D. D., Born, D. G., & Allen, C. K. (1963). Proactive inhibition and item similarity in short term memory. *Journal of Verbal Learning and Verbal Behavior, 2*, 440–445.

Wickens, D. D. & Engle, R. W. (1970). Imagery and abstractness in short term memory. *Journal of Experimental Psychology, 84*, 268–272.

■ **UNDERSTANDING WRITING STRATEGIES**

1. What is the relationship between the literature review and the introduction? What is the paper's thesis, or organizing statement?

2. Two kinds of literature appear in the review. What are they? What does each contribute to the study?

3. How does Jones-Waldinger order the literature review?

4. What is the experimental hypothesis?

5. How well does Jones-Waldinger explain her experiment's design?

6. What audience would benefit from this paper? Is the paper written for this audience? How do you know?

7. What conclusion does Jones-Waldinger reach?

8. What relationship exists between the conclusion and the data analysis section? ■

Personality Today Magazine *Presents: The Hiding of Anne Frank: A "Ghost Interview" with Karen Horney*

Dennifer P. Kann

By creating a distinctive audience, hypothetical *Personality Today Magazine*'s readers, and using the interview format to give both herself and psychologist Karen Horney individual voices, Dennifer Kann enlivens a potentially routine writing assignment for her psychology course, Theories of Personality. In this "interview" Karen Horney analyzes the personality of Anne Frank, the young Jewish girl whose diary chronicles her family's attempt to escape the Nazis.

Anne Frank was already "in hiding" by the time she and the others moved into the Annex to hide from the Nazis in July of 1942. This shocking contradiction of the widely accepted facts set forth in Anne Frank's diary is the result of Dr. Karen Horney's extensive psychoanalytical research into *Anne*

Frank: The Diary of a Young Girl and the Miep Gies book, *Anne Frank Remembered.*

"The juxtaposition of the Gies account and the content of the dated diary entries," Dr. Horney explained in a recent interview, "enabled me to conclude that Anne was psychologically 'in hiding' even before she started her diary on her thirteenth birthday. Her early diary entry on June 20, 1942, alerted me to this possibility since she referred to her previous inability to establish a close relationship with her peers, despite her apparent popularity. This reference, when considered with the other same-entry intimations of Anne's 'melancholy days,' lack of confidence, and inability 'to do anything about it' (Frank, 1952, pp. 2–3), indicated immediately that to understand this young girl, I would have to read between the lines. "

The significance of Anne's early psychological hiding or emotional withdrawal from others, according to Dr. Horney, is that it provided a clue as to the characteristic way in which Anne coped with the people and the world around her.

"The particular relevance here," Dr. Horney continued, "is that Anne's basic hostility and anxiety had already fostered the development of neurotic strivings that supported her tactics for dealing with her environment before she went into physical hiding. The conflicts that were entrenched in Anne's personality were not formed in the restrictive environment of the Annex, as a superficial reading of her document might imply. Rather, what happened in that restrictive environment was that Anne compulsively forced herself to focus upon those conflicts."

When asked to expand on the conflicts, Dr. Horney replied, "The converging conflicts Anne focused upon were the internally normal inner conflicts of an adolescent girl, compounded with her preexistent and growing inner conflicts, plus the simultaneous assaults by her external conflictual worlds within and without the Annex. By focusing on these conflicts, as she was doing in her diary writings, Anne was attempting to employ auxiliary approaches to solving the conflict within her pride system and later, between her pride system and her real self. But, the resulting egocentric intensity of these secondary defenses literally placed Anne in the midst of a psychic 'battlegound' (Horney, 1950, p. 259) between her superficial-expansive despised self and her purer-compliant ideal self. Then, according to Anne's experience, her only recourse was to withdraw 'from the inner battlefield and declare [herself] uninterested' (p. 259) by eventually solidifying her resignation solution. "

At this point in the interview, the verbose Dr. Horney took a much deserved break to get a glass of water while the interviewer tried to think of a tactful way to ask the doctor to please respond in a manner that the average reader might comprehend. Fortunately, she had a sense of humor, and, after a brief pause for her toothy smile, she ventured on.

"Let us go back to the basics," she said. "In the beginning Anne felt a basic hostility toward her parents for what she perceived to be their attitudes of rejecting indifference. This hostility was repressed only to evolve into a basic anxiety, which allowed Anne to project her hostility to the world in general, thereby sparing her the psychological discomfort of experiencing her true feelings for her parents. ''

Dr. Horney's assumption was that Anne's basic hostility probably resulted from her difficulties in taking her mother's attention away from Margot, Anne's older sister. In her diary entry of January 5, 1944, Anne wrote her still-painful memories of such an incident that took place only a few years before. Anne evidently retained her strong emotional reaction to the memory of this incident because it was too uncomfortably similar to her repressed childhood feelings of hurt, rage, and rejection.

"These were the feelings, in accordance with her neurotic needs," continued Dr. Horney, "that shaped Anne's 'early solution' (Horney, 1950, p. 21) for coping with other people and the world. To get what she thought was her fair share of attention, she built up her exuberant facade; and to protect her vulnerable sensitivities, she hid part of herself away. So, 'without realizing it, or at least without realizing the extent of it, [she lived] in two worlds—that of [her] secret life and that of [her] official life' (p. 40)."

After pausing for a sip of her water, Dr. Horney explained, "To maintain the balance between her two worlds, Anne's neurotic needs grew into neurotic claims to justify her frustration and indignation whenever her treatment by others did not 'cater to [her] notions' (p. 41). The 'over-all function' of Anne's claims was to 'perpetuate [her] illusions about [herself], and to shift responsibility to factors outside [herself]' (p. 63). So, as the world reacted to the 'superficial' Anne (Frank, 1952, p. 240) in ways she found unsatisfactory, Anne began to build the image in her mind of what the hidden 'better, deeper, purer' Anne (p. 240) 'should be able to do, to be, to feel [and] to know' along with the image of what she 'should not be' (Horney, 1950, p. 65). These inner dictates 'do not aim at real change but at an immediate and absolute perfection. They aim at making the imperfection disappear' (p. 72)." Then Dr. Horney emphasized the importance of the following as she leaned forward to make her point, " ' or at making it appear as if the particular perfection were attained. This becomes especially clear if . . . the inner demands are externalized. Then what a person actually is, and even what he suffers, becomes irrelevant. Only what is visible to others creates intense worries: a shaking of the hand, a blush, an awkwardness in social situations' (p. 72)."

"To clarify this in terms of Anne," she offered, "consider this example. In her second diary entry, that of June 15, 1942, before she even formally introduced herself to her diary, Anne wrote that she 'managed, without blushing or flickering an eyelid,' (Frank, 1952, p. 2) to keep her mother from knowing which boy she admired. The significance here is that Anne was already operating under a 'should' dictate to control, in the presence of her mother, both her feelings and her vascular system, either of which could have betrayed Anne with a threatening blush.''

"It is important to note that by this point in her life, a lot of Anne's energy was committed to the task of trying to control her reactions, as exemplified by this analogous blush. This was because the victory of self-control was crucial to the neurotic pride and self-hate conflict that operated within her pride system. Anne spoke proudly of her achievement in that early entry, and then in her entry of September 28, 1942, she contemptuously wrote about Mrs. Van Daan that 'people who blush get so hot and excited, it is quite a handicap in such a situation' (p. 30). Anne also wrote about blushing in a later entry that I will mention in a moment. What I found revealing though, was that I could almost measure Anne's neurotic progression by the content and intent of her writings related to blushing."

Dr. Horney then proceeded to point out that Anne's first blushing reference was before the Annex move and before there was any extra conflictual baggage to burden her. Or as Anne later described that time in her life: "I often felt deserted, but because I was on the go the whole day long, I didn't think about it and enjoyed myself as much as I could" (p. 152). The second blushing reference came after the Annex move when Anne began to feel and react to the pressures of her baggage along with that of the others. Of this time in her life, she wrote: "I couldn't understand it, I was taken by surprise, and the only way I could keep up some bearing was by being impertinent" (p. 153). The third blushing reference that Dr. Horney mentioned earlier was in Anne's diary entry of January 5, 1944. In it, Anne confessed to reading an article about blushing and wrote, "although I don't blush very easily, the other things in it [the article] certainly all fit me" (p. 116).

"Before I explain what Anne wrote about this time in her life," Dr. Horney interjected, "let me elucidate this blushing reference. The 'other things' in the article told of the thoughts and experiences of pubescent girls, and, in her corresponding entry, Anne wrote that she had had her third period and that it was her 'sweet secret' (p. 117). Anne made an important statement in this entry that she did not write down. This was one of the passages where it was important to read between the lines. At the beginning of this entry, Anne wrote how her mother considered herself a friend to her daughters. Then Anne added, 'a friend can't take a mother's place' (p. 116). In the next passage, Anne recalled the earlier-mentioned, painful childhood memory when she interpreted her feelings of rejection as rage. Of that experience with her mother, Anne wrote, 'I have never forgiven her' (p. 116). Then, as Anne wrote about and said she identified with the blushing article, she admitted to her 'sweet secret.' The message Anne did not write down, but implied between the lines was, 'There Mummy, I'm a woman now. I've made it all by myself—no thanks to you.' "

"I realize," continued the doctor, "that Anne also made references to homosexuality in this entry, but according to my past studies of female adolescents, I would not classify Anne in the group of those who develop homosexual tendencies. Anne's characteristics were more in line with the emotionally detached group (Horney, 1967, p. 235). But, we should not lose our train of thought here. This third blushing reference came at a time in Anne's life that seemed to show an intensification of her inner conflicts. I do not believe that it was merely coincidental that this came about near the time of Anne's menarche. My previous studies have shown that 'in analyzing adult women with neurotic troubles . . . the determining conflicts have arisen in childhood . . . [and] the first personality changes have taken place in adolescence . . . [and] the onset of these changes [coincided] approximately with the beginning of menstration' (Horney, 1967, p. 234). According to my calculations, Anne reached menarche around September of 1943, and from this point on in the diary, I saw a discernible increase of the symbolic and introspective elements in her writing. Now, we can return to our blush analogy for Anne's impressions of the changes that occurred at the time of the third blushing reference."

Dr. Horney pointed out that in her March 7, 1944, entry, Anne wrote, "Things improved slightly in the second half of the year (1943); I became a young woman and was treated more like a grownup . . . I wanted to change in accordance with my own desires . . . I didn't want to trust anyone but myself anymore. At the beginning of [1944]: the second great change, my dream . . . and with it I discovered my longing, not for a girlfriend, but for a boyfriend. I also discovered my inward happiness and my defensive armor of superficiality and gaiety . . . I quieted down and discovered my boundless desire for all that is beautiful and good" (Frank, 1952, p. 153).

"In this third phase, Anne was more intensely 'caught in the push and pull of pride and self-condemnation' (Horney, 1950, p. 170)," explained the doctor, "which further alienated her real self as she desperately sought the means to actualize her ideal self. To gain control over her raging inner conflicts, she relied more heavily upon her 'shoulds' and resorted more frequently to the secondary defenses which were voiced increasingly through her diary. This is exactly what her longing for a boyfriend was all about. Anne used Peter as a means to actualize her ideal self until she became so threatened by her self-condemning predictions of rejection that she rationalized in her March 12, 1944, entry that 'if [she] trusted someone completely, then [she] shouldn't want them hanging around [her] all the time' (Frank, 1952, p. 155). So, when the conflicts inherent in this situation became too uncomfortable for Anne, she solved them in her typical manner and withdrew."

This growing change in Anne was distressingly visible to Miep Gies, who wrote, "I'd seen Anne, like a chameleon, go from mood to mood, but always with friendliness. . . . But I saw a look on her face at this moment that I'd never seen before. It was a look of dark concentration, as if she had a throbbing headache. This look pierced me, and I was speechless. She was suddenly another person there writing at the table. . . . I was upset by Anne's dark mood. I knew that more and more her diary had become her life. It was as if I had interrupted an intimate moment in a very, very private friendship. . . . It wasn't Anne up there . . . it was another person" (Gies, 1987, pp. 186–187).

5. The appar
   ing techni

6. What kin
   terials?

7. How did I

8. How does
   argument

9. What pur
   her analy

10. Explain v
    What risl
    not be ap

A Co1
of Co.
Publi
Schoc

Janet M

In recent
observati
sociolog
teachers

I. INTRODl

A. Personal

As a prospe
cant amoun
This factor
specialty in
questions su
alleviate th

"By checking the details of the documents against each other," said Dr. Horney, "I surmised that the writing session Gies interrupted was that of July 15, 1944, when Anne wrote in her diary, '. . . I want to lay myself completely bare to you for once and defend myself against this attack' (Frank, 1952, p. 234). The perceived attack Anne disproportionately reacted to was from a book criticizing the youth of the day. Anne went on to write, 'I can watch myself and my actions, just like an outsider. . . . This "self-consciousness" haunts me . . .' (p. 234). Then Anne proceeded to bare her soul and used practically every possible secondary defense in doing so. This was the frame of mind that Gies intruded upon."

As Dr. Horney continued, her voice crescendoed, "And then, in Anne's final diary entry, that of August 11, 1944, she described herself as a 'little bundle of contradictions' and referred to her 'contradiction from without and contradiction from within' (Frank, 1952, p. 239). I found this self-description extremely appropriate, because, in layman's terms, Anne precisely described what is 'the essential characteristic of every neurotic: he is at war with himself. Actually, the foundation has been laid for two different kinds of conflicts. One of them is within the pride system itself. . . . the other, deeper conflict is between the whole pride system and the real self' (Horney, 1950, p. 112). And this is exactly where Anne was when she left us—in the midst of the latter conflictual battleground or the central inner conflict between the 'healthy and neurotic, constructive and destructive forces' (p. 113)."

"In the last lines of her diary, Anne wrote that she wanted to 'keep on trying to find a way of becoming what [she] would so like to be, and what [she] could be, if . . . there weren't any other people living in the world' (Frank, 1952, p. 241). This indicated to me," Dr. Horney concluded, "that Anne would have left us anyway, as she eventually grew more and more resigned to her inner, secret annex."

With her final statement, Dr. Horney looked to the interviewer and asked if there were any further questions. The one that immediately came to mind was, what the reaction of the psychological community had been to her findings. Openly she qualified, "Naturally, everyone is entitled to his own opinion, and you realize that personality theorists sometimes differ greatly as to what they believe to be the key determinants of human behavior. Generally, I would venture that most theorists familiar with the workings of my theory would agree that it allows an accurate portrayal of Anne's psychological hiding posture. The greatest strength in using my theory to view Anne is that it offers the opportunity to capture the essence of her 'moving away from people' tendency. It also, as in a series of snapshots taken from different angles, allows us to view the progression of her neurosis. Perhaps, in photographic terms, you could say that it offers an animated picture of Anne as opposed to a still shot."

"Not everyone, however, would agree with my theory or my conclusion." Then, with a chuckle, she added, "The Anne Frank Foundation was extremely upset that I characterized Anne Frank as neurotic! Some theorists

would r
fact, adj
for id-e
connota
a more
and stag
tude. O
younges
politica
that soi
ciencies
not to i
neuroch

"F
view, "I
Frank. 7
this hid

Frank, A
Gies, M
Horney,
Horney,
    pa
Horney,
Horney,
Monte,

■ THE

Using
he/she

■ UNI

1. Wi
   pai

2. Wł
   Hc

3. Fo

4. Ho
   to

---

retary, and principal use the lounge and the adjacent restroom facilities. Smoking is permitted.

The public school has a large teachers' lounge where most of the faculty spend their lunch breaks and free periods. I observed two aides also eating in the room. There is a small "janitor's room" where other aides and the janitors eat. Smoking is permitted in this room only, and several teachers meet there. Cafeteria personnel eat together in the kitchens.

The teachers' lounge was the most appropriate place to witness the teachers interacting. In this open setting without the presence of children and usually without supervisors, they acted spontaneously and seemed relaxed in their roles as work-mates.

I had slight concerns with the ethical question of being an unknown observer, but I felt comfortable with assuring anonymity in this paper, as well as in my field notes. Well known as a student, I was afforded the role of a "socially acceptable incompetent" and not only had certain matters explained to me as a newcomer, but was also comfortably ignored by many of the staff.[8] I believed my imposition in both these schools did not significantly alter the activities or conversations of the observed.

C. Intensive Interviewing

I developed my interview instrument by concentrating on the areas in which I believed teachers would reveal their problems, their desires, and solutions to difficulties. Many questions were repeated in varying contexts to ascertain the strength of conviction in their answers.

Topics in the instrument were experience; job satisfaction which included why they became a teacher, as well as their outside commitments; philosophy of education which revealed their attitudes on local issues and administrative support; their attitudes towards children, parents, and peers which addressed perceptions of capability; their commitment to the district in which they teach; stress and their coping strategies.

I purposefully chose my interviewees in an attempt to get a representative sample of new and long-experienced teachers, married and unmarried, male and female. I also interviewed the principal of each school, tailoring the interview instrument slightly. I had no difficulty in acquiring ten candidates for interviewing; however, I felt obligated to curtail the length of time in order to accommodate their busy school schedules. The majority of interviews were done at work during their free time, lasting an average of one hour.

I taped four interviews. Many of the other six requested I not tape them. Although I assured anonymity, I believed the tape recorder would have inhibited them from answering honestly. In retrospect, it is possible that at least two of the taped interviewees more carefully chose their words, and may have given me the "correct" answer rather than their "honest" answer.

The public
tion with their s
sension in some
teacher's proble
spreading that in
all sought outsi
other teachers "
solidarity among

The eleme
other, and inclu
tently both in m
ers. I believe the
which strongly p
sence of these e
tions among the

B. Specific Not

As stated earlier
mental sample
due to the vario
ferent. The inter
community con
teacher already
group's attendan
For several differ
others are not in
sciously separat
ity from profess

This incon
obfuscated the f
actual interviev
word itself. The
syncratic expect

Another fa
ness of the rese
ing to several va
the general clim
cooperation am
new principal.
grievances in th
many of the te
preted different
The sense

I estimate that my interviews were highly valuable in assessing the sense of community and understanding the perspectives of each teacher. However, to increase accuracy, it would be beneficial to interview a greater proportion of the staff. Particularly in the public school, I needed several more interview candidates to achieve some consensus, and be more assured that I had included most types of perspectives.

III. SUMMARY OF FINDINGS

A. General Evaluation

My main focus in this research was to assess the sense of community and how that was exhibited among the public and private school teachers. As Albert Hunter in his study of Chicago neighborhoods revealed, community is a multidimensional social organization and "rather than asking whether 'community' does or does not exist, we should approach the problem by asking whether this or that element of community is present and to what degree."[9] I attempted this approach when I did my participant observation, and again when I reviewed the data. The contrasting of one school to the other furthers this angle of examination.

With regard to the aspect of stress, there was much consensus among public and private school teachers about the causes of stress. Nearly all mentioned the deadlines, the paperwork, the frustration felt when a child is "unreachable," and the lack of some parents to support the goals of education. The unanimous response to the fact that these stresses are felt by many in the teaching profession signalled a chord of commonality among them. The fact that there was this consensus and that all ten admitted they liked teaching did not translate into a unified approach to alleviating stress, however. The majority, if they do not already feel peer support, want relations among faculty to improve and a cooperative spirit to develop.

In general, I found a stronger sense of community among the private school teachers than the public school teachers. My assessment was drawn from both the participant observations of the teachers' lounges and the interviewing, and I shall elaborate further.

My first discussion focuses on the information that participant observation revealed. The teachers' lounge in the private school was set up physically almost identically to the public school's. There were two tables and several chairs in the center of each room with couches and padded chairs around the perimeter. A refrigerator, soda machine, and microwave oven were present in each. Traffic flows around the tables to the various machines with the main center of activity being the center tables. In the private school there were enough seats for everyone to sit at the table, and thus, all were included in ongoing conversations.

In the public school, there were only nine chairs for the usual average of fifteen in the room. There was a definite preference for the seats at the ta-

ble as evi
empty sea
room con
ten occup
regular tea
pated in tl

A de
tain few t
were no bl
clude othe

In ad
tive comm
times the
change wi
this displa

The
related. C
school cle
derogatory
rarely per

Whil
public sch
ture, there
about hon
sumer pro
children ir

Birth
ties, each
ally each
teachers
share. The
such dem

The
cohesiven
teachers p
their admi
care of dis
for suppor
tions coul
inside and
faculty in
ing with s
from a tea
grated per

careful description of the present situation only and recognition of the element of transformation. This factor coupled with the personal needs and the private interpretation of community contributed to the complexity of this research.

IV. ANALYSIS OF THE FINDINGS

My finding regarding the sense of community as transitory and comparative is echoed by Joseph R. Gusfield in his sociological review *Community: A Critical Response*. Events "can only be described accurately as particular and nonrepeatable" due to the complex and fluid character of situations, and can be described as "specific associations as more or less communal."[10] Although Gusfield's thrust is to differentiate community from society, Hunter, as I have previously mentioned, recommends noting community's presence and the degree to which it is exhibited. The concept of community then, must be understood as a helpful analytical rather than empirical tool.

In this study, how one year differs from the next within the same school, and one school as compared to the other, provides the clearest qualitative representation of the sense of cohesiveness. The communal sharing among teachers is a vacillating process and not a rigid structure in the social organization of schools.

Gusfield makes another noteworthy point regarding the pre-conditions of community that are *perceived* to be vital but, in his opinion, are not necessary. A "homogeneous culture" is believed by many to be a requisite of community.[11] While none of the private school teachers commented on this point precisely, my interpretation of their remarks concerning the compatability of their faith commitment with the school families illustrates they believe their common background strengthens the ties to the students, parents, and each other. Gusfield emphasizes that "the perception among an aggregate of people that they constitute a community" and the "behavior governed by criteria of common belonging" is conducive to building a firm community feeling.[12]

This point correlates with the Coleman Report previously cited. Coleman defines a "functional community" as "one in which members not only share values but also actively participate in an interaction network."[13] Coleman insists that the greater strength of Catholic communities in these schools is proven by the higher achievements of these students over public school students.

The private school teachers believe that the similarities in their upbringing, their devotion and expression of their faith, their comparable socio-economic status, and for many, residence in the same school district represents a strong foundation on which to build solidarity.

The public school teachers do not perceive themselves as much alike in this regard. Their different economic levels were evident from the discussion of second homes, and the wide range of expensive to modest attire worn to work. They only appeared to be on common ground in their roles as teachers. If community is going to be fostered here, it must be directed at increasing awareness of the contributions and expertise of all, thereby highlighting their professional collegiality.

Max Weber carefully distinguishes between class and status: "class is unambiguously economic interest" and cannot in itself constitute a community.[14] "Status groups" on the other hand, "are normally communities, and refer to "every typical component of the life fate of men that is determined by a specific, positive or negative, social estimation of honor."[15]

School teachers are all afforded the same status because of their profession and are identified by the public as uniformly equal in this regard. Society has drawn the lines of distinction, and to the degree the teachers perceive a "them and us" sentiment, their community is fostered. But within ranks, recognition of the economic class differences creates a tension that undermines cohesiveness.

A second factor which enters into this issue is the complication that married women are often given the status of their spouses. As many of these teachers are married women, and particularly in the public school where much incorporation of private lives is included in lunch room conversation, they exhibit and often are given a higher status by the others if their husbands are professionals or are in higher economic income brackets. As Weber notes, "status groups are stratified according to the principles of their consumption of goods as represented by special 'styles of life'."[16] This stratification breaks down the solidarity that exists among the teachers.

Kai T. Erikson describes the tightly woven social fabric and fully integrated sense of community that existed in a small Appalachian area called Buffalo Creek in his book, *Everything in Its Path*. Erikson terms community as "communality" and defines it as the "network of relationships that make up their general human surround."[17] This communality is characterized by the deep bonds of commitments and obligations between neighbors, and the "almost perfect democracy" in which people are equal in status and "identical in temperament and outlook."[18] The collection of these people as community "cushions pain," "represents morality," and serves as the "repository for old traditions."[19] Erikson's interviews revealed that these people thought, felt, and expressed themselves similarly as a cohesive group. There is a blurring of the normal lines of division that usually separate people.

If the Buffalo Creek residents, private school teachers, and public school teachers were placed along a continuum, the Appalachians would be near the end showing the strongest sense of community, the private school teachers in the middle, and the public school teachers slightly further down the line. There is more equality and a larger degree of similarity among the private school teachers, but it is just not as strong or as fully accepted by all as the Buffalo Creek residents.

In reviewing the teachers' answers for elements of dependence and obligations to others, the private school teachers often do name another faculty member, but it is only one or two people on whom they depend rather than the entire group. A public school teacher, however, admits her peers "don't need help from me" and "don't listen to any of my new ideas." The feeling that their work atmosphere has been strained is obvious from this quote, "Teachers can perceive it's a bad place, and perceive administration doesn't support them, and then you get a hardened polarity and no support."

V. SUMMARY

I sincerely believe I was unbiased at the outset of this project. I had no clear idea as to exactly what I was researching and no pre-conceived opinion about the staffs. I thought both groups were friendly, and I had witnessed dedication to the teaching profession and children in both places.

It is possible that because I was a known observer in the private school, an accurate criticism could be made that teachers there may have been on their "best" behavior, and consciously avoided making derogatory statements. If this research were to be repeated, and it should be to increase reliability, the findings would be more precise if the observer was the same—either known or unknown—in both schools. Schools should also both be in the same neighborhood to help factor out some of the differences among student populations and the rural and urban perspectives I witnessed in this study.

I have gained a greater appreciation for the amount of time-consuming effort that is needed to conduct accurate research, and for the many difficulties that can arise which are not mentioned in the textbooks. I recognized quickly that I needed to interview many more people to be more assured of my findings, and to better grasp a common thread of opinions, particularly in the public school. It would have been very productive at this point in the research to return to the field and more carefully observe. This would afford me the opportunity to check and further elaborate on my findings.

One final brief note regarding what I believe the education system and future researchers need to ponder. The research to date suggests group social support and supervisors' concern is the preferred strategy for coping with stress. I question what I perceive to be a "feminine" solution, and challenge the research that it is fostering a continuance of the "learned helplessness" traditionally portrayed as a female characteristic.

Women were 83 percent of the national total of teachers in the United States in 1984, and yet men dominated the administrative, local, state and national education departments.[20] Perhaps if teachers were given more autonomy in the classroom, were permitted to do the work they are dedicated and trained to do, and were freed from the far-removed, male dominated bureaucratic directives of the "State" departments, teachers would not only feel less stressed, but would be able to rely on their own personal resourcefulness to resolve it.

Research needs to be alerted that, particularly in today's society, women teachers can not be viewed as one homogeneous grouping. Many women have multiple roles, and combinations of these such as wife, parent, single parent, dual or non-dual earner, and the variables such as race, ethnic origins, Master degree certified, and tenure prohibit any casual assessment of these people. I believe the changes that will result because the teaching profession has recognized the limitations of its present structure, and when equality in all the ranks of the profession is established, the professional status and satisfaction of teachers will increase.

Notes

[1]Joseph Gusfield, *Community: A Critical Response,* NY: Harper and Row, 1985, p. xv, xvi.

[2]Daniel W. Russell, Elizabeth Altmaier, and Dawn VanVelzen, "Job-Related Stress, Social Support, and Burnout Among Classroom Teachers," *Journal of Applied Psychology,* 1987, Vol. 72, No. 2, pp. 269–274.

[3]"Restructuring Teaching: A call for Research", *Education Digest,* September, 1987, p. 2.

[4]"Teacher 'Professionalization' versus Democratic Control," *Education Digest,* September, 1987, p. 15.

[5]G. K. Baruch, Lois Beiner, and Rosalind C. Barnett, "Women and gender in research on work and family stress," *American Psychologist,* February, 1987, Vol. 42, p. 131.

[6]Andrew M. Greeley, "Community As Social Capital: James S. Coleman on Catholic Schools," *America,* September 5, 1987, pp. 110–112.

[7]John Lofland and Lyn H. Lofland, *Analyzing Social Settings: A Guide to Qualitative Observation and Analysis,* (California: Wadsworth Publishing Company, 1984), p. 13.

[8]Ibid., p. 38.

[9]Ibid., p. 90, as quoted from Albert Hunter, *Symbolic Communities: The Persistence and Change of Chicago's Local Communities,* (Chicago: The University of Chicago Press, 1974), p. 4.

[10]Gusfield, op cit., p. 9.

[11]Ibid., p. 31.

[12]Ibid., pp. 32, 33.

[13]Greeley, op cit., p. 110.

[14]H. H. Gerth and C. Wright Mills, *From Max Weber: Essays in Sociology,* (New York: Oxford University Press, 1946), p. 183.

[15]Ibid., p. 187.

[16]Ibid., p. 193.

[17]Kai T. Erikson, *Everything in Its Path,* (New York: Simon and Schuster, 1976), p. 187.

[18]Ibid., p. 192.
[19]Ibid., p. 194.
[20]*Statistical Abstracts of the United States 1984*, (Washington D.C.: U.S. Department of Commerce, Bureau of the Census), p. 151.

Bibliography

Alpert, D. and A. Culbertson. "Daily hassles and coping strategies of dual-earner and non-dual-earner women," *Psychology of Women Quarterly*. September, 1987, Vol. 11, pp. 359–366.

Baruch, G. K., Lois Beiner, and Rosalind C. Barnett. "Women and gender in research on work and family stress," *American Psychologist*. February, 1987. Vol. 42, pp. 130–136.

Education Digest. "Restructuring Teaching: A Call for Research," September, 1987.

Education Digest. "Teaching 'Professionalization' versus Democratic Control," September, 1987.

Erikson, Kai T. *Everything in Its Path*. New York: Simon and Schuster, 1976.

Gerth, H. H. and C. Wright Mills. *From Max Weber: Essays in Sociology*. New York: Oxford University Press, 1946.

Greeley, Andrew M. "Community As Social Capital: James S. Coleman on Catholic Schools," *America*. September 5, 1987. pp. 110–112.

Gusfield, Joseph. *Community: A Critical Response*. New York: Harper and Row, 1975.

Lofland, John and Lyn H. Lofland. *Analyzing Social Settings: A Guide to Qualitative Observation and Analysis*. California: Wadsworth Publishing Company, 1984.

Russell, Daniel W., Elizabeth Altmaier, and Dawn VenVelzen. "Job-Related Stress, Social Support, and Burnout Among Classroom Teachers," *Journal of Applied Psychology*. 1987. Vol. 72, No. 2, pp. 269–274.

Statistical Abstracts of the United States 1984. U.S. Department of Commerce, Bureau of the Census.

Stoppard, Janet M. and Kim J. Paisley. "Masculinity, Femininity and Life Stress, and Depression," *Sex Roles*. May, 1987, Vol. 16, pp. 489–496.

Sylvia, R. D. and T. Hutchinson. "What Makes Ms. Johnson Teach? A Study of Teacher Motivation," *Human Relations*. September, 1985, Vol. 38, pp. 841–456.

■ UNDERSTANDING WRITING STRATEGIES

1. What is the value of LeRoux's study? How does she use the issue of value to introduce her paper?

2. What is the design of LeRoux's "experiment"? What kinds of limitations does this design impose?

3. How does LeRoux order her literature review? What criteria seem to govern the information she reports?

4. What categories does LeRoux use to present her findings? What else does she do with her data besides simply categorize it?

5. What external factors affected data gathering?

6. How does the essay make use of the literature in the section analyzing the data?

7. What does LeRoux indicate her conclusion will do? How effectively does it meet its own goals?

8. What else does the conclusion accomplish?

9. What argument strategies does this paper use? ■

■ SUGGESTIONS FOR WRITING

This paper combines theoretical foundations with practical observations in a traditional report format. Combine LeRoux's observations with your own research, and write an essay for a specific audience, a magazine for school administrators or one for teachers, on building "community" among teachers. ■

Simmel, Durkheim, and Marx: Three Views on the Individual in Contemporary Society

Patty Masters

Written as a response to a take-home examination question for an introductory sociology course, Patty Masters compares the theories of the great nineteenth-century social philosophers, Georg Simmel, Karl Marx, and Emile Durkheim, about the individual's role in society and the impact of the division of labor on social interaction.

INTRODUCTION

Georg Simmel, Karl Marx, and Emile Durkheim offer distinctive views on the nature of human individuality and the role of the individual in society. More divergent, however, are their assessments of the impact of the division of labor on social interaction during the early twentieth century and prognostications of the human future.

Simmel sees the individual as autonomous; though man functions within society, he retains a unique individuality. Thus, he is in the position to create new forms of social interaction that neutralize the human consequences of the division of labor. For Marx, man is engaged in constant conflict, both with his fellow man—the instrument and victim of economic forces—and with the mechanized environment that threatens to totally envelop him. Dialectical materialism has determined the history of the human race, but the creation of an egalitarian social system has the potential for creating a humanistic society. Durkheim sees man as the creature of society, formed by his environment, which includes not only human interactions, but also a strong biological component. The division of labor is an outgrowth of human evolution; it can be a source of organic solidarity if man chooses to make it so.

What was apparent to these theorists in the early twentieth century is, however, even more obvious today. The human social environment is fragmented; the individual exists in a world which is

> . . . Swept with confused alarms of struggle and flight,
>   Where ignorant armies clash by night.[1]

Presented in this paper are the underlying suppositions regarding the individual's relationship to society and the impact of the division of labor on social relationships as theorized by Simmel, Marx, and Durkheim.

SIMMEL'S DUALISTIC MAN

Simmel's theory of human individuality proposes the existence of aprioristic forms and the contents of individual experience. Forms are synthesizing principles, which select elements from the raw stuff of experience [contents] and shape these materials into determinate unities; they inform experience.[2] Forms are not only cognitive, but also affective. They may be modified in response to dynamic interactions with the social environment, but their modification proceeds slowly in comparison with the rapidly shifting perceptions of the individual. Forms are a stabilizing element in human existence, and only through forms is sociation between individuals possible. As Simmel writes:

> . . . . In any given social phenomenon, content and societal form constitute one reality . . . . Any social . . . process is composed of two elements which are in reality inseparable. A collection of human beings does not become a society because each of them has objectively determined or subjectively impelling content. It becomes society only when the vitality of these contents attains the form of reciprocal influence.[3]

Complete fusion of individual interests is not possible because each man retains within himself a unique "core of individuality"[4] that cannot be re-created by anyone else. Thus, human disjunction is inevitable in Simmel's view; man should not be submerged in society. His interests can be influenced and affected by social needs and interactions, but he cannot be expected to deny his individual aspirations because in doing so, he would sacrifice himself.

The requirement to act in the social interest and the compulsion to maintain his individuality is the source of tension in man's existence; but in the way this tension is resolved during the course of human interactions, man discovers his essential self.

Two of Simmel's essays focus explicitly on the division of labor and its implications for individual development: "The Metropolis and Mental Life" and "Subordination and Personal Fulfillment." In the former, Simmel states that the urban environment offers the least restrictive climate for the development of individual freedom. He observes:

> Cities are above all the seat of the most advanced economic division of labor . . . . The necessity to specialize one's product in order to find a source of income which is not yet exhausted and also to specialize a function which cannot be easily supplanted is conducive to differentiation, refinement, and enrichment of the needs of the public which obviously must lead to increasing personal variation within this public.[5]

But the negative aspects of the urban environment are also important. Simmel writes that where "quantitative increase of value and energy has reached its limits, one seizes on qualitative distinctions"[6] in order to differentiate oneself from the rest of society. This can lead to

> . . . eccentricities [and] extravagances of self-distantiation . . . the meaning of which is no longer to be found in the content of such activity itself, but rather in its being a form of "being different"—of making oneself noticeable.[7]

For this reason, the metropolis emphasizes striving for the most individual forms of personal existence "regardless of whether it is always correct or always successful."[8] Thus, the modern culture is obsessed with objective spirit, rather than emphasizing the subjective. The price society pays for this is evident in the lag between the development of cultural forms and the intellectual growth of the individual.[9]

> . . . This discrepancy is the . . . result of the success of the growing division of labor which requires from the individual an ever more one-sided type of achievement which . . . often permits his personality as a whole to fall into neglect.[10]

The far more serious consequence of this situation is the breakdown of social forms.

> . . . Perhaps less conscious than in practical activity and in the obscure complex of feelings which flow from him, he is reduced to a negligible quantity. He becomes a single cog as over against the vast overwhelming organization

of things and forces which gradually take out of his hands everything connected with progress, spirituality and value.[11]

Thus, life in becoming objectified, becomes formless.

In "Subordination and Personal Fulfillment," Simmel offers a contrasting perspective of the problem posed by the forms of sub- and super-ordination, an area that Marx and Durkheim view very differently. Subordination is, of course, necessitated by the division of labor. But, it offers some opportunities for growth of the personality, as long as one acknowledges that the individual is *not* defined by his function in society. While he observes that the individual and his work were originally fused,

> division of labor and production for the market . . . . have later permitted
> the personality to withdraw from work and to become based upon
> itself . . . . This differentiation of objective and subjective life elements
> whereby subordination is preserved as a technical-organizational value
> which has no personally and internally depressing consequences is . . . no
> panacea for all the difficulties . . . produced by domination and obedience.[12]

Nevertheless, what Simmel does propose is that man use his self-consciousness and objectivity to examine the social realities—of which the division of labor is one—and superimpose forms that are necessary to personal fulfillment.

MARX'S SOCIAL MAN

Karl Marx sees man as a species-being. He

> . . . not only makes both his own and other species into his objects, but
> also . . . relates to himself as the present, living species, in that he relates to
> himself as a universal and therefore free being.[13]

Unlike Simmel who sees man's work as only part of his existence, Marx believes that labor is an integral part of human creativity. Thus, the division of labor has devastating effects on man as an individual and man in the aggregate. Because the forces of production have been centralized in urban settings and the ownership of the means of production has been concentrated in the hands of one the bourgeoisie, transforming the proletariet into tools of the production machine, man no longer views his work as a creative activity. And,

> . . . an immediate consequence of man's alienation from the product of his
> work . . . his vital activity as a species being is the alienation of man from
> man. What is valid for the relationship of man to his work . . . is also valid
> for the relationship of man to other men and of their labor and objects of
> their labor.[14]

The division of labor is the culprit in Marx's scenario; only through a complete reorganization of society where the form of sub- and super-ordination is abolished can society attain balance.

[Marx's] paradigm for the future is found in the family or, to be more exact, in the relationship between the sexes. The unique pattern of these relationships has a systematic significance which makes it possible to project them as a general model for the structure of human relations in society.[15]

The ideal relationship between the sexes is egalitarian, with each partner realizing that his own fulfillment lies in the fulfillment of the other. So it should be with man once he attains his identity as "species-man." The realization of this ideal is to be found, Marx believes, in the communist structure.

DURKHEIM'S FUNCTIONAL MAN

For Emile Durkheim, man is pre-eminently a social organism. He is governed by concepts that reside within the collective consciousness, which Durkheim defines as

the totality of beliefs and sentiments common to the average members of society [which] forms a determinate system with a life of its own . . . . It is independent of the particular conditions in which individuals find themselves. . . . [it] links successive generations to one another . . . . [and] is totally different from the consciousness of individuals.[16]

The collective consciousness is the basis upon which humans can build organic solidarity. In contrast to Simmel, who believes that man retains a portion of himself that he does not invest in society, Durkheim sees the role of the individual within society as analogous to the role of an organ in an organism. Each organ performs a specific function that enables the entire organism to operate effectively. This interdependency and functional relationship is what necessitates the division of labor; the individual cannot lead a productive existence outside his social milieu.

To unleash the potential for societal progress, Durkheim believes it essential that each individual find his niche. This is something that humans sense intuitively. As he observes:

We are wary of those too volatile men of talent, who lending themselves equally to all forms of employment refuse to choose for themselves a special role and to adhere to it. It appears to us that such a state of detachment and indeterminateness is somewhat anti-social. We perceive perfection in the competent man, one who has a well-defined job to which he devotes himself and carries out his task. To perfect oneself . . . is to learn one's role . . . the yardstick for our perfection is . . . in the sum total of our services rendered and our ability to continue to render them.[18]

The division of labor is not the result of increasing density of society; instead the growth of societies which forces individuals into closer, more intimate contact, is the cause of the division of labor.[18] It is a positive force that enables individuals to compete; it is a gentle denouement of the struggle for existence.[19] The division of labor is a source of organic solidarity.

What is lacking in contemporary society is intermediate institutions that give the individual insight into his function within the whole societal organism. The division of labor, in its un-deformed state allows individuals to

> keep in constant contact with [their] neighboring functions becoming aware of their needs and the changes that take place . . . . The division of labor supposes that the worker, far from remaining bent over his task, does not lose sight of those cooperating with him, but acts upon them and is acted upon by them.[20]

In his preface to the second edition of *The Division of Labor in Society*, Durkheim discusses professional organizations and their potential for countering anomie. He sees the professional organization as capable of exerting a moral influence on social interaction.[21] It is not clear how this mechanism can work, and Durkheim, in fact, declines to speculate upon the rules which might govern its functioning. The division of labor has created a need for structures that can mediate between the individual and the reality of his economic existence.

Notes

[1]Arnold, Matthew, "Dover Beach," in *An Introduction to Literature*. Edited by Sylvan Barnet, Morton Berman, and William Burto. 5th Edition. (Boston: Little, Brown and Company, 1973), pp. 392–3.

[2]Simmel, Georg, *On Individuality and Social Forms*. Edited by Donald H. Levine. (Chicago: The University of Chicago Press, 1971), pp. xv–xvi.

[3]Simmel, p. 24.

[4]Simmel, pp. 9–10.

[5]Simmel, p. 335.

[6]Simmel, p. 336.

[7]Ibid.

[8]Simmel, p. 337.

[9]Ibid.

[10]Ibid.

[11]Ibid.

[12]Simmel, p. 341.

[13]Marx, Karl, *Selected Writings*, edited by David McLellan. (New York: Oxford University Press, 1977), p. 81.

[14]Marx, p. 83.

[15]Avineri, Shlomo, *The Social and Political Thought of Karl Marx* (London: Cambridge University Press, 1968), p. 87.

[16]Durkheim, Emile, *The Division of Labor in Society* (New York: The Free Press, 1984), p. 39.

[17]Durkheim, p. 4.

[18]Durkheim, p. 308.

[19]Ibid.

[20]Durkheim, p. 213.

[21]Durkheim, p. xliii.

■ **THE WRITER'S ASSIGNMENT**

Compare and contrast the ways Simmel, Durkheim, and Marx treat the themes of individuality and the division of labor, demonstrating how each theorist's treatment of these themes depends on a particular set of postulates about human nature, and in particular about the relation of self to society.   ■

■ **UNDERSTANDING WRITING STRATEGIES**

1. What does the introduction provide the reader?

2. How does the introduction relate to the rest of the paper?

3. What "postulates about human nature" does each of the thinkers hold?

4. How does each thinker view the individual?

5. How does Masters order her essay?

6. What other organizational options could Masters have used?

7. On what points does Masters see similarity among her authors? Where do they diverge?

8. Masters omits a conclusion. Why is this justifiable?

9. What kind of conclusion might she have used?

10. How well does the essay carry out the assignment?

11. For what audience is this written? What in the essay suggests this?   ■

NATO— A Credible Alliance?

Robin A. McDavid

> Robin McDavid evaluates the Reagan presidency's effect on NATO in this essay written for a modern history class. The essay relies on sources that emphasize Europe's perspective.

After nearly a decade of losing confidence in America's ability to conduct foreign policy in the world, the NATO allies finally breathed a sigh of relief due to the election in 1980 of Ronald Reagan as President. However, Mr. Reagan's foreign policy initiatives in his second term of office have again sent the NATO allies in search of some consistency and continuity in dealing with its American partner. In spite of his many accomplishments, in his first term of office (both domestically and internationally), Mr. Reagan has again put America on the defensive in its policy in dealing with NATO.

The decade of the 1970's saw a general decline of American will, of American spirit and of overall leadership in the world; both militarily and economically. The NATO alliance of this period was shaky at best. The events of the '70's—Vietnam, Watergate, the resignation of an American president, the invasion of Afghanistan, the Iran hostage crisis and the subsequent failed rescue attempt, all helped reduce European opinion of the United States to that of a seemingly helpless and stagnant superpower.

A change was imminent. Ronald Reagan was elected President of the United States in 1980. The optimism and anticipation of a new decade accompanied by a change in leadership brought hope to America and the NATO alliance. The Reagan doctrine was designed to rebuild America both economically and militarily and to change the European perception of America. A strong America would mean a strong NATO alliance.

In his first term, Mr. Reagan revitalized the spirit and resolve of America and gave its tarnished reputation in Europe a new luster. Mr. Reagan's tax recovery act helped stimulate the growth of America's economy. He increased military spending and for justification, increased European awareness of an overwhelming and definitive Soviet threat to the West. Mr. Reagan depicted the Soviets as the "Evil Empire" and such rhetoric helped him capitalize on many Soviet public opinion faux pas (i.e., shooting down KAL 007), due to the lack of Soviet leadership in the early part of this decade.

In spite of Mr. Reagan's early successes in his first term, the NATO alliance during this period was in a very precarious state. The Reagan administration was campaigning heavily for deployment of intermediate range nuclear weapons (Pershing II's and land based Cruise missiles) in Europe. At the same time, the Soviets were conducting a disinformation campaign against deployment. The Soviet plan was to infiltrate and support, monetarily, parties in Western Europe, such as the "Greens" in West Germany, to strengthen public support against deployment. The Soviet Union has always had an intent to split the Alliance, but deployment of intermediate range missiles became the rallying point to enable the Soviet Union to achieve the split in NATO from America.

Mr. Reagan achieved a huge step in both restrengthening and reuniting NATO with America due to his victory in Europe for deployment of the Pershings and Cruises. With this victory, Mr. Reagan seemed to announce to Europe and the Soviets a new beginning of unity, confidence, and credibility in policy with regard to NATO.

During Reagan's second administration, things started to fall apart. NATO began to lose confidence in the United States due to three specific issues. The first was the meeting with Mr. Gorbachev in Reykjavik, then the Iran-contra scandal and most importantly, the budget deficit.[1]

The Reykjavik summit meeting of October 11–12, 1986, between President Reagan and Soviet Secretary General Mikhail Gorbachev succeeded in alienating every sector of European opinion.[2] The forces of the right were horrified by Reagan's declaration for "complete elimination of all ballistic missiles, Soviet and American, from the face of the earth by 1996," and his aspiration to create "a world without nuclear weapons."[3] The left blamed him for making this aspiration unacceptable to the Soviets because of his insistence on retaining his Strategic Defense Initiative (SDI). Moderates in all countries, including political leaders and government officials, were disturbed by "the casual utopianism and indifferent preparation" of the entire exercise.[4]

Before the Reykjavik meeting, no Europeans and very few Americans were consulted. What was thought to be a simple meeting and discussion turned into a negotiation over issues which were vital to the security of the entire West. The Soviets produced proposals without warning and they were accepted without any preliminary examination by Western experts.[5] Reagan's stubbornness over SDI proposals could have caused great embarrassment to the U.S. had the Soviets accepted them. In the eyes of Europe, American leadership could no longer be trusted, because of the unprofessionalism displayed at the summit and Reagan's lack of consideration of the European member states of NATO.[6]

NATO leaders were uneasy about the extent to which the U.S. and Soviet leaders retained power to make decisions essential to their security, over the heads of European governments.[7] The United States, geographically separated by the Atlantic Ocean, is less likely to feel direct impact of poor judgment or hostile retaliation. President Reagan was perceived as a man who would do anything just to cut a deal with the Soviets, in order to assure his place in the history books.[8] The incident in Reykjavik so destroyed the faith of France that it caused them to take defense cooperation more seriously. They moved into close military contact with West Germany and revived the defunct Western Defense Union in order to provide a serious forum for the discussion of European Defense Cooperation.[9]

During 1986, another incident occurred, further diminishing European opinion of Reagan and his reliability. It was the Iran-contra scandal. The impact was worse than Watergate because it was not solely a domestic scandal. The discrepancy lies in the fact that the Europeans saw the Reagan administration as one that, "rallied the world against Iran's terrorism by describing it as part of a new international version of Murder, Inc. and consistently espousing the policy that neither America nor its allies will negotiate with any terrorist group," then secretly authorized weapons sales to the Iranians.[10] A string of laws were broken in the arms for hostages operation, including violation of the Boland Agreement which banned the use of U.S.

money supporting "directly or indirectly, military or paramilitary operation in Nicaragua by any nation, group, organization or individual," and prohibited the U.S. from persuading third countries to give military aid to the contras.[11] Europe's lack of trust in the U.S. parallels their lack of trust in our democratic system. Europeans question how the U.S. could bring to power a president quite ignorant in world affairs and enable him to delegate immense authority to others yet more ignorant, and make him solely responsible for the conduct of foreign affairs.[12] NATO and the European public question the power of the President. It is difficult to trust an ally whose leader seems unaware of the small, powerful cell of unqualified and irresponsible officials working in the White House basement, and making decisions about foreign policy that are vital to the West.[13]

As seen from a European perspective, Ollie North was depicted an American Hero. The television projected this handsome, bemedaled officer as a reminder of military men of the past, who seemed to believe that he had a higher conception of legality and greater insight into the national interest than the elected representatives of the people. This kind of man, historically, split France and Spain, and in the case of Germany, destroyed it.[14]

Europe felt that the United States, in supporting the contras, had acted immorally and illegally. The nature of the activities of the Irangate conspirators created great concern amongst the NATO allies. The policy which they implemented would not have won general approval (had they made the allies aware) in its approach to the questions of terrorism, or the Middle East or of Central America.

On the matter of terrorism, and the ransoming of hostages, the situation was clear. An international agreement achieved largely on the insistence of the U.S. stated that no ransom money, whatever the circumstance, should be paid to the terrorist groups for the release of hostages.[15] When it was revealed that senior American officials had done precisely that, NATO allies were justifiably outraged.

American 'leadership' in the Middle East has never carried much weight. The French and British have historically been involved and have a depth of understanding which Americans may never acquire. American attachment to Israel, and its devout hatred for Iran, makes it difficult for any administration to take a broader perspective of the Middle East and pursue Western interests with any kind of consistency.[16]

European opinion was not very supportive regarding the United States' policy towards Nicaragua. Few shared the view of the Administration that this was part of a global struggle against communism and should be given full support. Most denounced it as typical American imperialism. Policy towards Nicaragua seemed to parallel the U.S. approach used in reference to issues of the Third World as a whole, which was a lack of sympathy for nationalist movements and disregard for the complexity of the cultures within the region, and a blatant dismissal of the Third World as irrelevant except as a battleground against the forces of communism.[17]

This brings us, finally, to the problem of the American federal budget deficit. Europeans have watched with anxiety as the U.S. federal budget deficit has increased. True security in Western Europe depends on economic and social stability, thus exceeding dependency on military strength. European opinion blames mismanagement as the reason the U.S. debt has reached a nadir of that of Third World countries, and European confidence has been destroyed more so as a result of the national deficit than the Reykjavik summit or the Iran-contra affair.

The United States, instead of confronting the deficit problem, has denied responsibility for it and blamed Europe. When the other nations agreed to stabilize currencies and simultaneously reduce America's deficit, West Germany had the temerity to raise its interest rates, and prompted Treasury Secretary James Baker to announce on October 18, 1987 (the day before Black Monday), that the U.S., in response, would allow the dollar to fall. In other words, the economic strain was THEIR fault, and they were to be punished for it. West Germans are chronically afraid of inflation and are suspicious of Americans' spendthrift habits. European countries see the Reagan administration as unreasonable and hypocritical in blaming them for the deteriorating economic situation.[18]

It is true that the defense burden is unequally allocated. The United States is still acting the part of a creditor nation, contributing significantly more to NATO than any of its members. Our trading partners have never insisted that we bear this disproportionate share. This has been a price the U.S. has been willing to pay in order to contain what we have perceived to be the spread of communism (a concern shared by our allies, but rarely to the same degree), and to ensure our continued leadership in the defense of the free world.[19]

In future years, it may be necessary for our NATO allies to share a larger portion of the defense expense. Yet, such a move would have political consequences: America would no longer have the same position of leadership; our allies would be more independent of us, able and perhaps willing to seek different accommodations with the Soviets and other perceived threats. A more militarized West Germany would represent a substantial change in how we and they understand their power in the world. West European leaders are already talking of defense cooperation among themselves and of a greater European role in NATO decision-making, since the United States cannot be trusted to take their interests into account.[20]

The strength of any alliance between nations is the strength that is of an economic nature. It is up to succeeding American and European administrations to improve the economic well-being of the Alliance. It is profoundly important that Europe and America cooperate and coordinate their policies in order to keep the alliance credible into the 1990's and beyond. Through cooperation and coordination of economic, military, social, and foreign policies the NATO allies can help to lead the world towards a better union of nations, nations that are more concerned with internationalism than nationalism. America needs to take its natural lead here and become more understanding and concerned with Europe (both East and West) and its people.

Notes

[1]Michael Howard, A European Perspective on the Reagan Years, (Foreign Affairs, New York, Council on Foreign Relations, Inc. Editorial Offices, AMERICA AND THE WORLD 1987/88), p. 478.

[2]Ibid., p. 479.

[3]Ibid., p. 79.

[4]Sloan, NATO's Future, p. 73.

[5]Michael Howard, A European Perspective on the Reagan Years, p. 479.

[6]Ibid., p. 480.

[7]Further steps towards defence integration in Europe, Le Monde. (Manchester Guardian Weekly, Nov. 8, 1987).

[8]Michael Howard, A European Perspective on the Reagan Years, p. 481.

[9]Edward Cody, 7 West Europeans Plan Joint Strategy. (The Washington Post, Oct. 27, 1987).

[10]Michael Howard, A European Perspective on the Reagan Years, p. 484.

[11]John W. Mashek and Melissa Healy, Can they live up to the laws? (*U.S. News and World Report,* Reagan's Damaged Presidency, Oct, 1986) p. 25.

[12]Michael Howard, A European Perspective on the Reagan Years, p. 484.

[13]Ibid., p. 485.

[14]Ibid., p. 485.

[15]Ibid., p. 486.

[16]Ibid., p. 486.

[17]Ibid., p. 488.

[18]Robert B. Reich, The Economics of Illusion and the Illusion of Economics, (Foreïgn Affairs, New York, Council on Foreign Relations, Inc. Editorial Offices, AMERICA AND THE WORLD 1987/88) p. 517.

[19]Ibid., p. 519.

[20]Ibid., p. 519.

■ UNDERSTANDING WRITING STRATEGIES

1. What kinds of commitments does the introduction make?

2. Before McDavid focuses on Reagan's second term, what does the essay do?

3. What events shaped European opinion of Reagan?

4. Does McDavid have a bias? What in the essay supports your judgment?

5. How does McDavid conclude the essay?

6. How effectively does McDavid answer European criticisms?   ■

■ SUGGESTIONS FOR WRITING

Select one of Europe's criticisms of the United States. Begin with McDavid's information, but find out more about the criticisms and the United States' response. Write an essay objectively explaining both views; then evaluate the considerations motivating each position. Instead of merely reporting your sources' biases, help your reader understand the reasons for bias.　■

Transforming Stories
Elizabeth Rose

From Elizabeth Rose's readings about the educational experiences recounted in Richard Rodriguez's *Hunger of Memory*, Barbara Mellix's "From Outside, In," Plato, Robert Pirsig's *Zen and the Art of Motorcycle Maintenance*, and William E. Cole, Jr.'s *The Plural I—and After*, she develops a definition of education. This definition becomes the criteria for evaluating E. D. Hirsch's popular yet controversial book, *Cultural Literacy*.

In E. D. Hirsch's book *Cultural Literacy: What Every American Needs To Know*, Hirsch proposes a plan of education. This plan demands cultural literacy of students. "Cultural literacy" is defined as the "network of information that all competent readers possess." He further describes it as "background information, stored in minds" which enables a reader to understand both the stated and the unstated context which makes the literature meaningful. The importance of cultural literacy, Hirsch says, is that once it is part of America's educational system we will have greater "economic prosperity," greater "social justice," and "more effective democracy" (p. 2). The manner in which the plan for a culturally literate America would be incorporated into the school systems may vary. Hirsch believes that the current curriculum for kindergarten through eighth grade needs a "much stronger base in factual information and traditional lore." As of now heavy emphasis is placed on literature about "human feelings." He says "these texts convey information, but rarely the kinds most necessary for future literacy." A "higher proportion of factual narratives" are needed in the education system of a culturally literate America (p. 140).

　　Hirsch and two colleagues have put together a list of information and their explanation of the information that culturally literate Americans should know and they call this a "dictionary" (p. 135). Hirsch suggests that with this dictionary "only a few hundred pages of information stand between the literate and the illiterate, between dependence and autonomy" (p. 143). It is important to note that Hirsch is advocating memorization instead of learning the list of names, dates, and events in their contextual setting through reading. He cites several examples of how easily children memorize pertinent cultural stories. In assuming that children memorize easily, Hirsch fails to differentiate between the ease with which children memorize relevant cultural stories or folktales and the demand that they memorize lists of names, dates, and events. Overall Hirsch feels it is necessary to "devise an extensive curriculum based on the national vocabulary and arranged in a definite sequence," because an "explicit national vocabulary" is the "basis of a literate education" (p. 139).

As I read *Cultural Literacy* for the first time, I had very mixed feelings. I agree with the goal of cultural literacy, and I understand how important it can be when reading. My anger arose when Hirsch seemed determined to sustain an elite, the culturally literate who have power and control. I was not a part of this elite, and it frustrated me. I was angry with myself for not being well read to the extent of knowing all that Hirsch points out as important. So my public response was "this is not right." I really was not sure why it was wrong; however, I felt it was. It had to be wrong because I considered myself to be a part of an American culture, able to participate in our "democratic" political system and able to read important literature and understand it as well. I remember discussing it in class. Most of the other students thought Hirsch's proposal was a good idea. They must have been culturally literate. As they made comments on Hirsch, they would cite examples from their childhood that obviously connected them with the culturally literate. I resented their snobbery and figured they were agreeing with Hirsch because he was a well-educated man, working at a reputable school representing their very own white Anglo-Saxon male society. Most of the women in the class had no idea how this proposal of Hirsch's would restrict their lives and impede progress towards equality, as would be true of any minority. With all the pro-Hirsch discussion I began to doubt my own opinions; however, throughout the remainder of the course we have read many other books and articles which provided counter arguments for Hirsch's proposal for a culturally literate America.

In Richard Rodriguez's autobiographical account *Hunger For Memory*, I saw first hand how a young man responds to a life full of the "piling-up of knowledge and received opinions," the "acquiring of facts" and a "purely literate education." This Rodriguez says used "only a small part of the personality" and challenged "only a limited area of his being." He describes himself as the scholarship boy:

> The scholarship boy is a very bad student. He is the great mimic; a collector of thoughts, not a thinker; the very person in class who never feels obliged to have an opinion of his own. In large part, however, the reason he is such a bad student is because he realizes more often and more acutely than most other students—than Hoggart himself—that education requires radical self-reformation. As a very young boy, regarding his parents, as he struggles with an early homework assignment, he knows this too well. That is why he lacks self-assurance. He does not forget that the classroom is responsible for remaking him. He relies on his teacher, depends on all that he hears in the classroom and reads in his books. He becomes in every obvious way the worst student, a dummy mouthing the opinions of others. But he would not be so bad—nor would he become so successful, a scholarship boy—if he did

not accurately perceive that the best synonym for primary 'education' is 'imitation' (p. 67).

This "scholarship boy" is exactly the clone that Hirsch feels would create a better democracy, economy and society. Rodriguez's own account makes it clear just how undesirable the scholarship boy's mentality is. How effective will our democracy be if the entire population consists of dummies "mouthing the opinions of others"? What will happen to creation in the arts and sciences? The results are devastating. Rodriguez was externally motivated to please society and teachers in particular. He had no motivation for self-fulfillment.

> In fourth grade I embarked upon a grandiose reading project. "Give me the names of important books," I would say to startled teachers. . . . Each time I finished a book, I reported the achievement to a teacher and basked in the praise my effort earned. . . . When one of my teachers suggested to his drowsy tenth-grade English class that a person could not have a 'complicated idea' until he had read at least two thousand books, . . . I merely determined to compile a list of all the books I had ever read. . . . There was yet another high school list I compiled. . . . The article was accompanied by a list of the 'hundred most important books of Western civilization.' . . . I clipped out the list and kept it for the several months it took me to read all the titles (p. 61 and 64).

Rodriguez was aiming to complete a list of things to know that would make up his education. He was checking books off his lists as Hirsch suggests we should check names, dates and events from his dictionary of culturally pertinent knowledge. Rodriguez comments on his growth since his education and notes his "profound lack of self-confidence" (p. 66). He is the prodigy for Hirsch's proposal. Rodriguez's own remorse at having taken such a road exemplifies potentially damaging psychological effects of Hirsch's proposal.

In addition to Rodriguez's insecurities he has a hard time with the transition from his own culture, Mexican-American, to white Anglo-Saxon American. With all his hard work he concludes: "Here is no fabulous hero, no idealized scholar-worker. The scholarship boy does not straddle, cannot reconcile, the two great opposing cultures of his life" (p. 66). Hirsch does not take up the question of all the different cultures in America and the problems these cultures may have bridging the gap. When students must leave behind their entire first culture, a part of them is lost.

Barbara Mellix recounts a similar story of her own academic growth as a writer in "From Outside, In." Mellix reports various stages of her writing and what signifies the changes is her ability to speak from within, to find her own voice. She describes her own evolvement:

> Writing was an occasion for proper English. I was not to write in the way we spoke to one another. . . . In time, I learned to speak standard English with ease and to switch smoothly from black to standard or a mixture, and back again. . . . Each experience of writing was like standing naked and revealing

> my imperfection, my "otherness." And each new assignment was another
> chance to make myself over in language, reshape myself, make myself "bet-
> ter" in my rapidly changing image of a student in a college composition
> class. . . . I could not—in the process of composing—use the language of
> the old me, yet I couldn't imagine myself in the language of the 'others.' . . .
> improving upon my previous experiences with writing. I was beginning to
> think and feel in the language I used, to find my own voices in it, to sense
> that how one speaks influences how one means. But I was not yet secure
> enough, comfortable enough with the language to trust my intuition (p. 261,
> 262, 264, 266).

Mellix has become educated. But what crystallized the idea of writing for
her that brought her education? She says "my growing expertise, my power
to shape myself in language and share that self with 'others' " is what allows
her to "become" (p. 267). Mellix saw her education very differently from Rodriguez. Mellix sees knowledge as perpetual, continuous, an infinitely long
task. She says "I know that to seek knowledge, freedom, and autonomy
means always to be in the concentrated process of becoming" (p. 266). I find
this especially cogent: the infinity involved in knowledge is what makes the
process of becoming endless. Philosophies about the infinity of knowledge
have been around for a long time.

Socrates expands on the infinity of knowledge in Plato's many dia-
logues. In *Laches,* Socrates cleverly makes a deal with some less-than-clever
men. Socrates and four other prosperous and well-respected men are trying
to discover the best form of education for two of the men's sons. Socrates
knows there is no "best" form of education and that learning is endless. He
satisfies the other men while satisfying his own need to be constantly in a
state of becoming. He says:

> I say we ought to join in searching for the best possible teacher, first for our-
> selves—we really need one—and then for the young men, sparing neither
> money nor anything else. What I don't advise is that we remain as we are"
> (p. 49).

"Socrates" is on Hirsch's list; however, I do not see Socrates in any of
Hirsch's philosophy. His list of culturally relevant names, dates and events
defines education, what education should entail for every American. It
quantifies information and diminishes learning to a form of mimicry or en-
culturation, something I think Socrates would be very sad to see because it
makes no provision for self-fulfillment. Motivation holds in store for a student the same transforming powers that self-fulfillment does. Both are extremely important in the education process; motivation can be harmful if it
is not found from within.

In Plato's *Phaedrus,* Socrates outlines the "Decree of Destiny," the cycle of the souls (p. 31). The cycle of the souls shows the infinity of all humans' path in becoming. The two parts of the soul are motivated by
wholeness and self-knowledge. We evolve to higher beings as more of our

mortal self becomes immortal. Our mortal self represents growth constituted by external motivation. Our immortal self is growth with wholeness
and/or self-knowledge, which develops our souls. Socrates says:

> For every body that is moved from without is soulless; and every body that
> derives its motion from within itself has a soul, since that is indeed the
> soul's nature. But if this is so, that what really moves itself is not the body
> and is nothing else but the soul, then soul must necessarily be uncreated
> and immortal (p. 28).

Hirsch's proposal for cultural literacy is one such example of a set of restrictions that encourage external motivation. His plan advocates education
through acquiring knowledge not for self-fulfillment but for cultural-
fulfillment. The culture he talks about is not a culture that represents
wholeness, because everyone is not a part of his culture. Everything about
Hirsch is externally motivated: the education system he encourages, the
proposal he researches with funds from the Exxon Corporation and Hirsch
himself. It has been the goal of many people to try to discover just what education system would facilitate such philosophies as Socrates advocates.

Robert M. Pirsig in *Zen and the Art of Motorcycle Maintenance* has
his main character, Phaedrus/Narrator, describe what an ideal education
might be. Phaedrus calls the place for learning the "Church of Reason." The
narrator describes it:

> The primary goal of the Church of Reason, Phaedrus said, is always Socra-
> tes' old goal of truth, in its everchanging forms as it's revealed by the
> process of rationality. Everything else is subordinate to that. Their (church-
> men) primary goal never is to serve the community ahead of everything
> else. Their primary goal is to serve, through reason, the goal of truth (p. 133).

This last quote relates directly to Hirsch and his goal for "economic prosperity," greater "social justice" and a "more effective democracy." Truth is
deeply imbedded in these three goals. The problem comes when our society
loses sight of the truth and concentrates on the superficial benefits. Mellix
has seen the truth involved in these goals. She sees the infinity of knowledge and agrees with Socrates; thus she does not remain as she is. What does
Mellix have that Rodriguez did not have? How does one reach this advanced
state of mind?

This leads me to present a new type of literacy: spiritual cultural literacy. Spiritual cultural literacy is ultimately defined by each individual but
has standard components. It is based on that knowledge that makes us
"whole" and stresses "truth." Converse to Hirsch's argument that texts
with "human feelings" do not promote cultural literacy, I think that ethical
works discovering "human feeling" should be taught at an early age. It is
these types of literature that will encourage spiritual cultural literacy to be
discovered by each person.

William E. Cole, Jr. is an example of a student of life who lacked spiritual cultural literacy. In his autobiographical article "Writing as Literacy: An Alternative to Losing," Cole shows that it is not factual knowledge that drags him out of his drug addiction. Nor is it factual knowledge that teaches his students to write. As a professor of rhetoric and a former drug addict Cole says:

> You better have rules to get you where you are then, but when you're there you're going to need more than somebody else's rules to do what you ought to do. It's then you need something of your own that you can believe in, because without that . . .
>
> . . . Defining literacy as a form of powerlessness for our students, and showing in what ways powerlessness is an invitation to victimization, will not in itself be enough, of course. Indeed, without providing students with some vision of the transformation that can attend the attempt to become more responsible to one's self as a user of language, it is unprincipled to encourage him to see the inability to use it well as a kind of addiction, addiction as a kind of despair (p. 290).

Here again is the theme advocated by Socrates, Pirsig, Mellix and Rodriguez. One must be "responsible to one's self," one must seek truth for one's self. The spiritual development is seen in the use of "one's self" as opposed to "oneself."

Cole also describes the power of wholeness in his own experience as a drug addict. In his rehabilitation program some man was helping him out:

> He told me (Cole) I was going to have to learn how to believe in something bigger than I was, more than I was. That's just how he put it too, "you'll have to learn how to" (p. 293).

This "something" that is "bigger" than all of us is really most anything ethically good: quality, truth, peace, happiness. But it is always "something" and usually the "something" helps evolve us to "higher beings."

Truth is what Cole needed but how did he acquire truth if it was so far from him? Did a magical seed drop or did a fairy cast a spell on him? The magical seed was the stories he heard. The fairy was actually the man telling stories in his rehabilitation program. Cole explains his transformation:

> I couldn't get away from how sick I knew I was and from knowing he'd been there too and from seeing he wasn't there any more. I mean the way he talked about his own life I knew he'd been there. And he'd been clean for ten years, he told me that right off and I could see it (p. 294).

He learns in a way that no culturally literate dictionary of names, dates and events or school curriculum could have taught him. His search for truth with ethical guidance and discovery of self will certainly affect Cole's relationship with "economic prosperity," "social justice" and "democracy."

The literature by Pirsig, Plato, Rodriguez, Mellix and Cole are all stories. These stories are incorporated into my schemata and I in turn evolve and act on the stories in new ways. This dual subjectivity is often referred to as a labyrinth of mutual enclosure. Eugen Baer in *Medical Semiotics* explains that stories make up the world and the world is itself a story. He says "scientists as well as artists make us aware that the world tells the story of the self and that the self displays the story of the world" (p. 110). He dedicates many subchapters to the explanation of stories as cures and as diseases in the broader meaning of the words. The importance of stories in our world is essential to learning, and Hirsch ignores the mutual enclosure role of the story by stressing names, dates and events and disregarding the role of the actual story. By not reading *Alice in Wonderland* and just memorizing the key points as Hirsch suggests, one would lose the power of transformation Lewis Carrol originally intended the story to provide. The very power of transformation is illustrated as I read these books and gain a better understanding of who I am. I now understand why Hirsch is wrong. I would encourage Hirsch to read a few transforming stories filled with ethics and "human feelings." He should not bother with the "Decree of Destiny" because he is so externally motivated his face is a steering wheel.

I no longer resent not being a member of the culturally elite and feel for those who define themselves by elite groups. I have found sustenance in my life and am now a part of an expanding spiritually cultural, literate world.

Works Cited

Baer, Eugen. *Medical Semiotics.* Maryland: University Press of America, Inc., 1988.

Cole, William E., Jr. "Writing as Literacy: An Alternative to Losing." *The Plural I— and After.* New Hampshire: Boynton/Cook Heineman, (1988): 278–98.

Hirsch, E. D., Jr. *Cultural Literacy, What Every American Needs To Know.* Massachusetts: Houghton Mifflin Company, 1987.

Mellix, Barbara. "From Outside, In." *The Georgia Review* XLI (1987): 258–66.

Pirsig, Robert M. *Zen and The Art of Motorcycle Maintenance.* New York: William Morrow and Company, Inc., 1974.

Plato. *Laches.* Trans. Rosamond Kent Sprague. New York: Macmillan Publishing Company, 1973.

Plato. *Phaedrus.* Trans. W. C. Helmbold and W. G. Rabinowitz. New York: Macmillan Publishing Company, 1985.

Rodriguez, Richard. *Hunger for Memory: The Education of Richard Rodriguez.* Massachusetts: David R. Godine, Publisher, Inc., 1982.

■ THE WRITER'S ASSIGNMENT

Open topic. Develop a topic to synthesize the course readings.   ■

■ UNDERSTANDING WRITING STRATEGIES

1. How does Rose bring her seemingly diverse materials into focus?

2. What do the first few paragraphs do to create this focus?

3. How does Rose's use of personal experience contribute to this focus? What kinds of expectations does this set up?

4. What criteria does Rose use to evaluate the readings?

5. How does Rose move from one course reading to another?

6. Rose expands the definition of "cultural literacy" by referring to Plato. What is this expanded definition?

7. How effectively does this definition embrace the writers' experiences?

8. What importance does Baer have for the writers Rose has considered?

9. Where does the concluding paragraph leave the reader? Is this truly a conclusion for the essay?

10. How does this writer "synthesize"?   ■

The Case of "Luke"
Deborah M. Sanders

Writing for a Psychopathology of the Child course, Deborah M. Sanders presents Luke's case history. Drawing upon actual clinical encounters, her study describes Luke's behavior, relates this behavior to theoretical studies of childhood schizophrenia, relates interviews with Luke's parents, and recommends a course of treatment.

" 'Psychotic' means being so severely disturbed that one is 'out of contact with reality' or that one's 'reality-testing' is so poor that misinterpretations or ordinary situations grossly interfere with adaptation" (Achenbach, p. 414). Based on what I have learned in class and from reading *Developmental Psychopathology* by Thomas M. Achenbach, I believe Luke falls into the category we call *childhood psychoses;* more specifically, I believe an appropriate primary diagnosis for Luke is *Schizophrenia.*

In childhood psychoses, there is a big biologic input at the level of the autonomic nervous system. Reality testing has failed and there is massive separation from reality which may include hallucinations and delusions. There is almost always a mood disorder present and/or inappropriate or constricted affect—a bland personality. There also is some evidence of neurophysiological involvement: in Schizophrenia many experts have estimated that 50% is biologic and 50% is psychological or familial due to distorted communication patterns. It is important to stress though, that none of these involvements are completely causal. They are only components.

At first glance of Luke's case, I really didn't think he had a severe pathology. He seemed about as friendly as 11-year-old boys get. He was cooperative with the therapist and had no trouble separating from his father. I also was not very alarmed by Luke's parents' description of him. They said he had "temper tantrums" and that in school he always "wants to be the center of attention." Still, I thought Luke was a fairly average 11-year-old boy. What really worried me though, was Luke's own description of himself and his parents. He reported that he often hears voices that he knows are not there. His description of the incident when his parents told him he had a new bike waiting for him somewhere in the house and it turned out to only be a jogging suit appalled me; how could supposedly caring parents be so cruel? What frustrated me even more was the fact that Luke states that "my parents tease me a lot. But that's O.K.—I don't mind." Luke also reported that when he told his parents about the voices he hears, "they just laugh at me." They also laugh when he tells them about his wish to be a "truck driver." It scares me to think of what Luke's definition of love is . . . what is a child supposed to think about love and trust and caring when he is constantly the center of ridicule and humiliation by his parents? Luke seemed to be receiving very mixed signals from his parents with very little positive reinforcement of anything.

It is hard to "blame" Luke for any of the symptoms he has. His parents often appear to be "crazier" than he is. How else was he to turn out? Luke's parents appear to have a history of overprotectiveness in areas outside their present concerns about Luke's need for psychological help. They have high aspirations for Luke's success in school and life—possibly too high. Luke's mother is the most puzzling (she will be discussed later). She was not able to attend the sessions initially but did attend a brief closing interview. Luke's parents show outright signs of denial of the severity of their son's problems. They feel that somehow Luke's problem is related to his poor vision and the difficulty he was having transferring from eye-glasses to contact lenses. The therapists' impression of Mr. L was that he was far more concerned about Luke than he was able to communicate directly. Was this and his mother's absence from the sessions a type of avoidance? I seem to think that Mr. and Mrs. L have some unconscious guilt or knowledge of the damage they'd done to their son. I also think that Luke's parents were experiencing denial of the severity of their son's problems, like they really didn't want to know the truth or "have a finger pointed at them."

What really alerted me to the severity of Luke's pathology was the results of the tests administered to Luke. The WISC-R test of cognitive functioning showed a great deal of inter-test-scatter—a large degree of ups and downs. This discrepancy represents a combination of visual-motor impairment and psychopathology that affects logical, synthetic, integrative reasoning and thinking. These features suggest organicity and psychopathology intertwined. The degree of unevenness reflects the severity of cognitive invasion by either organic or psychogenic interference. Luke's Comprehension Subtest score (IQ: 69) indicates a relatively severe deficit in gradually acquired "socialization" learning and possible poor judgment for socially expected and interpersonally appropriate behavior. Luke's deficit in this area suggests the operation of chronic pathology in the area of self-monitoring and drive-regulation. It is very clear that Luke's reality testing is impaired based on the Picture Completion and Object Assembly Subtests. Luke's scores on these tests were very low. These tests require attention to detail and the ability to be critically analytical and synthetically integrative. Luke is unable to abstract or generalize spontaneously. Luke's Bender-Gestalt drawings are very alarming: they contain evidence of a mild perceptual difficulty and more compelling, evidence of psychogenic disturbance. However, Luke is definitely aware of the visual problems that he has. But the test results do not indicate any severe impairment stemming from either visual or motor deficits. Luke's Verbal Comprehension factor IQ and his Attention Concentration factor IQ scores are in the low average to average range which suggests that difficulties in thinking, difficulties in synthetic ego functioning, and in the application of sequential perceptual problem solving operation are somehow linked. According to the test scores, Luke evidences a severe unevenness of cognitive functioning, indicative of severe psychopathology. He appears to have the most trouble judging and foreseeing the consequences of his own behavior.

Luke possesses a quality of hauntedness, a sense, quite literally, of being invaded and injured. He has been raised in an environment where loving someone means psychologically abusing them and forcing them to question what is really real. Luke's projective figure drawings suggest three "transparencies" that suggest distortion of ego boundaries for self and others. Not surprising to me, Luke experiences himself as easily penetrable and likely to be seriously hurt. Because of Luke's long history of being ridiculed and hurt by his parents, Luke is guarded and naturally distrustful of others. To compensate for fears he has of being hurt, Luke has learned to deal with reality by attempting to ignore it; to pretend or convince himself that it's not really happening. In a discussion about school, Luke displays again a feeling of hauntedness. He possesses a sense of expected attack and retribution that probably reflects deep hurt and shame. The Rorschach and TAT responses evidence severe deficits in reality testing and, more specifically, Luke's capacity to trust his own judgment. Luke has learned to question almost everything he perceives: be it one of his own personal thoughts or a feeling possibly conveyed by his parents. According to the report, the Rorschach record contains additional evidence of defective reality testing—enough to warrant the diagnosis of psychotic cognition present. The tests' results, along with the therapist's description of Luke, show very clear evidence that Luke's reality testing is severely impaired, if not totally gone. Luke is not depressed though. He really is not "saddened," or extremely withdrawn. His personality style is more a constriction of affect . . . he shows some sense of emptiness, of blandness. He has a very fragile quality; he gives me the impression that he could very easily sink into a full-blown depression at the drop of a hat. He has serious ego-deficits, probably the result of his parents' perceived disappointment in him and his life's goals.

DSM III describes the essential features of schizophrenia as, ". . . the presence of certain psychotic features during the active phase of the illness, characteristic symptoms involving multiple psychological processes, deterioration from a previous level of functioning, onset before age 45, and a duration of at least six months . . . . at some phase of the illness Schizophrenia always involves delusions, hallucinations, or certain disturbances in the form of thought" (Achenbach, p. 439). If Luke in fact is schizophrenic, he most likely was born with a predisposition to mental illness, considering the pathology of his parents. This possible predisposition was likely compounded by the distorted communication patterns displayed by Luke's parents. Goldfarb (Achenbach, p. 445) portrays a model of childhood schizophrenia as caused primarily by parental inadequacy *and* organic abnormalities. He believes that the following characteristics are present in most children who are schizophrenic: parental inadequacies and perplexity, absence of positive reinforcements, stimulus confusion, deviant child, ego deficiency, and absence of normal guides for self-directed action and self-regulation; and defect in self-identity, diffusion of boundaries of self and nonself, absence of predictable expectancies; loss of referents and anchoring; catastrophic feelings of strangeness and unfamiliarity and panic with seeking for sameness. Luke definitely displays most, if not all of these qualities. There obviously are parental inadequacies and perplexities. The parents appear almost never to reinforce Luke positively for anything. They seem to give him a sense of worthlessness . . . that anything he says or does is absurd or ridiculous. Luke shows clear signs of ego deficiency in his discussions with the therapist and in the test results. The transparencies found in Luke's projective figure drawings suggest that the boundaries of self and others are diffused and distorted.

I do not think that Luke has become as severely schizophrenic or psychotic as he could become; although he does experience hallucinations, they have not taken over his life. He is aware of those experiences although he has been forced to question almost everything that happens to him. A diagnosis of schizophrenia for Luke is severe nonetheless. He is a very ill child who requires intensive therapy, first alone and eventually with his family. I expect Luke's therapy (together with his family) to last for at least four years and maybe more. I'm not sure though, that Luke will ever completely recover, especially since the possibility of organic dysfunction is very likely.

TREATMENT

I believe that no matter how much one-to-one therapy Luke receives with his therapist, the bulk of his problems will exist as long as his parents continue to raise him the way they have. I think at first, Luke needs intensive one-to-one therapy (possibly play therapy) to relieve some of the anxieties he has about himself and his abilities as a person. He needs to elevate his self-esteem or have someone else point out his good qualities (which may be very difficult to find). Next, I would begin conjoint family therapy, as described in our text on page 627. It is clear that Luke's family *must* be involved in his treatment; without them, treatment will go nowhere. Conjoint family therapy emerged in the 1950's and holds the view that the family is a social system in which each member's behavior is a function of pressures existing in the whole system. In this system, a child's problems and difficulties are viewed as symptoms of family stress and as serving a function for the family; the child is in a way informing the family of problems that exist. Without the child identifying these problems, the symptoms may recur in other family members and continue to cause problems for everybody. The family system is viewed as the target of treatment. Many therapists meet with the parents for a few sessions alone without the child to get family history and other facts relevant to the treatment. Other therapists place less emphasis on family history because they believe that this sets up the family for a pattern of the therapist asking questions and the family merely answering. (This is not favorable.) Almost all family therapists agree not to take sides with particular family members. In this case, I would not view Luke's parents statements as more valid simply because they are his parents. One key rule in the success of family therapy is that none of the family members have to say anything if they don't want to; similarly, the family members can say anything they want to without being punished. Conjoint family therapy obviously brings a family's attitudes and interactions into much broader focus. Also, family therapy might reduce the pressure on the child since he is not viewed anymore as the target of the therapy.

The problem arises though, with Luke's parents. I have mentioned previously that Luke's parents clearly deny Luke's problem and probably are also afraid of being blamed or held responsible for the problems that they do accept. I really think the only way to get Luke's parents actively involved in his treatment is to inform them very bluntly of the severity of Luke's problems. At first, they do not need to know how much of an impact they have had on his development; they should just be told that Luke has a lot of problems that need to be worked out with their help—that he is a very disturbed young man who will only get better if they participate actively in his treatment. If this approach fails and Luke's parents still refuse to attend the sessions, Luke should continue to receive counseling privately and at a school counseling service where he will learn to appreciate himself as a person and develop a higher self-esteem. Eventually, Luke will probably learn that his parents were largely responsible for his terrible feelings about himself. Hopefully with the help of a good therapist, Luke will learn to feel a little better about himself. Again, since the disorder is most likely organically based (at least 50%), Luke will probably not experience complete recovery; instead, he may just learn to deal with the negative feelings he has toward himself and his parents. I expect that therapy for Luke to last at least 3 to 4 years, but most likely much longer, based on the history of his symptoms. (It appears that this is not a sudden development in Luke's life; his parents did not suddenly notice Luke's peculiarities.)

PARENTAL PERSONALITY

I really believe that Mrs. L fits the old 1940's and 1950's description of a "schizophrenogenic mother" (Achenbach, p. 440). During this time, schizophrenia was blamed on mothers who were immature, narcissistic, over-intellectual, and incapable of mature emotional relationships. Although this label is not used any more, I believe Mrs. L really fits the description. It is also not held as true anymore that schizophrenia is primarily caused by the mother's attitude, although family communication and interaction is a key factor. Luke's mother seems to be obsessed with success. She, along with her husband, have very high expectations and aspirations for Luke. They seem to want Luke to be someone or something that he cannot possibly be. And even worse is the fact that they laugh at him and his own wishes to be a truck driver. Mrs. L never seems satisfied with anything her son does. She complains that he "gets too involved in television" and often forgets to zipper his pants." It is difficult to tell however, how often these situations actually occur, and if Mrs. L is just overly attentive (or unattentive) to Luke and his habits. She definitely seems to be on a "quest" for the perfect son. She is reluctant to admit that she and her husband had anything to do with Luke's problems, or for that matter, that Luke even has any problems. Freud believed (Achenbach, p. 628) that, "Children's developmental problems activate unresolved childhood conflicts of their parents so that when a parent seeks assistance from a therapist in relation to his child, he is also presenting a part of himself which seeks help." This may in fact be the case with Mrs. L. It is possible that deep down inside she knows she has done a poor job raising Luke. Maybe she knows she is partly at fault for her son's tragic development and seeks to remedy the situation by sending him to therapy and eventually finding help for herself. It also can be inferred (based on Freud's statement) that Mrs. L had a very disappointing childhood and is still disappointed with her life as it is now and is transferring those feelings to her son Luke because it hurts her less that way. By doing that she is avoiding the fact that she may have made mistakes in her life and it appears that Luke is actually the one with the problems.

In any case, Luke's mother most likely has as many problems as he does, if not more. She also requires intense therapy but in a different style.

■ UNDERSTANDING WRITING STRATEGIES

1. What kind of writing context does the first paragraph indicate?

2. What are the terms of the essay's definition?

3. Where do you find the terms identified with Luke?

4. What else does the writer offer about Luke besides identification with the terms?

5. How does Sanders's use of "I" affect you? Explain how this relates to the paper's purposes?

6. What balance exists between subjectivity and objectivity in Sanders's data about Luke?

7. What grounds does Sanders give for her proposed therapy? What objections might be raised to this based on the evidence Sanders has provided?

8. Sanders has chosen to address the three topics separately. How interdependent are these seemingly separate essays? On what do you base your conclusion? ■

■ SUGGESTIONS FOR WRITING

Integrate the three parts of Sanders's study into an integrated essay to which you add an introduction and conclusion that reaches a specific audience (professional journal, popular magazine, or a report to a superior or a diagnosis and treatment committee). ■

Thomas Merton's Long Climb to Freedom: The Seven Storey Mountain in Terms of Allport's Personality Theory

Susan Walton

Using Thomas Merton's spiritual autobiography, *The Seven Storey Mountain,* as a source for accessing Merton's personality, Susan Walton applies Allport's personality theory to Merton's religious experience. Her essay both illuminates Merton's experiences and critiques Allport in this essay written for the course, Theories of Personality.

To examine the Trappist monk Thomas Merton in the light of Gordon W. Allport's eclectic personality theory will be at the same time a gentle stroll and an arduous climb. This is entirely predictable given Merton's own consistent theme of paradox, both men's abiding concern for the faith of the individual, and each writer's long-windedness! Bearing in mind Allport's description of personality as "less a finished product than a transitive process" (Allport, 1955, p. 19), and noting that Merton's title alludes to Dante's allegory of Purgatory, let us now start to investigate Merton's personality as we take a look at the traits he revealed in his autobiography.

Merton himself, of course, chose what to reveal and what to conceal. And while he made a great show of telling everything, in minute detail, he hinted at more sins than he actually described. He was in the difficult position of being urged by his abbot to write (Merton, 1948, pp. 410, 413), yet having to pass "official censorship procedures" (Mott, 1984, p. 77) before publication. And we are in the awkward position of presuming to judge a world-renowned contemplative who was virtually licensed by his own Church hierarchy to proclaim his struggle toward true faith. Any negative comments about him might appear to be criticism of faith itself!

It should come as no surprise that Merton's cardinal trait appears to be his spirituality. His second and third sentences describe the paradoxical agony of being drawn to God and yet pushing Him away (Merton, 1948, p. 3), and thus declare the major theme of the autobiography. Despite a lack of formal religious training as a young child, Merton, at the age of ten, nonetheless grasped the primacy of faith in the village of St. Antonin: ". . . all focussed my attention upon the one, important central fact of the church

and what it contained." (Merton, 1948, p. 37) And he perceived the "root and
. . . foundation" (Merton, 1948, p. 57) of his father's friends', the Privats,
goodness to be their faith in God. The trip which he took to Rome at age
eighteen, prior to entering Cambridge and two years after his father's lingering death from a brain tumor, took on the aspect of a pilgrimage (Merton,
1948, p. 108). His conversion experience there involved a dream of his father's return to warn him about his sins (Merton, 1948, pp. 111, 112).

These early signs of spirituality in Merton later branched into mysticism—his sudden insight while in Cuba at Easter in 1940 that Heaven was a
present fact, not a future possibility (Merton, 1948, p. 285), for example. He
became aware of the action of grace within his life—his recovery from
blood-poisoning while at Oakham and, four years later, his awareness of his
own "emptiness" which opened him up to God's "free gift [of] . . . 'sanctify-
ing grace' " (Merton, 1948, pp. 99, 165, 169), to cite only two instances. His
ability to pray progressed from the Lord's Prayer through his spontaneous
prayers after Pop's and Bonnemaman's deaths, to the start of his real prayer
life with the purchase of his Breviaries (Merton, 1948, pp. 9, 160, 301). The
deaths of Pop and Bonnemaman marked a turning point for Merton: his sudden awareness of the "abyss" which would haunt him and propel him in his
progression towards Baptism as a Roman Catholic, his growing vocation to
be a priest, and his first retreat at Gethsemani, where the feared "abyss" began to take on the aspect of joyful surrender (Merton, 1948, pp. 161, 162,
181, 255, 323).

On the other hand, there were many doubts which Merton suffered.
Early on he noted hypocrisy in the Church of England, where he felt that St.
Paul's concept of charity was equated with gentlemanliness, and he became
disenchanted with his father's and mother's former places of worship because people there concentrated more on intellectual matters than on faith
(Merton, 1948, pp. 73, 115, 116). Allport would attribute this to "the doubt
engendered by visible hypocrisy and failure in institutional religion." (Allport, 1950, p. 120)

When considering Merton's many doubts about his vocation as he prepared to enter the Franciscan novitiate (Merton, 1948, p. 296), Allport would
remind us that "unless the individual doubts he cannot use his full intelligence, and unless he uses his full intelligence he cannot develop a mature
sentiment." (Allport, 1950, p. 116) Merton's doubts were like multiple small
adjustments to show him where his true direction lay (cf. references to com-
pass in chapter headings). And in a posthumous book of Merton's writings,
we find the fullest development of this theme of doubt's enrichment of
faith:

> Faith means doubt. Faith is not the suppression of doubt. It is the overcom-
> ing of doubt, and you overcome doubt by going through it. The man of faith
> who has never experienced doubt is not a man of faith (Merton, 1968; in
> Burton et al., 1975, p. 306).

This concentration of Merton's cardinal trait of spirituality makes him seem like a gaudy plaster saint, rather than the very human figure which the autobiography conveys. It is precisely this humanity which lends the account authenticity, and yet it is hard not to wonder whether Merton's intelligence and strong urge to proseletize engineered such an impression.

So now we turn to the central and secondary traits, which will help to round out this personality profile of Thomas Merton. A unique blend of perfectionism, the urge to communicate, and need for structure seem to dominate his central traits, attended by intellectualism, introversion, strong aestheticism, and a penchant for melodrama. Secondary traits include a slow-growing compassion, a humorous sense of the absurd, and a late-blooming interest in people.

The perfectionism best expresses itself in the restlessness and questing suggested by the Latin phrase at the end of the book, which can be translated loosely as "the book is over, the searching is not" (Merton, 1948, p. 423). It can also be seen clearly at the end of Part Two, with Tom praying to become a priest, and realizing that "[i]t was a moment of crisis, yet of interrogation; a moment of searching, but it was a moment of joy." (Merton, 1948, p. 255) It is important to remember that Merton's restlessness also led him to sample depravity at Cambridge, to flirt with Communism when first at Columbia, and to taste the life-styles of journalist, teacher, Franciscan, and lay-worker in Harlem. Sharing a contemplative insight, Thomas Merton wrote: "We cannot arrive at the perfect possession of God in this life, and that is why we are travelling and in darkness." (Merton, 1948, p. 419)

Merton's urge to communicate should be self-evident in the long list of his published works and letters, and all through his autobiogrpahy. Perhaps he began to write by mimicking his mother's diarist tendencies, but he scribbled early novels in French, confided his journalistic ambitions to Aunt Maud, worked on the Columbia publications, then wrote verse, book reviews, and numerous books once he had become a Catholic (Merton, 1948, pp. 52, 62, 150, 235, 236, 409).

Examples of Merton's articulateness abound, but a few stand out:

—the "moral fungus" of Cambridge,
—". . . Bellevue, where they collect the bodies of those who died of contemporary civilization, like Fred."
—"Day after day the round of the canonical hours brought them together and the love that was in them became songs as austere as granite and as sweet as wine."
—"The little children of Harlem are growing up, crowded together like sardines in the rooms of tenements full of vice, where evil takes place hourly and inescapably before their eyes . . ."
   (Merton, 1948, pp. 126, 153, 317, 346)

Merton's prayers, of course, reflected his urge to communicate with his Creator.

The restlessness which Merton manifested resulted largely from his need for structure, and his yearning for transcendence. He had a strong need to affiliate himself, and that need found expression in a wide range of activities from his bacchanalian behavior at Cambridge, to his brief associations with the Communist Party, and a Columbia fraternity. His M.A. thesis on William Blake gave structure to his sense of being out of step with his time, as he observed Blake to be (Merton, 1948, p. 190). At the moment of his Baptism, Merton felt caught up in "this immense and tremendous gravitational movement which is love . . . the Holy Spirit." (Merton, 1948, p. 225)

Still further evidence of Merton's affiliative urge appears in his use of the Breviaries, the structure of his teaching and meditation at St. Bonaventure's, and his first impression of Gethsemani: "The embrace of it, the silence! I had entered into a solitude that was an impregnable fortress." (Merton, 1948, p. 321) He admitted his need for support from the Christian missionaries at Friendship House, and he asked the gatekeeper-monk at Gethsemani to pray for him when he entered for the last time (Merton, 1948, pp. 349, 371). The most convincing evidence for Merton's achievement of transcendence occurs in Merton's Latin description of the Gethsemani monks in corporate worship: "Congregavit nos in unum Christi amor." (Merton, 1948, p. 414)

Gordon Allport's sensitivity to the religious personality enabled him to analyze these needs for affiliation and transcendence. He said: "For the great majority of people the solitariness of the religious quest becomes a burden. They long to fuse their religious insights with those of their fellows under a common set of symbols." (Allport, 1950, p. 153)

Merton's evident intellectualism won for him the chance to pursue independent studies at Oakham, and to wrestle with philosophy. He warmed to the appeal of the "master-mind element" of the Jesuits, and welcomed the mental discipline of the Spiritual Exercises of St. Ignatius (Merton, 1948, pp. 213, 270). His studies toward M.A. and Ph.D. degrees and his close analysis of the weaknesses of Communism reveal a nimble mind. Signs of intellectual snobbery appear in his contempt for the "jargon of transliterated French" in the novice handbook at Gethsemani (Merton, 1948, p. 374).

The keen awareness of paradox shown over and over by Merton can also be attributed to his intellect. From the start he declared that he was "free by nature" yet a "prisoner," and he amplified on that theme when he realized, after Baptism, that "conversion of the intellect" was not enough; conversion of the will was necessary too (Merton, 1948, pp. 3, 231). He remarked that the "logic of the Cistercian life was . . . the complete opposite to the logic of the world, in which men put themselves forward . . ." and imagined, at the close of the book, the Lord reciting a series of paradoxes to him, rather like the parables of the Gospel (Merton, 1948, pp. 330, 422, 423).

It appears that Thomas Merton was an introvert, from the scant evidence of any friendships right up until his Oakham years. In fact, only three friends are mentioned by name, Bill and Russ from Long Island, aged about seven, and Henriette in St. Antonin, aged eleven and a half. Merton mentioned going to Germany a few years later, "by myself as usual . . ." (Merton, 1948, p. 95) His love for the peace at Olean (in northwestern New York State), his meditations in his room in the city, and his sense of being recharged on his retreats, all reveal a rather solitary person. Near the close of the book, Merton referred to his long-term "aspirations for solitude and for a contemplative life" (Merton, 1948, p. 420).

The tendency towards introversion led directly to introspection, guilt and self-criticism, and awareness of his own sin. Merton portrayed himself as "a true citizen of my own disgusting century: the century of poison gas and atomic bombs." (Merton, 1948, p. 85) While at Cambridge he analyzed himself as being sexually repressed and in dire need of a conversion to extroversion, but only succeeded in becoming more of an introvert! (Merton, 1948, p. 124) He found fault with himself after Baptism for not going to daily mass, not engaging a spiritual director, for not praying enough (Merton, 1948, pp. 228, 229). Even after his entrance to the cloister, he exclaimed: "All my bad habits, disinfected, it is true, of formal sin, had sneaked into the monastery with me and had received the religious vesture along with me: spiritual gluttony, spiritual sensuality, spiritual pride . . ." (Merton, 1948, p. 387).

The benefits of Merton's introspection are the fruits of his contemplation, which he shares through his books. At Baptism his aloneness reminds him of "the singleness with which this Christ, hidden in the small Host, was giving Himself for me . . ." (Merton, 1948, p. 224). And shortly before he entered Gethsemani, his meditation in the chapel at St. Bonaventure's taught him that he no longer felt the need to receive, but to give (Merton, 1948, p. 356).

Love of language, art, landscape, literature—all these fit into Merton's aesthetic sense. His lyrical descriptions of France, of Cuba, of Blake and Hopkins, of performing the daily office on the trains to Olean and Gethsemani, of Advent liturgy and Gregorian chants, and of harvest time in Kentucky—all convey his joy in beauty, in a spiritual sense. He even declared that America's silent places must have been "made for contemplation" (Merton, 1948, p. 310).

When Merton got carried away, he wallowed in melodrama, and each reader will have to decide whether to take a charitable or a harsh view of his lapses. For example, his mention of his childhood "worship" of the gas light in the kitchen and his lurid description of the blood-poisoning episode are perhaps extreme. Arrogance shows itself when he speaks of not practicing his faith enough after Baptism: "All this would have been enough to an ordinary Catholic . . . but for me it could not possibly be enough" (Merton, 1948, p. 232). Envisioning his heroic future as a medic, if drafted, he daydreams: "I would be able to leaven the mass of human misery with the charity and mercy of Christ" (Merton, 1948, p. 313). All these episodes feature Merton as hero. Allport might comment here: "[M]ost neuroses are, from the point of view of religion, mixed with the sin of pride . . . As the focus of striving shifts from the conflict to selfless goals, the life as a whole becomes sounder . . ." (Allport, 1950, p. 107).

A quick examination of Merton's secondary traits reveals that for many years he had no real compassion, only self-pity when an unfortunate event happening to another person somehow left *him* bereft. Baroness de Hueck's arrival at St. Bonaventure's began to stir Merton's capacity for compassion, with her stories of the children of Harlem (Merton, 1948, pp. 339–344). But his compassion did not really flow until his brother arrived at Gethsemani, wanting instruction for Baptism. Teaching John Paul about God, and then mourning his death, was one of Merton's first real gifts of compassion, if one can safely judge by the record of his autobiography (Merton, 1948, pp. 394–404).

There are many instances of Merton's humor to choose from, but many of the earlier ones (Pop's whirlwind tours of Europe, the peculiar English faith) poke fun at others rather than at himself. Later, his amusement at performing Catholic meditations while "sitting like Gandhi," the irony that he had a cold while singing his first Gregorian chant, and his laughter at the absurd truth that he was finally exactly where he wanted to be when he was praying prostrate before the abbot—these instances of humor show maturity (Merton, 1948, pp. 269, 379, 421). And hand in hand with humor goes objectivity, such as this observation from the cloister: ". . . one of the most important aspects of any religious vocation . . . is the willingness to accept life in a community in which everybody is more or less imperfect." (Merton, 1948, p. 381) The Allportian view of humor is, of course, that it confers "perspective" (Allport, 1950, p. 57).

As for Merton's late-blooming interest in people, when it finally happened, at Columbia, within his circle of close friends Mark van Doren, Bob Lax, Ed Rice, Sy Freedgood, Bob Gibney, and Bob Gerdy, Merton regarded the friendship as a sacrament, which enabled him to reach out to God (Merton, 1948, p. 178). The Baroness, Father Edmund who counseled him on the Franciscans, and Dan Walsh, who urged him toward the Trappists, were three other major figures for Merton in his twenties. John Paul, time and again, seemed to show him who he really was, like a kind of mirror, most notably his sin of exclusiveness—at play in Douglaston, his spiritual emptiness—in the first year at Columbia, his flawed vocation for the Franciscan life, and his thirst for reconciliation and atonement—at Gethsemani (Merton, 1948, pp. 23, 151, 287, 394–397).

Now we must gather the threads of these traits and attempt to weave them into an Allportian explanation of why Thomas Merton was as he was. Allport would not consciously wish to leave out anything (for example, I am aware that I have not read all of Merton's writings, nor all of Allport's, and little commentary on either!), so he would wish to mention the external influences which helped to shape or intensify some of Merton's traits. Merton

himself gives us ample evidence of the chaos of the first part of his life—
born during the first world war and draftable during the second; losing his
mother to cancer at six and his father to a tumor at sixteen; living like a
gypsy in Bermuda and France while his artist father was alive; remembering
his father for his faith and talent and his mother for her disapproving perfectionism. He never had much opportunity to form a bond with his mother or
his brother in his early years, and he changed schools and cultures so often
that he made no real friends. His bombastic maternal grandfather made him
financially independent at the age of fifteen, but never was able to provide a
structure, other than his suspicion of the Catholic faith! So Tom, being curious, experimented with debauchery and irresponsibility until his rarified
English godfather forbade his return to Cambridge and sent him to America.
Add to the above at least twenty train- and boat-journeys in his first eighteen years. It is not hard to understand why Thomas Merton had such a
strong craving for security and stillness, and why he sought to transcend the
inadequacies of his life through union with God. It is little wonder that his
compassion, sense of humor, and genuine interest in other people took so
long to grow, or that he took to writing as a way to explain himself, to self
and others.

Allport would say that Merton saw the world as a beautiful but dangerous place, where you could not always rely on human relationships, and human sinfulness caused wars and unhappiness. He would say that Merton
saw himself as a sinner, but was able to make sense out of his life and continue his propriate striving because he believed himself connected to God
through grace. Once Merton focused his life through his faith, his dizzy
spells and general unhealthiness vanished, and he became robust. Allport
would say this answers his psychophysical riddle, how mind relates to body.

Merton's view of others, in an Allportian sense, changed according to
his stage of becoming. Thus in the early years, he sometimes viewed people
symbolically, as threats to his self-esteem and self-image. Later, as he had
developed a proprium enabling him to see himself and others as separate and
unique entities, he was able to establish genuine friendships and mentor-
ships, which in turn enabled him to know himself in the context of his Creator. The main, unifying threads of Merton's life are these thirsts for becoming, for developing his spirituality into faith, for finding a haven or base in
that faith, from which he could grow further, and for sharing his discoveries
with others (to bear witness, lend a hand . . .).

Merton's main conflicts are with himself; his intellect outstrips his
will and his self-esteem, and so he is frequently encountering conflict and
paradox and doubt. Merton needs affiliation and structure because of having
to adapt to all the changes of his early life, and because of his intelligence
and spirituality. He presents his story as a modern-day pilgrim's progress, to
show the way out of vicissitudes of sin and doubt, to help himself understand his own life better, and to please his abbot. Allport might apply his

sixth riddle of individuality here; Merton's life is consistant throughout in its constant changes and growth, which are nonetheless impossible to predict.

To round out the picture, Allport would mention other theorists' possible slants on Merton, because his eclectic theory can draw on all. To mention some briefly, Anna Freud's ego defences of turning against self, asceticism, sublimation, and rationalization could be found in Merton's story. Karen Horney's three solutions to the alienation which stems from insufficient affiliation with the mothering one could each be applied at different times in Merton's life. Harry Stack Sullivan's parataxic stage hangover into adult superstition could be detected in much of Merton's mysticism. And there would be room for discussion of Freud's theory that a person's belief in God is a direct projection of the relationship with the earthly father.

Allport's eclecticism makes it hard to fault his theory for any glaring omissions, but lends itself to one major criticism: the theory is unwieldy in its all-inclusiveness. Because Allport takes such care to take a sympathetic, detailed view of the person, he creates an open-ended situation which is nearly unmanageable. However, I believe that it is fair to the person in that it uses personal documents and the traits revealed therein, so it paints an impression rather than a hard-edged image. The lack of rigidity allows for a moving picture of the person's continuous change and growth. Allport's theory obscures nothing, because it is infinitely adjustable. This is why I like it so much, because it does not condemn or label, and it has a healthy regard for the existential aspect of what it is to be a human being.

Bibliography

Allport, Gordon W., *Becoming*; New Haven, Yale University Press, 1955.

————, *The Individual and His Religion*; N.Y., Macmillan Publishing Co., Inc., 1950 (1978).

The Asian Journal of Thomas Merton, ed. by Naomi Burton, Brother Patrick Hart, James Laughlin; N.Y., New Directions Publishing Corporation, 1975.

Letters from Jenny, ed. and interp. by Gordon W. Allport; San Diego, Harcourt Brace Jovanovich, Inc., 1965.

Merton, Thomas, *The Seven Storey Mountain*; San Diego, Harcourt Brace Jovanovich, 1948 (1976).

Monte, Christopher F., *Beneath the Mask: An Introduction to Theories of Personality*, 3rd Ed.; N.Y., Holt, Rinehart and Winston, 1987.

Mott, Michael, *The Seven Mountains of Thomas Merton*; Boston, Houghton Mifflin Company, 1984.

■ **THE WRITER'S ASSIGNMENT**

Using one personality theory studied in the course, evaluate a personality as he/she reveals it in a diary or autobiography. ■

■ **UNDERSTANDING WRITING STRATEGIES**

1. How does the introduction engage the reader and commit to the subject?

2. What central aspects of Merton's personality does Walton consider?

3. What are the central tenets of Allport's personality theory? How do you know this?

4. What distinction does Walton make between primary and secondary traits?

5. Is the discussion of Allport adequate for the reader's purposes? On what do you base your response?

6. What principles from Allport serve as organizing principles for Walton's essay?

7. How does Walton integrate her consideration of Allport and Merton?

8. What criteria does Allport provide for personality study?

9. What criteria does Walton employ for evaluating Allport?

10. To what audience is this addressed? What indicates this audience? How would you change this essay for a different audience? ■

■ **SUGGESTIONS FOR WRITING**

Read Thomas Merton's *The Seven Storey Mountain*. Write a review of Merton's biography for *Psychology Today*. Your review should include a clear but not too lengthy summary and an evaluation. Develop your evaluation using criteria from Walton's essay or, if you are familiar with another personality theory, from it. ■

NATO and the SNF Debate

Brad Werner

Brad Werner, writing here for a political science course, International Security and Arms Control, analyzes the role of short-range nuclear forces in European defense. Werner develops his essay by summarizing and integrating a substantial body of literature published in books and political science journals.

The principle behind a credible American strategic response is NATO's nuclear posture backed by the strategic might of the U.S. Since World War II, the security and peace of Europe has relied primarily on nuclear deterrence rather than on conventional deterrence. The two wars in which the U.S. has fought since signing the NATO agreement serve as examples of failed nuclear deterrence. In December of 1987, the INF treaty was signed and subsequently eliminated an entire class of missiles. This agreement of unprecedented magnitude, brought about by the strategies provided under the 1979 Dual-Track decision, is undoubtedly an historic step toward more effective arms control negotiations with the Soviets. But what does this mean for the future of NATO? How will this affect the strategy of deterrence for Europe, and what changes will need to be made?

The American missile deployment in Western Europe fortifies the underpinnings of deterrence. By doing this, the west is considered to have "coupled" Europe's defense to the U.S.'s strategic stance, extending its deterrent posture. Appropriately known as "extended deterrence," it has, more than anything else, guaranteed that the Soviet Union will not attack Western Europe.[1] This is based on the assumption that Moscow would believe in the possibility that a nuclear escalation would result from conventional war, especially in light of the Soviet conventional advantage; NATO's conventional inferiority would obligate it to use its short-range nuclear forces (SNF) to avoid losing the conflict.

Currently, though, the European climate is changing. The influence of Secretary Gorbachev's reforms extends beyond Soviet borders. _Glasnost_ is signalling that the Soviets appear to be leaning toward a more stable European climate. Critics of the Soviet mood fear that it may be lulling Western democracies. Despite Gorbachev's notion of a denuclearized Europe ("a false one" at that, says Bonn's Research Institute Director Karl Kaiser) strong Western opinion predicts his intention is "de-coupling" the U.S. from Europe. "We should above all, resist any tendency to achieve a 'triple zero-solution'," Kaiser warns because it would "bring to bear the conventional and the geopolitical advantage of the Soviet Union" while it maintains all of its nuclear options, "including strategic weapons that can be used in a tactical mode."[2]

Whether or not this is indeed an intention, it could certainly be a result. Soviet Foreign Minister Eduard Schevardnadze has recently stated that he believes SNF should be considered next on the arms control agenda, a plan that will itself create tensions within NATO. But what are the Soviet Union's intentions? How far should the West go in allowing this mood to influence the way we change our strategies? And how will it affect the interrelations of NATO countries? This paper's purpose is to investigate the current status of European security concentrating on SNF's role and importance. This can be done provided we have a background on: NATO and its military policy; the development of the "nuclear club" in Europe, France, and Great Britain; and the disparity of these weapons favoring the Soviet Union. Finally, I will touch upon what lies ahead for NATO and the role of SNF in it.

NATO AND ITS MILITARY POSTURE

The Structure of NATO

As a fundamental basis for strategy-making, NATO maintains a hierarchical structure of commands. This structure does not, though, limit the member nations to a dependence on a hierarchy of power. It is designed to provide a framework for maintaining both warfighting as well as peacetime strategies on behalf of the Allied members. Nonetheless, historical circumstances have caused the United States to take a more active role in both structure and strategy. Even when the treaty was signed in 1949, it was realized that the U.S. was the only member country with the military strength to provide a deterrence against the then-growing Soviet threat in Europe.[3] It can be noted, too, that the imbalance of power of the U.S. military in the NATO alliance has bred resentment among the various nations. This has been cited as a hinderance to the growth of independence of the European nations, and also as a factor in the failure of East and West Germany to unify since World War II.[4] But the military influence of the U.S. *is* of primary importance in maintaining deterrence against Soviet expansion in Europe. Thus, this gives the U.S. the responsibility of protecting the peace in Western Europe, which, in turn, helps to maintain peace throughout the world.

NATO's military structure is divided into specialty divisions which enable a smoother operation in its decision-making process. The highest organizational level in NATO is the North Atlantic Council. Comprised of representatives of each allied country, the Council oversees all aspects of the structure.[5] NATO also possesses a Defense Planning Committee and a Nuclear Planning Group (NPG) for treatment of more specific military and nuclear planning issues.[6] True military planning occurs on the level of the Military Committee, the section that advises the North Atlantic Council and the Defense Planning Committee as well as oversees the various strategic commands within the areas of the alliance.[7]

The actual existence of NATO is pointless without some form of military posture for implementing its goals. The need for strategy can be under-emphasized in the politics of many Western European nations. This relates to both fears and comforts on behalf of these nations. For example, the need for a nuclear deterrent posture tends to stir up fears regarding nuclear proliferation. Meanwhile, these nations tend to overlook the peace which has resulted from this extended deterrence for nearly forty years.[8]

Deterrence and Cooperation

The underlying goal of NATO is to provide a deterrent against war by maintaining a large and visible force. Although this is the best way to maintain peace from a military perspective, it also raises a number of questions. One important concern is the question of whether or not there is indeed a balance of conventional and nuclear capabilities between the NATO nations and the Warsaw Pact. Another concern is the extent to which the allied countries can cooperate to actually fulfill this goal.

The necessity for cooperation and coordination has been a primary issue throughout NATO's history. In order for its military posture to be effective, it must have cooperation in terms of nuclear arms procurement and deployment. Problems in this area have arisen in part because of financial concerns within the various NATO nations.[9] However, the real problem in nurturing international cooperation has been a political one.

Russell E. Dougherty warns that the effectiveness of future deterrence in Europe may be threatened if the members of NATO fail to understand the military, as well as political, significance of the Soviets. He warns that the failure to achieve full cooperation among the NATO nations is like allowing Soviet ideology to slip through its borders and that "the United States has failed to comprehend the totality of the political strategy of the Soviets toward the West and have underestimated the warfare doctrine they employ in consonance with that total threat."[10] To overcome this fault, the NATO nations need to become stronger in maintaining a system of deterrence, politically and militarily. In this regard, Dougherty continues,

> What is critical is that the democratic composition of the nations of the NATO Alliance demands that the concepts NATO espouses and the capabilities employed to implement the concepts be understood and supported widely by public opinion throughout the Alliance.[11]

Former Supreme Allied Commander Europe (SACEUR) General Bernard Rogers elaborates on this problem by noting that a deterrence policy cannot be effective without a sense of political unity among the NATO countries. This is important both for the strength of NATO itself and also for the credibility of a serious deterrent to the Soviet Union and the Warsaw

Pact. Lack of unity in NATO is a nagging element resulting from the fear of many in Western Europe of the pressures to modernize remaining nuclear arms. The United States needs to be in a position to understand this fear, but also Europe must understand that without a serious nuclear profile and without political unity, it will be impossible to negotiate positively with the Soviet Union over possible reductions in arms. Rogers indicates that nuclear arms' strength in Europe is a necessary deterrent against Soviet aggression, and that the NATO nations must be united in order to maintain a viable ethos in this arena.[12]

It is evident, then, that the military strategy of NATO depends on the cooperation of all members of the Alliance. Without this cooperation, the NATO strategy of deterrence will always lack its full potential for effectiveness. Yet there are indications that the NATO nations may be able to strive toward their common goal even without total agreement. As Ambassador Kirkpatrick has stated, "there is no perfect alliance."[13] Even if full political cooperation is not currently obtainable, and remains obstructed until the May summit when a decision is to be reached over modernization, that does not mean that the overall goals are beyond hope. The NATO nations simply need to be aware of the inherent problems they face and they need to reinforce their commitment to "struggle" together toward world peace.[14]

Flexible Response

The nature of NATO is defensive. In considering the importance of NATO's military posture, it is essential to take into account not only strategies for deterrence, but also strategies for flexible response in the event that deterrence fails. Its members must be willing and capable to retaliate immediately for Warsaw Pact aggression in order to firmly re-establish territorial peace in Europe.[15] Flexible response is most effective when continually combined with superior nuclear technology, hence providing a wider range of defense options. Yet, at the same time, deterrent strategies based on nuclear superiority will be lacking in effectiveness without the supplemented preparation of theater nuclear weapons and conventional forces. This aspect of strategy is outlined in NATO's plan MC 14/3 which states that these forces must be capable of deterring Soviet invasion on the battlefield. It is emphasized that the function of MC 14/3 is to reinforce deterrence by indicating the high probability of the appropriate employment of direct defense, deliberate escalation, or nuclear response to any level of enemy aggression.[16] General John Galvin, Commander in Chief, U.S. European Command defines these conditions:

> *Direct Defense* seeks to defeat aggression on the level at which the enemy chooses to fight. It rests on physically preventing the enemy from taking what he wants and places the burden of escalation on him.
> *Deliberate Escalation* seeks to defeat aggression by raising, in a controlled manner, the scope and intensity of combat, making the cost and risk

disproportionate to the aggressor's objectives, and the threat of nuclear response progressively more imminent.

General Nuclear Response contemplates the use of strategic nuclear strikes designed to destroy an enemy's capacity and will to continue the war.[17]

NATO's military posture goes beyond mere deterrence. It represents the fundamental need for having prepared forces in the case of an event of enemy aggression. There is also the serious concern for strategies which would be applicable in the event of limited conventional war in Europe. It is generally accepted that NATO's military capabilities would limit the possibility that this would escalate into a full-scale nuclear war. Also, it is important to consider that flexible response entails consideration of short-range nuclear force options as well as conventional force options. Therefore a primary NATO goal is to deter both conventional and nuclear aggression.[18] Soviet perception of NATO's SNF strength, and willingness to employ its SNF if necessary, are vital elements in making deterrence a credible strategy.

The additional views of Messrs. Warner, Thurmond, Gramm, and McCain given during hearings on the effect of the INF Treaty on NATO describe three important elements contributing to the requirement of a credible theater nuclear posture in Western Europe. First, as NATO policy is one of deterrence and defense instead of offense, they must have a "survivable" system to employ as a deterrent to a Soviet first-use. Second, a strong theater nuclear defense will disperse Warsaw Pact forces allowing for the success of a follow-on Forces Attack (FOFA). Third, given the successes of FOFA and conventional credibility, the viability of a survivable theater nuclear force would provide the time for NATO commanders to make rational decisions during a crisis. A release of pressure on commanders to use the weapons or not obviously carries with it the prospect for an increased nucler threshold.[19]

The strategic considerations of NATO's military posture must take into account the continued maintenance of military strength, in today's case this would call for the modernization of the *Lance* SSM missile. Maintenance such as this is necessary whether during conditions of peace or war. Military strategy, then, is vital to NATO's goals and must therefore concern not only arms procurement but also arms deployment.

CURRENT STATUS

Effect of the INF Treaty on NATO

Currently, the future of Western Europe's nuclear defense is undergoing uncomfortable debate. West Germany is faced with conflict over the modernization of short-range nuclear forces deployed there; it is a conflict that may entail heavy political ramifications on both intra-NATO and East-West relationships. While Great Britain, the U.S., and even France push for force modernization, West Germany is faced with domestic concern over new implications of deterrence.

Although many see the INF treaty as a lessening of East-West tension because of a reduction of the nuclear threat in Europe, others fear that it represents a possible trend toward the denuclearization of Europe. In the case of the latter, many fear the possibility of a withdrawal of U.S. troops and ultimately a disintegration of the Alliance. Those who subscribe to this theory, particularly defense experts and political conservatives, strongly believe that the elimination of INF may lead to the weakening of flexible response in Europe. Deployment of *Pershing* II's (PII's) and ground-launched cruise missiles (GLCM's) served as a bargaining block which has since disappeared. They served as medium-range nuclear deterrents aimed at targets inside the Soviet Union as well as a modernization effort in themselves aimed at replacing obsolescing NATO dual capable artillery and *Lance* missile batteries.[20] Also, contrary to strong supporters of the treaty, the second 'zero' in the zero-zero option (eliminating SRINF (500-1000 km) may inevitably lead to a third 'zero' that will eliminate SNF, and thus de-nuclearize Europe. They argue, too, according to the International Institute for Strategic Studies, that elimination of SRINF in NATO was unnecessary due to the possible chance of unilateral withdrawal of Soviet SS-12's and SS-23's, "which the USSR had argued in late 1983 and early 1984, had been deployed as a 'response' to the deployment of the *Pershing* II and the GLCM."[21]

We must take into consideration the INF Treaty's ramifications on Western Europe; first, the possibility of a nuclear conflict is by no means eliminated from the European theater. In fact, it may even be greater. The elimination of INF will leave a gap in NATO's range of flexible response. General Roberts elaborates that the treaty "reduces the range of NATO's nuclear weapons systems from 1,500 miles (GLCM's)/1,100 miles (PII's) to less than 300 miles, thereby making NATO's deterrent less credible to the Soviets."[22] Without these weapons serving as a profound deterrent to the Warsaw Pact, there is an increased possibility that nuclear war may "leapfrog" to a strategic confrontation.[23] Ambassador Kirkpatrick sees these missiles as representing a more "credible" deterrent since their existence "does not require the U.S. to take the ultimate step to strategic war."[24]

A second ramification of the treaty is that the elimination of the INF vehicles, about 3% of the Soviet nuclear warhead stockpile, does not diminish the Soviet nuclear threat to Europe. They can simply retarget strategic vehicles onto the same NATO installations. This leaves a strong disadvantage to the United States' allies since the U.S. would not have the weaponry of equal magnitude to deter such a Soviet attack.[25]

Third, the elimination of PII's and GLCM's severely exposes the great imbalance in conventional and theater nuclear forces. The Committee report states, "the INF Treaty, while succeeding in the removal of a number of nuclear weapons in the middle of NATO's deterrent spectrum, leaves an imbalance in conventional and theater nuclear forces on one side of the spectrum, and a strategic balance that is in rough parity on the other side."[26] This imbalance poses a true threat to the Alliance and should be looked at more closely.

Theater Nuclear Force Imbalance

Although the greatest challenge to NATO today may be its conventional disadvantage, more attention now must be placed on NATO's theater nuclear weapons. Both the Soviet Union and the Warsaw Pact show strong offensive capabilities in terms of theater warfare. Therefore, in addition to a need for continuous modernization of strategic nuclear forces, there is a need in the U.S. for maintenance of effective theater capabilities. The importance of SNF capability is evident in that NATO will not be able to provide an effective deterrent against the Warsaw Pact threat unless it is able to sufficiently follow up that threat with a flexible response. For this reason, NATO's military strategy calls for "a theater nuclear stockpile that provides NATO political leaders with a range of options to threaten both fixed and mobile targets, from those on or near the battlefield right through to those deep in Warsaw Pact territory . . ."[27]

While Gorbachev and the Soviets have made open comments regarding their desire to limit, if not eliminate, theater nuclear forces in Europe, they are not holding back on their deployment. In fact, in the report to the Senate Committee on Armed Services, Messrs. Warner, Thurmond, Gramm, and McCain say that since 1979, the Soviet Union has not only not decreased its theater nuclear arsenal, but it has dramatically increased it, "A quantitative, and in many cases, qualitative disparity exists today in favor of the Warsaw Pact in all categories of theater nuclear capability."[28]

Senator McCain, in an earlier hearing session with JCS Chairman Admiral Crowe and Secretary Carlucci, cites 1987's *Military Posture Statement* and edition of *Soviet Military Power* as showing the Warsaw Pact's 50% increase in short-range nuclear systems between 1980 and 1986. The report goes on to cite numbers of up to 10,000 nuclear-capable artillery weapons, over 500 *SCUD*'s, and over 500 *FROG*'s and SS-21's in Europe.[29]

The Additional Views report goes on to list examples of Warsaw Pact missiles and suggests that they have three classes of short-range ground-launched missiles compared to one NATO system, the *Lance*.[30] And the disparities are intense. According to Lucy Komisar, a foreign affairs writer based in Bonn, while NATO has 88 *Lance* missiles deployed in West Germany, the Soviet Union has 1,365 short-range weapons.[31]

The *SCUD*-B is the longest travelling short-range missile (300 km) which can cover most targets in the continental Western theater. NATO's *Lance* can only reach targets up to ranges of up to 130 km which means that NATO has no equivalent flexibility to stage "deep strike" missions of its own. This poses a serious threat to Western Europe's military strategy. In the shorter arena is the 70 km *FROG* and its successor, the very accurate

SS-21, with a range of 80-120 km. Since 1977, this weapon has been under a continuous deployment upgrade scheme unmatched by NATO. Such has been the case since the 1960's—NATO has not kept up with the Warsaw Pact's quantitative and qualitative modernization campaign and thus the effectiveness of its nuclear deterrent has eroded.[32]

A Western agreement to upgrade the *Lance* was all but set in stone at an October 1983 meeting in Montebello, Quebec. Specifically the agreement called for the reduction of 1,400 warheads on all existing SNF's to 4,600 in addition to the modernization of the obsolescing *Lance*. The 88 *Lance* missiles topped the priority list for modernization. Most of these are based in West Germany where 36 are controlled by U.S. forces, 26 by West Germans, while the remaining 14 are controlled by the British. Furthermore, during the INF debate Pentagon officials urged that the *Lance* be replaced by as many as 400 upgraded missiles with a range of up to 300 miles, 310 miles being the short-range ceiling established under the treaty.[33]

The Montebello decision also called for replacements for nuclear-tipped shells designed for 2,000 nuclear-capable NATO artillery pieces. These artillery-fired atomic projectiles (AFAP's) are dual-capable, meaning they can fire both conventional and nuclear-equipped mortars. Their range, though, is much shorter than that of the short-range missiles, requiring its operation at or near the forward troop line (FLOT).[34] If, however, SNF are eliminated these AFAP's can (and should) be modernized to do some of the *Lance*'s job. The 203 *Howitzers* can be modified to cover a range of up to 75 km. Its survivability would thus be enhanced since it could then be deployed away from the FLOT while still supporting front-line battle.[35]

In November 1988, a NATO nuclear planning group met in Monterey, California, to reconfirm the Montebello decision. Yet opposition, especially by the Federal Republic of Germany, emerged over the modernization of SNF. It must be noted that the Montebello agreement received support in 1983 when the U.S. and the Soviet Union were barely on speaking terms. Any INF negotiations were very far away from the "zero" option now solidified. At that point no one foresaw the elimination of missiles down to 500 km range. So now, after the agreement, Western European governments favor Montebello reinterpretation; the question now lies in whether the agreement is still a . . . discourage the possibility of a rash and discomforting decision. According to the *Washington Post*'s Karen De Young, the Soviets "have objected to NATO taking unspecified 'compensatory measures' in response to the INF treaty that would undercut the letter and spirit of the new agreement."[36]

West Germany

More than any other country in Europe, West Germany is in a solid predicament. It does not want the weapons on NATO's Western border because they will be employed in war on German territory. Yet at the same time, as

Sigal points out, if it were to loosen ties with the West and renounce the weapons on its soil, it would raise the fearful prospect of weakness and uncertainty in Central Europe.[37]

Due to its geography, West Germany is certainly in a unique political predicament. In this respect Clemmesen points out, "the increased vulnerability in Europe is not shared equally by all. It is primarily a West German problem. Both militarily and politically, the Federal Republic is the front line state of NATO."[38] Unlike the French and the British, the Germans have staged clear opposition to SNF modernization. Chancellor Kohl has called for the postponement of any decision until 1991 or 1992 due to concerns that a decision on his part could hurt his Christian-Democrat coalition in elections scheduled for December 1990. But domestic German attitudes are swaying. For the first time, nuclear weapons deployment is receiving criticism not just from the Left but also from the Center and the Center-Right.[39] Traditionally, political divisions over weapons' deployment on West German soil were sharp, the Left-leaning Social Democratic Party (SDP) strongly opposed. Now, however, Chancellor Kohl's CDP is leaning in the same direction, a disturbing matter to conservatives in Washington and in NATO. Prime Minister Thatcher as well as President Mitterand have urged missile modernization without delay on the basis that the Soviet Union has kept its missiles up to date. A delay such as the one Kohl has promoted would leave a gap in the operational effectiveness of nuclear deterrence. Since the *Lance* is operational until 1995, and the development and procurement of a follow-on to it is expected to take up to six years, any delay now could be costly. To postpone the modernization task may very well aggravate the problem (of conventional imbalance) such that flexible response may lose its flexibility.[40]

Soviet Initiatives

Western officials want to reach an agreement on the follow-on to the *Lance* by the NATO summit in May. But NATO's pressure has been weakened by some key, warm Soviet gestures to West Germany. In addition to the announcement of significant unilateral conventional cuts during a visit to Bonn in January, Soviet Foreign Minister Eduard Shevardnadze called for the dismantling of all the world's tactical nuclear arms.[41] Their proposed "triple zero" option described above has gained momentum in parts of Western Europe and although it is opposed by the U.S., Great Britain, and France, it may appear on the bargaining table before too long.

Another Soviet gesture has been Moscow's proposal for a partially demilitarized zone between East and West Germany, a move that, if accepted, could accommodate over 40 years of East-West tension.[42] But acceptance of this proposal would undoubtedly undermine NATO's strategy of deterrence in Europe, since it calls for the elimination of AFAP's as well as short-range nuclear missiles. Such an agreement would render NATO with *no* short-range deterrent in a most sensitive area and thus would not be in the interest of the Alliance.[43]

Not only is there a traditional yearning for national kinship between the two Germanys but there is an economic appeal in it as well. William Drozdiak of the *Washington Post* describes West Germany's interest,

> For Bonn, the renewed attractions of the opening toward the East, or *Ostpolitik*, are rooted in a constant desire to ease hardships for millions of fellow Germans living across the East-West divide, as well as in West Germany's growing satisfaction that it can wield more power and influence in Eastern Europe than anywhere else.
>
> At a time when the Bush administration is still sorting out its foreign policy agenda, Chancellor Helmut Kohl's government is pressing ahead with an Eastern Bloc strategy that rewards, even subsidizes, communist reforms that appeal to popular demands for trade union pluralism, multiparty elections or free-market economic policies . . .[44]

The Soviets have a very "strong mutual interest" in supporting the German efforts to nurture warmer relations with its Eastern partner. This would not only establish a more stable economic and political situation but also it could further draw West Germany toward neutrality and ultimately decouple it from NATO.

In addition to these Soviet initiatives has come a wave of unilateral arms-reduction measures on behalf of the Soviet Union. In December, Secretary Gorbachev told the U.N. that he would reduce Moscow's armed forces by 500,000 men. Shortly afterward, at the Paris Convention on Chemical Weapons, the Soviets pledged to unilaterally destroy their stockpile of chemical weapons even before an international agreement had been worked out. In continuing with its initiatives, Shevardnadze made public Moscow's intentions to withdraw "an unspecified number of short-range tactical nuclear weapons from Eastern Europe."[45] The foreign minister denounced the West's efforts to pressure West Germany into complying with the modernization. He claimed that nuclear-missile modernization would be "a step backward, not forward" and that any subsequent moves would depend on what the West decides.[46] In response to this I feel that attention should be called upon the fact that NATO's nuclear arsenal, even before the INF decision, was at its lowest level in 20 years.

A consistent policy of the Alliance has been in conducting analyses aimed at assuring that NATO's nuclear weapons are kept to the minimum number necessary for deterrence, taking into account any new conventional as well as nuclear force developments. In December of 1979 the Alliance decided that, unless obviated by the successful negotiation with the Soviet Union, the deployment of longer-range INF (LRINF) was necessary to maintain both the nuclear balance and the integrity of NATO's deterrence scheme. This is known as the "dual-track" decision.[47] At the time of the 1979 decision the NPG Ministers decided to reduce NATO's stockpile of warheads by 1,000 while maintaining a safe posture. Furthermore, in 1983 at the Montebello discussions, the NPG called on the withdrawal of 1,400 additional warheads thus bringing the total number removed to 2,400 since 1979.

Nonetheless, the Soviets have made some clear advances in warming up to the West in recent months. These moves, although appealing, have caused sheer anguish to the Alliance since they have managed to keep Bonn away from consenting to modernization.

France and Great Britain

While the U.S. *Lance* modernization issue dominates the European arena, France is already underway with its own $2.4 billion campaign to modernize its own SNF arsenal.[48] By 1992 France will be able to deploy the *Hades* SSM replacing the existing 32 *Pluton* SSM's. The *Hades* will have a range of up to 480 km and will be mobilized (each will be paired on truck trailers). Fired from France, these missiles will be able to stage an attack along the Inter-German border (IGB), thus it will have the primary purpose of protecting French forces as it will also have the capability of effectively hitting Pact battlefield targets.[49]

The progress of the *Hades* missile has incited less commotion because of France's NATO position. Although France is a member of the Alliance, it has been outside the military command since 1966, therefore it does not openly engage in the military debates such as that over the *Lance*. French nuclear capabilities became increasingly refined in the late 50's and early 60's and growing sentiment over a NATO commander—possibly an American—targetting and firing France's missiles led by de Gaulle to withdraw from the military branch insisting that only a French president would be able to do so. Also accompanying the move to become independent from NATO was de Gaulle's removal of all French troops from the NATO military system along with the removal of all military installations not controlled by France itself.[50] France wanted to gain independence from what they felt was a U.S. monopoly of allied leadership. Also leading to this attitude was the U.S. refusal to share any of its atomic secrets and materials as well as Washington's rejection of France's plan to form a NATO "global directorate." (This group consisting of the U.S., Great Britain, and France was to make collective military decisions.)[51]

The reasons for French nuclear development were several. First, with the friction between them and the other Western powers and especially their disgust over the increasing Anglo-American domination of NATO, France felt it would reverse the trend with prestigious nuclear capabilities. Second, due to this newly attained political leverage it would have a greater voice in East-West arms-control discussion. And third, after a sobering result of Diem Bien Phu and the ensuing political defeat in Indo-China, France felt it would be able to rebuild national confidence and morale. Also the growing mistrust in the U.S.'s willingness to strategically intervene in the case of European conflict, as mentioned in Pierre Gallois' *The Balance of Terror*, led to the desire for an independent French nuclear arsenal.[52]

By December 1956 the decision to proceed with nuclear development was solidified by the government of Guy Mollet. The move was accompanied by a firm within the Commissariat á l'Energie Atomique to go ahead with the program and a year later the decision was made public.[53]

Britain is also a nuclear force in Western Europe. The British emphasize a warmer relationship between their nuclear weapons and the Alliance. They subscribe to an interdependent rationale known as the "second nuclear decision center." Nuclear weapons' use is a right reserved to the Royal British Government when it feels it needs to protect national interest. However, since a decision by more than one NATO power to use the weapons would lead to a less calculable response, the chance for Soviet deterrence is greater. This rationale is based on the different possible needs for weapons' use by independent countries.[54]

Great Britain became the world's third nuclear power by 1957. Prime Minister Churchill and his government decided to proceed with a bomb project of their own. This decision emanated from the empire's willful desire to develop a tool for such immense military might. Churchill was envious of the bomb's destructive potential and his interest in it was heightened by several factors. First, he feared the massive military might of the Soviet Union paired with the unknown postwar behavior of its own ally, the U.S. This fear was later shared by Prime Minister Clement R. Attlee. Attlee recalls, "at that time we had to bear in mind that there was always the possibility of their [U.S.] withdrawing and becoming isolationist once again."[55] Another reason for Britain's nuclear desire was its inability to financially afford a standardized army dispersed across the globe to support the fading Royal Empire. Their reliance on the weapon soon became justification for an "across-the-board cutback in other military expenditures."[56]

The Parliamentary debate over whether to proceed with the program was long-fought yet successful for Churchill and supporters of the project. In his address before the 1955 debate he underscored the importance of its approval, "Then it may well be that we shall, by a process of sublime irony, have reached a stage in this story where safety will be the sturdy child of terror, and survival the twin brother of annihilation."[57]

Currently, Great Britain, too, is modernizing its nuclear forces. With some assistance from the United States, the British will have the capability of delivering about 500 nuclear warheads to the Soviet Union by the year 1995. With this capability they could extend considerable damage upon the Soviet Union, destroying about 40 to 50 percent of Soviet production capacity.[58] The addition of this force alone will raise the effectiveness not only of Britain's own deterrence strategy but also that of NATO.

In the political arena, Prime Minister Thatcher is openly urging Kohl and his government to accept the *Lance* follow-up proposal. The British leader met with Kohl to discuss the issue in February but to no immediate avail. Perhaps the tide will turn at Kohl's home in Oggersheim, where Thatcher will visit in April before the NATO summit in May.[59] It is by then that she and U.S. officials hope to have already reached a consensus over the issue at hand.

The nuclear capabilities of France and Great Britain are growing in size and strength. This factor of multi-party nuclear forces serves as a strategic plus for the NATO effort in its deterrence against a conventional attack. Wendt and Wilson explain that in the event of a Warsaw Pact conventional attack, "the Soviets would have no assurance that the battle had not involved France or Britain enough to prompt the employment of their nuclear weapons."[60] Thus, based on this independent level of nuclear deterrence by both France and Britain, it can be said that their progress in nuclear weapons development is indeed merited.

The Future of NATO

The heightening debate, along with recent East-Bloc initiatives toward what appears to be a fading of the cold war, is causing internal discomfort within NATO. However, it is my opinion that no radical changes will occur within the Alliance. But what are the choices for Western Europe and the U.S. in NATO? Although the increased nuclear arsenals of France and Great Britain are of significant importance to the European community, Western Europe will not replace the U.S. as far as the dominant force for nuclear deterrence. And if they were to try to replace it, there would most likely be extensive conflict over the sharing of nuclear arsenals. Instead Western Europeans should begin to share more of the military costs of deterrence, a problem the U.S. is experiencing with Japan.

Burden-sharing in the years to come is likely to breed serious conflict. With the exorbitant U.S. budget deficit, the U.S. Congress will demand more input on the part of the member nations. This will include a greater amount of defense spending, especially as both the U.S. and the U.K. reduced their defense budgets last year.[61]

Also it will become increasingly important for the member states to unify in working out problems. U.S. Secretary of State James Baker recently stated in a press conference on the modernization of SNF that the issue was an Alliance one, not a German-American one. He suggested that the group of members will resolve it "together in a spirit of cooperation."[62] The upcoming NATO summit in May will be a good opportunity to hear out dissenting opinions within the Alliance, and to come together on the top priorities on the future arms control agenda: START, Chemical Weapons, and Conventional Weapons. For the time being, however, NATO should remain committed to maintaining the updated quality and accuracy of its existing weapons.

The unity of NATO serves as an example of leadership throughout the free world. Thus, NATO needs firm military strategies in order to maintain its goals for peace in Europe. As I have discussed above, these strategies include policies of deterrence and flexible response. For the credibility of both of these strategies, a continuous upgrading of forces and equipment is absolutely necessary. Specifically, I would argue in favor of a follow-on to the *Lance* SSM.

Although it is easy for me to push for this, not being a West German, I still believe that the new tide of change within the Soviet Union is too young to trust completely. What would happen if Secretary Gorbachev were to die tomorrow? Who is to say what comes next, when political dissent within the Politburo is so rampant? In light of these changes, I believe it is important to be willing to accept them as well as to be determined to continue to take necessary actions to preserve NATO's security interests and to maintain the dignity of its inherently defensive forces.

Endnotes

[1]Jonathon Dean, "Military Security in Europe," *Foreign Affairs*, Fall 1987, 26.

[2]U.S. Senate Committee on Armed Services, "NATO Defense and the INF Treaty," *Hearings and Meetings: 100th Cong. 2nd sess: Part 4*, Feb. 17–8, 22–3, 1988 (Washington: GPO, 1988) 31.

[3]Lawrence S. Kaplan, *The United States and NATO: The Formulative Years* (Lexington: University Press of Kentucky, 1984) 170.

[4]Nancy L. Hoepli, ed., *Great Decisions 1988: Foreign Policy Issues Facing the Nation* (New York: Foreign Policy Association, 1988) 86.

[5]*NATO Handbook* (Brussels: NATO Information Service, August 1980) 31.

[6]*NATO Handbook*, 32.

[7]*NATO Handbook*, 33–4.

[8]Jeane J. Kirkpatrick, "The Atlantic Alliance and the American National Interest," *Current Policy* 30 April, 1984: 13.

[9]Christian Brumter, *The North Atlantic Assembly* (Dordrecht, Netherlands: Martinus Nijhoff, 1986) 136.

[10]Russell E. Dougherty, "Concepts and Capabilities," The Atlantic Council's *Strengthening Deterrence: NATO and the Credibility of Western Defense in the 1980's* (1982) 1. Air War College Associate Programs Supplementary Text, Air University, ATC, Maxwell AFB AL, December 1983.

[11]Dougherty, 1.

[12]U.S. Senate Committee on Armed Services, "NATO Defense and the INF Treaty," *Hearings: 100th Cong., 2nd sess: Part 2*, 29 Jan., 1–2 Feb. 1988 (Washington: GPO, 1988) 100–7.

[13]Kirkpatrick, 17.

[14]Kirkpatrick, 17.

[15]*Hearings: Part 2*, 163.

[16]David N. Schwartz, *NATO's Nuclear Dilemmas* (Washington: Brookings Institution, 1983) 187.

[17]*Hearings: Part 2*, 163.

[18]James C. Wendt and Peter A. Wilson, "Post-INF: Toward Multipolar Deterrence," (Santa Monica: RAND/P-7407, Feb. 1988) 3.

[19]Report, 42–3.

[20]U.S. Senate Committee on Armed Services, "NATO Defense and the INF Treaty," Report, 1 April, 1988 (Washington: GPO, 1988) 47.

[21]International Institute for Strategic Studies, Strategic Survey 1987–1988, (London: IISS 1988) 34–5.

[22]Hearings: Part 2, 116.

[23]Report, 75.

[24]Hearings: Part 2, 72.

[25]Report, 71–2.

[26]Report, 72.

[27]Michais J. Legge, "The Future of the Theater Nuclear Stockpile," RAND Report, no. R-2964FF (Santa Monica: The Rand Corporation, 1983) 44.

[28]Report, 41.

[29]U.S. Senate Committee on Armed Services, "NATO Defense and the INF Treaty," Hearings: Part 1. Jan. 25–7, 1988 (Washington: GPO, 1988) 121.

[30]Report, 41.

[31]Lucy Komisar, "Short Range, Dead Germans," Progressive Nov. 1988: 15.

[32]Report, 42.

[33]Karen DeYoung, "Nuclear Issues Linger for NATO," The Washington Post 23 Dec. 1987, A12.

[34]Wendt, 10.

[35]Wendt, 10.

[36]DeYoung, A12.

[37]Leon C. Sigal, Nuclear Forces in Europe: Enduring Dilemmas, Present Prospects (Washington: Brookings Institution, 1984) 3.

[38]Hans-Henrik Holm and Nikolaj Peterson, eds., The European Missiles Crisis: Nuclear Weapons and Security Policy (New York: St. Martin's Press, 1983) 203.

[39]Komisar.

[40]Hearings and Meetings: Part 4, 30.

[41]Robert J. McCartney, "Soviet Calls For Further Arms Cuts," The Washington Post 19 Jan. 1988, A10.

[42]Michael R. Gordon, "Behind the Arms Plans, a Clash of Visions," The New York Times 12 March, 1989.

[43]Wendt, 11.

[44]William Drozdiak, "Soviets Back Bonn Strategy in East Bloc," The Washington Post 18 March, 1989, A1.

[45]Peter Gumbel, "Soviets To Pull Some Missiles Out Of Europe," The Wall Street Journal 29 Jan., 1989, A1.

[46]Gumbel, A1.

[47]NATO Nuclear Planning Group, "The Montebello Decision," Press Release M-NPG-2 (83) 22, 27 Oct., 1983 (NATO/OTAN Press Service) 1.

[48]Edward Cody, "France Moves To Modernize Missiles," The Washington Post 10 March 1989, A36.

[49]Wendt, 15.

[50]Lawrence S. Kaplan and Robert W. Clawson, eds., NATO After Thirty Years (Wilmington: Scholarly Resources, 1981) 52.

[51]Kaplan, NATO After 45.

[52]Schwartz, 38–9.

[53]Schwartz, 39.

[54]Wendt, 17.
[55]Schwartz, 29.
[56]Schwartz, 47.
[57]Schwartz, 47.
[58]Wendt, 19.
[59]McCartney, "NATO Allies Still Divided On Missiles," *The Washington Post* 22 Feb. 1989, A26.
[60]Wendt, 20.
[61]International Institute For Strategic Studies, *The Military Balance 1988–1989* (London: IISS, 1988) 57.
[62]European Press Guidance, "Short-range Nuclear Force Modernization," 6 March 1989.

Works Cited

Brumter, Christian. *The North Atlantic Assembly*. Dordrecht, The Netherlands: Martinus Nijhoff Publishers, 1986.

Cody, Edward. "France Moves to Modernize Missiles." *Washington Post* 10 March 1989, A36.

Dean, Jonathon. "Military Security in Europe." *Foreign Affairs* Fall 1987, 22–40.

DeYoung, Karen, "Nuclear Issues Linger For NATO." *Washington Post* 23 Dec. 1987.

Dougherty, Russell E., "Concepts and Capabilities." *The Atlantic Council's Strengthening Deterrence: NATO and the Credibility of Western Defense in the 1980's* 1982.

Drozdiak, William. "Soviets Back Bonn Strategy." *Washington Post* 18 Mar. 1989, A1.

Foreign Policy Association. *Great Decisions 1988: Foreign Policy Issues Facing the Nation*. New York: Foreign Policy Association, 1988.

Gordon, Michael R., "Behind the Arms Plans a Clash of Visions." *New York Times* 12 Mar. 1989.

Gumbel, Peter. "Soviets to Pull Some Missiles Out of Europe." *Wall Street Journal* 20 Jan. 1989, A18.

Holm, Hans-Henrik and Nikolaj Peterson, eds., *The European Missiles Crisis: Nuclear Weapons and Security Policy*. New York: St. Martin's Press, 1983.

International Institute for Strategic Studies. *Strategic Survey 1987–1988*. London: IISS, 1988.

International Institute for Strategic Studies. *The Military Balance 1988–1989*. London: IISS, 1988.

Kaplan, Lawrence S. and Robert W. Clawson, eds. *NATO After Thirty Years*. Wilmington: Scholarly Resources, 1981.

Kaplan, Lawrence S. *The United States and NATO: The Formulative Years*. Lexington: University Press of Kentucky, 1984.

Kirkpatrick, Jeanne J., "The Atlantic Alliance and the American National Interest." *Current Policy* no. 581 30 April 1984.

Legge, J. Michael. "The Future of the Theater Nuclear Stockpile." RAND Report, no. R-2964FF, Santa Monica: The RAND Corp., 1 1983.

McCartney, Robert J., "NATO Still Divided On Missiles." *Washington Post* 22 Feb. 1989, A26.

McCartney, Robert J., "Soviet Calls For Further Arms Cuts." *Washington Post* 19 Jan. 1988.

NATO Information Service. *NATO Handbook.* Brussels: NATO Information Service, 1980.

OTAN/NATO. NATO Nuclear Planning Group: *The Montebello Decision,* Brussels: Press Service, Oct. 1983.

Schwartz, David N., *NATO's Nuclear Dilemmas.* Washington: Brookings Institution, 1983.

Sigal, Leon V., *Nuclear Forces in Europe: Enduring Dilemmas, Present Prospects.* Washington: Brookings Institution, 1984.

United States Senate. Committee on Armed Services *Hearings on "NATO Defense and the INF Treaty".* 100th Cong., 2nd sess. parts 1,2,4. Washington: GPO, 1988.

United States Senate. Committee on Armed Services *Report on "NATO Defense and the INF Treaty".* 100th Cong., 2nd sess. Washington: GPO, 1988.

United States Dept. of State. Office of Public Affairs. Press Release. *NATO Nuclear Planning Group Final Communique.* 26 Oct. The Hague, The Netherlands, 1988.

■ THE WRITER'S ASSIGNMENT

Develop a topic broadly related to the course using approaches we have studied. This 10–12 page paper should use bibliographic sources other than those assigned in the course. Endnotes should be used to indicate sources, and you should include a bibliography if you have consulted sources that are not indicated in notes.   ■

■ UNDERSTANDING WRITING STRATEGIES

1. What kinds of writing strategies does Werner use in his opening paragraphs?

2. How do the first four paragraphs relate to the rest of the essay?

3. What is Werner's thesis?

4. How well does Werner explain NATO? How necessary is this explanation for understanding the subsequent discussion?

5. What kind of assumptions does Werner have about Soviet military policy in Western Europe? To what degree do these assumptions influence his choice of source materials?

6. According to Werner, what problems exist in the NATO alliance? How do these relate to NATO's military role in Europe?

7. What ramifications does the INF Treaty have for NATO's defense of Western Europe against Soviet aggression?

8. What evidence does Werner offer for disparity between Soviet and NATO nuclear strength? How do you evaluate both his evidence and his sources?

9. What is West Germany's position on nuclear forces? What impact does this have on NATO?

10. What conclusions does Werner make about NATO's future? How well do these conclusions grow out of the evidence Werner has presented? ■

■ SUGGESTIONS FOR WRITING

1. You are Brad Werner, and you plan to submit this paper to an undergraduate research conference. They request a 500-word abstract rather than the paper itself. Write an abstract that shows the paper's full scope and depth.

2. Write a position paper that opposes Werner's views. Be certain to outline his opposition and answer his main points by either reevaluating his evidence and arguments or introducing new evidence. ■

Native Americans and the Reservation System

Angela M. Womack

Writing for her English composition course, Angela Womack's research paper presents evidence opposing the reservation system and advocating Indian self-sufficiency. By taking a position, the essay develops an argument from evidence derived from secondary sources instead of piecing together summaries.

It is July 7th and 10,000 Navajo Indians make ready to leave land in Arizona that they have called home for generations. Their land has been assigned to the Hopi tribe by the United States government to settle a dispute between the two tribes over the land in question (Johnson 15). Ella Bedonie, a member of the Navajo tribe says, "The Navajo and the Hopi people have no dispute. It's the government that's doing this to us. I think the Hopis may have the land for a while, but then the government . . . will step in," (Johnson 17). The Hopis are receiving 250,000 acres to compensate them for the 900,000 acres they will lose in this land deal; however, the groundwater on this land is questionable due to possible contamination by a uranium mine upstream.

To offset this unappealing aspect the government sweetened the deal with incentives of livestock (Johnson 16). This was the fate many Indians had to face as western expansion swept across the continent. Now consider that the incident mentioned occurred not on July 7, 1886, but on July 7, 1986. Indian relations with the government are as alive and problematic today as ever before, for the federal government's administration of the reservation system both promotes and restricts the development of the native American culture.

Perhaps it would be best to define exactly what a reservation is. It is simply an area of land reserved for Indian use. There are approximately 260 reservations in the United States at present (Williams 28). The term reservation can be traced back to the time when land was "reserved" for Indian use in treaties between whites and Indians. Figures from 1978 by the Bureau of Indian Affairs show that 51,789,249 acres of land are in trust for Indians; 41,678,875 acres of this are for tribes, and 10,110,374 acres are for individuals (U.S. Bureau of Indian Affairs 6). The Indians are by no means restricted to these areas, although this assumption is commonly made. They are free as any other citizen to leave these areas. The reservation system provides benefits which promote the development of the Indian culture, and many are not offered to the general public. These benefits were established to encourage Indian acceptance to living on the reservation by guaranteeing that the Indians' ways of life would be altered as little as possible. For instance, each reservation has its own form of tribal government and tribal laws (Williams 28). Although a few federal laws for crimes such as murder take precedence, most crimes committed on the reservation are under the jurisdiction of the tribal court (U.S. Bureau of Indian Affairs 6).

This exemption from outside regulation by the state and federal governments has provided many benefits for the Indians, most of which have only recently been recognized. One benefit is that the Indians on the reservation are exempt from paying state or federal taxes on land, cars, or income obtained from the land (Williams 29). Thus the income obtained from the sale of timber and mineral rights is tax free. Also, since the reservation is independent from outside regulation, many tribes have established gambling, such as bingo and blackjack, on their reservation (Arrandale 129,130), activities which often are illegal outside of the reservation. The revenue from such activities is also tax free just as any tourist business on the reservation is. Besides exemption from taxation, protection from outside regulation also excludes the participation by the reservation Indian in hunting and fishing guidelines. Many Indians can hunt and fish without licences or adherence to set limits (Williams 29) on the reservation. Some tribes have taken this one step further and, as Tom Arrandale says, "have been claiming priority rights to harvest Pacific Northwest fish . . . ," in his report on the economic development of the American Indians (140).

The Indians on the reservation are also entitled to many programs offered by the government. These include job training programs, education programs for small children (Battise), Indian scholarships, health services, welfare assistance, economic development aid (Horswell 11), and housing projects (Martin 2). However, these programs are not as important as the right to self-government, because it is self-government that eases the burden of assimilation felt by the Indians, and even encourages the continual development of their unique culture.

Most positive aspects, however, tend to lose value in the presence of the more unfavorable ones which in turn add to a loss of the Indians' culture. Examples of unfavorable conditions include the Indians' dependency on the federal government and the changing policy towards the reservation system by the federal government and in turn contribute to the poor standing of the American Indian on the reservation. The average income of an Indian on the reservation is under $7,000, with an average unemployment rate of 35 percent ("Adrift in Their Own Land" 89). It is important to note that these are averages, and thus, some reservations are far worse than others. James Cook refers to the American Indians as being, "among the most disadvantaged minorities . . . ill educated, unhealthy and poor," (68). The reservation has even been referred to by Dillion S. Myer, Head of the Bureau of Indian Affairs in the 1950's, as resembling "Japanese-American detention camps." He is more than qualified to make this comparison since he was also in charge of dismanteling the detention camps after World War II (Philip 41).

On November 30, 1984, the Presidental Commission on Indian Reservation Economics issued a report stating that the United States government was the major obstacle in the economic growth of Indian reservations (Williams 30). Many Indians agree and assert that the dependency on the government is directly related to the fact that the government holds all reservation land in trust for the Indians. The only way this land can be sold or used as collateral is with permission of the Secretary of the Interior, or an authorized representative, based on his determination "that he (the Indian) is capable of managing his own affairs," (U.S. Bureau of Indian Affairs 2). Since this permission has been granted only sparingly, it is evident the government does not view the Indians as competent to manage their own affairs. Due to the fact that economic development requires capital and that the Indians have been denied access to the only capital they possess, economic development on the reservation screeches to a halt (Arrandale 138). Thus, dependency is encouraged.

Also encouraging dependency on the government are such federal programs as job training, welfare assistance, and economic development aid which contrary to their intended purpose may be more harmful than beneficial. It was perhaps said best by James Watt, former Secretary of the Interior, "If you want an example of the failures of socialism, don't go to Russia—come to America and go to the Indian reservations," (Williams 29). From infancy to old age the Indian is greeted by one federal program after another. Even with job training and placement programs, the isolation of most reservations prevents any meaningful results. Most have developed a "learned helplessness" when referring to their dependency (Williams 29). They have stopped making any efforts because they know the government will be there regardless of if they try. Grace Goedal, a full-blooded Yakima, says, "I love my people, but they're like children. They've been pampered for such a long time" (Williams 29). Another Indian, Verna Lawrence, a member of the Sault Ste tribe, also expresses this feeling by saying, "Intelligent human beings are exiled for a lifetime and conditioned to be totally dependent on the handouts from taxpayers" (Williams 30).

What could be worse than this dependency on the government for handouts? The ways in which the government has tried to solve it. Just when the Indians had become accustomed to the policy of the government and felt comfortable on where they stood, the policy would change. The history of the government has been to alternate from encouraging self-sufficiency on the reservation to fostering assimilation into society (Arrandale 133), moving from one extreme to the next.

Indians were greeted early with the instability of the government's policy, especially in the 1800's. A good example would be the removal of Indians from the areas of Florida and Georgia by the Jackson Administration. This removal became known as the "Trail of Tears" by the Indians due to the high number of Indian deaths suffered along the way. The Indians of these areas had been assured that they would be undisturbed if they were to adopt the white man's ways, to assimilate. The Cherokees were especially successful at this, closely resembling the white farmers of the area in housing and agricultural activities, only to be forced from their land to reservations in Oklahoma (Young 175). They went from a friendly policy under the government to a hostile one of total removal and separation.

The government's policy would change yet again in 1887 with the passing of the General Allotment Act by Congress. It split up reservation land and handed out tracts of land to Indians as a way to once again assimilate them into society. Since many Indians were dependent on the reservation system, they were unable to maintain the individual lots on their own. This resulted in a dramatic loss of land. Between the years of 1887 and 1934, tribal lands dropped from 138 million acres to 48 million acres (Arrandale 134).

Realizing that they had made a great mistake, the United States government once again changed its policy. In 1934, the Indian Reorganization act was passed by congress to forbid the parcelling out of land and to establish tribal governments on the reservation (Arrandale 134). At this point both the Indians and the government [assumed] that the game of "ping pong" had come to an end. The Indians felt comfortable that the government's policy would stabilize and survive this time. The government also felt that it had matured with its dealing of the Indians and could keep its promises.

This feeling of safety was to be short lived. Just as the government of the 1990's will be different from the government of the 1980's, so was the government of the 1950's from the government of the 1930's. There was to be a changing of the guards in the Bureau of Indian affairs with the appointment of Dillon S. Myer as its new head in 1950 (Philp 37). This change of personnel was to also cause a change in the policy established in 1934. In 1953 congress approved new legislation which called for the relinquishment of government supervision on the reservation, and called for the equal status of Indians without special privileges (Arrandale 134). Fortunately this decision would be overturned, but it would forever emphasize fear of impending change among the reservation Indians (Arrandale 134).

The government was trying to help in both its policy of assimilation of the Indian into our society and separation of the Indian culture to the reservation, but the key problem with both policies was that they were extreme responses when a more moderate course might have served better. Either the government would establish a parent-child relationship, supporting the Indians' every need, or it would sever the relationship abruptly, leaving the Indians without the experience of where or how to begin to take care of their own affairs.

What can be done to solve the problems of the reservation to make the overall development of the Indian culture promising? Basically, the Indians are going to have to take matters into their own hands and stop waiting for someone to do this for them, and they are. For instance, the Native Americans Right Fund in Colorado is set up specifically to handle such issues as funding, approval of funding, and to represent Indian tribes in lawsuits against the government (Battise). The tribes are winning many lawsuits brought against illegal land seizure by the government, including a recent suit resulting from the denial of reservation status for the Alabama Coushattas by the State of Texas. Another important achievement by the Indians is what they do with victory settlements from these lawsuits. A growing number of tribes are investing their cash awards for long-term economic development instead of in such short-term gains as dividing it among the tribe members ("A New Band of Tribal Tycoons" 56). Still other tribes are taking their exempt status from outside regulation to further themselves economically such as with commercial fishing and gambling as stated earlier.

All of these examples show how the Indians are becoming effective when dealing with the government and with their own money. Perhaps when the next change in government policy comes, the Indians will have achieved greater self-sufficiency and will no longer be so greatly affected by the government's whim. Better yet, maybe the government will recognize its past history of extremes, and take a more conservative middle stand.

Works Cited

"Adrift in Their Own Land." *Time* 6 July 1987: 89.

Arrandale, Tom. "American Indian Economic Development." *Editorial Research Reports* 17 Feb. 1984: 127–142.

Battise, Carol. Personal interview, 25 Sept. 1987.

Cook, J. "Help Wanted—Work, Not Handouts." *Forbes* 4 May 1987: 68–71.

Horswell, Cindy. "Alabama-Coushattas See Hope In U.S. Guardianship." *Houston Chronicle* 26 May 1987: 11.

Johnson, Trebbe. "Indian Land, White Greed." *Nation* 4 July 1987: 15–18.

Martin, Howard N. "Alabama-Coushatta Indians of Texas: Alabama-Coushatta Historical Highlights." Brochure, Alabama-Coushatta Indian Reservation: Livingston, Texas [n.d.].

"A New Band of Tribal Tycoons." *Time* 16 March 1987: 56.

Philp, K. R. "Dillon S. Myer and the Advent of Termination: 1950–1953." *Western Historical Quarterly* Jan. 1988: 37–59.

[U.S. Bureau of Indian Affairs.] "Information About . . . The Indian People." Mimeographed flier, March 1981: 1–6.

Williams, Ted. "On the Reservation: American's Apartheid." *National Review* 8 May 1987: 28–30.

Young, J. Williams T. *American Realities: Historical Realities From the First Settlements to the Civil War.* Boston: Little Brown, 1981.

■ UNDERSTANDING WRITING STRATEGIES

1. How does the conflict between the Hopi and the Navajo over land and the government's role in the conflict prepare the reader for the essay's position?

2. What kind of information follows the introduction? How necessary is this for the rest of the paper?

3. How do the reservation system's advantages weigh against the disadvantages? Are these inherent in the system or in Womack's presentation?

4. What role does the federal government assume toward the Indians in its administration of the reservation system?

5. What kind of evidence does Womack offer in support of her criticisms of reservation policy? How convincing is this evidence?

6. How does Womack organize this evidence? How relevant is this organization to the current situation?

7. What proposals for change does Womack make? What kind of evidence does she present supporting these proposals? ■

■ SUGGESTIONS FOR WRITING

Consider Womack's essay in relation to Scott Mersch's essay, "Edward F. Beale: Conflict of Interest in California Indian Policy." Focusing on audience, purpose, objectivity, and the quality of information, write an assessment of these essays' relative merits. ■

Locarno Diplomacy, Germany and the West, 1925–1929

David Woolner

Writing for a seminar, Topics on Modern German History, David Woolner reviews Jonathan Jacobson's book on German foreign policy during the Weimar Republic.

The period in European history which began at Locarno in 1925 is often viewed as the beginning of a new era, a time in which Germany and the Allies tried resolutely to put the lingering hatred of the First World War behind them. "The Spirit of Locarno" became the saying of the day. But like "The War to End All Wars" and so many other optimistic phrases that followed the turn of the century, "The Spirit of Locarno" was in fact ephemeral: a short-lived blossoming of hope that did not reflect the real and very deep divisions of Europe in the 1920's. Nowhere is this made more clear than in Jonathan Jacobson's excellent book, *Locarno Diplomacy, Germany and the West, 1925–1929*.

Central to Jacobson's book is his observation that each state pursued the Locarno agreement with its own particular goals. As such, each party allowed itself to interpret the treaty in a manner best befitting its national interests. Thus, while Locarno did bring about an atmosphere congenial to frank discussions and negotiations, it did not in fact change the basic positions of each of the parties involved.

Stresemann, the German Foreign Minister, for example, saw the Locarno agreement as a means by which Germany might obtain a revision of the Versailles treaty. Germany's aims included the removal of all foreign troops from her soil, the return of the Saar, the prevention of a hostile French and British alliance, an end to disarmament inspections and an assurance of the unity and territorial integrity of the Reich. Implicit in these goals, however, was Stresemann's hope that the Locarno agreement would eventually allow for the redrawing of Germany's eastern frontier. This he hoped to accomplish by a negotiated settlement, but force was not ruled out. In Stresemann's view, either eventuality was enhanced by the Locarno talks. With France assured of her security, and with all her troops out of Germany, Stresemann felt that the likelihood of a French attack on Germany in the event of a war between Germany and Poland was greatly reduced. Moreover, with the British elevated to the role of "honest broker," Stresemann felt that it might even be possible for Germany to elicit considerable British sympathy for her desire to redraw her eastern borders. Finally, Stresemann was also concerned that Germany not become too dependent on Moscow for support. An agreement with the West insured that this would not happen.

The French view of Locarno was quite different. Their aim was to secure entente with Great Britain, while simultaneously pursuing the promise of detente with Germany. Detente, however, did not mean that the French were willing to revise the Versailles treaty. Quite the contrary; in their view, the Locarno agreement was not a means by which the treaty of Versailles might be revised, but rather a means by which it might be implemented. Paramount to France was her right to reparation and security. Promises of goodwill meant nothing. Foreign Minister Briand therefore, knowing full well that under the terms of Versailles he would have to pull his troops out by 1935, pursued the Locarno talks with the aim of securing for France further assurances of German compliance. If Germany were willing to propose some method of anticipatory payment, France might be willing to talk about an early withdrawal of her troops—provided of course, that continued verification of the demilitarized status of the Rhineland could be assured.

To the British, the Locarno agreement provided a method by which Britain could guarantee French security without alienating Germany. The Locarno pact, in the eyes of the Baldwin government, was a deterrent to war since it removed any uncertainty about British involvement should war break out. It was not, however, a blank check with respect to French interests on the Continent. Britain was not committed in any way to France's "little entente." Central Europe was not seen by the British Foreign Minister, Chamberlain, as a vital concern of H.M. government. Of far greater concern was the threat of Germany falling into camp with the Soviets—a threat that Stresemann skillfully manipulated to his advantage through his "Rappallo bluff." For this reason, Britain could not afford to be seen as wholly in support of French concerns. To do so would jeopardize Germany's rapprochement with the West. Furthermore, there were still many within and outside of the government who felt that England should be very cautious with respect to her commitments on the Continent. Chamberlain, well aware of this, sought to assure continued British support of France by committing her to an agreement least likely to arouse the objections of those opposed to British continental entanglements. The Locarno treaty, which excluded any discussion of Germany's eastern frontier and which involved England only in the unlikely event of a war on Germany's western borders, suited these concerns perfectly.

In spite of the different aims and concerns of each of these states, the initial talks of October–November 1925 did produce some positive results. Germany, for example, promised to maintain her western borders, to arbitrate disputes in the east, and to join the League of Nations. In return, Britain and France agreed to exempt Germany from League sanctions against Russia, to evacuate Cologne, and to leave open to question the status of Germany's eastern borders. Subsequent talks were also agreed to, in which issues such as the abolishment of the IMCC and the reduction of troops in the occupied zones would be discussed.

Despite these initial successes and the tremendous optimism they generated, the later talks were to prove much more difficult. Germany now pressed for the complete withdrawal of all allied troops. But Briand, ever mindful of France's right to reparation and security, refused to consider the idea. The impasse that resulted was further complicated by the nature of Chamberlain's policy. To him, nothing the Germans could say or do would justify a break-up of the French and British entente. And, although Chamberlain often encouraged Stresemann to not give up his efforts, he nevertheless felt it important that the Germans never lose sight of this. It was his policy therefore, to always present a united front at the negotiating table— even when he privately sympathized with Stresemann's position. He was willing, behind the scenes, to pressure the French towards a compromise with the Germans, but his pressure was never strong enough to move Briand. In Chamberlain's opinion, the importance of the entente simply did not justify any action on the part of the British that might jeopardize their relations with the French.

As long as Chamberlain's attitude prevailed at the Foreign Office, the chances for a break in the long stalemate that now settled in over the Locarno powers seemed unlikely at best.

As the talks entered their final year however, two factors would alter completely Chamberlain's carefully constructed policy. The first was the election of Britain's first Labour government; the second was money.

The new British government was much less patient with the French than its predecessor. To Henderson, the new Foreign Minister, Briand had been dragging his feet over the issue of the evacuation of the Rhineland. According to the Labour government, German pacification was dependent on reconciliation. This meant the prompt removal of all foreign troops from Germany. The new government also felt that it had a right to an increase in its share of the recently negotiated Younge annuity so that it could make up for past shortfalls in the money it received to pay its war debt. This new demand, which the British planned to introduce at the Hague conference without notifying the French in advance, was sure to upset them. As far as France was concerned, the Younge plan was a *fait accompli* and not subject to revision.

The difficulties these two issues were to cause at the Hague conference did indeed prove disruptive. Snowden's demands for a revision of the Younge plan infuriated Briand and nearly brought the conference to a close. But it was the issue of evacuation which proved to be most divisive. Here, Henderson, frustrated with the obstinance of the French, decided to act unilaterally and to conclude a separate withdrawal agreement with Stresemann. This, in effect, brought the British-French entente to an end and signaled the close of the Locarno era.

That the Locarno talks failed to produce a settlement that would stand the test of time should not come as a surprise to the serious student of history. The gulf that separated the French and German people in the late 1920's was still very wide. The foul taste of Versailles still permeated the German palate, and the memory of Verdun has clung to French consciousness to this day. Jacobson's book is a vivid reminder of this. The difficulties that each of these statesmen faced are all too clearly brought to light in this work. Indeed, it seems remarkable that Briand, Stresemann, and Chamberlain were able to accomplish anything at all, given the lingering hostility that existed on both sides of the Rhine. Jacobson's book stands as a kind of testament to these men and their noble efforts. It is well written and well documented and this writer recommends it highly.

Work Cited

Locarno Diplomacy, Germany and the West, 1925–1929, by Jon Jacobson, Princeton University Press, 1972.

■ THE WRITER'S ASSIGNMENT

Using the tone of *The American Historical Review* or the *New York Review of Books*, write a 5–7 page review reflecting your own opinion of one of the assigned history books. The review should present an overall impression of the book and indicate how it adds to the historiography in the field. You should write *as* historians *for* historians; the review should be fairly formal with no contractions or use of the first person. ■

■ UNDERSTANDING WRITING STRATEGIES

1. How does the first paragraph create a context for Woolner's discussion of the book?

2. What is the review's thesis?

3. How does the thesis organize the summary or overview of the book?

4. How does Woolner fulfill the thesis's commitments in his summary?

5. Is the "overall impression" of the book adequate to engage the reader's interest? Why or why not?

6. What does Woolner do to indicate the book's contribution to the historiography of the period? How well does he do this?

7. Explain how the essay's tone fulfills the assigned "*as* historians *for* historians"?

8. Where do you see Woolner's opinion? How adequate is this for a review's purposes? ■

■ **SUGGESTIONS FOR WRITING**

Read several reviews from *The American Historical Review* and/or the *New York Review of Books*. Considering what these reviews do—writing strategies, summary contents and lengths, opinions and judgments, tone and style—develop criteria for a good book review, particularly for historical studies. Then write either a paper explaining what constitutes a good book review, or your own good book review.　■

Business

11

With the exception of letters and memoranda, nearly all business writing takes the form of reports, and business reports, regardless of their subject, conform to a highly conventional format. In business courses, as in other disciplines, students learn to write in their discipline's professional voice. All but three of this section's essays use the format of a professional business report. You will better appreciate the reports in this section if you are familiar with the business report's conventions.

Business reports are a management tool used to apprise senior executives of organizational activities and proposals for activities, or to communicate between sectors of an organization. Consequently a business report writer has a clear idea of his report's purpose and audience. Usually a business report begins with a letter of transmittal addressed to the executive who asked for the report. This letter describes the report's purposes, its sources of information, and the project's constraints. The report itself follows an organization more like a book's than a journal article's with a table of contents, headings demarcating topic shifts, and appendices. For the benefit of a busy executive the business report's initial pages, with an executive summary and a section on conclusions and recommendations, are some of its most important features. Usually, then, a business report will contain the following components in the specified order:

Title page
Table of Contents
Executive Summary
Conclusions and Recommendations
Introduction
The body of the report with topic and subtopic headings
Appendices
Notes
Bibliography

The reports in this section, while they all use the same format, reflect some of the business report's different purposes. In "What the Trade Deficit

Means to Americans," "The Robotics Revolution in the Automotive Industry: Will Workers Become Obsolete?" and "Discrimination in the United States Tax System: Punishing the Poor for Being Poor" Clare Macy, John Barnickel, and David Leathers respectively write informational reports. William Goodwin examines a specific business's management problem and proposes a solution in "Employee Turnover at Kragen Auto Parts." Susan Magoulas, also considering a specific business's needs, argues to change phone systems in "Proposal to Convert Horizon Telephone System to Merlin Communication System." Finally, Laura Frings reports her own research in the feasibility study, "The Value to Corporate America of Outdoor Experiential Training: Is It Worth the Cost?"

This chapter's remaining papers' purposes differ little from those in reports, but they do use different formats. In an interoffice memorandum Glenn Homesley proposes a stock investment strategy in "Recommendation for Investment in Common Stocks." Denise Bolduc and Charlotte Locklear-Enquist write position papers in "Selling to Society: Sexual Images in Advertising" and "The Burzynski Clinic Controversy."

The essays here represent work done for courses in technical and business writing, English composition, and business management. Despite the clear format differences, these essays represent students developing criteria and evaluating information and institutions, analyzing data, summarizing and incorporating secondary sources, and constructing arguments just as do the essays in other disciplines.

The Robotics Revolution in the Automotive Industry: Will Workers Become Obsolete?

John Barnickel

Writing for a marketing class, John Barnickel analyzes the United States auto industry's implementation of robotics. This report, like many written for business, synthesizes secondary sources to provide a corporate reader with a necessary overview of a problem.

TO: Ce Ce Iandoli

FROM: John Barnickel

DATE: November 30, 1988

SUBJECT: Transmittal of Final Report

The attached report is the result of a research project you assigned on November 14, 1988. It explores the use of robotics in the United States automotive industry. You will find my conclusions and recommendations included in this report.

The purposes of the study were to examine:

(1) The reasons for using robotics in the automotive industry

(2) The expected use of robotics in the future

(3) The resulting displacement of automotive workers due to robotics

Several articles drawn from current periodicals were used for the primary research. In addition, books on the topic were used for secondary research.

This project was both a challenging and informative undertaking. Considering the time constraints, the demands of simultaneously taking 3 other university courses, and working part-time, I believe my findings highlight the issue of robotics in the United States automotive industry quite well.

If you have any questions, please feel free to call me at (415) 939-0430.

THE ROBOTICS REVOLUTION

IN THE

AUTOMOTIVE INDUSTRY:

WILL WORKERS BECOME OBSOLETE?

Presented

to

Ce Ce Iandoli
Professor of Marketing 4495

California State University, Hayward

Submitted

by

John Barnickel
Student in Marketing 4495

California State University, Hayward

November 30, 1988

TABLE OF CONTENTS

EXECUTIVE SUMMARY

Worker displacement due to robotics in the United States automotive industry is a growing concern of many. In recent years, misleading reports have drawn catastrophic conclusions for assembly line workers. This report analyzes (1) the reasons for using robotics, (2) future automation plans, and (3) resulting worker displacement due to robotics.

The results of the study indicate the following:

1. Rising labor costs, increased international competition (primarily from Japan), and concerns over quality control contribute to the popularity of robotics.
2. As long as cars sales remain strong, Chrysler, Ford, and General Motors will continue committing tremendous dollar amounts to automated manufacturing technology.
3. Though future demand for some positions will decline, worker displacement among those currently employed in the auto industry may not be as severe as previously forecasted. The United Auto Workers Union has obtained retraining rights for robot maintenance, programming, and management positions. No outside hiring will take place for these newly created positions.

INTRODUCTION

In recent years, professionals have been predicting the consequences of the robotics revolution in the automotive industry. We have read articles about workerless, robotized factories that operate in cold and dark warehouses, where cafeterias and parking lots are not needed. It was assumed that by the mid-1980s, tens of thousands of automotive assembly line workers would be consulting unemployment offices. Robots have arrived in the automotive industry, but without the disastrous implications. Is the worst still yet to come for Detroit's blue collar workers, or were past predictions false alarms?

Purpose of Report

This report will analyze (1) the reasons for using robotics in the United States automotive industry, (2) expected use of robotics in the future, and (3) the resulting displacement of automotive workers.

Definition

To provide a common reference perspective, the following definition of "robot" is supplied: Robots are machines that operate autonomously and are capable of moving materials, parts, tools, and specialized devices through variable programmed motions for the performance of a variety of tasks.

DISCUSSION

No other industry has pursued robotics to the extent and with the speed of the automotive industry. Robot purchases by auto manufacturers account for well over half of the entire robotic industry's dollar volume (Rutigliano, 1986). Since 1979, U.S. automakers have spent at least $40 billion to build highly automated plants. This "pedal to the metal" approach stems from an attempt to stay innovative and competitive. Attention is once again being concentrated on manufacturing. According to Stephen Cohen, director of the Berkeley Roundtable on the International Economy, "to stay innovative, you need mastery and control of the production process." Along with the concern to stay innovative in production, the push toward automation is in response to concerns over rising labor costs, and competition in international markets.

Rising Labor Costs

United States automakers face one of the highest average wage rates in U.S. manufacturing industries. Auto manufacturers in 1981 found it possible to operate robots for $6 per hour, well below the $20 per hour required for the pay and benefits of a worker doing the same tasks (Levitan, Johnson, 1982).

Robots, like any machine, have the advantages of precision, speed, untiring availability, reliability, and relative imperviousness to hostile environments. A robot won't call in sick because of a hangover, and never demands overtime pay. Unfortunately, robots today cannot react to unforeseen circumstances or changing conditions, and they can't improve performance based on prior experience. While robots surpass humans in terms of dexterity, they lack intelligence and sensitivity. A robot is in no way a total human replacement, but may replace the routine, highly paid employee.

International Competition

By the end of 1982, the United States, with twice Japan's population, had fewer than one third as many robots (Lynn, 1982). The growing use of robots by Japanese automakers will not increase their advantages over the U.S. industry, so long as we keep pace with them.

Some U.S. managers who visit auto assembly plants in Japan are often disappointed with what they see. Many of Detroit's plants are at least as sophisticated, but productivity is far short of expectations. The facilities have the potential to elevate American car companies to absolute leadership in manufacturing technologies, but we first need to figure out how to make them work. "They're now discovering that if you don't have good management, you'll end up with a rotten automated plant," concludes David Cole, director of the University of Michigan's Office for the Study of Automotive Transportation (Mitchell, 1986). At any rate, U.S. automakers plan to continue spending tremendnous amounts on robotics in the future.

Expected Use of Robotics in the Future

The General Motors corporate forecast is presented below in Table 1. General Motors plans to increase the number of robots in use from its 1980 total of 302, to 14,000 in 1990, for an average annual growth rate of 47 percent (Hunt, 1983).

TABLE 1. Projected Robot Applications in General Motors

Application	Number of Robots in use				
	1980	1983	1985	1988	1990
Welding (Arc and Spot)	138	1,000	1,700	2,500	2,700
Painting	47	300	650	1,200	1,500
Assembly	17	675	1,200	3,200	5,000
Machine Loading	68	200	1,200	2,600	4,000
Parts Transfer	32	125	250	500	800
Total	302	2,300	5,000	10,000	14,000

Source: GM Technical Center, Robotics Display, April 1982

In 1982, there were reports of a slowdown in robot acquisitions at General Motors and other auto firms due to a lack of financial capital. Car sales must remain strong before any further expansion can occur.

Neither Ford nor GM is retreating from its commitment to advanced manufacturing technology. For the long haul, automation remains Detroit's main weapon. "I don't want to go into a competitive manufacturing battle without the best technology," says Gerald Elson, GM's executive director for artificial intelligence. "If we're not going to win it on technology, then what are we going to win it on?" Automakers remain convinced that automation will eventually pay off. "The act is coming together," insists John Durstine, assistant general manager at Ford's Body & Assembly Operations. "You're just seeing the first rehearsal" (Mitchell, 1986).

Displacement of Automotive Workers

If this is the "first rehearsal," what will "opening night" bring in terms of employee displacement? In the automotive industry, overall displacement does appear significant. By 1995, 50 percent of automobile assembly will be done by automated machines. Seventy-five percent of job loss in Michigan is expected to be in the auto industry (Hunt, 1983). The hardest hit will be routine laborers such as painters and welders. Considering these statistics, researchers still contend the overall displacement will not be a problem.

Actual Displacement May Be Less Than Expected

Many argue that the chief goal of automation is not to eliminate direct labor costs. Quality control costs are the main issue. Quality control costs for a typical factory represent 25–35 percent of the total manufacturing costs—robotics can sharply reduce this figure.

The jobs will not disappear all at once, and robot programming, management, and maintenance will provide some new jobs. Since robots are production equipment, and all production equipment is maintained by members of the United Auto Workers Union, these jobs will remain within the UAW. The UAW has successfully obtained advance notice and retraining rights from auto manufacturers in an effort to gain protection from sweeping automation.

The high cost of robotics, and delayed start-up times can quickly erode some of the expected cost savings. At present, American industry lacks trained personnel to implement, and maintain robotics technology. The implementation of robotics, and the resulting worker displacement will not occur overnight.

CONCLUSIONS

People are starting to see that, rather than dehumanizing the work place, robots, by taking over the simplest, most tedious, dirtiest, and most hazardous jobs, have done the opposite: they have helped employees at the low end of the labor ladder "upscale" their working lives, moving them to work assignments surely more worthy of human capabilities and aspirations (Rutigliano, 1986). No doubt some workers will become obsolete, though it should be noted that the arrival of the robot may have saved many jobs by enabling the department to remain competitive. The displacement of 28,000 workers in General Motors due to robotics should be compared to the approximately 140,000 workers who were laid off in the past due to lagging sales, poor economy, and foreign competition.

Young people seeking jobs in the future will have to learn marketable skills other than welding, painting, and other operative tasks that are now being robotized. The automated factory will depend more, rather than less, on the people in it. While there will be fewer engaged in direct production, there will be more people in supportive functions.

RECOMMENDATIONS

Human resource planners in the automotive industry should: (1) develop and implement a policy for retraining workers displaced by robots, (2) communicate the retraining policy to all employees, (3) solicit and encourage a high level of employee participation in the decision-making process concerning robots, and (4) evaluate employee reactions to the change process, and try to reduce or minimize resistance to change (Verney, 1986).

Bibliography

Barrett, F. D. "The Robot Revolution." *The Futurist* 19 (October, 1985): 37–40.
Fey, Carol. "Working With Robots: The Real Story." *Training: The Magazine of Human Resource Development* 23 (March, 1986): 49–56.
Hunt, H. Allan. *Human Resource Implications of Robotics.* Kalamazoo, MI: W. E. Upjohn Institute For Employment Research, 1983.
Levitan, Sar A. "The Future of Work: Does It Belong to Us or to the Robots?" *Monthly Labor Review* (March, 1982): 105–114.
Miller, Robert J. *Robotics: Future Factories, Future Workers.* Beverly Hills, CA: Sage Publications, Inc. 1983.
Mitchell, Russell. "Detroit Stumbles on Its Way to the Future." *Business Week* (June 16, 1986): 103–104.
Rutigliano, Anthony. "Robots to Invade U.S. Industries." *Management Review* (September, 1986): 50–53.
Verney, Thomas P. "HR Planning for Robots in the Work Place." *Personnel* (February, 1986): 8–9.

■ THE WRITER'S ASSIGNMENT

Using standard business report format, write a report using secondary sources on some issue challenging American business. ■

■ UNDERSTANDING WRITING STRATEGIES

1. According to Barnickel, what is robot technology's major advantage for business? What is its major disadvantage?

2. In what ways is the displacement of workers by the increased use of robotics not as great as first anticipated? How do workers benefit by increased robotics?

3. What plan for this essay does the "Executive Summary" indicate? How effectively does the report carry out this plan?

4. If you omitted the topic headings, how clearly is this essay's information presented?

5. Do the report's conclusions follow logically from the evidence presented?

6. Do you agree with Barnickel's position and recommendations? What in the report affected your agreement or disagreement? ■

■ SUGGESTIONS FOR WRITING

Beginning with information Barnickel has provided in his report, write a position paper on robotics' value for American business. Before you write, consider the different purposes inherent in a business report and a position paper. How will your audience differ? How will your argument differ? What will you need to do in your introduction and conclusion to appeal to your audience and to shape your argument? ■

Selling to Society: Sexual Images in Advertising

Denise Bolduc

> In this position paper written for an English composition course, Denise Bolduc justifies businesses using sexually oriented material in advertising.

As Americans, we live in a sexually oriented society. Ever since the sexual revolution of the 1960's, sex has become more accepted and sex in the mass media has become more widespread. Magazines, television, and movies display this fact well. Now another branch of the media, advertising, is being criticized for its use of sexual images. This criticism is unnecessary because advertisers are not venturing forward to change people's ideals about sex. There is a big difference between "selling sex" and "selling with sex." Advertisers are merely selling their products to a society that is already sexually oriented. Advertising does not lead society; it follows.

The fundamental principle of advertising is to sell products in a way that is appealing to the majority of the people in that product market. The 1980's are an era where people are primarily concerned with their attractiveness. People improve their bodies through fitness programs and dieting, and then they need soaps, perfumes, cosmetics, and clothing in which to present themselves. So advertisers sell these products using sexual themes. The human mind thinks that sex is glamorous; people like to look at other people. It's natural to want to be more desired, and that is the message these ads want to express.

Advertisers began to use the device of sexual images for one simple reason. On any given day, the average consumer is exposed to over 2,000 different advertisements. If exposed to the same types of things over and over, the consumer gets bored; he becomes immune to the familiar. Advertisers began to use sexual images to grab the attention of their audience. Everyone has some sort of interest or opinion of sex, so there is a greater chance that people will read the ad and remember it. Memory is a key factor here. The more time the consumer spends looking at the ad, the better the chance of his remembering the product, and in turn, buying it.

Although sexuality in advertising has become a heated issue only in the past five or six years, it is not a "new" method of advertising. Actually, there is not usually anything new to say in advertising, only new ways to say it. "Sexy" ads can be traced back as far as 1902. In this year, Coca-Cola ran an ad featuring a very attractive woman. Although she was fully clothed, at that time the ad was considered very sexy.

The 1950 campaign for White Rock soda is another good example. In these ads, a topless "White Rock" girl is kneeling by a stream looking down at her reflection. Sex in advertising is nearly as old as advertising itself.

For a sexual ad or ad campaign to be successful, of course, it must be marketed properly. The most important marketing techniques in question are that the ads be in good taste and appropriate, or relevant to the product. If the ads are promoting a sensuous product (suntan lotion, lingerie, fragrances) then some types of sensuous images should appear in them. But in some cases, sex is irrelevant to the ad. The classic example is the woman in a bikini trying to sell a sportscar. This is called "lazy advertising." The sexual image of the woman has nothing to do with the car, and this makes the ad tasteless. When advertisers use sexual images to sell a product, these images must be relevant to the overall image of the product, otherwise the ad is considered tasteless.

Some people would argue that any ads dealing with sexuality are tasteless and offensive; that is their perogative. Granted, there will always be objection when sex is involved, but sexual ads are not stating morality messages, nor are they exploitative. These ads do not say that sex is good or bad, and they are not encouraging sex, or "selling sex." They merely use it as a device to convey the image of the product.

This same rule holds as far as the question of exploitation goes. The images in sexual ads are not pornographic; they do not portray people in unnatural or demeaning ways. Also, men and women are given equal status in the ads. Gone are the days when a woman was treated as an object or a target. Equality is stressed in sexual ads.

As with any issue, there will always be those who are against any hint of sex in advertisements. The important thing is not to offend the majority. If an ad campaign gets enough negative reaction, it will stop. Advertisers walk in great dread of offending potential customers.

Famous designer Calvin Klein has undoubtedly been the leader in sexual advertising, and the sales that go with it. His campaign began back in 1980 with a commercial for his denim jeans. In this TV spot, a teenage Brooke Shields boasted how "nothing comes between me and my Calvins."

These ads created quite a stir among American consumers. They were the spark that ignited the fire of sexual advertising as it is known today. Through this ad campaign, Klein established a name and a reputation for himself which he still holds today.

After much success with jeans, Klein, whose firm produces its own ads, set out to sell his new lines of underwear for men and women. The ad for men's showed a tanned and muscular Tom Hintnaus (member of Brazil's 1984 pole vaulting team) reclining in the sun wearing nothing but a pair of Calvin Klein briefs. The women's underwear ad shows a model with her undershirt pulled up to reveal her breasts (In magazines for younger people, her shirt is pulled down.). She is also wearing nothing else but Calvin Klein briefs.

Obviously, Klein was marketing his products correctly because in their first five days at Bloomingdale's, 400 *dozen* pairs of Klein's men's underwear were sold, and today the women's briefs are selling at a rate of five million dollars per month.

Of course, Klein's latest and most successful campaign is for his new line of Obsession fragrances. These black and white print ads show naked bodies semi-intertwined, usually one woman and two men. These ads are in no way meant to be pornographic; rather, they are designed to show the sensuality and allure of the product.

Klein says that his commercials are a chance to create a new art form. He considers himself an artist who sells, and he gives you his vision of what things should be. Klein's purpose for creating sensual ads is to make people stop and think. He says, "I don't want women flipping through 600 pages of Vogue and not even noticing my ads. I'm not trying to exploit anyone, I'm trying to create something sensual, new and amusing."

Despite any consumer criticism, Calvin Klein's erotic Obsession ads have sold his product right off the shelves. In its first year on the market

(1985) it became the number two selling perfume (behind only Giorgio), and today it is among the top three sellers in every major department store in the nation.

Calvin Klein products are only one line among a great many who use the selling device of sexual images, and use it successfully.

Over the last 25 years, virtually every barrier (law or regulation) has fallen concerning what can be written, printed, or filmed about sex in the mass media. The success of sexual advertisements means that advertising has finally crossed that barrier also. As fast as it has grown in the past five years, experts expect the trend to continue in the next five.

Joe Kilgore, the executive creative director at Ogilvy & Mather Advertising Agency in Houston, Texas, remarked, "In the 1960's a commercial had to be funny or it wasn't considered a good commrcial. Now the trend is that it has to be sexy or it's not a good commercial."

There will always be people who want to be more desirable to members of the opposite sex, or those who need attention, or those who like to dwell in fantasies. Advertisers must market their products in the way that the public responds best to. As long as sex is a popular issue or concern among the American people, ads will continue to reflect this, and people will continue to buy.

■ UNDERSTANDING WRITING STRATEGIES

1. What is Bolduc's justification for sexually oriented advertisements?

2. What distinction does Bolduc make between appropriate and "tasteless" sexually oriented advertisements? Where is this distinction made?

3. What is the author's implied definition of pornography? In what ways do you agree or disagree with this definition?

4. How does Bolduc shape her argument? What kind of argumentative or persuasive strategies does she use?

5. Does Bolduc persuade you of her position? Why or why not?

6. What kinds of evidence does Bolduc give to support her position?

7. What other kinds of evidence might she have used?   ■

■ SUGGESTIONS FOR WRITING

Feminists have strenuously objected to sexual imagery in advertising because, like pronography, it identifies women principally as sexual objects concerned only with physical appearance and sexual allure. Collect eight to ten magazine advertisements for products from like categories (for example, toiletries, beverages, or automobiles) that use both men and women in their advertising. Analyze how advertising presents men and women in these ads.

For example, do designer jeans ads use both men and women? If so, are they portrayed differently? Do alcoholic beverage ads portray men differently from women? Are there differences between beer and wine ads, or between these ads and ads for hard liquor? Write a response to Bolduc's essay using specific evidence derived from your investigation. ■

The Value to Corporate America of Outdoor Experiential Training: Is It Worth the Cost?

Laura Michele Frings

In this report written for an administrative communication class, Laura Frings analyzes outdoor experiential training's long-term value in improving employee performance. Since her own primary research forms an important part of the presentation, this business report involves some of the scientific report's writing strategies for presenting experimental findings.

THE VALUE TO CORPORATE AMERICA

OF

OUTDOOR EXPERIENTIAL TRAINING:

IS IT WORTH THE COST?

Submitted by:

Laura Michele Frings
Administrative Communications
Section 03

November 30, 1988

TABLE OF CONTENTS

LIST OF TABLES

Table 1   Significant Differences in Perceptions Between Harness Event
Participants and Non-Participants

Table 2   Significant Differences Between Men and Women's Perceptions
of the Outdoor Experiential Training Program

EXECUTIVE SUMMARY

Many large corporations are utilizing experiential outdoor learning activities as a training tool. Participants take part in activities that appear dangerous, but are actually very carefully managed. The goal is for these experiences to help break down barriers established in the work groups at the office. The hope is that the participants come back to their work environments more willing to take risks, more willing to work as a team. In theory this is commendable, but do participants find these experiential learning adventures worthwhile? Do participants feel safe in the hands of the coordinating staff? And probably even more important, do these adventures effect any positive change in the office?

To answer these questions, I conducted a partial census mail survey, interviewed two "Ropes Course" participants, and researched secondary information pertaining to this subject in journals and magazines.

The census mail survey was conducted in conjunction with Action Associates—a company that provides an experiential outdoor learning adventure they call "The Ropes Course." Action Associates provided the names of participants in the Ropes Course learning experience between 1986 and 1988. The questionnaire that was utilized included eleven statements that the respondents were asked to rate on a five-point Likert scale (5 = Strongly agree through 1 = Strongly Disagree). Of the 1050 questionnaires mailed out, approximately 29% were returned. This is a favorable rate of return for a mail survey.

After editing and coding the surveys, the information from 280 surveys was input into the computer. A program called SPSS.RAW was used to generate the statistical findings in this report.

In general, the data obtained from the survey was quite supportive of experiential outdoor learning. Some of the most noteworthy statistics were the following: 63% of the participants felt that the staff was experienced; 46% of the participants thought the course has a positive impact; 49% of the participants strongly agreed that they would recommend the experience to others; 41% of the participants evaluated the course as a long lasting learning experience. The study showed that those who participated in the harness events (81%) expressed more satisfaction with the program as compared to those who did not participate (19%).

Telephone interviews were conducted six months after participants responded to the questionnaire. I found that most of the enthusiasm for outdoor learning had dwindled to almost nothing. It appears outdoor experiential learning is effective for the short-term, but long-term effectiveness is doubtful.

I believe the beneficial short-term effects can be sustained if the program is monitored correctly. Corporations cannot expect a day or two of outdoor experiential learning to affect permanent changes in their employees. These corporations must be willing to dedicate time and money to necessary follow-up in order to sustain changed behavior.

Secondary research provided the elements considered necessary to make the program work optimally and to continue the desired effects. These elements include the following:

- Orientation meetings with key participants to calm fears, instill positive attitudes, and establish realistic expectations
- A preliminary assessment of the participating work group or individual's needs and what they hope to accomplish with the training
- Ongoing tie-ins and metaphors linked to the work environment
- Carefully facilitated discussion among the participants during the course of the training
- Development of action plans before returning to the work place
- Follow-up by both the provider and the participants
- Commitment from top management (Gall, 1988)

INTRODUCTION

Background

Action Associates is a company that provides an experiential outdoor learning adventure for people—usually employees of large corporations. The participants take part in activities that may appear dangerous; however, physical danger is not the intent; physical challenge is. The theory is that if you can get people to risk attempting something that they know they can not do, and demonstrate to them that they can succeed at these challenges, then their whole attitude about how they approach life, work, and managing others will change. It seems the riskiest part for most participants is learning to trust other people and to work together. Experiential learning provides the opportunity for people to take the kinds of risks they avoid in the office. They must take the chance of showing their vulnerability to others, looking foolish in front of others, or asking help from others. These experiences help to break down barriers established in the work groups at the office. This, of course, is a primary objective of the experience. Companies such as "Action Associates" would like to convince corporate America that they can help participants achieve the stated objectives. Of course, the key question is whether participants find the experience worthwhile, and whether the learning transfers back to the office.

Primary Research Strategy

In order to answer these questions, I conducted a mail survey in conjunction with Action Associates. I surveyed people who had participated in the Ropes Course Training in 1986, 1987, and 1988. Participants were selected by Action Associates. A Likert style questionnaire to measure the participant's attitudes and feelings about the Ropes Course was utilized.

I sent out a total of 1050 questionnaires and accepted responses for two weeks. A total of 296 questionnaires were received and 16 were discarded for incompleteness, leaving 280 surveys to complete our study. The response rate was 29%—average for a mail survey.

I also conducted telephone interviews with four participants from the Ropes Course learning experience six months after they responded to the survey.

METHODOLOGY

To conduct the research project, I used a sample census mail survey. In this way, I could gather primary data from participants in the Ropes Training Course from 1986 through 1988 at a minimal cost and optimal efficiency for Action Associates.

Test Variables

The independent variable of the study was the Ropes Training Course itself. The dependent variable used was the effects of the training. This was measured through the answers the respondents gave on the questionnaire. The classification variables used were gender, age, and occupation—all factors which could influence the dependent scores.

Sampling Plan

Action Associates composed a list of participants in the Ropes Training Course from 1986 to 1988. Therefore, the sample selection for this study was not random. The sample was large though, consisting of 1050 subjects. Of the 1050 subjects, 280 were qualified respondents. Of this 280 total, 176 were male and 104 were female.

The Questionnaire

I used a 20-item questionnaire (See Appendix A which is a copy of the questionnaire). Eleven of the items were rated and nine were categorical (questions that ascertain demographic characteristics). Subjects were asked to rate each statement based on a five-point Likert scale, which ranged from "1" (Strongly Disagree) to "5" (Strongly Agree). At the end of the questionnaire, I asked questions concerning certain rope events and the financing of the training program. Also, respondents were given the opportunity to write in any additional comments on their questionnaires (Appendix C—Comments). Respondents were assured that the comments would remain confidential unless they authorized their permission for use.

Test Procedure

The questionnaire was distributed to 1050 potential subjects through the mail. Respondents were given approximately two weeks to reply. They were provided self-addressed, stamped return envelopes for their convenience and to facilitate a speedy return of the questionnaires. At the end of my deadline, 296 of the 1050 questionnaires had been received. Out of the 296, I had to disregard 16 for missing information, incompleteness, or failure to follow directions.

Coding

A code book was designed to match the questionnaire. Each correctly completed questionnaire was coded and this data was entered directly into the computer.

The columns of the code book were labeled as follows:

Columns # 11-12   Age

Column #13   Gender
1 = Male   2 = Female

Column #14   Occupation
1 = Professional
2 = Managerial/Executive
3 = Technical
4 = Secretarial/Clerical
5 = Other

Columns #15-17   Date course was taken
Column #15 = last digit of the year
Columns #16-17 = Month

Column #18   Ropes Course Location
1 = La Honda
2 = Any other location

Columns #20-30   Respondent's opinions regarding the Ropes Course
Columns #20-30 were completed by the respondents. Eleven questions were asked regarding the ropes course; the respondents were asked to provide answers based upon the provided scale. A copy of the questionnaire is included in Appendix A.

Columns #31-34   Additional Information
Column   #31 = Did your group do harness/belayed events?
Column   #32 = Were you project coordinator?
Column   #33 = Did you financially authorize the course?
Column   #34 = Permission to use additional comments in publications.

For columns #31-34   1 = yes   2 = no

Columns #40-42   Identification Number
Each correctly completed questionaire was assigned a three-digit number beginning with 001.

Limitations

I discovered two limitations to the research study. First of all, 50 (18%) of the respondents did not fill in Columns #11–18 (age, sex, occupation, date course was taken, location where course was taken) completely. Consequently, a non-response rate was assigned for any question in this section left unanswered. The second limitation was a result of the questionnaire design. A column on the right side of the questionnaire was provided for coding most of the questions; however, no such provision was made for the categorical information at the top of the questionnaire. This increased the time needed to code each questionnaire.

Editing

The first step in the editing process was to check each questionnaire to verify that it had been completely and correctly filled out. The chief concern was that each question in the main body of the questionnaire (Columns #20–30—the questions regarding the Ropes Course itself) was completed correctly. I accepted all questionnaires that had correctly and completely filled out the main body whether or not the categorical questions were answered. My objective, of course, was to accept as many returned questionnaires as possible. Of the 296 questionnaires received, sixteen were rejected.

After each questionnaire had been coded and edited, I entered the data into the computer. I printed a hard copy of the data to verify information from the coded questionnaires.

DATA ANALYSIS

After editing and coding the surveys, the information from all 280 surveys was input into a computer. This was done with a program called SPSS.RAW. The input was then checked by comparing a hard copy of the input against the surveys. A statistical computer program generated both descriptive statistics and the hypothesis tests. The findings follow:

(N = total number of respondents)
- The average age is 39.
- The ages range from 18 to 63.
- One hundred seventy six (63%) were males.
- One hundred four (37%) were females.
- Occupations fell into these categories:
  (Appendix B, Figure 1)
  N = 278   • Professional—0   (0%)
  - Managerial—166   (60%)
  - Technical—59   (21%)
  - Clerical—12   (4%)
  - Other—41   (15%)
- Date the course was taken:
  N = 230   • 1986—2   (1%)
  - 1987—131   (57%)
  - 1988—97   (42%)
- Location the course was taken:
  N = 275   • La Honda—126   (46%)
  - Other—149   (54%)
- Only 13 (5%) of the respondents were project coordinators. (Appendix B, Figure 2)
- Only 20 (7%) of the respondents were the ones who financially authorized the course. (Appendix B, Figure 2)

In evaluating questions (Q) one through eleven, I specified a 95% confidence level. This meant that the true population mean (average) should lie within this interval 95 out of 100 times.

Q 1—Ropes course met my expectations.
  (Appendix B, Figure 3)
  - Mean = 3.875   Confidence interval = 3.765—3.985
  - Strongly disagree—6   (2%)
  - Disagree—21   (7%)
  - Neutral—42   (15%)
  - Agree—142   (51%)
  - Strongly agree—68   (24%)

Q 2—Ropes course met my team's expectations.
    (Appendix B, Figure 4)
- Mean = 3.946   Confidence interval = 3.855—4.038
- Strongly disagree—2   (1%)
- Disagree—8   (3%)
- Neutral—56   (20%)
- Agree—151   (54%)
- Strongly agree—63   (22%)

Q 3—The services were appropriate to my needs.
    (Appendix B, Figure 5)
- Mean = 3.961   Confidence interval = 3.850—4.079
- Strongly disagree—8   (2%)
- Disagree—14   (5%)
- Neutral—40   (14%)
- Agree—137   (49%)
- Strongly agree—81   (29%)

Q 4—The services were appropriate to my team's needs.
    (Appendix B, Figure 6)
- Mean = 4.007   Confidence interval = 3.915—4.100
- Strongly disagree—4   (1%)
- Disagree—8   (3%)
- Neutral—37   (13%)
- Agree—164   (59%)
- Strongly agree—67   (24%)

Q 5—The course had a positive impact.
    (Appendix B, Figure 7)
- Mean = 4.125   Confidence interval = 4.024—4.226
- Strongly disagree—3   (1%)
- Disagree—12   (4%)
- Neutral—34   (12%)
- Agree—129   (46%)
- Strongly agree—102   (36%)

Q 6—The course was a long lasting learning experience.
    (Appendix B, Figure 8)
- Mean = 3.511   Confidence interval = 3.395—3.626
- Strongly disagree—11   (4%)
- Disagree—28   (10%)
- Neutral—87   (31%)
- Agree—115   (41%)
- Strongly agree—39   (14%)

Q 7—The course was a long lasting team learning experience.
   (Appendix B, Figure 9)
   • Mean = 3.275   Confidence interval = 3.152—3.362
   • Strongly disagree—13   (5%)
   • Disagree—28   (10%)
   • Neutral—131   (47%)
   • Agree—90   (32%)
   • Strongly agree—18   (6%)

Q 8—The staff demonstrated expertise.
   (Appendix B, Figure 10)
   • Mean = 4.589   Confidence interval = 4.520—4.659
   • Strongly disagree—1   (0%)
   • Disagree—0   (0%)
   • Neutral—9   (3%)
   • Agree—93   (33%)
   • Strongly agree—177   (63%)

Q 9—The staff demonstrated expertise.
   (Appendix B, Figure 11)
   • Mean = 4.571   Confidence interval = 4.502—4.641
   • Strongly disagree—1   (0%)
   • Disagree—0   (0%)
   • Neutral—8   (3%)
   • Agree—100   (36%)
   • Strongly agree—171   (61%)

Q10—The staff demonstrated integrity.
   (Appendix B, Figure 12)
   • Mean = 4.546   Confidence interval = 4.469—4.624
   • Strongly disagree—2   (1%)
   • Disagree—0   (0%)
   • Neutral—14   (5%)
   • Agree—91   (32%)
   • Strongly agree—173   (62%)

Q11—I would recommend your services/use it again.
   (Appendix B, Figure 13)
   • Mean = 4.923   Confidence interval = 4.187—4.399
   • Strongly disagree—8   (3%)
   • Disagree—4   (1%)
   • Neutral—24   (9%)
   • Agree—106   (38%)
   • Strongly agree—138   (49%)
   • Harness events: (Appendix B, Figure 2)
   N = 280   • GROUP 1—Participants—226   (81%)
               • GROUP 2—Non-participants—54   (19%)

I decided to do a cross tabulation to see if a significant difference existed between the experience of the harness event participants and the non-participants. To do this, I used an F-Test. I checked the yes/no answers of the harness event question against the responses to questions one through eleven.

Hypothesis: In comparing the group that did the harness events with the group that did not do the harness events, there will be no significant difference in their perceptions of the Ropes Course.

I looked for an alpha level of .05 or lower to tell whether or not there was a significant difference in the perceptions of the two groups. In nine out of eleven questions there was a significant difference between the perceptions of the two groups. Those who participated in the harness events expressed more satisfaction with the program overall. I therefore rejected the null hypothesis. To measure the significant differences between perceptions, I looked at the mean answer for each group for each question (1–11).

TABLE 1. Significant Differences in Perceptions Between Harness Event Participants and Non-Participants

Question #	Group 1	Group 2	Significant Difference
1	3.94	3.59	Yes
2	4.02	3.65	Yes
3	4.02	3.72	Yes
4	4.06	3.78	Yes
5	4.14	4.06	No
6	3.57	3.26	Yes
7	3.29	3.13	No
8	4.64	4.37	Yes
9	4.64	4.30	Yes
10	4.61	4.28	Yes
11	4.35	4.06	Yes

I also wanted to see if there were any significant differences in the way men and women perceived the program. Again, I did a cross tabulation. This time I compared men and women's answers to each question (1–11). I also utilized an F-Test here to check for any significant differences between the two groups.

• GROUP 1 = Female—104   (37%)
• GROUP 2 = Male—176   (63%)

Hypothesis: There will be no significant difference between the way men and women view the Ropes Course.

Once again, I looked for an alpha level of .05 or lower to tell whether or not there was a significant difference between the perceptions of the two groups. To accomplish this, I looked at the mean answer for each group. I found that there was no significant difference in the way men and women viewed the program. I, therefore, rejected the null hypothesis.

TABLE 2. Significant Differences Between Men and Women's Perceptions of the Training Program

Question #	Group 1	Group 2	Significant Difference
1	3.85	3.92	No
2	3.93	3.97	No
3	3.97	3.94	No
4	4.05	3.94	No
5	4.12	4.13	No
6	3.47	3.58	No
7	3.26	3.26	No
8	4.56	4.64	No
9	4.55	4.62	No
10	4.53	4.57	No
11	4.27	4.34	No

Basic Findings

Based on this survey, I concluded that overall the participants had favorable opinions of the Ropes Course experiential learning experience. Moreover, I found that those who participated in the harness events (81%) expressed more satisfaction with the program as compared to those who did not participate (19%). To me, this was an indication that participants need assurance that they are truly safe, in order to enjoy the program. The harness seemed to play a crucial role as a physical sign of safety and security.

There was no significant difference between the perceptions of men and women who participated in the Ropes Course. This was an important finding because many corporate executives theorize that this type of outdoor learning experience would be distasteful to most women. On this note, however, the comments did indicate men and women who did not like the athletic prowess required (or at least perceived by the participants to be required) for the training.

TELEPHONE INTERVIEWS

Research Strategy

Six months after completion of the mail census questionnaire, I telephoned four of the respondents. I wanted to check to see if their impressions of the training had been altered by time. I called the participants at their homes in the evening. I did not want to call them at their offices for fear they might feel pressured in the office environment to give only favorable impressions. All four of the participants I selected had responded very positively to the training when they were first surveyed. I spoke to two women and two men. All of the telephone respondents listed their occupation under "managerial/executive."

Findings

The results of the telephone interviews, although a very small sampling, were enough to make me seriously doubt the benefits of this type of outdoor experiential training for corporate America. Not one of the four felt that the training had had any enduring positive change in their work performance or in their relationships at work. Linda T. summed up the experience this way, "If the company wanted to give us a thrill, they could have sent us to Great America a lot cheaper than this!" Bob B. said, "I wish the company would give me the money they waste on these types of activities!" I found this attitude surprising considering I spoke only to people who had responded very positively at the time of the survey. One woman said that she enjoyed the training and felt it had been a personal growth experience; she did not, however, feel that the training improved her relationships with her co-workers. Bob B. made another informative remark that I believe is quite revealing. Bob said that they were told the Ropes Training Course was a team building experience, yet the corporate climate at his company is completely against teamwork. He said the competition for promotions, raises, and good accounts pits the workers against each other every day. It is obvious that a short training course is not going to undo the corporate climate.

CONCLUSIONS AND RECOMMENDATIONS

Although the responses on the questionnaire were quite positive overall, I think the comments on the backs of the questionnaires (Appendix C— Comments) and the telephone interviews reveal some real problems with outdoor experiential learning.

Some of the comments spoke of fear and peer pressure. I am concerned that, with the best of intentions, companies may be causing their employees to experience physical and psychological trauma. It was clear to me that many people felt coerced. Do corporate employers have the right to make such activities mandatory? And are people's actions under such peer pressure genuine? I fear not. It is clear to me that even structured properly this training is *not* for everyone. I do not feel comfortable with management making such activities mandatory. I suggest that employees be given an orientation to the outdoor training. In this way, people could decide whether or not they would feel comfortable participating.

A proper orientation would also have the benefit of increasing the potential for learning. Many participants did not know what they were supposed to be deriving from the training. An orientation course would have solved this dilemma. Management needs to do a preliminary assessment of the participating work groups' or individual's needs and determine what benefits they hope to derive from the training. As I stated above, this training is simply not for everyone.

The companies that provide outdoor experiential learning, like Action Associates, must work closely with each corporate client. It is important for the experiential learning provider and the corporate client to set objectives. What does the corporate client hope to achieve with this training? Without established guidelines and direction, agreed upon by corporate client and provider, the chances are it will simply be a day of employee fun. And fun can be purchased for much less than these courses. As Linda T. stated in my telephone interview, "If the company wanted to give us a thrill, they could have sent us to Great America a lot cheaper than this!"

Finally, management must be willing to commit much more of their time and resources to preliminary and follow-up activites if outdoor experiential learning is to be successful. Management cannot simply send employees to outdoor training providers to be "fixed" in a brief training session. This also brings to mind the area of corporate climate. Management must realize that a mere training session will not foster a feeling of camaraderie and team among employees if the corporate climate is doggy-eat-dog.

In conclusion, outdoor experiential learning has possibilities if the following guidelines are followed:

GUIDELINES

1. Orientation meetings with key participants to calm fears, instill positive attitudes, and establish realistic expectations.

2. A preliminary assessment of the participating work group's or individual's needs and what they hope to accomplish with the training.
3. Ongoing tie-ins and metaphors linked to the work environment.
4. Carefully facilitated discussion among the participants during the course of the training.
5. Development of action plans before returning to the work place.
6. Follow-up by both the provider and the participants.
7. Commitment from top management. (Gall, 1988)

My secondary research has shown me that corporations in America are not following the guidelines above. Therefore, I would have to say that outdoor experiential training, currently, is not worth the cost. A day of employee fun at an amusement park, like Great America, would probably accomplish as much, and it would be cheaper!

Bibliography

Flaschner, Alan B, and Robert F. Hartley. *Essentials of Marketing Research.* Oklahoma: The PennWell Publishing Company, 1983.
Gallagan, Patricia. "Between Two Trapezes," *Training & Development,* (March 1988): 40–48.
Gall, Adrienne L. "You Can Take the Manager out of the Woods, but . . .", *Training & Development,* (March 1988): 54–59.
Long, Janet W. "The Wilderness Lab Comes of Age," *Training & Development,* (March 1988): 30–39.

Telephone Interviews

Bob B., age 48, male, manager, divorced
    November 18, 1988
Sharon L., age 31, female, manager, married
    November 21, 1988
John F., age 46, male, manager, married
    November 21, 1988
Linda T., age 38, female, manager, married
    November 22, 1988

APPENDIX A

Survey Questionnaire and Scale presented to the participants.

Age _____ Sex _____ Occupation _____

Date Course Was Taken _____
Please Circle Ropes Course location   1 = La Honda   2 = Other _____

ROPES COURSE SURVEY

This short questionnaire is designed to gather information about your opinions of the Ropes Course learning experience. Your responses will remain confidential and anonymous. Please answer the questions accordingly, based upon the following scale. Mark your answers in the spaces provided.

Strongly Disagree	Disagree	Neutral	Agree	Strongly Agree
1	2	3	4	5

Col.

1. The Ropes Course learning experience met my highest expectations.   _____ 20

2. The Ropes Course learning experience met my team's highest expectations.   _____ 21

3. Your services were appropriate to my needs.   _____ 22

4. Your services were appropriate to my team's needs.   _____ 23

5. The Ropes Learning Course had a positive impact in my relationship with the team. (ie, communication, support)   _____ 24

6. The Ropes Course has been a long lasting learning experience that has transferred to my own work environment.   _____ 25

7. The Ropes Course has been a long lasting learning experience that has transferred to my team's work environment. _____ 26

8. Your staff demonstrated experience.   _____ 27

9. Your staff demonstrated expertise.   _____ 28

10. Your staff demonstrated integrity.   _____ 29

11. I would recommend your service.   _____ 30

Did your group do harness/belayed events?
        1 = Yes   2 = No   _____ 31

Were you the project coordinator for your Ropes Course day?
        1 = Yes   2 = No   _____ 32

I am the one who financially authorized such a Ropes Course
training project.
       1 = Yes   2 = No   _____   33

Please make additional comments on back of questionnaire form.
If you have made any additional comments, may we have your
permission to use them in our publications?
       1 = Yes   2 = No   _____   34
If yes, please sign below.

Signature X _____   Date ___/___/___

Thank you for your help!

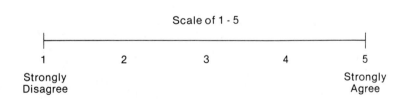

Scale of 1 - 5

1   2   3   4   5

Strongly   Strongly
Disagree   Agree

APPENDIX B

Graphs for Questions 1 through 11.

FIGURE 1. (Categorical Information)

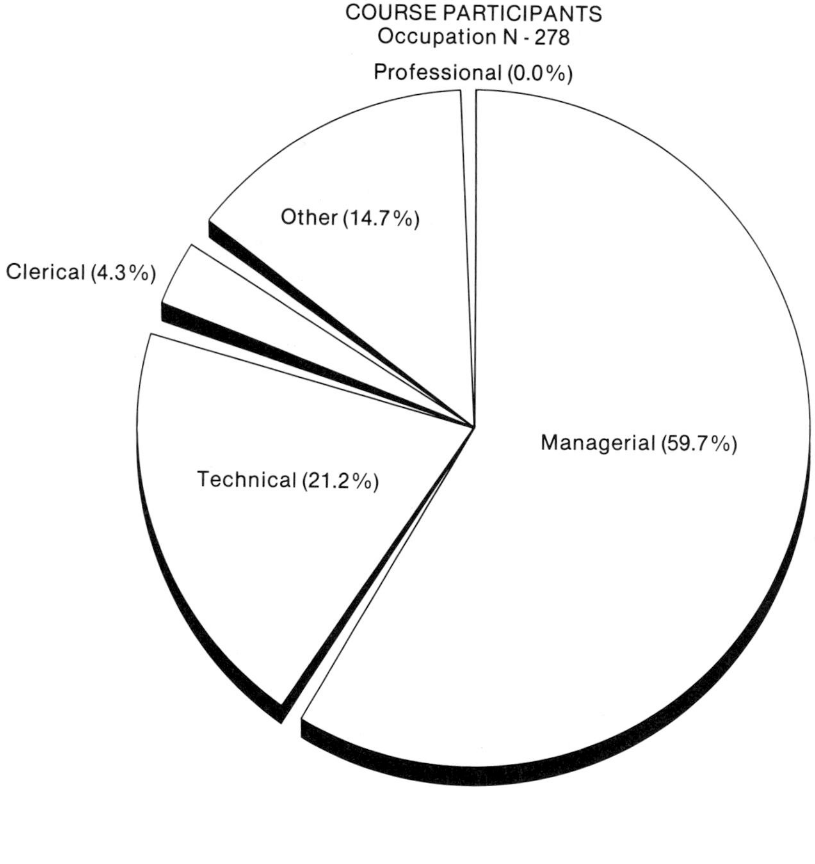

COURSE PARTICIPANTS
Occupation N - 278

FIGURE 2. (Categorical Information)

ACTION ASSOCIATES

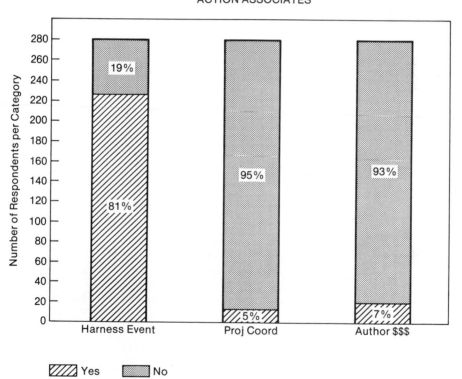

FIGURE 3. Question 1

ACTION ASSOCIATES

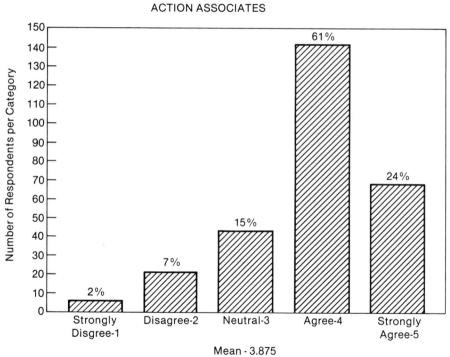

Mean - 3.875

FIGURE 4. Question 2

ACTION ASSOCIATES

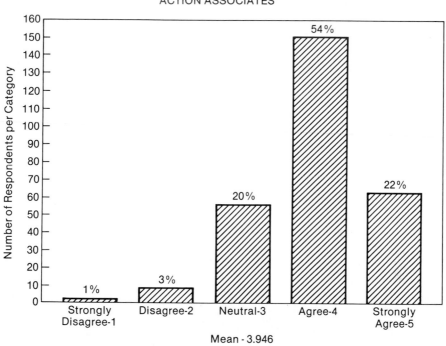

Mean - 3.946

FIGURE 5. Question 3

ACTION ASSOCIATES

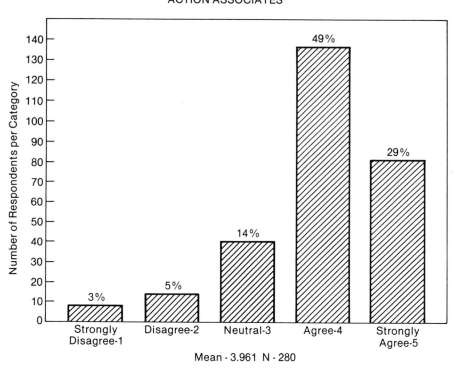

Mean - 3.961 N - 280

Approp To Needs - 1

FIGURE 6. Question 4

ACTION ASSOCIATES

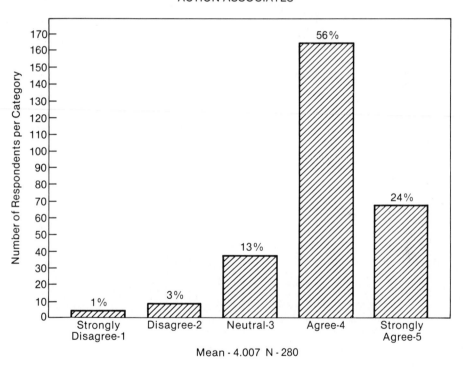

Mean - 4.007 N - 280

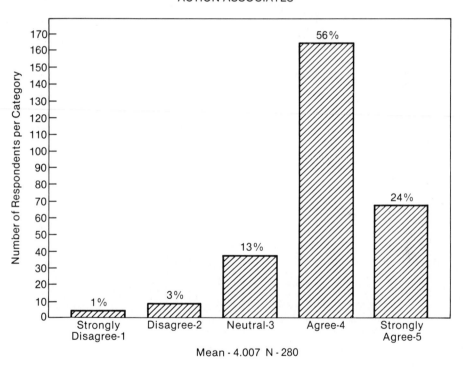 Approp To Needs - 2

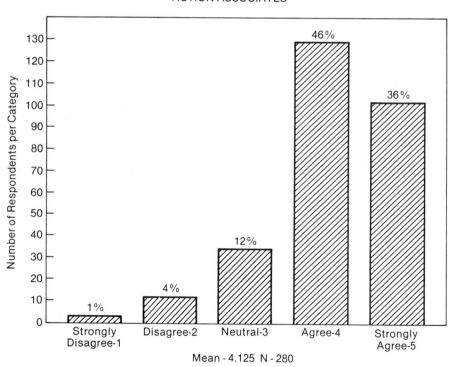

FIGURE 7. Question 5

ACTION ASSOCIATES

Mean - 4.125 N - 280

Positive Impact

FIGURE 8. Question 6

ACTION ASSOCIATES

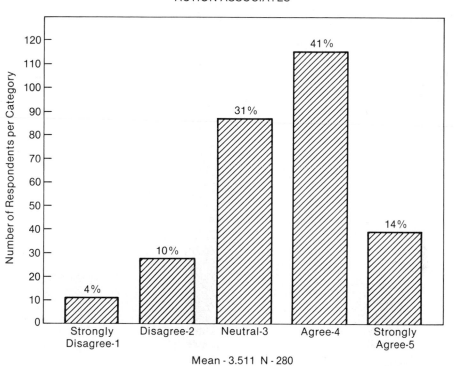

Mean - 3.511 N - 280

Long Lasting Exper.

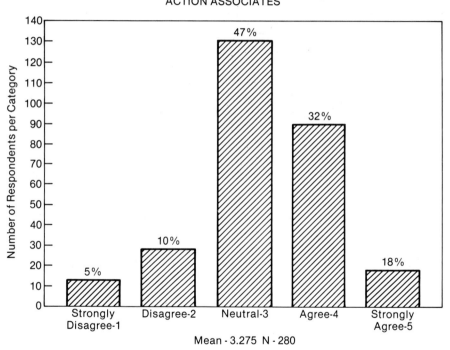

FIGURE 9. Question 7

ACTION ASSOCIATES

Mean - 3.275 N - 280

Long Lasting Exp - 2

FIGURE 10. Question 8

ACTION ASSOCIATES

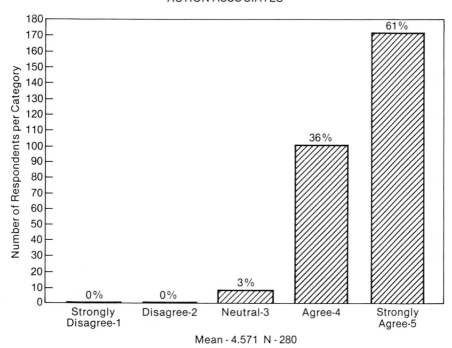

Mean - 4.571 N - 280

Staff - Expertise

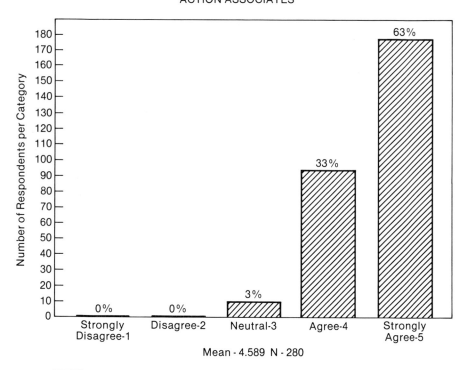

FIGURE 11. Question 9

ACTION ASSOCIATES

Mean - 4.589 N - 280

Staff - Experienced

FIGURE 12. Question 10

ACTION ASSOCIATES

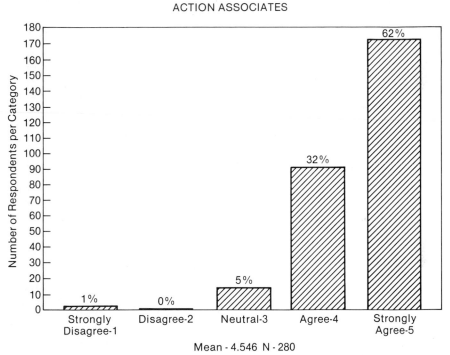

Mean - 4.546 N - 280

Staff - Integrity

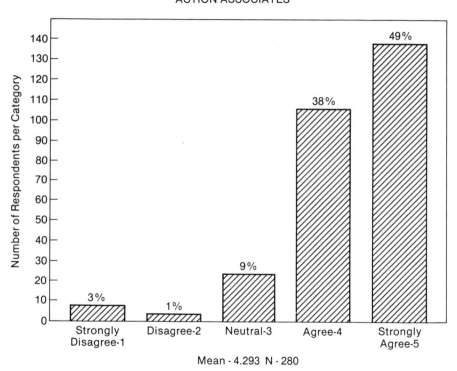

FIGURE 13. Question 11

ACTION ASSOCIATES

APPENDIX C

Comments from the participants. The comments are reproduced exactly as they appeared. No changes have been made to correct spelling, grammar, or punctuation.

*Asterisks indicate the comments where consent was given for Action Associates' use in publications or advertisements.

COMMENTS

Service/Benefit

*　An ongoing curriculum of 2–4 classes, each of 2 days duration, would be a helpful method of both reinforcing the learning, and integrating new employees into the group—I would appreciate more pro-active follow up marketing—

*　I recall hearing comments later such as: "It's the first time or opportunity that I really got a chance to know her. You know, she's really not such a bad person." "What a wasted day." "Great Experience!!" There were quite a few mixed viewpoints as to the value or lack there of on the day.

*　I felt the course was a great exercise in team effort to keep each other from physical harm and accomplish team goal. However I don't feel it helped to apply to our work environment. It did help relieve some of the job pressures for a few days and bring us together as a team.

*　The most interesting aspect of the day was the realization that our team was not operating as a unit. We were trying to solve a problem as a group of individuals. The ropes staff pointed this aspect out to us, and more importantly they asked us if we tended to also work as individuals without supporting one another. This was a major revelation. It's like the nose on your face that you over look. This lack of team work on the job realization was singularly worth the price of the whole day!

*　The ropes course not only related to team building, but is pertinent in individual confidence building.

For me the effect was seeing myself rather differently than I'd seen me before. In terms of team, I believe I saw an aspect of our team interaction through some of the activities but I really don't feel I gained any additional skill to make team interaction more effective and satisfying. I found the experience enriching but saw how for some it wasn't so I'm not sure I could enthusiactictly recommend this to others.

*　Working together as a team on the ropes course was a 1000 times more valuable than "talking" about teamwork in a seminar.

*　I did not feel it was a reflection on your course or staff, but I did not feel that the beam and ring exercises contributed in any way to a business application. I felt we wasted a half-day of an expensive seminar on this. It may have seen fun and interesting but not useful. On the other hand, the group exercises were applicable and helpful in letting us get to know each other and to see different management and coping styles in controlled situations. At very least, this portion of the program should have happened first.

I believe that the course helped me, individually unfortunately, I was hoping for more emphasis on team building that was lacking.

I didn't feel that it was a teamwork event. There were individual experiences that expanded my capabilities, but they were not a result of a teamwork exercise.

* The quality of this "team building" experience exceeded my expectations. The mental and physical exercises complimented each other. I left the courses with a head full of valuable learning experience, rather than a stack of literature to shove into my desk drawer. I strongly recommend it to others.

* This element of a one-week course was handled in an outstanding, professional fashion that also was great fun! My only reservation is that team learning could have been reinforced by some group discussion following each event.

* The Ropes Course was a marvelous allegory for the principles of teamwork and leadership; I would highly recommend the experience to any group—project team to upper management—which could benefit by better communication, cooperation, and achievement.

Use more pre-action discussion to enhance learning.

* The course put me on a first-name basis with co-workers who would not normally be met "informally." I now feel a physical as well as social comfort among previously intimidating managers. Consequently, I feel freer in my dealings, comfortable enough to express opinions which may be contrary to prevailing ones. This may not seem such a good thing but our organization is now under incredible pressure in a competitive business environment and unusual and creative solutions to old problems can be very valuable.

I am not any longer a part of the same team with whom I took the ropes course. Nevertheless, I feel that as a team-building exercise it was one of the best that I have seen. I have recommended it to my current business team but find resistance to try it. I'm beginning to sound like a stuck record—every time I hear the need for teamwork I say "Ropes Course." I know what individual resistance is about as I was very apprehensive, too. I believe what I have said here shows that apprehension unnecessary.

* For a one day experience, the course provided an excellent teaming environment. The opportunity for people to extend, trust, support and experience success individually, and as a team, made it very worth while. For some, the experience will provide the springboard to expand successes in life, and certainly, higher self-esteem.

To get more people involved I think there should have been another alternative to the pole/platform trapeez exercise.

* This experience has been one that will definately assist me in individual/team and professional/personal relationships for my lifetime! It was terrific. I would strongly recommend this training for any group of individuals who have a responsibility to move forward as a workgroup.

* The experience that every manager should go through to gain an insight into the inter relationships that exist in every facit of life. Communications of all types are to be understood, and respected. In a short, team leaders based on strengths where identified, clearly indicating that leaders of people change with knowledge and ability.

The Ropes course has been a experience that I would and do recommend to build understanding respect of individuals and their contribution in a highly physical (for some people) and challenging environment. Not dissimular to the challenges of life and business. "Thank you for the experience."
*   I thought the experience was a good one for demonstrating that teamwork is more effective than individual effort—the encouragement from others was very powerful.
    The lack of follow up course work is a problem, because this was a peak experience that faded over time. I don't see a good way to recommend that follow-ups be done—there doesn't seem to be a practical way to integrate this into on-site training.
    I did enjoy it very much, and would recommend it to others, because body experience is so much more powerful than mental training alone.
    The actual events were terrific and well worthwhile for my team. I have happily recommended your course to other departments in my company. I felt it to be more of a fun, challenging reward for my staff, rather than a deep learning experience.
*   My personal experience in the harness/belayed events approached some of my life's *great experiences*. The translation of those emotions into day-to-day living is a much more "challenging" experience.
*   I was some what concerned by inadequate medical attention considering strenuous nature of events and peer pressure causing inadvisable behaviour.
    I found you course stimulating and an excellent team building exercise.
*   We used the ropes course in conjuntion with a "breakthrough thinking" course the following day. We had 2 follow-up "breakthrough thinking" sessions. This increased the effectiveness of the team's ropes experience.
    The team had a wonderful experience—it was talked about for many weeks, and actually increased teamwork on the project.
*   The rope course provided me the opportunity to learn about my fears and confidence levels. It provided insight into my strength as an individual and as a <u>participating</u> group member. Great Experience!
*   I found the Ropes Course to meet my personal and professional challenges, however, many of my teammates were not willing to meet the challenges. I believe this was partially due to the fact they were not forewarned in any way of what to expect. It would have been/caused more productive teambuilding and bonding if only those who truly wanted to participate did so.
*   If I seem somewhat neutral in my reactions, it's less due to any deficiency in the course content or execution, but rather is more a reflection of my company's work environment. As individuals, I think everyone in the group had a chance to experience dealing with some type of fear. For some, it was the physical and mental challenge of the events. For others like my-

self who have been with groups in real potentially life-threatening situations (while climbing, of course), the chance to test one's ability to suppress fear of failure in front of one's peers was intriguing. As seems to usually be the case, the people who expected the least probably took home the most.

The course did help bring some of the fringe people into the team. However, most of these people have since left the company. The people outside the team who would have benefited the most were also the people who failed to show for the course. Unfortunately, this is something over which you obviously have no control. It might however pay to stress to the company organizer that the persons whose participation is most required. Along the same lines, it is also valuable encourage those unable to participate in the athletic events to least come along for the hike. We had one severely overweight person who came along, took pictures, cheered us on, and by vicariously living through the events, obtained as much individual and group satisfaction as the rest of the participants.

* I feel that the course helped bring out the ability of the individual in accomplishing a task that was totaly alien to their nature. It promoted team building among all of us, and a respect for others in that they relied up you to help them through their fears. Very important part of building a good relationship with your fellow co-workers.

Teamwork continue in the Business environment, however, some have let it die. Business pressures frequently override the relationships we established.

* The course was not voluntary for my group; attendance was mandatory. Rumors about it caused significant anxiety among the less athletic in our group.

I myself was rather out of shape, and somwhat anxious about my back. I've had several herniated discs, and surgery about five years ago.

But my negative reaction was more intellectual than physical. I am sceptical about "miracle new approaches", and the presentation about "Ropes" failed many of the tests I put to such ideas.

I tried hard (but unsuccessfully) to hide my scepticism and "play along".

My initial assessment was not changed by the course.

I stand by my assessment: the course had a few good ideas, a few good messages, and some good team building. But not enough to justify all of the hoopla.

One aspect disquieted me a lot. In any group, there are likely to be a few genuine acrophobes. Ours was no exception (I'm not one of them).

The group pressure on our acrophobes reminded me of the pressure which lures kids into drugs and other illegal activity. I wanted to shout "Just say no!" I didn't, though, and I am ashamed of myself.

Learning, I assert, need not strip us of our dignity.

I believe the bonding would have been stronger if we had used your facilities—more challenges/more rewards.

The ropes course we attended was a regional sales meeting. We were not told where we were going or what we would be doing so their really were no expectations to be met. A very strong attempt was made to tie the learning experiences of each event to a sales situation and "break thru thinking." Long term I believe this correlation has failed for two reasons.

1) To substantially forge teams and change established behavior patterns, groups of people must be subjected to stress and strange surroundings and events for a longer period of time than we allocated.

2) Tektronix as a company did not follow thru and reinforce their commitment to break thru thinking. Clearly, these two items are beyond the direct control of Action Associates.

Personally, I enjoyed the experience and learned some truths I had previously only paid lip service to.

1) The worst that can happen if you try is to break even.

2) Seemingly overwhelming tasks are actually quite easy, if you take it one step at a time and pay attention to the present not the future.

Like we say in AA—there are no big deals!

Thank you for you time and I hope to meet you again.

The ropes course taught teamwork skills and interpersonal problem solving as I've never before experienced. Learning to support as-well-as lead, learning to encourage as-well-as direct, the ropes course balances the teamwork equation.

* I left the company shortly after taking the course. The morning was dull as dog shit—the afternoon was excellent and the 60 foot climb, to walk across a small log will never be forgotten!

■ THE WRITER'S ASSIGNMENT

Using standard business report format, write a report using primary and secondary sources on some issue challenging American business.   ■

■ UNDERSTANDING WRITING STRATEGIES

1. What is outdoor experiential training, and what is it designed to do for companies with large work forces? According to the author, are these programs successful?

2. Describe the methodology used to collect and analyze information used in this report.

3. How objective is the author's methodology? What indicates this?

4. What is the thesis the report seeks to prove? Where is this thesis proven?

5. Are the conclusions the author reaches reasonable based on the data reported? Why or why not?

6. Do you agree with the interpretation of data (including the telephone interviews)? Why or why not?

7. To make outdoor experiential training more effective, what guidelines does the author suggest? Why?

8. This report contains complex statistical data. How clearly is the information presented? What affects this clarity?

9. Why does the author place the information she does in the appendices? How useful is this information? ■

■ **SUGGESTIONS FOR WRITING**

Write a memorandum to the president of your company recommending whether or not your company should adopt outdoor experiential training. Use Frings's report as a source, but be certain to relate her findings to your own company's needs. (Please design your own company.) ■

Employee Turnover at Kragen Auto Parts
William F. Goodwin

Seeking a change in management design, William Goodwin's report analyzes Kragen Auto Parts's management hierarchy, establishes the hierarchy's effect on management dissatisfaction, and proposes a course of action to the company's personnel director. Despite the apparently "real" audience, this report fulfills a writing requirement for an administrative communication course.

RELIANCE RESEARCH, INC.
38163 Parkmont Drive
Fremont, California 94536
November 30,1988
(415) 793-0592

Mr. Dan Siewart III
Personnel Director
Kragen Auto Parts
1507 Charcot Avenue
San Jose, California 94717

Dear Mr. Siewart:

Attached are the results of a study on employee turnover you requested at our meeting on November 2, 1988. This report is based on the ideas of leading behavioral scientists and managerial theorists.

The purpose of the study is to:

* determine the cause of the high turnover rate among senior employees.

* determine the cause for the high rate of voluntary demotion among in-store management.

* to provide definitive actions to be taken.

The central problem here (and all of the other problems that derive from it), stems from the tall, centralized structure of the management hierarchy. Flattening the structure and improving communication is the solution.

The main limitation in the study was the lack of sufficient time to completely research the problem. Additional comparisons and correlations could have been examined to test the findings in this report.

I am confident the information in this report will help you maintain your workforce and improve the prospects of future employees. If you have any questions or desire a more thorough study, feel free to contact me anytime.

Cordially yours,

William F. Goodwin
Chief Researcher

EXAMINATION OF

EMPLOYEE TURNOVER

IN

KRAGEN AUTO PARTS

Submitted

to

Dan Siewart III

Personnel Director

Kragen Auto Parts

Submitted

by

William F. Goodwin

Chief Researcher

Reliance Research Inc.

November 30, 1988

CONTENTS

SUMMARY

Despite the success Kragen Auto Parts has achieved in the last eight years, the company's senior employees have become increasingly dissatisfied. Their dissatisfaction is demonstrated by the high rate of turnover and voluntary demotion among them. (See Appendix A which graphically represents the turnover rate over the last eight years.)

The problem is the loss of the senior employees who have the most experience and training. Many of these employees have reached in-store management levels and are dropping down to clerk status. They are now being replaced by employees with less experience and training. The repercussions of this trend have finally begun to be noticed. The increase in customer complaints is a prime indicator. The effects will only intensify as time goes on unless changes are made.

The problems affecting the employees all stem from a basic problem in the structure of the management hierarchy—it is too tall and greatly impedes the flow of information. A change in the structure of the management hierarchy is, therefore, the primary step to take in solving these problems. The change would allow communication to move more freely in all directions, and it will allow individuals and departments to work with each other instead of against or through one another.

Immediate action should be taken to prevent any further damages to the company. The changes prescribed will help the company become more efficient, and as a result, more profitable.

CONCLUSIONS

1. There is a high rate of employee turnover and voluntary demotion among the senior employees. This is due to their dissatisfaction with the company.
2. The senior employees are being replaced by younger employees with less experience. As a result, customers have become increasingly dissatisfied with the service.
3. Dissatisfied customers will begin to shop at the competitors' stores, and there will be a resulting loss in income.
4. The main step in alleviating these problems is to change the structure of the management hierarchy—to make it more flat so information can flow more freely between departments, and between levels of management. This will bring all levels closer to one another and the focus of each other's goals will become much clearer.

RECOMMENDATIONS

1. Immediate action should be taken to flatten the management hierarchy. This will physically bring the groups closer together, and it

will provide a shorter, more direct path for information to flow between levels and departments.

2. Give the store managers a direct channel to the president. Allow them to air their ideas and opinions regarding decisions being made. This will simultaneously increase the employees' feeling of worth and decrease the workload on upper management.

INTRODUCTION

Background Information

When Kragen Auto Parts started some thirty years ago it was a privately owned store. The owner, Al Kragen, was also the store manager. Even though he began to open up new stores, the management structure remained fairly flat. A diagram of the original structure is presented below in Figure 1. Note that there were only two levels present: president/owner and store managers. Also note that the two were directly linked to one another. Because they were so closely linked, communication was quick and easy. Vertical flow of information was cut to a minimum by the short vertical distance between top and bottom levels. This is important because it has been found that vertically flowing information tends to be more threatening when coming from the top downward, and it tends to be less accurate when flowing from the bottom upward (Rogers & Rogers, 1976). Downward communication is perceived as more threatening because the messages conveyed are often demanding and impersonal. Upward communication is not very accurate because subordinates tend to tell their superiors what they want to hear and will avoid communicating what they think upper management does not want to hear.

FIGURE 1. Kragen's Management Structure, circa 1960.

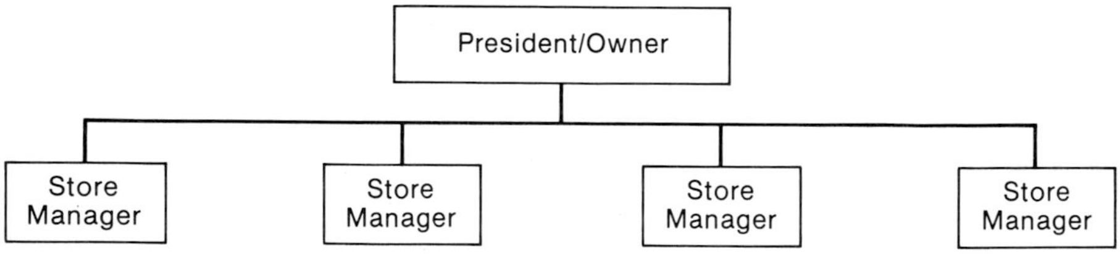

Source: Company Files

Horizontal communication is more frequently used than vertical communication in organizational settings since people feel more open and free communicating with peers than with superiors and subordinates (Downs, 1967). Because peers share a common frame of reference, message distortion is less likely (Steers, 1988).

In recent years, Kragen's has grown rapidly. Many activities once carried out by Al Kragen are now done by entire departments of people. The management hierarchy has grown as large and complex as the company. As you can see in Figure 2, there are no longer two levels of management, but rather, several. The structure is highly centralized—that is, the decisions are still made at the top. But, there is little, if any chance for feedback by the store managers who are usually the ones most affected by the decisions.

FIGURE 2. Segment of Kragen's Management Structure, 1988.

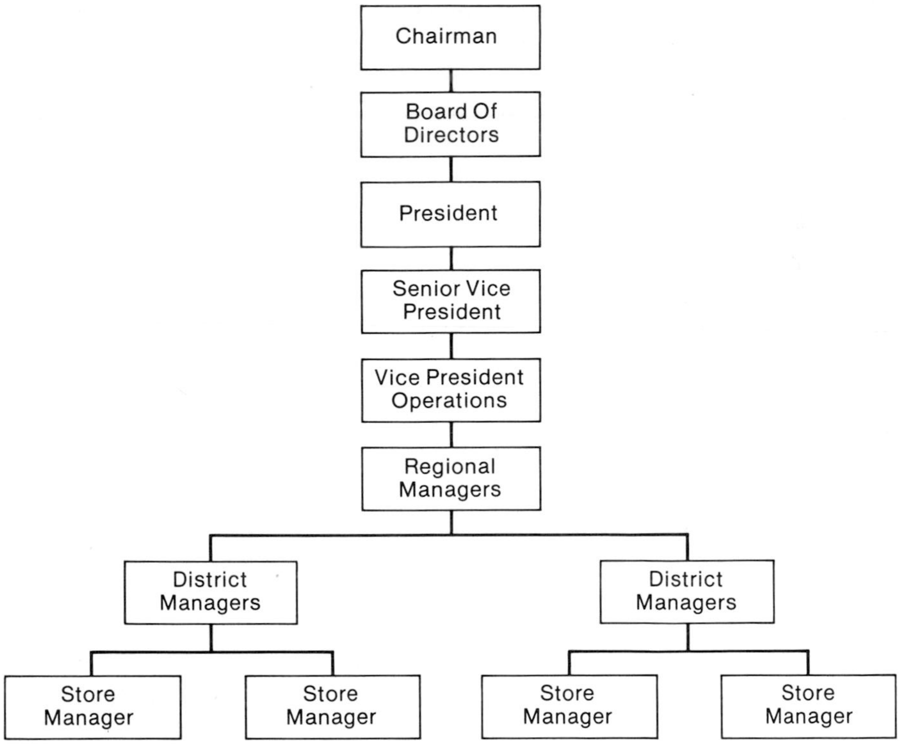

Source: Company Files

Central Problem

The main problem affecting Kragen Auto Parts today is the high turnover rate of its senior employees. This is a critical problem because the company is losing its most experienced workers, and they must be replaced. Unfortunately, it is forced to replace them with less experienced, and often untrained employees. This decreases the company's efficiency because the new employees do not have the benefit of on the job training under skilled, experienced salespeople. The less they know to begin with, the less they can help the customers. This problem is compounded by the fact that these new employees must immediately assume the role of the senior clerks. This includes training new employees—a difficult thing to do since they did not receive proper training themselves. One can easily see the domino effect created by this situation.

In order to increase employee and customer satisfaction, action must be taken to keep the senior clerks from quitting or stepping down in rank. To do this, changes must be made in the hierarchical structure to allow them more voice in the decisions that affect them. This would entail flattening the structure and decentralizing the authority.

Research Limitations

Careful attention was payed to the choice of theories used to describe the phenomenon taking place. However, because of the time constraint, a complete study was not possible.

An important concept to be investigated would be to see if there is a correlation between the exodus of senior employees and the simultaneous drop in unemployment. If could be concluded that the increase in other available jobs is the reason for employees' quitting. However, it does not explain those who have taken a voluntary demotion from a management position to a clerk.

It would also be advantageous to search for another firm with similar demographics as Kragen's, but with a flatter, more decentralized structure. Then a comparison study could be done to see if the difference in structure leads to a difference in employee satisfaction. This would be the best way to test the hypothesis put forth in this report. These concepts would be thoroughly examined in a study of more depth and time.

ANALYSIS

Structure and the Flow of Communication

Put in simplest terms, the taller the structure, the slower the flow of information. The most obvious reason is that there are so many different levels that the message must go through to get from the top to the bottom and vice versa. Figures 1 and 2 illustrate this concept very well. In Figure 1 there are only two levels. Communication was rapid during this period. The group meetings Al Kragen had with the store managers were the vehicles used to exchange information. Because of the closeness of the two levels, these meetings were comfortable and effective. According to A. D. Szilagyi, an expert in the field of behavioral science, the group meeting is among the most effective methods of communication from the standpoint of both parties involved. (See Appendix B which lists and ranks the most effective methods for upward and downward communication.)

In the present structure, the president is far removed from the store managers. Although there are monthly meetings between the president and the regional managers; between the regional managers and the district managers; and between the district managers and the store managers, there are seldom any group meetings with the president and the store managers both in attendance. In fact, such meetings have occurred only six times in the last eight years. To further the point, the company's implementation of bulletin boards, pay envelope inserts, suggestion forms, and the employee newsletter as effective means of communication is really ineffective. The study by Szilagyi ranks these techniques among the poorest in effectiveness. But, under the present structure, these are the most convenient.

Also, the tall structure inhibits an upward flow of information. Store managers often feel there is too much red tape between them and the upper management, and they do not even try to communicate upward. This is detrimental because the upward flow of information is the only internal, accurate source of feedback from the store level.

Many of the senior employees have begun to feel as if they have no say in their job. This feeling has led them to quit or put themselves in a position where they have as little responsibility as possible. This is a problem that could have been avoided for the most part by integrating and flattening the structure to bring all of the groups closer together.

Structure and Centralization of Power

The taller the management hierarchy, the more centralized is the authority. Kragen's is highly centralized—all of the decisions are made at the top. Again, a problem arises because of the great distance between the president and the store managers. The impact of decisions made at the top almost always affect the store managers the most. But, the structure does not allow them into the decision-making process—a mistake, because the store managers often have more first-hand knowledge of an idea being tested by upper management. Allowing them to feed back information will help the company as well as give them a sense of worth and achievement.

The rationale behind a flatter, more decentralized structure is best summed up by Michael H. Mescon, management theorist at Georgia State University:

- Extremely large organizations cannot be managed centrally because of the quantity of information required and the resulting complexity of decision making.
- Decentralization gives decision-making authority to the manager closest to the situation and therefore most knowledgeable of its details.
- Decentralization stimulates initiative and identification with the organization. Under decentralization the largest full unit of organization is small enough for its manager to fully understand, fully

control, and feel part of. The manager, thus, may feel the same enthusiasm for his or her unit that an independent entrepreneur feels for his or her own business.

- Decentralization helps train younger managers for top posts by exposing them to making important decisions early in their career.
- Since the distance from the bottom to the top is shorter, decentralization encourages the aggressive young manager to stay with the firm and advance within it.

The basic right every individual wants to exercise in their life is the right to make the decisions that affect them. People build up frustration when decisions regarding their life or their job are made by someone else. When the frustration becomes too much they do something to relieve it. In the case of the senior employees, they either quit and look for a job where they feel they will have more control, or they demote themselves to a position where they do not expect to have any say in decision making.

ACTIONS

Recommended Courses of Action

The primary recommendation for retaining the senior employees is to flatten the structure to make it a more decentralized organization in which communication travels easily and is encouraged. The easiest and fastest way to flatten the structure is to combine some of the middle management departments like Inventory, Shipping & Receiving, and Advertising into one separate level under the control of one manager. This allows for better horizontal communication between these departments—resulting in fewer mistakes, and thus, fewer complaints by both employees and customers. Figure 3 shows an example of a flattened structure applicable to Kragen's. The arrows indicate a direct channel of communication that employees are encouraged to use. This action helps flatten the structure without adjusting so much the physical make-up of the hierarchy. The senior vice president can be pulled from between the president and the regional managers and concentrate more time and effort on the other middle management departments. Having one person coordinate these departments will increase their efficiency as a team.

Also highly recommended is allowing the store managers to examine executive decisions, and to voice their opinion before any decisions are made. This will not only make the employees more satisfied, but it will make the entire organization more efficient.

A final recommendation is to examine the techniques for effective communication in Appendix B, and try to utilize the most effective methods possible. The most direct and effective is a regularly scheduled informal meeting between the president and the store managers; one that occurs at least bi-monthly.

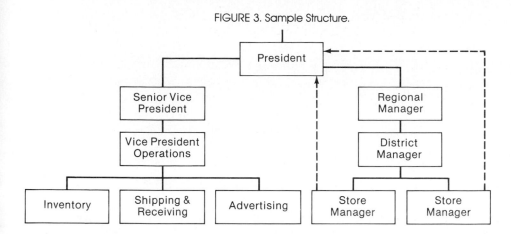

FIGURE 3. Sample Structure.

Source: Primary

Fiscal Impact of Recommended Actions

The actions prescribed here do not entail expensive changes in store design or inventory. Nor do they call for the addition or deletion of any departments. All that is really needed is a reshuffling of departments and chains of command to make the overall structure as flat as possible. This will allow an unrestricted atmosphere of communication. Under such conditions, many of the senior employees would be retained. This would give the next generation of employees the chance to be properly trained by experienced co-workers.

APPENDIX A

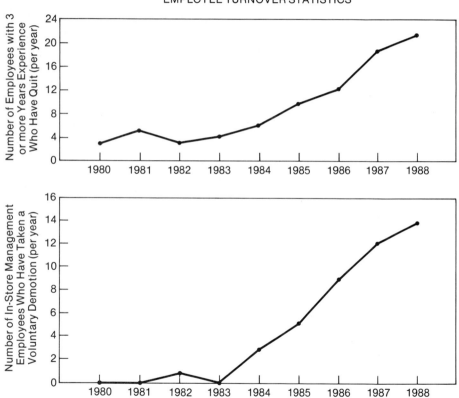

EMPLOYEE TURNOVER STATISTICS

APPENDIX B

EFFECTIVE COMMUNICATION TECHNIQUES

Rank	Upward Communication Techniques
1	Informal discussion
2	Meeting with supervisors
3	Attitude surveys
4	Grievance procedures
5	Counseling
6	Exit interviews
7	Union representatives
8	Formal meetings
9	Suggestion boxes
10	Employee newsletter

Rank	Downward Communication Techniques
1	Small group meeting
2	Direct organizational publications
3	Supervisory meetings
4	Mass meetings
5	Letters to employees' homes
6	Bulletin boards
7	Pay envelope inserts
8	Public address system
9	Posters
10	Annual reports, manuals, media advertising

Bibliography

Downs, A. *Inside Bureaucracy.* (1967): 377–385.

Mescon, Michael H. *Management.* (1988): 371–372.

Rogers, E. M., and Rogers, R. A. *Communicating in Organizations.* (1976): 95.

Steers, Richard M. *Introduction to Organizational Behavior.* (1988): 377–392.

Szilagyi, A. D., and Wallace, M. J. *Organizational Behavior and Performance.* (1983): 168–170.

Company Files: Personnel and Public relations.

■ THE WRITER'S ASSIGNMENT

Using conventional business report format, prepare an analysis of a business's management with recommendations for changes. ■

■ UNDERSTANDING WRITING STRATEGIES

1. According to Goodwin, what is the primary cause of management turnover at Kragen Auto Parts?

2. Does the information Goodwin provides confirm his hypothesis for management turnover? What other conclusions might be reached from this evidence?

3. What changes does Goodwin advocate to correct Kragen's management problems? What reasons does he offer supporting these changes?

4. How relevant is the discussion of communication flow to Goodwin's analysis of the company?

5. How clearly and completely does Goodwin present Kragen's structure and problems? How well are these related to his theoretical materials?

6. For what audience is this written? What parts of this report would be most useful to this audience?

7. What parts of this report seem inappropriate for its audience? Why?

8. Review the "Appendices" to this report. Is this information relevant? What are the advantages of putting this information in appendices rather than in the body of the report? ■

■ SUGGESTIONS FOR WRITING

Compare this report with those by Barnickel and Frings. Write a pamphlet for business students on writing effective business reports. Consider style, format, and purpose. ■

Recommendation for Investment in Common Stocks

Glenn Homesley

Writing for a business management course, Glenn Homesley here writes a position paper recommending an investment strategy for a company's stock portfolio. Since this would be an "in-house" communication, he uses the form for an interdepartmental memo.

SENTRY INCOME GROWTH FUND
2010 Capital Boulevard
Dallas, TX 75222

To: Mr. Tracy McFarland
          Portfolio Management Supervisor

From: Glenn Homesley
          Investment Analyst

Date: October 10 1988

Subject: Recommendation for Investment in Common Stocks

RECOMMENDATION

As you requested, I have researched common stocks to include in our mutual fund portfolio. I used investment service reports and business periodicals to select two securities which I believe will meet our objectives of maximum growth and a high rate of return on current income.

I recommend investing 63 percent of our portfolio in Pfizer Inc., which has a high dividend yield and will provide our shareholders with current income. Thirty-two percent of our portfolio should be invested in COMPAQ Computer which is experiencing a strong growth trend in earnings and will give us high capital gains through price appreciation. Five percent of our portfolio assets should be held in cash to give us enough liquidity to carry out transactions.

PFIZER INC. (PFE)

I selected Pfizer Inc. as the fund's income stock because of its high dividend yield and superior dividend growth. *Moody's Handbook of Common Stocks* (1988) lists PFE as one of its dividend achievers. Moody's reports that PFE's dividends have increased 13.8 percent per year over the last 20 years (*Moody's*, 1988, p. DA3). The following graph shows the annual increase in dividends per share for the past five years:

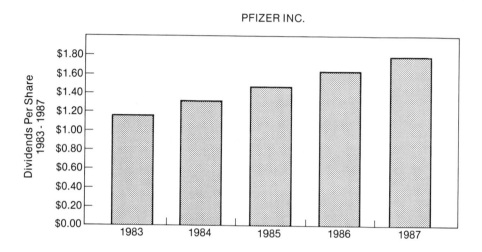

PFIZER INC.

The dividend for 1988 was increased to $2.00 per share. At a current share price of $50.50 this results in 4 percent dividend yield, which is 0.6 percent above the most recent S&P 500 index yield. An increase in the quarterly dividend is also likely in early 1989 (*Standard & Poor's NYSE Stock Reports*, 1988, p. 1810).

COMPAQ COMPUTER (CPQ)

I recommend investing in COMPAQ because of its high potential for growth. CPQ's net sales have increased 143 percent from 1985 to 1987. Earnings per share are estimated to be $5.20 this year, up 45 percent from 1987, and are projected to be $6.25 in 1989 (*SEP*, 1988, p. 596C). These gains in sales and earnings have helped CPQ's share price increase from an average of $11.60 in 1983, the first year CPQ's stock was listed on the exchange, to $48.87 in 1987. The share price also reached an all time high of $78.50 last year. The following graph shows CPQ's average price per share for the last five years.

COMPAQ COMPUTER

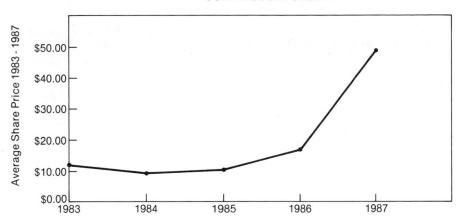

PORTFOLIO DISTRIBUTION

To achieve our objectives of current income and growth while limiting the fund to two securities. I recommend the following portfolio diversification.

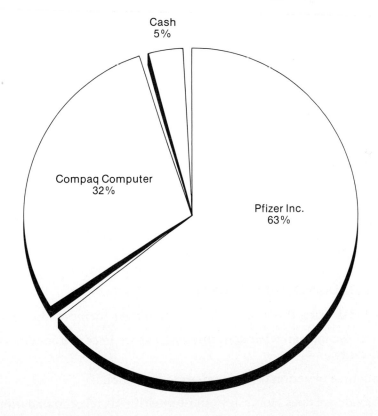

I feel that our shareholders will use our mutual fund as a source of income, so I would invest most of our assets in Pfizer. With a beta of 0.99 (*S&P*, 1988, p. 1810), Pfizer is also a safe stock and we shouldn't expect large unexpected changes in its price which might erode our principal investment.

Putting approximately 32 percent of our assets in COMPAQ will provide us with the required growth without cutting into our shareholders current income. I would also hesitate to invest more than this in COMPAQ right now because it is a volatile stock and present market conditions are very uncertain.

Finally, I would leave the rest of our assets in cash and short-term marketable securities. I feel that five percent would give us enough liquidity to carry out routine transactions without seriously decreasing our total rate of return.

CONCLUSION

Judging from the research I have done, I believe that this is the best investment strategy to follow. I feel that this portfolio will give us the best total return if current trends continue. Please consider this recommendation and let me know if you approve.

Reference List

Dun & Bradstreet. (1988). *Moody's Handbook of Common Stocks.* (Spring). DA3-DA20. New York: Dun & Bradstreet.

Standard & Poor's Corp. (1988). *Standard & Poor's NYSE Reports,* 55 (160), 596C, 1810 New York: Standard & Poor's Corp.

■ THE WRITER'S ASSIGNMENT

Write a two- to three-page memo recommending a feasible course of action justified by evidence. Use memo format with content-specific headings and include two secondary sources cited in-text. ■

■ UNDERSTANDING WRITING STRATEGIES

1. From considering this essay, what characterizes memorandum format?

2. Ignoring the format, what does this essay share in common with conventional essays?

3. What course of action does the memo recommend?

4. What evidence does Homesley offer to justify his recommendation?

5. What do the graphs and charts contribute to the essay? Where are they described in the text?

6. Precision and brevity are key elements in business communication. How effectively has Homesley exercised these attributes?

7. Would expanding this memo make it more or less effective? Why? ■

Discrimination in the United States Tax System: Punishing the Poor for Being Poor

David E. Leathers

David Leathers, an accounting student, presents this position paper identifying inequities in taxation and recommending changes in the tax code in business report format for an administrative communication course.

TABLE OF CONTENTS

EXECUTIVE SUMMARY

The United States tax system unfairly treats the low income earner in the following ways:

- The federal government's minimum survival level income not subject to tax is too low.
- Most federal and state tax deductions require a large income.
- The sales tax increases the poor's overall tax rate at too fast a pace.
- The social security tax takes away money needed immediately. The low income earner cannot afford to wait until age 65 to collect.

Tax measures must incorporate the needs of all the citizens and treat each one fairly. Low income earners may be paying their share, but that is more than they can afford.

Congress has been working toward tax reform, but they have not gone far enough toward a fair system. They seem to be moving in two directions at once. They are progressing forward by increasing the capital gains tax and eliminating some of the tax shelters, but they are falling behind by lowering the upper level income tax rates.

The tax system could be improved by implementing the following:

- Eliminate the sales tax in most cases
- Double the standard deduction
- Limit use of tax incentives for the wealthy
- Eliminate the interest deduction for second mortgages
- Limit the interest deduction on primary mortgages over $200,000

INTRODUCTION

Discrimination against various income groups is incorporated in the body of the United States tax system. The concepts of progressive and regressive taxes will be discussed to demonstrate exactly who is paying how much. Ethical questions, such as whether or not the poor should be taxed and who gains the benefit of taxation, will also be dealt with.

This discussion will be limited to personal taxes (including federal income tax, state income tax, social security tax, and sales tax).

DISCUSSION

Ability to Pay

Dean Erwin Griswold of Harvard Law School, in an article in the *Atlantic Monthly* (1952), noted that "ability to pay" has been the principal justification for a progressive tax system. (Taubman, 1978).

A progressive tax system is one in which those who earn more income pay a higher rate of taxes than those who earn less. A straight tax imposes the same rate on everyone, and a regressive tax (opposite of the progressive tax) charges a higher rate to the poor than the rich. The concept of "ability to pay" has always been important in the United States. We consider it proper to tax those who can afford taxes more than those who cannot afford it.

The poverty line was invented to aid the theory. It marks the minimal survival income level. This income level must be protected, and any income above this line is available for taxation.

Protected Income

The Internal Revenue Code of the United States (IRC, 1988) has set limits which cannot be taxed called the standard deduction. The amount which is not subject to taxation is subtracted from net income to arrive at taxable income. The standard deduction amount depends on the classification of the taxpayer.

$3,000	single individuals
$5,000	married couples
$4,400	single heads of households

The code also allows personal and dependency exemptions of $1,950 per person. The taxpayer can deduct a personal exemption for himself and all individuals classified as dependents of the taxpayer. Dependents generally include the spouse, children, and elderly parents supported by the taxpayer.

For example, a single mother with one dependent child has been granted a reprieve of $8,300 (4400 + 1950 + 1950). This income is the level below which the government considers improper to tax—at least improper to tax directly.

The current standard deduction amounts are not high enough. A single individual living alone earning $4,950 (3000 + 1950) would not be able to pay for food, clothing, and the rent. This income is clearly below the sustenance level and should not be taxed.

An argument has been made that if the poor are not taxed they would not feel they have contributed their share toward the operation of the government. To counter this, a poor tax of $15 dollars should be imposed just like the board game Monopoly. A foolish argument deserves a foolish answer, but we shall see that the poor are paying in other ways besides the income tax.

Social Security

President Roosevelt started the Social Security Tax in 1935. This tax is not subject to the standard deduction. Even extremely low income earners must pay this tax of seven percent. The justification for this straight tax is that it really is not a tax but a retirement plan. The money is an investment for the future and will be returned with interest upon the individual's retirement at age 65. In this vein, the government decided that this tax should not be imposed on income above $45,000. These taxpayers probably do not need the benefits of social security, so why should they pay for a retirement plan they do not need?

For the low income earner, the Social Security Tax is a great financial burden. The security of having an income after age 65 is very important to some, but the money is needed right now. With $4,950 a year to spend there is very little room for such luxuries as retirement benefits, and for a family of four, earning $12,800 a year is not enough for food, clothing, and the rent.

Sales Tax

The next culprit is the sales tax. This tax is doubly abusive. Like the social security tax, it is a straight tax. But unlike the social security tax, it has a strongly regressive element. The poor pay a higher rate because they spend a larger percentage of their income on goods subject to the tax than do high income earners. There is no sales tax on investment purchases whether they are stocks and bonds or gold bars. So far the government has not chosen to tax most food items, but there are other items of importance, such as clothing, which they do tax.

The Internal Revenue code also discriminates against some states by not allowing taxpayers to deduct sales tax against their net income. States such as Oregon do not have sales tax. They collect entirely through income and property taxes both of which are entirely deductible. Taxpayers of California do not get this benefit so their net real tax rates are higher.

Income Tax Deductions

The tax code is riddled with deductions which low income earners cannot hope to receive. The government refers to them as tax breaks or incentives. Only high income taxpayers can benefit. Home mortgage interest is deductible on original loans of $1,000,000 or less. They also allow a deduction of interest on second mortgage loans of up to $100,000.

This second feature allows the wealthy to borrow up to $100,000 against their home to buy a Ferrari and deduct the interest. The lower income earner who does not own a home cannot deduct the interest on their less expensive Honda.

President-elect George Bush has proposed a reduction of the capital gains tax. Currently the tax rate on gains made buying and selling stock and other investment type commodities is the same as the income tax rate. It would seem unfair to tax people who work for a living more than those who buy and sell stock for a living, but Bush sees it as another tax incentive. He wants to encourage stock trading. Those who cannot afford the rent much less play in the stock market are not encouraged.

Pechman and Okner found that in 1966 the combined federal, state, and local tax rates were partly regressive and partly progressive (Pechman and Okner 1974).

> The tax burden is very high at the bottom of the income scale and then drops abruptly until the $3000 income level is reached. Between $3000 and $25,000, the effective rates change from 20 to 25 percent of income and then diverge above the $25,000 level.

See Appendix A for the effects of taxation on income distribution. A progressive tax is designed to create greater income equality while a regressive tax does the opposite. A regressive tax widens rather than decreases the gap between rich and poor.

CONCLUSION

The United States currently uses an unjust tax system. The U.S. Congress passed the Tax Reform Act of 1986 in response to a general outcry against the system, but the results are less than was hoped. They raised the capital gains tax to make it the same as the income tax. This is a positive step toward reform, but they also lowered the tax rates for high income earners and have not disposed of all the "loop holes." Congress seems unwilling to pass a real tax reform. They consider a truly progressive tax a socialist trap and are unwilling to offend the wealthy.

It may be impossible to find a non-biased taxpayer to devise a fair tax system, but the American people are entitled to something better than what we have now.

The sales tax needs to be eliminated except for cases where the tax is imposed for a specific purpose such as the gas tax which pays for road repair. Items which should not be taxed include everything from toothbrushes to clothing.

A fair tax system must not tax the poor. The current standard deduction amounts are not high enough. They should be doubled to ensure that low income earners are able to pay for the necessities of life. It is abominable that working citizens should be taxed when they make less than someone on welfare who is completely subsidized by the government.

The deduction for interest on second mortgages should be eliminated, and the interest deduction on primary mortgages over $200,000 should be limited. The current cut off point of $1,000,000 for primary mortgages is too high.

APPENDIX A: LORENZE CURVE BEFORE AND AFTER TAX

The Lorenze Curve depicts the distribution of income among members of a population as illustrated in Figure 1. Notice the diagonal line. This line, called the line of equal distribution, indicates perfect income equality (everyone has the same income). The curved lines beneath the diagonal are the after tax and the before tax lines. The tax differential shown here includes federal, state, and local taxes. It is significant that the after tax line is slightly closer to equality than the before tax line. This indicates that the tax system in the United States is slightly progressive. The rich are taxed at higher rates than the poor.

FIGURE 1. Lorenze Curves of the Distributions of Adjusted Family Income before and after Federal, State, and Local Taxes, 1966.

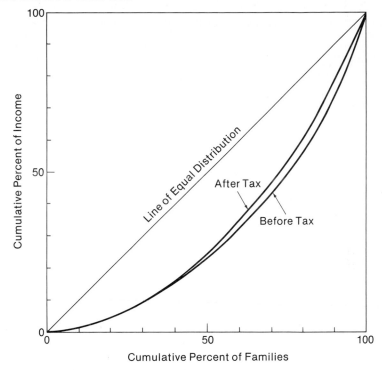

SOURCE: Pechman, Joseph A. and Benjaamin A. Okner. Who Bears the Tax Burden? Washington, D.C.: Brookings, 1974. 5,7

Also significant is the fact that the lowest 35 percent are taxed at about the same rate. The before tax and the after tax lines are the same indicating that taxes have not changed their relative positions.

Sources

Batchelder, Alan B. *The Economics of Poverty.* New York: John Wiley & Sons, 1966.

Blum, Walter J. and Harry Kalven, Jr. *The Uneasy Case for Progressive Taxation.* Chicago: University of Chicago, 1963.

Internal Revenue Code as of June 23, 1988. Chicago: CCH, 1988.

Pechman, Joseph A. and Benjamin A. Okner. *Who Bears the Tax Burden?* Washington D.C.: Brookings Institute, 1974.

Taubman, Paul. *Income Distribution and Redistribution.* Reading, Mass: Addison-Wesley, 1978.

■ THE WRITER'S ASSIGNMENT

Using secondary sources, write an informational report, but one that takes a position. Please use business report format. ■

■ UNDERSTANDING WRITING STRATEGIES

1. What is the difference between a "progressive" and "regressive" tax? Which system does Leathers feel would most benefit the poor and why?

2. The author argues for eliminating tax deductions for second mortgages and placing a cap on the deduction for primary mortgages. How will this create greater equality in the tax code?

3. What would be the direct and indirect benefits to the poor of changes in the mortgage deductions?

4. How are the benefits derived from tax changes described in this essay?

5. What changes could Leathers make to strengthen his argument for the benefits?

6. Leathers uses highly connotative language in some of the descriptions. Find examples of connotation and analyze the effect this language has on the reader's response.

7. Leathers uses specialized vocabulary, often called jargon, in his discussion of the tax code. Are these terms adequately defined and clearly explained? Find examples that support your conclusion. ■

■ SUGGESTIONS FOR WRITING

1. Select a section of this essay that uses highly connotative language. Replace the connotative words with denotative or neutral words. Write a brief explanation of how this change in language changes the essay.

2. Select one of the proposals for tax changes that Leathers addresses. Write a position paper about this change that considers both the advantages and disadvantages and objectively evaluates the arguments on both sides. Use secondary sources. ■

The Burzynski Clinic Controversy

Charlotte Locklear-Enquist

For her Writing for the Organization class, Charlotte Locklear-Enquist in this formal position paper supports keeping a controversial cancer treatment center open. She writes in the persona of a public relations officer preparing colleagues for press releases.

In 1977, Dr. Stanislaw R. Burzynski, M.D., Ph.D., founded the Burzynski Research Institute in Houston, Texas. Since then he has treated over 1,400 advanced cancer patients with the cancer growth inhibiting peptides he named Antineoplastons (1).

Antineoplastons are an alternative treatment for incurable cancer patients who have found that conventional treatments (radiation, chemotherapy) do not help. Controversy surrounds Burzynski and his clinic because the Antineoplastons have not yet been FDA approved. The Texas State Board of Health Examiners is now threatening to close the clinic because of pressure from the FDA and other medical associations.

Burzynski's constant harassment indicates that FDA approval seems to be more a political matter than a scientific or medical process. Exhaustive investigations have been conducted by the Harris County Medical Society (no charges were brought), the Texas Board of Medical Examiners, and the FDA (these are still in progress). Currently, Burzynski is suing the FDA for false statements made to insurance companies which attempted to discourage them from paying patient claims (2). In January 1983, the American Cancer Society "slammed Antineoplastons as an Unproven Method in a statement to the half million medical readers of its official journal" (3).

In April 1983, the FDA filed suit against Burzynski to stop all further research, development, manufacture, and administration of Antineoplastons. The ruling permitted Burzynski to continue research and testing in Texas only, and prohibited interstate shipment until FDA approval (4). In 1985, the FDA raided the Burzynski clinic with an illegal search warrant looking through scientific, medical, financial and personal records for unspecified violations (5).

The Burzynski Research Clinic insists that it must be allowed to remain open for the following reasons:

1. Dr. Bruzynski has operated in Texas for the past 11 years with the approval of the Board of Health and the State Legislature.

2. Many patients are already receiving Antineoplastons and have obtained great benefits from them. If their treatments were suddenly stopped, their condition could deteriorate severely, or they could die.
3. Other countries enthusiastically support the Antineoplaston research and treatment. These countries include England, Japan, China, Germany, and Italy.

Once the Antineoplaston treatment is understood and the arguments are explored, one recognizes the need to permit the Burzynski Clinic to continue operation.

The Antineoplaston Treatment

Burzynski has studied cancer growth inhibitors for more than 20 years. He discovered peptides and amino acid derivatives naturally found in the human body that control cancer, not by destroying cancer cells, but by correcting them.

Normally, when new cells develop they become specialized, into tissue or bone for example. Once they are specialized they no longer divide to form new cells. But, when the human body is in a weakened state, some cells become misguided and never specialize. These cells keep dividing and finally overwhelm the normal cells. In this way a tumor develops.

What Burzynski discovered is that the body can, and does, guide these cancer cells back onto their normal path by sending "messenger" peptides, which bond to cancer cells and reprogram them with the correct information they need to normalize and fulfill their original function.

Instead of destroying the "bad" cancer cells, Antineoplastons restore the cancer cells to a healthy condition without interfering with normal cells. Chemotherapy and radiation are foreign poisons to the body and their function is to kill cells, both bad and good. According to Null, the "beauty of the treatment is that harmful drugs, radiation, and surgery are not required. The body virtually heals itself" (6).

The Antineoplastons are produced by a separate biochemical defense system that is completely different from the immune system. According to Burzynski, without this "corrective system everyone would succumb to the cancer-causing forces that are constantly triggering abnormal cell development" (7). His research indicates that there is a severe shortage of the Antineoplastons in cancer patients.

The Antineoplaston treatment is self-administered orally or intravenously on an out-patient basis and is normally free from side effects. Within three to six weeks Burzynski can tell if a cancer patient will benefit from the Antineoplastons. Burzynski stresses that Antineoplastons are not effective in treating all types of cancer, nor for all patients. He has had "astounding results" with brain tumors, malignant lymphomas, and bladder cancer, while having little success with cancer of the testicles and childhood leukemia (8).

THE ARGUMENTS

A Member in Good Standing

Burzynski is a member in good standing with both the American and World Medical Associations. While he was a researcher and Assistant Professor at Baylor College of Medicine in Houston, his research was sponsored and partially funded by the National Cancer Institute (9).

Burzynski has operated in Texas for the past 11 years with the approval of the Texas State Board of Health Examiners and the Texas State Legislature. Because the Antineoplaston research has been performed in Texas, he has been granted approval to administer the treatment in that state only. This is why interested patients must travel to Texas to receive the treatments.

Burzynski has presented his research at nineteen international and national conventions (10). At least five independent groups have verified Burzynski's research and continue their own work with Antineoplastons:

1. the Medical College of Georgia
2. the Imperial College of Science and Technology of London
3. the University of Kurume Medical School in Japan
4. the University of Turin Medical School in Italy
5. the Shandong Medical Academy in China (11)

In 1986 Burzynski was a featured speaker at the 14th International Cancer Congress, the most prestigious congregation in cancer research. In 1987 Burzynski was the subject of a special session of the International Congress on Chemotherapy (12). It is shameful that Burzynski's research is so accepted and honored on an international level, but remains taboo in the United States. Ironically, Burzynski fled Communist Poland to seek more scientific freedom in the United States (13).

In 1983 Burzynski filed for FDA approval of the Antineoplastons, and has been cooperating with the FDA's testing and publishing requirements. Whether he is processing medication for hundreds or only three patients, Burzynski follows the "exhaustive FDA routine for insuring that his medications meet the highest pharmacological standards" (14). He and his associates have "published over 90 papers validating the safety and effectiveness of Antineoplastons" (15). But still the FDA has a "clinical hold" on Burzynski's Investigative New Drug application filed in 1983 (16). And now, the Texas State Board of Examiners is threatening to shut the clinic down. How will the research be completed to the FDA's satisfaction if the clinic is forced to close? Surely there has been enough evidence to prove that the treatment is beneficial to some cancer patients, and that should be enough to keep the clinic open.

Burzynski has been so closely monitored by the State of Texas that if any patients had been severely harmed or if they had died directly from the Antineoplaston treatment, his license would have been revoked immediately. He has been operating for 11 years without a single damaging incident to a patient, and there are no harmful side effects. He has made it possible for many patients to go into remission and helped many others to have a better quality of life than they would have had if treated with radiation and/or chemotherapy.

Dependent Patients

Many patients are already receiving Antineoplaston treatments, which have significantly improved their lives. A five-year follow-up study of Antineoplaston therapy in patients with advanced cancer showed the following results: 60% obtained objective remission, 47% experienced completed remission, and 20% survived over 5 years without cancer (17). In many cases, tumors shrank in size or disappeared after the treatments began.

One example is Vicky. She was diagnosed in February 1988 as having incurable cancer, adenocarcinoma (malignant tumor originating in glandular tissue) of unknown origin in the lungs. She was told by her medical doctor that it was the "most common and least treatable of the known cancers and that there was no cure." Vicky did not wish to be subjected to the pain of four different chemotherapy and radiation treatments, which would also be experimental. She instead sought another alternative: Antineoplastons. She contacted Burzynski, and after reviewing her medical records he thought he could help her. When Vicky first saw him she was in a wheelchair and on oxygen, a result of several hospitalizations to remove fluids in her lungs. She was so ill that she did not think she would survive the trip to Texas. After three weeks of the Antineoplaston treatments she began feeling better. "My pain diminished considerably, and the X-rays showed a decrease in lung fluids. I'm off oxygen and am able to do things around the house and go shopping" (18).

What would happen to Vicky and the hundreds of other Antineoplaston treated patients if the clinic were closed down? Incurable cancer patients should have the right to seek natural treatments other than toxic radiation and chemotherapy. The majority of Antineoplaston patients have not experienced any side effects, and those reported are minimal: excessive stomach gas, slight skin rash, slightly changed blood pressure, chills and fever (19). These minor effects are much more desirable than the side effects from chemotherapy and radiation, which include severe headaches and nausea, hair loss, and drastic weight loss.

In fact, some desirable side effects of Antineoplastons have been proven: a decrease of plasma triglyceride and blood cholesterol levels, and an increase in white and red blood counts (20).

International Approval

The Burzynski Research Institute's two major objectives are to "obtain independent replication of our research and to generate wide international interest" (21). The contributions of the Japanese and Chinese have been especially helpful in meeting these goals.

Japanese scientists have proven that Antineoplaston A10 is effective in mice, which enabled the Texas clinic to administer higher doses to patients. They have also proven the Antineoplaston A2 to have strong activity against liver cancer in tissue culture. Japanese doctors are planning clinical trials by April 1989 (22).

China has made a tremendous breakthrough and will soon be manufacturing the Antineoplastons for use. A clinic is planned to open in July 1989, and future plans include another clinic in the Philippines and exportation of Antineoplastons to countries in southeast Asia (23).

England and Italy are also actively supporting and pursuing the research. Wide international interest and acceptance should influence the FDA to quicken approval, but unfortunately, the American medical community has been resistant and even hostile to Burzynski and his treatment. "International medical interest in some alternative cancer therapies has produced increasing prestige in Europe for American scientists still beleaguered at home" (24).

Recommendations

It is strongly recommended that the Burzynski Clinic be allowed to remain open for the following reasons:

1. Burzynski is a highly qualified and respected cancer researcher who is internationally acknowledged to have a proven cancer treatment. He and his associates have been trying to meet the FDA requirements for five years, and despite the overwhelming publications, studies, and evidence, the approval is withheld.

2. Hundreds of patients are currently receiving Antineoplastons, which have greatly improved their condition. It would be a tragic and unnecessary mistake if these treatments were denied them.

3. Burzynski has received much support and acceptance internationally. It is hard to understand why he is receiving so much resistance in the United States. This treatment is proven effective for some cancer patients and has no harmful side effects. It should be FDA-approved immediately so its benefits can be available to thousands more cancer patients.

Notes

1. Burzynski Introduction Booklet, p. 4.
2. Townsend Letter, Feb/March 1988.
3. Townsend Letter, July 1988.
4. Townsend Letter, July 1988.
5. Townsend Letter, July 1988.
6. Null, Gary, p. 96.
7. Burzynski Introduction Booklet, p. 6.

8. Null, Gary, p. 103.
9. Burzynski Introduction Booklet, p. 4.
10. Burzynski Facts Sheet.
11. Burzynski Facts Sheet.
12. Townsend Letter, July 1988.
13. Townsend Letter, July 1988.
14. Townsend Letter, Feb/March 88.
15. Townsend Letter, July 88.
16. Burzynski Press Release.
17. Townsend Letter, July 88.
18. Riley, Vicky.
19. Burzynski Introduction Booklet, p. 10.
20. Null, Gary, p. 99.
21. Burzynski Stockholders Newsletter #2.
22. Burzynski Stockholders Newsletter #2.
23. Burzynski Press Release, October 1988.
24. Townsend Letter, July 1988.

Bibliography

Burzynski Research Institute, Inc. *Facts Sheet.* October 1988.
Burzynski Research Institute, Inc. *Introduction Booklet for Perspective Patients.* August 1988.
Burzynski Research Institute, Inc. *Press Release:* "Taiwanese to Benefit from U.S. Biotechnological Breakthrough Regarding Cancer." October 1988.
Burzynski Research Institute, Inc. *Stockholders Newsletter #2.* August 15, 1987.
Null, Gary. *When Traditional Medicine Fails . . . Gary Null's Complete Guide to Healing Your Body Naturally.* December 1987.
Riley, Vicky. Personal interview. October 1988. Howell, Michigan.
Townsend Letter for Doctors. February/March 1988.
Townsend Letter for Doctors. July 1988.

■ THE WRITER'S ASSIGNMENT

Imagine yourself as a staff member in a small public relations office, taking a position helpful to your organization. Prepare a clipping file containing issues relevant to your organization. You will use this file to update the organization's position from time to time so that the company will be ready when necessary to "meet the press." Prepare a position paper that will be suitable for writing press releases or for other publication.   ■

■ UNDERSTANDING WRITING STRATEGIES

1. Describe this essay's format. How does the format contribute to clarifying the position?

2. How does this format compare with that used by Frings?

3. What is the paper's position? How does Locklear-Enquist structure the arguments advancing this position?

4. Is this essay objective or biased? What indicates this?

5. How well is the Antineoplaston treatment explained? Does this help to clarify or explain the author's position?

6. For what audience is this written? What in the essay indicates this?

7. In what ways could this position paper be useful to business?

8. How does this paper meet the assignment's goals? ■

What the Trade Deficit Means to Americans

Clare Macy

Clare Macy's business report analyzes the current trade deficit causes and its impact on the United States' living standard.

TABLE OF CONTENTS

SUMMARY

The average American is largely unaware of how the trade deficit affects him or what he can do about it. This report's purpose is to explain the factors that have contributed to the deficit which threatens America's standard of living.

The research done for this report has revealed two major causes of the deficit: America is no longer an industrial economy but is instead a service economy, and Americans and their government are purchasing more imported than domestic products.

This report concludes that Americans need to buy American products and press their government into enacting policies that combat the deficit.

CONCLUSIONS AND RECOMMENDATIONS

It is this writer's opinion that the trade deficit is an issue that the United States government as well as each American citizen should attend to. It threatens us with the devaluation of our dollar and increases both interest rates and recession.

I, therefore, urge Americans to purchase American products to strengthen our industrial economy. I also encourage the American people to let our government know we are concerned about the trade deficit and that we expect some positive action taken toward reducing the deficit. To begin this feat, American citizens must educate themselves about the deficit and its solutions.

INTRODUCTION

"The trade deficit and its financial consequences hang like a sword of Damocles over the U.S. economy," says C. Fred Bergsten, Director of the Institute for International Economics.[1] This threatening proclamation invites us to ask the questions: How did we get to this state of affairs? What effect does it have on the American citizen? How can American citizens correct this situation?

This report proposes to answer these questions beginning by putting the trade deficit into the perspective of the history of the American economy. It will then examine the trade deficit's effects on the average consumer. Finally this report will explore ways in which we can correct or improve the deficit situation.

GOODS-PRODUCING VERSUS SERVICE INDUSTRY

The question of the trade deficit did not appear suddenly when Ronald Reagan gained office as President. In fact, it can be traced back to when

---

[1]C. Fred Bergsten, "Debtor America and the Budget Deficit," *USA Today,* Vol. 117, July, 1988, p. 17.

America underwent its industrialization. "Farmer, laborer, clerk—this is a brief history of the United States. Farmers, who as recently as the turn of the century constituted more than one-third of the total labor force, now are less than 3 percent of the workforce."[2]

The transition from farmer to laborer to service-oriented professions caused America to slowly rise to the most productive country and then fall below other countries a fraction of its size. As seen in Figure 1, Japan and Germany have now far surpassed the U.S. in manufacturing in a matter of a few decades. In the span of 15 years, America went from a healthy, growing economy, as shown below:

- For two decades after World War II, American productivity growth increased more than 3 percent per year.
- In 1960 the United States had about 25 percent of the world market share in manufacturing.

FIGURE 1

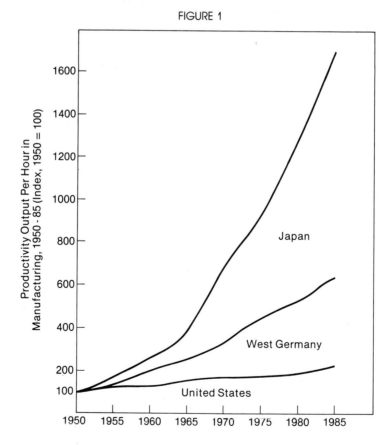

Source: Bureau of Labor Statistics

[2]Naisbitt, John, *Megatrends*, New York, NY: Warner Books, Inc., 1982, p. 5.

- In the important U.S. market, American companies produced 95 percent of the autos, steel, and consumer electronics sold in 1960.

to an economy clearly in decline, as shown here:

- Between 1973 and 1981, productivity growth decreased to about .4 percent per year. And in 1979, productivity growth declined 2 percent.
- In 1979 the U.S. share of world manufacturing slipped to just over 17 percent.
- In 1979 American companies' share of the domestic market dropped to only 79 percent of the autos, 86 percent of the steel, and *less than 50 percent* of the consumer electronics sold in the United States. These slippages continued into the 1980s.[3]

ENTER: JAPAN

Japan's relatively recent industrialization has had quite an effect on our trade deficit. In the 1970s, when the oil crisis struck, "America's love of small foreign automobiles" blossomed.[4] Japan was able to import our knowledge of management tactics, such as our famous quality control circles, while we imported their products.[5] Japan and other countries are accused of colluding "to bar American products from their markets and to invade traditionally American markets with below-cost pricing,"[6] so-called "dumping." In simple terms, this means these countries are closing America off from exporting to their countries while they are exporting products at below cost to squeeze our companies out of business, thereby eventually raising their prices to America. So far, our government has been unable to curtail Japan and others from circumventing our trade laws to prevent "dumping." The loophole that these countries use is they sell their below-cost products to third-country markets with the knowledge that the products eventually find their way to the American market.[7]

THE TRADE DEFICIT DEFINED

The balance of trade is the difference in value over a period of time between imports and exports of commodities, services, and remittances.[7] Currently America imports more goods, services, and remittances than it exports, creating a deficit. Simply put, America is buying more than it is selling. Econo-

[3]Naisbitt, John, *Megatrends*, New York, NY: Warner Books, Inc., 1982, p. 53.
[4]Naisbitt, John, *Megatrends*, New York, NY: Warner Books, Inc., 1982, p. 56.
[5]Ibid.
[6]Glazer, Sarah, "Industrial Competitiveness," *Editorial Research Reports*, Issue No. 0013-0958, March 20, 1987, p. 133.
[7]Gove, Philip Babcock, et al., *Webster's Third New International Dictionary*, G. & C. Merriam Co., 1961.

mist George Gilder is quoted as saying, "America has a trade deficit because it's the only country that can't export to America."[8]

As it stands now, the trade deficit has been growing at a rate of $138 billion a year.[9] "In manufactured goods alone, the United States went from a $15.5 billion surplus in 1981 to a $137.7 billion deficit in 1987."[10]

THE DEFICIT COMES HOME

With the increased deficit, the American standards of living has decreased, and the economy has gone into a decline. It has been forecasted that the markets for service exports will become scarce and that the standard of living will fall "as America grows to depend on imports in areas in which it once manufactured its own goods."[11]

In real terms, the trade deficit is the culprit in the American ever-increasing budget deficit. The United States is now the largest debtor in the world, now totaling approximately $400,000,000,000.[12] "The proximate cause of this historically unprecedented deterioration—which will render both American economic and foreign policy exceedingly vulnerable to decisions made abroad for the indefinite future—is, of course, our massive trade deficit."[13]

Because we are so dependent on foreign countries' investing in our economy, we are vulnerable to their actions. "Whenever foreign investors perceive that correction of the patently unsustainable trade imbalance will require another downward move in the exchange rate of the dollar . . . they simply cut back, or totally stop, their investments in dollar assets."[14] It is believed that such cutback or cessation of foreign investment "could produce a rise in real U.S. interest rates of as much as three–five percentage points, which, in the current state of the economy, almost certainly would push it into a sharp recession."[15] What this illustrates is the direct link between our trade deficit, rising interest rates, and the imminent recession.

What Can We Do About It?

The average American often feels helpless and victimized, as though he has no power over his life, his home, his neighborhood, or his country. This is

---

[8]Kasten, Robert W. Jr., "Deficit Monster or Deficit Mouse?" *USA Today*, Vol. 117, July, 1988, p. 20.

[9]Best, Eric, "Economists Waiting for a Fall," *San Francisco Chronicle*, November 20, 1988, A-1.

[10]Ibid.

[11]Glazer, Sarah, "Industrial Competitiveness," *Editorial Research Reports*, Issue No. 0013-0958, March 20, 1987, p. 133.

[12]C. Fred Bergsten, "Debtor America and the Budget Deficit," *USA Today*, Vol. 117, July, 1988, p. 20.

[13]Ibid.

[14]Ibid.

[15]Ibid.

the same American who often does not vote because he feels ineffective. Combatting the deficit, however, lies in his power.

Buy American

We may be unable to regain our position as the leader of the industrialized world, but we can support our existing industries by buying American products. As consumers we need to be aware that prices between American and foreign goods do not differ significantly, and even when they do, buying foreign products is a short-sighted way of thinking. Knowing that the trade deficits affect our declining living standard, Americans must not support foreign manufacturers at the expense of American manufacturers.

Appeals to Government

Another way Americans can influence our economic destiny is to encourage our leaders to adopt more stringent laws to protect us from Japan and other countries "dumping" their products onto our markets. We can influence our government to further its attempt to break down the trade barriers foreign countries impose upon America as an exporter. We can also encourage government to place tariffs on imports into America, thereby making our own products more competitive within the American market.

Furthermore, we can educate ourselves about the trade deficit and support those views we feel are beneficial to us and defeat views we feel are detrimental to us. Letters can be sent to government officials voicing our concerns and opinions.

CONCLUSION

The trade deficit is a winding road which has no easy end in sight. However, to understand the problem, we must look back at history and trace the movement of our economy. Only then can we define what the problem is and how it affects us. Once defined, the problems can be analyzed to determine the most plausible solutions to correct or slow the progression of the trade deficit. We must act as we feel: Proud to be American.

Bibliography

Bergsten, C. Fred, "Debtor America and the Budget Deficit," *USA Today*, Vol. 117, July, 1988.

Kasten, Robert W., Jr., "Deficit Monster or Deficit Mouse?" *USA Today*, Vol. 117, July, 1988.

Glazer, Sarah, "Industrial Competitiveness," *Editorial Research Reports*, Issue No. 0013-0958, March 29, 1987.

Naisbitt, John, *Megatrends*, New York, NY: Warner Books, Inc., 1982.

Best, Eric, "Economists Waiting for a Fall," *San Francisco Chronicle*, November 20, 1988.

Gove, Philip Babcock et al., *Webster's Third New International Dictionary*, G. & C. Merriman Co., Publishers, 1961.

Silk, Leonard, *Economics in Plain English*, New York, NY: Simon & Schuster, Inc., Publishers, 1978.

■ THE WRITER'S ASSIGNMENT

Using standard business report format, write a report using secondary sources on some issue challenging American business. ■

■ UNDERSTANDING WRITING STRATEGIES

1. What is Macy's distinction between an industrial and a service economy? What effect has the change from one to the other had on the trade deficit?

2. What solutions does Macy propose to counteract the trade deficit? How well are they explained?

3. What is the correlation Macy makes between the trade deficit and recession? What other factors might affect both the trade deficit and recession?

4. How does Macy structure this essay? Where do you see this?

5. How well has Macy met the commitments indicated in her summary? Where do you see this?

6. Why does the business report present its recommendations and conclusions, as well as its summary, at the beginning?

7. Why is this paper's format effective for business communications? Could it be adapted to other types of writing? Why or why not? ■

Proposal to Convert Horizon Telephone System to Merlin Communication System

Susan Magoulas

As part of her business report that proposes converting phone systems, Susan Magoulas analyzes Cravens Management Company's phone needs and compares the Horizon phone system's ability to meet those needs with Merlin's.

MEMORANDUM

TO: Hartley D. Cravens, Vice Chairman

FROM: Susan Magoulas, Executive Assistant

DATE: December 5, 1988

SUBJECT: Conversion of Cravens Management Co. Telephone System

The attached report is the result of a research project that Budd McCormick requested in his memo to me of November 15, 1988. It is a study of the conversion of Cravens Management Company's Horizon telephone system to Cravens & Company's Merlin Communications System. You will find my conclusions and recommendations included in this report.

The purpose of the study was to determine:

1) Why we need one phone system

2) How one phone system will improve office efficiency

3) How much the conversion will cost to implement

The primary resource used was the Spring 1988 AT&T Source Book, which is the most current catalog of AT&T products. In addition, I contacted AT&T to get additional information regarding the cost and installation of the communication system. I also used the Merlin Communications System Guide and the Horizon brochures we had on file.

I learned quite a bit about office phone systems by working on this project. I believe you will agree after reading this report that it will be cost effective for the Company to convert Cravens Management Company to Cravens & Company's Merlin system as soon as possible. If you have any questions, please let me know and I will be happy to answer them.

attachment

cc: H. P. McCormick, Vice President, CMC
     E. W. Tuescher, President, CCSIS

Proposal
to
Convert

Horizon Telephone System

to

Merlin Communications System

Presented
to

Hartley D. Cravens
Vice Chairman

Cravens Management Company, Insurance Services

Submitted
by

Susan Magoulas
Executive Assistant

Cravens Management Company, Insurance Services

December 5, 1988

SUMMARY

The most important part of any business is its communication with its clients. When communication is disrupted or problematic, then something should be done.

There is a problem with Cravens Management Company's phone communications system which must be resolved. For the last year Cravens Management Company's letters to clients, agents, brokers, etc. have been going out with the Cravens & Company, Special Insurance Services phone number on them. This was done in anticipation of Cravens Management Company changing phone systems. However, economic considerations prevented this change from occurring. Calls continue to come in for Cravens Management Company on Cravens & Company, Special Insurance Services phone system. This has created a problem for our switchboard receptionists as well as clients, agents, brokers, etc.

This proposal explains why the phone system should be changed, as well as the approximate cost to convert the phone system. The conclusion is that it will cost slightly more than $5,000 to convert the system. It would be timely to convert the system now before the prices go up again next year.

Since communication is so important to Cravens Management Company, I recommend that we implement the conversion of Cravens Management Company's Horizon phone system to the Merlin Communications System as soon as possible, in order to increase the efficiency of our office in general.

INTRODUCTION

Background Information

Cravens & Company, Special Insurance Services (CCSIS) converted its old AT&T phone system to the AT&T Merlin Communications System on July 21, 1986. CCSIS's phone number was also changed at this time. Cravens Management Company (CMC), a subsidiary, was still in the early stages of development. CMC's portion of CCSIS office space had just been renovated and there were only two employees. CMC shared an AT&T Horizon phone system with Cravens Re Facultative Facilities (CRFF), another entity sharing CCSIS office space.

The Current Situation

CMC has since grown into a ten-person operation in San Francisco, with two other offices in Los Angeles and Seattle. CRFF has downsized to only three employees who are left to work on any CRFF claims that may come in (these employees also work part-time for CMC). If CRFF's remaining claims are transferred to the Highlands' office at the end of the year, as has been suggested, CRFF will be inactive. This means only ten people will be left on the Horizon phone system, which is capable of handling up to forty stations. CCSIS's Merlin System, on the other hand, is capable of handling ninety stations and at present handles twenty-two.

As of January 1, 1988, in anticipation of CMC converting to CCSIS's Merlin System, all new and renewal orders of stationary and business cards were sent in with CCSIS's phone number. All correspondence currently going out to agents, brokers, clients, and insurance companies, etc. has CCSIS's phone number on it. To that end, the Merlin Communications System is being answered by the receptionist as "Cravens Companies." Unfortunately, the conversion was never done due to cost considerations and this has created some problems.

Purpose of Report

The purpose of this report is to: 1) Discuss the problems of having two different phone systems, 2) Explain how having one phone system will improve office efficiency, 3) Determine the approximate cost of converting CMC to the Merlin Communications System.

DISCUSSION

Problems and Improvement of Office Efficiency

There are several problems associated with having two separate phone systems. The major problem is that since all stationary and business cards for CMC list CCSIS's phone number, calls come in for CMC on the Merlin System continuously. To get around this problem for the past year, our receptionists have had to "conference call"[1] calls coming in on the Merlin System by using another line to call the Horizon System, putting that call through the Horizon System to the person at CMC and then "conferencing" the call on the Merlin System into the call on the Horizon System. If this sounds confusing to read about, imagine how confusing it is to do! Not only is this confusing and inconvenient, but it also ties up two of the Merlin System lines, lines that could be used for other clients, agents, etc. to call in on.

Having two systems is confusing for the receptionist. There are many times when she is answering a call on one system when another call comes in on the other system. She has to go back and forth between the different consoles and if the Merlin System has a call come in for CMC she has to conference it over to the Horizon System. When we have a temporary come in to substitute for the receptionist, there is a real problem training her to handle both consoles. This has happened several times in the past and when clients and others are cut off on phone calls accidentally, they are not happy about having to call back (especially when it's a long distance call).

Due to a bookkeeping error, AT&T has no record of our Horizon system besides the console. We have never bought or paid rental on the Horizon phones, except for the console, since moving to the Bank of America building. We aren't sure how this error occurred. However, this means that if there are any problems with the Horizon System, we can't get service on it without questions being asked, as has happened several times in the past. We could possibly be liable for five-year's rental on the Horizon phones which could be very expensive as we currently pay $67.62 a month just for rental of the Horizon console.

Last Opportunity

The five-button phone sets that were originally desired for CMC were $225 each.[2] When I phoned AT&T to check on the prices, I was told that the five-button sets had been discontinued in May, 1988. Now our only alternative is the 10-button set which sells for $355 each.[3] Because we waited to convert CMC to the Merlin System it will now cost us $130 more per set, increasing the cost of the conversion by a minimum of $1,300 or 25% of the total cost of the conversion. This figure is based on ten phones—the minimum number of Merlin sets CMC needs. This does not include any extra phones for expansion. However, with no price break for a volume purchase, new phones should be purchased when needed.

Present Mode of Operations

Our current method of using both systems is adequate but most inconvenient. The problem is the longer we wait to convert the system the more CMC's conversion to the Merlin System is going to cost. AT&T would not indicate whether their new January catalog would include price increases or not. Abandoning the Horizon for a single phone system will make it easier on the receptionists, as well as save time. Other than the initial expense to convert the system, there won't be much difference in the operation cost of the system.

Merlin Communications System Features

The Merlin System offers the following features not on the Horizon System:

- Station Message Detail Recording
- Page
- Conferencing
- Privacy
- Call Coverage
- Automatic Line Selection
- System Speed Dialing
- Programmable Line Ringing

For details on these features and other information, please see Exhibit I attached.

Cost

When CCSIS expanded personnel last year, four additional 10-button sets were bought for $370 each. The only reason the price on the 10-button sets dropped to $355 per set in May, 1988, was because the five-button sets were no longer offered.[4] One useful feature that has been added to the 10-button sets is a built-in two-way speaker phone. This feature was added because AT&T felt customers should get more for their money since the less expensive five-button sets were no longer available. When CCSIS originally purchased their 10-button sets, the two-way speaker phones were an additonal $333 each. Since the two-way speaker phones are now included, CMC will be saving over $300 per set.

Another useful feature that should be added when we convert CMC to the Merlin System is Station Message Detail Recording (SMDR).[5] This provides a complete record of all calls by station number. The cost for this feature is $520 for the SMDR[6] and $595 for the printer.[7] This will allow the phone bill to be split up appropriately between CCSIS and CMC.

Overall, it will cost approximately $5,050 to convert CMC to the Merlin System (see attached Exhibit II). After ordering the phones it takes approximatley seven to ten working days for the phones and wiring to be installed.[8]

CONCLUSIONS

It will be well worth the money for CMC to convert to the Merlin System as soon as possible. Problems with conferencing calls between systems and training staff will continue if we keep both systems. In addition, if anything goes wrong with the Horizon System we will be in a bind as we cannot get servicing on it.

Cost will continue to be an issue. It is unlikely that AT&T will lower the cost of the 10-button phones again as that was a special deal in response to their dropping the five-button sets.

There will no doubt be some problems when CMC converts over to the Merlin System, but with all the advanced features it offers, the Merlin System will greatly increase office efficiency and ease training requirements. In time everyone will become accustomed to the system.

RECOMMENDATIONS

I recommend that we order the Merlin 10-button sets CMC needs now to secure the price of $355 per set.[9] I also recommend that we purchase the Station Message Detail Recording (SMDR) from AT&T for the Merlin System. This will provide us with a complete record of all outgoing calls by station number that will enable us to correctly allocate phone charges betewen CMC and CCSIS.

EXHIBIT I. The Merlin Communications System—Features

The MERLIN Sytem Models 1030 and 3070 come with certain *Standard features*. *Custom features* are assigned to the System's programmable buttons by you (or by your System Administrator) and programmed into the System's memory. *Dial Code System features* or enhancements to individual phones can be added to further customize your MERLIN System. (The System comes with a User Guide and an Administration Manual, which provide detailed information on all features, functions, programming and troubleshooting procedures.)

Standard Features

These are standard with every telephone and are in your set at installation. They include:

- **Call Park**—places an active call in a holding state at one phone for answering at another.
- **Call Waiting**—provides a brief ring or voice announcement from the speaker and a flashing green light to indicate another call.
- **Conference**—add up to two outside and two inside people to a call.
- **Distinctive Ringing**—provides different ringing patterns for incoming, transferred and intercom calls.
- **Drop**—disconnects a person from a conference call.
- **Group Listening**—user can turn on the speaker so caller's voice is heard in office.
- **Hold**—lets you place a call on hold; the green light next to the line button will flash rapidly.
  - **Automatic Hold Release**—green light goes off, indicating that the person has hung up.
  - **Automatic Hold Reminder**—a brief ring every minute reminds you that the call is on hold.
- **Intercom**—signals a called party with a distinctive intercom ring.
  - **Intercom Voice Announcement**—signal a called party with a voice message.
  - **Intercom Auto Dial**—program buttons with intercom numbers for quick signalling.
- **Line Request**—reserves a line that is busy; the System notifies you when it is free.
- **Message Waiting**—lets user know a message is waiting.
- **Monitor-On-Hold Speaker**—if user is on hold, this lets you turn on the speaker and hang up the handset until the other person returns.
- **On-Hook Dialing**—user can turn on the speaker and dial without lifting the handset until the call is answered.
- **Recall**—provides a timed switchhook flash for use of the MERLIN System with Centrex or PBX systems.

- **Ringing Line Selection**—automatically selects the ringing line when the call comes in and handset is lifted.
- **Send Message**—lets attendant notify a person that a message is waiting by touching the Send Message button.
- **Transfer**—lets user pass outside calls to any phone in the System.
- **Test/Program Switch**—tests System functions and program in custom features.
- **Voice Terminal Programming**—enables you to program custom features onto individual phones.
- **Voice Terminal Testing**—use the T/P switch to check that all lights and ringing mechanisms are working properly.
- **Volume Control**—adjusts the sound level of phone's ring and speaker.

Custom Features

- **Automatic Answering**—for outside lines or intercom. Allows the Hands-Free-Unit to automatically answer calls. (When used with the Automatic Multi-Purpose Adapter, enables automatic answering of modems and answering machines.)
- **Automatic Line Selection**—System automatically selects a free line when handset is lifted. (The order of line selection is programmable.)
- **Button Access to Line Pools**—access any line pool by touching a button.
- **Call Coverage**—lets a user at one phone receive calls directed to another.
- **Call Forwarding**—lets you have calls ring at a different phone when necessary.
- **Call Restrictions**—allows the restriction of specific phones according to your needs.
  - **Outside Call Restriction**—restricts some phones to incoming calls only.
  - **Outside Toll Restriction**—restricts some phones to incoming and local calls only.
  - **Allowed-List Call Restriction**—allows toll restricted phones to make toll calls to a specific list of area codes and/or exchanges. (not available with FM1)
- **Dial Access to Pools**—allows access to line pools using dial codes.
  - **Dial Access to Pools Restriction**—restricts some phones from dial access to certain pools.
- **Do Not Disturb**—prevents a phone from ringing for a temporary period; lets you conduct business uninterrupted.
- **Group Paging**—allows assignment of phones to paging zones so people can page others through phone speakers. (not available with FM1)

- **Line Administration**—enables the System Administrator to assign combinations of pooled or personal lines to any phone.
- **Last Number Redial**—automatically stores last number dialed; redials by pressing appropriate button or dialing a simple code.
  Saved Number Redial—stores saved number for later redialing by touching a button or dialing a code.
- **Manual Signaling**—touching a dedicated intercom auto-dial button will generate a beep at the called phone.
- **Multiple Line Pools**—assigns outside lines to different line pools so similar services are pooled together (e.g. regular, WATS, etc.)
- **Outside Auto-Dial**—lets you program buttons for one-touch dialing of frequently called numbers.
- **Personalized Ring**—select one of eight different ringing signals.
- **Privacy**—prevents others from joining a call (automatic on intercom.)
- **Programmable Line Ringing**—lets you program outside line buttons, pool buttons and cover buttons to ring immediately, after a delay or not at all.
- **Station Message Detail Recording**—provides complete records of all incoming and/or outgoing calls by station number and type of line, with time, date and length of call. Account codes are optional. (not available with FM1)
- **Touch-Tone Enable**—allows the System to temporarily generate Touch-Tone signals when connected to lines that carry rotary signals.
- **Touch-Tone/Rotary Option**—enables System to work with either Touch-Tone or rotary phones or both.
- **Voice Announcement Disable**—lets you program phones to block intercom voice announcements and to ring automatically to signal intercom calls.

Dial Code Features

- **Call Pickup**—allows the answering on one phone of a call you hear ringing at another.
- **Personal Speed Dial**—stores outside numbers for easy dialing using a three-character code (for 5- and 10-button phones only.)
- **System Speed Dial**—allows assignment of System Speed Dial codes to up to forty phone numbers. (not available with FM1)

Optional Features and Equipment

Optional equipment is available which can even further increase your MERLIN System capabilities. Several items are listed here. We recommend that you discuss your potential needs with your AT&T representative or call us at 800/247-7000.

- **Automatic Multi-Purpose Adapter**—allows the attachment of modems, cordless phones or automatic answering machines.
- **Extra-Alert Devices and Accessories**—for noisy or remote areas. Bells, horns, chimes and strobes available.
- **Hands-Free Unit**—provides top quality speakerphone service.
- **Headset Adaptor**—lets you plug in a standard headset for hands-free operation.
- **Manual Multi-Purpose Adaptor**—allows the connection of manually operated accessories to any MERLIN System.
- **Loudspeaker Paging System**—a three-zone paging system with plug-connected modular components.
- **Background Music**—provides background music through the loudspeaker paging system.
- **Music-On-Hold**—provides music to parties on hold.

Merlin Communications System Models 1030 and 3070 Specifications

Registration:
AS 593M-64884-MF.E (FM1 and 2)
Ringer Equivalence 0.8A
Loop Start

Power:
117 VAC grounded outlet required
Model 1030—150 WATTS
Model 3070—400 WATTS

Environment:
40° to 104° F.
Maximum Humidity: 80%
Ventilation: 6 inches top and sides
Air: free of moisture, dust, chemicals

Space:
Tabletop or shelf
Wall mounting requires Wall Mount Kit

Weight:
35 lbs per control unit (fully equipped)

Power Failure:
Four CO lines

Paging:
Contact closures for 3 zones and all zones
Suitable for Pag Pac® 20

Extra Alerts:
Maximum of 3 line driven

Attendant Positions:
Five

Voice Links:
22 Analog Links, 22 simultaneous conversations, including conferences

Intercom:
2 Intercom paths per station module, maximum of 6 intercom paths with Model 1030, 14 intercom paths with Model 3070.
2 buttons per terminal, one selects voice announcement, one selects tone announcement.
NOTE: FM3 Registration is not yet available, but will allow its use as key behind (fully protected key as opposed to multi-function)

SOURCE: AT&T, Merlin Communications System, Attendant's Guide, Models 1030 and 3070 with Feature Module 4. Issue 1, Sept., 1985.

EXHIBIT II. Cost to Convert CMC to the Merlin System

10—Ten-button Phone Sets at $355 each	$3,550
3—Additional Merlin Lines approximately	$385
(Added to existing box including installation of ten wire runs + $30 for AT&T Technician visit + $70 per Technician Hour)	
1—Station Message Detail Recording Card (SMDR)	$520
1—AT&T #475 Dot Matrix Printer	$595
	———
Approximate Total	$5,050

Footnotes

[1]AT&T, *Communications System, Attendant's Guide Models 1030 and 3070 with Feature Module 4*, Issue 1, September, 1985, pp. 28–29.

[2]AT&T, *Source Book*, Spring, 1988, p. 4.

[3]AT&T, Phone conversation with Andrea Miller, November 22, 1988.

[4]*Ibid.*

[5]AT&T, *Communications System, Attendant's Guide Models 1030 and 3070 with Feature Module 4*, Issue 1, September, 1985, p. 38.

[6]AT&T, *Source Book*, Spring, 1988, p. 9.

[7]*Ibid*, p. 12.

[8]AT&T, Phone conversation with Andrea Miller, November 22, 1988.

[8]*Ibid.*

Bibliography

AT&T. *Direct Source Book*. Spring, 1988.

AT&T. *Merlin Communications System, Attendant's Guide, Models 1030 and 3070 with Feature Module 4*. Issue 1, September, 1985.

AT&T. *Merlin Communications System, User's Guide, Models 1030 and 3070, with Feature Module 4*. Issue 1, September, 1985.

Horizon CS. *Attendant's Guide to CAP*. Issue 2, April 1982.

Horizon CS. *Reference Manual*. Issue 4, April, 1982.

■ THE WRITER'S STRATEGIES

1. Describe this report's format. How does it compare with other reports in this section?

2. What are Magoulas's main arguments favoring conversion to the new phone system?

3. How persuasive are these arguments? Why?

4. According to Magoulas, is the conversion cost justifiable? Why or why not?

5. What is the essay's tone? How objective is it?

6. How would the reader use the information provided in the "Exhibits"?

7. Should Magoulis have included information on the Horizon System as well for comparison purposes? Why or why not? ■

Humanities and the Arts

Writing for humanities and the arts does require some distinctive writing tasks, which we will look at in a moment, but it also shares some writing approaches in common with the sciences, social sciences, and business. Humanities and arts students need to develop criteria and write evaluations, but instead of evaluating scientific or historical data or a management style, they evaluate photography (Eileen Coppola's "Dance Photography"), philosophy (Faun Ryser's "Idealism and Materialism," Daren Di Nicola's "Clear and Distinct Ideas in Descartes' *Meditations*," and Cynthia Stuffman's "The Order of the Proofs for the Existence of God in Descartes' *Meditations*"), critical arguments (McKeel Hagerty's " 'More' or Less Reality?"), and other critical studies (Nathan Turner's "Shaping the Young American Mind: *The American Pageant*"). Comparative analysis leads as much to understanding literature in Stephanie Hodde's "The Body," Doris Brewster's "Comparison of the Gilgamesh and Noah Flood Stories," and Laurie Loftus's "Valenzuela and Kafka: The Word 'Killer' and the Word Killer" as comparing experiments leads to scientific understanding. Finally, like students in all disciplines, students in humanities and the arts write using secondary sources. Although the style may not be as clearly defined as for a review of the literature in the sciences and social sciences, student research essays in the arts and humanities summarize, respond to, and quote from books and articles published in professional journals. Audrey Peake goes to secondary sources for information about T. S. Eliot and the world in which he lived as background for her literary analysis in "The Hollow Men of Eliot's Time" just as Kathy Silvey bases her study of Shakespeare's comic heroines on work done by literary historians and scholars. Two history papers integrating research from primary and secondary sources are Karim Manassa's "Joe Crail: On the Dam Bandwagon" and Scott Mersch's "Edward F. Beale: Conflict of Interest in California Indian Policy."

While writing shares common tasks across the disciplines, writing about literature also calls upon special knowledge of literary devices—theme, point of view, character, structure, and special uses of language. A paper about literature may study a work's theme as do Lauren Burke's "Dante's *Inferno*," Lisa Hacken's "Past as Present in John Fowles's *The Magus* and *The French Lieutenant's Woman*," Sarah Hanna's "Of Johnson's *Rasselas*," and Karen Hyman's "The Interdependence of Sanity and Social Life." Brett Nelson's "Modern Victimization" and Susan Seehaver's "Myra Henshaw: A Look at Choices" study novels through their important characters, while Randy Coppinger analyzes the narrator and his point of view in "The Narrator as God."

The essays comprising this section represent students writing for classes in philosophy, dance history, history, literature, classics, and English composition. While class assignments shape these essays, many of the students write for distinctive audiences beyond their instructors. As in the sciences and social sciences, students writing in the arts and humanities learn the voice of professional journals in their disciplines. This clear professional voice appears in Nancy Hale's "T. S. Eliot's Aims for Drama and *Murder in the Cathedral*" and McKeel Hagerty's " 'More' or Less Reality? (An Old Platonic Argument)." Karim Manassa's "Joe Crail: On the Dam Bandwagon" and Scott Mersch's "Edward F. Beale: Conflict of Interest in California Indian Policy" consciously conform to history journal writing both in content and style. Jessica Sollee's descriptive dance review, "Jim Self's Lookout: Heed His Warning!", Brendan Cole's humorous analogy in "The Pizza Guy" and Brian Zug's personal voice in "Sensible Words" engage a wider, more popular audience. Whatever the subject, approach, or tone, this section's essays show students meeting education's challenge in thoughtful, perceptive, and often original writing.

Dante's Inferno

Lauren Burke

For the Great Books Colloquium, Lauren Burke read, discussed, and wrote about western civilization's major writers and philosophers for four semesters. Written for the Colloquium, this essay traces one of Dante's *Inferno*'s central themes, confronting the sins of worldliness on his journey through hell.

HELL, A LEARNING EXPERIENCE

In the first Canto of Dante's *Inferno* we find our narrator "astray from the straight road and / alone in a dark wood" (I.3–4). Dante was chased into the woods by a She-Wolf after attempting to climb the "Mount of Joy." By the time Virgil appears, Dante is in dire need of some guidance. After identifying himself, Virgil tells Dante that in order for him to reach the summit of the "Mount of Joy" he must take another route:

> He must go by another way who would escape
> this wilderness for that mad beast that flees
> before you there, suffers no man to pass.
>   (I.89–91)

Virgil offers to guide Dante along "another way," around the She-Wolf to the mountain.

Therefore, one of the purposes of Dante's journey through hell is to get past the Three Beasts of Worldliness (the Leopard, the Lion and the She-Wolf) so that he may continue on the "straight road" toward heaven (Mount of Joy). Dante encounters the sins which these beasts represent throughout his entire journey. It is through the recognition of and confrontation with these sins that Dante learns to overcome his own sinful tendencies.

Dante's most important confrontation with sin in *The Inferno* is his personal conflict with his loyalty to God. In the onset of this glorious tale Dante's loyalty toward God is not his first priority. Dante's misguided loyalties seem to be his most conspicuous flaw. A good example of Dante's misplaced loyalty is evident upon his recognition of Virgil:

> . . . you are my true master and first author,
> the sole maker from whom I drew the breath (13)
> of that sweet style whose measures have brought me (13)
> honor.
> (I.82–84)

These verses contain praises that belong solely to God. Yet, it is to Virgil that Dante gives credit. He is crediting Virgil for giving him the gift of prose when such a splendid gift could only be divine. A man who does not even recognize that this gift is heaven-sent is surely not pious enough to reach heaven, the very origin of his gift. (Knowledge of God's justice will bring him that much closer to heaven's gates and that much further from the sins of his fellow men.) Dante discovers many of his earthly idols in the halls of hell and comes to realize that he cannot put his strongest faith in men. However, I do not believe Dante ever redirects his faith from men to God while he is in hell.

The irony of *The Inferno's* depiction of hell is that the sinners who inhabit hell are granted control over what their punishment will be. Each sinner is punished on the basis of the sins he chose to commit. Whatever a man's sin was on earth it is distorted and enlarged by God's justice and transformed into the sinner's punishment. This way, each sinner chooses not only his sins, but his punishments. Virgil tells Dante in Canto I how the most ferocious beast, the She-Wolf, came into being: "Envy first released her on the world" (I.104). Surely by "Envy" Virgil must have meant man since God is not capable of envy. (How could He envy anything when He created everything?) Since it was man who created sin, it was also man who created a need for hell.

To best describe how hell came to be and what God's role is in its existence, one must imagine God as an awesome mirror. Upon a man's death, his soul and his deeds are reflected in this mirror. Whatever the contents of that man's soul, be they virtuous or base, they will be magnified by how much they contradict God's Nature. The resulting image of himself that the soul sees in the divine mirror will reflect what his eternal fate will be.

The pattern between the sins and punishments of the damned in *The Inferno* is perfectly consistent. Although man created the sins by his own accord, God brings justice to those sins by creating a pattern between punishment and sin. The sins of which the men in hell are guilty are all more or less sins against God himself. So, just as the sinners distorted the beauty God granted them, God distorts their image in His mirror.

I have chosen Circle Seven, Round Three of hell to illustrate with more detail the concepts which have been introduced above. This Round of Circle Seven is the eternal habitat of The Violent Against Nature. These sinners took the gift of fruitfulness and distorted it beyond recognition to serve their own grotesque desires. Their punishment is to wander eternally in burning rain. The rain itself reflects the unnaturalness of their sin. Because these sinners were violent against nature during their sojourn on earth, nature is now exercising her power to revenge herself. The rain which falls on sinners' hides scorches their soft skin and bakes their features beyond recognition. The hideous result of each sinner's appearance is no more hideous than their violent distortion of the act of reproduction. And so, while earth's rain brings fruitfulness and new life, hell's rain brings nothing but pain and the wrath of nature whom the sinners violated on earth.

The sinners of this particular station in hell are of a higher earthly stature than the majority of hell's sinners. In Dante's conversation with Ser Brunetto Latino, Ser Brunetto describes the lot of sinners which the circle contains: "We were all clerks and men of worth, / great men of letters, and scholars renowned" (XV.106–107). Dante shows more love toward these sinners than any others he encounters in the course of his journey. It is in this circle that he meets up with his dearest earthly friend, Ser Brunetto Latino. The reunion between the two is a classic example of Dante's misplaced loyalties. Dante had at one time held Ser Brunetto Latino in tremendous regard and apparently still does. However, the eyes with which the Lord sees Ser Brunetto contrast so sharply with Dante's vision of him that Dante can barely recognize his dear friend now that God's judgment is evident to mortal eyes:

> I searched his baked features closely, till at last
> I traced his image from my memory
>
> In spite of the burnt crust, and bending near
> to put my face close to his, at last
> I answered: 'Ser Brunetto, are *you* here?'
> (XV.26–30)

Dante's obvious surprise at Ser Brunetto's presence in hell proves how blind his faith has been. This surprise shows that Dante would not have placed Ser Brunetto in hell if it had been his decision. The multitude of respected figures which Dante stumbles across in hell serve the purpose of uprooting the faith he places in mortals and relocating that faith in the more secure abode of God. It is for this reason that Dante's journey begins in hell. If Dante will abandon his earthly loyalties and ambitions and leave them in hell early on, he will be capable of accepting God completely during the later part of his journey with Beatrice.

I do believe that Dante makes progress as *The Inferno* develops. However, this progress does not develop consistently. The best way to illustrate his progress is through his feelings toward the sinners. The more he tends to sympathize and identify with those whom God has "banished," the more he doubts God's judgment and the closer he comes to sin. The more he tends to reject the sinners, and therefore praise God's justice, the more he progresses toward God. At the onset of his journey Dante was so impressed by the Virtuous Pagans that he thought them to be more worthy than himself:

> And they honored me far beyond courtesy,
> for they included me in their own number,
> making me sixth in that high company.
> (IV.100–102)

Not only was Dante honored to be included with people whom God had placed in hell, but he was honored to be placed below them as sixth in a company of six. By the Seventh Circle Dante's attitude toward the sinners has changed some and he is now less eager to join their pitiful ranks, even those of his close friends:

> I did not dare descend to his own level
> but kept my head inclined as one who walks
> in reverence meditating good and evil.
> (XV.43–45)

This attitude toward Ser Brunetto shows Dante's progression away from the sinners. However, in the next Canto he is once again eager to join the sinners: "I would have thrown myself to the plain below / had I been sheltered from the falling fire" (XVI.46–47). Although Dante seems to have regressed since the former Canto, he has clearly progressed since his encounter with the Virtuous Pagans. He is obviously not *so* eager to join the Sodomites that he actually does. In fact, the only sinners he *does* join in all of hell are those which he comes in contact with in the First Circle when he was most ignorant of hell's justice. In the First Circle he considered the sinners to be better than himself, but in the Seventh Circle he illustrates what he has learned about his relationship with the sinners by placing himself high upon a dike. Because of Dante's position on the dike the sinners are forced to walk on the same level with the hem of his robe. The sinners which he spoke to were forced to "stare up at my (Dante's) height" (XVI.25). This illustration indicates that Dante now knows himself to be superior to the sinners. This opinion is clearly one which Dante has developed during the course of his voyage.

This Circle more than any other teaches Dante that earthly fame and prestige mean nothing to God. The men in this Circle, as I mentioned earlier, were revered tremendously on earth. However much pleasure their fame may have brought them on earth, it means very little where it counts the most, in eternity, and these great men now grovel in hell:

> This peeled and naked soul who runs before me
> around this wheel was higher than you think
> there in the world in honor and degree.
>   (XVI.34–36)

The contrast between this sinner's position on earth and his position in hell is sharp. The message is very clear; a man's status on earth means nothing once he is dead. While Dante is learning to accept this truth, the sinners refuse to believe their lack of status. They to hold onto their fame on earth with a tight grasp. It is almost as if they believe their great works on earth, whatever they may have been, will keep them alive and famous eternally. Ser Brunetto's last words to Dante show the hope and faith that he places in his work: " 'Remember my *Treasure*, in which I shall live on: / I ask no more' " (XV.118–119). The sinners, well, at least Ser Brunetto, do not seem to be aware that something as mortal as the written word cannot bring one eternal grace. They believe they can find eternal grace in the memories of men. As Ser Brunetto scampers away across the floor of hell Dante paints the image of one who thinks he has won but has really lost:

> He turned then and seemed,
> across that plain, like those who run
>
> for the green cloth at Verona; and of those,
> more like the one who wins, than those who lose.
>   (XV.119–122)

This is the last hope of the sinners of hell, that they will be remembered on earth. But even this hope is in vain since they know that one day the Second Coming will arrive and all traces of any virtue they possessed will vanish. After this time, the only trace of them will be their eternal pain in hell.

Dante's relationship with Virgil is one of the most important symbols in *The Inferno*, for it represents his relationship with reason. Behind this relationship lies the path which led Dante out of the woods in the first Canto. Although the road of reason can easily lead Dante out of the woods, it can just barely bring him to the foot of the "Mount of Joy." As I mentioned earlier, one of Dante's major conflicts in *The Inferno* is where his loyalties lie. After observing his relationship with Virgil throughout their voyage it is not difficult for one to realize that Dante's strongest bond is with reason. I believe that it is because of this bond that Virgil is chosen to be Dante's guide. Dante would surely need someone he trusted a great deal to lead him across such a terrifying landscape.

Although I believe it is healthy for Dante to have a strong bond with reason, reason is merely a stepping stone to a more significant bond, a bond with God. Dante can utilize his relationship with reason as a means for forming a relationship with God. Although Dante learns a great deal in *The Inferno* about reason, sin, punishments and the sinners themselves, I do not believe he ever crosses the line away from reason to God. Many details in the two Cantos of Circle Seven indicate this lack of connection between Dante and God. Although Dante is midway through his journey by the time he reaches this Circle, he has not yet recognized God's hand at work in hell. While commenting about the basic geography of hell, he is not sure whom he should credit with its construction: "The engineer, whoever he may have been, / designed the margin we were crossing by" (XV.11–12).

Another indication that Dante depends more on reason than on God is his constant turning toward Virgil for advice. There are many instances where he will not act without Virgil's consent: "Let us sit together, if it pleases him / who is my guide and leads me through this pit" (XV.41–42). Although Dante is sometimes wise to depend on Virgil, Virgil's advice is not always the best advice. In Canto XVI Virgil orders Dante to obey the wishes of the sinners:

> "Do as they ask," he said,
> "for these are souls to whom respect is due.
>
> If it were not for the darting flames that hem
> our narrow passage in, I should have said
> it were more fitting you ran after them."
>   (XVI.14–18)

The words which Virgil utters above reflect the reason why Virgil is in hell. It is obvious from his statement that he does not truly know God. If these words *did* come from one who knew God, surely they would be words of blasphemy. No sincerely pious man would ever refute God's judgment by praising sinners which He damned. In the quotation above, Virgil says that the only reason Dante should not run after the sinners is because of the danger of the flames. This same attitude is reflected in Dante's reaction to the sinners:

> I would have thrown myself to the plain below
> had I been sheltered from the falling fire;
> and I think my Teacher would have let me go.
>
> But seeing I should be burned and cooked, my fear
> overcame the first impulse of my heart
> to leap down then and there.
>   (XVI.46–51)

The only thing preventing Dante from joining the sinners above is his fear that he will suffer their fate. In order for Dante to truly escape sin, he will need more motivation than fear of punishment; he will need to abstain from sinning, not out of his fear of God, but out of his love for God. It is only through loving God that Dante can be saved. It is for this reason that Virgil will be left behind at the foot of Paradiso. Reason can only bring one so far. In *The Inferno* reason brings Dante through the depths of hell. There he learns to accept the gravity and unnaturalness of sin and he learns to detect those who do sin. However, Dante still has much to learn and he has yet to abandon Virgil for a more worthy Guide.

■ THE WRITER'S ASSIGNMENT

Select one of the *Divine Comedy*'s themes and explain how Dante develops it in one part of the *Inferno*. ■

■ UNDERSTANDING WRITING STRATEGIES

1. What does the introduction contribute to the essay?

2. What is this essay's focus, and where does Burke indicate it to her reader?

3. How does Burke structure this essay?

4. What evidence does Burke offer to convince the reader? How well are you convinced?

5. What kinds of assumptions does Burke make about her audience? What in the essay indicates this?

6. What changes would you make in this essay to better engage the reader in the essay's argument?

7. What is this essay's purpose? On what do you base your response? ■

Comparison of the Gilgamesh and Noah Flood Stories

Doris Brewster

In this research paper written for an English composition class, Doris Brewster compares the flood stories in *The Epic of Gilgamesh* and *Genesis*. Placing each story in its historical context, Brewster sees similarities that might indicate influence.

From the best information available to scholars, there is a gap of about 1,000 years between the writing of the *Gilgamesh Epic* and the setting down of the early books of the Bible. These scriptures are credited to Moses but there is evidence that there may have been several authors over a span of years.

In the Bible, the early verses find God saying, "We shall make man in our image" (Gen.1:26), giving rise to the idea that the Hebrews were polytheistic in their early culture, as was common in the Mesopotamian area. Many peoples inhabited this fertile area and there surely was an overlapping of lifestyles, diet, customs and religion.

The Hebrew people were nomadic for the better portion of their history, coming into contact with peoples of many cultures and beliefs. In addition, they suffered captivity on at least two occasions and necessarily had foreign customs forced on them. This melding of histories may account for the many legends and oral traditions that bear striking similarities, culture to culture, era to era.

The similarities between the flood story according to the *Epic of Gilgamesh* and that recorded in Genesis indicate a carry-over of ideas from the Sumerian-era tales to the Hebrew version. Both accounts have enough overall similarity to cause the observer to suspect a common base.

In the beginning, according to the Bible, God created man in his own image and pronounced His human creation, as well as the entire universe, "good." His pleasure was not long to endure as man exercised his own creative spirit by becoming sinful and evil. God regretted His creation of man and planned his destruction by flood. There was one exception to this general evil condition of mankind and that was Noah, whom God regarded as a righteous man and undeserving of destruction.

God gave Noah instructions for the saving of himself and his household as well as for the collection of sufficient breeding stock to repopulate the earth after the flood. Noah had every reason to believe God's words because they came in the form of a Covenant that bound God to fulfill His promises as well as binding Noah to obey His instructions.

As was always the case, Noah followed God's instructions scrupulously; setting about to preserve his life and that of his family.

Within this same theoretical time frame, the flood story, as related in the *Epic of Gilgamesh*, finds the god Enlil enraged with mankind because they disturbed his rest and determined to destroy them by an all-encompassing flood. The prevailing Sumerian view of their gods as superstrong, immortal, but thoroughly "human" beings, makes such a callous decision understandable and not totally unexpected. In this same vein, we find that Enlil made no provision for the saving of even one human, nor for repopulation of the earth after the flood waters receded. An "assistant" god, Ea, favored one mortal, Utnapishtim, and determined to save him, albeit for selfish reasons.

He gave his favorite human specific instructions which were promptly embellished and modified, and, in some portions, totally ignored. Fortunately, this did not seem important to Ea and the saving of Utnapishtim's household proceeded.

Both accounts of the flood tell of the respective families' days aboard their crowded vessels and of massive outpourings of water both from heaven and from underground. Many days were spent in storm and many more helplessly adrift until both boats were said to come to rest on mountain tops; Noah's on Mt. Ararat and Utnapishtim's on Mt. Nidir.

From his safe resting place on Mt. Ararat, Noah sent out birds to search for some indication, dry land or the return of green growth. His early attempts proved fruitless but eventually his diligence was rewarded and a recently released dove returned bearing a green branch.

As instructed, Noah released his animals and prepared sacrifices to God in thanksgiving for the safe journey of himself and his family (Gen.8:17–20). God was pleased with Noah's sacrifices and determined "never again to curse the ground for man's sake" (Gen.8:21). He spoke to Noah and made, again, a Covenant with him in which He promised never again to destroy the world by flood. To seal this Covenant, which bound both God and man, He set a rainbow in the clouds as a sign (Gen.9:16–17).

Meanwhile, so to speak, Utnapishtim's boat rested on Mt. Nidir. Birds were also sent out and eventually conditions were right for the animals and people to disperse out into the world. Utnapishtim prepared a sacrifice to express his gratitude for being spared as well as to appease the angry Enlil who had originally engineered the destruction of mankind.

The gods were induced by Utnapishtim's sacrifice into a mood of good will and forgot their differences with mankind and rejoiced at his ultimate survival.

The lengthy span of time between the recording of the two versions of the flood story, along with other factors, gives rise to the very real possibility that the earlier tale may have influenced the later one. This is not an unacceptable assumption when one considers that both peoples occupied the same lands in overlapping groups for many centuries and would quite possibly have shared some stories and legends.

Oral traditions, such as carried the stories of Utnapishtim or Noah, were doubtlessly subject to interpretation, amplification and even editing, by virtue of having been repeated by many people over many years' time.

The majority of the differences in the two tales center around their descriptions of the attitudes and actions of "God." Evidence indicates that the Hebrews evidently regarded their God as somewhat "plural" at an earlier time, as did the Sumerians at the time of the writing of the *Epic of Gilgamesh*. One can only speculate as to the tone and the texture of the Noah flood story had it been written at the same time. As it was, the ensuing years, exposure to other cultures, suffering captivity, and wandering in the wilderness surely served to modify, solidify and generally mature the Hebrew's attitude toward their relationship to God.

By the time Moses set about to record the early books of the Bible, the prevailing concept of God was likely quite different from that of the Hebrews 1,000 years earlier. He was, conceivably, looking backward in time and describing events handed down through oral tradition with the only perceptions available to him, those of a people who now believed in one God, omnipotent and self-sufficient rather than working in concert with others; caring and merciful, rather than capricious; committed and trustworthy rather than responding to sacrifices solely to satisfy his whims; in touch with man's daily life rather than viewing his "servant" from a distance; and a God who was bound by His own laws, as well as binding man.

In short, God, through the more sophisticated, morally-oriented eyes of Moses, had become a more sophisticated, morally oriented God. We may, in fact, be witnessing the interpretation of an earlier story by an author, or authors, insulated and influenced by the passage of vast amounts of time.

■ UNDERSTANDING WRITING STRATEGIES

1. According to Brewster, what are the main differences between the Gilgamesh and the Noah flood stories?

2. To what does Brewster attribute the differences?

3. What conclusion does Brewster reach about the two stories after comparing them?

4. What generalizations is Brewster able to formulate in her conclusion? What kind of a logical pattern does the relationship between the comparison and the conclusion suggest?

5. Describe the writing strategies Brewster uses to compare the two stories. How else might she have approached this problem? ■

The Pizza Guy

Brendan Cole

For his classics course, Ancient Comedy, Brendan Cole turns a rather ordinary request to analyze the relationship between Platus's *Menaechmi* and Shakespeare's *Comedy of Errors* into an enjoyable essay by making a rather unusual analogy of the plays with bread and pizza. Each contains the same ingredients, but the pizza and Shakespeare add spice to the old basics.

I feel compelled to relate a story to you so alarming and uncanny that it overshadows my urge to simply convey in more formal terms the comparison between William Shakespeare's *Comedy of Errors* and Plautus's Menaechmi.

It begins on a cold night just after I had finished reading both plays. I was stumped on the many questions I wished to answer in the paper. I left the library and began to walk, preoccupied with these complex and intimidating dilemmas. What are the differences between the two plots and how does each relate to what is funny or comic? What differentiates one from the other or are they simply the same plays written by two separate authors? What is the role of character development in relation to these plot changes and in what way do they affect the comic theme? I suspected that the comic themes were the same for both plays, but I was having trouble distinguishing exactly what made each unique.

With these questions in mind it is no wonder I became unbearably hungry for some sort of unhealthy food. Luckily my wanderings had taken me to the front door of a pizza parlor. I stepped inside. The place was empty except for myself and the two cooks Bill and Mike. They knew me from my outstanding patronage and I knew them for their superb baking abilities. I ordered a pizza and sat down at a table. After a few minutes Bill came over and sat down next to me. He said that I looked troubled and wondered what the problem was. I looked at him desperately and asked if he knew anything at all about Shakespeare. He looked at me a moment and smiled a huge, brown-toothed smile and said, "Boy, Shakespeare is my specialty. In fact, not just Shakespeare, but all comic plays before the mid seventeenth century A.D." What luck, my pizza man is a literary critic. I quickly related my previously mentioned dilemmas to him and anxiously waited for his assessment.

At that time, my pizza was brought over by Mike. Bill told me not to eat the pizza but to begin looking at it carefully. He then told Mike to bring out some fresh Italian bread. I told him I only had enough money for the pizza, but he said that it was on the house. The bread came and he ordered me not to eat that either but to closely scrutinize it as well as the pizza. I did the best I could considering my overwhelming hunger. After a moment, Bill straightens in his chair, points to the bread, and states grandly, "That is the *Menaechmi* and the pizza is the *Comedy of Errors.*" I tell him the pizza doesn't look that bad. Bill laughed and began to speak:

"Each of these baked goods have the same basic ingredients. For the bread you have flour, water, and salt, and for the pizza dough you have basically the same things but in different proportions. Now let us view the bread and dough as the comic plot for the two authors. The comic plot underlies the whole theme for each play and is the basic driving device behind whether or not we deem the comedy successful. Like the bread, nearly all of Plautus's comedy is based on the ingredients of the plot. Through all the mistaken identities and loss of material possessions from one character to that character mistaken for a twin, Plautus must keep the balance of reality and the fantastic in strict proportion. We must all agree that the idea of two brothers with the same name, in the same town, being so exactly alike that close friends and relations mistake them for the other, is slightly fantastic, but, held together with the congealing power of reality displayed through a closely scrutinized sense of time, area and character relation, the comedy somehow works. Just like the bread, we are not exactly sure why this combination of ingredients appeals to us but we do know that we like it. Eat some bread."

I ate some bread and thought about what Bill had told me. I wondered if he would tell me about the *Comedy of Errors* soon so that I could dig into my pizza that was getting cold. As if on cue he began to speak again:

"Although we see the crust of the pizza, it is easy to understand that crust alone does not make a good pizza. What Shakespeare has done is taken the older concept of bread and reformed and changed it to fit a style that is, at the same time different but reminiscent of the older tradition. What is the sauce then, and what are these pepperonis here? First, we can say that generally they are all considered spices. They enhance the pizza in much the same way Shakespeare uses character development, added plot structure, as well as the good old romantic twist to enhance his plays for the audiences of the Elizabethan Era. If Shakespeare offered them the same old bread that they had been chewing on for hundreds of years, his plays would have been unsuccessful. The people of that era want spicy sauce and extra onions. For Shakespeare's reality and fantasy to remain balanced, he has more factors to contend with. By developing his characters more completely, he brings the audience into closer involvement with the play. No longer is the audience watching, they are living the experience of the characters. We can more closely identify with the lovers, Luciana and Antipholus of Syracuse, with far greater ease than with Erotium and Menaechmus of Epidamnum. Because Shakespeare has taken the fantasy that much farther by including a second set of twins, so also must he take reality a commensurate step further through character development and plot structure. Also, by bringing the audience closer to the characters, a bit of the farcical nature is left behind, and a more dramatic urgency arises. I believe that much of the comedy lies in the audience's knowledge of the ensuing conflict over the obvious ignorance of all characters as to what exactly is going on. Shakespeare sprinkles his literary pie with a dash of cheese from the most ancient form of humor. He doesn't rest the taste of his pizza solely on the crust and spices alone. He uses other techniques of humor to supplement his comic theme. This will often help the inferior crust seem more appealing by detracting from its specific flavor. The cheese represents the low humor surrounding the bodily excretion of gastric waste. You can obviously see why cheese is the most adequate analogy. But, my hungry people, I can see that I begin to deviate from your questions.

I will end this discussion with a very important idea. It is exceedingly easy to look at this bread and this pizza and hastily deem the pizza superior in all ways to the plain bread. That would be just as wrong as saying Shakespeare's play is superior to Plautus's based on the intricacy of each play. A pizza may be superior, but not on the basis of looks. All these frills are meaningless if the actual taste in your mouth does not delight you. You know what I say if you have ever paid for a beautiful but horrid tasting pizza. In contrast, just as most people will enjoy a piece of well-made bread, fewer will enjoy a pizza with all the trimmings because of its overwhelming nature. However, I think those people who do enjoy the pizza will enjoy it more than those who enjoy the bread."

Our conversation was interrupted by a weary group of college students yearning for a tasty snack and some advice on Pre-Cambrian societies in southern central Asia. Bill said that he is only the pizza guy and couldn't be expected to know everything. As I thanked Bill and began to eat my cold pizza, to my great surprise I watched as Mike came from around the counter with a huge stone axe and a plate of spaghetti. From here on the story doesn't concern me, Shakespeare, or Plautus and so I conclude.

■ THE WRITER'S ASSIGNMENT

Select either Moliere's *Misanthrope* or Shakespeare's *Comedy of Errors*. Compare the later play with its earlier principal source (Menander's *Dyskolos* for Moliere, and Plautus's *Menaechmi* for Shakespeare), and focus your comparisons on developments in the form of comedy over time. You will need, for a paper this length, to select one or two aspects of the play, rather than attempt an overall treatment. Don't forget to cite sources, and to support your thesis with clear references to the plays' texts. ■

■ UNDERSTANDING WRITING STRATEGIES

1. On what aspects of the plays does Cole focus his paper? How well does the thesis indicate this focus?

2. How does Cole structure his comparison?

3. What is this essay's tone? How does this enhance or detract from the ideas Cole is presenting?

4. Is the essay's argument clear and precise? How well is the argument supported by textual references?

5. What is this essay's purpose in relation to its audience? What elicits your response?

6. Is this essay's argument "objective" enough to support its underlying purpose? ■

The Narrator as God in Fowles's The French Lieutenant's Woman

Randall Coppinger

Randy Coppinger finds that novelist John Fowles plays god when he gives his narrator omniscience and the power to intervene in human affairs. Fowles's use of inertia theology and the Trinity, and creation and free will reinforce the analogy between God and the narrator that Coppinger presents in this essay for his writing course focusing on literature.

Nietzsche's declaration of God's death has strongly influenced many twentieth-century writers. John Fowles, playing with a century's traditions, revived God for his own writing purposes. In *The French Lieutenant's Woman* Fowles equates himself with God. We can see this more clearly if we examine some basic ideas about God—omniscience, intervention, inertia, the Trinity, creation, and free will.

The claim for his omniscience and ability to intervene is not made directly by Fowles. These attributes, nevertheless, are very clear in the novel and play an important part in the analogy between Fowles and God. Omniscience and the power to intervene in human affairs are unique characteristics of God. Only God, not mortals, can be everywhere at once, seeing everything and intervening at will. How is the novelist like this? His omniscience appears in his description of Mary on page 64. The narrator compares Mary to her twenty-two-year-old great-great-grandmother, making the narrator either impossibly old or omniscient. Another example of omniscience occurs in chapters 10 and 11. Both chapters occur at the same time (according to chapter 11's introductions) and the narrator saw the events of both. He was both at the Undercliff and in Aunt Tranter's Lyme Regis house simultaneously.

The narrator also can see into more than one character at a time. The conversation between Ernestina and Mary at Aunt Tranter's house shows this. The "tiny light" in Mary's eyes goes unnoticed by Mary, yet is seen in the text. And in the same situation the narrator shares Ernestina's observation that Mary had "won the exchange" even though Mary is unaware.

These examples illustrate omniscience, but how does the narrator "intervene"? The previous examples also show the narrator intervening in the story to share the omniscient information. This is especially true of the comparison used to describe Mary. In another instance where the narrator intervenes, he reminds readers of their own time for reasons of comparison. The narrator describes the servant Sam by pitting him against previous servants and the kind of servants who would follow him (39). The intervention reminds us that we have historical perspective on the situation, something the novel's characters lack. Likewise, they alone participate in the experiences of their time in a way we cannot. Another example of time intervention includes statistics about Victorian brothels and the twice-suggested notion that Sarah is a lesbian.

These examples lead us to the God Analogy, Fowles's identification with God. The novelist possesses characteristics unique to God. In much the same way that we believe that God is everywhere and that He can intervene (with historical insight), Fowles asks us to believe that the narrator possesses these same abilities. Fowles does not stop and say, "Now look here, I'm onmiscient and have divine power to intervene," but the fact that he takes such liberties as a novelist, is to possess divinity by fiat. Not only does he grant himself these abilities, he uses them extensively to make clear his superiority.

The terms "narrator" and "novelist" are interchangeable here only to an extent. This limitation brings us to the second terms of the analogy: inertia theology and the Trinity. Both concepts serve as descriptions of God. Inertia theology, or the great clockmaker theory, states that God initiated all things, and that all things continue without needing further maintenance. The Trinity describes God as having three independent members that make up the whole. In *The French Lieutenant's Woman*, Fowles presents himself in much the same way.

Inertia theology first appears when Fowles actually uses the term "malevolent inertia" to describe Charles's interpretation of Fowles's intervention into his world (267). Charles was also described as having felt the route of his life as "an inexorable onward direction as fixed as that of the train which drew Charles along. While this may seem to be an image of destiny, the key here is that Fowles laid the track. He set the characters in motion, and they behave relative to this motion. Once the track is laid, the course is set and "god" sits back as the world continues.

The concept of the Trinity is perhaps more abstract, but appears in two separate passages. First, the entire Trinity can be construed in the presence of the "bearded man" flipping a florin on the train (318). This man is Fowles himself yet in the novel's world. As suggested earlier, the narrator and novelist are related, specifically because they are both Fowles. The novelist can be seen as "God the Father" since he created the world and set it in motion. The narrator's "among us" and "a comforter" in this world, yet not seen by mortals, thus exemplifying "God the Holy Spirit." Finally, "God" becomes flesh in this world as witnessed by Charles on the train. "God the Christ" completes the Trinity of Fowles's godhead.

The presence of the Trinity and inertia theology strengthen the God analogy. The novelist describes himself in ways we commonly describe God. The detail in which the reader "discovers" Fowles strengthens his "faith" in the God analogy, and thereby in the narrator/novelist. We are very close to omnipotence here that Fowles has himself both invoked and denied. Fowles seemingly dispells omnipotence early in chapter 13. Or does he? Fowles's use of creation and free will, characteristics shared by both God and man, give further insight into Fowles's use of the God analogy.

Fowles claims creative powers from the beginning of chapter 13, although he does not label it so until the middle of the third paragraph on page 81. He states that the wish to create is foregoing proof that we actually can create. The link with God is made later when he says, "The novelist is still a god, since he creates . . ." (82). We, of course, identify Fowles as the "novelist" since this is the world we are in. Just after having revealed his creation idea, Fowles links creation with free will.

> We also know that a genuinely created world must be independent of its creator; a planned world (a world that fully reveals its planning) is a dead world. It is only when our characters and events begin to disobey us that they begin to live (81).

This says that evil is necessary for good to exist. If characters are not allowed to disobey, then there can be no true obedience. Because the reader is led to identify creation and free will, and because these are part of Christian ontology, Fowles has prepared his reader for chapter 13's bold identification of the novelist with God.

What conclusions does the God analogy lead us to make about the novel? To answer this we need to consider that Fowles's identification with God has a definite pattern. First of all Fowles merely suggests he possesses characteristics unique to God. Later in chapter 13 he comes right out and argues that he is like God because he possesses abilities that all humans share with God. Finally, at the end Fowles's identification with the Trinity in the way he presents himself in the novel, and the God-game he plays with the novel's multiple endings, engages the reader in the novel's thematic treatment of fiction, reality, and belief.

A close observer might notice inconsistencies in the God analogy. How can God/Fowles have divine intervention and still allow the created world to continue on inertia? How can a creature have free will and yet obey "divine" intervention? Or how can one have free will and also be directed by inertia? These questions seem to pop Fowles's little bubble, don't they? Not true. We have the same conceptual problems with understanding God. We have not been able to explain the relationship between these concepts in our own theology. It seems that the more we try to dispel Fowles's God analogy, the closer the novel's world and our world converge.

So that we will not feel compelled to worship Fowles, let us move away from the analogy's implications for readers to a consideration of its implication for the novel's characters. Of free will, Fowles seems to suggest that Mrs. Poulteney has foregone hers. Possessing little sin in her own mind, Mrs. Poulteney has nothing to contrast with her self-righteousness. She frequently refers to her age, death, and expected salvation, yet the narrator, playing God, consigns her to damnation for her self-righteous choices. Charles, too, must contend with the tension between God's omnipotence and his own free will. Charles, like us, questions his creator (Fowles) when he keeps finding himself in situations that deny the exercise of his free will. Charles asks if this is real. Fowles wants us to ask the same question on two levels. First of all, is Charles's experience real? Is the book real? Is fiction real? Is Fowles god? On the second level, the novel demands that we question reality. Charles only knew of one way to verify reality—science. He also realized that science did not explain his misery or limited choice. The other way he (and we) can explain reality is by discourse theory which basically states that things are real only if they can be experienced although not necessarily measured. Returning then to the first level. Can the book's events be scientifically measured? No, therefore they are not real. Can the book's events be experienced? We have just experienced them so the answer is yes. The next logical step would be to say that the book is therefore real and Fowles is a god. But is this true? This is the ultimate question the book leaves us hanging with, much like the question of which of the book's three endings is real. Do we measure reality or experience it? Did Charles stay with Sarah or leave?

Unlike Nietzsche, a recent movie, *Time Bandits*, allowed for a God, calling Him the Supreme Being. At the film's end Satan had been burned and his remains put in a barrel. When the young protagonist returned to his present time, his house was on fire, caused by something in the toaster. When his parents opened the toaster, the boy recognized the burned object as a piece of Satan. He shouts, "Don't touch that! It's evil!" They touch it, they explode, and the movie ends. The end of *The French Lieutenant's Woman* is much less conclusive. This, however, is not a disappointment; it *is* the point.

■ THE WRITER'S ASSIGNMENT

Write a paper giving insight into John Fowles's *The French Lieutenant's Woman* by explaining how John Fowles "plays" with some nineteenth-century novel convention—the omniscient narrator, romantic characters, class distinctions, religion, or Darwinism. ■

■ UNDERSTANDING WRITING STRATEGIES

1. What is the paper's central position, or thesis?

2. How does Coppinger support this thesis?

3. How does Coppinger organize his argument? How well is the argument supported by reference to the text?

4. Does the author adequately explain the aspect of the novel he discusses? What audience does his explanation indicate?

5. Considering the criteria presented in chapter 1 for good analogies, evaluate the essay's governing analogy.

6. What kind of insight does this essay offer into Fowles's novel?

7. Does the conclusion effectively leave the reader with a clear sense of the insight gained?

8. Why does Coppinger allude to the movie, *The Time Bandits*? How well is this allusion explained? ■

■ SUGGESTIONS FOR WRITING

Rewrite the introduction and conclusion to appeal to a distinct audience and engage them in the essay's subject. ■

Dance Photography

Eileen Coppola

Writing for a dance history course, Eileen Coppola critiques photographic strategies for presenting dance movement. The essay's historical perspective gives the reader background on dance necessary to appreciate the evaluation.

"Dance Photography" is a deceivingly simple term, which actually encompasses a wide range of images and philosophies, and expresses them in these two seemingly uncomplicated words. It is a term which refers to the constantly changing perceptions of many artists working under different circumstances at different points in time. Throughout the history of photography, photographers have been motivated to use the dance form as subject matter for their medium for widely different reasons, with varying degrees of importance unevenly distributed between the two artistic mediums of photography and dance.

Some photographers have taken an "informational"[1] approach, photographing dance and dancers more for historical documentation of the dance itself than for the sake of producing photographic art. This is closely related to a photo-journalistic approach, and often these photographs may capture the very essence of a dance or dancer, since a single publicity shot may be required to communicate the feeling of a dance, or the choreographer's specific message. Quite the opposite approach to dance photography has been referred to as "incidental."[2] In this type of photograph, the most important aspects of the image are those which apply to the photographic medium. This photographer does not seek to serve the dance, rather he is thinking more of his own medium as a form of artistic expression, and dance happens to be the subject matter for his photographs. Some photographers are not concerned with communicating what is the dance, for example movement, although often accidents do occur in which images do happen to convey movement. An effective way to express this type of dance photography is to say that dance is the "landscape"[3] of the photograph, which for the photographer evokes something other than the dance itself. Yet another variation of dance photography, which in some ways combines elements from the previous two discussed, involves communication of an emotional message, inherent in the dance. The most important element is the emotion which is expressed by the dance, and then communicated through the photograph.

These somewhat over-simplified categories of dance photography provide a degree of insight into this complicated field, and begin to present questions about the collaboration between the two mediums. As in any collaboration, I think something of each medium is sacrificed, because the emphasis must be placed on either one or the other, and compromises must be made. While those who photograph to provide information about the dance seem to place more importance on the dance form than on the photographic form, which becomes merely a vehicle of documentation, others maintain photography as an art form in its own right, and dance becomes a subject matter like any other. One may begin to question whether images produced by photographers who want only to document the dance can actually be accepted as art form at all, since many special artistic and creative qualities of the photographic medium become secondary to the dance. This work "seems to express less of the photographer and his medium than the subject of his images."[4] One can also philosophize that dance photographers for whom dance is only incidentally a subject matter may not produce photographs that express the dance at all, since many of their images seem to be mere expressions of the photographer's psyche, which only happens to be triggered by dance or dancers. These images evoke for the photographer something other than the dance. I feel these questions can be further understood, if not finally answered and dismissed, by examining the relationship of dance and photography, as it has been developed by artists throughout history.

The idea of expressing dance through pictures was accepted long before the invention of photography. Dance and dancers were often depicted by draftsmen for newspapers or magazines, or through the medium of lithography. With the invention of photography began many new and exciting experiments, for example photographer Edweard Muybridge began to experiment with photographs of posed people and animals, which when viewed in quick succession conveyed an appearance of movement. Though these photographs were not of dancers and Muybridge was primarily interested in motion picture films, these photographs represent some of the first known attempts by a photographer to convey movement through his medium, and a fascination with this phenomenon that was and is shared by many photographers.

Although Muybridge was pursuing his movement studies as early as 1880, subsequent dance photographs were not so much photographs of dance movement as they were photographs of dancers, or portraits. Some sterling examples of this type of photography which prevailed are the photographs of the legendary ballerina, Anna Pavlova, stretching from the late nineteenth century into the nineteen thirties. These are highly stylized and posed photographs which reveal little of Pavlova as a woman, or of dance, for various reasons. In the early days of photography long exposures prohibited movement shots, because they would be blurred. Sometimes wooden supports were used to hold the dancer in a fixed position simulating movement, but the essence of dance was more often than not absent. One of the more innovative attempts to feign movement was the photographing of dancers posed lying down on a black floor. These photographs were taken from some point above, and were supposed to create the impression of dancers in flight, but unfortunately did not appear natural. Therefore many still posed photographs were taken of dancers, rather than movement shots. Pavlova preferred photographs that presented her as a sort of super-human woman, idealized, heavily made up and always in costume. She preferred that photographs taken of her be retouched, often by herself, to ensure that she looked perfect. She was not concerned with presenting herself or the dance, but rather a calculated and other-worldly image used mainly for publicity. Interestingly, this attitude toward what a dancer should be, the image or character which should be projected, is characteristic of the classical ballet style, in which Pavlova danced. Photographs of Pavlova reveal little about the movement of the dance, yet say something to us of the classical balletic style. There is not much evidence of artistic photographic expression in these photographs; the dancer is simply placed in front of the camera, yet it must be noted that to merely achieve this was an accomplishment for a photographer. These photographs of Pavlova exist as precious documents, and represent the prevalent mode of dance photography during that era.

The first dancer that is known to have consciously collaborated with a photographer on a more artistic level was Vaslov Nijinsky, and the photographer was Baron Adolphe De Meyer. Nijinsky and De Meyer worked together around 1910, and the photographs produced are not only expressive of Nijinsky and the dance, but also are successful as independent works of art. These photographs are most incredible because without showing actual movement they successfully "suggest previous and subsequent action."[5] De Meyer did not need to literally depict leaps, or to blur the dancer's movement in order to convey, or confuse, the feeling of movement. He managed to capture the essence of movement in very sensitive and subtle ways. What's more, De Meyer managed to capture the spirit of the dance, particularly in "Scheherazade," and the personality of Nijinsky. De Meyer's photographs were not intended for publicity, but rather to exist as works of art. De Meyer "invented nothing, merely saw Nijinsky as a creature of force and externalized a modicum of his motion."[6] He did not try to change or invent his subject, but seemed to respect it, and like it, and react to it in an artistic manner. Nijinsky was a subject matter that moved De Meyer to photograph him, and through the special nature of his medium De Meyer used him to create works of art. These photographs of Nijinsky stand in striking contrast to the photographs of Pavlova, even though many of them were taken during the same period of time, in the early nineteen hundreds. They clearly represent two contrasting approaches to dance photography. One, a historical and documentary approach, in which the image of Pavlova was recorded for publicity purposes, as opposed to the creative and artistic approach of Baron De Meyer, who viewed his medium as an art form, and the dance as the subject matter which moved him to create works of art.

The next step forward in dance photography was made by Arnold Genthe, who also photographed during the early nineteen hundreds. Genthe was primarily a portrait photographer, who also worked with dancers, such as Isadora Duncan. In many ways he was able to successfully apply his beliefs about portrait photography to his dance photographs. For example, he felt it essential that his subject not be aware of the exact moment the photograph is taken, in order to capture the true essence of the subject, and he felt that a posed portrait could never give the convincing impression of life or movement. These attitudes were exemplified in one unusual photograph of Anna Pavlova. When Pavlova came to Genthe to have her portrait taken, Genthe managed to photograph her while she was warming up, moving and dancing without realizing that she was being photographed. The one successful photograph of the series is the only existing shot of Pavlova in action, totally abandoned in the ecstacy of the dance. The photograph is about an extraordinary dancer engrossed in dynamic movement, in total contrast with the typical Pavlova picture, and the key principle was the dancer's oblivion to the moment of being photographed. The success of the photograph lies in the depiction of movement, and in the capturing, to some degree, of Pavlova's personality.

Arnold Genthe's favorite dancer to photograph was Isadora Duncan, who objected to being photographed until she worked with Genthe, and re-alized that she could be photographed while dancing, and without thinking of the camera. Genthe's many photographs of Isadora and the Isadorables are lovely outdoor shots, often taken of the women dancing by the sea shore. Here Genthe was able to express the movement of the dancers, and also deep emotional meaning, particularly the association with nature that was the essence of Duncan dancing. In his photographs the dancers are in har-mony with their environment, and seem to be dancing freely, oblivious to the camera. These photographs are a joy to view, and convey a wonderful feeling of carefree abandonment. Genthe's ability to photograph actual movement rather than implied movement was due largely to technical ad-vances in photography which allowed for shorter shutter speeds and there-fore motion with minimal blur. Yet he felt that it was not only important to simply photograph the action, but also that "unless the pose indicates the preceding and following movement, motion is not conveyed."[7] While taking a step forward in being able to photograph motion, Genthe also took a differ-ent approach than photographers of Pavlova. When one looks at Genthe's images, an overwhelming natural and spontaneous feeling is conveyed, as though we are able to capture a precious glimpse into the lives and dancing of these women who move oblivious to the camera, and there is a refreshing quality in this, that the photographer is unconcerned with everything but recording this private moment of truth. Genthe was unconcerned with pos-ing the dancers and creating something specifically for the camera. Rather his motivation to shoot dance "came about as a result of the desire to cap-ture its rhythm and suggest it adequately for the camera."[8] Genthe's photo-graphs of dance capture and suggest rhythm in addition to being delightful records of Duncan, and adequately capturing movement. His love for the dance form seemed to be as great as his mastery of his photographic medium.

John Lindquist belongs to a particular breed of dance photographers, for whom love of the dance is the primary motive for pursuing dance pho-tography. Lindquist's life-long interest in dance eventually prompted him to photograph many well-known modern dancers, such as Ted Shawn and Ruth Saint Dennis. Later Lindquist became the official photographer for Ja-cob's Pillow, the dance company which Ted Shawn founded after the con-clusion of Dennishawn. Many of these photographs were taken outdoors, on platforms built specifically for the purpose of photographing, set against backgrounds of trees and open skies. In all of Lindquist's photographs, the dancers seem to be at their most expressive moment, both at the peak of their dance movement, and at the height of personal expression. Lindquist managed to have "caught the moment of genius, the uniqueness of each art-ist."[9] In fact, the individual personality of each dancer seems to be projected from these photographs. For instance, his photographs of Ruth Saint Dennis convey the theatrical monumentality that "Miss Ruth" certainly exuded, and quite different feelings are conveyed through photographs of other dancers. Lindquist prefers not to pose the dancers, but to view the dance before shooting it, and then feel the peak moments when he shoots the second time around. In fact, Lindquist attributes his ability to capture the peak moments of the dance to his kinesthetic sense of movement, which helps him to feel the photographic image in his body.

Lindquist is a photographer whose "life has been no less dedicated to the art of dance than the dancers in his photographs."[10] Indeed Lindquist's very unique talent stems from his kinesthetic sense, a feeling of movement in the body, which is a basis for dance. He seems to be a man more dedicated to the dance as an art form than to the photographic art form. His involvement in photography existed only as a result of and in relation to dance, and for him, it seemed to be important only when dancers were the subject matter. With this sort of philosophy toward photography, one may not expect that the images produced would be works of photographic art, but rather mere document of dance. Yet John Lindquist's attitudes toward these two art forms has allowed him to produce images which exist as works of art in their own right. He has managed to do what few photographers before him had done, in a way that no other photographer has done. He has captured the dance and the dancer in motion, at the height of expression and movement and nobility. This glorification of the dance form is yet another type of dance photography, and certainly a valid expression of one individual's attitudes and beliefs about the collaboration between the arts of dance and photography.

While Lindquist's main motive to photograph was dance, quite a different approach to dance photography was taken by Thomas Bouchard. Bouchard photographed the "generation" of modern dancers who broke away from Dennishawn, most importantly Doris Humphry and Charles Weidman, along with Hanya Holm. Bouchard seemed to be aware of some of the problems involved in the collaboration between two art forms, and honestly and consciously addressed them. He recognized that two different artistic mediums could not combine and produce pure artistry. Certainly there must be a degree of compromise on either side. One such example is that dance as seen through the camera is against the very nature of dance movement. Suddenly an art form which explores and moves through space is confined to a fixed rectangular space, motionless, and a three-dimensional, transient art becomes fixed in a two-dimensional paper form. Bouchard realized and verbalized the concept that one "must use the inventive and imaginative qualities of the camera to recompose the entire event,"[11] for our purposes, the dance. Here Bouchard consciously addressed his own role as the photographer, and here is where he placed importance, on the special qualities particular to his own medium of expression. He felt that his artistic vision went beyond the desire to preserve steps, and aimed at the depth and message of his subject matter. He was interested in the human and expressive aspects of the dances he photographed, and fortunately the early modern dancers were very interested in expressing emotion through their medium as well. By looking at his photographs, it is evident that Bouchard was successful in capturing the emotional qualities of his subject matter. Photographs of Hanya Holm and her dance "Trend" convey a strong intensity, a feeling of something looming, pending, and an energy that is held taut, ready to spring forth. Photographs of Doris Humphry and Charles Wiedman communicate quite a different sensation, a much lighter feeling of suspended motion, a moment of breathlessness between movements. From viewing these photographs in succession, it becomes strikingly apparent that Doris is a very different person from Hanya, so successful is Bouchard in capturing emotions expressed through dancers, and by dance.

Often Bouchard's photographs are of still moments, sometimes with only a flip of a skirt to suggest movement, or at times so still that the dancer appears statuesque. In these instances, Bouchard has managed to convey the meaning of the dance without movement. These still photographs are the epitome of his unique artistry, for with them he has managed to use his artistic medium to the full extent of its capacity. He has used the qualities unique to photography in order to successfully express the essence of the dance, the emotional qualities of the dance, ironically, without photographing movement. Bouchard was not only a great dance photographer, but also unquestionably an artist.

A photographer very similar in philosophy to her contemporary Thomas Bouchard is Barbara Morgan, who chose Martha Graham as the subject matter for her photographs. Morgan worked closely with Graham, and the majority of their collaboration took place between 1936 and 1941. She is an artist who believes that:

> The dance photographer expresses the spirit of the movement in terms natural to photography . . . By this positive control, the photographer graduates from the status of a passive machine accepting accidental picture conditions and becomes a conscious photographic director who senses the dance potential of his subjects and transforms their actual movements into the photographic image on paper.[12]

Barbara Morgan seeks not to capture a movement of the dance, but to find the elements which make photographic sense, which are important and unique to the photographic medium. She believes that this is the manner in which the dance can be most adequately expressed through photography. She suggests that the photographer seeks to produce "not merely a document of dance, but the dance or section of the dance recreated,"[13] by the photographer. Morgan also addresses the issue of accident and passivity, and believes that by consciously selecting what and when to photograph, as well as controlling the technical aspects of photography, such as lighting, camera angle, shutter speed, or film processing, the photographer becomes an active artist. Morgan realizes that technical skill is important, but only as a means to an end, in the service producing works of art. Characteristically, Morgan's manner seems always deliberate, and she always takes much time, se-lecting and editing with her camera, rather than shooting and hoping for the best.

Morgan's photographs use abstract qualities to convey human emo-tionalism. In fact, many of her photographs are valid when viewed upside down, but she has never been interested in design or pattern for their own sakes. In her photographs they must always be used to convey meaning on a deeper level. Fortunately, Martha Graham has much the same attitude about her dancing, and her movements always convey some deeper, human meaning, beyond the motion of dance, beyond dance for dance's sake. Mor-gan's photographs are all intensely emotional, as are Graham's dances, and she has managed to perfectly express the universality of Graham's themes. Again, like Bouchard, her photographs are often of that still moment, when for a fraction of a second the dancer reaches her peak of emotional expres-sion, and for a fleeting moment stands freed and enabled by her art. Barbara Morgan and Thomas Bouchard have very similar understandings about the relationship between photography and dance, and yet their photographs are strikingly dissimilar, beyond the different dances as subject matter. I believe this is due to the concept of individual artistic expression inherent in their philosophies. The dance photographer as active artist, who employs his or unique talents within the photographic medium, to produce images that are as much an artistic expression of individuality as they are expressions of dance. Barbara Morgan's photographs are certainly moving studies of Martha Graham, but they are also artistic expressions of Barbara Morgan herself, as well as works of art which stand on their own, apart from the sub-ject matter of dance.

Thus far, the photographers which I have discussed have been inter-ested in photographing dance for a variety of personal reasons. More re-cently, many photographers of dance have made this field their livelihood, or at least part of it, and in order to earn a living, this often means photo-graphing for publicity purposes. It is interesting to explore how individual photographers have managed to combine the two artistic mediums for a more commercial purpose, for example the press, and the images that result. One commercial theater photographer who managed to retain the original passion for art that first drew him to his profession is Marcus Blechman. He maintained an understanding of dance photography which far surpassed just documenting dancers for the press. For instance, he believed that:

> When you try to take an action shot, you are freezing a moment which should never be frozen. It is the picture itself which must move and give the feeling that it extends beyond the frame.[14]

Blechman seemed to understand that it is not merely a great dance mo-ment captured which makes a great photograph, but the picture itself, the photographic qualities of the image, which can give a feeling of dance.

Blechman preferred to photograph in his studio, where he had maximum control of the photographic elements, and he had the dancers improvise to express their personal individuality.

Another theatrical photographer who also preferred to photograph in the studio was Max Waldman. Waldman returned dance photography to the studio at a time in the nineteen sixties and seventies when many of his contemporaries were more concerned with action photography, usually shot during performances. Waldman preferred the controlled environment of studio photography, which is a popular feeling among dance photographers today. The result was dance photography which incorporates a sense of portraiture, and movement, similar in concept to Arnold Genthe's approach. Like Blechman, Waldman also used improvisation in the studio to capture the personality of the dancers. This technique seems to be very effective, because in Waldman's photographs there is a personal, almost intimate feeling with the dancers. Again in the manner of Arnold Genthe, Waldman preferred to capture the action of the dancers which suggest both the preceding and following movements. Hence, his photographs give the feeling of not single great dance moments captured, but of delightful dance phrases, which make the photographs express a flow of movement.

Waldman had a very specific style of photography which successfully combines the movement of the dance with a sense of portraiture which provides insight into the personality of the dancers. As I have noted, there are many similarities between the approach of Arnold Genthe and that of Max Waldman to dance photography. Yet there is also a difference between the two which suggests separate motivations for their work in dance photography. Genthe was concerned with recording the dance and its movement, without creating something specifically for the camera. Waldman, through his work in the studio, employed all of his talents in his own medium to consciously create a work of photographic art, especially for the camera. Whereas Genthe strove to adequately document the dance, Waldman was more concerned with the photographic elements of his images.

Two photographers who present strikingly different attitudes toward dance photography, and who were both contracted by the New York City Ballet, are George Platt Lynes and Martha Swope. Lynes, like Waldman, preferred to work in the studio, where he was afforded maximum control. George Balanchine would pose the dancers for the camera, while Lynes would control the photographic elements, such as lighting, to enhance the dance pose for the camera. In this way, Lynes functioned as a craftsman in the service of the ballet, yet he and Balanchine deliberately composed for the camera, for Lynes' particular artistic medium.

Quite contrary to this manner of photography is that of Martha Swope, who succeeded Lynes as New York City Ballet photographer. If it could be said that Lynes followed an "artistic" approach to dance photography, by concentrating on the unique technical qualities of his medium, then it might also be said that Swope follows a more journalistic approach. She "faithfully follows the dance, with her camera, as it unfolds before her on stage."[15] Swope prefers to shoot during performances, and uses no artificial light, no posing, no optics, no special photo-chemistry. Rather, she reports the dance through action photography. Through her photographs she attempts, successfully, to capture and communicate the reality of dance, the danger, the excitement, of what dance is, in a word, the event. These are not the beautifully set and perfectly lighted photographs of composed and quiet dancers typical of George Platt Lynes' photographs. Rather we seen the reality of the New York City Ballet, the work, sweat, and action.

Despite one common motive which brought both Lynes and Swope to photograph the New York City Ballet, which was to produce publicity photographs for the company, each photographer chose to do their job in an entirely different way. Lynes maintained a more craftsman-like approach, and his main concerns as a photographer were the photographic elements of his images, such as gorgeous lighting. Hence, his dance photographs are elegant studies of dancers, with every technical detail perfectly controlled, he is certainly a master of the photographic technique. Contrarily, Martha Swope's photographs reflect a fascination less with photography, more with dance, and her photographs capture all the vitality and energy of performances, including not only the peak moments of movement, but also the quiet reflective moments. Clearly the dedications of these two fine dance photographers are unevenly distributed between the two arts, as necessarily seems to be the case. Lynes' contemplative technique is focused on his own medium while Swope's journalistic manner reflects her fascination with dance. Another interesting aspect about their work is that they have each dealt with dance photography from the point of view of a publicist, hired for commercial and advertising reasons. Yet they have both done this without sacrificing their own personal passions about dance photography which motivated them to photograph dance originally.

Today there seems to be two major trends in dance photography, exemplified by George Platt Lynes and Martha Swope, those photographers who prefer the control of shooting in the studio, and those who take a more journalistic approach to dance photography. Max Waldman was an artist who preferred the control of studio photography, but this was at a time when most of his contempories were moving in quite another direction, specifically, toward realism and reportage of dance. Though this major trend in dance photography began in the nineteen sixties, it has been more widely recognized recently, and is a direction that more and more dance photographers, such as Martha Swope, are exploring today.

In the nineteen sixties modern dance took a new and definite direction, which many young photographers were eager to document with their cameras, often more for historical than for publicity reasons. Two most notable dance photographers from this era were Peter Moore and James Klosty. Peter Moore photographed the dance events of the Judson Church dancers, where modern dancers such as Trish Brown, Yvonne Rainer, and Lucinda

Childs rebelled against the established techniques of their mentors. These young dancers perceived dance to be simply movement in space, which could be engaged in by anyone at anytime, anywhere. Moore was fascinated by this new avant-garde dancing, and it was his objective to be a witness to dance, and to present it as undistorted and objectively as possible through the photographic medium, undistorted meaning as much as possible unchanged by photographic qualities. He was working in a journalistic fashion, as a photographer in the service of the dance. Yet his photographs are subjective. Despite his efforts to the contrary, they exemplify the fact that:

> Distortion occurs anyway by what action was not recorded, or by the technical limitations of the photographic chemical process, or by the subjective editing that occurred later . . .[16]

So that even when it is a photographer's purpose to be an impartial witness and documentor of dance history, the qualities and nature of his medium always require him to be subjective, for he must choose what, where, and how to photograph. Furthermore, even if he has deliberately tried not to express the individual personalities of the dancers, he unwittingly has expressed much of his own individual personality, at the very least through the photographic qualities of his images. Moore's photographs have a distinct quality to them, a bizarre and somewhat eerie feeling, as telling and representative of Moore's work as his signature.

James Klosty was a dance photographer who followed his passion for recording modern dance in another direction. He totally immersed himself in the Merce Cunningham Dance Company, with the intention of producing a record of Cunningham's life in the late nineteen sixties and early nineteen seventies. Although Merce Cunningham was the major company against which the Judson dancers rebelled, I have chosen to present Klosty after Moore because Klosty seemed to carry his photography a step further, from the viewpoints of both documentation and objectivity. His photographs provide records not only of the company dancing, but also of the company life itself, an area previously passed over by most photographers. What's more his photographs appear less subjective than Moore's, they are more realistic and simple images of dancers, with less of Klosty's personality apparent, and less of the unique "distortions" of the photographic medium peeking through. Surely Klosty was a degree more successful in the aim to be objective.

The philosophy toward dance photography taken by Peter Moore and James Klosty reiterates certain recurring questions about the roles of dance and photography combined. To what extent can this sort of photography be accepted as photographic art, when it seems that the photographer does not merely ignore his medium of artistic expression, but actively tries to supress the qualities which we understand to give it validity as an art form, in order to present a realistic representation of dance? Can photography exist as an art form only in relation to, and in the service of another art form? I think that at the very least it can be said that no matter how hard the photographer may try to be an objective observer of his subject matter, in this case dance, it is impossible for him to exist separately from his medium, and he must address the limitations and special qualities of the medium, at least subconsciously, in order to photograph. For example he must choose what to photograph and when, and decide what looks good enough, or right, to photograph. This is clearly demonstrated by the photographs of Peter Moore, which are highly subjective despite his efforts to be an objective observer. This is also evident in the photographs of Martha Swope, who, much in the manner of Klosty and Moore, is motivated by a desire to follow and record dance. Often her photographs capture very touching and emotional moments, not just the peak moments that most photographers would select. For example, one very strong photograph of Galina Ulanova curtseying at the end of a performance is a very touching and powerful image. This is not because the curtsey is especially lovely, but because of the vast black space to which she bows. It is not dance which makes this photograph successful, but a feeling evoked by the photographic element of a black empty space. This communicates a surreal feeling, that does not really report much about the dance at all. Despite Swope's effort to simply follow and record the dance, she too incorporates more personal elements into her photographs.

There are many dance photographers today who choose to work in their studios, as opposed to the performance photography of Klosty, Moore, and Swope. Among the best of these photographers are Jack Mitchell, Kenn Duncan, and Herbert Migdoll. These photographers work for specific ballet companies, for example Duncan for the American Ballet Theater, and Migdoll for the Joffrey Ballet, much in the same way as Lynes worked for the New York City Ballet. In their studios, these photographers are able to control every photographic element of their images, such as lighting, camera angle, or dancers' pose or movement. All of these photographs are technically perfect, so much so that, in my opinion, they all seem to look very much alike. These photographers are directly addressing the elements of their medium and using their craftsmanship to produce photographs which are technically correct, sharply focused, well lighted and precisely posed. However it seems to me that through directly addressing these photographic elements, they have established very definite criteria for what makes a "good" dance photograph. Herbert Migdoll even goes so far as to suggest that the proper angle to shoot dance from is at the waist or below. In my opinion this leaves little room for the photographer's personal expression, the freedom to be creative in decision making, determining what, when, and how to shoot. However Kenn Duncan feels that this manner of photography is the most creative and that the "less creative aspect of photography is shooting from the wings during a performance."[17] With this rationalization he places more weight on the photographic aspects of dance photography, and this philosophy is also applicable to Jack Mitchell's style of photography.

Characteristically, Jack Mitchell's photographs speak more of a perfect photographic situation in a studio than of the energy, vitality, or emotions of the dance, or of the photographer. Rather than capturing the dance, these photographs are more portraits of dancers, looking posed and waiting for the click of the camera. It is my contention that when Max Waldman returned dance photography to the studio situation and incorporated a sense of portraiture into his photographs, he also captured a feeling of a spontaneous and natural movement, an energy, which Jack Mitchell's photographs seem to lack. It appears that in the case of these studio photographers, such strong attention to, and preoccupation with the photographic elements of the image have brought about a more crafty and less artistic approach to dance photography. The results are beautiful, but common images, which in my opinion lack both the essence of dance, and individual artistic creativity.

One current dance photographer who does not conform to either of the two major trends I have just presented is Lois Greenfield. She has managed to successfully combine photography and dance, in that she uses the unique qualities of her medium, and also captures the essence of dance in her photographs. Unlike Martha Swope or James Klosty, Greenfield is not motivated by a desire to document dance, although her photographs are often used in newspapers. She prefers to work in her studio, where she can work with dancers to control and create her photographs, as opposed to a performance situation, where she has no control over photographic elements. This preference is a common feeling among photographers today, yet Lois Greenfield's work does not comply to the standards of her contemporaries. Nor are her photographs just "great dance moments captured."[18] Greenfield captures the movement, the essence of dance without photographing the peak moments of the dancers. Rather she conveys the dynamic feeling of dance through qualities of her own artistic medium. For example, in one of her photographs movement is conveyed by the path of the dancer's skirt. The photographic quality of the skirt is the element that makes the photograph successful, or interesting, rather than the dancer. In this manner Greenfield has captured the movement and lyrical quality of the dance, but expressed it in photographic terms. In fact, Greenfield refers to the fact that her photographs capture the essence of the dance as a "wonderful, fortuitous coincidence,"[19] and actually has no interest in conveying what is dance, unless she's hired to do so. She directly addresses the problematic situation that arises when making photographs of someone else's art, specifically the choreographer's, which has been a recurring theme throughout the history of dance photography. To what extent does photography serve the dance? Is it the dance which dominates the photographer's vision and makes the photograph itself? Or does dance serve photography just as any other subject matter does? Lois Greenfield states:

> If I like a photograph, it is because it evokes, for me, something other than what it is . . . Dance just happens to be my landscape.[20]

As I have explored, many of the great dance photographers have taken opposing points of view on this matter. I have not attempted to create any definitive answers, but rather to present the many facets of the issues by examining dance photographers, the ways in which they work, their motivations, and their images.

It is my belief that dance photography can be made to serve many different purposes, depending upon the motivations and inclinations of the photographer. Clearly in some instances, photography is employed in the service of dance, by such as John Lindquist, Peter Moore, and Martha Swope. To what extent the images produced exist as works of photographic "art," I feel is up to each individual to determine for himself. Surely there are many different levels that these works can be evaluated on, for instance, how well the dance movement is conveyed, or how powerful is the emotional content? However it is my opinion that the more artistic approach, from the point of view of the photographer, is that in which dance serves as a landscape for the photographic medium. Yet this philosophy cannot be readily accepted as the unequivocal and correct approach to photographing dance, because these photographs may be successful works of art without accurately expressing the dance. An extreme example of this is Jack Mitchell's work. As Thomas Bouchard expressed many years ago, the two mediums of photography and dance cannot be combined in the hopes for pure artistry; collaboration necessitates a certain degree of compromise. This compromise between photography and dance has been dealt with by many photographers, with varying, and exciting results.

Footnotes

[1]Tobie Tobias. "Fleeting Gestures: Treasures of Dance Photography," *Dance Magazine*, Feb. 1979, p. 26.

[2]Tobias, p. 26.

[3]David Linder. "More Than Just Dance," *Dance Life*, with Lois Greenfield, vol. 4, 1979, p. 21.

[4]David Linder. "Dance Photography Review," *Dance Life*, vol. 4, 1979, p. 9.

[5]Lincoln Kirstein, *Nijinsky*, (Alfred A. Knopf, Inc., 1975), p. 47.

[6]Kirstein, p. 47.

[7]Arnold Genthe, *As I Remember*, (John Day in Association with Reynal and Hitchcock, 1936), p. 196.

[8]Genthe, p. 196.

[9]Iris M. Fanger. "Catching the Feeling of the Dance: John Lindquist," *Dance Magazine*, Aug. 1972, p. 58.

[10]Fanger, p. 58.

[11]Thomas Bouchard. "The Camera's Eye as Choreographer," *Dance Magazine*, Nov. 1951, p. 15.

[12]Doris Hering. "Barbara Morgan, One of America's Great Photographers Reflects a Decade of Dance," *Dance Magazine*, Int. with Barbara Morgan, July 1971, p. 43.

[13]H. B. Kronen. "Books/The Dancer's Image," *Dance Scope,* June 1981, vol. 15, series 2, p. 63.

[14]Anna Kisselgoff. "The Dance in Photographs," *New York Times,* 15 Jan. 1978, p. 18.

[15]Linder, "Dance Photography in Review", p.3.

[16]David Linder. "Salon de Refuse," *Dance Life,* vol. 4, 1979, p. 17.

[17]Marion Horosko. "Getting Photographed," *Dance Magazine,* Int. with Kenn Duncan, May 1981, p. 34.

[18]Linder, "More Than Just Dance," p. 21.

[19]Linder, p. 21.

[20]Linder, p. 21.

Bibliography

Books

Barnes, Clive. *Waldman On Dance.* New York: William Morrow & Co., Inc., 1977.

Genthe, Arnold. *As I Remember.* New Jersey: John Day in Association with Reynal and Hitchcock, 1936.

Kirnstein, Lincoln. *Nijinsky.* (USA), Alfred A. Knopf, Inc., 1975.

Morgan, Barbara. *Martha Graham: Sixteen Dances in Photographs.* 194; rpt. (USA), Morgan & Morgan, 1981.

Periodicals

Ackerman, Mildren. "Dialoge: On Dancing and Dancers." *Impulse,* 1961, pp. 4–6.

Bouchard, Thomas. "The Camera's Eye As Choreographer." *Dance Magazine,* Nov. 1951, pp. 14–15, 45.

Fanger, Iris M. "Catch the Feeling of the Dance: John Lindquist." *Dance Magazine,* Aug. 1972, pp. 48–58.

Hering, Doris. "Barbara Morgan, One of America's Great Photographers Reflects a Decade of Dance." *Dance Magazine,* July 1971, pp. 43–56.

Horosko, Marion. "Getting Photographed." *Dance Magazine,* May 1981, pp. 32–34.

Jowitt, Deborah. "Books: Morgan Looks at Graham." *Ballet Review,* Spring 1981, vol. 9, #1, pp. 109–112.

Kronen, H. B. "Books/The Dancer's Image." *Dance Scope,* June 1981, vol. 15, series 2, pp. 57–63.

Lazzarini, John and Roberta. "Images of Pavlova: The Fanciful Photo Legacy." *Dance Magazine,* Jan. 1981, pp. 59–64.

Linder, David. "Dance Photography Review." *Dance Life,* 1979, vol. 4, pp. 1–15.

Ibid., "Salon de Refuse." pp. 17–20.

Ibid., "More Than Just Dance," pp. 21–28.

Ibid., "Dramatizing the Dance." pp. 40–49.

Tobias, Tobi. "Fleeting Gestures: Treasures of Dance Photography." *Dance Magazine,* Feb. 1979, pp. 24–30.

Newspapers

Daria, Irene. "Images That Dance." *New York Photo District News,* Dec. 1983, vol. IV, Issue I, p. 1, col. 2–3, p. 30, col. 1–2–3.

Kisselgoff, Anna. "The Dance in Photographs." *New York Times*, 15 Jan. 1978, Arts and Leisure, p. 6, p. 18.

■ UNDERSTANDING WRITING STRATEGIES

1. What is the distinction Coppola makes between the "informational" and "incidental" approaches to dance photography?

2. What are the most striking differences between photographs of Pavlova, Nijinsky, and Duncan? How do the differences reflect the development of dance photography?

3. In what ways are Genthe and Waldman similar? In what ways do they differ? Are the differences indicative of progressive movement in the art of dance photography? Why or why not?

4. What is Coppola's main criticism of dance photography? How does her criticism reflect the dilemma in the genre as a whole?

5. How does Coppola order her lengthy essay? What other kinds of ordering approaches might she have taken?

6. How does Coppola enable her reader to "see" the photographs she discusses? How else might she have approached this?

7. How does Coppola engage her reader's interest? Where do you see this? ■

■ SUGGESTIONS FOR WRITING

Using Coppola's distinction between informational and incidental photography, critique the work of any art photographer who interests you. You might review a book of Ansel Adams photographs, or the photographs by a single photographer for a sports magazine. You might wish to evolve other criteria besides informational and incidental. ■

Clear and Distinct Ideas in Descartes' Meditations

Daren Di Nicola

Di Nicola worked with Cynthia Stuffman throughout their modern philosophy course refining their understanding of Descartes' *Meditations*. This paper resulting from their work represents a "term" paper in the best sense of the word. The work began with a class discussion that led to tutorials in the professor's office and a shorter initial study. Di Nicola and Stuffman then expanded their own interpretations of Descartes by reading other philosophers and interpreters. Although they worked through the ideas together, their papers reflect independent work. Stuffman's paper entitled "The Order of the Proofs for the Existence of God in Descartes' *Meditations*" also appears in this section of the anthology.

In the following, I will define Descartes' usage of the terms "clear and distinct" and then proceed to show the significance of these terms, properly understood, for the arguments Descartes sets forth in the *Meditations*.

In order to begin, we must first discover what Descartes means by "clear and distinct ideas." An answer may be found in his *Principles*. An idea which is clear is that "which is present and open to an attentive mind," and that which is distinct is that which is "so precise and separated from all others that it contains within itself absolutely nothing but what is clear."[1] According to these definitions, an idea may be clear without also being distinct, but an idea which is distinct must also be clear.[2]

How is it then, that we arrive at ideas which are both clear and distinct? The answer to this may be found by examining Descartes' *Rules*. The aim of the *Rules* is to supply one with the method in which true knowledge may be obtained. In Descartes' view, the way to true knowledge is not to be found through sense experience, but rather through the workings of our intellect alone; as he states in Rule II, "our inferences from experience are frequently fallacious." Arithmetic and Geometry, in his view, are sciences that reflect the truth and certainty one can arrive at through the process of pure reason; in other words, they may be grasped purely by the intellect alone. In Rule III, he further narrows the boundaries for acquiring knowledge when he proclaims that there are only two ways to arrive at the knowledge of things, "intuition and induction." The following will help clarify the connection with clear and distinct ideas:

> intuition is the undoubting conception of an unclouded and attentive mind, and springs from the light of reason alone; it is more than deduction itself, in that it is simpler, though deduction, . . . cannot by us be erroneously conducted. (Rule III)

At this point, we may begin to understand more fully that which Descartes is undertaking in the *Meditations*. In the first Meditation, the premise of a malignant demon is proposed, raising doubts about all that Descartes had previously assumed to be true. This includes all external sense data as well as (at this point) the mathematical truths. However, once the *Cogito**** is presented in Meditation II, it becomes clear that it is through reason that certainty and knowledge may be obtained.

The *Cogito* illustrates several important facts concerning clear and distinct ideas. First, the formation of the idea of one's own existence, and the infallibility of that notion, confirms that there is at least one thing which can be known that cannot be doubted. In other words, the malignant demon (or what is also known as hyperbolic doubt) cannot be extended to include doubt of one's own existence.[3] The idea I have of my existence is clear; that is, it is present to my attentive mind each time I affirm that I exist, and it is distinct, in that the conception of my existence does not depend on the conception of any other object. Finally, the "assumption" of the general truth of clear and distinct perceptions, based on what has been learned from the *Cognito*, is presented at the beginning of Meditation III. At this point, however, Descartes has shown only that the *Cogito* withstands the hyperbolic doubt and therefore, it would be a hasty generalization to conclude that all clear and distinct perceptions are necessarily true.

Before proceeding on to Meditation III, we may find it necessary here to further examine Descartes' notion of "idea." In the Second Replies, Definition 2 he defines ideas as "the form of any thought, that form by the immediate awareness of which I am conscious of that said thought." This does not require that the idea be an "image" of a particular thing, but rather a conception of the nature of a thing grasped through the intellect alone. It is in this way that he will define the idea he has of God in Meditation III.[4]

In Meditation III, Descartes further draws a distinction between ideas, stating that those ideas which represent substance, or the essence of a particular thing, are of a different nature than those representing external sensible objects. This was proven earlier in Meditation II with the example of the piece of wax, where it was demonstrated that nothing certain could be said of the wax by considering merely its sensible qualities, but rather the wax (or its essence) ultimately must be grasped by the intellect alone. A further discussion of the essence of material things is offered in Meditation V. Again, this coincides with what was stated earlier about the role of intuition in Descartes' method as presented in the Rules.

At this stage, however, there is only one substance which can be known to exist, that is, myself as a thinking thing, and it is by examining this notion that Descartes will seek to find whether or not the existence of any other being can be inferred. Meditation III sets out to prove the exis-

*Cogito ergo sum: Descartes' important philosphical statement, "I think; therefore I am."

tence of God by way of considering the nature of oneself and finds in it proof that a being more perfect must necessarily exist.

The proof for the existence of God rests on two main assumptions; these are that, the idea of perfection entails reality and a cause must contain at least as much reality as its effect. To demonstrate the latter proposition, Descartes considers his ideas of external objects and notes that there is nothing of those ideas which could not possibly be found also within the idea he has of himself (i.e., the idea of extension, length, breadth, etc.). In addition, Descartes asserts that ideas vary in regard to the degree of objective reality which they possess, those representing substances containing more objective reality than those "that represent only modes or accidents." An idea which contains more objective reality than another is defined as participating "by representation in higher degrees of being or perfection."[5]

The idea of God as eternal and infinite, in turn has more objective reality than any other idea. Thus, as I am aware that I am a finite and imperfect being, and that I have an idea of a being which is infinite and perfect, it follows that that idea could not have been caused by me (for that which is perfect could never be caused by that which is imperfect) and therefore, God must exist. As Descartes states:

> if the objective reality [or perfection] of any one of my ideas be such as clearly to convince me, that this same reality exists in me neither formally nor eminently, and if, as follows from this, I myself cannot be the cause of it, it is a necessary consequence that I am not alone in the world.[6]

Further, the idea of God which I have is completely clear and distinct from any other idea which I may possess, for there is only one idea of both perfection and infinity.

An important consequence arises from the proof of God's existence. The perfection which the idea of God contains does not at the same time allow Him to be a deceiver, for in Descartes' view, "it is a dictate of the natural light that all fraud and deception spring from some defect"[7] and God, being perfect, has no such defect. This revelation is important for two reasons. First, it confirms the reliability of our faculty of memory which will allow us to assume that that which was previously clearly and distinctly apprehended as true remains true when it is again apprehended (since we are no longer susceptible to deception).[8] Secondly, it directs us to look for error in our judgments not from without, but from within our own nature. The question may be asked then, how is it that false judgments are possible?

To answer this question, we may look to Meditation IV. Descartes states that error arises from the "concurrence of two causes . . . the understanding and the will."[9] By "understanding" he means that which enables one to apprehend the ideas used to form certain judgments. There is no error in the process of understanding because there is no affirmation or denial taking place. The error then stems from the will (also referred to as "freedom of choice"), which allows us to either "affirm or deny" without being cognizant of any external influence affecting our judgments. Errors then occur when "I do not restrain the will, which is of much wider range than the understanding, within the same limits but extend it even to things I do not understand."[10] "Things I do not understand," are meant to refer to those things which I do not clearly and distinctly perceive. In other words, they are confused ideas, not clearly apprehended by the intellect alone. Thus, Descartes removes once and for all the final obstacle which had prevented him from asserting with utmost certainty that all clear and distinct ideas are necessarily true.

In Meditation V, Descartes launches into a consideration of the ideas which he has of the essence of material things as well as offering another proof for the existence of God. In regards to the former, he remarks that he has very distinct ideas of such qualities as extension, breadth, and depth, in addition to other qualities usually attributed to objects such as figures, numbers, and motion. He further admits that these qualities have a very distinct relationship to mathematical truths and as such, may be grasped intuitively. In other words, by directing his attention to these notions, he may view them with perfect clarity and distinctness. From this observation he determines that there are in his mind "innummerable ideas of certain [like] objects."[11] What is more important is the realization that these objects may exist independent of his thought. When considering the form "triangle" for example, he admits that although there may never have existed a triangle outside his own thought;

> it remains true nevertheless that this figure possesses a certain determinate nature, form, or essence, which is immutable and eternal, and not framed by me, nor in any degree dependent on my thought.[12]

Thus, the triangle is not an object of his own invention nor a product of any sense experience. Instead, it is a real entity grasped solely by the intellect.

In addition, he can demonstrate diverse properties of other objects (in the same manner as those of the triangle), and since these do not depend on him for their existence; he draws the general conclusion that since these are objects that are clearly and distinctly perceived and therefore true (Meditation IV), "it is highly evident that all that is true is something [truth being identical with existence]." He then recalls how the intuitive knowledge of arithmetic and geometry (such as the propostion $2 + 3 = 5$) seemed most certain to him even at the outset of the Meditations.

Following the above demonstration, Descartes undertakes a new proof for the existence of God based on the same principles which assured him of the existence of triangles and other like objects. The proof is, that which I clearly and distinctly perceive to pertain to an object, in other words, its attributes, does in fact belong to that object. An example of this may be found in the manner in which Descartes perceived that the nature or essence of a triangle was distinct (i.e., that its three angles are equal to two right, etc.). One main attribute which Descartes can conceive of as pertaining to God is that of existence, and this in turn is joined with the notion of God's perfection. The fact that I can clearly and distinctly perceive of this attribute of

God leads Descartes to assert, "because I cannot conceive God unless as existing, it follows that existence is inseparable from him, and therefore that he really exists."[13]

What has been stated in Meditation V, paves the way for the pursuit of all knowledge. The general truth of clear and distinct perceptions (Med. IV), the reliability of memory (as God is not a deceiver, Med. III), and the judgments we may make with certainty of those objects whose nature we clearly and distinctly perceive made possible through our knowledge of God. As Descartes asserts at the end of the Meditation:

> the certitude and truth of all science depends on the knowledge alone of the true God . . . now that I know him, I possess the means of acquiring a perfect knowledge respecting innumerable matters.[14]

All that remains then is to prove that material things exist and this is accomplished in Meditation VI. The argument begins by examining the difference between that which is called imagination, and that of pure intellection (or conception). Imagination being likened to that of a "mental picture" as when one imagines a pentagon, its sides, and the area contained by those sides. Whereas the essence of the pentagon, that it is a five-sided figure, can be understood by the process of reason alone.

Here Descartes makes the distinction between a "thinking substance" and "corporeal substance."[15] The latter contains the attribute of extension which, as we have seen, is not essential to the nature of a thinking thing (yet is capable of being conceived by it). Imagination further has a unique relation to that which is known as sense perception, for those objects which affect the senses often cause one to imagine certain objects in connection with those sensations. Those "objects" are then said to exist, for I am aware that they must be something as I must admit that I am sometimes affected by them (in that I have certain ideas concerning their existence), and the only reason that would remain that would cause me to believe that they do not exist is that I am somehow being deceived. Therefore, as it has been proven that God is not a deceiver and that the only way that these ideas could have been produced in me is by something external to me (as my essential nature does not include extension and the like), corporeal objects must exist.

This proof of the existence of external objects does not however, affect any of the previous pronouncements on the truth of our clear and distinct ideas or the method by which the ideas come to be known. It is only by grasping the essential nature of corporeal objects that true knowledge may be found and our ideas of those objects can be said to be really clear and distinct. Our notions of corporeal objects remain confused and indistinct when we rely solely on sense perception to explain their nature (as for example, when we "see" the sun and imagine it to be small in size, when reason dictates that it is considerably larger).

Descartes' notion of clear and distinct ideas and their role within the

Meditations has not escaped criticism. Although it was my intention to merely define his usage of these terms and then show their importance throughout the Meditations, an examination of some of those criticisms will prove useful in gaining an even deeper understanding of his philosophy and some of its inherent difficulties.

To begin with, there is the problem of circularity. In brief, the argument consists of the fact that Descartes seems to assert the following:

1. The only reason that we can be sure of the truth of our clear and distinct ideas is that God exists.
2. We can be sure that God exists because we can clearly and distinctly perceive this to be true.

The problem with this argument is that it does not properly reflect that which Descartes is asserting in the order of his *Meditations*. The truth of our clear and distinct perceptions is proven prior to Meditation III (where the first proof for the existence of God is offered). The proof stems from the *Cogito*, which remains true whether or not God exists (as a deceiver or otherwise).[16] As was mentioned earlier as an effect of Meditation III, the main function of the proof for the existence of God at this point concerns the reliability of our memory and not the indubitable nature of clear and distinct perceptions (at that moment which we perceive them to be true). Further, the passage by Descartes in the Fifth Meditation which prompted the objections (and the stating of his argument in the form noted above, #1) was intended for the purpose of establishing the orderliness of the universe which would in turn allow for scientific knowledge.

Thus by carefully following the intended order of the Meditations, we may avoid any circularity. The above mentioned changes of circularity arise only when particular later passages are interspersed with material found in earlier Meditations.[17]

A more difficult problem is proposed by Hobbes in the Third Set of Objections (Objection IX). The problem seems to rest on the way in which Descartes uses the term idea. As was stated earlier, Descartes intends the term idea to refer to "the form of any thought, that form by the immediate awareness of which I am conscious of that said thought." (Second Replies, Def. 2) However, in his initial proof for the existence of God, he seems to resort to using the term idea more as an "image," which carries with it all sorts of visual connotations. In fact, Descartes himself states in Meditation III, "Of my thoughts some are, as it were, images of things, and to these alone properly belongs the name idea."[18] He then further classifies his ideas as either innate, adventitious, or factitious. However, in considering innate ideas (such as the idea of God), it remains to be explained how those ideas which Descartes states represent substances or essences grasped through pure intellect can at the same time be classed as "images of things."

Even if we accept the use of the term idea as meaning a particular way in which the mind represents some object other than itself to the understanding (and not as an actual image, or "picture" of a thing) an even greater problem arises when Descartes wishes to prove that his idea of God contains in it more "objective reality" than any other idea he might have. As Hobbes points out,

> how can it be maintained that the ideas which reveal substance to me are anything greater or possess more objective reality than those revealing accidents to us? Does reality admit of more and less?[19]

It may be noted that this problem did not arise when considering the *Cogito*. In this argument there was nothing which was proposed which could not be grasped through purely intellectual means (without arousing any sensual imagery). However, in order to convince us that the infinite idea of God possesses more objective reality than the idea we have of finite substances, he must evoke an image which lends itself to sensual, rather than intellectual comprehension. Our ideas, if truly innate, cannot admit to some being more real than others unless we form some sort of visual representation of that idea. Thus, the proofs on which the crucial Third Meditation depends are not as solid as they first appear.

Descartes must be able to prove God's existence in Meditation III by way of the purely intuitive means used in arriving at the *Cogito* if he is to be able to assert that anything besides himself can be known for certain by the sole virtue of its being clearly and distinctly perceived. However, it is my opinion that he does not fully accomplish this task; for although I may be able to grasp intuitively an idea of the infinite nature of a being like God, I cannot in the same way grasp the causal principle that states that a cause must contain in it at least as much reality as its effect. Therefore, I am likewise unable to see how I may infer from the premise that I am aware of my own existence as a finite being to the existence of a being greater than myself as existing based on that principle.

The difficulty that Descartes ultimately has with the term "idea" in Meditation III can be seen as part of a greater problem inherent in trying to explain the universe by purely rational means. The problems usually arise in trying to fix some point of reference to one's ideas. Finally, it is evident from the preceding that Descartes does not remain true to his method of acquiring knowledge (as stated at the outset of this essay), but rather goes outside the boundaries in order to proceed with the remainder of his proofs. It is for this reason that Descartes cannot be said to have accomplished all that he set out to prove in the Meditations.

Notes

1. AT. viii 22, 3–9
2. A further definition of distinct is offered by Jonathan Ree: "The meaning of 'distinct' is thus very close to that of 'separate' and 'independent'; and what makes an idea or perception confused is that it combines elements which ought to be kept separate." p. 88. *Descartes*. (New York: Pica Press). 1975

3. As L. J. Beck asserts: "The force of the hypothesis of the Malignant spirit breaks on the rock of the Cogito." p. 143. *The Metaphysics of Descartes.* (Oxford: Oxford Univ. Press). 1965
4. The actual definition he gives an idea at this point is that of an "image." The problems this definition raises are treated later in this essay. For now, we assume the definition he gives in the *Replies* in order to show the uninterrupted progression of the *Meditations*
5. p. 38. Descartes. *Meditations.* 1641
6. Ibid., p. 39.
7. Ibid., p. 44
8. This point is perhaps better stated by Jefferey Tlumak; "When one clearly and distinctly proves that God exists, that theorem is immediately converted from a momentary certainty to a fully irreversible one—persuasio to scienta." p. 63. Hooker, M. (ed.) *Descartes. Critical and Interpretive Essays* (Baltimore: Johns Hopkins University Press). 1978 Article, Tlumak
9. p. 46. *Meditations*
10. Ibid., p. 44
11. Ibid., p. 57
12. Ibid., p. 50
13. Ibid., p. 51
14. Ibid., p. 53
15. The subject was actually first approached in Meditation II with the "wax example," but it is here more fully treated
16. This position is supported by Beck as well. p. 146. *Metaphysics*
17. Again, Beck treats this position on circularity with sufficient detail: see pp. 139–147 *Metaphysics*
18. p. 36 *Meditations*
19. Ibid., pp. 69–70

Bibliography

Beck, L. J. *The Metaphysics of Descartes. A study of the* Meditations. Oxford: Oxford University Press. 1965

Butler, R. J. (ed.) *Cartesian Studies.* Oxford: Basil Blackwell. 1972

Gueroult, Martial. *Descartes' Philosophy Interpreted According to the Order of Reasons:* II The Soul and the Body, Chpt. XXI. Translated by Roger Ariew. Minneapolis: University of Minnesota Press, 1985

Hooker, Michael (ed.) *Descartes. Critical and Interpretive Essays.* Baltimore: The Johns Hopkins University Press. 1978. Essay: "Certainty and Cartesian Method." Tlumak, Jeffery

Ree, Jonathon. *Descartes.* New York: Pica Press, 1975

Rorty, Amelie Oksenberg (ed.). *Essays on Descartes'* Meditations. Berkeley: University of California Press. 1978. Article: "Analysis in the *Meditations*: The Quest for Clear and Distinct Ideas," Curley, E. M.

Williams, Bernard. *Descartes: The Project of Pure Enquiry.* New Jersey: Humanities Press, 1978

(Descartes, Rene. *Meditations.* 1641, *Principles of Philosophy.* 1644)

■ **UNDERSTANDING WRITING STRATEGIES**

1. What kinds of resources does Di Nicola use to define *clear* and *distinct*? What is the definition? Why is this important?

2. What relationship does Di Nicola identify between Descartes' *Cogito* and clear and distinct ideas?

3. How does Di Nicola use summary in his essay?

4. How does Di Nicola move from the definitions of *clear* and *distinct* to the argument for God's existence?

5. Explain how deductive logic operates in Di Nicola's discussion of Descartes' second proof for the existence of God.
   "that which I clearly and distinctly perceive to pertain to an object [its attributes] does, in fact, belong to that object."
   One main attribute that pertains to God is existence.
   "Because I cannot conceive God unless as existing, it follows that existence is inseparable from him, and therefore, that he really exists."

6. How does Di Nicola account for the logic in his critique?

7. What objections have been raised to Descartes' proofs of God's existence? How does Di Nicola use these objections in his essay?

9. Consider this essay as a "critical analysis." Explain how the critique operates in terms of criteria and evaluation. ■

■ **SUGGESTION FOR WRITING**

Read Cynthia Stuffman's essay on Descartes. Write a critique of these two papers explaining their strengths and weaknesses. Establish clear criteria for your own evaluation and carefully summarize each essay. ■

The Past as Present in John Fowles's The Magus and the French Lieutenant's Woman

Lisa J. Hacken

A Modern British Literature class so interested Lisa Hacken in novelist John Fowles that she read all of Fowles's novels. Then as part of an independent studies project she wrote this paper that focuses on the thematic use of time in two of the novels.

In *The French Lieutenant's Woman* and *The Magus* the relationship of the past to the present as well as to the future is an important concern of John Fowles. Many other characteristic and pervasive themes in Fowlesian fiction are related to this central concern with time. In particular, time is related to escape, mystery, and freedom. The characters attempt to escape time; the future is a mystery; and the protagonists' freedoms hinge upon an acceptance of the time past. The growth and discovery of self of the protagonists in *The French Lieutenant's Woman* and *The Magus* involves an inquiry into the nature of time. The protagonists' recognition of the eternal presence of the past is an important theme in both novels. During their individual experiences, both Charles Smithson and Nicholas Urfe must ascertain the relation and influence of their pasts to the present and to the future. Furthermore, the protagonists' reactions to history depict the reality of the past and the fundamental importance of the past in influencing the present and determining the future.

Each of the protagonists becomes involved with the quest for his personal past. Studying their quests reveals the relevance of the past to the present, and the importance of history and its effects upon human existence. In the forward to *The Magus* Fowles asserts that novelists must "range the full extent of their own lives freely. The rest of the world can censor and bury their private past" (10). Ultimately Fowles will also show the same for his protagonists as they will learn that the past is inescapable. In order to achieve the unity and freedom in human experience, Fowles suggests, one must be able to accept, understand, and thereby conquer his "private past."

In *The French Lieutenant's Woman* Fowles' focus on time is clear in the setting, structure, narrative perspective, and endings, as well as in the character development. One obvious classification for Fowles' *The French Lieutenant's Woman* is as an historical novel. The structure and narrative technique of this work suggest a variety of possible interpretations. Yet on the simplest level the novel is written and set in the style of a literary past, Victorian England. The perspective of the novel, however, is that of the twentieth century. The dichotomous relationship between the novel's nineteenth-century historical landscape and the contemporary narrative style therefore suggests a connection between the past and the present. One way in which the narrator demonstrates the "presence" of the past is through allusions to literary works and prominent figures of the preceding century. The endings of *The French Lieutenant's Woman* also demonstrate Fowles' belief in the presence of the past. *The French Lieutenant's Woman* contains the typical Fowlesian open, ambiguous ending. The first possibility consists of a "thoroughly traditional ending" and the marriage of Charles and Ernestina (290–94). The second possible ending culminates in the romantic reunion of Charles and Sarah (375–93); and the third, a more modern conclusion, ends in the separation of Charles and Sarah and the preservation of Charles's individualism and his ability to endure life (394–99). Be presenting three possible endings to the novel, Fowles suggests the nature of time's continuum. Offering a traditional eighteenth-century ending, an ending for the narrative present, and a modern twentieth-century ending allows Fowles to demonstrate his theory that the past, present, and future are united and are inseparable.

In *The French Lieutenant's Woman* time is also represented in the protagonist's search for an understanding of self. The past is depicted as the central conflict in this quest as Charles struggles to make sense of his existence by escaping not only his past but also his present. Part of Charles' main dilemma in his trial for selfhood is the need to discover where, in time, he belongs; Charles knows he is just as much a product of his grandfather as he is a product of his father and uncle—he cannot ignore the bond with his past (19). Charles is literally devoted to studying the past in his paleontological avocation. However, instead of making any constructive connections between the remnants of the past and any relevance they may have for the present or might have on the future, Charles merely collects the fossils as inert artifacts.

Charles fails to notice the futility of his efforts; instead, he blames his own sterility on the sterility of his era. As a Victorian, Charles is a victim of social convention that has been established by years of ancestry. The limitations of society cause him constantly to feel the pressure of "duty, agreeable conformity to the epoch's current . . ." (48). These constrictions necessitate his search for an outlet for his individuality, an outlet he finds in Sarah Woodruff. His relationship with the mysterious, "scarlet woman of Lyme" represents this need to escape the reality of his surroundings—to create a microcosm for himself (107). Charles' engagement with Ernestina, on the other hand, is something Charles embraces in order to "blend into his surroundings." Yet caught in his own indecisive dilemma, Charles will later repeat to himself, "If I could only escape, if I could only escape . . . he mur-

mured the words to himself a dozen times; then metaphorically shook himself for being so impractical, so romantic, so dutiless" (254). His responsibility to Ernestina represents the duty and commitment the age demands of
him.

As the treatment of time presents various tensions between past and
present, the whole question for Charles becomes one of how and where to
integrate himself. Fowles depicts the Victorian era as one of transition—trying to liberate itself from past influences while also battling the forces of the
present and of the unknown future. New scientific, religious, and social theories began to undermine established conventions, and these changes were
likely to have a profound effect on the individual. Charles, like the age itself,
exists in a state of transition: caught between the old and the new—the past
and the present. Charles is no longer in a well-defined position on the Chain
of Being; he must adhere to the Darwinian philosophy of learning to survive
by blending with his surroundings, yet he has trouble adapting.

Charles' relationships with both Ernestina and Sarah are closely connected with the concern for time. For Charles, Ernestina represents the old,
and Sarah represents the new. The way Charles views Ernestina demonstrates the sharp contrast between Ernestina and Sarah:

> Her humour did not exactly irritate him, but it seemed unusually and un-
> welcomely artificial. . . . She was very pretty, charming . . . but was not that
> face a little characterless, a little monotonous with its one set paradox of de-
> mureness and dryness? . . . In this vital matter of the woman with whom he
> had elected to share his life, had he not been only too conventional? . . . and
> his mind wandered back to Sarah, to visual images. . . . it unsettled him and
> haunted him, by calling to some hidden self he hardly knew existed. (113–
> 14)

Brooding over his relationship with Ernestina, Charles is allured by the new
and mysterious Sarah. Charles attempts to escape the reality and convention of Ernestina by fleeing to Sarah. Sarah, an enigma, is a social outcast
who has flouted traditional morals. She is referred to as "Poor Tragedy" and
"the French Lieutenant's whore" because of her supposed relations with a
French lieutenant (12). Realizing the moral problems involved in his relations with Sarah, however, Charles' "one thought now was to escape from
the appalling predicament he had been landed in; from those remorselessly
sincere, those naked eyes" (126). In the present, Sarah becomes for him not
only a form of escape but also a someone to escape from. Charles has nowhere to turn. Sarah's presence constantly reminds him of his struggle to
adapt; he also struggles to define his desires in a world that does not admit
sexual desire: "In Charles' time private minds did not admit the desires
banned by the public mind," yet Charles finds himself irresistibly preoccupied by such desires (154). Moreover, he is struggling to be an individual, to
make free-will choices. But one must remember that his era is still haunted
by religious zealots of the past who "believe in hell" and are eager to damn

free-will sinners (23). Mrs. Poulteney, whose "one obsession is Immorality," is a character who lives in this religious past (22). The past and the present weigh ominously on Charles and he is forced to preserve whatever vestige of self-identity he may find in the midst of his war with himself.

In the conflict between past and present, the past becomes more and more a burden for Charles, and his compulsion to escape becomes more insistent. He becomes driven, even haunted by the imperative to escape the trammels of time. Rather than confront the past, to try to understand it in order to overcome it, Charles continues to escape to something or someone more ideal—Sarah: ". . . to Charles the openness of Sarah's confession . . . seemed less to present a sharper reality than to offer a glimpse of an ideal world" (154). Yet, Charles will not be happy in any dream world because the reality of his past will haunt him:

> He would have liked to be sailing once again through the Tyrrhenian; or riding, arid scents in his nostrils, towards the distant walls of Avila; or approaching some Greek temple in the blazing Aegean sunshine. But even then a figure, a dark shadow, his dead sister, moved ahead of him. (155)

Fowles' choice of words here is important. Dark shadows and dead sister symbolize Charles' past. These figures and forms of the past exist in the present and move ahead in the future. Here the particular dilemma for Charles lies in the shadows of the past, for as the narrator states, "he is a man struggling to overcome history" (257). From the narrator's modern perspective, however, this definition of Charles is acceptable; all human beings are guilty of the need to escape as the narrator tells the reader in one of his many intrusions:

> You do not even think of your own past as quite real; you dress it up, you gild it or blacken it, censor it, tinker with it . . . fictionalize it, in a word, and put it away on a shelf—your book, your romanced autobiography. We are all in flight from the real reality. That is the basic definition of Homo Sapiens. (87)

Charles seems to have a choice between reality and mystery (or the unknown). In *The French Lieutenant's Woman* Sarah embodies the mystery intrinsic to Fowlesian fiction. Charles begins to realize that to break off his engagement with Ernestina and to seek Sarah means to explore the mystery in himself. In his desire for freedom, Charles breaks off his engagement with Ernestina; in his desire for mystery, Charles devotes himself to the quest for Sarah. Charles associates freedom with the mystery of Sarah and the unknown of the future; he associates imprisonment with Ernestina and the past. Charles likes to believe that his real duty is to be a type of Odysseus— to seek the unknown and to reject the domestic responsibility and commitment manifest in his engagement vows with Ernestina: "But to recall them [vows] was to be a prisoner waking from a dream that he was free and trying to stand, only to be jerked down by his chains back into the black reality of his cell" (266). Charles feels burdened by the reality of his past, and yet he does not know where to turn in the present. His lack of freedom causes frustration and sterility as he becomes "one of life's victims, one more ammonite caught in the vast movements of history, stranded now for eternity, a potential turned to a fossil" (288). He is merely rocklike and impotent. While trying to reject his age, Charles instead succumbs to the repression of his era and the conservatism of the past. The Darwinian influence constantly reminds him of his need to "adapt" and "survive"; he is "trapped" between the past and the present as "he [stands] . . . against the vast pressures of his age . . ." (257).

In addition to the escape and mystery motifs, the theme of freedom is related to the treatment of time. Charles' rejection of the past as well as of the present denies him the freedom he seeks from the past. When he thinks of the past, images of entrapment are often contrasted with those of freedom. In rejecting the monetary and business offers from Ernestina's father, Charles rejects the prevailing values of his age. Charles' apprehensiveness in this scene somewhat foreshadows his later rejection of Ernestina:

> . . . [he] felt intolerably excited by the proximity of the moment of choice.
> He had not the benefit of existentialist terminology; but what he felt was really a very clear case of the anxiety of freedom—that is, the realization that
> one *is* free and the realization that being free is a situation of terror. (296)

Clearly, if Charles honestly confronts everything his age represents and chooses to reject its convention, then he must outwardly reject his past. During painful moments of introspection Charles tells himself that he must make a choice whether to ". . . stay in prison, what your time calls duty, honour, self-respect. . . . Or [to be] free and crucified" (314). Ultimately, Charles views "his age, its tumultuous life, its iron certainties and rigid conventions, its repressed emotion . . . as the great hidden enemy of all his deepest yearnings. That was what deceived him; and it was totally without love or freedom . . ." (315). Charles believes his happiness will not be met in his acquiescence to his age. He strives to conquer history while at the same time making sense of his present and future.

The image of the past as a burden also accompanies the images of entrapment and freedom. Charles begins to achieve personal freedom as he begins to understand himself and his desires. Yet the focal point of his self-awareness seems to come at a time of rejection—when he relieves himself of burdens:

> Charles's whole being rose up against those two foul propositions; against
> this macabre desire to go backwards into the future, mesmerized eyes on
> one's dead fathers instead of on one's unborn sons. It was as if his previous
> belief in the ghostly presence of the past had condemned him, without his
> ever realizing it, to a life in the grave. (316)

Charles' only approach to freedom, he thinks, is being rid of the omnipresent shadow of the past. Only after breaking his engagement with Ernestina does "he [feel] as if a burden had been lifted off his shoulders; a defeat suffered, and yet he had survived it" (343).

Even though Charles has always viewed his past as a burden, even though he is the man "struggling to overcome history," he is now acutely aware of the nature of time and history. While seemingly rejecting his past, he actually accepts it. He knows he will never be "free" from his past, per se, but he can conquer it. In the following comment to Dr. Grogan, Charles echoes the medieval "felix culpa" motif; he demonstrates his faith in being able to learn from the old in order to improve on the new and the unborn: "I don't see where good is to spring from, if it is not out of that evil. How can one build a better self unless on the ruins of the old?" (340). Fowles suggests here, as he does in many of his works, that resolution does not come without conflict: true freedom cannot be achieved without suffering. Further, in the third "optional" ending of the novel, Fowles asserts that Charles "has at last found an atom of faith in himself, a true uniqueness, on which to build . . ." (399). Charles' past is a crucial component of his "true uniqueness." Though he is free of the burden of history, Charles' past and future will always be present. Past, present, and future, then, comprise Charles' whole being, and he cannot escape them. Thus Fowles proves his ultimate intent: Charles now can walk confidently and fearlessly towards his future while also looking back; he is both "prospective and retrospective" (398).

Ultimately, the novel asserts that one must admit the power and reality of the past in understanding the present and in shaping the future. Ironically, the individual's victory in the war with time is the understanding of the inability to escape, for each time there is an ending, there is also a beginning. Charles realized this process when reading the account of La Ronciere: "the day that other French lieutenant was condemned was the very same day that Charles had come into the world . . ." (204). With the understanding of what has brought him to where he is Charles can embrace the future anew: ". . . the future made present . . . it was as if he found himself reborn, though with all his adult faculties and memories" (399). At last Charles has achieved a sense of selfhood and purpose; and *The French Lieutenant's Woman* achieves a unity with Charles as the link between historical past, narrative present, and the responsive reader's future.

The same unity of time is a dominant theme in *The Magus*. This novel details how Nicholas reaches the "point of fulcrum" which Conchis mentions (111). Like Charles, Nicholas must reach a point at which he understands and accepts himself in relation to his personal past. Ultimately, he will learn that the influence of the past upon the present is inevitable and in fact his "past will merge into [his] future" (111). As in *The French Lieutenant's Woman*, the escape, freedom, and time themes are here interrelated; but the unity of time past and present is something Fowles aims to achieve in *The Magus*.

Fowles' treatment of time in *The Magus*, as in *The French Lieutenant's Woman*, can be examined in light of the novel's setting and the protagonist's reaction to time—past, present, future. The first evidence of a connection between the past and the present lies in the setting of the novel—specifically, the classical landscape of Greece. The moment Nicholas encounters Phraxos, he is aware of the continuity and "timelessness" of time on the island. Nicholas often describes the solitude of Phraxos (to which he frequently escapes), but he also recognizes the "agelessness" of Greece itself; perceptively he realizes "that on the island one was driven back into the past . . . one too easily saw out of the present, and then the past seemed ten times closer than it was" (78). The reader must remember that the setting of the novel at the beginning and ending is London, yet the novel's major portion, centered in Greece, drives both Nicholas and the reader to the past. Nicholas is immediately aware of the mythical quality of Greece and the island as he describes

> . . . the feeling of having entered a myth; a knowledge of what it was like physically, moment by moment, to have been young and ancient, a Ulysses on his way to meet Circe, a Theseus on his journey to Crete, an Oedipus still searching for his destiny. . . . As if the world had suddenly, during the last three days, been re-invented, and for me alone. (160)

Here, Fowles' classical, literary allusions suggest an eternal connection with the past. Nicholas' awareness that past events may repeat themselves in the present and in the future also enhances the idea of the continuing presence of the past.

Ultimately Nicholas will realize the possibility of "fission and fusion" with time: fission represented by the futile desire to evade one's past or present; and fusion represented by the integration of past, present, and future (666). In his quest for freedom Nicholas frequently attempts to avoid responsibility and commitment—whether to the past or the present. For instance, he admits that he "was forced to go frequently for walks to escape the claustrophobic ambience of the Lord Byron School" (53). Aside from evading the responsibility of his supposed profession, Nicholas' relationship with Alison offers the best study of his efforts to separate and escape. During the intensity of a fight with Alison before Nicholas leaves for Greece, Nicholas' only thought is "remembering with intense relief that [he] should soon be free of all this" (43). Nicholas deceives himself in thinking that by escaping his present, sweeping events and persons of the present into the past, that he will be free. Even though he subconsciously realizes that he can avoid the past no more than he can avoid the present, he still attempts to escape the reality of both. Once in Greece, Nicholas acts as if Alison is a part of his personal past from which he has separated; she becomes emblematic of a past—a huge responsibility—that he tried to avoid. When given opportunities to make any lasting commitment with Alison, Nicholas absconds. Early in the novel Nicholas states that "always [he and Alison] edged away from the brink of the future. [They merely] talked about *a* future . . ." (37). Later, when they are reunited in Athens, Nicholas is still unable to react constructively to Alison; he can only think of himself (and the intrigue of his experience on Phraxos), and the only thing he knows for certain is "[he] did not want . . . this eternal reattachment to the past" (257). When Alison gives Nicholas the choice between her and the mystery of the godgame (surely a foreshadowing of the identical choice Nicholas will give Alison at the end of the novel) Nicholas chooses the latter confidently. He has convinced himself that "[he] had to be free to be enchanted" (284).

Like Charles, Nicholas "needs the existence of mysteries," and he will discard Alison for those mysteries (240). All of Nicholas' experience on the island is a form of mystery; it is this element of mystery which so attracts Nicholas. Like Charles, he associates the mystery (of Bourani) with his freedom. He would rather reject what he views as a predictable future with Alison and pursue the alluring present contained in the godgame. Whatever choice he makes, however, the future is still a mystery. Like Charles, Nicholas seeks to reject "hardcore" reality in favor of experiences and persons associated with mystery. Fowles does not condemn his protagonists; in fact, he defends their motivations on the grounds of what he terms a "hunger" for mystery, but he does not allow them to escape their pasts.

Nicholas still possesses the problem of denying reality and his past. Only slowly does he realize that "he had tried to turn life into fiction, to hold reality away . . ." (549). (This realization echoes the narrator's intrusion into *The French Lieutenant's Woman* where he states that all of humanity fictionalizes the past in order to escape its reality.) This self-awareness is a pivotal point in the discussion of time. Nicholas will begin to approach the point of fulcrum to which Conchis has led him all along.

The unity of time is depicted largely in light of Conchis' theory of the point of fulcrum: the moment at which one understands the nexus of the past, present, and the future. Many scenes in the novel portray the influence of the past upon the present to depict further a "fusion" of the two. During his initial conversations with Conchis, Nicholas is aware that Conchis' story is "all past" yet Conchis "make[s] it seem all present" (156). By means of both narrative and staged drama Conchis plunges Nicholas into an episode from his past war experience, and Nicholas apprehends that he "was back in 1943" (384). The significance of this and the other of Conchis' narrative portions in the novel lies in "the oddness of this weaving of the past and the alleged present" (305). Still, at the time Nicholas has a hard time believing that the past can affect him in any way. However, the mere fact that Nicholas narrates the novel in retrospect, with a certain objectivity, suggests that he has indeed been affected by the past. He would prefer to think that "once more [he] was a man in a myth, incapable of understanding it" (388). This solution carries the notion of mystery which appeals to Nicholas. Nicholas sees only Conchis, not himself, as "a victim of the past" (431). Part of the meaning to be derived from Conchis' narratives lies in the fact that every individual is a victim of his or her "private past." Like Charles, Conchis is also "struggling to overcome history." Yet he understands and will try to guide Nicholas to understand that "all that is past possesses our present" (317).

Only at the trial does Nicholas confront the recognition of what he already knows: his past will always be with him during any endeavors to create his own, individual, unique world. Freedom for Nicholas, as well as for Charles, means the freedom of choice and will. But before one can choose freely and successfully he must accept the evolution of his self. At the trial scene in the novel, Conchis and the members of the godgame offer Nicholas an opportunity to avenge their cruelties by whipping Lily's back. However, Nicholas will not whip Lily because it is impossible for him physically to destroy his past. During this crucial scene, when he is given the important opportunity to choose, Nicholas finally understands the meaning of freedom:

> . . . I was in a sunlit square ten years before and in my hands I held a German sub-machine gun. And it was not Conchis who was now playing the role of Wimmel. Wimmel was inside me, in my stiffened, backthrown arm, in all my past; above all in what I had done to Alison.
> *The better you understand freedom, the less you possess it.* (526)

Nicholas knows that he has caused Alison emotional pain because of his selfish inability to devote himself to her; now, frustrated, he torments himself with this knowledge. Nicholas does not truly *possess* freedom because, like Charles, he will never be "free" from his past. Until he reaches the moment of acceptance, Nicholas' past will burden him. Now he understands, however, that his past is a part of his being, a part of the experience of life. The past, present, and future complete Nicholas' being. When he tells Alison that "[he] will never be more than half a human being without [her]", he insinuates that he will never be complete if he does not regain his past (667). Nicholas' emotional reaction to all that he has learned thus can be only one of "multiple sadness, for the past, for the present, for the future" (563).

As *The Magus* concludes with a typical Fowlesian open ending, Fowles leaves his reader with a final image of the merging of time in human experience. Nicholas and Alison are "frozen in the present tense" (668) as they stand "trembling, searching between all [their] past and all [their] future; at a moment when the difference between fission and fusion lay in a nothing" (666). They both are at the point of fulcrum; their future, together or apart, hinges on the present moment, and the past infuses the present.

The conclusion of the novel presents not only a clearer image of the influence of the past upon the present but also the continuous nature of time. Several incidents at the end of the novel suggest a certain timelessness. First, Nicholas, apparently at the end of his experience, finds himself again with Alison, in a parallel situation, as he was at the novel's start. The quote from T. S. Eliot's "Little Gidding" which Nicholas found during his first trip to the island foreshadows the scene at the end of the novel:

> We shall not cease from exploration
> And the end of all our exploring
> Will be to arrive where we started
> And to know the place for the first time. (71)

So history may repeat itself; or, at least, Nicholas's "private past" is forever present and inescapable. By leaving "all past, present and future suspended" at the novel's conclusion, Fowles demonstrates his ultimate belief in the fusion of time past, present, and future in human experience—past, present, and future will coexist at some point in human experience. For Fowles, in these two novels, there are no definite endings; and the past is no less real than the present or the inevitable future. The continuing presence of the past theory shows that the past is inseparably part of the present, and the flux of the past and the present into the future is also likely. Just as Fowles, through his fiction, hopes to "range the full extent of his life by not burying his private past," so also must his protagonists range the full extent of their lives, no matter the burden (10).

■ THE WRITER'S ASSIGNMENT

This paper's subject and approach evolved through conversations about the novels with the professor. ■

■ UNDERSTANDING WRITING STRATEGIES

1. According to Hacken, what relationship does Fowles see in the past, the present, and the future in *The French Lieutenant's Woman*? How does Charles choose to deal with his past?

2. According to Hacken, how does the setting of *The French Lieutenant's Woman* relate to the novel's thematic concerns?

3. How does Hacken compare both the use of time and setting in *The French Lieutenant's Woman* and *The Magus*?

4. What does this comparison contribute to the essay's overall purpose?

5. How does Hacken explain the metaphor of "fission and fusion" in relation to *The Magus*? How well does this explanation assist her reader to understand Fowles's novel?

6. How could the same metaphor be applied to *The French Lieutenant's Woman*?

7. How does Hacken order her essay? How well does this order give the reader insight into the two novels' relationship?

8. What is the essay's main idea or ideas? Are these clearly stated in a thesis statement?

9. What does Hacken do as a writer to develop her main ideas? ■

■ SUGGESTIONS FOR WRITING

Write a critique comparing and evaluating Hacken's and Coppinger's treatments of *The French Lieutenant's Woman*. You may wish to consider their audiences and purposes as well as their essays' writing strategies and contents. ■

The Body

Stephanie Hodde

In José Donoso's short story, "Chattanooga Choo Choo," the body is a symbol for identity loss. Stephanie Hodde's essay, written for a literature course on the comparative gothic, compares Donoso's symbolic use of the body with Luisa Valenzuela's equation of the body and the literary text in *Other Weapons*.

The human body is a subject often dismissed and repressed by society as unpleasant and unapproachable, rendering it an exemplary and central theme in many gothic texts. How an author individually chooses to address the human anatomy (i.e., form, shape, function, presence, absence) in his or her work, however, is left to be considered. In his macabre short story, "Chattanooga Choo Choo," José Donoso presents the body as a symbol for a society that has dismissed the personal, physical experience for a plastic, inanimate reality where the human form, like life, loses its identity and its value; thus, the body represents the absence, not the presence of human life. In contrast, the final section of Luisa Valenzuela's work, "Other Weapons," reveals that the body is an active, powerful presence synonymous with the literary text, the South American war-territory, and the sensory experience of the main character as she bravely confronts her painful reality.

In Donoso's story, both the actual text and the real human form appear spineless, lacking depth and meaning beyond their material surfaces. Through their lifeless, physical presences, the narrator and his companions sustain an altered, frivolous existence where even human history is only repeated in jest. For instance, the narrator's wife, Magdalena, and Ramon's wife Sylvia re-enact a forgotten 1940's tune, "Chattanooga Choo Choo," at a cocktail party: ". . . the two women's gestures and grimaces, the pursed, dark lips, the stridency, the hair floating with the dance, the glitter of teeth in sudden, broad smiles, were unquestionably those of the Andrew sisters" (10). This ghostly act suggests that the characters can only physically identify with dead events, even in the present. The narrator is frustrated with his wife's unemotional obsession for ". . . transforming herself into an empty, vulgar Forties doll, of representing the reality of that Period, naive and cruelly American, to those who had not actually lived it . . ." (12). Yet, the narrator, who controls the physical and emotional body of the text, is eventually transformed by his wife into a singing replica of the 1940's to warm the cold ambiance of a party. Thus, the body is seen as a shell of a missing text, a surface reality; one which avoids experiencing the present and can only unbury the past.

Donoso exhibits the human body as an artificial form which is inconstant and worthless as it is unable to express any sensation common to a "real-life" experience. This idea is emphasized through the appearance and reactions of a central character, Sylvia Corday. Sylvia's face is described as perfectly egg-shaped, ". . . plastic, polished, inert" (1). Her physiognomy is not altered by the passage of time, nor emotional expression, but is constantly erased by her husband Ramon and recopied from beautiful faces on the cover of Vogue. Her torso inhabits an equally lifeless form from which, as it appears too thin to give birth, she can never experience her own life for it is constantly disassembled and immobilized without ever letting blood. At several points in the story Sylvia's attempts to act and communicate have no effect on her situation—her comments remain unrecognized in conversation, and the handicap of missing arms often keeps her from obtaining what she wants; in this case, a red paper mouth to replace her absent one. She is merely "an outline of an idea searching for something to complete it and give it access to life: ears, arms" (23). Though her endless faces and easily constructed body live for all Ramon's friends to enjoy, she ceases to exist in her own body as it is never fully complete.

Finally, "Chattanooga Choo Choo" expresses the absence of the human body and its disconnection with life as certain characters try to escape their ordinary existence by manipulating and transforming themselves and their loved ones. Here, the body expresses the theme of domination and submission between men and women. For instance, the narrator, although first disgusted by Ramon's dismemberment of Sylvia, desires to manipulate her puppet-like body as he remarks,

> The power of civilized man . . . who knows how to compel a woman's submission by removing or putting on her arms, . . . her eyes in the form of false eyelashes, eyebrows, removing her sex itself so she can use it only when he needs her. . . . (26)

Yet, as the narrator secures his reality in his physical and sexual control over Sylvia and his wife, his body is, in turn, dismantled. Sylvia, "that collapsible, foldable woman . . .," (46) removes his genitals with Elizabeth Arden Vanishing Cream as they engage in remarkably clean, unemotional, and soundless sex. Since his sex had explained his entire, socialized existence, his new androgyny erases him both bodily and mentally; ironically, though, the remaining "pressure-clasp" leaves much to be desired as to significance of his original manhood. Also, Magdalena reverses roles in her marriage by taking apart her husband, neatly packing him in a suitcase small enough for luncheons. Yet this victory only secures her surface existence. Again, the bodies' interactions completely deny life: sex does not result in reproduction, but in elimination, and marriage problems are not resolved by divorce, but by dismemberment.

Although the body plays an equally significant role in "Other Weapons," here it resembles a living text which involves the physical and emotional experiences that occur in an active, ongoing history. The body enlivens the narrative, the characters and the territory they inhabit with positive, physical imagery. Luisa Valenzuela stresses a need to incorporate the significance of the body in our experience of the text and our understanding of South American crises. Thus, the body becomes an actual record for the main character's personal encounters. For instance, we see the physical effects of Laura's long struggle in South America in her mirror image:

> . . . rather sad, pointy knees; in general, not much is rounded. Then there's that long inexplicable scar that runs down her back that she can only see in the mirror. A thick scar, apparent to the touch, sort of tender even though it's already healed and doesn't hurt . . . A beaten back. (110)

In addition, her body continues to express the preoccupations of her existence in the present and in her past memories: "So-called anguish tightens the opening of her stomach and makes her want to shriek a *bocca chiusa* . . ." (107). Finally, her body also gives life to the violence and frustration of the war experience as her nameless lover threatens physical life. "I could have sliced you into little pieces, I only broke your nose, I could have broken all your bones, my bones, anything" (134).

Yet in the midst of her difficult experience, Laura is in touch with her body which intensifies, not minimalizes, her existence. Unlike the characters in "Chattanooga Choo Choo" who are satisfied with their paperweight bodies and transient faces, Valenzuela's characters are not satisfied with their mirror images and must substantiate their bodies in order to survive and enjoy their survival. For instance, no personal connection exists for Laura between her wedding picture and her present appearance as she critically analyzes the photograph:

> A subtle veil that follows the line of her nose (the same nose she now sees in the mirror, which she touches but doesn't recognize at all, feeling like it just appeared above her mouth a second before. The mouth is rather hard, made for a nose that wasn't quite so light). (11)

Here the author suggests that her body has changed as she lives through experience, therefore her physical sensations are far more significant than this still-life of a past event. Likewise, we witness evidence of her tears, vomiting, and physical pleasure from sexual contact which are all living sensations that help her to verify her reality. This is illustrated in an encounter with her nameless man: ". . . she starts to know that leg is hers because she can feel it's alive under his tongue and suddenly the knee she sees in the mirror is also hers, and most of all the curve of the knee . . ." (114).

Even as Luisa Valenzuela illuminates the theme of domination and manipulation in her text, the body is not mutilated but strengthened as it becomes even more aware of its wholeness as it struggles through personal and public relationships. For instance, in numerous scenes, Laura's nameless lover (or memory of her dead boyfriend) tries to manipulate her, yet "she refuses to be pliable, changing, and her inner voices howl in rage and hit against the walls of her body while he molds her at leisure" (129). This active struggle reveals that she is enduring the loss of her man by trying not to give in to his memory, thus her body is a significant part of her survival. Furthermore, her body becomes a weapon, even when she seems to be sexually and verbally violated: "The moments when she makes love are the only ones that really belong to her . . . to this body right here, the body she's touching, that gives her shape, all of her" (120). Finally, as her lover forces her to undress and appear naked in the living room for the benefit of One and Two beyond the "Peephole," this exposure only reemphasizes that she must accept the reality of her female body and her female existence in South America. Thus, her physical existence develops as her whole experience, her whole means of survival, and not as a spare appendage that must be dragged along.

José Donoso and Luisa Valenzuela have created an utter contradiction in their individual concerns with the human body. As "Chattanooga Choo Choo" reveals the insignificance and absence of the human body in an entanglement of physical forms, *Other Weapons* lauds the presence of the human body as it validates its characters and the actual text. I tend to believe that Luisa Valenzuela's approach is the least Gothic of the two writers because the body remains so complete through the whole text. However, if one recognizes that the entire work of *Other Weapons* is a story about countless, missing, and harmed bodies, any doubts as to her integrity as a Gothic writer should be discounted.

■ **THE WRITER'S ASSIGNMENT**

Write an essay comparing and contrasting any two of the readings we have had in the course.   ■

■ **UNDERSTANDING WRITING STRATEGIES**

1. What exactly is being compared?

2. How does Hodde focus and develop her comparison?

3. What kind of assumptions is Hodde making about her audience's knowledge of the works? How do you know this?

4. What kind of evidence does Hodde use? How effectively does she use it? Explain whether or not this use is convincing.

5. How would you describe the paper's overall writing strategy?

6. How well is each story incorporated into the paper as a whole?

7. Explain how the conclusion brings the paper's different ideas together. ■

■ SUGGESTIONS FOR WRITING

The author refers to the idea of "the gothic" in her discussion of the body. Write a paper in which you define and illustrate from your own reading experiences the concept of "the gothic;" then take a position using specific references to Hodde's study on whether she effectively demonstrates the role of "the gothic" in the two stories she discusses. ■

"More" or Less Reality?
(An Old Platonic Argument)
McKeel O. Hagerty

McKeel Hagerty considers critical studies of Shakespeare's *A Midsummer Night's Dream* that see the play's dream world and reality as antithetical. Plato wrestled with the nature of illusion and reality. In this paper written for his Shakespeare class, Hagerty uses criteria derived from Gregory Vlastos's study of Plato to counter the literary critics' assumptions.

Given the development of thought in the twentieth century, it is very difficult to examine a play such as *A Midsummer Night's Dream* and not use terms such as existential and existentialism. But, in the case of this Shakespearean play, a problem arises when critics suggest that the supremacy of the dream world over the waking and tangible world makes the dream world "more real" than the other. A good example of this "more real" argument is shown in Marjorie Garber's *Dreams in Shakespeare*:

> For *A Midsummer Night's Dream* is a play consciously concerned with dreaming; it reverses the categories of reality and illusion . . . to touch upon the central theme of the dream which is truer than reality. (Garber, 59)

Although arguments concerning degrees of reality have their roots in Plato, the very methodology of dividing dreams and waking into two worlds suggests that critics are using the more modern existential analysis. Suggesting such analysis seems to present either an inexcusable anachronism or another plug for Shakespeare's visionary genius, but it can be shown as an ontological flaw. Understandably, literary critics cannot be judged by the same criteria as philosophers; the two fields are uniquely different and likewise necessary. Nevertheless, it seems that some perspective is needed to see the reasons for such anachronistic critical analysis and how it is likely flawed ontologically. But, more importantly, if such questions of existential schisms can be raised about the play, some attempt must be made to show unity.

The premises for such ontological arguments are not unfounded. Shakespeare hints of such possibilities as he develops a complex paradigm of antitheses. The most important of these antitheses is the opposing development of the dream world of the forest and the "real" world of Athens. The dream world is that of fairies, fantasy, irrationality, passion, and darkness or night. The world of Athens is characterized as the world of reason, law, order, decorum, and light or day. In this broad perspective, these antitheses are easily kept in perspective existentially; they are merely different. However, a problem arises—which we will examine later—when we examine how this antithetical paradigm affects the characters and the play's outcome. We must also examine why the reader is easily swayed into seeing the folly of one of these worlds and choosing the other as superior and hence "more real." A closer look at the characters of these two worlds is necessary to gain some perspective on these antitheses.

As with most Shakespearean plays, only the audience is privileged with the knowledge of the antitheses taking place. Therefore the characters are left alone to act as their own nature and world dictates. Both worlds have parallel hierarchical structures. Each world has a king and queen—or its equivalent—and a group of mechanicals. In the fairy world everything submits to the will of Oberon and Titania. In one of the most famous speeches of the play, Titania tells of the influence of her passions and will on nature:

> . . . the spring, the summer,
> The childing Autumn, angry winter, change
> Their wonted liveries; and the mazed world,
> By their increase, now knows not which is which.
> And this same progeny of evils comes
> From our debate, from our dissension;
> We are their parents and originals.
>   (II.i.111–17)

We see that the very seasons are changed by the folly of Oberon and Titania. However, the negative side of the fairies' influence is not emphasized so the reader's perspective becomes obscured by the Phantasamagoric and exotic side of this world. The following passage is a fine example of fanciful reality of the fairy world:

> Be kind and courteous to this gentleman,
> Hop on his walks and gambol in his eyes;
> Feed him with apricocks and dewberries,
> With purple grapes, green figs, and mulberries;
> The honey bags steal from the humble-bees,
> And for night-tapers crop their waxen thighs,
> And light them at the fiery glow-worm's eyes,
> To have my love to bed and to arise. . . .
>   (III.ii.164–71)

After hearing Titania tell of these exotic realities, the reader can easily become lulled to sleep logically, only seeing the fairy world as a world of "dances and delight" (II.ii.254). But passion and emotion also have a negative side; Oberon and Titania can just as easily bring "Whistling wind" (II.ii.86) and "Contagious fogs" (II.ii.90) as they can "dances and delight" (II.ii.254). The fairies only exist to experience their own passions and influence the "merely real" world through the medium of dreams and imagination. This influence will become more important later in the discussion of the supremacy of the dream world over the "merely real" world.

The dream world is contrasted with the world of Athens, a most appropriate place for the world of reason to exist, given great philosophical writings from that city. The nature of this world of reason is best described by Lysander in his often quoted passage:

> The will of man is by his reason swayed
> And reason says you are the worthier maid.
> Things growing are not ripe until their season:
> So I, being young, till now ripe not to reason.
> And touching now the point of human skill,
> Reason becomes the marshal to my will,
> And leads me to your eyes, where I o'erlook
> Love's stories, written in love's richest book.
>   (II.ii.115–22)

Athens is characterized by order and reason but scorns fantasy and fiction. The irony of Lysander's speech is that, at the time, he is under the influence of Oberon's love potion. Thus Lysander is explaining his position in the only terms he knows; those of reason and rationality. The highest proponent of reason in Athens is its Duke, Theseus. Garber argues that Theseus is "The apostle of reason against imagination" (70). This emphasis on reason over fantasy is shown in Act V when Theseus cynically compares the world of fantasy, love and art with Athens:

> More strange than true. I never may believe
> These antic fables, nor these fairy toys.
> Lovers and madmen have such seething brains,

Such shaping fantasies, that apprehend
More than cool reason ever comprehends.
The lunatic, the lover, and the poet
Are of imagination all compact.
    (V.i.2–8)

Interestingly, Theseus makes this speech after the previously unresolved lovers return to Athens in complete harmony. Theseus unquestioningly changes his previous stance on this issue and condones the lover's changes, but still makes this speech, not giving any real credit to the transformations. Thus Theseus and Athens remain diametrically opposed ideologically to the fictive world of Oberon and Titania.

Moving beyond the primary structural differences of the two worlds, the notion of transformation and how it distinguishes the fairy world from Athens becomes important. Garber refers to the dream world as "The gateway, not to folly, but to revelation and reordering" (Garber, 60). In essence, those who enter the fairy world come out changed by the influence of the fairies. As previously mentioned, Titania's speech in Act II (II.i.111–17) creates its own logical problem; Titania and Oberon's passions are just as likely to bring negative changes to the world as positive ones. Nevertheless, the positive transformations do occur structurally. It is these transformations that cause critics to declare the dream world superior to Athens. Sheldon Zitner, in his essay "The Worlds of *A Midsummer Night's Dream*," suggests that Shakespeare argues for "the supremacy of the 'unseen world' over the 'world of sense' " (Zitner, 397). A closer look at the nature of these transformations is needed to give some perspective to Zitner and Garber's arguments.

The most prominent of these transformations is the resolution of the conflicts surrounding the lovers: Hermia, Helena, Demetrius, and Lysander. The transformation is brought about by Oberon and Titania's chief agent Puck. Puck is sent by Oberon to "anoint" the eyes of Lysander so that he would awaken and fall in love with the first person he sees which was ostensibly supposed to be Hermia. Oberon's plan backfires at first, but, after several similar attempts and many humorous scenes with Puck and the confused lovers, the proper combinations are eventually brought together. To avoid more plot summary, it is obvious that the significance of this resolution is in the fact that the transformation and resolution of the lover's conflicts could not have occurred in Athens; Hermia and Lysander were running away from Athens for this very reason. The lovers left Athens at odds and, as a result of the fairy love ointment, their problems were resolved.

The other key transformation brought about by the fairies is shown in Bottom's revelation speech in Act IV. Bottom represents the mechanicals of Athens and is a unique recipient of transformation given his supposedly unsophisticated nature. In this passage he describes his experience with the fairies as a dream:

> I have had a most rare vision. I have had a dream, past the wit of man to say what dream it was. Man is but an ass, if he go about to expound this dream. . . . the eye of man hath not heard, the ear of man hath not seen, man's hand is not able to taste, his tongue to conceive, not his heart to report, what my dream was. (IV.i.204–14)

Despite Bottom's simplemindedness, he captures the very essence of the distinction between the two worlds; one world cannot be described in the terms of the other world. Bottom says that man, using the senses, cannot describe his dream. This problem of description was previously shown in Lysander's speech (II.ii.115–22) when he, under the influence of the fairy love ointment, uses terms of rationality to describe his change of heart. For Bottom, he is transformed with his new insight into the world of dreams and wishes it to be expounded in writing: "I will get Peter Quince to write a ballet of this dream" (IV.i.214–15). In making this statement, Bottom offers the medium between the two worlds: art. Nevertheless, the structural value of his transformation cannot be overlooked; it could not have occurred in Athens.

Overall, it is quite clear why critics such as Garber and Zitner assert the world of dreams to be supreme; it brings transformation and delight that could not have occurred in Athens. On this level I cannot strongly disagree with Garber and Zitner; the transformations do occur. But is Garber justified in asserting the dream world to be of a higher reality than Athens? This starts to have many similarities with Plato's discussion of the Cave in *The Republic* (Rep. VII); perhaps a look at this will help.

Plato asserts that certain types of reality are more real than others. He says that one world (the world of forms) is "Far more real" (Rep. VII.515D) than the world which he asserts to be "Only a dim adumbration in comparison with reality" (Rep. X.597B). In Gregory Vlastos' article *Degrees of Reality*, he concludes that Plato confuses the notion of degrees of reality with types of reality. In essence the two worlds may have different qualities but they cannot possibly have different degrees of reality only different types of reality. But most importantly, Vlastos argues that, in order for Plato's universe to exist at all, the two worlds must exist simultaneously: existential unity. In the broadest possible sense, Plato's error seems to parallel the criticism surrounding the two worlds of *A Midsummer Night's Dream*. Ultimately the world of dreams seems to have the more noble qualities; it transforms those who enter it, whereas the world of Athens is stifling to young energetic love and fantasy, openly rejecting it. Similarly, Oberon and Titania are much more interesting poetically, artistically, and aesthetically than the boringly rational and decorous Theseus and Hippolyta. And though the differences between the two worlds exist, as Vlastos would no doubt conclude, these two realities are at best different and must be viewed as merely different. Thus it seems conclusive that Garber is not justified in making an assertion for greater reality in the fairy world. But does Vlastos' argument hint of a higher elegance of thought in this schism of the two worlds? This elegance would seem to be in the notion of existential unity.

Vlastos' argument for the necessity of coexistence or existential unity of the two worlds is similar to a statement made by Zitner: "The autonomy of its diverse worlds relieves the action of the play of the burden of causes and consequences" (Zitner, 402). This unity is first implied in Bottom's dream speech as he tries to bridge the gap between the two worlds using art. This type of unity is ideologically rejected by Theseus throughout the play (V.i) but is ironically supported later when he states " 'tis almost fairy time" (V.i.364). The irony of his statement is shown at the end of the play when the fairies invade the sleeping Athens; Oberon says:

> Now, until the break of day,
> Through this house each fairy stray.
>   (V.i.401–2)

Despite the two worlds' apparent disdain for each other, they both give in to each other and unite in the end. This unity seems to suggest that even the most rational minds dream and dreams require a rational world to play out their existence upon.

I do not feel that the play was intended to have any didactic purpose, but the preceding argument seems to bring a very oblique one to the surface: any world in excess is a problem in its own right. The world of Athens represents civilization and order but it can also stifle true love and artistic expression. Likewise, the fairy world can bring about miraculous transformation and delight but also has the potential to be dangerous when the passions of Oberon and Titania are not positive. Certainly asserting one world to be "more real" than the other is logically flawed, but more importantly, it missed the quintessential purpose in Shakespeare's antithetical development: existential unity. The two worlds must exist simultaneously. However, Shakespeare never does "get off the fence" to admit the necessity of this unity in *A Midsummer Night's Dream*. I guess, as in most Shakespearean problems, this unity is for the audience to recognize and enjoy.

Bibliography

Arthos, John. *Shakespeare's Use of Dream and Vision.* New Jersey: Rowman and Littlefield. 1977.

Evans, G. Blakemore, ed. *The Riverside Shakespeare.* Boston: Houghton Mifflin, 1974.

Garber, Marjorie B. *Dream in Shakespeare.* New Haven: Yale University Press, 1974.

Vlastos, Gregory. "Degrees of Reality". *Plato: A Collection of Critical Essays.* Vlastos, ed. New York: Anchor, 1971.

Zitner, Sheldon P. "The Worlds of *A Midsummer Night's Dream.*" *South Atlantic Quarterly* 1 (1960): 397–403.

■ THE WRITER'S ASSIGNMENT

Your paper should focus on some aspect of Shakespeare's drama and give insight into his work from an external perspective (philosophical, historical, or critical). This paper should use recent criticism for framing and substantiating *your own* arguments about the play(s). ■

■ UNDERSTANDING WRITING STRATEGIES

1. What context does the introduction give for Hagerty's study of *A Midsummer Night's Dream*?

2. Besides indicating the general problem the essay will study, what kinds of commitments does the introduction make? How well do these engage the reader?

3. What are the two worlds of *A Midsummer Night's Dream*? What philosophical (ontological) problems do these two worlds present?

4. How does Hagerty's assessment of these two worlds differ from Marjorie Garber's and Sheldon Zitner's?

5. What does Hagerty mean by existential unity? How does it differ from Plato's concept of degrees of reality? What does Hagerty see as the ontological problem of discussing *A Midsummer Night's Dream* in terms of existential reality?

6. What is the essay's central position? What does Hagerty offer to convince the reader? How convincing is the argument?

7. How does Hagerty structure the essay?

8. How does this essay "use" secondary sources? ■

■ SUGGESTIONS FOR WRITING

For a literary work you are studying, read two critical essays on a similar aspect of the work. Write an essay in which you give an overview of each essay, compare these essay's similarities and indicate where they differ. Tell which essay gives better insight into the literary work and why. Give textual support for your argument. ■

T. S. Eliot's Aims for Poetic Drama and Murder in the Cathedral

Nancy S. Hale

For an independent study project on modern drama, Nancy Hale read T. S. Eliot's theoretical and critical essays on drama to establish what he values in dramatic writing. This essay uses the criteria derived from Eliot's own dramatic theory to study his play *Murder in the Cathedral.*

The recent centennial of T. S. Eliot has helped to refocus, in both the public and academic arenas, the achievement of and influence of one of the century's most controversial practitioners and theorists of poetry. However, the poetic works which occupied most of his last twenty to thirty years, the stage dramas, have remained in many ways anathema. They are not widely performed and are not studied critically as much as his lyric poems. But what is more intriguing is that Eliot left behind a large body of criticism on the drama, essays on both individual dramatists (Elizabethans in particular) and dramatic theory. The inquiry which follows—into the relationship between his plays and criticism—reveals not only some of Eliot's techniques for writing his own dramas, but also his deep concerns for art, in the form of poetry, and the effect it has on its audience. This paper, in reviewing some of Eliot's views on the drama from 1920 to 1951, will demonstrate how they are evidenced in *Murder in the Cathedral* (1935), which has been called the "most successful integration of his dramatic theories" (C. Smith 110). Eliot attempted to achieve a form, both in language and subject matter, that would fulfill his conception of the poetic drama, whose purpose is to create a vision of reality and ultimately have a transcendent effect on the audience.

I

It is "poetic drama," or drama in verse, that becomes Eliot's overriding concern in the criticism. His earliest dramatic essays from the 1920s spring from his dissatisfaction with the playwriting of the contemporary stage, particularly the scarcity of plays in verse. He opens "The Possibility of a Poetic Drama" (1920) by bringing up the questions of "why there is no poetic drama to-day (and) how the stage has lost all hold on the literary art" (*Sacred Wood* 80). Shakespeare and the other Elizabethan and Jacobean dramatists who had earlier developed a successful form in verse were the subject of intense study by Eliot, and were held up by him, along with Aeschylus, as the prime examples of what drama could achieve. But the tradition of verse drama they had developed had somehow become lost by the twentieth century. Prose dramas, such as those of Ibsen, Chekhov, and Shaw, had come to dominate the state under the aegis of "realism." (The outstanding verse exception in English was by Yeats and the Abbey Theatre in Dublin.) Eliot's distaste for the realistic dramas stems from his perception that these works failed to live up to the standard of art: "Where you have 'imitations of life' on the stage, with speech, the only standard that we can allow is the standard of the work of art, aiming at the same intensity at which poetry and the other forms of art aim" (*SW* 80). He saw the "dramas of ideas" of Shaw, Ibsen, and Maeterlinck (whose plays were in verse) as misusing the stage for the purpose of displaying particular popularized philosophies. For art he saw that

> (t)he essential is to get up on the stage (a) precise statement of life which is at the same time a point of view, a world—a world which the author's mind has subjected to a complete process of simplification. I do not find that any drama which "embodies a philosophy" of the author's . . . or which illustrates any social theory (like Shaw's) can possibly fulfill the requirement. . . . And the worlds of Ibsen and Tchehov (sic) are not enough simplified, universal. (*SW* 68–69)

The lack of simplification or universality he attributes to Ibsen and Chekhov is due largely to their strict adherence to a stark realism in form and language, which is devoid of the abstraction Eliot saw necessary to the creation of art (*Selected Essays* 93). However, as Ronald Peacock points out, Eliot's preference for and dedication to the cause of verse over prose in drama may have caused him to overlook the merits of a skillful prose ("Eliot's Criticism" 92).

Behind Eliot's championing of verse drama is the recognition of a basic lure for the poetic in the individual: ". . . The majority, perhaps, certainly a large number of poets hanker for the stage; and . . . a not negligible public appears to want verse plays. Surely there is a legitimate craving, not restricted to a few persons, which only the verse play can satisfy" (*SW* 60). The human need that poetic drama fulfills especially well is first an emotional one. One of the speakers in his watershed "Dialogue of Dramatic Poetry" (1928) disputes the modern attitude, put forward by such figures as William Archer in *The Old Drama and the New* (1923), that verse represents a "restricted and artificial" emotional range, and that prose does a more effective job of expressing human feelings. The speaker maintains the contrary position:

> The human soul in intense emotion strives to express itself in verse. It is not for me, but for the neurologists to discover why this is so, and why and how feeling and rhythm are related. The tendency, at any rate, of prose drama is to emphasize the ephemeral and superficial; if we want to get at the permanent and universal we tend to express ourselves in verse. (*SE* 34)

It is poetry that possesses the ability to express more completely and intensely the kind of material that drama (or at least the best drama) intends to communicate—human action that results in a revelation of emotion or some kind of truth. Peacock remarks that "if verse, or poetry, makes the expression of the drama more complete it makes it more dramatic" (*Art of Drama* 225). Another of the participants in the dialogue asks, "What great poetry is not dramatic? . . . Who is more dramatic than Homer or Dante? We are human beings, and in what are we more interested than in human action and human attitudes?" (*SE* 38) Another speaker clarifies the concept by suggesting that poetry simply makes for better drama. In the case of Shakespeare, "the same plays are the most poetic and the most dramatic, and this is not by a concurrence of the two activities, but by the full expansion of one and the same activity" (*SE* 39).

Having established poetry as the most effective medium for the drama, the problem that remained for Eliot—and the critical point that was the most complex for him to deal with—was the question of the means in which poetry specifically relates the action of the drama and the voices of the characters. It is basically a question of language and meter. In a much later essay, "Poetry and Drama," (1951) he puts forward the proposal that

> if poetry is merely a decoration, an added embellishment, if it merely gives people of literary tastes the pleasure of listening to poetry at the same time they are witnessing a play, then it is superfluous. It must justify itself dramatically, and not merely be fine poetry shaped into a dramatic form. . . . And from this it follows . . . that the audience, its attention held by the dramatic action between the characters, should be too intent upon the play to be wholly conscious of the medium. (*On Poetry and Poets* 76)

The poetic language and meter need to complement the dramatic situation to enable the whole scene to be more effective. The fault of many of the poet/dramatists of the nineteenth century who attempted to produce plays in verse (such as Shelley and Browning) was, in Eliot's opinion, that they tended to write dramas with exquisite poetry tacked on as an impressive decoration, regardless of its context in action. The poetry may have been fine to listen to or read, but it tended to distract from the drama at hand. In the space of the stage, Eliot felt, it is necessary for the language to be suited to the dramatic situation and not be "self-conscious" of the fact that it is indeed poetry. The verse and action must work hand in hand, so to speak, to create a unified design or order that will engage the audience. Late in "Poetry and Drama" he describes what he feels poetic drama should strive for:

> I have before my eyes a kind of mirage of the perfection of verse drama, which would be a design of human action and words, such as to present at once the two aspects of dramatic and musical order. . . . To go as far this direction as it is possible without losing that contact with the ordinary everyday world with which drama must come to terms, seems to me the proper aim of dramatic poetry. (*PP* 93–94)

It is Eliot's goal in poetic drama—and also his goal in all art—to create a meaningful order out of ordinary physical existence. The verse dramatist makes use of such poetic devices as imagery and metaphor to establish patterns and designs within the drama that are able, by enhancing the action, to bring out deep and universal truths that are both spiritual and emotional. *Murder in the Cathedral* is Eliot's first fully realized attempt to create, from the integration of stage action and the language in which it is presented, such a design by means of an historical event. He uses Christian and other traditional imagery and patterns in the story of the martyrdom of St. Thomas at Canterbury to represent an ideal, divine order working in an ordinary world.

II

The origin of drama as an extension of a religious ritual had long been a vital consideration to Eliot. In the "Dialogue" he mentions the work of anthropologists Cornford and Harrison, who had identified the origins of Greek tragedy as an offshoot of mystery religions (*SE* 32). He comments in a theatre review in the *Criterion* of 1922 that "the stage, not only in its remote origins but always, is a ritual, and the failure of the contemporary stage to satisfy the craving for ritual is one of the reasons it is not a living art" ("Dramatis Personae" 305–306). Although he will point out that literature cannot be a substitute for religion and vice-versa (*SE* 36), he does recognize the power of formalized religious ritual to crystallize certain truths and emotional experiences central to a culture, a power that is shared by literature, especially drama. Indeed, one of the discussants in the "Dialogue" observes that the performance of a High Mass makes for one of the few truly "dramatic" performances one could attend (*SE* 34). It is no small coincidence, perhaps, that these comments were made in 1928, the year after Eliot had been confirmed into the Church of England. The ritual nature of drama was able to reflect the "sense of the supernatural order in the natural world," an element of his personal "religious concern to integrate the real with the ideal" (C. Smith 31).

The choice of Becket's martyrdom as a subject for verse drama was not wholly Eliot's own—he was basically working to order, having been asked to create some kind of appropriate work to be performed inside Canterbury Cathedral for the 1935 Canterbury Festival. Rather than depict the entire career of Becket, Eliot chose to focus on the assassination itself, covering only a few episodes in the brief period of time between his return from exile in France on December 2, 1170, to his murder by four knights under order of Henry II on December 29. In addition to the actual historical characters of the Knights, Eliot surrounds Becket with other groups of characters for him to interact with—the chorus of Women of Centerbury, three Priests, and four anonymous Tempters.

The martyrdom motif presents a type and perpetuation of Christ's life, which is in turn a duplication of the myths involved in the origin of the Greek tragedy—the passion, death and rebirth of a god. Francis Fergusson has identified the structure of *Murder in the Cathedral*'s events with the basic structure of Greek tragic form. Part I, Thomas' return and temptation, corresponds to the Agon, which portrays the hero's struggle with a central spiritual issue. Part II, Thomas' confrontation with the knights and his death, corresponds to the "catastrophe," the violent, climactic consummation of the hero's life (Fergusson 28–29). In addition to this ancient pattern Eliot also draws parallels to Christ's passion in Thomas' last days. His progress to Canterbury is thronged by enthusiastic, leaf-throwing crowds, as in the Palm Sunday procession; he endures multiple temptation; and those who carry out his violent death deny their responsibility as did Pilate.

Thomas' chief struggle is not so much the political one with the king and his knights as much as it is an inner struggle of how he is to face his martyrdom. In the atmosphere of agitated anticipation set by the Chorus and Priests who fear for his safety, Thomas in his initial appearance explains that he must recognize how his life is to be directed: "The substance of our first act / Will be shadows, and the strife with shadows" (*Complete Poetry and Plays* 183). The "shadows" refer to the nameless, shadowy Tempters who provide Thomas with the various alternatives that "shadow" his life. Like the first two temptations of Christ, the first three Tempters offer Thomas sensual pleasure (the carefree spirit of his younger days from the first) and political power (the authority of his office as Chancellor from the second and the leadership of an insurrection against the king from the third). But as these all represent temporal desires, they are rejected by Thomas easily: "No! Shall I, who keep the keys / Of heaven and hell, . . . / Descend to desire a punier power?" (187) The fourth, however, offers true temptation to the Archbishop, in seeking personal, eternal glory in the service of God by his own actions:

> What can compare with glory of Saints
> Dwelling forever in the presence of God?
> . . . .
> Seek the way of martyrdom, make yourself the lowest
> On earth, to be high in heaven. (192)

At these words, which he does admit as representing his own desires, Thomas realizes that he has become subject to willful pride, the chief among sins:

> Is there no way, in my soul's sickness,
> Does not lead to damnation in pride?
> I well know that these temptations
> Mean present vanity and future torment.
> Can sinful pride be driven out
> Only by more sinful? Can I neither act nor suffer
> Without perdition? (193)

Thomas' concern for acting and suffering brings out the paradox that leads to his central crisis—though enduring martyrdom should be a matter of passive suffering, he secretly fears seeking martyrdom as a deliberate act, one decided by his own will. The fourth tempter sums up Thomas' dilemma with one of the play's key speeches:

> You know and do not know, what it is to act or to suffer.
> You know and do not know, that acting is suffering,
> And suffering action. Neither does the actor suffer
> Nor the patient act. Both are fixed
> In an eternal action, an eternal patience
> To which all must consent that it may be willed
> And which all must suffer that they may will it,
> That the pattern may subsist, that the wheel may turn and still
> Be forever still. (193)

Thomas had spoken these very words in his first speech to the Women of Canterbury, who feared the consequences they would suffer upon his return to England. Now it is Thomas who must realize the true nature of suffering, that it is part of an eternal pattern. The image of the turning wheel with its still center had been used by Aristotle (G. Smith 46–47) and Dante (Jones 65) to describe the process of the unmoved mover giving motion to a receiver at the rim. Eliot's circular, repetitive language further underscores the design of an endless motion. Thomas now recognizes his role in the eternal pattern, that he must align his will accordingly to achieve God's end, for "The last temptation is the greatest treason / To do the right deed for the wrong reason" (196). Having achieved the understanding of his role in God's design, Thomas explains the motives of true martyrdom to his faithful in the prose Christmas sermon which serves as an interlude between the play's two acts:

> A martyr, a saint, is always made by the design of God, for his love of men, to warn them and to lead them, to bring them back to His ways. A martyrdom is never the design of man; for the true martyr is he who has become the instrument of God, who has lost his will in the will of God, not lost but found it, for he has found freedom in submission to God. (199)

The martyr's compliance corresponds to that of Christ, who prayed that "*Thy* will be done." In Part II, Thomas refuses to have the doors of the cathedral barred against the invading Knights, proclaiming, "We have only to conquer / Now by suffering. This is the easier victory. / Now is the triumph of the Cross. . . ." (212)

But as Christ suffered for all men, Thomas, continuing Christ's pattern, has his own people within the play that his suffering affects, the Women of Canterbury. As God's will acts upon Thomas, Thomas' suffering acts, in turn, upon the Women to bring them, as the sermon indicates, back towards God, to a fuller realization of His presence. The Women have led an undisturbed existence in Thomas' absence, observing the same seasons pass, "keeping (their) households in order" (176), "Succeed(ing) in avoiding notice / Living and partly living" (180). They fear for Thomas' life on his return not only for his sake but their own, that his death will destroy their peaceful routine, bringing a "disturbance of the quiet seasons" (180). Their language of impending doom and disorder is largely one of nature imagery, waste-land motifs of barren landscapes needing renewal—"And the world must be cleaned in the winter, or we shall have only / A sour spring, a parched summer, an empty harvest" (201). This language intensifies and becomes more violent as the threat to Thomas increases, climaxing at the point of the murder: "Clear the air! clean the sky! wash the wind! take store from stone and wash them. / The land is foul, the water is foul, our beasts and ourselves defiled with blood" (213–214). The catastrophe is one that is beyond ordinary existence, unlike any other in their typical human experience:

> Every horror had its definition,
> Every sorrow had a kind of end:
> In life there is not time to grieve long.
> But this, this is out of life, this is out of time,
> An instant eternity of evil and wrong. (214)

Yet the women do not immediately realize that the disaster, the "rain of blood" will refresh the earth, symbolically bringing them spiritual renewal, leading their lives back to God. They need to be taken "out of time" through what befalls Thomas in order to be reminded of the timeless reality of God. In their final chorus the Women give their thanks to God for His grace given through blood: "We thank Thee for Thy mercies of blood, for Thy redemption by blood. For the blood of Thy martyrs and saints / Shall enrich the earth, shall create the holy places" (221).

Eliot had, after writing *Murder in the Cathedral*, remarked that he felt the purpose of the Greek chorus was to "mediate between the action and the audience" and to "intensify the action by projecting its emotional consequences, so that the audience see(s) it doubly, by seeing its effect on other people" ("Need for Poetic Drama" 995). The intense emotional voice that the chorus gives to their need for Thomas' sacrifice strikes a chord within the audience for our need for such symbolic actions. Like the Women of 1170, we the audience need to be reminded of the eternal patterns of desolation, death, and renewal. Eliot's desire to involve the audience with the events of Thomas' death is further underscored by the prose speeches of the Knights following the murder. Directly addressing the audience, the Knights use the language of modern political rhetoric to explain away their actions and blunt the effect of the martyrdom. The effect of the speeches is jarring, and forces us to consider our own reaction to Thomas. The decidedly twentieth-century flavor of their arguments serves to remind us that the martyr and those who persecute him will probably always be with us.

Thomas' sacrifice, horrific as it is, brings the women out of their superficial, "unreal" existence and into a brief contact with the real, the timeless. The playwright, in a similar fashion, uses his poetry to bring the audience into an awareness of an eternal reality as well. It is not simply the action, but also the poetry in which it is expressed, that is able so effectively to convey the experiences which may go beyond ordinary emotions. In closing "Poetry and Drama" Eliot describes where poetry may lead us: "For it is ultimately the function of art, in imposing a credible order upon ordinary reality, and thereby eliciting some perception of an order in reality, to bring us to a condition of serenity, stillness and reconciliation. . . ." (*PP* 94). The quiet ending of *Murder in the Cathedral* brings us back to a quiet, everyday world, a world that has yet been transformed, if briefly, into a more percipient one. In Eliot's view, the awareness of the sense of reality, like Thomas' realization of his role and its effect emotionally and spiritually, is the goal to which the poetic drama strives.

Works Cited

Eliot, T. S. *Complete Poems and Plays, 1909–1950.* New York: Harcourt, 1952.
———. "Dramatis Personae." *Criterion* 1 (1922–23) 305–6.
———. "The Need for Poetic Drama." *The Listener* 14 (1936) 994–95.
———. *On Poetry and Poets.* New York: Farrar, 1957.
———. *The Sacred Wood.* 1928. London: Methuen, 1960.
———. *Selected Essays.* 1951. New York: Harcourt, 1964.
Fergusson, Francis. "*Murder in the Cathedral:* The Theological Scene." *Twentieth Century Interpretations of* Murder in the Cathedral. Ed. David R. Clark. Englewood Cliffs, NJ: Prentice-Hall, 1971. 27–37.
Jones, David E. *The Plays of T. S. Eliot.* London: Routledge, 1960.
Peacock, Ronald. *The Art of Drama.* London: Routledge, 1957.
———. "Eliot's Criticism of Drama." *The Literary Criticism of T. S. Eliot.* Ed. David Newton-De Molina. London: Athelone P, 1977. 89–110.
Smith, Carol H. *T. S. Eliot's Dramatic Theory and Practice.* Princeton: Princeton UP, 1963.
Smith, Grover. "Action and Suffering: *Murder in the Cathedral.*" *Twentieth Century Interpretations of* Murder in the Cathedral. Ed. Clark. 38–53.

■ THE WRITER'S ASSIGNMENT

Use T. S. Eliot's literary criticism to give insight into some aspect of his work.   ■

■ UNDERSTANDING WRITING STRATEGIES

1. How does Hale's introduction engage both the subject and the reader's interest?

2. For what audience is this essay written? What indicates this?

3. What is Eliot's major objection to modern prose drama?

4. Why does Eliot prefer verse drama to prose drama?

5. What does Eliot see as the central task in using poetic language and meter in effective drama?

6. What criteria for evaluating Eliot's drama does Hale develop from Eliot's criticism?

7. What aspects of Eliot's drama does Hale examine? How do these relate to the critical criteria?

8. How does Hale structure her essay? What is her governing idea? Where do you find this?

9. How does the essay's first part relate to the second?

10. What does Hale tell her reader about *Murder in the Cathedral*? How sufficient was this for following Hale's argument? ■

■ SUGGESTIONS FOR WRITING

Do you agree with the position Eliot makes in *Poetry and Poets:* "For it is ultimately the function of art, in imposing a credible order upon ordinary reality, and thereby eliciting some perception of an order in reality, to bring us to a condition of serenity, stillness and reconciliation. . . ."? Support your position by demonstrating how a piece of literature you have been studying either does or does not order "ordinary reality" and whether or not it brings "serenity, stillness and reconciliation." ■

Of Johnson's Rasselas

Sarah Hanna

Sarah Hanna writes here about the dangers in unshared thoughts, limited companionship, and narrow intellect in Samuel Johnson's *Rasselas* in a paper for the course, Restoration and Eighteenth-Century Literature.

In his book *The History of Rasselas, Prince of Abissinia*, Samuel Johnson develops a premise in which he maintains that without adequate intercourse with society, a person will retreat into fanciful ideas and turn that fancy into reality in his or her mind. He shows dangers in unshared thoughts, limited companionship, and narrow intellect.

Johnson begins by suggesting that continual lone reflection is the enemy to action. Prince Rasselas spends months and then years meditating on his unhappiness with his life in the Happy Valley. It is only in conversation with his old teacher that he realizes that he wants to leave the Happy Valley (p. 45). But once he makes this decision, he returns to his solitary reveries and procrastinates even longer. He is so delighted with his dreams of escape that he spends years envisioning what he will see and do on the outside (p. 46). Even while he searches for an escape path he allows himself to be distracted for another ten months: "He met a thousand amusements which beguiled his labour and diversified his thoughts" (p. 49). Only in the company of the poet, Imlac, does Rasselas follow through on his intentions to leave. Imlac, with the stories of his travels and experiences, is the personification or Rasselas' dreams (pp. 54–69). The reality of Imlac's life jars the prince out of his reveries. Finally, together with his sister Nekayah and her companion Pekuah, Rasselas and Imlac leave the Happy Valley.

They begin their search for the best choice in life. Thinking that in "pastoral simplicity" they might find the answer, they observe some shepherds. But the travellers found little to envy or admire:

> . . . they were so rude and ignorant, so little able to compare the good with the evil of the occupation, and so indistinct in their narratives and descriptions, that very little could be learned from them. (p. 82)

Then they find the hermit who is reputed to have found wisdom and happiness in retreat from society. However, though the hermit believes that to live a good life one must "remove from all apparent evil" (p. 85), he asserted that solitude was not a valid means to achieve this end:

> I have been for some time unsettled and distracted: my mind is disturbed with a thousand perplexities of doubt, and vanities of imagination, which hourly prevail upon me, because I have no opportunities of relaxation or diversion. . . . My fancy riots in scenes of folly, and I lament that I have lost so much, and have gained so little. In solitude, if I escape the example of bad men, I want likewise the counsel and conversation of good. . . . The life of a solitary man will be certainly miserable, but not certainly devout. (p. 86)

In the months after Pekuah was kidnapped by Arabs during their visit to the pyramids, Imlac chides Nekayah to return to life from the solitude of her grief: "Do not suffer life to stagnate; it will grow muddy for want of motion; commit yourself again to the current of the world" (p. 115). He implies that she could lose touch with reality and reason by remaining stuck in her sorrow.

When Pekuah is returned to her companions, she describes the Arab women as childish and ignorant:

> They had seen nothing; for they had lived from early youth in that narrow spot: of what they had not seen they could have no knowledge, for they could not read. They had no ideas but of the few things that were within their view . . . (p. 124)

Johnson suggests that those who live their lives in limited space and companionship will become retarded in spirit and character.

Years of solitary study and reflection had a profound, almost devastating effect on the astronomer the travellers met in Cairo. In his lone contemplation of the heavens, he formed the belief that he indeed controlled the movement of that which he studied. In his comments on the astronomer's delusion, Imlac ruminated on the dangers of fancy:

> To indulge the power of fiction, and send imagination out upon the wing, is often the sport of those who delight too much in silent speculation. . . . He then . . . amuses his desires with impossible enjoyments, and confers upon his pride unattainable dominion . . . By degrees the reign of fancy is confirmed; she grows first imperious, and in time despotick. Then fictions begin to operate as realities, false opinions fasten upon the mind, and life passes in dreams of rapture or of anguish. (p. 133)

Later, after the astronomer had shared many hours of conversation with Nekayah and Pekuah, reality creeps back into his mind. His delusion disappeared until he was alone again:

> The sage confessed to Imlac, that since he had mingled in the gay tumults of life, and divided his hours by a succession of amusements, he found the conviction of his authority over the skies fade gradually from his mind, and began to trust less to an opinion which he never could prove to others, and which he now found subject to variation from causes in which reason had no part. . . . I am like a man habitually afraid of spectres who is set at ease by a lamp, and wonders at the dread which harassed him in the dark, yet, if his lamp be extinguished, feels again the terrours which he knows that when it is light he shall feel no more. (p. 141)

Johnson thus implies that, to avoid not only narrow-mindedness but eventual subjugation to fancy, a person must sustain community with the world outside himself, outside his family, even outside his country. He suggests, therefore, that no one alone can reason; that reason can only be synthesized from the experience and observation of all.

■ THE WRITER'S ASSIGNMENT

Writing's purpose is not merely a means of assessment but rather a means to a pedagogical end encouraging you to read carefully and critically and to formulate explicit judgments of what you read and not settle for vague, inarticulate impressions. Considering this, explain Johnson's beliefs as to the relationship between sanity and social life. What pattern do you notice? How does Johnson see these related? How does all this relate to the issue of Reason? ■

■ UNDERSTANDING WRITING STRATEGIES

1. What is the essay's thesis? How does this relate to the assignment of explaining Johnson's beliefs about the "relationship between sanity and social life"?

2. How does the essay expand its thesis? How does this relate to the further questions in the assignment?

3. What does Johnson see as the danger of solitude?

4. Compare this essay with Hyman's essay, "The Interdependence of Sanity and Social Life." How are their interpretations of *Rasselas* similar? How do they differ?

5. Every main idea in an essay needs explanation and "proof" by references to primary or secondary sources. Are this essay's explanations adequate for the reader to understand the main ideas? How well do references to the text of Rasselas "prove" the main ideas? ■

The Interdependence of Sanity and Social Life

Karen Hyman

Writing for a course entitled the Age of Tormented Reason, eighteenth-century survey of British and American literature, Karen Hyman considers the tension between reason's role in defining both sanity and social good and passion's moderating force in Johnson's *Rasselas*.

In *Rasselas* Johnson's beliefs about the relationship between sanity and social life are that they are interdependent; without sanity, social life breaks down; and without social life, sanity breaks down. This contextual and comparative definition of the relationship leads to complexities and uncertainties, not simple absolutes. Johnson resolves this which-came-first-the-chicken-or-the-egg paradox by emphasizing individual responsibility for action as the logical response. He supports the idea that both individual sanity and social good are defined by Reason, but admits the necessity and inevitability of moderating total rationalism with consideration for unavoidable human passion. Johnson's refusal to simplify the scope of the issue serves to stimulate the reader's own consideration of the matter, and indicates that he believes the topic deserving of every thinking person's scrutiny.

The first part of the pattern that was noticeable was that unless social life is based on and conducive to sanity, it will tend to break down. This is illustrated by Rasselas' rejection of Happy Valley. The community was not governed by rational premises, just the opposite. Its enforced isolation from the rest of the world, its emphasis on "pleasure and repose" (41), the propagandizing and lack of productive employment (41–43) resulted in the residents' unhappiness and alienation, and finally the escape of several of its members. Rasselas finds out "not one of all your attendents . . . does not lament the hour when he entered upon this retreat" (68). Those who remain are not members of a cohesive, cooperative community, but bits of a crowd torn with selfish and divisive sentiments.

The second part of this pattern of relationship between sanity and social life is that without social life, sanity breaks down. This is foreshadowed briefly in the chapter on the hermit, who admits "I have been for some time unsettled and distracted . . . and resolve to return to the world tomorrow" (86). It is illustrated more definitively in the episode of the astronomer. Imlac explains: "too much . . . silent speculation . . . when we are alone . . . (on) some particular train of ideas" (133) and soon,

> the fictions begin to operate as realities, false opinions fasten on the mind, and life passes in dreams of rapture or anguish. This is one of the dangers of solitude (134).

These obsessions become madness when they become "ungovernable, and apparently influence speech and action" (133); in other words, when they manifest in the social life. This can be corrected, Johnson urges, by exposure to the rational social consensus of the body politic. Rasselas and Company do this for the astronomer, and he gains back his "reason (which) had been so long subjugated by an uncontrolable and overwhelming idea" (142). The function of social life as emotional support that contributes to mental stability is articulated by the astronomer: "I rejoice to find my own sentiments confirmed by yours" (143).

Reason is used by Johnson to define sanity, as Imlac says: "All power of fancy over reason is a degree of insanity" (133). Nevertheless, he admits that "there is no man whose imagination does not sometimes predominate over his reason" (133). And he seems to suggest that there are indeed human needs which rationality cannot address: " 'What comfort,' said the mourner, 'can truth and reason afford me?' " (81). Even reasoned goodness is discussed as merely a vehicle for achieving that deepest of human longings: "Whether perfect happiness would be procured by perfect goodness . . . this world will never afford an opportunity of deciding" (97). Despite his strong support for Reason, Johnson admits that it is no panacea: "what reason did not dictate, reason cannot explain" (146).

In the end, the only certainty is "the uncertainties of our present state"

(132) and "the shortness of our present state" (149). Beyond that, "philosophy can tell no more" (148).

■ THE WRITER'S ASSIGNMENT

Writing's purpose of not merely a means of assessment but rather a means to a pedagogical end encouraging you to read carefully and critically and to formulate explicit judgments of what you read and not settle for vague, inarticulate impressions. Considering this, explain Johnson's beliefs as to the relationship between sanity and social life. What pattern do you notice? How does Johnson see these related? How does all this relate to the issue of Reason?   ■

■ UNDERSTANDING WRITING STRATEGIES

1. What is this essay's position statement? How well does it reflect the assignment's guidelines?

2. How does Hyman develop her ideas?

3. The assignment limited the student to two pages. How well developed is the essay given the limitation? Are the ideas clearly expressed? Is textual support adequate?

4. What specific details does Hyman give to support her generalizations?

5. Compare this essay with Hanna's essay, "Essay of Samuel Johnson's *Rasselas*." How are their interpretations of *Rasselas* similar? How do they differ?

6. If you were given a similar assignment limited to a maximum of two pages, what kinds of writing strategies would you use? What kinds of prewriting techniques would be helpful?

7. How might this essay be expanded to a longer paper through using both secondary sources and further reference to the text?   ■

Valenzuela and Kafka: The Word "Killer" *and the Word Killer*

Laurie Loftus

Laurie Loftus compares Valenzuela's "The Word 'Killer' " to Kafka's "In the Penal Colony" from the perspective of how they subvert order and language in this essay for a course on comparative gothic literature.

The more conscious we become of our power to exploit and do violence to the human spirit in the name of civilization, the greater is our need to express it. We become painfully aware that to use the language handed down to us is to become implicated in its system of repression and oppression. The Gothic is aware of the intricate interworkings of violence and language; the darkness which surrounds the Gothic letter is the presence of the repressed. To acknowledge the underside of consciousness is perhaps an attempt to liberate it. But the extent to which we can feel liberation in language varies drastically. Both Kafka and Louisa Valenzuela mean to subvert the given order and to question the power of language to subvert itself. But "The Word 'Killer' " and "In the Penal Colony" are nearly inversions of each other in the way they "execute" these themes.

From the onset of her story, Valenzuela situates herself within the text; it feels alive with a full range of human emotions and sensations. "One can desire. One can always desire . . ." (63) gives us the sense that, for the Valenzuela of this story, sex becomes bound up with language and imagination in an act of rebellion against the uncertainty of the everyday. But after he confesses to having killed in cold blood, her lover connects her to "the notion of death" (66). Which side, then, is she on? Does a woman involved in a heterosexual relationship necessarily bind herself to the patriarchal order under which she has been subjugated? In a way, hearing from Valenzuela's narrator is like hearing from the "ladies" in Kafka's text who, from the officer's mention of them, seem to get a kick out of Fascism, groupies of the Commandant who flock to his side to witness the spectacle of torture. Kafka's aim is of course, to speak against this.

Kafka's narrative and its obsession with detail help image the machinization of torture in his text. In the way that his absence is as obvious as Valenzuela's presence, his machine of death and torture needs no human touch to perpetuate it. "Up till now a few things still had to be set by hand, but from this moment it works all by itself" (141). Kafka imitates the autonomy of the system of evil in his textual structure, and in doing so draws us into it. Reading, we become physically ill with his detailed descriptions of the instrument of torture, that which in the penal colony executes "the death sentence." With his tongue planted firmly in his cheek, Kafka plays on the authority language would have were it not for the structure in which it exists. His attempts to subvert that structure, then, become in his text mock participations in it. Communication becomes torture; the accused, without a trial, without notice even, becomes the victim of language as violence. The message is literally bored into him: "There would be no point in telling him. He'll learn it on his body" (145).

Like Kafka's prisoner, Valenzuela's woman learns the difference between the thing and the word that signifies it through the body, her lover's. At first, when she can only acknowledge the word killer to herself, in her mind, she participates in the kind of self-alienation which seeps through Kafka's text but which seems so out of place in Valenzuela's; "She feels outside her own skin, out of place" (73). She also perceives from him his need to see himself in her, to seek self-affirmation in the act of sex. The fusion of Thanatos and Eros becomes a mechanization not unlike Kafka's:

> . . . he drops sentences that move mechanisms and set off pulleys that move cogs which interconnect until an entire system of questions comes alive. A general mobilization which helps him to recognize himself in her (71).

At the interface of love and death lies the uncertainty of language from which Valenzuela attempts to furnish an escape. But her narrator understands that the more she represses the reality of her lover's identity, the further she travels from herself. The crisis threatens her to the extent that even "the words betray her and collapse. She's even banished from her own kingdom, language" (77).

In the end we sense that Valenzuela, perhaps because she "loves life so" like her narrator, forces to bring language to its place of full redemptive value, where truth and experience mesh. Because she knows herself, she recognizes that, though not an easy one, the flight from repression involves the utterance of a free word. Kafka couches his subversion in another sort of system, that given by the allegory in its extended travel away from mere utterance. At this point we should pose another huge question generated by the contrast of voices: to what extent does the difference owe itself purely to the difference of gender? From what place in Valenzuela does her immense strength come, and why does Kafka not journey to that place?

With Kafka, subversion takes the form of silence, silence creeps into collective consciousness horrifically but quietly. "Because it was working so silently the machine simply escaped one's attention" (164). Kafka is dangerously close to the hierarchical fascism he indicts; indeed, it was Hitler himself who claimed that there are no more words. We can believe that Kafka redresses this in his choice to devote his life to writing. But in order to show the violence done to language in the violence done in the world, Kafka needs to imitate it in his story: he forces onto us a condition of illness in reading as though there were no other way to depict suffering than to duplicate it. But perhaps this comes more as a representation of his own personal agonies than a search for a way out of them. If there is at least a shred of truth in this, then we can better understand where the two writers split. For in Valenzuela is the raging desire to speak against the given order only as she displaces it with her voice, the acutely personal and universal voice of the oppressed. Refusing to maintain a safe distance from her text, Valenzuela screams out against the deep silence at her center, at the center of language: " 'KILLER', she shouts. And the voice finally manages to bolt out of her and she isn't calling out or accusing; in fact, she's giving birth" (78).

In his bitter condemnation of the system-within-a-system, Kafka leaves no hope for what is on the other side of death. Perhaps the end of Valenzuela's story reveals what happens when one woman speaks out from the place where death and desire commingle, where she refuses subjugation: she gives birth to language, to hope, and to herself *ad infinitum*.

■ THE WRITER'S ASSIGNMENT

Contrast any two of the assigned readings we've had in the course. ■

■ UNDERSTANDING WRITING STRATEGIES

1. How does the essay's title relate to its central thesis?

2. For what audience is Loftus writing? What indicates this?

3. Which story does Loftus prefer and why? Where does she indicate this preference?

4. In what ways are the two stories compared? How clear is the comparison?

5. How does Loftus order her essay's components? In what other ways could the comparison have been structured?

6. What insights does the comparative approach used here give to the literature? ■

■ SUGGESTIONS FOR WRITING

Write an essay comparing two short stories. Emphasize in your essay how some aspect of one story clarifies the second story. ■

Joe Crail: On the Dam Bandwagon

Karim Manassa

"Joe Crail: On the Dam Bandwagon" represents Karim Manassa's research using both historical documents and written histories. Employing the professional historian's research strategies and professional historical journal style, Manassa's essay, written for a historical methodology course, relates California Representative Joe Crail's role in the conflict surrounding building Boulder Dam.

The breathtaking seven hundred and twenty-six foot tall Boulder Dam, known today as the Hoover Dam, resulted from nearly a decade of spirited debate and political maneuvering in the 1920's. Much controversy surrounded the legislating of the Boulder Dam in regard to the necessity, feasibility, location, type, water and power rights, and constitutionality of this project. The state of California became particularly interested in this project due to power and water needs caused by its rapid growth. Republican California Representative Joe Crail, from the booming city of Los Angeles, served his district's interests in Congress from 1927 to 1933. Previously serving on the Republican State central committee for southern California from 1918 to 1920, Crail became intimately aware of the lack of power and water in his area. He actively pursued construction of the Boulder Dam, and controversial publicity against its opponents, to reap benefits for the state as well as his political career.

The need for a dam along the Colorado River became apparent during the 1920s in light of the flood, water reserve, power, and irrigation problems and the availabile construction technology. Seven states partook, from beginning to end, both in the controversy and the construction: California, Arizona, Nevada, Utah, New Mexico, Colorado, and Wyoming. These states were in some way physically associated with the Colorado River and felt they had direct interest in the Boulder Dam project.

A number of problems plagued California; these could only be solved with the construction of a tall, power-producing dam along the Colorado. Since California's problems were typical with those of most of the other states involved, and were the impetus for Joe Crail's involvement, a brief synopsis is in order.

Drought and water were a paramount problem to the people of the Imperial Valley in the southeast region of California.(1) Irrigation from the Colorado River was badly needed to aid the farmers in agricultural work. In addition, flash floods from the Colorado River menaced the vulnerable Imperial Valley in southeast California, and the federal government had pulled out of its unsuccessful flood control project in the area in 1915.(2) Finally, Los Angeles power needs doubled every four years, making demands that local power companies could not meet. Hydroelectric power could meet these needs.(3)

Although the need for a dam was clear, the location of it and the water rights of each state were not. By 1922, the seven states involved were grouped into an upper basin (Colorado, Utah, New Mexico, and Wyoming) and a lower basin (California, Arizona, and Nevada) according to location and water contribution via runoff. The controversy in the lower basin began when California laid claim to half of whatever the water rights in the lower basin were, despite the fact it failed to contribute any flow of water to the Colorado River.(4) In contrast, Arizona drained 95 percent of its runoff into the Colorado River.(5)

Meanwhile, the controversy did not end with water rights. In fact, it continued with whether to build a short dam up the river for $30 million that would only serve for irrigation and flood control, or to build a tall dam down the river for $70 million that would produce electricity as well.(6) Thus, power became the key question involved, and California was its chief proponent due to the tremendous output potential of hydroelectric power and Southern California Edison's desire to harness it.

For several years before 1921, Southern California Edison had planned to build several dams for power production.(7) By 1921, however, it was clear that the federal government was to pay for Boulder Dam because its proponents viewed this project as a federal duty and under federal jurisdiction. Thus the new question was that if the tall dam were built, should the public or private sector tap the power? "There were disagreements about the distribution of the power as well as about its production. And Herbert Hoover was not sure that there should be power produced at the dam at all."(8)

By now, a tall, power-producing dam built on Arizona soil seemed to be the best alternative. Arizona Governor George Hunt made it clear, however, that Arizona would only sign a compact when the power issue was resolved in favor of private, independently operated interests under his state's jurisdiction.(9) If the federal government were to handle the power production and distribution, it became certain that it would sublet its interests to Southern California Edison in light of its lobbying efforts. Not only would Los Angeles get the power it needed (since it was the only large electrical market), but also California would have a monopoly on the hydro-electric power for which Arizona would have nothing to gain. This came to the forefront when California proposed the Swing-Johnson bill, as we shall see later.(10)

By 1922, the contrast between the interests of California and the other six states became clear. California's growth and development was tremendous; it created an "inflated economic complex" which outpaced its own resources by virtue of its ever increasing water and power needs. The other states remained undeveloped and sought to maintain this status in light of low immigration.(11) At this point, Secretary of Commerce Herbert Hoover set up a commission to study the proposed Boulder Dam. This commission suggested a 50–50 split in the annual water flow between the upper and lower basin states.(12)

In 1922, the Colorado River Conference was held in Santa Fe to address and solve both proposals and problems. Out of this conference came a compact establishing the division between the upper and lower basins with a 50–50 water split, and the need for a tall, hydro-electric dam built downstream at Arizona.(13) Since Nevada's land was mostly unarable and state leaders only wanted 2% of the lower basin's 50% water allotment, the battle lines were drawn between California and Arizona.

Arizona was the only state not to ratify the compact because it insisted that a water distribution agreement be made first with California. A second conference was called in August of 1927 to uncover the roots of the situation.(14) Arizona had much arable land that could rival California's production of citrus fruits and subtropical crops and felt that an equal split of the remaining 48% would be unfair in light of its runoff contribution.(15) As a result of this, California withdrew its support from the compact as well.

At this point, Republican California Representative Phil Swing came forth. His long political and judicial career forcused on the endangered Imperial Valley and its people. Swing's support went far beyond this base when he announced the Swing-Johnson Bill in response to the failure of the Colorado River Compact. This bill officially proposed the federal government's construction of the tall, hydro-electric dam in Arizona. In addition, the initial $58 million estimate was to be fully repaid with interest in fifty years by an electricity tax.

This bill ignited a fierce battle in Congress that would last the next several years. Arizona became defensive of the Swing-Johnson Bill, and contended that it violated its state rights. Arizona produced a statement with twenty-six reasons why it and the other five states should object to the Swing-Johnson Bill. These objections included: ". . . that irrigation demands are sacrificed to power prospects; that the bill utilizes the natural resources of Arizona and Nevada to develop California; that the bill initiates the taking of natural resources from one state to another without compensation."(16)

The aforementioned background set the tone for the heated debates in Congress from 1927 to 1930, despite the adoption of the Swing-Johnson Bill on December 21, 1928. One such participant in the House of Representatives was California congressman Joe Crail. Not only did he wage a political debate, but a public war against Arizona as well.

Joe Crail served in the House of Representatives from March 4, 1927, to March 3, 1933, in the 70th, 71st, and 72nd Congresses.(17) He was a Republican from Los Angeles whose support did not extend beyond it, and who eventually lost in his attempt to become a U.S. Senator in 1932. He had served in Congress on several House committees including Public Buildings and Grounds, Roads, World War Veterans' Legislation, and Elections. He introduced Bills and Resolutions for pensions, relief for widows, awarding military honors, erecting public buildings in Culver City and Hollywood, building of Pacific Coast Highway, etc.(18)

For a congressman who never served on the Flood Control Committee nor the Irrigation and Reclamation Committee, Joe Crail was very outspoken both in Congress and in public on those matters. His use of the media and threats against Arizona would suggest that Crail not only sought his constituents' interests, but also his own senatorial ambitions.

His media campaign for the dam began when the Swing-Johnson Bill was rumored to exist even before the second Santa Fe conference began in August, 1927. That June, Crial announced that he expected a serious flood situation very soon, and that the water problems and solutions associated with the Colorado River should be treated as national issues, not local ones. (19) Then, after the second conference in August where Arizona had been giving everyone a hard time about its state rights being violated, he spoke to a prominent men's club and the newspapers regarding the "bad" attitude of Arizona toward the Boulder Dam.(20)

Among other things, Crail openly attacked Arizona suggesting that it be made a territory again. He maintained that its stand on the Colorado River amounted to rebellion. In addition, he pointed out that when Arizona entered the union it pledged to the federal government that it would disclaim all right to ungranted public land, that it would not tax such land, and that it would let the government carry out any reclamation work it saw fit. (21) Arizona had agreed to this and made it part of its Constitution, but on May 31, 1927, voted to delete this via two amendments.(22) Crail saw this as an act of rebellion.

A. W. Crawford, speaker of the Arizona House of Representatives, replied to Crail by wire stating there was not a single instance when one state was obliged to procure consent of another state to change its constitution. (23) Thus, he accused California of trying to evoke a federal response against the state rights of Arizona. This charge inspired Crail to give an immediate response, not only reiterating the aforementioned charges, but also stating that Arizona was directly holding up immense water projects until Southern California (via Edison) agreed to pay Arizona taxes on the power that the federally owned hydro-electric plants would be producing.(24) Although Arizona had suggested this at this time as a matter of compensation, by no means was it approved by the federal government.

Up to the introduction of the Swing-Johnson Bill, this media battle was waged primarily in the Western newspapers. By September 1927, however, it had reached national proportions. The *New York Times* announced Joe Crail's "plan" to delete Arizona from the United States on grounds that it had not met her agreement upon entering the union.(25) The article clearly criticized Crail's threat as ludicrous and unpatriotic, arousing sympathy for

Arizona and hindering the efforts to build the much-needed Boulder Dam.

The place that had the most heated and insulting debates surrounding the Boulder Dam was the U.S. Congress. Here, the *Congressional Record* detailed the battles between Joe Crail and the Arizonians. From the way Crail talked about the project, it appeared he finally had an issue, besides pensions and PCH, that he could really get involved with and become known for.

Interestingly enough, Crail began calmly talking about the three duties of the federal government in the Colorado River region and the benefit it would have even for Arizona. "The first duty is river regulation and flood control. Control of the Colorado against floods is vital to the people of the Imperial Valley, the Palos Verdes Valley, and the Coachella Valley in California. It is also of great interest to the people of the Yuma project in Arizona."(26) Crail pointed out in this same speech the duty of the federal government under the Constitution to maintain navigable rivers, which part of the Colorado was not. Finally, he pointed to the duty of reclamation and irrigation for the benefit of arid areas, such as Arizona.

Crail elaborated upon the conditions necessitating these duties. He pointed to the Imperial Valley as being hundreds of feet below sea level which created a serious flood hazard not to mention the build-up of silt around the area.(27) In fact, Crail insisted that in just this one instance, the government had an obligation to build a dam, even if it would have no returns from the community at large.(28) As we shall see, the beauty of the Swing-Johnson Bill provided for complete repayment of the dam's cost within fifty years.

Joe Crail concluded that: ". . . these duties of the government on the Colorado River can be taken care of properly only by a high dam at Boulder Canyon. There is no other way that it can be properly done."(29) Not only would a high dam, he insisted, manage water better, but also would provide for hydro-electric power, which would help conserve our oil resources.(30)

One key point Crail constantly reiterated was the feasibility of the whole project. He sought to answer the critics by declaring the dam was necessary, feasible, practical by engineering standards, and constitutional by legal authorities of the day.(31) When asked by a fellow Representative by what authority the government could build this dam, Crail responded by insulting him for not listening and then reiterating the three duties incumbent upon the federal government.(32)

Unfortunately for Crail, Representative Lewis W. Douglas of Arizona was a bit more skeptical and challenged Crail on several points. The Swing-Johnson Bill denied state's rights, he said, supported an economically unfeasible power plant, appropriated too much for the construction of a flood control dam, and would ultimately stunt the growth of the Southwest because it was a wasteful project that would only give more water to Mexico. Moreover, he was: ". . . bitterly opposed [to the measure] . . ."(33) Failing to account for the natural ecological replenishment of water systems, Douglas went on: "Irrigation and navigation are absolutely incompatible. One defeats the other. You can not leave water in a stream and still take the water out of the stream."(34)

The opposition went on to point the finger directly at California as the sole instigator of the Swing-Johnson Bill (which it was) to further its own ends not only in regard to water, but also power. Douglas pointed out that Los Angeles was the only really large market for electricity and that it could never absorb the amount of power that was proposed the Boulder Dam could produce.(35) In addition, Representative Elmer O. Leatherwood of Utah contended that this was not an irrigation project, but rather a massive power project, dreamed up by California, that would never repay the federal government.(36) Douglas added that if Los Angeles had to put up bonds for the power project, it would not do it.(37)

At this point, Crail stood to defend California. He stated California could well afford the entire cost of the dam by itself, but could not legally build it nor fund it because that was left up to the federal government.(38) He then accused his opponents of unfair criticism of Los Angeles as being consumed by self-interest. "Los Angeles has done nothing in this matter to be ashamed of," he claimed, "and it has nothing to conceal or to apologize for."(39)

The main line of defense for Crail was the provision in the Swing-Johnson Bill requiring the repayment to the federal government for the construction of the dim via the hydro-electric power produced. He said that the cities who purchased the power would have to have a contract with the government to buy it at a fixed price and for a long period of time until the costs to the government were repaid. These included the costs of operations, construction, carrying charges, and even interest.(40)

Crail continued to point out the economic advantages of this undertaking. First, he maintained, the economic security of the project: "It is not often that the Government is asked to undertake a development where the return of the money expended is guaranteed in advance."(41) Next, he assured Congress that the power companies the government would contract were secure and reliable; granted, he had Southern California Edison in mind when he said this. By 1930, when the appropriations for the dam were finally being considered, Crail even brought up the fact this public works project would employ five thousand men during the Depression when jobs were needed.(42)

The debate between Crail and Arizona intensified to the point of literal shouting matches and insults. Throughout the debates, Crail insisted upon the legality and legitimacy of the dam. He did not convince the Arizonians. Crail, still on the receiving end of Douglas by 1930 (for appropriations), finally insisted: "It would serve no useful purpose for me to discuss the validity of these contracts which my friend from Arizona dcrides."(43) No matter how legal the Attorney General found these contracts to be, Arizona was still going to oppose them on the grounds they violated states' rights.

In spite of all opposition, Crail gave an impassioned speech to Congress on December 18, 1928, just before the Swing-Johnson Bill was brought up for vote. He emphasized this was not a visionary scheme of California that was going to violate the rights of Arizona. He stressed the urgent need for a dam, and he promised: "Not a shovel full of dirt is to be turned, nor a stick of dynamite discharged, nor one dollar expended in the enterprise until the Secretary of the Interior is satisfied that responsible parties have contracted in writing to reimburse the Government . . . with interest."(44)

Arizona continued to receive the brunt of California's criticism from Phil Swing, the California Representative who was the key instigator of the Boulder Dam project. On the same December 18, he sought to discredit Arizona and her efforts as being unpatriotic and self-seeking. He insisted that no matter how the bill was worded or amended, that Arizona would not find it acceptable. He also pointed out that as soon as this bill would be passed, Arizona planned to file suit in the Supreme Court claiming the bill was unconstitutional. Douglas ignored these charges and merely responded that the bill was a dishonest one.(45)

Though the bill passed 167 to 122, the battle was not over yet. While Arizona began to appeal her case to the Supreme Court, appropriations to implement the legislation were considered in 1930. Douglas was as determined as ever to block the first installment of $10 million (out of $49 million) by rekindling all of the old accusations against California. Crail took the forefront in defending the bill and its appropriations.

Joe Crail began a scathing speech of Douglas and the state of Arizona. He reiterated what Swing had said two years earlier, that Arizona would never agree under any circumstances to the Boulder Dam. In addition, he criticized Douglas for asking questions that were answered two years before, and that Arizona wanted to tax the utility companies that were there. Douglas, he sarcastically concluded, was: ". . . sure that the Government, and particularly the State of California, are going to despoil the weak state of Arizona and rob it of its birthright. Woe, woe, woe."(46)

In wake of the passage of the Swing-Johnson Bill and the first $10 million installment of the appropriations bill that had been passed, Arizona filed suit in October, 1930. After a series of hearings, dismissals, retrials, etc., the Supreme Court ruled against Arizona on grounds the federal government, under the Constitution, had authority over navigable streams.(47) After the success and start of construction of the Boulder Dam in 1930, Joe Crail's dance in the spotlight ended.

For the next two years, Crail continued business as usual in the House of Representatives. He failed to get the Republican nomination for Senator in 1932 because his support died outside of Los Angeles. Swing did not run for any election in 1932 since he felt his mission of the Boulder Dam was over in light of the initial appropriations approval. Crail returned to Los Angeles where he practiced law until his death on March 2, 1938.

In conclusion, California Representative Joe Crail tried to take a lead role in actively promoting the construction of the Boulder Dam. Despite the fact he was never formally assigned to any congressional committee dealing with the project, Crail gave fervent support and debate in Congress in favor of it. In addition, Crail waged a public battle with Arizona and its representatives who were bitterly opposed to the dam. The outrageous demands for revocation of Arizona's statehood, made by Crail, indicate his play upon the popular controversy possibly to promote his own senatorial ambitions in addition to those of California.

Endnotes

1. Beverly Bowen Moeller, *Phil Swing and Boulder Dam* (Los Angeles: University of California Press, 1971), 9.
2. Ibid., 11.
3. U.S. Congress, *Congressional Record*, 70th cong. 1st sess., Vol. 69, Pt. 9 (1928), 9629.
4. Mary Austin, "The Colorado River Controversy," *The Nation*, 125 (November 9, 1927), 510.
5. Marshall Trimble, *Arizona: A Panoramic History of a Frontier State* (New York: Doubleday and Company, Inc., 1977), 364.
6. Moeller, *Phil Swing and Boulder Dam*, 70.
7. Ibid., 21.
8. Ibid., 32.
9. Ibid., 109.
10. Austin, "The Colorado River Controversy," *The Nation*, 511.
11. Ibid., 510.
12. Moeller, *Phil Swing and Boulder Dam*, 33.
13. Austin, "The Colorado River Controversy," *The Nation*, 510.
14. Ibid., 511.
15. Ibid., 511.
16. Ibid., 511.
17. *Biographical Directory of the American Congress 1774–1971* (Washington, D.C.: U.S. Government Printing Office, 1971), 796.
18. U.S. Congress, *Congressional Record*, 70th Cong. 1st sess., Vol. 69, Pt. 11, Index (1927–28), 122–123.
19. *Los Angeles Times*, June 11, 1927, Index.
20. *Los Angeles Times*, August 9, 1927, Index.
21. *Los Angeles Times*, July 1, 1927, Index.
22. Douglas D. Martin, *An Arizona Chronology* (Tucson: The University of Arizona Press, 1966), n/a.
23. *Los Angeles Times*, July 2, 1927, Index.
24. Ibid., July 2, 1927, Index.
25. *New York Times*, September 18, 1927, Section E.
26. U.S. Congress, *Congressional Record*, 70th Cong., 1st sess., Vol. 69, Pt. 9 (1928), 9510.
27. Ibid., 9510.
28. Ibid., 9511.
29. Ibid., 9510.
30. Ibid., 9512.
31. Ibid., 9513.
32. Ibid., 9511.

33. U.S. Congress, *Congressional Record*, 70th Cong., 2nd sess., Vol. 70, Pt. 1 (1928–29) 836.
34. U.S. Congress, *Congressional Record*, 70th Cong., 1st sess., Vol. 69, Pt. 9 (1928), 9767.
35. Ibid., 9628.
36. U.S. Congress, *Congressional Record*, 70th Cong., 2nd sess., Vol. 70, Pt. 1 (1928–29), 836.
37. U.S. Congress, *Congressional Record*, 70th Cong., 1st sess., Vol. 69, Pt. 9 (1928), 9629.
38. Ibid., 9511.
39. Ibid., 9510.
40. Ibid., 9511.
41. Ibid., 9511.
42. U.S. Congress, *Congressional Record*, 71st Cong., 2nd sess., Vol. 72, Pt. 10, 1930, 11264.
43. Ibid., 11264.
44. U.S. Congress, *Congressional Record*, 70th Cong., 2nd sess., Vol. 70, Pt. 1 (1928–29), 836.
45. U.S. Congress, *Congressional Record*, 70th Cong., 1st sess., Vol. 69, Pt. 9 (1928), 9767.
46. U.S. Congress, *Congressional Record*, 71st Cong., 2nd sess., Vol. 72, Pt. 10 (1930), 11264.
47. Trimble, *Arizona: A Panoramic History of a Frontier State*, 365.

Bibliography

Primary Materials

Congressional Record, Dec. 5, 1927–June 21, 1930.
Los Angeles Times, annotative Indexes, June–August, 1927.
New York Times, Sept. 18, 1927.

Secondary Materials

Austin, Mary. "The Colorado River Controversy." *The Nation*, 125 (November 9, 1927), 510–512.
Biographical Directory of the American Congress 1774–1971. Washington, D.C.: U.S. Government Printing Office, 1971.
Martin, Douglas D. *An Arizona Chronology*. Tucson: The University of Arizona Press, 1966.
Moeller, Beverly Bowen. *Phil Swing and Boulder Dam*. Los Angeles: University of California Press, 1971.
Trimble, Marshall. *Arizona: A Panoramic History of a Frontier State*. New York: Doubleday and Company, Inc., 1977.

■ THE WRITER'S ASSIGNMENT

Using both primary and secondary sources, analyze a person's role in an historical event. The paper should conform to professional historical journal style and format. ■

■ UNDERSTANDING WRITING STRATEGIES

1. How does the introduction engage the reader's interest?

2. What kind of commitment does the introduction make about the subject matter?

3. How does Manassa organize the synopsis? How does this integrate with the rest of the paper?

4. What was the nature of the conflict about building the dam?

5. How does Manassa characterize Joe Crail? What evidence does he offer to support this characterization?

6. What reasons did Crail cite for federal involvement in the dam project? On what grounds did the opposition counter these?

7. How objective is Manassa's presentation of the two sides? What passages indicate this?

8. Is the principal writing strategy here explanation, argument, or narration? How is this developed?

9. What material does Manassa draw from other writers (secondary sources)? What does he add from newspapers and the *Congressional Record* (secondary sources)?

10. To what degree does Manassa shape his historical facts into historical writing and to what degree does he merely report the facts? ■

■ SUGGESTIONS FOR WRITING

Beginning with Manassa's paper, research and explain either California's case for or Arizona's case against building Hoover (Boulder) Dam. ■

Edward F. Beale: Conflict of Interest in California Indian Policy

Scott Mersch

Scott Mersch's paper presents research into both historical documents and written histories done for a historical methodology class. Employing the professional historian's research strategies and professional historical journal style, Mersch's essay analyzes the difficulty Indian Superintendent Edward F. Beale had in developing a policy that actually benefited California Indians.

With the signing of the Treaty of Guadalupe Hidalgo on February 2, 1848, California became a territory of the United States. Part of the federal government's increased responsibility from this new acquisition was the administration of Indian affairs in California and in the other territories of the Mexican Cessation.[1] In none of the new territories, however, was the administration of Indian affairs as important as in California. In the same year as the signing of the peace treaty with Mexico, the great California Gold Rush began as thousands of miners and settlers poured into California, overrunning the land inhabited by Indians.

In the following year, another important change with federal Indian policy occurred. The Bureau of Indian Affairs was transferred from the Department of War to the newly created Department of the Interior. Perhaps the most significant aspect of this change was the argument used by the officials of the Interior Department to effect this transfer. They argued that it was impossible to civilize and educate the Indians while Indian affairs were managed by military leaders.[2] Thus, this administrative change was to be the first step in a policy that was to be more favorable to the Indians.

The Indian policy in California was primarily developed by California's first Indian superintendent, Edward F. Beale. The efforts of Beale and of those who followed his policy, however, demonstrated how difficult it was to develop a policy that actually benefited the Indians. Although the promises and goals of the general policy were for the protection and subsistence of the Indians, the details of the policy did not result in fulfillment of these objectives. Instead, there was a critical conflict of interest in the Indian policy developed by Beale, and the confused priorities resulted in a policy that sought to benefit the Indians only within the context of what would best protect and benefit the whites.

In March, 1852, Congress established the independent superintendency of California with Edward F. Beale as the superintendent. No definite policy was established, but Beale was sent to California to investigate the situation and to make a proposal regarding what further action the government should take. Congress appropriated $14,000 for his salary and $100,000 to be used to preserve peace with the Indians.[3]

Beale first traveled in the northern part of the state and on October 29, 1852, he sent a letter with his suggestions to the Commissioner of Indian Affairs. His proposals were as follows:

> In the first place, I propose a system of "military posts" to be established on reservations, for the convenience and protection of the Indians; these reservations to be regarded as military reservations or government reservations. The Indians to be invited to assemble within these reserves.
>
> A system of discipline and instruction to be adopted by the agent who is to live at the post.
>
> Each reservation to contain a military establishment, the number of troops being in proportion to the population of the tribes there assembled.
>
> The expenses of the troops to be borne by the surplus produce of the Indian labor.
>
> The reservations to be made with a view to a change in location, when increase of white population may make it necessary.
>
> A change of present Indian laws to be made, so as to suit the condition of the State and the proposed policy.[4]

These proposals became the basis of the Indian policy in California. They also demonstrated the conflict of interest that shaped Beale's actions and administrative policies.

Beale stated that the reservations were for the convenience and protection of the Indians. The brief details he presented, however, put much emphasis on the military, an aspect that was more directed at protecting the whites. Also the possible need for moving reservations because of white settlement was emphasized. This aspect of the policy clearly would not have been beneficial to the Indians but much more beneficial to land-greedy whites.

After writing to the commissioner, Beale traveled to southern California for the first time. During this visit he became convinced of the necessity of concentrating all his efforts and the funds appropriated by Congress in this part of California. He presented his argument for this plan in his letter of November 22, 1852.[5]

The influence of factors not related to the Indians' welfare appear in this letter. Beale argues that there was not enough money appropriated to help all the Indians in the state. He insisted that he needed to concentrate all the funds in one district of California if any of the Indians were to benefit. "If . . . I take one district and expend this amount," he wrote, "I may succeed in saving great suffering to the Indians and preserve peace to the whites."[6] While Beale indicates concern for saving the Indians' suffering, preserving peace for the whites and protecting their interests were the more important goals.

Beale does explain why he selected Southern California as the area in which to concentrate his efforts. He argued that the isolated white settlers on the ranchos were the most defenseless settlers in the state, and that they needed protection from the Indians more than the whites in the other parts of the state. He said:

> You will naturally ask, if there are so few people there, why protect them, to the neglect of the more populated portions of the country? Because it is from this quarter that we draw our supplies of beef cattle entirely. Los Angeles county is the cattle market of the State.[7]

Thus, the protection of the white's cattle interest became a major factor in shaping Indian policy.

Beale's letter also revealed other priorities. When writing about the Indians in the districts that he was not going to be able to help, he stated:

> I know that they starve; I know that they perish by hundreds; I know that they are fading away with a startling and shocking rapidity, but I cannot help them. Humanity must yield to necessity. They are not dangerous; therefore they must be neglected.[8]

This policy of neglecting the Indians that were not a threat to the whites was characteristic of general United States Indian policy for almost three quarters of a century, and this factor was certainly very significant in the policy developed by Beale, even though he wrote in the same letter, "It is a crying sin that our government, so wealthy and so powerful, should shut its eyes to the miserable fate of these rightful owners of the soil."[9]

In March, 1853, Congress acted on the proposals that superintendent Beale had submitted. Congress gave the president the authority to establish five military reservations in California or in the bordering territories of Utah and New Mexico. To cover the expenses of removing and subsisting the Indians, Congress appropriated $250,000. The president approved the plan, and he directed that Beale should execute it.[10]

Secretary of the Interior, Robert McClelland, informed Beale that the president approved the plan and instructed Beale to return to California to implement the plan. McClelland gave Beale precise instructions:

> In your journey to California, and other movements connected with the execution of the plan adopted in relation to the Indians in California, their security, subsistence, and protection, should constitute your sole object, and no other subject must be permitted to engage your time or attention.[11]

The intent of the secretary of the interior was for the Indian policy in California to be centered on the needs of the Indians. During his superintendency, Beale tried to help the Indians, but he intended to pursue a policy that had white interests as a higher priority than the interests of the Indians.

On September 2, 1853, Beale arrived in California's Tejon Pass area. He held a council with the Indians of that region and convinced them of their need to assemble and live at a place where the government would watch over them. He spoke of the advantages of farming and explained that the government wished to protect them from the whites while protecting the whites, too. The terms he offered them were:

> The government should commence with a system of farming and instruction, which would enable them in a few years to support themselves by the produce of their own labor.
>
> That for this purpose the government would furnish them with seed of all kinds, and with provisions sufficient to enable them to live until the produce of their own labor should be sufficient to support them.[12]

Beale also promised the Indians that the reserve would be in the area where the council had been just held as it was near where most of the Indians were from.

The Los Angeles *Star* also presented an account of this two-day council with the Indians. Its description substantiates how Beale and others perceived the situation with the Indians. The *Star* described how Beale explained to the Indians that "while mingling with the whites they could never rise to an equal station with them; but among themselves a firm feeling of friendship and equality could exist." He also emphasized how on the reservation "they could build up a city and educate their children for future usefulness." What future usefulness the children could expect was not explained but the *Star* did report that Beale had told them the alternative to this plan: "acquiesence in the will of the Government, or extermination by disease and mixture with the white race."[13]

Thus, a segregation policy emerged without considering alternatives. Integration never seemed to be an option although the Commissioner of Indian Affairs, Luke Lea, in his annual report of 1851 had said that the incorporation of the Indians into the citizen population was necessary for an attempt to civilize the Indians to be successful.[14] This conclusion was not a common assessment of the situation, and Lea never followed it up.

Another statement by Commissioner Lea was very significant because it typified the common white attitude toward Indians. In his annual report of 1852, Lea wrote:

> In the long and varied conflict between the white man and the red—civilizations and barbarianism—the former has often been compelled to recede, and be destroyed, or to advance and destroy. The history of the contest, however, bears witness to the fact that that the victor has, in general, manifested a generous desire, not only to spare the vanquished, but to improve his condition.[15]

Often the categories of civilization and barbarism were equated, in an absolute sense, with the whites and Indians, and any effort to aid the Indians was seen as a gracious act.

Before submitting his decision to open a reservation at Tejon Pass, Beale consulted with several other people to get their opinions and support. United States Army Lieutenants George Stoneman, R. S. Williamson, and J. G. Parke were in California surveying possible routes for the Atlantic and Pacific railroad, and Beale wrote them to get their opinion. They responded positively to Beale's questions regarding the Tejon Pass area, and they wrote that they knew of no better spot in the southern portion of the state for a reservation. They were impressed especially with the isolation of the Tejon reservation, the good farming land in the area, and its ideal location for a military fort that would protect the interests of the whites and the Indians.[16]

The isolated nature of the Tejon Pass area was certainly a key factor. Others also commented on and emphasized this aspect of the reservation's location. For example, Congressman John B. Weller expressed his support for Beale's reservation plan emphasizing the need to isolate the Indians from the whites.[17] The superintendent who followed Beale, Thomas Jefferson Henley, also agreed that the location was excellent, due in part to its isolation.[18]

If the Los Angeles *Star* adequately reflected it, public opinion supported Beale. "Mr. Beale," editorialized the *Star* on June 24, 1854, "is a man of untiring energy, and is entirely unselfishly devoted to the work. Let him have a fair trial, and he will make the miserable wild Indians of California the happiest people in the state."[19] Demonstrating attitudes toward both Beale and the Indians, this was very representative of attitudes of many of the people in California.

The paper also reported on the cattle situation. On October 20, 1855, it credits the Tejon reservation with helping to stop Indians from stealing horses and cattle.[20] This aspect of the reservation was very important, not only because it was part of the motivation for establishing the reserve, but also because it may have kept it in existence.

There were many factors involved in the continuation of the Tejon reservation, but the protection it provided for white interests was probably the most significant. In his letter of November 22, 1852, Beale wrote: "It is through the very pass of the Tejones that all our cattle are driven to this market, and through this pass also that the Indians descend on their winter forays. It has been well said that 'the Tejones' is the key to Los Angeles."[21] The most significant white interest that needed to be protected was cattle, and this concern continued throughout the existence of the Tejon Reservation.

Even when there were major problems with drought, the reservation was not abandoned. Nor was it abandoned when it cost much more to maintain it than the commissioner of Indian affairs and Congress had originally planned on. In a letter to B. D. Wilson, dated January 17, 1856, John Weller wrote:

> There is no disposition whatever on the part of the Com. Indian Affairs to abandon that reserve [Tejon]. Although it has not been as prosperous as was

desirable so far as Collecting the Indians is Concerned, yet it has given peace & security to our people in that region and it would certainly be very unwise to abandon it. Knowing as I do the importance of that reservation to the protection of the people of Los Angeles, San Bernardino & San Diego I can never Consent to its removal.[22]

The reservation was suffering from several problems at the time that this letter was written: drought, whites selling liquor to the Indians, and land ownership. In spite of all these problems the reservation was not closed during this time period because it was still useful to the whites.

Beale and the other superintendents in California who sought to establish reservations faced a problem that was not so dominant elsewhere, the problem of finding enough federal land to put a reservation on. Most of the land was either owned by the state or was part of one of the Spanish land grants. Because of this shortage of federal land, all of the California reservations during the 1850's were on land that was not public. Most of the reservations had to rent their land from private owners. For the Tejon reservation this land problem was acute and ultimately contributed to the 1864 closing of the reservation.

The first mention of the government land shortage was made by Beale when he first considered the Tejon pass area for a reservation. In his November 22, 1852, letter he wrote that Congress needed to look into buying the land. In a letter to W. B. T. Sanford, B. D. Wilson also wrote that the Tejon reservation, while the only suitable location, would encounter a problem over land ownership. There was confusion over whether some of it, or none of it, was owned by the government, but several people recommended that Beale go ahead with his plan anyway. Congressmen Gwin and Latham were two who supported the plan to establish the reservation regardless of the land situation.

Land was not Beale's only difficulty in trying to administer California Indian policy. As he wrote constantly to the commissioner of Indian affairs, he found it difficult to keep up with his accounts.[23] At one point, Commissioner William Manypenny reprimanded Beale and suggested that it was better for Beale to postpone his operations rather than not follow instructions he had been given.[24]

Beale had significant support in California, but lacked support in Washington. Because he was a Democrat, Beale faced bitter opposition from the Whig politicians, and this combined with his confused account led to his being replaced by Thomas Jefferson Henly in 1854.[25] People in California, who were generally supportive of Beale, and even the Indians, were unhappy about his removal from office. The Indians' displeasure was reported in a letter to B. D. Wilson: "The Indians are very much displeased at the idea of Mr. Beale leaving them, and I think they will give 'Uncle Sam,' a great deal of trouble if steps are not taken with them."[26]

At the Tejon reservation, Beale had developed almost a paternal identity among the Indians. He maintained strict discipline with the Indians, but he also referred to them as "My people" when he described in a 1854 letter how his feelings of compassion for the Indians were changing to a deep interest in their welfare.[27] His descriptions of the reservation were very positive in this letter; however, he may have been exaggerating and creating an ideal image to try to get more funds appropriated for the reservation. He ended the letter with a description of an Indian boy who had made some garters for him. He stated that he was sending them with the letter as an example of the ingenuity of the Indians under his charge. He closed the letter by writing: ". . . and I repeat that such ingenuity, (for this is but one instance in many I could mention) and such constancy in labor, deserve and should receive the fostering care of a government which possesses in its treasury so many unappropriated millions."[28]

After his removal from the superintendency, Beale successfully defended himself against the charges of financial mismanagement which had been leveled at him by his political opponents. J. M. Broadhead, second comptroller, wrote the Secretary of the Treasury James Guthrie about the investigation of Beale's financial records. Broadhead reported that the auditor had suggested an investigation before the Secretary of the Treasury because of the large amount of funds involved. Broadhead, however, then wrote:

> My own views of the case coincide, to a great extent, with those expressed by the Auditor. No disposition has been shown by Mr. Beale to evade scrutiny; on the contrary, the commendable promptness and candor with which he has proffered explanation, his ready and unembarrassed replies, and his urgent request that you, as head of the department, will thoroughly examine him upon the points in dispute, have tended to confirm the confidence in his honesty and uprightness that an acquaintance with him from his boyhood has justified me in entertaining.[29]

Thus, Beale was cleared primarily because of his general reputation and his friendship with Broadhead. How Beale spent the funds was never clearly determined, but he was credited as being an honest man by those conducting the inquiry into his financial matters as superintendent.

Even after his dismissal from the superintendency, Beale played another important role in California Indian policy. This role also demonstrates the conflict of interest in the California Indian policy, perhaps even more than Beale's efforts while superintendent. In 1864 the Indians at the Tejon reservation were moved to the Tule River.[30] Among the several factors involved in this move were drought and local white influence. One of the primary reasons, however, that the move was made was because the owner of the land wanted the Indians off. Ironically, the owner of the land at that time was Edward F. Beale.

Albert Hurtado in *Indian Survival on the California Frontier* tells how Beale acquired this land. During the Civil War Beale had been appointed by President Abraham Lincoln to the position of U. S. Surveyor General for California. He used this position to acquire the title to Rancho El Tejon, which encompassed the area containing the Tejon reservation and other lands. He then rented the land for the reserve to the government for $1,000. a year.[31] Thus, in 1864, when he decided he wanted the Indians off, the man who had started the Tejon Reserve became the one who caused it to close. The primary motive for stopping the reservation from continuing on his land was indicated by his letters: to protect his cattle.

The attitude expressed by Beale in his correspondence with J. P. H. Wentworth, California Superintendent for Indian Affairs in 1863, over this matter was much different than the attitude he had expressed ten years earlier. By August 11, 1863, his attitude was distinctly negative:

> I do not choose to go before the public as desiring to rent to the government, as your letter, without explanation, might lead any one to believe. On the contrary, if I rent at all it will only be as a great favor, and one only reluctantly granted. I require the whole of my ranch, and have purchased it for a purpose which would be altogether disarranged by such a disposition of it.
>
> I now inform you that I will on no account rent to the hostile and vicious Indians [the Indians from the Owens Valley] whom you have lately removed there, and whose presence endangers at all times the lives of my people and neighbors. Those savages, fresh from the experience of last summer, in which they once or twice defeated the soldiers sent against them by the government, and committed the most atrocious murders and outrages, may at any time break out again into open mutiny, one hour of which might cost me my entire stock of sheep, horses, and cattle, and the lives of valuable employees and neighbors. I therefore request you to remove these dangerous and hostile Indians from my property immediately.
>
> As for the very large number of Indians who were there before, and who have occupied this place under the government protection for twelve years without paying their rent, all of whom I know, while I would prefer their removal I shall not urge it, but request you to regard my reply of July 29, consenting, at your request, to rent a portion of the ranch as a reserve, as relating to them alone.[32]

William Brewer visited Beale in 1863 and reported on the size of Beale's property: 87,750 acres. When Beale was superintendent, he claimed to have a deep interest in the Indians' welfare. However, now he was unwilling to share his land with them.

In general, most people have considered Edward F. Beale to have been a good developer and executor of Indian policy in California. The viewpoint of Edward Everett Dale when he referred to Beale as one of the few able and honest officials in the Indian affairs of California, was the common viewpoint among historians. Perhaps in comparison to other Indian agents he was more honest and effective; however, in terms of what he did, or did not do, for the Indians, Beale's reputation was over-inflated.

Beale represented an Indian policy that, at best, sought to benefit the Indians only when it coincided with what was favorable for the whites. He was caught up in the conflict of priorities that the government in general had difficulty with. The government was to be the protector of the Indians while being responsible for the interests of its citizens—interests that usually left no room for any Indian interests. Beale became caught up in this conflict, and this conflict was mixed up with his personal interests and greed as well. Thus, in addition to the Indian policy he developed, he was significant as one who represented the conflicts of interest in U.S. Indian Affairs.

Notes

[1]Edward E. Dale, *Indians of the Southwest; A Century of Development Under the United States* (Norman, 1979), 3.

[2]Ibid., 6–7.

[3]Ibid., 35–36.

[4]33rd Congress, special session. *Senate Executive Document No. 4*, 373–374.

[5]Ibid., 377.

[6]Ibid.

[7]Ibid., 377–378.

[8]Ibid., 378.

[9]Ibid.

[10]33rd Congress. 1st session. *Senate Executive Document No. 1*, 464–465.

[11]Ibid., 465.

[12]Ibid., 469–472.

[13]John Walton Caughey, ed., *The Indians of Southern California in 1852: The B. D.Wilson Report and a Selection of Contemporary Comments* (San Marino, 1952), 110–113.

[14]32nd Congress, 1st session. *Senate Executive Document No. 1*, 265.

[15]32nd Congress, 2nd session, *Senate Executive Document No. 1*, 293.

[16]33rd Congress, 1st session, *Senate Executive Document No. 1*, 478–479.

[17]Ibid., 476–477.

[18]33rd Congress, 2nd session. *Senate Executive Document No. 1*, 511.

[19]Caughey. *The Indians of Southern California in 1852*, 135.

[20]Ibid., 147.

[21]33rd Congress, special session. *Senate Executive Document No. 4*, 378.

[22]Caughey, *The Indians of Southern California In 1852*. 147.

[23]33rd Congress, 1st session, *Senate Executive Document No. 1*, 467–469.

[24]Ibid., 480–481.

[25]Dale. *Indians of the Southwest*. 39.

[26]Caughey. *The Indians of Southern California in 1852*, 136.

[27]33rd Congress, 2nd session, *Senate Executive Document No. 1*, 507.

[28]Ibid., 508.

[29]34th Congress. 3rd session, *Senate Executive Document No. 69*, 7.

[30]See 38th Congress, 2nd session. *House Executive Document No. 1*, 269–270 and 275.

[31]Albert C. Hurtado, *Indian Survival on the California Frontier* (New Haven, 1988), 148.

[32]38th Congress. 1st session. *House Executive Document No. 1*, 221–222.

Bibliography

Primary Sources

Caughey, John W., ed. *The Indians of Southern California in 1852: The B. D. Wilson Report and a Selection of Contemporary Comment.* San Marino: Huntington Library, 1952.

House of Representatives. *Executive Documents.* 38th Cong., 1st sess., 1863–64, doc. 1. 38th Cong., 2nd sess., 1864–65, doc. 1.

Senate. *Executive Documents.* 32nd Cong., 1st sess., 1851–52, doc. 1. 32nd Cong., 2nd sess., 1852–53, doc. 1. 33rd Cong., 1st sess., 1853–54, doc. 1. 33rd Cong., 2nd sess., 1854–55, doc. 1. 33rd Cong., spec. sess., 1853, doc. 4. 34th Cong., 3rd sess., 1856–57, doc. 5.

Secondary Sources

Dale, Edward E. *The Indians of the Southwest: A Century of Development Under the United States.* Norman: University of Oklahoma Press, 1949.

Hurtado, Albert L. *Indian Survival on the California Frontier.* New Haven: Yale University Press, 1988.

Rawls, James J. *Indians of California: The Changing Image.* Norman: University of Oklahoma, 1984.

■ THE WRITER'S ASSIGNMENT

Using both primary and secondary sources, analyze a person's role in an historical event. The paper should conform to professional historical journal style and format.   ■

■ UNDERSTANDING WRITING STRATEGIES

1. What do the first two paragraphs do? Why is this important for a historical essay?

2. What is the essay's thesis? What kinds of evidence does Mersch offer to support this?

3. How did Beale justify centering his Indian policy in Southern California?

4. What was Beale's attitude toward the relationship between Indians and whites? How does Mersch regard this? What indicates this?

5. Why did the Tejon Reservation receive wide support? What was the nature of that support?

6. How does Mersch integrate the information from the letters (his primary source) into the essay? Pay particular attention to the way he introduces the letters.

7. What conclusions does Mersch reach about Beale? What evidence leads to this conclusion?

8. How well does Mersch argue his case against historians' conventional view that Beale was a good developer and executor of Indian policy? ◼

◼ SUGGESTIONS FOR WRITING

Beginning with Mersch's study of Beale, write a position paper on the American government's attitudes toward Native Americans. ◼

Modern Victimization
Brett Nelson

Written for his second semester composition class, Introduction to Literature, Brett Nelson's essay studies fictional characterization by comparing the protagonists' victimization in Conrad's *Heart of Darkness*, Faulkner's *Light in August*, and Fitzgerald's *The Great Gatsby*.

There are essentially two schools of belief which have resulted from man's propensity to question the nature of his innate soul. The first, and perhaps more archaic of the two, espouses that man, from his very conception, is tainted by an evil presupposition. Under this auspices, a society which imposes values and establishes structure is requisite to prevent his primal drives from consuming him. For, in the absence of such imposed order, man would necessarily succumb to his "inner darkness;" having no restraining order save his own, which, at its core, is spoiled.

The second belief holds that man, at his basal center, is utterly replete with goodness. Thus, his own innate moral code is sufficient enough to secure his goodness. His society's code, on the other hand, would displace or leech him of his own code. Or it might impose such an austere set of restraints upon him, that his own restraints would be shattered, and he, like his rearing society, would emerge utterly destroyed. In either scenario, there would necessarily be victims, for it is difficult to speak of evil without the medium of corruptible goodness for it to act upon. Great modern writers, who have addressed this fundamental question as their thematic concern, have fittingly realized the integral illustration a victimized entity offers. Hence, it is appropriate that William Faulkner's *Light in August*, Joseph Conrad's *Heart of Darkness*, and F. Scott Fitzgerald's *The Great Gatsby* all deal with man's victimization. And although Conrad's victim, Kurtz, illustrates that man is innately evil, while both Faulkner's Joe Christmas and Fitzgerald's Jay Gatsby illustrate that it is society which corrupts man, all utilize the medium of victimization to explicate their respective thematic drives.

Each character then, while serving to illustrate his author's point, must also operate within certain governing parameters. The first stipulation is that the victimized protagonist exude a certain uniqueness which is uncharacteristic of his ultimate corrupter. This requisite serves to separate him from his victimizer, bolster our awe in his presence, and heighten the emotional appeal of his eventual devastation. This particular element, should not, however, elevate him to such a level that he readily escapes our own grasp of emotional identification with him. Secondly, he should exist in a cosmos which is at once chaotic, violent, and absurd. This turbulence may radiate outward from within, as in Kurtz's dilemma, or it may be savagely projected upon innocent man by his corrupt society, as in Joe's and Gatsby's victimization. Lastly, and consequently, he must somehow embody the greater perpetual human victimization this cosmos casts on us all, thus being destroyed as a result of his failure to assert himself aptly in relation to his circumstances, as we ourselves might do.

Conrad's central victim, Kurtz, is primarily unique in his moral purpose, and the reverence it garners. Marlow, the book's narrator, wonders "whether this man who had come out equipped with moral ideas" will be able to assert them in a savage jungle (33). Kurtz's "ideas" are perhaps best surmised in his own writings: "by simple exercise of our will we can exert a power for good practically unbounded" upon the natives (50). Marlow, reveling in the tremendous breath of Kurtz's noble purpose, compares him to "an exotic Immensity ruled by an august Benevolence" and later concludes Kurtz is "a universal genius" (50; 71). Ultimately Marlow most aptly describes Kurtz, when he asserts, "I am unable to say . . . which was the greatest of his talents" (71).

But despite the uniqueness of Kurtz's intentions, all is blurred when he enters the immense jungle, which hastily forces the wheels of his corruption into motion. Here, "all that mysterious life of the wilderness that stirs in the forest, in the Jungles" and "in the midst of the incomprehensible which is also detestable" had "closed around him" (10). Here the very elements bespeak of an underlying evil current: "The forest, the creek, the mud, the river—seemed to beckon with a dishonouring flourish before the sunlit face of the land a treacherous appeal to the lurking death, to the hidden evil, to the profound darkness of its heart" (35). Kurtz, thus, was utterly encompassed by a primal evil, which to a man that, "All Europe contributed to the making of" must have seemed violent and chaotic (50).

Yet although Kurtz's surroundings are obviously brooding, it is his inability to assert his moral purpose extraneous of society's order, and not his mere surroundings, which solidifies his corruption. Kurtz "lacked restraint in the gratification of his various lusts, that there was something wanting in him—some small matter which when the pressing need arose could not be found under his magnificent eloquence" (57). Essentially, his soul had gone mad: "being alone in the wilderness, it had looked within itself and by Heavens, I tell you, it had gone mad!" (65). Marlow, in fearful thought, grapples with the notion that Kurtz had allowed his inner savagery to surface; allowed himself, with its prodding, to be utterly consumed by its presence:

> The wilderness had patted him on the head, and behold, it was like a ball—an ivory ball; it had caressed him and lo! he had withered; it had taken him, loved him, embraced him, got into his veins, consumed his flesh, and sealed his soul to its own by the inconceivable ceremonies of some devilish initiation. He was its spoiled and pampered favorite (49).

In essence, then, the wilderness "echoed loudly within him" because he was always hollow at the core (57). Kurtz, when ultimately realizing that all men are innately savage, is left only to cry, "The horror! The horror!" (72). Thus, he, with this statement, is forced to embrace all humanity's, "heart of darkness" or, as Marlow notes, to "embrace the whole universe" with a stare that is "piercing enough to penetrate all the hearts that beat in the darkness" (69).

Faulkner's thematic victim, Joe Christmas, similarly possesses a uniqueness of character, yet unlike Kurtz, his inspires a contemptuous awe, rather than reverence. Joe's distinction lies in the unbridled strength of his proud, ruthless, cold self-sufficiency. His prowess shines in the midst of a society that draws false strength from a sterile religion. He is described as wearing his hat, "cocked at an angle arrogant and baleful above his still face" and later as possessing a "quality ruthless, lonely and almost proud" (33). Moreover, Joe possesses a "gaunt" face, with a countenance that, ". . . had been molded in a still and deadly regularity and then baked in a fierce oven" (37). Joe's fellow workers view him in an almost jealous awe: "We ought to run him thorough the planer . . . Maybe that will take that look off his face" (34).

Yet despite the self-sufficiency of his character, Joe, like Kurtz, is unable to assert himself in a corrupt society. As a white Southerner convinced that he possesses a trace of Negro blood (He asserts, "I think I got some nigger blood in me" [216]), Joe is consequently alienated from both white and black communities; the result of a society which has placed distinctions between the two. Joe is thus forced never to truly have roots, or even a foundation in his society; as Bryon Bunch states, "there was something definitely rootless about him, as though no town nor city was his, no street, no walls, no square of earth his home " (33). Joe's lack of heritage is clearly visible when he walks the streets of both white and black parts of Jefferson. In the white man's world, he appears "a phantom, a spirit, strayed out of its own world and lost" (125). Then he passes down the hill into the Negro quarter. It lies "lightless hot wet primogenitive Female" and assumes the shape of a "black pit" ready to engulf him (124–125). In symbolic terms, Joe travels both streets at once with his "steady *white* shirt and *dark* pacing legs" (126). Joe, at one point, even attempts to purge himself of the society imposed color distinction. Living with a Negro woman in the northern city, Joe lies in bed breathing hard and deep: "trying to repel from himself the white blood and the white thinking" (248). Yet Joe, like Kurtz, cannot escape the corruption, and even though he tries to make the "dark odor" of the Negroes his own, his white mentality writhes "with physical outrage and spiritual denial" (248).

In representing the black community, Joe is consistently victimized by his society's religiously justified prejudice. This prejudice is most evident in Percy Grimm's belief that, "the white race is superior to any and all other races" (498). So racially biased is Joe's society, that his own father was killed because his face bared "the black curse of God Almighty" (423). Joe's grandfather thinks Joe the very "teeth and fangs" of Satan because of his mixed blood (426). As a result, he feels God has "put the mark" of Cain on Joe to show his contempt of his race (409). Even as a child in the orphanage, the children ran about him calling "Nigger! Nigger!" which again Joe's grandfather believed was the showing of "God's will" (422). Lastly, Joe's name is equated, by his grandfather, with "sacrilege" (422).

Ultimately, Joe's victimization results in his crucifixion as a "martyr." As one character notes, it appeared as if Joe had, "set out and made plans to passively commit suicide" (489). Hightower acknowledges the society's corrupt religion as being the culprit of his death: "Pleasure, ecstasy, they cannot seem to bear: their escape from it is violence . . . in praying . . . And so why should not their religion drive them to crucifixion of themselves and one another?" (405). They must crucify Joe in order to stifle their own consciences: "since to pity him would be to admit self doubt and to hope for and need pity themselves. They will do it gladly, gladly. That's why it is so terrible, terrible" (406). Perhaps this is why Joe embraces all humanity in death, almost as a Christian Martyr, having "eyes open and empty to everything save consciousness and with something of a shadow about his mouth. For a long moment he looked up at them with peaceful and unfathomable and unbearable eyes" (513).

Fitzgerald's victim, Jay Gatsby, is unique unto himself. For, in a spiritually void and corrupt morass which calls itself society, Gatsby exudes a pure, unbridled vitality of character. Nick, the novel's narrator, asserts, "there was something wonderful about him, some heightened sensitivity to the promises of life" (2). Later, Nick muses over Gatsby's "extraordinary gift for hope, a romantic readiness which I have never found in any other person" (2). Moreover, Gatsby's own physical features bespeak of his imitable vitality. Nick says Gatsby's very smile had "a quality of eternal reassurance in it" which you "may come across four or five times in your life" (48). But perhaps the best indication of Gatsby's vitality is found in Nick's comment that "Gatsby . . . sprang from his own Platonic conception of himself. He was a son of God . . ." (99).

Gatsby's victimization results from his attempt to attain a position in upper East Egg society; a society which consequently destroys him. Thus,

Gatsby, much like Joe Christmas, is doubly victimized by a society which seemingly beckons him, yet refuses to accommodate him. As a child, Gatsby dreamed of the splendor of upper society, creating "a universe of ineffable gaudiness" in his mind (99). Each night he "added to the pattern of his fancies until drowsiness closed down upon some vivid scene" (100). In short, Gatsby's aspirations are based upon the "promise that the rock of the world was founded securely on a fairy's wing," or the fear, as he would later say to Nick, that he might be viewed as, "just some nobody" (100; 67).

In the pursuit of his dream, Gatsby focuses his tremendous energy on Daisy Fay (fay, ironically meaning "fairy") and becomes lost in the drive for his dream. To Gatsby, Daisy represented all that he strived for: "For Daisy was young and her artificial world was redolent of orchids and pleasant, cheerful snobbery and orchestras . . ." (151). To him, her "inexhaustible charm" was the fact that "her voice was full of money" (120). Yet Gatsby fails to realize that he has created an illusion in Daisy, for:

> Daisy tumbled short of his dreams—not through her own fault, but because of the colossal vitality of his illusion. It had gone beyond her, beyond everything. He had thrown himself into it with a creative passion, adding to it all the time, decking it out with every bright feather that drifted his way. No amount of fire or freshness can challenge what a man will store up in his ghostly heart (97).

Consequently, Gatsby is ignorant of the fact, nearly to the end, that he does not belong in East Egg society. Gatsby "possessed some deficiency" which made him "subtly unadaptable to Eastern life" (177). To the East Egger's, Gatsby represents "Mr. Nobody from Nowhere" (130). He is additionally ignorant of their unspoken laws and customs; as Tom notes when Gatsby accepts a rhetorical invitation to dinner, "My God, I believe that man's coming, doesn't he know she doesn't want him?" (104). Furthermore, the East Egg populous is unable to accept his emotion and vitality and thus they must ruin him to satiate their own corruption. East Egg society, just as Tom and Daisy, "smashed up things and creatures, and then retreated back into their money" (180).

Gatsby's ultimate victimization, then, comes in the wake of his realization that his dream, itself a result of society, is based on a false illusion. As Nick notes, "He had been full of the idea so long, dreamed it right through to the end, waited with his teeth set . . . at an inconceivable pitch of intensity. Now, in the reaction, he was running down like an over-wound clock" (93). Ultimately, Gatsby, like Kurtz and Joe, accepts his victimization, and realizes the broader implications his own victimization casts upon others:

> Gatsby was overwhelmingly aware of the youth and mystery that wealth imprisons and preserves, of the freshness of many clothes, and of Daisy, gleaming like silver, safe and proud above the hot struggles of the poor (150).

As Nick uneasily concludes, "he must have felt that he had lost the old warm world, paid a high price for living too long with a single dream" (162).

What I am suggesting, then, is that Kurtz, Christmas, and Gatsby were all victimized to express their authors' thematic points. Kurtz, representing the prodigy of English civilization, comes face to face with his primal animal nature, and in its presence, casts off the very ideals of humanity. He transcends the facade of his society, which was destroying African soil to serve its own ends, and quite literally destroys the Africans themselves. Thus he illustrates the inability of man to exist peacefully in the absence of social structures. Christmas and Gatsby, on the other hand, offer the opposing view. Their victimization stems from the corrupt society which has violated their otherwise innocent essence. Joe's rigid determination to counter the society forces which compulsively attempt to shape his will to their own, eventually facilitates his destruction. Gatsby, while illustrating the same point, essentially attempts to exist within the parameters that society has inspired in him, but since these are nearly contrary to his own, he is helplessly destroyed. In any case, all three victims are utterly effective in their respective ends, for each raises to the surface our remote kinship with their plight. Thus, regardless of an individual's personal standing on man's innate nature, the element of victimization surely offers a new dimension to man's propensity for question.

Works Cited

Conrad, Joseph. *Heart of Darkness.* Ed. R. Kimbrough. New York: Norton, 1963–1988.
Faulkner, William. *Light in August.* New York: Random House, 1985.
Fitzgerald, F. Scott. *The Great Gatsby.* New York: Charles Scribner's Sons, 1925.

■ THE WRITER'S ASSIGNMENT

Compare the treatment of a particular theme or point of view in Conrad's *Heart of Darkness*, Faulkner's *Light in August*, and Fitzgerald's *The Great Gatsby*. Your 8–10 page essay should develop and explain a clear relationship (a thesis) and should support this with thorough references to the literary texts appropriately introduced and explained. ■

■ UNDERSTANDING WRITING STRATEGIES

1. What does Nelson see as the essential difference between Faulkner's, Conrad's, and Fitzgerald's view of man in his natural state?

2. How does Nelson describe Kurtz, Joe Christmas, and Jay Gatsby as victims?

3. How does Nelson structure his study of the three novels?

4. How well does this structure help the reader keep both Nelson's thesis and the themes he discusses clear?

5. Effective comparisons require some commonality in the objects of study. What commonality exists in this essay? Where do you find it?

6. How is each author's vision distinctive? How does Nelson show this?

7. What conclusions does Nelson reach? Are the arguments adequately developed and supported to justify the conclusions? Where do you see this?

The Hollow Men of Eliot's Time

Audrey Peake

The students in Audrey Peake's English composition class did group research projects on the historical, critical, and literary backgrounds of major poets. This essay analyzes T. S. Eliot's poem "The Hollow Men" using the information Peake gained from her group's research.

Thomas Sterns Eliot was a man whose talents included journalism, literary and social criticism, drama, and poetry (his greatest talent). His poetry consists of the group of poems written during his first years in England, commencing in 1914; his darkest poetry beginning in 1919; and his Christian poems. Out of the period in which he wrote his darkest poetry comes "The Hollow Men." The Hollow Men is in five parts, all of which were published separately before Eliot collected them into one whole poem. Eliot's personal life, as well as the history of his era, both surface frequently in this particular poem. Thus it is through certain aspects of Eliot's life and his time period that the theme of "The Hollow Men" is developed; "Combining the history of the civilization [and] its present condition, 'The Hollow Men' portrays a civilization unable to face reality, as well as a civilization devoid of hope" (Pearce 22).

The epigraphs at the beginning of "The Hollow Men" give the first hint of Eliot's attitude toward the state of his civilization. Eliot took the quotation "Mistah Kurtz—he dead" from Joseph Conrad's *Heart of Darkness*. This quotation is a contemptuous announcement by a black servant that the exceptional white god of the Congo has expired. "A penny for the Old Guy" is a common English children's saying when they use a stuffed effigy of Guy Fawkes to beg pennies for fireworks on Guy Fawkes Day, No-

vember 5. With this connection between Kurtz and Guy Fawkes, Eliot introduces the history of "lost/Violent souls" of past civilizations. In addition to
using the epigraphs as an introduction to his poem's hollow, stuffed men,
Eliot attempts to reduce the worth of his own civilization's hollow men; for
unlike the hollow men described later in his poem, both Guy Fawkes and
Kurtz at least recognize their situation, and one of them actually engages
himself in action (Smith 103).

Part I of "The Hollow Men" describes the hollow men Eliot sees in his
world. The speaker of the poem depicts himself, as well as others, as merely
scarecrows or dummies with "headpiece[s] filled with straw." Along with
this emptiness comes brokenness. For example, the hollow men's voices are
meaningless like "rats' feet over broken glass." And they have shape but no
"form," as well as "gesture without motion." Some critics such as Ronald
Bush believe that the images of brokenness reflect Eliot's marriage at the
time he wrote "The Hollow Men."According to Bush, Eliot lived through
the worst year of his marriage because of his wife's near death and his own
illness caused by exhaustion (Bush 82). Most critics agree instead that these
images of brokenness and shallowness seem to portray the emptiness and
narrow existence of the people Eliot saw around him. Eliot believed that
it was better to be either completely good or bad rather than hesitate to
commit any action at all. Thus Eliot protrays in the last verse of Part I a civilization which will be remembered only for "hollow men" instead of "lost/
Violent souls" like Guy Fawkes and Kurtz, who at least were "failures of
success, not of will" (Schneider 106). It is in this last verse that Eliot also introduces what he considers "death's dream Kingdom." "Those who have
crossed / With direct eyes, to death's other kingdom," according to Robert
Fleissner, represent the dead, who unlike Eliot's hollow men, at least face
the reality of death (Fleissner 40).

In Part II of the poem Eliot continues to describe death's dream kingdom. Again Eliot employs the image of brokenness. He writes that the eyes
in this kingdom are "sunlight on a broken column" and the voices are
"more distant . . . / Than a fading star." The speaker desires to distance himself from this kingdom as well as wear "deliberate disguises." According to
Grover Smith, Eliot here portrays his civilization as one which cannot even
face this kingdom of death in its dreams, so men take refuge in disguises in
which they "shrink from everything but concealment among other hollow
men" (Smith 104–05). Eliot reemphasizes the civilization's fear of "that final meeting / In the twilight kingdom" in the last verse or Part II.

Part III of "Hollow Men" begins with a relationship between the "dead
land / . . . cactus land" and the people of this land. With this expanding image of emptiness, Eliot seems to make the situation's horror more significant by applying this deadness to the whole civilization rather than to a few
hollow men. In the second verse, Eliot returns to a broken image to describe
the civilization's helplessness. Here we literally see Eliot's concern for the

spirituality of his time. According to some critics, this concern stems from Eliot's own spiritual progress at the time he wrote "The Hollow Men," for he was in between the stages of spiritual desperation and spiritual peace.

The hollow men's actual entrance into death's kingdom, "which has been shunned" throughout the poem, is depicted in Part IV (Williamson 158). In this waiting place, which according to Smith, represents purgatory, the eyes which were direct, then broken, earlier in the poem are no longer present at all. This represents the people's complete despair. Eliot describes the hollow men as they "grope together / and avoid speech." However, Eliot touches on a kind of hope in the next verse for the eyes appear once again. According to Smith, this symbolizes salvation. Again his hope might stem from Eliot's release from his own spiritual desperation for he seems to convey the idea that there is hope for civilization. Yet he ends the verse with the thoughts that perhaps it is "the hope only / Of empty men."

The last part of "Hollow Men" is devoid of hope. Instead it portrays an "eternal going round in the cactus land, enclosed in time and place" (Drew 97). To convey this cycle, Eliot employs the nursery rhyme, "Here we go round the mulberry bush." However, the hollow men "circle the cactus of the desert instead of the mulberry bush in the garden" (Schneider 104). This echo, according to Smith, portrays a civilization in which "there [is] no beginning and middle, only an end (103). And it is in this cycle that Eliot brings in "the shadow" which falls "between the idea / And the reality / Between the motion / And the act." Schneider says that this seems to represent the failure of energy and will (105). "For thine is the kingdom" breaks up the image of the Shadow in each verse in order to portray a failure of completion. Then the avoidance of these failures is excused by the fact that "Life is very long." Thus the Shadow triumphs and "the world ends / Not with a bang but a whimper." This relates back to the epigraph of Guy Fawkes who attempted to blow up parliament but failed thus ending his life with a whimper rather than a bang.

Clearly, Eliot's concern for the state of civilization appears in each part of "Hollow Men." A consistent lack of action, as well as a lack of spirituality, in Eliot's opinion, was causing an emptiness or hollowness to spread throughout the entire society. One could make a similar argument relating to today's society. Those of us who go through life avoiding reality, failing to commit ourselves to action are exactly like Eliot's "hollow men." We are only stuffed dummies, not good or bad, but somewhere in between. Thus we are a part of Eliot's cycle, going around the prickly pear, consumed by the Shadow, incapable of making decisions and acting on those decisions. And, according to Eliot, if we continue to follow this cycle, we too will soon have little hope of salvation on that final meeting, and we will be unable to complete even the Lord's Prayer. Thus perhaps Eliot was not only warning his own civilization of this emptiness, but all future civilizations as well, for we too are in danger of leaving this world "Not with a bang but a whimper."

Works Cited

Bush, Ronald. *T. S. Eliot: A Study in Character and Style.* New York: Oxford University Press, 1983.

Drew, Elizabeth. *T. S. Eliot: The Design of His Poetry.* New York: Charles Scribner's Sons, 1949.

Fleissner, Robert. "T. S. Eliot's 'The Hollow Men'." *The Explicator.* Summer 1984: 42.

Pearce, T. S. *T. S. Eliot.* New York: Arco Publishing, Inc., 1969.

Schneider, Elisabeth. *T. S. Eliot: The Pattern in the Carpet.* Los Angeles: University of California Press, 1975.

Smith, Grover. *T. S. Eliot's Poetry and Plays: A Study in Sources and Meaning.* Chicago: University of Chicago Press, 1956.

Williamson, George. *A Reader's Guide to T. S. Eliot.* New York: H. Wolff Books Manufacturing Co., 1966.

■ THE WRITER'S ASSIGNMENT

Analyze T. S. Eliot's poem "The Hollow Men" with reference to the work's historical and critical contexts and the author's life. Develop your essay from an organizing principle or thesis. ■

■ UNDERSTANDING WRITING STRATEGIES

1. What is this essay's thesis? How is this thesis developed throughout the essay?

2. What kinds of evidence does Peake offer to support the thesis? How have they been incorporated in the body of the paper? Explain whether or not this is effective.

3. Peake makes the distinction between failure of success and failure of will. What is the distinction? How does Peake use this distinction to shape her material?

4. For what audience is Peake writing? What kind of assumptions does she make about their knowledge of the subject?

5. Is there a sufficient overview of the poem for the audience to follow Peake's arguments? On what in the essay do you base your response?

6. How well does this essay provide historical, critical, and biographical contexts for its insights into the poem?

7. How do these contexts increase your understanding of the poem?

8. Compare the first and last paragraphs. Which is the most effective and why? ■

■ SUGGESTIONS FOR WRITING

1. Write an introduction for this essay that engages the reader's interest and makes full commitments about the paper's content. Try to engage your reader's interest in Eliot's importance and his poetry's relevance, and make your reader desire to know more about this poem. Look back to the suggestions for introductions in this book's first part.

2. Write an essay arguing whether or not biographical and historical backgrounds help in our understanding of literature. Refer to one or two specific works and biographical and historical information about them to support your position. ■

Idealism and Materialism

Faun Ryser

> Writing for Introduction to Philosophy, Faun Ryser writes about the basic tenets of philosophical idealism and materialism and which philosophical system she prefers.

As I first considered idealism and materialism, I felt sure I would choose materialism over idealism as a belief system, but as I reflected on both of these theories, I realized that if I must choose one or the other, it would have to be idealism. Since the question I must answer is, "Which position makes most sense to me?" I must admit that idealism makes more sense. To be honest, however, I feel much more comfortable with a position somewhere in between these two extreme ideas since both theories pose their own set of problems.

Perhaps it would be best to briefly look at both theories before comparing their inherent differences and similarities. Because idealism and materialism are simply very radical ways of solving the mind–body problem, I will consider this first. Mind and matter are two essentially different entities. Once we define them as entirely different, how do we get them back together in a causal relationship? Many theories have been proposed such as interactionism, but one of the ways of dealing with this problem is by simply denying the existence of one or the other. This is exactly how idealism and materialism address this issue.

IDEALISM

Idealism is a "metaphysical theory that all things are constituted by mind and its ideas." It is a theory about the ultimate nature of things. It defines mind as the *sole* reality. There are two types of idealists: the objective idealist and the subjective idealist. An objective idealist believes that all things are made of mind and ideas, but that things can also exist independent of our knowing them. The subjective idealist believes that all things are made of mind and ideas but that these things cannot exist unless perceived by someone.

MATERIALISM

Materialism is actually a form of naturalism. Naturalists believe that the only things that exist are those things which can be scientifically investigated. Materialism is the "metaphysical doctrine that matter with its motions and qualities is the ultimate reality." It denies the reality of mind and supernatural and spiritual things. Mechanistic materialism says that all matter is governed by fixed physical laws. This brings up the problem that if man is a machine governed by fixed physical laws, is moral responsibility or creative thinking possible? Therefore the question of causality and determinism becomes a central concern. While not all materialists believe in causal determinism, these two beliefs do usually occur together. Therefore if all things are governed by a set of predetermined physical laws, then the free will of man and the belief in immortality are total absurdity.

One of my basic problems with either theory is: why is a radical solution to the mind–body problem needed at all? To drop half of the problem seems to be a rather inadequate attempt at solving the dilemma. Of course since I am living in 1988 and understand how the physiology of the nervous system and mind work in a harmonious interaction with the body, I cannot quite understand the philosopher's difficulty in rectifying such a situation. Descartes' explanation of interactionism seems to be a fairly logical attempt to explain this away. However, I tend to agree with Gilbert Ryle that this is not a real problem but simply a categorical mistake made by many philosophers when considering the "dualism problem."

Considering all of this, I would have to consider myself an objective idealist. I believe with Locke that what is directly known by the mind are ideas which themselves correspond to things in the external world. To know what something is in the material world, one must recognize those properties and the corresponding ideas that exist in our minds. I, along with Locke, trust my senses to produce ideas and believe there is a real world of experience independent of my mind's perception of it. My ideas are like mental copies of the real thing. As my common sense tells me, ideas are always going on in my mind but other things can exist outside of my mind which I can easily perceive. This idea is reminiscent of Plato's theory of forms. Platonic forms or ideas exist apart from our mind. They exist out there independent of our mind and will; therefore, Plato could be considered an "objective idealist." Aristotle's idea that "No form without matter, and no matter without form" makes a lot of sense to me. In other words, ideas and matter exist simultaneously in the same object. Therefore, I guess I am also a materialist. For the subjective idealist to say that a door only exists in the mind of the perceiver seems ridiculous. Even a blind and deaf person would not be able to walk through a door if he has no perception of it. Thus, primary qualities do exist independent of any observer.

I feel that any theory taken to its extreme can become absurd. My personal belief is that things do exist in the material or physical world because I, along with millions of other people, have experienced them. There are also, I believe, other entities which exist but cannot be measured in the same way as matter. Such things as love, honesty, dishonesty, and knowing do actually exist everywhere, everyday, in everyone but they are mental or intangible nonphysical things. How can I or anyone living in a physical and intellectual world go off the deep end and deny the existence of either physical evidence or nonphysical evidence when we can see, hear, feel, and experience all of these everyday?

■ THE WRITER'S ASSIGNMENT

Does idealism or materialism make more sense and why?   ■

■ UNDERSTANDING WRITING STRATEGIES

1. How does the introduction present the essay's topic and engage the audience? How effective was this in engaging your interest?

2. This analysis largely depends upon the definitions of materialism and idealism. How effectively are the terms defined? What kind of examples does Ryser use to develop her definition?

3. Based on Ryser's definition of idealism and materialism, which would you prefer and why?

4. Why does the author frequently use "I" (the personal voice) here? How does it enhance or detract from the arguments?

5. Ryser frequently uses rhetorical questions. How is this technique useful in persuading a reader to share the author's position? What drawbacks do rhetorical questions have?   ■

■ SUGGESTIONS FOR WRITING

Rewrite this essay directing it to a wider audience and using a formal tone. Before you begin your revision, picture your audience and write a brief profile of its characteristics. List changes you plan on making in the introduction and conclusion, as well as the style, to appeal to that audience.   ■

Myra Henshaw: A Look at Choices

Susan Seehaver

This essay written by Susan Seehaver for an American literature class, examines the choices made by the character Myra Henshaw in Willa Cather's novella, My Mortal Enemy.

Willa Cather's novella, *My Mortal Enemy*, provides a fascinating study of the choices people must make and how these choices affect the rest of their lives.

Myra Henshaw is such a person. Orphaned at an early age, she has grown up in the care of an over-indulgent uncle whose self-made money has provided Myra with all the glitter of material wealth. In addition, her uncle has purchased the respect of the town of Parthia and of the local Catholic church. Like many nouveau rich, John Driscoll has contempt for people without money. At one point he warns Myra of his plan to disinherit her saying, "I've tried both ways and I know. A poor man stinks and God hates him" (p. 915).

What a shock it must have been for him to learn that his wonderful niece was in love with the son of an Ulster Protestant. It's bad enough that Myra has fallen in love with someone outside the Catholic church, but this Oswald person is the son of a man Driscoll has had a falling out with sometime in the past and the resentment on Driscoll's part is still very real. John Driscoll's stubbornness forces Myra into an extremely difficult situation.

At this point Myra is faced with a choice which will shape the rest of her life. On one hand she loves the wealth and splendor of being the most fashionable family in Parthia. On the other hand she is in love with Oswald Henshaw and nothing, not even the threat of being disinherited, is going to stop her from marrying the man she loves. John Driscoll's stubbornness is certainly matched by Myra's.

Myra makes her decision and leaves her home with only the clothes she wears. She walks out without looking back. More importantly, she leaves without looking into herself. At this point in Myra's life she does not indulge in introspection. Had Myra been able to take an honest look at herself and her values, her choice may have been a very different one. However that is not to be.

The choice Myra makes is a noble one in theory. She believes she can walk away from John Driscoll's money, into the arms of Oswald Henshaw, be married and live happily ever after. However Myra is a romantic only as far as philosophy and theory are concerned. In the cold light of reality she is a practical person with worldly tastes, who values the things money can buy.

The story continues several years later. Myra's choice has changed both her lifestyle and her outlook on life. She has begun to realize that her life is not what it might have been if she had heeded her uncle's warnings.

The Henshaws live in a small but lovely second story apartment in an old brownstone on the north side of Madison Square. While this is not exactly like living in poverty, it is a far cry from the house that she grew up in. Her status is clearly lower than what she had become accustomed to as a young lady. At this point Myra sees no connection between her present circumstances and her choice of Oswald in preference to her uncle's offerings of wealth and status. She attributes her place in life "to the kind of bad luck which befalls women who fall in love" (p. 920).

Oswald Henshaw has matured from the love struck young man who returned to Parthia to claim Myra as his bride. He is now a kind, considerate, and somewhat boring businessman and husband, perhaps boring only by comparison to Myra's exciting friends from the artistic worlds of theatre, literature, and art. Myra's obvious preference for these friends is apparent as she dashes off to meet Lydia's train in the company of a handsome young man from the Chicago stage, leaving Oswald at home sipping a whiskey and soda (p. 920).

Myra's outlook on life is beginning to change. She has become a suspicious, jealous, and two-faced woman. She can be friendly, even charming with her toney friends, and sees nothing wrong with spending time with young unmarried men. However when it comes to Oswald and his business associates, she presents quite a different side of herself. Her jealousy and suspicion of Oswald surface for almost no reason at all. The reader cannot imagine Myra affording Oswald the liberty of single female companions in spite of that fact that she has her male friends. She becomes angry and upset over little things such as an unidentified key on Oswald's chain or the gift of sleeve buttons from a young acquaintance.

As for Oswald's business associates, they bring out the worst in Myra. When she must be around them she is challenging and difficult. Even though they seem to respect or even fear her, she is irritated by them. They are rich and powerful and seem to remind Myra of what she has given up. Or perhaps being with them irritates her because she senses that Oswald hates the kind of work he does and "went into an office only because we were young and terribly in love" (p. 924). Whatever the reason, the result is obvious. Myra feels no connection between her place in life and the choices she has made. Her circumstances are the result of the people around her, never her own responsibility.

Part II of the story rejoins the Henshaws and Nellie Birdeye ten years later. Nellie finds the Henshaws living in a rundown apartment-hotel. They have all moved down life's ladder of success since the last time they were together. Myra is dying of cancer. Oswald has taken a humble position in a city office. He is poorly paid and must not only work to provide for their basic needs, but also serve as Myra's nurse. There is certainly no money to hire a nurse for Myra's care.

Myra has continued to grow bitter and hostile. However her physical appearance reflects a dual nature which causes Nellie to remark that Myra "looked strong and broken, generous and tyrannical, a witty and rather wicked old woman who hated life for its defeats, and loved it for its absurdities" (p. 933). While the circumstances of Myra's life may have changed drastically, so has she. She has grown or more correctly she is growing. On the surface her bitterness and anger seem to be the main change in her, but on a deeper level the change is profound. Myra has begun to examine her life in terms of the choices she made for herself. Frequently she slips into the old style of blaming others or looking at fate or luck to explain her present circumstances. Each time she comes back to an attitude of introspection which she lacked at younger ages.

Perhaps it seems too late for this to be of any value for Myra but she needs to find the value in it and she does. As Myra lies dying, she speaks into the darkness, "Why must I die like this, alone with my mortal enemy?" One may wonder who Myra is referring to as her mortal enemy. On the surface it seems to be Oswald, however on a deeper level Myra is speaking of herself. She finally seems to recognize that she has been her own worst enemy. She is facing the reality that her life is a result of the choices she has made and that no one else, not even fate is responsible for her misery. Yet in addition to confronting this awful truth Myra, in her final hours, finds a way of reconciliation.

When Myra hires a cabman to take her out to the cliffs of Glouchester to spend her final hours, she finally finds the forgiveness of her sins which she has been seeking. Just a few weeks before her death Myra visited this place with Nellie and commented that "the great sinners always came home to die in some religious house, and the abbot or the abbess went out and received them with a kiss" (p. 936).

When her time to die has come Myra returns to the cedar trees by the sea and allows the first cold bright streak of dawn to kiss her and give her absolution (p. 936).

Her life is finished. The end is similar in some respects to the way she lived. She has made a choice about her death and she stubbornly takes care of the logistical details. In one respect her death is very different from her life. Through her suffering, and the growth it allowed her to experience, she has gained insight. That insight allows her to put her bitterness behind her and die in peace. The very peace that eluded her in life was hers in death.

■ THE WRITER'S ASSIGNMENT

Write an essay about a literary work that argues for a thesis, your "angle." The body of the essay should offer ample detail, evidence, and commentary to persuade your reader that your thesis's assumptions are valid. Write for an audience that includes more people than your teacher. Don't adopt a stuffy style. Use a voice that is natural to you, but don't use slang. Provide enough information so that someone who is not familiar with the literature you discuss can appreciate your essay's purpose. ■

■ UNDERSTANDING WRITING STRATEGIES

1. What is the essay's thesis? How well is it explained or developed? Where do you find this?

2. What overview does Seehaver give to Cather's work? How well does this enable some one "not familiar with the literature" to appreciate her essay's purpose?

3. How does an overview differ from a plot summary?

4. How does Seehaver demonstrate her thesis? How does she use support from Cather's text?

5. Where does Seehaver develop her arguments?

6. Seehaver argues that Myra undergoes a significant change in her perspective about herself and the choices she has made. Is the reader simply told that these changes have taken place or has Seehaver shown the reader the changes? What is the difference between showing and telling?

7. For what audience is this written? What suggests this?

8. How well does Seehaver meet the assignment guidelines? How would you revise this essay to better conform to these? ■

Shakespeare's Drag Queens
Kathy Silvey

In Shakespeare's theatre young boys played women's roles. Many of Shakespeare's comic heroines disguise themselves as boys to create the delightful ironies this paper studies when boys playing girls play boys. Writing for a Shakespeare class, Kathy Silvey draws on recent critical studies for background to analyze Shakespeare's comic women characters.

> The tragic personality is dominated by . . . a fatal predisposition to one mode of behavior while comic heroes are versatile, dynamic, and resourceful. They demonstrate a vast repertoire of behavioral modes, varying from formal to informal, rational to emotional, masculine to feminine. . . . While the majority of Shakespeare's tragic heroes are men, his comic heroes are women, whose intelligence, wit, and versatility transcend conventional gender stereotypes and provide new models of adulthood.[1]

Shakespeare probably had several reasons for dressing some of the female heroes of his comedies as men. The fact that only men were allowed to act on the Elizabethan stage definitely had some bearing on this idea. He obviously enjoyed giving his audience the spectacle of a man playing a woman playing a man, who might at some point in the play opt to play a woman. Yet beyond this obvious delight in sexual crosses and, one might say, double crosses, Shakespeare, by dressing his comic heroines in men's clothes, mirrored a trend of his time, foiled the defined sexual roles of the courtly literary tradition, challenged accepted sexual and marital roles in general—not to mention an entire patriarchical social structure—and extended the Renaissance value of the balanced psyche to include the androgynous balance of masculinity and femininity. Most importantly, in the characters of Julia, Viola, Rosalind, and Portia, he introduced models of strong, independent women, whatever they happened to be wearing, to his world and ours.

Androgyny wasn't anything new to the Elizabethans. From about 1580 onward, a rather significant transvestite movement began around London. As F. G. Emmison points out, "A sexual sidelight rarely noticed by other writers bears on the wearing of men's clothes by females of lewd or lively disposition."[2] There was never any serious protest against women wearing men's clothes until the trend reversed itself and men began to wear skirts. It was then the Puritans under King James began to oppose the entire movement.

> Since the daies of Adam women were never so Masculine; Masculine in their genders and generations, from the Mother, to the youngest daughter; Masculine in Number, from one to multitudes; Masculine in Case, even

from head to the foot; Masculine in Moode, from bold speech, to impudent action; and Masculine in Tense: for (without redress) they were, are, and will be still most Masculine, most mankinde, and most monstrous.[3]

And this was exactly how androgyny was perceived, as "monstrous." Like centaurs or satyrs, women in men's clothing were "monsters," half one thing and half another, in heretical rebellion against the entire Great Chain of Being. Shakespeare himself uses the monster image when one of his comic heroines begins to regret her disguise. When Viola discovers Olivia has fallen in love with her as Cesario she says,

> How will this fadge? My master loves her dearly, And I (poor monster) fond as much on him
> (*Twelfth Night*, II.ii,33–35).

But despite the common Puritan perception of this lifestyle, historical evidence suggests that "the male disguises of Shakespeare's plays, Beatrice's wish to be a man, or Rosalind's shrewish lines to Orlando probably accord . . . well with women's behavior in Shakespeare's own time."[4] This should come as no surprise, since England in the sixteenth century had a better androgynous female role model than just about any society before or since in Queen Elizabeth. The very existence of a strong, independent female monarch, especially one who was worshipped as Elizabeth was, would have naturally encouraged other women to assert their own independence.

And Elizabeth was not only such a ruler, she also maintained control of her own destiny in ways which most women of the time could only dream of. There were, after all, but few areas of an Elizabethan woman's personal life that she had much say in. Probably the most vitally important of these was courtship. Elizabeth used her spinsterhood and the fact that she had many poweful suitors to great political advantage, and while the average Elizabethan woman naturally would not have gained any political power through courtship, she generally wielded more power in her relationship with her suitors than with any other man in her life.

One reason for this was that, in Shakespeare's day, it could be very important for a young man to make a profitable match. If he needed money, or was in a socially undesirable position, a rich or socially superior woman could be his ticket to prosperity and social standing. Shakespeare realized this, and also realized how much of the power that would generally be reserved for the man situations such as these gave the woman who was being courted. It is no surprise, then, that his more independent comic heroines are courted by men who are either financially or socially inferior to them. Portia, in *The Merchant of Venice*, wields this type of control. Eric W. Stockton believes "A woman can be powerful in *Merchant* because of the importance of wealth in the play. In Venice wealth transcends or threatens social boundaries, and Portia is wealthy,"[5] and Bassanio is in debt. Orlando, in *As You Like It*, is the younger son of the duke, and as such he courts two people to advance his social state; he is Duke Senior's courtier and Rosalind's suitor. According to Stockton,

> As You Like It, The Merchant of Venice, and Twelfth Night present the courtship and marriage of a socially superior woman and a relatively impecunious man, a fantasy which would have been deeply appealing to Shakespeare's own generation.[6]

But a woman did not have to be wealthy or of a high social rank to be in control of a courtship. The language of the courtly love tradition gave and attributed to women a great deal of power over men, especially in the metaphors which describe the beloved as a landlord, a conquering foe, a patron, or, most often of all, a ruler of the lover's heart.[7] In Shakespeare's day, the literal holders of these powerful positions were usually male, but the roles were reversed in the courtship. Although Shakespeare used the courtly love tradition in his comedies, his more androgynous characters never took part in it. He pokes fun at both the cold, distant women and the melodramatic, languishing men of the tradition. Rosalind puts down Phoebe for accepting the abusive "ice-goddess" role, and her own relationship with Orlando stands in marked contrast with Phoebe and Silvius's extremes. In *Twelfth Night*, Viola chides both Olivia and Orsino for succumbing to the courtly ideals. In both cases the result is the same. Phoebe and Olivia fall madly in love with Rosalind and Viola, recognizing something admirable in the women's straightforwardness that they don't see in the men, who are too caught up in convention to reveal their honest selves.

But whatever advantages women had during courtship they traditionally lost at the altar. The reins of power over a typical woman's life would often simply be passed from the father to the husband. Of course, this kind of translation of power has no place in the life of an independent woman like Rosalind or Viola, but Shakespeare had to find some way to deal with the transition of devotion from father to husband if not that of authority. Linda Bamber sees this transition as key to an understanding of the comic heroine as compared to her tragic counterpart. She believes that tragic women, when they leave their fathers and cleave to their husbands, are forced to make choices that eventually undo them. When Cordelia says, "Surely I shall never marry like my sisters, To love my father all" (*King Lear*, I.i.102–03) she is choosing—and her choice is both correct in its logic and tragic in its outcome. Paradoxically, the moment Desdemona abandons her father for Othello, she loses her husband's trust. She has betrayed the man who up to that point had been paramount in her life. Othello has no way of knowing she won't do it again, and is thereby prepared to believe she will be unfaithful to him. Shakespeare's comic heroines are spared that choice.[8] Portia's and Viola's fathers are both conveniently dead, Rosalind has been separated from her father by banishment, and although Julia's father is mentioned in the present tense twice, she never comes in contact with him. Each one is able to avoid the choice between father and husband because Shakespeare has seen to it that there is no father for his androgynous heroine to choose for or against. Portia is even able to follow her heart and her father's will simultaneously, and although Rosalind gives herself in marriage (twice, once as Ganymede and once as herself), her father obediently gives his blessing at her prompting. Diane Elizabeth Dreher notes, "Interestingly enough, Shakespeare's fatherless daughters are the most androgynous. Free from the dilemma of domination or defiance, they are able to express themselves in other, more creative directions."[9] Even between fatherless tragic heroes and these comic heroines the contrast is striking.

> Shakespeare's plays . . . demonstrate the effect of the missing parent upon the children. Unlike Hamlet or Coriolanus, Shakespeare's daughters are not traumatized by the loss of their fathers. Rosalind, Viola, and Portia incorporate their father's talents, strength, and character into their own personalities.[10]

So to create truly independent, androgynous female characters, Shakespeare had to deal not only with the woman herself, but with her relationships to her father and her husband. She had to be separated from her father in some way before she could realistically travel about dressed as a man, and her dependence on her father had to be broken before she could take important steps on her own, like arranging her own marriage and giving herself to the man she chose. She would also have to tame her own future husband. This was no easy task, since he would probably not be as balanced a person as she. He might be hopelessly melancholy, or lecherous, or apt to value male friendships over love, or unrealistic about the nature of women. Whatever the case, these women not only had their own individual strength to utilize, they also had the element of disguise on their side.

Viola's challenge is to take a man who is absorbed in his melancholy despair over unrequited love and make him see the beauty that is right under his nose. Duke Orsino "exhibits the most extreme case of courtly excess"[11] in the middle comedies. Since she can approach him as a man, she is able to gain his friendship and respect without the conventions which have helped to limit his relationship with Olivia. She also must convince him that not all women are as cool as the Countess. "Viola teaches him, man to man, about how men make brave vows they seldom keep and how women 'are as true of heart as we' (II.ii.106)."[12] Her lesson has validity because she is a woman, and it is taken seriously because the Duke believes she is a man.

Rosalind has a few things to teach Orlando about women which are best said in disguise as well. Orlando's misconception is the exact opposite of Orsino's. While the Duke doesn't trust women enough, Orlando gives Rosalind too much credit. As Ganymede, Rosalind is able to be realistically objective about herself.

> She warns Orlando of his Rosalind's potential for shrewishness or fickleness to let him know she will not always meet his expectations. Reserving the right to remain herself, she rejects the traditional feminine stereotype . . . affirming a new kind of partnership.[13]

As Ganymede, Rosalind is able to be Orlando's friend, confident, and equal, roles that women of her day would not generally have a chance to play with men. This is an extremely important part of the role playing all these women do as men because it gives them a chance to be seen as people first and as women second.

But one of these women establishes herself as an independent person and an equal before ever deciding to dress as a man. When Bassanio firsts decides to court Portia, he is a fortune hunter. But when he meets her, he learns to accept her as an equal as she gains his love and respect.

> Portia's concept of marriage is partnership . . . She gives herself, not to be dominated by Bassanio, but to share with him . . . Portia is assertive and androgynous during the entire courtship and marriage . . . She has consistently played the male role: in managing her household, arranging her marriage, and later, in administering justice.[14]

And it is through this Portia, the young lawyer who administers justice, that we see the extent not only of Portia's equality compared to the men, but of her superiority. Normally, the woman would be expected to be ruled by her emotions and the man would be expected to act according to his superior male reason, but here again, the roles are reversed. "With the wisdom of androgyny, Portia enters the courtroom in dignity even as the men around her are reduced to passionate extremes of fear, grief, or sadistic vengeance.[15] Portia also competes against men both as a man and as Bassanio's wife. She is not Julia, who is dealing with a sexually promiscuous husband, or Viola, who hopes to transfer Orsino's emotions from Olivia to herself. "As the young doctor, Portia takes a place among the male rivalries and accents her competition with Antonio for Bassanio's loyalty,"[16] finally winning it with the ring trick. In this sense, if no other, she is probably the most androgynous of Shakespeare's drag queens.

It is also important to realize that, although all these comic heroines are in love and must be dealt with in terms of the men they will marry, none of them are presented as half of a person. They demand treatment as ends in themselves.

> In Shakespeare's comedies, and only in the comedies, we see the feminine Other face to face. In the tragedies we respond to the women . . . on the basis of our interest in the hero . . . In the romances the loss and recovery of the feminine is experienced through our sympathy with the male Self who has lost and found his feminine Other . . . But our response to the comic heroine is direct and unmediated by her father, lover, or husband.[17]

The fact that they are dressed as men adds a great deal to this reaction, and the audience isn't exempt from viewing them differently from other women when these heroines adopt men's attire either. Even in the comedies,

> Assertive female behavior becomes more acceptable in doublet and hose. Audiences enjoy Rosalind and Viola's saucy wit but often perceive the as-

sertiveness of Beatrice and Katharina as hostile and aggressive. Paradoxically, for women to express themselves fully, they must do so in disguise.[18]

But just as these disguises aren't merely for the men's benefit, they aren't merely for the benefit of the audience either. The women themselves learn, grow, and mature in their disguises. They allow them "greater expression and development. Once liberated from her long skirts, boned stays, and farthingales, the comic heroine can move about freely in the Forest of Arden or the law courts of Venice, manifesting greater physical and psychological freedom."[19]

And this kind of psychological freedom is healthy. When Lady Macbeth denies her sexuality, it is a sign of a tragic character imbalance. But in the comedies, sexual ambiguity can lead to a better balanced persona. The comic heroines are still completely women when they are in disguise, but they become stronger women. All of them still cry, and Julia and Rosalind still faint, but in general they become more complete people through their experiences.

Viola's balanced personality, in particular, is conspicuous by its absence in the other main characters and in its contagiousness. Olivia and Orlando,

> are arrested in extremes: she in defensive defiance, he in masochistic emotionalism . . . she has become cold and rational, he has succumbed to passive emotionalism. Viola, however, unsettles them both, tempering Orsino's emotional excess with witty companionship, and invoking from the cold Olivia a heated rush of passion.[20]

Unfortunately, this result of her men's weeds causes her to regret having worn them. "Unlike Rosalind who grows more vigorous as she likes her disguise, Viola feels that she and Olivia are victims of hers."[21] When she finally reveals herself for what she is, she frees both Olivia and herself. She also elicits a balanced response from the Duke, who expresses the respect he has gained for her by knowing her as a man in the same breath that he expresses his wish to see her dressed as a woman. Her masculinity impresses him, and now her femininity fascinates him as well.

Rosalind's disguise seems to have a more transforming effect than any of the other women's. Viola remains constantly feminine and Portia has a masculine strength about her from the outset. But at the beginning of *As You Like It*, Rosalind "is fearful and depends on Celia to suggest a refuge in Arden; only then she decides to disguise herself as a man and the disguise helps her control her fears."[22] Just as Orlando and the audience react differently to Ganymede than they would to Rosalind, she begins to act differently as she becomes accustomed to her role.

> The role of Ganymede . . . helps Rosalind develop greater strength of character. When she enters the forest . . . she comforts Celia, her doublet and hose summoning courage and resolution. . . . As psychological studies have shown, playing a role actually develops similar tendencies within the individual.[23]

She uses her disguise to achieve the same kind of balance that Viola strikes between her emotions and her reason. "Rosalind is both realistic and romantic. She controls her romantic excess beneath the mask of Ganymede, giving reign to her emotions with Celia."[24] And this balance, like Viola's, shines all the brighter in light of the extreme natures of the people she encounters. "Her friendship with Celia saves her from the isolation and excessive subjectivity of Jaques; her romantic idealism is in contrast to both Touchstone's earthiness and Silvius's Petrarchan excess."[25] This psychological balance is the balance of androgyny, which she develops through her disguise. "She is a creative balance of masculine and feminine that anticipates Jung's concept of individuation."[26]

Shakespeare created strong, androgynous, balanced female characters in Viola and Rosalind, but when he created Portia, he created a feminist.

> While other women in Shakespeare adopt men's attire to protect themselves or follow their lovers, Portia . . . leaves the domestic realm . . . to enter the law courts of Venice, the world of men . . . Portia's brilliant success represents a direct accusation of the traditional social order. . . . Strong, precise, and intellectually creative, Portia can see more justice in the law than any man in Venice.[27]

So besides the dramatic and literary effect of having these women dress as men, Shakespeare makes important social and psychological statements. His women may have a dramatic convention in common, but they remain individuals throughout. Julia, at first but a child, the comic equivalent of Juliet, gains maturity from her experience as a man. Viola, the determined survivor of a shipwreck, takes on the image of her brother and activates the masculine side of her nature. Rosalind, banished from home and scared to tears, learns to take control of her emotions and of her life. Portia, angered at first by her necessary contraction to her father's will, comes to see the wisdom of his judgment and to utilize it in her own judgment at Antonio's trial. Competing directly against the men both in the trial and in her relationship with her husband, she proves herself to be the wisest man in Venice.

Shakespeare's hand in the creation of these characters is not merely that of a technically consummate author, it is also that of a supremely sensitive man and a feminist. He seems to realize, more than most of his contemporaries, that though the sexes each have their strengths and weaknesses females are as capable of strength, independence, deep feeling, and keen reason as males. No other conclusion can be drawn from the wisdom and power of Shakespeare's drag queens.

Footnotes

1. Diane Elizabeth Dreher, *Domination and Defiance* (Lexington: The University Press of Kentucky, 1986), 115.

2. F. G. Emisson, *Elizabethan Life: Morals and the Church Courts* (Chelmsford: Essex County Council, 1970), 18.
3. Hic Mulier, *On The Man-Woman: Being a Medicine to Cure the Coltish Disease of the Staggers in the Masculine-Feminines of our Times* (London: G. Purslowe for J. Trundle, 1620), SigA3.
4. Marilyn L. Williamson, *The Patriarchy of Shakespeare's Comedies* (Detroit: Wayne Street University Press, 1986), 41.
5. Ibid, 30.
6. Ibid, 25
7. Ibid, 28.
8. Linda Bamber, *Comic Women, Tragic Men* (Stanford: Stanford University Press, 1982), 110–15.
9. Dreher, 116.
10. Ibid, 117.
11. Williamson, 35.
12. Ibid.
13. Dreher, 121.
14. Ibid, 132.
15. Ibid, 134.
16. Williamson, 50.
17. Bamber, 109.
18. Dreher, 117.
19. Ibid.
20. Ibid, 125.
21. Williamson, 31.
22. Ibid, 30.
23. Dreher, 121.
24. Ibid, 122.
25. Ibid.
26. Ibid, 123
27. Ibid, 133–34.

■ THE WRITER'S ASSIGNMENT

Your paper should focus on some aspect of Shakespeare's drama and give insight into his work from an external perspective (philosophical, historical, or critical). This paper should use recent criticism for framing and substantiating *your own* arguments about the play(s).   ■

■ UNDERSTANDING WRITING STRATEGIES

1. How did the title affect you? Is the title appropriate for the paper? Why or why not?

2. What is the essay's central focus? Where is this indicated?

3. How does Silvey order the essay?

4. What was the Elizabethan attitude toward androgyny? Why is this attitude prevalent in Shakespeare's plays?

5. What distinction does Silvey make between Shakespeare's tragic heroines and comic heroines?

6. How do the differences between tragic and comic heroines reflect on women's role in Elizabethan society?

7. For what audience is this paper written? What has Silvey assumed about her audience? Where do you see this?

8. What kinds of changes would you make if the audience were a class of freshman students? ∎

Jim Self's "Lookout": Heed His Warning!

Jessica Sollee

Writing for a dance history class, Jessica Sollee's solid description recreates a dance performance in this review of Jim Self's postmodern dance concert.

Jim Self's latest work "Lookout" was performed at the Dance Theater Workshop's Bessie Schönberg Theater on February 18, 19, 20, and 22. Jim Self, a former member of the Merce Cunningham Company, performed the self-choreographed dance in solo. "Lookout" is made up of five sections entitled "Les Egouts de Paris," "Goose on a Sidewalk," "The Vision of Guy," "A Shoebox Edge," and "A Mean Cat and a High Line." The dance is at first quite intriguing and unusual but loses its interesting quality by unnecessary repetition and fragmented movement themes. Self saves his dance from total failure by his exceptional performance abilities as a dancer. He maintains a constant level of deep concentration and executes difficult moves with agility and ease. Overall, however, Self's work is unsuccessful because he does not communicate his ideas clearly enough to the audience. Much of the dance seems to be a bizarre display of idiosyncratic movements which lack continuity, fluidity, and meaning.

In the first section of the dance, Self is dressed in black and wears a pair of large fisherman rubber boots which squeak with each step he takes. In silence Self maintains a slow sustained quality in his movements that are occasionally interspersed by sudden sharp gestures with his arms and head. At times, Self creates strange animalistic sounds with his voice. He repeats the same series of movements horizontally as well as to the diagonals of the stage. This section drags on for a lengthy period of time and the repetition is useless and destructive to the dance.

In the second section the use of props, jazz music by Bruce Lieberman, and story written by Richard Elovich and read aloud all add rich flavors to the dance. The props used were four large triangular shapes filled with either oranges, bread, water, or sand. The story was the major focus in this scene. The story is written in monologue form and is narrated by two off-stage male voices. The main character is a man who is involved in an affair with a married woman named Lucy. Just as the story becomes interesting it takes on a fragmented repetitive style similar to that of Self's movement pattern in the first section. The tale is read in an undramatic child-like manner that simplifies a complicated human experience. Like the dance, it completely lacks emotion and has no ending. At the climax of the dance a phrase from the story is repeated and accompanied by music. Self adapts a movement theme to fit the present rhythmic phrase. Although the unified rhythmic phrases work well together, they are repeated several times and, like much of the dance, lose their initial dynamic quality.

The only key to understanding this dance can be found in this one-sentence description presented in the program: "A man watching television tries to sort out the mistaken identities of two intruders." Self in no way helps the audience to comprehend his ideas. In fact he makes the task quite difficult. By combining this one-sentence description with the dance one can be led to believe that Self is making a statement about the ill effects of television. The dance seems to show how television portrays the complicated situation of human life as entertaining and simplistic. Which, in turn, transforms the audience into emotionless, passive recipients of life.

Whether Self is working purely on the intellectual level or is trying to fit into the "dance nouveau" (experimental dance), he falls short of his attempt. For while he vigorously strives to satisfy his personal goals as a choreographer, he loses sight of his audience, often leaving them dangling in confusion.

■ UNDERSTANDING WRITING STRATEGIES

1. What kinds of commitments does the introduction make about the subject? How does it indicate that the essay is a review?

2. With what criteria does Sollee evaluate the performance?

3. What are the criticisms? How do these criticisms relate to the criteria?

4. Are the criticisms specific or general? In what way?

5. In what ways does the review help the reader "experience" the performance?

6. Where do you see evidence of either objectivity or bias?

7. How does this review differ from the often heard evaluation, "I don't know art, but I know what I like"?

8. What should a review accomplish? How well do you feel this review meets your own criteria? ∎

∎ SUGGESTIONS FOR WRITING

Meet the challenge of writing about movement by observing an athlete or a dancer and writing notes recording both large general movements and specific details. First write an objective description of the movement you have observed. Pay attention to action verbs, and concrete and specific language. Rewrite the paragraph, this time adding your own evaluation to the description. ∎

The Order of the Proofs for the Existence of God in Descartes' Meditations

Cynthia Stuffman

> Written for a course surverying modern philosophy, this paper reflects a "term" paper in the fullest sense of the word. Stuffman worked with Daren Di Nicola throughout the course refining their understanding of Desartes' *Meditations*. The work began with a class discussion that led to tutorials in the professor's office and a shorter initial study. They then expanded their own interpretations of Descartes by reading other philosophers and interpreters. Although they worked through the ideas together, their papers reflect independent work. Daren's paper entitled "Clear and Distinct Ideas in Descartes' *Meditation*" also appears in this section of the anthology.

The question of the relative merits of the three proofs for the existence of God in Descartes' *Meditations* is an issue of no small controversy, from Descartes' own time to the present. The question of the order of these proofs has, as well, given rise to many articles and sections of critical works on the *Meditations*. It is to this issue of the positions of the proofs that my research has been directed; however, the value of the proofs has also been considered insofar as it has contributed to an understanding of the main question.

Preparatory to dealing with possible positions for the ontological proof,

I feel it would be helpful to examine several things: its actual position in Meditation V, and in what way certain aspects of the preceding Meditations may or may not determine that position; its alternate position in the Geometrical Exposition in the *Second Set of Replies*, and why this may or may not be significant; and, additional material from the *Meditations* and the *Replies* that may be pertinent to this question.

At the conclusion of Meditation II, Descartes' only certainties are the existence of himself and his ideas. Descartes' way out of this solipsistic condition is to establish in Meditation III that, among his ideas, there is one that could not exist unless there also existed a being other than himself. This idea is the idea of God as an infinitely perfect being and Descartes argues that this idea can only have been caused by such a being. His argument rests on a principle which he takes to be self-evident: "Now it is manifest from the natural light that there must be at least as much reality in the efficient and total cause as in the effect of that cause." (AT.VII,40) Descartes then applies this principle to his ideas in asserting that every idea in the mind must have a cause with at least as much formal reality as there is objective reality in the idea. While Descartes acknowledges that he cannot, in general, validly infer from the objective reality of an idea to the formal reality of that of which it is an idea, the idea of God is fundamentally different. Descartes, himself, possesses sufficient formal reality to be the source of his other ideas; his formal reality as a finite and imperfect being is, however, insufficient as the source of his idea of an infinitely perfect being. He concludes that only God could be an adequate cause of his idea of God, and that, therefore, God exists.

There are several consequences of this first proof for the existence of God. In addition to giving Descartes some manner of escape from solipsism, the existence of a perfect being is used to free him from the possibility of a deceiving demon, in that the notion of perfection must necessarily be incompatible with a desire to deceive. Thus, at the conclusion of Meditation III, the existence of a veracious God allows Descartes to assert, at least in general, the credibility of his clear and distinct perceptions. If this is the case, however, then the question arises of how he can account for error.

This, then, is the crux of Meditation IV: how to explain human error in such a way that it does not call into question either the nature of God or the truth of clear and distinct ideas. Descartes described the nature of judgments, erroneous or otherwise, as dependent upon two things: ". . . namely on the faculty of knowledge which is in me, and on the faculty of choice or freedom of the will . . ." (AT.VII, 56) It is not these faculties, as given by God, which lead to error, but rather the manner in which they are used by man: ". . . the scope of the will is wider than the intellect; but instead of restricting it within the same limits, I extend its use to matters which I do not understand." (AT.VII,58) Descartes' errors, then, follow not from God, but from himself; and these errors can be avoided by suspending judgment in the absence of clear and distinct perceptions.

It would seem that, on the basis of divine veracity shown in Meditation III and the manner of avoiding error shown in Meditation IV, Descartes might proceed directly to the establishment of an external reality. However, in Meditation V he returns to the idea of mathematical truths or essences. The truth of such ideas is shown to be independent of any material reality; in fact, the dependence seems to work in the other direction. Descartes uses the example of the property of a triangle such that the sum of its angles is equal to the sum of two right angles. That this essential truth is unaffected by the possible nonexistence of triangles is fairly obvious; what is equally true, but perhaps a little less obvious, is that were any triangle to exist, it must conform to this essential truth. Thus, existence is shown here to depend on essence; and, for Descartes, it seems to follow that the truth of our clear and distinct ideas is tied to our knowledge of essences. This is the springboard to the consideration of God's essence and the ontological proof. Where the essence of a finite thing has been shown to involve only possible existence, the essence of God, as infinite and perfect, involves necessary existence. Crucial to this argument are the assumptions that existence is a property which can be predicated and that non-existence is an imperfection.

Towards the end of Meditation V, Descartes seems to anticipate some of the later objections, both to the merits and the position of his ontological proof:

> . . . as regards God, if I were not overwhelmed by preconceived opinions, and if the images of things perceived by the senses did not besiege my thought on every side, I would certainly acknowledge him sooner and more easily than anything else. For what is more self-evident than the fact that the supreme being exists, or that God, to whose essence alone existence belongs, exists? (AT.VII, 69)

What Descartes implies in response to anticipated objections is consistent with, and in a sense serves as a prelude to, his discussion prior to the geometrical presentation of his arguments in the *Second Set of Replies*. In the above excerpt from Meditation V, he implies that the order of the proofs in the *Meditations* is following the order of discovery, of moving methodically from what is easily established to that which is more difficult. This intention is also clearly stated in the third rule of the *Discourse on Method* (AT.VI,18). In the *Second Set of Replies*, he contrasts this method of demonstration with that of the Geometrical Exposition; and, in so doing, he sets out to explain why the positions of the causal and ontological proofs are reversed.

Descartes states that the method of demonstration in the *Meditations* follows the analytic order, ". . . the true way by means of which the thing in question was discovered methodically." (AT.VII, 155) The synthetic order of the Geometrical Exposition, by contrast, begins with what is discovered last in the analytic order; the propositions are shown as following from the definitions, axioms, and postulates which precede them in the exposition.

Descartes is rather emphatic about his choice of the analytic order for the *Meditations*, and his reasons are clearly stated: the analytic method is more instructive and satisfying to the reader; and, because of this, it is both more appropriate and more effective for a metaphysical inquiry.

However, Descartes also discusses a factor common to both methods, and that is the order of reasons; that is, the arguments demonstrated first must be logically independent of those that follow, while the later arguments must be demonstrated as logically dependent upon those that precede them. He goes onto state that, "I did try to follow this order very carefully in my *Meditations*." (AT.VII,155)

There are additional references to the proofs for the existence of God in the *First Set of Replies*. In responding to objections against the ontological argument, Descartes states that,

> . . . it is the kind of argument which may easily be regarded as a sophism by those who do not keep in mind all the elements which make up the proof. For this reason I did have considerable doubts to begin with about whether I should use it . . . But there are only two ways of proving the existence of God . . . and since I expounded the first method to the best of my ability in the Third Meditation, I thought that I should include the second method later on. (AT.VII, 120)

In the *Fourth Set of Replies*, while discussing the importance of the notion of cause in demonstrating God's existence, Descartes states that it is ". . . the primary and principal, if not the only way, that we have of proving the existence of God." (AT.VII, 238)

There appear to be quite a few confusing aspects in these, as well as other, sections from the *Replies*. This becomes even more apparent in how they are used by various critical authors to support not only differing, but directly opposing, views on the proofs for the existence of God. From a number of cogent opinions on this subject, I have (reluctantly) restricted myself to presenting and commenting on several which I found to be most pertinent to the question of the order of the proofs.

The first of these is from Jonathan Rée, who takes the position that the ontological argument is ". . . simply a restatement, or an explanation, of the causal argument."[1] The main textual support for this viewpoint seems to be the section, quoted above, from the *Fourth Set of Replies*. His interpretation of this passage is that Descartes is asserting that there is, in fact, only one proof for the existence of God. If one were to agree with Rée, then the position of the ontological proof in Meditation V would appear to be quite arbitrary. However, Rée's position can be contested in several ways. His interpretation of Descartes' remarks in the *Fourth Set of Replies* is extremely narrow, and can hardly be reconciled with statements in the *First & Second Set of Replies*, quoted above. It seems that Rée has simply overlooked or dismissed any evidence that might conflict with his view. Since the main point that Rée wishes to pursue appears to be that Descartes' arguments are not religious at all, but rather ". . . an elucidation of his theory of ideas . . .",[2] his equation of the two proofs may have been a hasty assumption that merely served to allow him to get on with what he saw as a more interesting question.

The same quotation from the *Fourth Set of Replies* cited by Rée to support his early conclusions seems to have been used somewhat more objectively by Norman Kemp Smith.[3] While both authors hold the opinion that that relationship of the ontological to the causal proof is one of dependence, Smith's view does not jump to a conclusion of equivalence. He refers to the ontological argument as an ". . . additional, simpler, and more direct demonstration of God's existence . . .",[4] while still holding that this argument is not one that is self-sufficient outside of the context of the *Meditations*. Smith asserts that the conclusions of the ontological argument, while justified, would still have no metaphysical validity without the previous demonstration that ". . . our faculties are divinely conditioned, and that all given essences can therefore be relied on as being archetypal in character."[5] In other words, the position of the ontological proof, far from being arbitrary, is determined by those portions of Meditations III & IV.

By far the most prolific opinion on the relationship between the two proofs is expressed by Martial Guéroult, not only in his two-volume work on the *Meditations*,[6] but also as the sole topic of a smaller volume, *Nouvelles Réflexions Sûr la Preuve Ontologique de Descartes*. This viewpoint is also espoused, somewhat less prolifically, by L.J. Beck.[7] Beck states that ". . . my point of view is akin to that of M. Guéroult . . . which I find convincing and have on the whole followed."[8] The conclusions of Beck and Guéroult regarding the order of the proofs are essentially the same as Norman Kemp Smith's; however, the arguments are far more intricate in illustrating their view of the whole order of the *Meditations* as a ". . . system of chains of reasoning . . . a strictly logical order."[9] Guéroult counters opinions that the position of the ontological proof is capricious by insisting that the order of the *Meditations* is ". . . not a disconcerting succession of fortuitous discoveries, but an *order* . . . the necessary and rigorous production of reasons one by the other."[10] It seems that the view of Beck and Guéroult can be briefly summarized as follows: The general validity of clear and distinct ideas guaranteed by a veracious God in Meditation III, the universal validity of clear and distinct perceptions obtained through the notions of truth and error in Meditation IV, and the connection between those perceptions and knowledge of essential natures in Meditation V are all seen as essential steps on which the validity of the ontological argument depends. All the intricacies of this logical dependence involve detailed interpretations, the length of which render them beyond the scope of this paper. However, Guéroult sums up the implications of their view in the following excerpt from his concluding chapter:

> Once we perceive the true complexity of reasons, we understand the truth of the Cartesian statement that if one element were lifted from the doctrine, the doctrine would be destroyed completely.[11]

With regard to the different order of the proofs in the Geometrical Exposition, both Guéroult and Beck point to Descartes' remarks on the different methods of analysis and synthesis which precede the exposition as being sufficient explanation. Beck also interprets some of Descartes' comments in a letter to Mersenne as implying that ". . . the *Replies* are to be valued as notes or glosses upon the main text, but not as essential links in the main argument."[12]

It is interesting to note that, throughout their argument, both Beck and Guéroult refer to the same passages from the *Replies* which have inspired opposing interpretations for others. While many of these critical authors seem unwilling to accept ambiguity in these quotations, the interpretations of Guéroult and Beck seem, perhaps, the least flexible.

Two of the more suspect instances are worth mentioning. Beck, in arguing for the dependent nature of the ontological proof, cites a portion of the quotation from the *First Set of Replies* where Descartes stresses that it is important to "keep in mind all the elements which make up the proof." (AT.VII, 120) Beck interprets this phrase as referring to ". . . all that has been acquired previously."[13] Isn't it equally plausible that Descartes is referring, not to the arguments which preceded it but, the premises of the argument itself? Guéroult makes repeated reference to the quotation from the *Fourth Set of Replies*, where Descartes describes the argument from cause as the ". . . primary and principal . . . not to say the only . . ." manner of proving God's existence. Guéroult interprets this to mean that the ". . . validity of the ontological argument is conditioned by the proof from effects."[14] Again, isn't it equally plausible that the phrase, "not to say the only," might mean that there are in fact other proofs which may be indepenent of this "primary" proof?

These are some of the questions that are also of interest to E. M. Curley.[15] Curley's main concern involves the relative merits of the proofs for the existence of God; however, he acknowledges that the order of the proofs and the possible reasons for this order have a direct bearing on their merit. He states that the two causal proofs, in attempting to explain some contingent facts by positing the existence of God, are ". . . not much better than their reputations."[16] The main difficulty with the second causal argument is that it requires us to accept the notion that something can be self-caused; yet, Curley feels that this particular notion is what is dealt with in the ontological argument. The first causal argument is seen by Curley as having other serious defects; but he emphasizes that, because "Descartes tends to fall back on the second argument when the first is questioned,"[17] it may in fact be the case that they both depend in some way on the ontological argument. It is this third argument that Curley finds most plausible, although he is well aware that it may be far more difficult to evaluate and interpret. From this perspective, Curley sees the view of Guéroult and Beck as a kind of death knell for the ontological argument.

In their view, the ontological argument only has value if we have already confirmed the existence and veracity of God. If one were to accept this view then, according to Curley, the argument is ". . . made to depend on arguments which are implausible in themselves and, in any case, arguably dependent on the ontological argument."[18] Curley also implies that their view rests precariously on a kind of blanket rule for interpreting Descartes: since logical order was of utmost importance for Descartes, one may conclude that, where one proposition follows another, it may be taken for granted that the one that comes first is a necessary condition for that which follows.

Even if this were granted, we must still account for the different order of the proofs in the Geometrical Exposition. Curley feels that the explanations given by Beck and Guéroult ". . . put more weight on the distinction between analysis and synthesis than it can bear."[19] While Descartes goes to some length to distinguish between the two methods of presentation, he also stresses that common to both methods is the "order of reasons." This raises the following question: if the order constrains Descartes to present arguments as following only from those which precede them, then how can he possibly justify even having presented the proofs in different orders? This is one of the discrepancies that Curley points to in questioning the narrow implications of Guéroult's view; and, I agree with Curley that this point alone is sufficient to cast doubt on theories claiming that the position of the ontological proof in the *Meditations* is logically entailed.

However, in rejecting such view, I do not feel that I am thereby committed to what Guéroult saw as the only alternative view—namely, that the placement of the ontological argument was "fortuitous." It is quite possible to take Descartes' statements from the *Meditations* and the *Replies*, interpret them consistently, and derive from them a view that is neither as narrow as that of Smith, Beck, and Guéroult, nor as precipitate as that of Rée. Some of Curley's conclusions have, I believe, derived such a view. He states that Descartes' causal arguments may have been put forward first because ". . . he thought the most natural way to prove God's existence . . . would be to proceed from common assumptions of the causality of our ideas."[20] On this point, I agree with Curley; yet there may be some additional points worth clarifying.

On the question of any of the proposed dependent relationships between the causal and the ontological proofs, I remain thus far unconvinced. The passages from the *Meditations* and the *Replies* used to support these views seem to be not only confusing but often contradictory. That many of the very same passages have been used to argue for the dependence of the ontological proof on the causal proofs, for the dependence of the causal proofs on the ontological proof, and for the equivalence of the proofs, simply boggles the mind. Some of these critical authors, when faced with Descartes' circumlocutions, seem to have no compunction in interpreting the ambiguities to fit their theses, irrespective of other passages which contradict their interpretations. It is the presence of just such ambiguities that make me hesitate in asserting any definite relationship between the proofs.

As to the position of the proofs, I think it may be helpful to keep in mind Descartes' main objective: to lay the foundation for scientific knowledge. That he felt the possibility of such knowledge was to be found in God makes his proofs for God's existence of paramount importance. To have given precedence to the proof whose validity would appear more obvious, and be less open to misinterpretation, makes a kind of practical sense. Although Descartes felt the ontological argument to be self-evident, he was under no illusions as to the difficulties involved in its comprehension.

My conclusion, then, is that the position of the ontological proof was determined by pragmatic, rather than logical, reasons. And, if my conclusion seems less than emphatic, it is because I am well aware that I have but scratched the surface of this question. Thus, I offer it with the following qualifications:

> For although probable conjectures may pull me in one direction, the mere knowledge that they are simply conjectures, and not certain and indubitable reasons, is itself quite enough to push my assent the other way. (AT.VII, 59)

Notes

1. J. Rée, *Descartes*; p. 137.
2. Ibid.; p. 139.
3. N. K. Smith, *New Studies in The Philosophy of Descartes*.
4. Ibid.; p. 304.
5. Ibid.; p. 305.
6. M. Guéroult, *Descartes' Philosophy Interpreted According to the Order of Reasons, Vols. I & II*.
7. L. J. Beck, *The Metaphysics of Descartes*.
8. Ibid.; p. 231.
9. Ibid.; p. 26.
10. Guéroult, Vol. I; p. 242.
11. Guéroult, Vol. II; p. 216.
12. Beck; p. 26.
13. Ibid.; p. 237.
14. Guéroult, Vol. I; p. 243.
15. E. M.Curley, *Descartes: Against the Sceptics*.
16. Ibid.; p. 125.
17. Ibid.; p. 141.
18. Ibid.; p. 157.
19. Ibid.; p. 159.
20. Ibid.; p. 160.

Bibliography

Beck, L. J., *The Metaphysics of Descartes: A Study of the Meditations*. Oxford: Clarendon Press, 1965.
Curley, E. M., *Descartes: Against the Sceptics*. Oxford: Basil Blackwell, 1978.
Guéroult, Martial, *Descartes' Philosophy Interpreted According to the Order of Rea-

sons; *Vol. I: The Soul And God* & *Vol. II: The Soul And The Body*. (Translated by Roger Ariew) Minneapolis: University of Minnesota Press, 1985.

Rée, Jonathan, *Descartes*. New York: Pica Press, 1974.

Smith, Norman Kemp, *New Studies in the Philosophy of Descartes*. London: Macmillan, 1966.

All textual references are from the following translation and are indicated in the body of the paper by the volume and page number of the Adam and Tannery edition, on which the translation is based:

Cottingham, John, Dugald Murdoch, Robert Stoothoff.
Descartes: Selected Philosophical Writings, Vol. I & II. Cambridge: Cambridge University Press, 1988.

■ UNDERSTANDING WRITING STRATEGIES

1. How do paragraphs 1 and 2 combine to create an introduction? What commitments does this introduction make?

2. How does Stuffman use summary in her essay?

3. What does *solipsistic* mean? Why are Descartes' certainties about his own existence solipsistic?

4. How does Stuffman summarize Descartes' first proof for God's existence? What audience does this summary suggest? What does the essay's vocabulary contribute to your understanding of the essay's audience?

5. What is this essay's primary purpose? What shows this?

6. What is the relationship between Descartes' order of his proofs of God's existence and his *Discourse on Method?*

7. How does Stuffman use outside critiques of Descartes? How does she present them in her essay?

8. How does Stuffman synthesize the ideas of Descartes with those of his critics? How does this synthesis inform Stuffman's critique? ■

■ SUGGESTION FOR WRITING

Read Daren Di Nicola's essay on Descartes. Write a critique of these two papers explaining their strengths and weaknesses. Establish clear criteria for your own evaluation and carefully summarize each essay. ■

Shaping the Young American Mind: The American Pageant

Nathan Turner

A few years ago journalist Frances Fitzgerald's book, *America Revised*, documented the subtle bias and altered view of American history in social studies textbooks after the sixties. Nathan Turner looks for historical bias when he examines a high-school history textbook's chapter on President William Howard Taft.

"William Howard Taft and the Progressive Revolt," a chapter taken from the high school history text *The American Pageant*, considers how Congress affected the presidency of Taft. It examines influences of both the "Old Guard Republicans" and the reformist wing of the Republican Party. It also discusses the after-effects of former President Roosevelt's "vigorous progressivism," the Republican party's unity problems in 1908–1912, and the emergence of President-to-be Dr. Woodrow Wilson.

The Payne–Aldrich Tariff is the chapter's first major issue. The Republican presidential platform of 1908 promised to revise tariff levels generated by the Dingley Tariff of 1897. Whether the revision would be up or down was not specified, and Taft soon confronted conflicting congressional forces. The conservatives, or "Old Guard," were led by Speaker of the House Joseph Cannon. A shrewd and powerful man, Cannon feigned friendship with Taft in order to manipulate the president's potential legislative influence. Cannon advocated very minimal reductions and was pleased with the 600 upward revisions to the Payne bill, engineered by Senator Nelson Aldrich and his followers. The insurgent faction of Congress, under the leadership of Senator Bob LaFollette, had faith that Taft would remember his campaign promise and veto the renamed Payne–Aldrich Bill. Taft supported his new "friends" and signed the bill, setting off political fireworks all across the country. To quiet things down, he travelled by train to several major cities and made speeches defending his decision.

Conservation of natural resources was another controversy in which Taft involved himself. President Roosevelt's policy had been to keep all natural resources from being developed by private industry. He maintained that they should be saved for the people of America's future. Taft was against premature depletion of resources also, but his dedication to the letter of the law allowed private industry to develop those resources under government supervision. This was the beginning of the split between Roosevelt and Taft.

In 1910, Taft supported the Mann–Elkins Act, a "mildly progressive" interstate commerce bill. He was forced to veto it, however, when the insurgents in the House of Representatives added too many harsh restrictions. This was more than they could handle, and the Republican party split right down the middle. Other contributing factors to the division are mentioned by the author, but Taft is regarded as the situation's catalyst.

Taft generated ninety legal actions against trusts during his term. The author compares this favorably to Roosevelt's forty-four actions in eight years, but maintains that most of Taft's important legal victories were originated by the previous administration rather than his own.

Tariff troubles plagued Taft again in 1911. Taft engineered and then pushed through the congressional red tape a mutual tariff reduction between the United States and Canada. Unfortunately, he stepped on a few too many representatives' toes in the process, and Canada began to hear rumors that the U.S. planned to make her an economically dependent colony. They decided the treaty was not in their best interest and rejected it.

Other issues this chapter discusses include the policy known as "Dollar Diplomacy," in which American dollars were pumped into foreign economies in order to secure political leverage, and the conflict between Roosevelt and Taft prior to the 1912 presidential election. Considerable attention is given to the aspects of both men and their battle for the Republican nomination. Taft won it, but the struggle divided the already factionary party and did much to put Dr. Woodrow Wilson in the White House. Wilson's background, including his New Jersey governorship, is discussed, as is the campaign platform he used to win over voters who were tired of the Republican candidates' antics. He received 435 electoral votes versus 88 for Roosevelt and 8 for Taft.

The selection ends with a retrospective of the Taft administration in which mistakes far outweigh successes. An anti-Taft viewpoint is very evident throughout the chapter, especially here at its end.

The author wastes few words describing the good things Taft did for the U.S., but has plenty to say about his shortcomings. Phrases such as "poor judge of public opinion" and "fatal political handicaps" are used to describe him. The author writes for a captive audience, the high school student, and is guilty of assuming his readers to be ignorant of this subject. The average student, equipped with a blind faith in his textbook and no previous specific knowledge of Taft, would probably accept this chapter's bias.

The chapter assumes that its readers are well acquainted with Teddy Roosevelt and his presidency. Roosevelt's contempt for the limits of the law is presented as an understood principle, as is his anti-third-term sentiment in the 1908 presidential election. While both may be considered factual by other historians, further explanation would have lent more credibility to these assumptions.

Finally, the chapter frequently refers to Taft's considerable legal background without sufficient factual support. These instances would be tolerable, if they were not used to explain Taft's decisions so often. As the text stands, we must trust that the author has not merely invented correlations to support his statements.

Interpretation plays a minimal role in this chapter. The basic facts about the Taft administration have been consistent for at least the past two decades, and few authors are willing to make drastic changes to accepted ideas. Two other historical books, *The Presidency of William Howard Taft* and *William Howard Taft: An Intimate History*, back up this author, statement for statement. It is evident that he has done little more than carry a few of the older interpretations out to a slightly greater degree. The authors of the comparison sources, Judith Anderson and Paolo Coletta, found fault with Taft, but not as often as this text's writer. This becomes more evident as we examine his writing style.

The colorful descriptions and analogies the author includes make this chapter enjoyable. Though rarely positive, comments about Taft compel and often shock. His writing style allows the piece to flow from one Taft criticism to the next. "Oddly enough, the floundering President had meanwhile been gaining some fame as a smasher of monopoly" describes Taft's trust legislation. "Though ordinarily lethargic, Taft bestirred himself to use the lever of American investments to boost American diplomacy" introduces Dollar Diplomacy. Another example describes Taft's foreign policy: "A luckless Taft could point to a few diplomatic triumphs. . . ." The use of words such as "floundering," "smasher," "lethargic," and "luckless" paint a dim picture of the President, but nevertheless one which sticks in the reader's mind. The tone of the chapter is set by the first subtitle, which reads: TAFT—A ROUND PEG IN A SQUARE HOLE. Taft did not fit into the post-TR White House very well, a fact he himself admitted. He once wrote "Politics make me sick!", and the author conveys the message that William H. Taft's presidency was not healthy for politics either.

The historical accuracy of this selection is acceptable. Cross-examination with two randomly selected sources yielded no discrepancies, only varying degrees of negativism towards Taft. Further research should show that very few historians disagree with the views expressed in this chapter. The writer's first concern is to capture and hold his reader's attention, and he does not abandon or falsify facts to do so. He is able to mate historical truth to lively narrative, a practice which many modern historians never master.

American freelance journalist Francis Fitzgerald, after comparing today's history books to those of the 50's, maintains that current texts are enjoyable and interesting at the expense of accuracy. The boring, concretely structured and detailed textbooks of old, though often dry, were at least dependable. Furthermore, the factual interpretations were uniform from book to book, and authors stressed objectivity above style. According to Fitzgerald, these characteristics have been pushed aside, and historians can no longer be trusted to related the past as it actually was. She is correct to say that history books have changed drastically; her mistake is correlating writing style with accuracy.

The American Pageant is an ideal example of a text which relates decades'-old views in a colorful, new way. Fitzgerald writes, ". . . each generation of children reads only one generation of school books. That transient history is . . . their particular version of America." This chapter meets all her criteria for modern history, except that it perpetuates the same views as we find in her favorite textbooks from the 1950's. Though *The American Pageant* is not without its faults, it exemplifies enjoyable as well as accurate history writing. At least in this case, modern history can be judged to be responsible and valuable.

■ THE WRITER'S ASSIGNMENT

Do high-school history textbooks present either a negative or positive bias about America to young readers? Write an essay reviewing part of a history text that answers this question. ■

■ UNDERSTANDING WRITING STRATEGIES

1. How well does the introduction lay the groundwork for the essay?

2. How does Turner organize his chapter summary? How else might such a summary be organized?

3. What criteria shape Turner's judgment of the chapter?

4. What kind of evidence does Turner present supporting his evaluation?

5. How does Turner use Frances Fitzgerald? How effective is this?

6. How well does Turner's essay meet the assignment's guidelines?

7. Would this review be acceptable for a special interest magazine or journal? Why or why not? ■

■ SUGGESTIONS FOR WRITING

Is it possible to write history without bias? Write a paper on the relationship between fact, interpretation, and language in history writing. Support your position by referring to examples of historical writing among the selections in this chapter, in textbooks, or in books or journals. ■

Sensible Words

Bryan Zug

Bryan Zug explores the sensory world of William Carlos Williams' language in this essay on three poems, "This Is Just to Say," "The Great Figure," and "Poem," done for his writing course focusing on literature.

What if it were possible to eat words? Of course the concept sounds silly, but what if it were really possible? There would be no more food shortages in the world. The sentences of politicians alone could serve as the staples of the planet. Now take the situation a step further. Imagine a time and a place where words could not only satisfy the basic need of human hunger, but also could cater to taste, any taste. Sipping a hearty chocolate soda or dining on shrimp scampi would all be available at the tip of a tongue. Unfortunately contemplations like this are only dreams, right? Well maybe, just maybe, the plan is a bit more feasible than we might ever think. Though words have never been able to supply the energy a human needs to survive, words can spark our senses. Words can make us taste. They can create smells within our mind. They can make us see things in a world of detail. William Carlos Williams is a poet who has the ability to do this. Throughout his poetry Williams concerns himself with the short description of a scene. It makes no difference what the subject is. Each word he applies to paper works to trigger a sensory perception in the minds of his audience. This is the common bond among all of Williams' poetry. In his poem "This Is Just to Say" Williams concentrates on the sense of taste. The subject of Williams' "The Great Figure" brings out a world of sights and sounds, while his creatively titled "Poem" focuses on a scene of silent action.

William's poem "This Is Just to Say" is a confession. The speaker in the poem has done something terrible. He has gone and eaten some plums from his icebox. This would seem to be no real disaster, but he realizes that the plums he ate were probably meant for breakfast. Though the subject of snacking on plums meant for something else has never been a hot social topic, it is a topic that many people can relate to very well. I recall times in high school when I would get home and mom was still at work. I'd be hungry and would open the refrigerator to locate something to satisfy my hunger pangs. No matter what I removed from the fridge, whether a piece of pie or leftover casserole from the week before, it always seemed that I would get it when mom got home. No matter what I ate, it was always for dinner tonight, breakfast tomorrow, or lunches for the whole week.

Williams' speaker writes the poem in first person and does not specifically describe himself. It's easy for me to picture the scene in Williams' poem set in an average American household. I see the speaker as a husband and the receiver as his wife. The husband has left a short note, the poem, to his wife on the kitchen table following a midnight snack or something similar. The man feels guilty for acting on his instincts and not thinking things through. The poem is his expression of guilt and his request for forgiveness. Williams' speaker is also very clever. The poem's descriptiveness makes the listener feel compassion for the speaker by creating the same gustatory temptation the speaker faced.

Williams gives full attention to his technique in "This Is Just to Say." He combines his choice of words with his own personal pattern of rhythm in order to make his listeners taste the plums which have caused his speaker the trouble. Williams' last two lines are examples of his best descriptive style: "so sweet/ and so cold" (11–12). "Sweet" and "cold" are both ordinary words that give strong feelings. My tongue chills at their sound. Not only does Williams choose these words for this specific reason, but he places them in a rhythmic pattern which emphasizes their meaning even further. The way these last two lines are set up in the poem gives them a great deal of visual prominence and when read out loud their syllabic accents heighten the gustatory image. "So sweet" (11) has two stressed syllables in a row and "and so cold" (12) has an unstressed syllable followed by two stressed syllables. Williams concentrates on sight, sound, and taste to make the listener identify with the speaker in the poem.

Williams triggers his readers' tastebuds in "This Is Just to Say." No matter how many times I read this poem I always end up wanting to rush to the store to buy a few ice cold plums. The real trick behind Williams' poem is the fact that he packs so much information into so few words. He does this by creating a picture for us. He doesn't say the plums are ice cold, but his words and rhythm create the image of the icebox opening up and the speaker pulling out a plum. This image leads the reader to see the plums in the icebox and, amazingly enough, by using the word "delicious" (10), the reader can even taste the plums that the speaker has eaten. The imagery is the factor that completes Williams' purpose. The point of the whole poem is to draw sympathy to its subject. To do this it is necessary for the reader to identify with the speaker and his reasons for doing what he did. What better way to identify with the speaker than understanding the motives for his crime? Williams knows the power of this and acts on it by creating the same desires in the mind of the reader. By creating these same desires and tastes, Williams makes his reader identify with the temptation that sat before the speaker. Without letting us know it, we are coaxed into the same decision that the speaker was faced with. This, in turn, leads us to the realization that if we were faced with the same decision, we would have also eaten the plums that sat in the icebox. If the whole purpose of the poem is for the reader to forgive the speaker for his actions, then Williams has achieved his purpose by making us feel like we would have committed the same crime.

He knows that it is hard to convict people of a crime that we have also committed. This is an interesting human trait that was probably first recognized when Jesus confronted the adulterous woman and her accusers who were about to stone her. In the same way, Williams seems to force those who would not have eaten the plums to throw the first plum pit.

Williams' poem "The Great Figure" deals with a subject completely different from the subject of "This Is Just to Say." In "The Great Figure" Williams focuses on the number five. The entire poem is nothing more than a statement. The speaker of the poem sees the number five in the midst of a great commotion. As he stands outside in the pouring rain, his attention is caught by the shape of the number five that appears on the side of a red firetruck as it races by. This simple fact is the focus of the entire poem. Here Williams' subject doesn't lend itself to anything but its literal meaning. His technique of description does show us the figure of the number five in a way we may have never seen before. The purpose of the poem is to make Williams' listeners see the situation through the speaker's eyes.

Williams doesn't narrow down the possibilities of the speaker's identity in "The Great Figure" as he did in "This Is Just To Say." In this second poem, he has created a speaker who does nothing more than describe the action of the poem: "I saw the figure 5" (3). This line where the speaker says what he saw in first person is the only clue we have to the identity of his speaker. Williams does this intentionally so that even more people can identify with this poem than with "This Is Just to Say." As far as the speaker's audience is concerned, Williams doesn't mention any audience within the poem and he gives no indication that there should be a defined audience. I see "The Great Figure" as a one-sentence poem that is a literal photograph. Its audience is made up of all the people who take the time to look at the image Williams has described.

In "The Great Figure" Williams uses his talent of creating an image to spark different senses than he did in "This Is Just to Say." Instead of whetting our appetite, he focuses our eyes and thrills our ears. Williams describes the circumstances of his literary picture with bright visual and auditory imagery. He makes the figure stand out by using colors that contrast and a rhythm that magnifies this contrast: "I saw the figure 5 / in gold / on a red / firetruck" (3–6). As in "This Is Just to Say," Williams' words carry a distinct denotive meaning. The words "red" and "gold" are colors that I quickly recognize as contrasting, but Williams once again adds to the existing contrast through the use of rhythm. He has placed these words in the poem so that the syllabic emphasis is the same on both words. This gives the listener the sense that the terms are of equal strength. This whole contrast is the reason the number five stands out so brightly. This visual contrast is the reason the scene caught the speaker's eye. Following the sight of the figure, the speaker describes the rush of the engine going by. Here Williams incorporates the tool of onomatopoeia in describing the way the firetruck passes: "to gong clangs/ siren howls/ and wheels rumbling" (10–12). Williams makes us hear the firetruck as it passes. He makes his imagery so loud that his listener can't ignore it.

In the midst of what seems to be a chaotic uproar, the speaker describes the visual picture that caught his eye. This reminds me of times when I've been looking up a word in a dictionary. While flipping through pages on the way to a definition my eye will catch on a word just for a second. For some reason or another it will stick in my head even though I saw it for only a split second. I always end up going back to look it up; I don't know why. The same thing happens with newspaper headlines. Some words are eye catchers for some odd reason. This freezing of action for a split second is the very focus of "The Great Figure." From the first line, "Among the rain" (1), noise belts out from around the speaker. Then the speaker says that he saw the figure five, an action which stands in silence. There is no noise in looking at things. Following this segment in the middle of the one-sentence poem, the speaker describes the rush of the fire engine. Combining sight and sound Williams creates a scene that makes me feel the rush of the fire engine as it passes. In a flash of flurry a red firetruck drives by and the millions of other things that would usually run through people's minds are bypassed because this is a special instant. The speaker doesn't wonder where the firetruck is going or if someone might be hurt. Instead he is caught in an unguarded moment just contemplating the figure five that was painted in gold on the red firetruck. Williams captures this moment by creating a scene with words.

Williams tackles the subject of how a cat walks in his poem titled "Poem." With style similar to "The Great Figure," he uses his art of description to capture an entire moment in time. Once again, Williams chooses a subject that is not very deep and brings depth to it through his poetry. He is able to give meaning to the way a cat walks by capturing its living beauty in words. Williams's subject doesn't do anything out of the ordinary. The cat merely walks along in the way it has all its life. The only difference between this and any other point in the existence of the cat is the fact that Williams captured this moment. In doing so he captured more than just the picture of a cat walking. He has recorded the essence of a cat's existence for the entire world. The subject of "Poem" parallels the subject of "The Great Figure" because in both instances Williams' technique of description is the only factor that gives the subjects depth and meaning. These two creations are not poems that do anything. They are simply poems that exist for the sake of being.

Williams doesn't identify the speaker in "Poem" at all. Unlike the previous two poems where different speakers are evoked, here we don't know who is talking. As in "The Great Figure," however, we see that the audience is not identified either. It would seem that we have a picture that is just existing. It isn't coming from anywhere and it isn't going anyplace. It is probably safe to say that the speaker is William Carlos Williams himself and that the audience is the world at large.

Williams gives his listeners a close-up look at what it is to be a normal housecat in "Poem." His description is better than a *National Geographic* report because it combines a few carefully chosen words to create a living picture. Not only do we see the picture of a cat, we know and feel the manner of its stride: "As the cat / climbed over / the top of / the jamcloset / first the right / forefoot / carefully / then the hind / stepped down / into the pit of / the empty / flowerpot." This is the entire poem. Williams' description is one that is difficult to dissect and analyze because it exists as one continuous thought. Williams chooses specific words that give little or no connotative meaning. This characteristic is present throughout the three poems we have touched on. In the case of "Poem," Williams uses specific words in open poetic form to create a rhythmic pattern which accomplishes his purpose exactly: "first the right / forefoot / carefully" (5–7). "First the right" (5) and "forefoot" (6) both begin with the letter "f" and end with the letter "t." This contributes to the unity of the poem by making the two lines similar but expressing different portions of the same thought. The way these lines are placed in the text of the poem helps to add to the motion the cat makes. "First the right" (5) falls naturally into a medium paced tempo because it has three syllables. When the reader goes to the next line and reads "forefoot" (6), he is forced to slow down because the line is one syllable shorter than the preceding line. In the same way, I get the picture that the cat also slows down a bit as he carefully places his front right paw on the top of the jamcloset. Williams doesn't place too much emphasis or too little emphasis in any one area of his description. This is the descriptive detail that is present in all three of Williams' poems.

In "Poem," Williams' imagery creates depth impressions on the senses of sight and sound. He uses these to instil in his listeners the memory of what a cat is like. Williams describes the flowing agility of a cat's stride: "first the right / forefoot / carefully / then the hind" (5–8). This line makes me think of the times I have spent playing with the many various cats that my family has had over the years. Williams makes me picture my favorite calico walking on a shaky sofa arm quietly testing each step with his front paw before trusting it with the weight of his rear leg. The amazing fact is that with the use of one sentence full of carefully chosen words placed in a rhythm scheme Williams is able to create the picture of something I have noticed many times. Williams does even more than this in his poem. He captures the whole person of this specific cat and cats in general. Lines nine through twelve describe the cat as he walks indifferently into a flowerpot. This is a visual image no doubt, but it somehow goes further. It outlines a cat's naturally curious and nonchalant personality. Williams again lets his sensory images take his subject to new heights with the most ordinary of tools.

William Carlos Williams is a master of description. The common bond among all of Williams' poetry is the fact that he favors a descriptive form of poetry. His subjects and literary tools vary from poem to poem, but his sense-sparking imagery is present in all of his poems. Williams often achieves his goal by keeping the speaker and audience vague so that more people can identify with his subject matter. He puts together scenes that are easy to see, taste, hear, or feel. Williams' technique is the only thing that does not vary from poem to poem. I see the cat and hear its silence in "Poem." I watch the still figure of the number five amidst the middle of a noisy, contrasting, and artificially lighted scene in "The Great Figure." I can taste the plums and sympathize with the guilty party in "This Is Just to Say." For each of Williams' poems memories of similar situations from my own life pop into my head.

No, it's not possible to eat words except when you make a mistake, but that is never very satisfying. It is possible, however, to trigger our tastebuds and get our mouths watering. William Carlos Williams knew this fact and his mastery of this skill is very evident in his poetry. His poetry has the ability to trigger our senses into seeing and feeling things that are not real, but are only images. Williams uses these images to look at some very common things. He puts a frame of words around everyday events and hangs them on the wall so that we can look at them in our free time. Williams uses his ability of description to point out the beauty of everyday situations that might otherwise pass us by.

Works Cited

Williams, William Carlos. "The Great Figure." *Literature: An Introduction to Fiction, Poetry, and Drama.* Ed. X. J. Kennedy. Boston: Little, Brown, and Company, 1987. 498.

Williams, William Carlos. "This Is Just to Say." *Literature: An Introduction to Fiction, Poetry, and Drama.* Ed. X. J. Kennedy. Boston: Little, Brown, and Company, 1987. 445

Williams, William Carlos. "Poem." *Literature: An Introduction to Fiction, Poetry, and Drama.* Ed. X. J. Kennedy. Boston: Little, Brown, and Company, 1987. 621.

■ THE WRITER'S ASSIGNMENT

Write an analysis of poetic language that increases your reader's appreciation of the poem or poems you consider. Be certain to keep your readers in mind and write to engage and maintain your readers' interest. ■

■ UNDERSTANDING WRITING STRATEGIES

1. How does Zug capture the reader's attention in the first paragraph?

2. What is the tone of this essay?

3. What do the introduction and the tone suggest about Zug's audience?

4. What is this essay's central insight into Williams's poems?

5. How does Zug demonstrate this position?

6. One way Zug develops his essay is through several analogies from personal experience. How effective is this approach?

7. How has Zug objectified his personal experience so that the reader can relate his own experiences to them?

8. What are some of Williams' poetic devices Zug considers? What does his discussion of these devices contribute to our understanding of the poems?

9. How does Zug weave together the diverse strands of his argument at the paper's end? How effective is the conclusion? On what do you base this? ■

■ SUGGESTIONS FOR WRITING

How does Zug's writing compare with "professional" writing about literature? Examine a poetry review in a literary magazine, a study of Williams' poetry in a scholarly journal, and a popular magazine poetry review. Write a paper for fellow undergraduate students explaining how to write effectively about literature. Be certain to consider tone, content, and the effective use of both text and personal observations. ■